North·South Center
UNIVERSITY OF MIAMI

Drug Trafficking in the Americas

Edited by

Bruce M. Bagley
and William O. Walker III

Transaction Publishers
New Brunswick (U.S.A.) and London (U.K.)

The mission of the North-South Center is to promote better relations and serve as a catalyst for change among the United States, Canada, and the nations of Latin America and the Caribbean by advancing knowledge and understanding of the major political, social, economic, and cultural issues affecting the nations and peoples of the Western Hemisphere.

Library of Congress Cataloging-in-Publication Data

Drug Trafficking in the Americas / edited by Bruce M. Bagley and
   William O. Walker.
      p. cm.
   Includes bibliographical references.
   ISBN 1-56000-752-4 (acid free paper)
   1. Drug traffic--United States. 2. Drug traffic--Latin America.
3. Narcotics, Control of--United States. 4. Narcotics, Control of
--Latin America, I. Bagley, Bruce Michael. II. Walker, William O.,
1946-   , III. University of Miami. North-South Center.
HV5825.D77693 1995
363.4'5'097~~dc20

                                                              94-24418
                                                              CIP

ISBN 1-56000-752-4

Printed in the United States of America

00 99 98 97 96 95 94 7 6 5 4 3 2 1

Contents

Mexico

Central America and the Caribbean

International Dimensions

Contributors

Xavier Andrade is an anthropologist affiliated to the Facultad Latinoamericana de Ciencias Sociales (FLACSO) in Ecuador. He has directed several research projects related to the social effects of narcotrafficking. Mr. Andrade received his degree from the Pontificia Universidad Católica del Ecuador. Some of his published titles include *Pequeños Traficantes* and *Violencia Social y Pandillas*. He is a contributor to the book *La Economía Política del Narcotráfico: El Caso Ecuatoriano*.

Bruce Michael Bagley is the Associate Dean of the Graduate School of International Studies (GSIS), University of Miami. Dr. Bagley is also Director of Interamerican Studies at GSIS and Director of the North-South Center Drug Trafficking Task Force. Among his recent publications are *En Busca de la Seguridad Perdida: Aproximaciones a la Seguridad Nacional Mexicana*, co-edited with Sergio Aguayo Quezada (Mexico City: Siglo XXI, 1990); *Economía y Política del Narcotráfico en Colombia*, co-edited with Juan Gabriel Tokatlián (Bogotá: Universidad de los Andes y CEREC, 1990); and *Economía Política del Narcotráfico en el Ecuador*, co-edited with Adrián Bonilla and Alexei Páez Cordero (Quito: FLACSO, 1991). He also prepared an interview with President César Gaviria Trujillo (Colombia) for the inaugural issue of the North-South magazine (June 1991) and authored a monograph entitled *Myths of Militarization: The Role of the Military in the War on Drugs in the Americas* (Coral Gables: North-South Center, 1991).

Professor Bagley has been a Visiting Professor at ICESI (Instituto Colombiano de Estudios Superiores de INCOLDA), in Cali, Colombia. He has presented papers at professional conferences or symposia sponsored by Boston University, MIT, The National Defense University (Washington, D.C.), University of Texas (Austin), the University of Virginia (Charlottesville, VA), the Latin American Studies Association (Washington, D.C.), the Inter-American Dialogue (Washington, D.C.), the Institute of the Americas (La Jolla, CA), the GSIS Institute of Soviet and Eastern European Studies, and the University of Miami's North-South Center on facets of U.S.-Latin American relations in the 1990s.

i

Recently, Dr. Bagley served on the Miami Coalition for a Drug Free Community's International Task Force and on the Inter-American Commission on Drug Policy (sponsored by the Institute of the Americas and the Center for Iberian and Latin American Studies, University of California, San Diego).

X. Adrian Bonilla is a political scientist. He is a Ph.D. candidate at the Graduate School of International Studies of the University of Miami. At present he is a researcher at Facultad Latinoamericana de Ciencias Sociales (FLACSO) in Ecuador. Mr. Bonilla is the author of *En Busca del Pueblo Perdido* (FLACSO: Ecuador, 1991) and co-editor, with Bruce M. Bagley and Alexei Páez Cordero of *La Economía Política del Narcotráfico: El Caso Ecuatoriano* (FLACSO: Ecuador and North-South Center, 1991).

Alvaro Camacho Guizado, a sociologist from Universidad Nacional de Colombia, received his Ph.D. from the University of Wisconsin. He is a professor of sociology at Universidad Nacional de Colombia (Bogotá) and Universidad del Valle (Cali) as well as a visiting professor at the Institut des Hautes Etudes de l'Amerique Latine in Paris. Some of his publications include *Capital Extranjero: Subdesarrollo Colombiano* (Bogotá: Punta de Lanza, 1976); *El Frente Nacional: Ideología y Realidad* with Humberto Rojas (Bogotá: Punta de Lanza, 1972); *La Organización Social de la Centralización del Capital en Colombia* (Cali: Universidad del Valle, 1977); and *Droga, Corrupción y Poder: Marihuana y Cocaína en la Sociedad Colombiana* (Cali: CIDSE-Universidad del Valle, 1981).

Fernando Cepeda Ulloa has been Colombian Minister of Interior (1986-1987); Minister of Communications (1987-1988); and Vice Minister of Economic Development (1972). He served as Plenipotentiary Minister in Washington (1980-1982) and as Ambassador to the Court of St. James (1988-1990). He was Permanent Representative of Colombia to the United Nations and is currently Colombia's Ambassador to Canada. He received a law degree at the Universidad Nacional and did graduate work in political science at the New School for Social Research. In 1988, he was made a fellow of St. Anthony's College, Oxford University. He was president of the Joint Latin American Program in International Relations (RIAL) and a founding member of the Andean Interuniversity Center (CINDA).

Dr. Cepeda taught political science at the Universidad de los Andes, Bogotá, where he also served as acting president, vice president, dean, head of department, and research director. He promoted the creation of the political science department, the school of Law, and two research centers: the Center of Regional Studies and the Center of International Studies. He has written and published essays and books in the field of political development and international affairs.

Jorge Chabat is a professor at Centro de Investigación y Docencia Económicas (CIDE) and the Universidad Iberoamericana (Mexico City). He received his degree in international relations from El Colegio de México and is currently pursuing a Ph.D. in international relations at the Graduate School of International Studies, University of Miami. He has published regularly on the topics of Mexican foreign policy and U.S.-Mexican relations.

Eduardo A. Gamarra, who has taught at Universidad Católica Boliviana and at the University of Pittsburgh, is currently an associate professor of political science at Florida International University. He received his Ph.D. in political science from the University of Pittsburgh in 1987. Dr. Gamarra is the author of *Revolution and Reaction: Bolivia 1964-85* and co-editor of the series *Latin America and Caribbean Contemporary Record*, a third volume of which is forthcoming. He has also published over thirty articles and book chapters, most of which deal with Bolivian politics, international relations, and Bolivia's involvement in the international drug trade.

Kevin Healy was a Peace Corps volunteer in the late 1960s in the Lake Titicaca region of Peru. He subsequently participated as a social science advisor from Georgetown University in an assistance program for the Universidad Católica of Asunción, Paraguay. In the mid-1970s, Healy conducted field work for his rural development study in Bolivia which was later published. Since 1978, Healy has been a grant officer for the Andean region with the Inter-American Foundation and frequent public speaker. He has written on socio-economic development issues. Healy has an undergraduate degree from the University of Notre Dame and graduate degrees from Georgetown and Cornell universities.

Antoinette Khan-Melnyk is currently a Ph.D. candidate at the University of Miami, Graduate School of International Studies. Her area of interest is the Caribbean and her specific focus is economic development. She is assistant editor of the *Journal of Interamerican Studies and World Affairs*.

Gabriela D. Lemus is a North-South Center graduate fellow at the Graduate School of International Studies, University of Miami. Currently, Ms. Lemus is focusing on U.S.-Mexican relations with a special emphasis on the impact of Mexican-Americans on U.S. foreign policy toward Mexico.

Donald J. Mabry is professor of history and senior fellow at the Center for International Security and World Affairs, Mississippi State University. He is the editor of *The Latin American Narcotics Trade and U.S. National Security*.

Anthony P. Maingot is professor of sociology and editor of *Hemisphere*, a magazine of Latin American and Caribbean studies at Florida International University (FIU). A past president of the Caribbean Studies Association, he is a member of the Board of Contributors of *The Miami Herald*, the Board of Directors of *Caribbean Affairs*, senior vice president of the Caribbean Resources Development Foundation (CARDEV), contributing editor, Caribbean politics, *The Handbook of Latin American Studies*, The Library of Congress. He is a co-author of *A Short History of the West Indies* (St. Martin's Press), now in its fourth edition. His most recent book is *Small Country Development and International Labor Flows: Experiences in the Caribbean* (Westview Press, 1991).

William B. McAllister is a Ph.D. candidate in modern European history at the University of Virginia. His dissertation concerns international aspects of drug control. He is the author of "Conflicts of Interest in the International Drug Control System," which appeared in *The Journal of Policy History* (Fall 1991). Mr. McAllister has previously taught in a juvenile crime and delinquency prevention program in Oklahoma that focused on drug- and alcohol-related issues.

Frank O. Mora is assistant professor of international studies at Rhodes College, Memphis, TN. He has conducted research and published articles on several aspects of Paraguayan politics and foreign policy. He is the author of *Política exterior del Paraguay: 1811-1989* (1993). He recently served as an observer for the Latin American Studies Association (LASA) in the May 3, 1993, Paraguayan elections. He is currently working on issues dealing with new roles of the Latin American armed forces in the post-Cold War period.

Edmundo Morales, a native of the Andes of Peru, teaches sociology at West Chester State University of Pennsylvania. He studied at Universidad Nacional San Marcos, Lima, Peru, received his M.A. in sociology from New York University and his Ph.D. from the Graduate School of the City University of New York. He is the author of *Cocaine: White Gold Rush in Peru* and many articles on drug trafficking and Andean culture. He is a self-taught photographer whose work has appeared in *National Geographic Magazine*, book covers, and text illustrations. His most recent photographic work, "Growing Old in Spanish Harlem," a collection of 30 photographs documenting life of Hispanic elderly, has been on exhibition in the Museum of the City of New York.

Alexei Paez Cordero received an M.A. in political science from the Facultad Latinoamericana de Ciencias Sociales (FLACSO) in Ecuador, where he is presently a researcher. He has published *El Anarquismo en el Ecuador* (CEN-

INFOC, 1986) and co-edited *La Economía Política del Narcotráfico: El Caso Ecuatoriano*. He has written several articles on the topic of narcotrafficking.

David Scott Palmer is professor of Latin American politics and United States-Latin American relations at Boston University. He holds a B.A. in international relations from Dartmouth College, an M.A. from Stanford University in Hispanic American studies, and a Ph.D. from Cornell University in comparative government. His research and writings include works on Peru, the Latin American military, democracy and authoritarianism, U.S. policy toward Latin America, Latin American guerrilla movements, and Sendero Luminoso. Among his publications are "Rebellion in Rural Peru: The Origins and Evolution of Sendero Luminoso," *Comparative Politics*, January 1986 and "Peru: The Authoritarian Legacy," in *Latin American Politics and Development* (Wiarda and Kline, eds., Westview, 1985).

Raphael F. Perl is a specialist in international narcotics policy in the Division of Foreign Affairs and National Security of the Congressional Research Service (U.S. Library of Congress). He is author of *International Narcotics Control and Foreign Assistance Certification: Requirements, Procedures, Timetables, and Guidelines* (U.S. Senate Committee on Foreign Relations, 1988) among numerous other congressional publications.

Pola Reydburd received her B.A. in English from Southern Illinois University (Carbondale) and her M.A. in educational administration and leadership from the University of Alabama's International Programs. She is currently enrolled at the Graduate School of International Studies, University of Miami. From 1984 to 1988, she was executive director of B'nai B'rith International for District 23 (the Caribbean). In 1990-1991, she served as executive director of CAP: Colombian Accuracy Project, an organization created to improve the image of Colombia and Colombians in the United States; presently, she is a member of its Board of Directors.

Alejandro Reyes is a sociologist from the Universidad Nacional, Bogotá, Colombia.

Linda Robinson is the Latin America correspondent for *U.S. News & World Report*. Based in Miami, she travels frequently throughout the region. Her book on Central America and Panama, *Intervention or Neglect: The United States and Central America beyond the 1980s*, was published in August 1991 by the Council on Foreign Relations. Prior to joining the staff of *U.S. News & World Report*, Ms. Robinson edited and wrote for *Foreign Affairs* and *The Wilson Quarterly* magazines. Her articles have also appeared in *The New York*

Times, The Los Angeles Times, Survival (U.K.), *Nexos* (Mexico), *Commonweal,* and other newspapers and magazines. The Congressional Research Service commissioned her to write a study of the Central American peace process and U.S. policy, which was published in the House Foreign Affairs Committee's annual report, *Congress and Foreign Policy 1987.* A graduate of Swarthmore College, Ms. Robinson is a member of the Council on Foreign Relations.

José Luis Simón is a Paraguayan journalist and sociologist. He is director of the international relations program of the Centro Paraguayo de Estudios Sociológicos where he is also the executive editor of the international relations journal *Perspectiva Internacional Paraguaya.* Mr. Simón has published a number of books and articles on topics dealing with international relations, civil-military relations, human rights, and Paraguayan foreign relations. Some of his works include *Política Exterior y Relaciones Internacionales del Paraguay Contemporáneo* (1990), *La Dictadura de Stroessner y los Derechos Humanos,* vols. 1 and 2, and "Del Aislamiento a la Reinserción Internacional: El Paraguay de la Inmediata Transición Post-stronista." Mr. Simón is also editor of the international news section of the Paraguayan daily *Hoy.*

Juan Gabriel Tokatlián is a sociologist from the University of Belgrano in Buenos Aires, Argentina. He has an M.A. and a Ph.D. in international relations from Johns Hopkins University's School of Advanced International Studies (SAIS) in Washington, D.C. Dr. Tokatlián is currently the director of the Center for International Studies at the Universidad de los Andes in Bogotá, Colombia. He is the author of *Política Exterior Colombiana: De la Subordinación a la Autonomía?* and the co-editor of various texts, among them *Teoría y Práctica de la Política Exterior Latino-americana, Relaciones Internacionales en la Cuenca del Caribe y la Política de Colombia,* and *Narcotráfico en Colombia.* He has also written several essays on international politics and Colombia's foreign policy.

Francisco E. Thoumi is a research consultant in Washington, D.C. He is also a former professor of economics at California State University-Chico, prior to which he served as section chief at the Inter-American Development Bank. He is the author of several books and articles on economic problems of Latin America.

William O. Walker III is professor and chair of the history department at Ohio Wesleyan University. He received his Ph.D. from the University of California, Santa Barbara, and in 1988 was awarded the John D. and Catherine T. MacArthur Foundation Fellowship in International Peace and Security. Dr. Walker has been a visiting professor, Graduate School of International Studies, University of Miami. He specializes in U.S. foreign relations, narcotics control, and interamerican relations. He is the author of *Drug Control in the Americas*, and his most recent book is *Opium and Foreign Policy: The Anglo-American Search for Order in Asia, 1912-1954*, University of North Carolina Press, 1991.

Carol Weir has studied at the University of South Carolina, Warwick University (Coventry, England), and Universidad de los Andes (Bogotá, Colombia). She completed her Masters of Interamerican Studies at the University of Miami's Graduate School of International Studies. She is interested in social movements and Central America.

Introduction

During the last two decades, drug trafficking emerged as one of the fastest growing industries in Latin America (valued at an estimated $100 billion annually). Not only does it pose serious threats to public health, institutional development, and political stability in much of the hemisphere, but it has become a contentious issue in U.S.-Latin American relations. Despite its undeniable significance, U.S. and Latin American scholars have only recently begun to explore this complex issue and its consequences seriously. With a few notable exceptions, the limited work that has been done has generally focused on specific countries, regions, or communities or on bilateral relations with the United States. It has therefore lacked the comparative and interregional scope that is fundamental to a comprehensive understanding of the drug trade.* Without the background information and in-depth analysis necessary to do so effectively, both U.S. and Latin American policy makers have frequently found themselves obligated to formulate and implement policies to combat the explosive growth of drug trafficking. Thus, despite the billions of dollars spent over the last 20 years by the United States and other governments in the region to control this illicit trade, the results have often been disappointing and, at times, counterproductive.

This study undertakes to explore in detail the political economy of the drug trade in the hemisphere in order to understand better its subnational, national, and international dynamics and implications. The Andean subregion and Mexico were selected as the primary focus of the project because they

---

* Few academic studies have been undertaken to examine the pervasiveness of the drug trafficking phenomenon. As a result, the Graduate School of International Studies (GSIS) and the North-South Center of the University of Miami, in collaboration with the Centro de Estudios Internacionales (CEI) of the Universidad de los Andes in Bogotá, Colombia, co-sponsored a two-year research project (March 1992-September 1994) on the economic, social, political, legal, and international dimensions of drug production and trafficking in the hemisphere. The Andean republics (Colombia, Ecuador, Peru, and Bolivia), Mexico, Central America and the Caribbean, Paraguay, and the United States constitute the primary focus of the study.

comprise the principal producing-processing-exporting countries in the Americas for the marijuana, cocaine, methaqualone, and heroin entering the United States.

By political economy, we mean that the economics and politics of the drug trade should be studied in tandem, as a unit rather than in isolation. In addition, special attention is given to the patterns and dynamics of production, distribution, and consumption characteristic of the drug trade in the region, as well as the economic, social, and political implications in producing, transit, and consuming countries. In short, the purpose of this project was to focus on both the supply and demand sides of the drug equation and on the public policy responses that drug trafficking has elicited (or failed to elicit) from individual countries and regional organizations.

We are, of course, aware that the term "political economy" encompasses multiple, and often contradictory, theoretical and methodological, Marxist and non-Marxist, radical, liberal, and conservative perspectives. We are not in a position to resolve these long-standing theoretical disputes, nor do we have any intention of attempting such a task. The selection of a political economy approach is dictated by a conviction that the economic dimensions of the drug trade must be studied in the social and political contexts within which they occur and which, in turn, they transform. We believe that application of the variegated tools of political economy will focus our collective attention on the interrelationships between economics and politics that lie at the heart of the drug trade, while providing ample opportunities for the individual scholars affiliated with the project to pursue their own lines of research using established disciplinary methodological techniques.

The core premise underlying this volume is that drug trafficking cannot be properly studied or understood in the context of any.single country; it is a multinational phenomenon involving intimately connected supply and demand factors, an international market, and intense government "regulations." These factors are integral components of a single process and deserve to be studied accordingly. Drug producing and drug consuming countries are, in the most literal sense of the term, interdependent. Depending on the country, transit states are often equally so. A corollary to this premise is that the drug trade cannot be usefully viewed as merely an economic (or social or political) phenomenon; it is rather a process that has ramifications at each of these levels of society and that must be examined in terms of their interrelationships.

The State of the Art Conference on Drug Trafficking Research was held in Miami, Florida, on March 13-16, 1992. It was sponsored by the North-South Center's Drug Trafficking Task Force and the Universidad de los Andes' Centro de Estudios Internacionales. The conference brought together a multidisciplinary group of academics and other experts to examine the impact of drug trafficking on society and the political economy of the Western Hemisphere (with special attention to political stability and processes of democratization) and to assess the current social science literature on the subject. The result of this effort is the collection of 28 essays divided, by country and region, into nine sections presented in this volume.

In the first section, *U.S. Drug Policy Toward Latin America*, William O. Walker III reviews the historical logic and practice of U.S. policy in Latin America and examines U.S. drug control policy by focusing on the Andean drug strategy. In his essay, Walker argues that the result of the U.S. strategy is paradoxical. U.S. traditional efforts at democratic institution-building stand at odds with the reality that drug control in source countries can have a destabilizing effect. He contends that this behavior is reflective of a "quick-fix mentality" and has been proved, empirically, not to work. In the second essay, Raphael F. Perl examines the Andean strategy and issues relevant to the policy-making process, evaluates U.S. government assessment reports, and concludes that policy makers are confronted with a series of problems and contradictions that bring into question the effectiveness of the strategy itself. Next, Donald J. Mabry examines the U.S. and Latin American militaries' role in drug control efforts and concludes that military involvement in eliminating the drug supply at its source places the armed forces in a potentially dangerous position because of the possibility of corruption, breakdowns in the chain of command or in military and internal preparedness for other missions. At the same time, this approach belies the larger issue of the drug problem which is social control. The final essay on U.S. policy was written by Bruce M. Bagley who reviews the 1992 San Antonio summit and its aftermath from a historical and policy context and poses a series of questions that serve as guidelines to determine the success or failure of the hemisphere's war on drugs.

The second section of the book contains five essays by Colombians regarding their country's role in the drug war. The first essay, by Francisco Thoumi, analyzes the factors leading to the growth of drug trafficking as a business in the country and examines the roots of domestic difficulties in the context of modern Colombian politics. Alvaro Camacho Guizado addresses Colombia's central role in the drug trade and explores the effects that the drug trade has had on Colombian society, economy, culture, and politics as well as the international impact of the issue. Alejandro Reyes' essay explores drug-related violence in rural areas and the linkages between drug trafficking organizations and the guerrilla groups. He also evaluates the social impacts of state counterinsurgency operations and the problems of pacification in drug producing areas. The last two essays in this section are contributions from Juan Gabriel Tokatlián. In the first, Tokatlián evaluates the effect of the war on drugs on U.S.-Colombian relations, questions the basis for the current international narcotics regime, and suggests that cooperation has been elusive because of the lack of conceptual convergence on the issue. The second essay evaluates the impact of the aerial spraying of the herbicide glyphosate on the Colombian countryside and the shift from the cultivation of marijuana to opium poppies.

The third section of the book contains two essays on Peru. In the first, Edmundo Morales reviews the social and anthropological aspects of the capitalist transformation of Peru and calls for a new model of economic development to aid the integration of coca farmers into the international market economy, in light of past policy failures. David Scott Palmer then explores Peru's policy options vis-à-vis drug cultivation and drug trafficking. Specifically, he looks at the interplay between drug trafficking and the Shining Path guerrilla movement and discusses the limitations that this relationship places on the Peruvian state.

The fourth section examines Bolivia. Kevin Healy first reviews the literature on coca consumption, coca production, and the illegal cocaine industry in Bolivia. Eduardo Gamarra then explores the internal and external pressures deriving from drug trafficking in Bolivia in the midst of economic crisis and a fragile transition to democracy. Gamarra notes that there are serious problems with "alternative development" programs and that interdiction measures and repressive strategies have proven futile; since U.S. pressure is potentially destabilizing, he believes that attempts should be made to "decocainize" U.S.-Bolivian relations.

The fifth section addresses the impact of drug trafficking on Ecuador, basically a transit country and a relative "island of peace" when compared to the other Andean nations. Alexei Paez evaluates Ecuador's current position within the political economy of Andean drug trafficking and analyzes the evolution of state policies, as well as the impact of drugs on the country's financial and penal systems. Xavier Andrade examines the societal effects of the war on drugs as it has been fought in Ecuador. The essay by Adrian Bonilla reviews U.S. policy toward Ecuador, as well as Ecuador's own antidrug efforts, focusing on treaties and international agreements signed by the Ecuadoran state. Bonilla systematizes the information on state structural reforms and the social effects these reforms have had, especially with regard to U.S.-sponsored interdiction policies.

The sixth section studies Paraguay's role in the political economy of drug trafficking in the hemisphere. In the first essay, José Luis Simón discusses how the drug issue is addressed in Paraguay's contemporary politics and attempts to determine how drugs have influenced both state and society in Paraguay. The second essay, by Frank Mora, is historical in nature and reviews the periodization of Paraguay's relation to the international drug trade which is rooted in the infamous "French Connection" of the 1970s.

The seventh section takes up the case of Mexico. Jorge Chabat examines the historical role of drug trafficking in U.S.-Mexican relations and points out that as the United States increased emphasis on drug interdiction in the mid-1980s, levels of conflict between the two countries were greatly intensified. Finally, he contends that, in the recent era of more open cooperation under President Carlos Salinas de Gortari, it became evident that drug trafficking was a secondary issue in U.S.-Mexican relations overshadowed by economic concerns. William O. Walker then provides a look at U.S.-Mexican relations following the death of U.S. DEA agent Enrique Camarena. Finally, Gabriela Lemus looks at drug trafficking and the U.S.-Mexican border. Her paper provides a case study of Operation Alliance and concludes that drug interdiction policy along the border between the United States and Mexico has only a limited impact on the overall status of the bilateral relationship.

Section eight includes four essays on drug trafficking issues in Central America and the Caribbean. Linda Robinson reviews Central American involvement in drug trafficking and concludes that the region is incapable of responding effectively to the threats inherent in the rapid expansion of drug trafficking owing to extensive corruption and weak political institutionalization. Carol Weir focuses on Costa Rica and its primary role as a transshipment point for drugs coming from South America. Anthony Maingot provides a general overview of the drug trade in the micro-states of the Caribbean. Finally, Antoinette Khan analyzes the impact of drug trafficking on Jamaica, focusing on marijuana production, eradication policies, and interdiction efforts jointly sponsored by Jamaica and the United States.

The concluding section emphasizes additional international dimensions of drug trafficking. In the conference's keynote address, Ambassador Fernando Cepeda Ulloa depicts an optimistic scenario: Because of the new thinking about drug trafficking responses, an evolution that uses coalition-building approaches and consensus to establish a global strategy has ensued. William B. McAllister examines international treaties and U.N. agencies and concludes that the drug regime, as it has evolved, is a system that is reflective of Western cultural, social, economic, and religious biases. In the last essay, Pola Reydburd analyzes the images and concepts that are being disseminated by popular literature and concludes that these stereotypes have a negative impact and generate prejudice by linking drug dealers and corruption with all Latinos.

U.S. Drug Policy
Toward Latin America

Chapter One

The Bush Administration's Andean Drug Strategy in Historical Perspective

William O. Walker III

Introduction

In South America the administration of U.S. President George Bush put to the test the very credibility of its drug control strategy. If control at the source, the mainstay of U.S. drug policy, could not succeed in the Andes, then the almost century-long war on drugs would be lost. Objectively, the chances for victory in this most recent phase of the global drug war appeared remote even as the formidable power of the Medellín cartel ebbed. From within the U.S. Congress, the House Committee on Government Operations clearly labelled the administration's Andean strategy a failure, arguing that fundamental flaws in the drug strategy would preclude its successful implementation at any time in the foreseeable future. The committee's finding echoed similarly pessimistic conclusions of other analyses by U.S. government agencies as well as independent researchers.[1]

At the same time, and to casual observers of antinarcotics policy, this must have seemed a remarkable paradox; failure in the Andes probably would not deter U.S. policy makers from pursuing a comparable strategy in the future. Such has been the historic logic and practice of U.S. narcotics foreign policy toward Latin America. It is not the purpose of this chapter to detail tactical changes in U.S. drug strategy from its inception through the two drug summits held in Cartagena, Colombia, and San Antonio, Texas, in February 1990 and February 1992, respectively. Suffice it to note that governmental appraisals of the strategy on the eve of the latter meeting remained highly critical.[2]

The Andean drug strategy did not appear all of a sudden in the aftermath of the cocaine summit, held at Cartagena, Colombia, in February 1990. It had originated earlier, in late August 1989 after the assassination of presidential

1

candidate Luis Carlos Galán in Colombia, and formally became part of the National Drug Control Strategy which the White House subsequently announced in September 1989. The Andean strategy amounted to a broad, triadic program composed of military support, law enforcement advice, and economic assistance for the coca-growing and cocaine-producing countries of Bolivia, Colombia, and Peru.[3] As first designed, the strategy represented the culmination of more than a decade of U.S. anticoca efforts in the region. These various programs had been systematically impaired, however, by political instability — evident on occasion in each of the countries, by economic and social inequities, by a lack of will, by corruption, and also by dubious planning by policy makers in Washington, D.C.[4]

At the time of this writing in late 1992, evaluating the drug war seems almost a surreal undertaking. There is a timeless quality to the defining events in the struggle against drugs in the Andes. The litany is a familiar one. The government of Peru is charting a precarious course in Andean affairs, its attention divided between drugs, societal decay and economic chaos, and guerrilla war; President Alberto K. Fujimori's "auto-golpe" of April 5, 1992, and the capture of Abimael Guzman Reynoso, the leader of Sendero Luminoso, merely underscores this assessment. Bolivia pleads with the United States for further development assistance, knowing that the price will probably be greater militarization of peasant coca-growing regions in the countryside and additional political instability in the capital. Colombia lurches with great uncertainty toward political pluralization but fears that drug-related violence, exacerbated by the July escape from jail of Medellín cartel chief Pablo Escobar Gaviria, will undermine this latest effort at democratic institution building. And the United States, as it has since at least the mid-1980s, urges the three nations to stay the course, although with less public fanfare than in the past.[5] It was a situation that some day will require its own Gabriel García Márquez to render it explicable. In the meantime, it is possible to uncover the roots of the Bush administration's Andean strategy.

Roots of the Andean Strategy

As the Andean strategy evolved, considerable emphasis was placed upon a military response to the cocaine trade. Calls for militarization of the hemisphere's war on drugs emanated from the U.S. Congress as early as 1981, notably from the House Select Committee on Narcotics Abuse and Control, which was created in 1976. Also, the House Foreign Affairs Committee, then under the leadership of Rep. Larry Smith (D-FL), took up the call for a militarized drug war.[6] And although certain officials in the Department of State's Bureau of International Narcotics Matters (INM) were receptive to the idea of an active drug war, as seen in the earlier development of INM's air wing and other assistance programs, the Reagan administration's Department of Defense (DOD) viewed the matter in an altogether different light. Fighting the drug war was not then seen as part of DOD's mission, essentially because it could not be won in any acceptable definition of the term. Further, the ongoing cold war with the Soviet Union and its allies still commanded the nation's defense priorities. As I previously argued in *Drug Control in the Americas* and elsewhere, President Ronald Reagan was quick to attack drugs with powerful rhetoric but was reluctant to make the drug war a policy priority of the first order as some members of Congress were urging him to do.[7] For the Reagan White House, the struggle against communism and the Left in Central America dominated hemispheric policy.

Indications of a change did come, however, on April 8, 1986, when President Reagan declared in National Security Decision Directive No. 221 that drug production and trafficking comprised a threat to the security of the Americas. Simultaneously, the White House began to up the ante in the war on drugs. Responding to an appeal from Bolivia, U.S. officials initiated planning for what became known as Operation Blast Furnace, a joint military effort from July through November 1986 against cocaine-processing facilities. In the short term, Blast Furnace was a resounding success. The formerly lucrative cocaine trade out of Bolivia was severely disrupted for several months. For a nation that had fallen victim to a "cocaine coup" in July 1980, Bolivia had come a long way.[8] To policy makers in Washington, the easy success of Blast Furnace indicated the likely rewards, in foreign policy and domestic politics, of an uncompromising approach in the future to the South American drug trade.

If Operation Blast Furnace was the progenitor of Bush's Andean strategy, then the *Tranquilandia* raid must be viewed as the operational precursor to Blast Furnace. In March 1984 Drug Enforcement Administration (DEA) personnel and select Colombian authorities, assisted by the satellite capabilities of the U.S. National Security Agency, raided a major cocaine-processing facility in the southern province of Caquetá. Although the raid was a dramatic, if short-lived success, the political costs to Colombia were high. By mid-November 1985, the two officials most responsible for the raid — Justice Minister Rodrigo Lara Bonilla and Colonel Jaime Ramírez Gómez of the narcotics unit of the National Police — were dead, evidently murdered by assassins in the pay of the Medellín cartel.[9]

What Tranquilandia and Blast Furnace had in common was the psychology of the "quick fix." This perspective was based upon the unfounded assumption that the enemy — in this case, cocaine producers and their operatives — would, in effect, surrender in the face of a dramatic show of force. This "raid now, reflect later" mentality proved to be counterproductive to the kind of political stability that the Reagan administration wistfully hoped anticocaine activity would engender. Instead of helping to build viable political institutions conducive to the growth of democracy in Andean South America, the drug control strategy of the United States ironically was contributing to institutional deterioration. What was needed, some U.S. policy makers correctly reasoned, was a strategy that looked at the drug problem in the longer term, a strategy that over time could be integrated into other central aspects of hemispheric relations.[10]

As mentioned, the Andean strategy did not emerge all at once after the Tranquilandia and Blast Furnace raids. Instead, U.S. officials designed and began implementing a plan they designated "Operation Snowcap," an elaborately conceived multinational effort to halt the export of cocaine from South America. Snowcap was beset, however, by a series of debilitating problems almost from its very inception in April 1987. The operation was overly ambitious from the outset in assuming that twelve South American nations viewed the cocaine problem with a comparable degree of seriousness, let alone from an angle of vision similar to that of the United States. Even more telling, the lines of operational authority for Snowcap were far clearer on paper than in practice. How, for instance, did DEA and INM divide responsibilities and apportion the myriad of tasks associated with Snowcap? What role would the U.S. military play when Snowcap was activated? What funding was available for Snowcap, and which agency would control the expenditure of funds? Furthermore, did Andean leaders share the enthusiasm of the White House for the inevitable paramilitary operations that would be conducted on their soil?[11] No official in the Reagan administration could respond to these concerns with a high degree of certainty as critical evaluations of the program later demonstrated.

That Operation Snowcap ultimately was applied to only three nations (Bolivia, Ecuador, and Peru) indicated that its original objectives were overly optimistic and that its basic problems were fundamentally structural in nature. It was one thing for U.S. officials to encourage Andean governments to use their best endeavors to curb illicit coca growth, to prevent the refining of cocaine, and to regulate the import of precursor chemicals, but was quite another for U.S. personnel to participate in local law enforcement activities and even to engage in counterinsurgency operations. Moreover, it was highly offensive to governments, not just in the Andes but throughout Latin America, for the White House and the State Department to certify how well these putative client states, if that is not an inelegant characterization, were meeting objectives more or less established by the United States. Policy makers in Washington argued that this extensive level of involvement in the internal affairs of especially Bolivia and Peru was crucial for the success of Snowcap. David L. Westrate, assistant administrator for operations of the DEA, was notably forthcoming in that regard.

The real problem was that U.S. authorities meant something quite different than their Andean counterparts when they spoke of institution building. To policy makers in the DEA and at INM, institution building under Snowcap referred not so much to the durability of political institutions in the

Andes but rather to the enhancement of law enforcement capabilities so far as coca and cocaine controls were concerned.[12] It remained unclear, though, whether support from Washington for the gradual process of democratization should precede or follow the realization of effective controls. Whatever its shortcomings, Snowcap exists in late 1992 as a component of U.S. anticoca efforts, even while remaining dwarfed by the focus of the Bush administration on its Andean drug strategy.[13] Operation Snowcap was thus overrun, it seems, both by events and by the need for a more visible response to the Andean cocaine trade. As President-elect Bill Clinton prepared to take office, the fate of U.S. drug policy remained uncertain.

U.S. Narcotics Control Policy in Historical Perspective

The evolution of U.S. narcotics control policy into the quasi-military approach that marked the Andean strategy cannot be explained solely with reference to developments in the 1980s. Only a much longer perspective can provide clear understanding. Bush's strategy must, therefore, be seen in the broadest possible context, one that incorporates historical, programmatic, and conceptual factors. To comprehend the origins of the Andean strategy is to know something about the place of Bolivia, Peru, and, to a lesser extent, Colombia in the history of drug control in the Americas. At the same time, a knowledge of past efforts to control coca — or other drugs — is not sufficient for a full understanding of Bush's strategy. As we shall see, other aspects of U.S.-Latin American relations, in general, have an explanatory role to play as well.

To begin, since the first world antiopium conference, held at The Hague in 1911-1912, the United States has encouraged other nations to adopt antinarcotics policies of strict control at the source. In the Andes this naturally meant limits on coca leaf production, particularly on the part of Peru, at that time the world's leading exporter of coca leaves. Yet Bolivia and Peru were reluctant to enforce any international antidrug agreement because of the negative effects of controls on their respective economies. Officials in the two countries suspected, with some justification, that adherence to a broad treaty would ultimately serve to undermine their licit domestic coca markets.[14] This interpretation of global antidrug conventions did not change substantially in Lima or La Paz for more than seventy years.

Control at the source, as advocated by the United States, was a deceptively simple approach to drug control. The basic assumption was that if the few identifiable producers of raw materials could be persuaded to curtail production, then the international drug problem would virtually disappear. But with the world capitalist economy built upon a foundation of supply and demand, commodities that in one culture served a licit ceremonial purpose might well serve less acceptable purposes elsewhere. Hence, demand for coca's chief by-product, cocaine, fostered the growth of one aspect of the illegal drug business. Control at the source never became the answer to international drug problems because U.S. policy makers essentially saw it in isolation from the greater social and political context in which, in this case, coca leaves were cultivated and marketed. As early as 1924, drug-producing nations, already on the defensive at international gatherings, warned that production controls would be impossible unless these source countries received what is now termed development assistance.[15] Putting their own citizens at risk, proponents of controls on opium and coca, the substances basic to the maintenance of an effective drug control regime, have long ignored such warnings from producer states.

For a number of reasons, reducing coca production in the Andes did not become a central theme in U.S. narcotics foreign policy until fairly recently. First of all, the use of cocaine declined sometime after the First World War and did not enjoy a significant revival until the 1950s. Even then, the extent of usage greatly paled in comparison to the perceived cocaine epidemic of the late 1970s and 1980s.[16] Furthermore, opiates, more than any other narcotic substance, captured the attention of the global antidrug movement between the two world wars. Drug restrictionists focused on the huge market in China for morphine, heroin, and smoking opium — whether of domestic or foreign origin. Of considerable, if not comparable, concern for U.S. narcotics control officials at both the Department of State and the Federal Bureau of Narcotics (FBN), one of the DEA's predecessor agencies, was the drug traffic across the border with Mexico.[17] Mexico served as both a major source- and transit-country for all kinds of drugs destined for the United States. And in Central America, the situation in Honduras concerned U.S. officials, who watched, as they also were doing in China, drugs play a significant role in national politics. The barter of drugs for guns nearly helped topple from power the legitimate Honduran government.[18]

Authorities in Bolivia and Peru never seriously considered restricting coca production in the 1930s despite some public interest in the adoption of controls. Debates were conducted at a low level about the effects of coca chewing, or *el coqueo,* upon traditional users of coca *(coqueros).* In Peru, corruption in the Bureau of Health reportedly cut short incipient discussions about controls. And in Bolivia, in something of a prologue to more modern developments, an organization of growers in the coca-rich Yungas region solidly opposed the imposition of restrictions on coca cultivaton.[19] The influential Peruvian newspaper, *El Comercio,* became an especially strong advocate of controlling coca but acknowledged that little could be accomplished in that regard until alternative crops were produced with access to a stable market.[20] This same consideration, a persistent theme in current debates over drug control, was raised in Bolivia where extensive discussions about the efficacy of el coqueo concluded that the chewing of coca leaves, a long-entrenched custom, was a relatively harmless activity for the habitual coquero.[21]

Of greater importance for present purposes is to determine why the United States did not put greater pressure on Bolivia or Peru to adopt a program of control at the source. Although the answer to this question must necessarily remain speculative for lack of conclusive evidence, one plausible hypothesis reveals a great deal about the intermittent nature of coca control as a foreign policy priority. In short, there existed little public demand in the United States, or for that matter in Europe, for rigid controls on coca; hence, little could be gained politically from holding either nation to strict accountability.

It is also necessary to consider reasons unrelated to drugs. Concern in the United States by the late 1930s about hemispheric security in the face of a mounting Axis threat far outweighed the importance given to illicit cocaine traffic. The December 1938 Declaration of Lima promised consultation in hemispheric affairs and thus held out the prospect of reciprocity in future inter-American relations.[22]

Seen in that perspective, undue pressure to control the growing of coca could have undermined stability in the region as European nations edged closer to war. As was the case at other times and in other places, U.S. drug control officials accepted the limits of what they could accomplish given other, overriding security concerns.[23] This deference to arguably more compelling foreign policy objectives would be far less constraining in the 1980s and early 1990s when U.S. security was increasingly linked to the overplanting of coca bushes in the Andes.

Cocaine use alone, no matter how extensive in the United States, could never have become a sufficient reason to turn the quest for coca control into a foreign policy issue of major importance. Yet usage, let alone abuse, when considered in combination with other, unrelated factors of greater magnitude for U.S. policy makers, could and did transform control of coca and cocaine into a national security matter. Yet for such a development to transpire, policy makers had to incorporate drug control into the general spectrum of security concerns and then link, over time, the promotion of controls on coca with broader issues in inter-American relations.

The first task, joining drug control and security policy, had been accomplished as early as July 1937 with the outbreak of the Sino-Japanese war.[24] By the time the United States became involved in the Second World War, narcotics were deemed to be an important strategic commodity that ought to be kept out of the hands of the Axis powers as a matter of policy. The head of the FBN, Harry J. Anslinger, formerly a consular official in the State Department, worked assiduously to accomplish that goal.[25] Anslinger's particular genius for management, manifested during his thirty-two years as commissioner, enabled him to play well the bureaucratic game in Washington.[26] As a result, he acquired for the FBN by 1950 a minor but important role in the operations of the new national security state. By the time he retired from his post in 1962, he had all but guaranteed that the FBN and its successor agencies would be included as appropriate in the making and implementation of national security policy.[27]

Linking coca and cocaine control with previously unrelated issues in inter-American relations would not be accomplished as easily or as quickly. Nonetheless, such an effort was begun in the 1940s. During the Second World War, Peru supplied cocaine for medical needs to the Allies under the Lend-Lease program. The government in Lima also acted at that time to curtail the illegal traffic in cocaine and agreed, after consultation with U.S. officials, to restrict the incipient cultivation of opium poppies despite appeals to the contrary by several Peruvian firms. After 1945, most international drug control activities came within the jurisdiction of the Commission on Narcotic Drugs (CND) of the United Nations. The United States resumed, at that forum and in bilateral relations, its earlier effort to bring about control at the source in the Andes.[28]

Helpful as well in creating a climate in which coca control could be discussed in Peru was the National Institute of Andean Biology. Established in 1940, the institute was empowered to investigate the effects of el coqueo on habitual chewers. The task would be a daunting one; throughout the Andes, el coqueo was apparently on the rise in the 1940s. A reassessment of the role of coca in society was not out of the question by the end of the decade, however. In 1947 there appeared a study by two Peruvian experts on coca, *Estudios Sobre La Coca y La Cocaina en el Perú,* which posited that scientific evidence did not support the idea that coca was indispensable to the well-being of the traditional coquero.[29] Armed with this information and also bolstered by the apparent willingness of Peru to study the effects of el coqueo, the CND sent a Commission of Inquiry on the Coca Leaf to Bolivia and Peru in 1949, but the results of the inquiry were inconclusive and disappointed U.S. authorities. Significantly, Andean officials — most notably, Manual A. Odria in Peru — were not then prepared to enact the radical kind of social and economic reforms that would alter traditional reliance and dependency on coca leaves.[30]

The purpose of this overview has been to suggest that the efforts to identify coca controls with other U.S. interests in South America accomplished little from the late 1940s through the late 1970s. Indeed, Peru and Bolivia effectively ignored for some time the 1961 Single Convention on Narcotic Drugs, a major agreement which gathered previous global antidrug accords under one instrument. Indeed, the government of Bolivia failed to sign the Single Convention until 1975. Also, the domestic policies of Peru's Fernando Belaunde Terry in the mid-1960s scarcely augured well for placing limits on coca leaf cultivation. Hence, the creation in Peru in 1969 of a national coca monopoly, *Empresa Nacional de la Coca* (ENACO), did little to inspire confidence in Washington that actual controls on coca were at hand. U.S.

drug officials had long denounced drug monopolies as obstacles to control, which made ENACO suspect in their eyes — as had been the many opium-smoking monopolies their predecessors had encountered earlier in Asia. Meanwhile, Colombia began to play a much more prominent role in the international cocaine trade, and the traditional chewing of coca continued unabated in Bolivia.[31]

A Threat to Hemispheric Security?

How, then, were U.S. officials going to promote drug control in the Andes as a foreign policy priority? In order to do so, the production of cocaine would have to be perceived as a threat to the security of the United States, the producer nations, or both. Yet how, it must further be asked, could cocaine possibly undermine hemispheric security? Answering this question requires seeing the political economy of the cocaine business in a larger context. Understanding both U.S. policy toward Latin America throughout the cold war and recognizing the historic U.S. claim of hegemony in the hemisphere provides an appropriate framework.

It is no surprise that Latin America was not spared the ideological ardor of the cold war. After 1945, the United States had basically followed a two-pronged policy toward Latin America: opposition to the spread of communism and support for the growth of a free-market economy.[32] As needed, these twin pillars of U.S. policy have included the fashioning of economic development programs through both private and public investment and reliance on counterinsurgency tactics — about which more later — to overcome perceived threats to political stability from anticapitalist, Leftist revolutionaries. Political scientist D. Michael Shafer aptly noted in his important study, *Deadly Paradigms: The Failure of U.S. Counterinsurgency Policy*, that U.S. policy increasingly emphasized the interdependence of development and security.[33] Without such an explanatory context, it is not possible, for example, to understand U.S. tolerance of the Bolivian Revolution in 1952, the unrealistic expectations that shaped Washington's response to selective democratic reform in Colombia in the early 1960s, or U.S. alarm at the revolutionary military regime in Peru in the late 1960s and the 1970s.[34]

By 1969, U.S. policy makers realized that programs to control the traffic in illegal drugs could help maintain U.S. hegemony over Latin America.[35] Hence, Operation Intercept at the Mexican border served both domestic and foreign policy objectives of the administration of President Richard M. Nixon. Intercept enabled the White House to secure political control of the drug issue, which was commanding the attention of the public because of heroin addiction among U.S. soldiers returning from Indochina, and simultaneously to assert its authority in the hemisphere.[36] In due course, U.S. policy makers would employ the political and economic instability of the 1980s in the Andes to their advantage in inter-American relations, even if the extensive, illegal coca cultivation and the traffic in cocaine were only symptoms of that instability. They accomplished this feat programmatically by joining drug control assistance with the established practice of providing aid for military, police, or counterinsurgency forces.

On this latter point, additional information is in order. The Kennedy administration had raised counterrinsurgency policy to the level of doctrine. In doing so, the vigorous men of the New Frontier were merely building upon a tradition that reached back to pre-Revolutionary days, found considerable expression in the Indian wars of the nineteenth century, and then manifested itself abroad for the first time in the Philippines at the turn of the century. [37] Working on the assumption that the revolution of rising expectations could not fully be met, U.S. policy makers in the cold war shouldered the daunting burden of forcing demands for development and modernization into acceptable channels. In operational terms, this effort entailed, in part, the creation of the Office of Public Safety (OPS) in the Agency for International Development (AID), the extension of miliary assistance abroad in order to contain the spread of communism, and the establishment of the International Military and Education Training program (IMET) in an attempt to reshape the frequently negative attitudes of Third World military personnel toward development.[38]

The Andean nations of Bolivia, Colombia, and Peru received a significant portion of this development-cum-security funding. The Public Safety Program of OPS, which became the most notorious of these assistance programs, dispensed funds liberally for the purpose of enhancing local law enforcement capabilities.[39] This objective closely resembled the goal of U.S.-style institution building that would define Operation Snowcap some twenty-five years later. The United States also extended military assistance to each of the three countries under a variety of programs and trained under IMET several thousands of their military personnel in the first thirty years of the cold war.[40]

Providing this assistance set the stage, as Michael T. Klare has shown, for the extensive paramilitary aid that has dominated U.S. drug-control funding in Latin America since the early 1970s. Indeed, when the U.S. Congress denounced and abolished the Public Safety Program as of July 1, 1975, the International Narcotics Control (INC) program had already been in place for nearly four years. The Nixon administration designed INC as a means of going to the source of illicit drug production. Although Mexico at first benefitted the most from the program, Bolivia, Colombia, Peru, and Ecuador were no less vital to its ultimate success.[41]

INC programs failed to achieve desired results in South America in the late 1970s and early 1980s despite, for that time, extensive funding.[42] Funds appropriated for Colombia's antidrug program compared favorably with funding for Mexico. But as the commerce in marijuana and cocaine gradually turned into a multi-billion-dollar business, corruption among the drug police and the military and indecisiveness in Bogotá limited the effectiveness of U.S. aid. Similar problems compromised U.S. programs in Bolivia, Ecuador, and Peru, where the smuggling of coca paste and cocaine became highly organized. The presence in the Andes of DEA agents in a training capacity had little discernible impact on the illegal trade. Incipient local efforts to restrict coca cultivation were largely without effect; coca remained the most lucrative and, in some areas, the only cash crop. And as the global inflation of the late 1970s made both fiscal planning and reliance on monetary policy impossible, dependence on cocaine for foreign exchange coincided nicely with the large drug appetites of North Americans.

Officials in Washington, realizing that available resources were not sufficient for controlling coca and cocaine, were forced to reconsider their policy options. General Luis García Meza's cocaine coup in Bolivia on July 17, 1980, made that decision all the more necessary. INC programs, military assistance, and some AID projects directly related to coca control were subsequently put on hold or sharply curtailed throughout the Andes. INM, DEA, and other U.S. agencies, nevertheless, decided not to revise their traditional response to the drug problem. Turning once again to control at the source, as if it were some modern Holy Grail, the United States resumed assistance to Bolivia and Peru. By late 1983, both countries had established mobile narcotics enforcement units, known as UMOPAR (Unidad Movil de Patrullaje Rural). The Bolivian government of Hernán Siles Zuazo signed in August 1983 a series of coca control agreements with the Department of State, whereas Peru accepted U.S. financing for a coca eradication project, known as CORAH (Control y Reduccíon de Cultivos de Coca en el Alto Huallaga).

Needless to say, these anticoca efforts generated great opposition among peasants whose livelihood, usually for want of an alternative, depended upon coca. In Colombia, too, INM was insisting upon the use of force as an appropriate response to the cocaine traffic out of Medellín and Cali. In short order, the drug war had become a hot war — Low Intensity Conflict as it was designated in the United States — and a highly controversial issue in hemispheric relations, symbolized by the Tranquilandia raid, Operation Blast Furnace, and Operation Condor Six in Peru — all of which were immediate antecedents of Operation Snowcap and Bush's Andean drug strategy.[43]

What had taken place, therefore, in the mid-1980s was the nexus of development programs, however inadequately funded they may have been, and security policy. Indicative of this linkage was the suspension in mid-1985 of military and economic aid to Bolivia for lack of progress in controlling the planting of coca bushes. Narcotics control finally had become a foreign policy priority for the United States, or so the White House wanted the public to believe.[44] As discussed earlier, Reagan gave meaning to the union of development and security in April 1986 when he declared cocaine to be a security threat to the Americas. For the Reagan administration, it, therefore, logically followed that what threatened security and development programs could eventually undermine U.S. hegemony.

Maintaining Hegemony

The preceding narrative and analysis of events inevitably raises the question: Was George Bush's Andean drug strategy essentially a device designed to maintain U.S. hegemony, where possible, in Latin America? To answer such a question as this in the affirmative is to suggest that U.S. drug policy was, at base, profoundly cynical and concerned less with drug control per se than with U.S. power and prestige. Unfortunately, the history of U.S. relations with Latin America, generally, and narcotics control strategy, specifically, indicates that such a conclusion may, indeed, be valid. Only if presently unavailable documentary evidence shows otherwise at some future date will the present analysis need revising.

Should any new evidence produce additional support for a critical analysis, then the following basic hypotheses about past and present drug control strategy and post-1945 U.S. relations with Latin America may well be further validated:

1. The Western Hemisphere was the one part of the world in the early 1990s where cold war assumptions about foreign policy under went the least revision. (U.S. policy in the Middle East transcends cold war assumptions in basic ways.)

2. Since 1945 U.S. policy makers operated on the belief that economic development and security policy were interdependent.

3. Following Operation Intercept in 1969, drug control increasingly became a major domestic and foreign policy issue in the Americas.

4. U.S. antidrug policy of control at the source, not to mention interdiction, remained predicated upon the belief that drug problems were primarily foreign in origin.

5. The poor record of drug control in the Americas was more indicative of a flawed U.S. strategy than a lack of political will in producer nations.

6. Because of conceptual or structural problems with their strategy, U.S. officials needed an identifiable adversary in order to justify the continuation of unproductive policies.

7. Linking drug control and hemispheric security precluded indefinitely a thorough revision of U.S. drug control strategy.

8. Imposing a security framework on the politics of drug control contributed to political and economic instability in the Andes.

9. Bolivia, Colombia, and Peru tacitly accepted instability as the difficult short-term price in exchange for possible future reciprocity over drug policy and other matters of mutual concern with the United States.

Thus, it was not surprising that the drug summit at Cartagena validated the Andean drug strategy and presented no challenge to U.S. leadership in the war on drugs. Yet the ostensible promise of reciprocity contained in the Cartagena Declaration turned out to be an illusion. Neither President Bush nor Secretary of State James A. Baker III, who said all the right things at Cartagena and after about the need to curb domestic demand for drugs, went so far as did President Franklin D. Roosevelt in January 1940, when he said to reporters about Latin Americans: "Give them a share. They think they're just as good as we are, and many of them are."[45] The share, if that is the right word for it, that U.S. policy makers offered to Andean leaders following Cartagena resembled old wine in old bottles. Assistance was selective, not always appropriate, and generally offered with a carrot-and-stick approach.[46]

What is worse, if that is possible, is that an historical perspective on the Andean strategy suggests that more of the same might be forthcoming before the dire need for substantive change is taken seriously in Washington. More than an appreciation of the history of drug control in the Andes and a knowledge of U.S. economic and military aid programs as applied to drug control are involved. The very conceptual framework of U.S. drug control policy has traditionally served Washington's quest for power and prestige in the Americas. That is, except in the cases of Japan in the 1930s and the People's Republic of China in the 1950s, U.S. officials could assume that those nations most in thrall to illicit drugs were disposed to adopt control policies similar to those of the United States but were prevented from doing so by circumstances largely beyond their control.[47]

Attributing benign intentions to producer nations began to change dramatically in the late 1960s, however, as drugs flowed freely into the United States from Mexico, and Bolivia and Peru failed to put into effect the 1961 Single Convention. From the late 1970s through the mid-1980s, U.S. policy makers acted on the assumption that commitments to effective drug control on the part of producer and processing nations were, at length, disingenuous. In order, therefore, to deal with the drug scourge in the United States, the Reagan administration, mindful of both congressional pressure and the domestic political benefits that a tough stand against drugs would bring, reasserted Washington's authority in hemispheric affairs by equating drugs and security.[48]

Put more bluntly, the existing linkage between development and security gave the Andean countries scant room for maneuver in American narcopolitics. To receive U.S. economic assistance, ultimately, was to accept the Andean drug strategy. Although its various limitations were transparent, and perhaps dangerous to democratic institution building, the Bush administration's drug strategy could not be rejected out of hand without jeopardizing far more vital interests throughout the Andes. The Andean drug strategy, viewed in historical perspective, ought to come under reconsideration in the early months of Bill Clinton's presidency.

Notes

1. U.S. Congress. House of Representatives, Committee on Government Operations, *Thirty-Eighth Report by the Committee on Government Operations,* "United States Anti-narcotics Activities in the Andean Region," 101 Cong., 2nd sess., November 3, 1990 (Washington, D.C.: Government Printing Office, 1990); see also *Thirteenth Report by the Committee on Government Operations,* "Stopping the Flood of Cocaine with Operation Snowcap: Is it Working?," 101 Cong., 2nd sess., August 14, 1990 (Washington, D.C.: Government Printing Office, 1990); U.S. Department of State, Office of Inspector General, *Report of Audit: International Narcotics Control Programs in Peru and Bolivia,* Memorandum No. 9CI-007, March 1989; and Bruce M. Bagley, "Myths of Militarization: Enlisting Armed Forces in the War on Drugs," in *Drug Policy in the Americas,* ed. Peter H. Smith, (Boulder, Colo.: Westview Press, 1992), 129-50.

2. U.S. General Accounting Office, *Drug War: Observations on Counternarcotics Aid to Colombia,* GAO/NSIAD-91-296 (Washington, D.C.: Government Printing Office, September 1991); see also *Drug War: U.S. Programs in Peru Face Serious Obstacles,* GAO/NSIAD-92-36 (Washington, D.C.: Government Printing Office, October 1991); U.S. Department of State, Office of Inspector General, *Report of Audit: Drug Control Activities in Bolivia,* Memorandum No. 2-CI-001, October 1991; U.S. General Accounting Office, *The Drug War: Counternarcotics Programs in Colombia and Peru:* "Statement of Joseph E. Kelley, Director, Security and International Relations Issues, National Security and International Affairs Division before the Subcommittee on Terrorism, Narcotics and International Operations, Committee on Foreign Relations, U.S. Senate," GAO/T-NSIAD-92-9, February 20, 1992 (copy in author's possession).

3. Government Operations Committee, "United States Anti-narcotics Activities in the Andean Region," 1-3.

4. Government Operations Committee, "United States Anti-narcotics Activities in the Andean Region," 3-10; William O. Walker III, *Drug Control in the Americas,* rev. ed. (Albuquerque: University of New Mexico Press, 1989), 204-13; Kevin Healy, "Coca, the State, and the Peasantry in Bolivia, 1982-1988," *Journal of Interamerican Studies and World Affairs* 30 (Summer/Fall 1988): 105-26; Cynthia McClintock, "The War on Drugs: The Peruvian Case," *Journal of Interamerican Studies and World Affairs* 30 (Summer/Fall 1988): 127-42; Juan Gabriel Tokatlían, "*Seguridad y drogas: su significado en las relaciones entre Colombia y Estados Unidos,* in *Economia y Politica del Narcotrafico,* eds. Juan Gabriel Tokatlián and Bruce Michael Bagley (Bogotá: CEREC, 1990); and Marc W. Chernick, "The Drug War," *NACLA: Report on the Americas* 23 (April 1990): 30-38, 40.

5. During and in the wake of the Persian Gulf War, coverage in U.S. newspapers of drug-related difficulties in the Andes declined; yet it was evident that prior patterns in U.S.-Andean narcotic relations persisted with little discernible change. For Peru, see *New York Times,* January 14, 1991, A2; *Washington Post,* January 24, 1991, A15; *New York Times,* February 27, 1991, A12; *Washington Post,* March 2, 1991, A8; and *New York Times,* June 19, 1991, A7. For Bolivia, see *Washington Post,* April 23, 1991, A10; *Washington Post,* April 27, 1991, A12; *Washington Post,* May 7, 1991, A24; *Washington*

Post, May 19, 1991, A28; and *Washington Post,* June 9, 1991, A31. For Colombia, see *New York Times,* January 13, 1991, 5; *Washington Post,* January 26, 1991, A10; *New York Times,* February 27, 1991, A9; and *New York Times,* June 20, 1991, A1, A4 on Escobar's surrender. For a critical analysis of U.S. policy by journalist Douglas Farah, based in Bogotá, see *Washington Post,* February 24, 1991, B2.

6. U.S. Congress. House of Representatives, *Annual Report for the Year 1981 of the Select Committee on Narcotics Abuse and Control,* 97 Cong. 1st sess. (Washington, D.C.: Government Printing Office, 1982); U.S. Congress. House of Representatives, *Hearing before the Committee on Foreign Affairs,* "The Role of the Military in Narcotics Control Overseas," 99 Cong. 2nd sess., August 5, 1986 (Washington, D.C.: Government Printing Office, 1986). See also Bagley, "Myths of Militarization."

7. Walker, *Drug Control in the Americas,* 221-22; Walker, "U.S. Drug Control Policy and Drug Trafficking in the Americas: An Unwitting Alliance," Paper: American Society of Criminology Annual Meeting, Reno, Nevada, November 1989. For an assessment of INM's air wing in Mexico, see U.S. General Accounting Office, *Drug Control: U.S.-Mexico Opium and Marijuana Aerial Eradication Program,* GAO-NSIAD-88-73 (Washington, D.C.: Government Printing Office, January 1988).

8. Walker, *Drug Control in the Americas,* 199-201, 203, 207. On Operation Blast Furnace, see also Michael H. Abbott, "The Army and the Drug War: Politics or National Security?," *Parameters* 18 (December 1988): 95-112. Abbott argues that Blast Furnace did not necessarily follow directly from Reagan's National Security Decision Directive. Yet, there was an important convergence of operations and thinking about security that well served future policy purposes. See also Lt. Col. Sewall H. Menzel, U.S. Army Ret., "Operation Blast Furnace," *Army* 39 (November 1989): 24-32.

9. Walker, *Drug Control in the Americas,* 211.

10. See the comments about the need for economic assistance to producer nations as an element of U.S. antidrug aid by then-Deputy Assistant Secretary of State for Inter-American Affairs Michael Skol in *Washington Post,* June 8, 1989, A4. See also U.S. Congress. House of Representatives, *Hearing before the Committee on Foreign Affairs,* "Operation Snowcap: Past, Present, and Future," 101 Cong., 2nd sess., May 23, 1990 (Washington, D.C.: Government Printing Office, 1990), 53.

11. For a probing review of Operation Snowcap, see Foreign Affairs Committee, "Operation Snowcap."

12. U.S. Congress, 1990, *Thirteenth Report by the Committee on Government Operations,* "Stoping the Flood of Cocaine with Operation Snowcap. Is It Working?" August 14.

13. For evidence that the Andean strategy has replaced Operation Snowcap as the centerpiece of the Bush administration's anticocaine effort in South America, see *Washington Post,* June 13, 1990, A35.

14. Walker, *Drug Control in the Americas,* 20-22.

15. Walker, 50-51. Especially prescient were the comments of Arturo Pinto-Escalier, Bolivia's delegate to the Second Geneva Opium Conference of 1924-1925.

16. The best-known exponent of a cyclical theory of drug use is David F. Musto, M.D. His *The American Disease: Origins of Narcotic Control,* expanded ed. (New York:

Oxford University Press, 1987) remains the seminal study on drug usage and control in the United States. It does Musto's pioneering scholarship no disservice to suggest that a spiral metaphor may be more precise in explaining patterns of drug use.

17. On narcotics in China, see William O. Walker III, *Opium and Foreign Policy: The Anglo-American Search for Order in Asia, 1912-1954* (Chapel Hill: University of North Carolina Press, 1991), Chap. 2-6; Walker, *Drug Control in the Americas*, Chap. 6. The Federal Bureau of Narcotics was created in 1930.

18. Walker, *Drug Control in the Americas*, 86-92, 140-51; Walker, *Opium and Foreign Policy*, 62-132.

19. Walker, *Drug Control in the Americas*, 92-93, 138-39.

20. *El Comercio* (Lima), December 17, 1937.

21. Walker, *Drug Control in the Americas*, 136-37, 139.

22. Walker, *Drug Control ...*, 138-39; Irwin F. Gellman, *Good Neighbor Diplomacy: United States Policies in Latin America* (Baltimore: Johns Hopkins University Press, 1979), 74-80.

23. In deferring their own policy objectives to other ostensibly more important foreign or security policy goals, U.S. drug officials established a precedent that they and their successors would follow in areas as diverse as Iran, French Indochina, the Golden Triangle of Southeast Asia, Afghanistan, and Central America. See note 44 below for citations concerning specific instances of this kind of behavior.

24. Walker, *Opium and Foreign Policy*, 109-31.

25. Walker, *Opium...*, 132-53; Douglas Clark Kinder and William O. Walker III, "Stable Force in a Storm: Harry J. Anslinger and United States Narcotic Foreign Policy, 1930-1962," *Journal of American History* 72 (March 1986): 915-16, 919-21.

26. Douglas Clark Kinder, "Bureaucratic Cold Warrior: Harry J. Anslinger and Illicit Narcotics Traffic," *Pacific Historical Review* 50 (May 1981): 169-91; John C. McWilliams, *The Protectors: Harry J. Anslinger and the Federal Bureau of Narcotics, 1930-1962* (Newark: University of Delaware Press, 1990).

27. McWilliams, *The Protectors*, Chap. 7; Walker, *Opium...*, Chaps. 8 and 9; and Kinder, "Bureaucratic Cold Warrior."

28. Walker, *Drug Control ...*, 156-61.

29. Walker, *Drug Control...*, 137, 156, 175-76; Carlos Gutiérrez-Noriega and Vicente Zapata Ortiz, *Estudios Sobre La Coca y La Cocaina en el Perú* (Lima: Ministerio de Educacíon Pública, 1947).

30. Walker, *Drug Control...*, 177, 189-90; Thomas E. Skidmore and Peter H. Smith, *Modern Latin America*, 2nd ed. (New York: Oxford University Press, 1989), 206-7.

31. Walker, *Drug Control*, 190, 195-97; Walker, *Opium and Foreign Policy*.

32. David Green, *The Containment of Latin America: A History of the Myths and Realities of the Good Neighbor Policy* (Chicago: Quadrangle Books, 1971), 255-90; and Roger Trask, "The Impact of the Cold War on United States-Latin American Relations,

1945-1949," *Diplomatic History* 1 (Summer 1977): 271-84. See in general, Skidmore and Smith, *Modern Latin America*, 348-71; Stephen G. Rabe, *Eisenhower and Latin America: The Foreign Policy of Anticommunism* (Chapel Hill: University of North Carolina Press, 1988), 16-25, 63-68, 77-83, 126; and Jerome Levinson and Juan de Onís, *The Alliance That Lost Its Way: A Critical Report on the Alliance for Progress* (Chicago: Quadrangle Press, 1970).

33. D. Michael Shafer, *Deadly Paradigms: The Failure of U.S. Counterinsurgency Policy* (Princeton: Princeton University Press, 1988), 79.

34. Rabe, *Eisenhower and Latin America*, 126; Levinson and de Onís, *The Alliance That Lost Its Way*, 204, 207, 239-42; John Sheahan, "Economic Forces and U.S. Policies," in *Exporting Democracy: The United States and Latin America*, ed. Abraham F. Lowenthal (Baltimore: Johns Hopkins University Press, 1991), vol. II: *Case Studies*, 219-20; Skidmore and Smith, *Modern Latin America*, 209-13.

35. On hegemony, see Guy Poitras, *The Ordeal of Hegemony: The United States and Latin America* (Boulder, Colo.: Westview Press, 1990); and in general, Robert O. Keohane, *After Hegemony: Cooperation and Discord in the World Political Economy* (Princeton: Princeton University Press, 1984).

36. Edward Jay Epstein, *Agency of Fear: Opiates and Political Power in America* (New York: G.P. Putnam's Sons, 1977), 81-85; Walker, *Drug Control...*, 192, 202; Richard B. Craig, "Operation Intercept: The International Politics of Pressure," Paper: Organization of American Historians Convention, Atlanta, Georgia, April 1977.

37. The present analysis draws upon the classic study by Richard S. Slotkin, *Regeneration Through Violence: The Mythology of the American Frontier, 1600-1860* (Middletown: Wesleyan University Press, 1973).

38. Shafer, *Deadly Paradigms*, 79-96.

39. On the Public Safety Program generally, see A.J. Langguth, *Hidden Terrors: The Truth about U.S. Police Operations in Latin America* (New York: Pantheon Books, 1978). Specifically, see Michael T. Klare, *Supplying Repression: U.S. Support for Authoritarian Regimes Abroad* (Washington, D.C.: Institute for Policy Studies, 1977), 7-25.

40. Klare, *Supplying Repression*, 31-32, 36, 40, 44.

41. For more on aid to Mexico, see Walker, *Drug Control...*, 192-95; Richard B. Craig, "La Campaña Permanente: Mexico's Antidrug Campaign," *Journal of Interamerican Studies and World Affairs* 20 (May 1978): 107-31. On the INC program itself, see Klare, *Supplying Repression*, 25-30.

42. The following account of the late 1970s and early 1980s is largely taken from Walker, *Drug Control...*, 193-203, 205-13.

43. Walker, *Drug Control....* See also Rensselaer W. Lee III, *The White Labyrinth: Cocaine and Political Power* (New Brunswick, N.J.: Transaction Publishers, 1989); Edmundo Morales, *Cocaine: White Gold Rush in Peru* (Tucson: University of Arizona Press, 1989).

44. Although the extent to which drug control has become a foreign policy priority for the United States remains unclear, it is safe to say that larger security interests no longer eclipse entirely the objective of drug control. For more on the

unequal relationship between security policy and antidrug activities in Iran, in Southeast Asia and the Golden Triangle, in Afghanistan, and in Central America, see Walker and Kinder, "Stable Force in a Storm," 923, note 45; Walker, *Opium and Foreign Policy*, Chap. 9; Alfred W. McCoy, *The Politics of Heroin: CIA Complicity in the Global Drug Trade* (Brooklyn: Lawrence Hill Books, 1991) [McCoy's book is a greatly revised and expanded edition of his classic study, *The Politics of Heroin in Southeast Asia* (New York: Harper & Row, 1972, 1973)]; and Peter Dale Scott and Jonathan Marshall, *Cocaine Politics: Drugs, Armies and the CIA in Central America* (Berkeley and Los Angeles: University of California Press, 1991).

45. Quoted in David Green, "The Cold War Comes to Latin America," in *Politics and Policies of the Truman Administration,* ed. Barton J. Bernstein (Chicago: Quadrangle Books, 1970), 151-52.

46. See note 5 above. And see *New York Times*, January 27, 1991, 12, on the Andean drug trade and Ecuador. See also Bruce Michael Bagley, "After San Antonio," *Journal of Interamerican Studies and World Affairs* 34 (Fall 1992): 1-12.

47. For more on the conceptual framework behind U.S. drug policy, see William O. Walker III, "Decision-making Theory and Narcotic Foreign Policy: Implications for Historical Analysis," *Diplomatic History* 15 (Winter 1991): 31-45.

48. Walker, *Drug Control...*, 203-16, 220-23; Bruce Michael Bagley, "U.S. Foreign Policy and the War on Drugs: Analysis of a Policy Failure," *Journal of Interamerican Studies and World Affairs* 30 (Summer/Fall 1988): 189-212.

References

Abbott, Michael H. 1988. "The Army and the Drug War: Politics or National Security?" *Parameters* December: 95-112.

Bagley, Bruce M. 1992a. "Myths of Militarization: Enlisting Armed Forces in the War on Drugs." In *Drug Policy in the Americas,* ed. Peter Smith. Boulder, Colo.: Westview Press.

Bagley, Bruce M. 1992b. "After San Antonio." *Journal of Interamerican Studies and World Affairs* 34(3): 1-12.

Bagley, Bruce M. 1988. "U.S. Foreign Policy and the War on Drugs: Analysis of a Policy Failure." *Journal of Interamerican Studies and World Affairs* 30(2-3): 189-212.

Chernick, Marc W. 1990. "The Drug War." *NACLA: Report on the Americas.* April.

Craig, Richard B. 1977. "Operation Intercept: The International Politics of Pressure." Paper presented at the Organization of American Historians Convention, Atlanta, Georgia, April.

Craig, Richard B. 1978. "La Campaña Permanente: Mexico's Antidrug Campaign." *Journal of Interamerican Studies and World Affairs* 20(2): 107-131.

Epstein, Edward Jay. 1977. *Agency of Fear: Opiates and Political Power in America.* New York: G.P. Putnam's Sons.

Gellman, Irwin F. 1979. *Good Neighbor Diplomacy: United States Policies in Latin America.* Baltimore: Johns Hopkins University Press.

Green, David. 1971. *The Containment of Latin America: A History of Myths and Realities of the Good Neighbor Policy.* Chicago: Quadrangle Books.

Green, David. 1970. "The Cold War Comes to Latin America." In *Politics and Policies of the Truman Administration,* ed. Barton J. Bernstein. Chicago: Quadrangle Books.

Gutiérrez-Noriega, Carlos, and Vicente Zapata Ortiz. 1947. *Estudios Sobre la Coca y la Cocaina en el Peru.* Lima: Ministerio de Educacíon Pública.

Healy, Kevin. 1988. "Coca, The State, and the Peasantry in Bolivia, 1982-1988." *Journal of Interamerican Studies and World Affairs* 30(2-3): 105-26.

Keohane, Robert O. 1984. *After Hegemony: Cooperation and Discord in the World Political Economy.* Princeton, N.J.: Princeton University Press.

Kinder, David Clark. 1981. "Bureaucratic Cold Warrior: Harry J. Anslinger and Illicit Narcotics Traffic." *Pacific Historical Review.* May.

Kinder, David Clark, and William O. Walker III. 1986. "Stable Force in a Storm: Harry J. Anslinger and United States Narcotic Foreign Policy." *Journal of American History.* March.

Klare, Michael T. 1977. *Supplying Repression: U.S. Support for Authoritarian Regimes Abroad.* Washington, D.C.: Institute for Policy Studies.

Langguth, A.J. 1978. *Hidden Terrors: The Truth about U.S. Police Operations in Latin America.* New York: Pantheon Books.

Lee, Rensselaer W. III. 1989. *The White Labyrinth: Cocaine and Political Power*. New Brunswick, N.J.: Transaction Publishers.

Levinson, Jerome, and Juan de Onís. 1970. *The Alliance That Lost Its Way: A Critical Report on the Alliance for Progress*. Chicago: Quadrangle Press.

McClintock, Cynthia. 1988. "The War on Drugs: The Peruvian Case." *Journal of Interamerican Studies and World Affairs* 30(2-3): 127-42.

McCoy, Alfred W. 1991. *The Politics of Heroin: CIA Complicity in the Global Drug Trade*. Brooklyn: Lawrence Hill Books.

McWilliams, John C. 1990. *The Protectors: Harry J. Anslinger and the Federal Bureau of Narcotics, 1930-1962*. Newark, N.J.: University of Delaware Press.

Menzel, Lt. Col. Sewall H. 1989. "Operation Blast Furnace." *Army*. November: 24-32.

Morales, Edmundo. 1989. *Cocaine: White Gold Rush in Peru*. Tucson: University of Arizona Press.

Musto, David F. 1987. *The American Disease: Origins of Narcotic Control*. Expanded ed. New York: Oxford University Press.

Poitras, Guy. 1990. *The Ordeal of Hegemony: The United States and Latin America*. Boulder, Colo.: Westview Press.

Rabe, Stephen G. 1988. *Eisenhower and Latin America: The Foreign Policy of Anticommunism*. Chapel Hill: University of North Carolina Press.

Scott, Peter Dale, and Jonathan Marshall. 1991. *Cocaine Politics: Drugs, Armies, and the CIA in Central America*. Berkeley and Los Angeles: University of California Press.

Shafer, D. Michael. 1988. *Deadly Paradigms: The Failure of U.S. Counterinsurgency Policy*. Princeton, N.J.: Princeton University Press.

Sheahan, John. 1991. "Economic Forces and U.S. Policies." In *Exporting Democracy*, ed. Abraham F. Lowenthal. Baltimore: Johns Hopkins University Press.

Skidmore, Thomas E., and Peter H. Smith. 1989. *Modern Latin America*. New York: Oxford University Press.

Slotkin, Richard S. 1973. *Regeneration Through Violence: The Mythology of the American Frontier, 1600-1860*. Middletown: Wesleyan University Press.

Tokatlián, Juan Gabriel, and Bruce M. Bagley. 1990. *Economia y Politica del Narcotrafico*. Bogotá: CEREC.

Trask, Roger. 1977. "The Impact of the Cold War on United States-Latin American Relations, 1945-1949." *Diplomatic History*. Summer: 271-84.

U.S. Congress. House of Representatives. 1982. *Annual Report for the Year 1981 of the Select Committee on Narcotics Abuse and Control*. Washington, D.C.: GPO.

U.S. Congress. 1986. *Hearing Before the Committee on Foreign Affairs*. "The Role of the Military in Narcotics Control Overseas." August 5.

U.S. Congress. 1990. *Hearing Before the Committee on Foreign Affairs*. "Operation Snowcap: Past, Present, and Future." May 23.

U.S. Congress. House of Representatives, Committee on Government Operations. 1990. *Thirty-Eighth Report by the Committee on Government Operations*. "United States Anti-narcotics Activities in the Andean Region." November 30.

U.S. Congress. 1990. *Thirteenth Report by the Committee on Government Operations.* "Stopping the Flood of Cocaine with Operation Snowcap: Is It Working?" August 14.

U.S. Department of State, Office of Inspector General. 1991. *Report of Audit: International Narcotics Control Programs in Peru and Bolivia.* Memorandum no. 9CI-007. March.

U.S. Department of State, Office of Inspector General. 1991. *Report of Audit: Drug Control Activities in Bolivia.* Memorandum no. 2-CI-001. October.

U.S. General Accounting Office. 1991. *Drug War: Observations on Counternarcotics Aid to Colombia.* GAO/NSIAD-91-296. Washington, D.C.: Government Printing Office. September.

U.S. General Accounting Office. 1991. *Drug War: U.S. Programs in Peru Face Serious OBstacles.* GAO/NSIAD-92-36. Washington, D.C.: GPO. October.

U.S. General Accounting Office. 1992. *The Drug War: Counternarcotics Programs in Colombia and Peru.* GAO/T-NSIAD-92-9. February 20.

U.S. Government Accounting Office. 1988. *Drug Control: U.S.-Mexico Opium and Marijuana Aerial Eradication Program.* GAO-NSIAD-88-73. January.

Walker, William O., III. 1989. *Drug Control in the Americas.* Rev. ed. Albuquerque: University of New Mexico Press.

Walker, William O., III. 1989. "U.S. Drug Control Policy and Drug Trafficking in the Americas: An Unwitting Alliance." Paper presented at the annual meeting of the American Society of Criminology. Reno, Nevada. November.

Walker, William O., III. 1991. *Opium and Foreign Policy: The Anglo-American Search for Order in Asia, 1912-1954.* Chapel Hill: University of North Carolina Press.

Walker, William O., III. 1991. "Decision-making Theory and Narcotic Foreign Policy: Implications for Historical Analysis." *Diplomatic History* Winter: 31-45.

Chapter Two

U.S.-Andean Drug Policy

Raphael F. Perl

Background

Andean Initiative as Part of Emerging Overall Drug Strategy

In September 1989, President George Bush outlined a comprehensive, multifaceted drug control strategy with both national and international dimensions. The strategy focused on reducing both the demand and supply of illicit drugs through treatment, prevention/education, research, law enforcement, and international efforts. An important goal of the strategy was to reduce the amount of illicit drugs illegally entering the United States by 15 percent within two years and by 60 percent within ten years. The president refined the strategy and forwarded it to Congress on January 25, 1990 (US-ONDCP 1990, 49-52, 120-121). The following year, in February 1991, policy makers modified goals to a 20 percent reduction by 1993 and a 65 percent reduction by the year 2001 (US-ONDCP 1991, 15). In January 1992, predetermined fixed percentage reductions were eliminated and respective goals for 1994 and 2002 became "reduction below a (to-be-established) baseline level in estimated amounts of cocaine, marijuana, heroin, and dangerous drugs entering the United States..." (US-ONDCP 1992, 26).

The president's 1989 national drug control strategy contains a number of ongoing international elements which differed from those of preceding years. These international components 1) provide for limited antinarcotics-related economic assistance to major cocaine-producing countries, 2) concentrate more on disrupting the activities of trafficking organizations (i.e., on seizing processing labs, chemicals, and assets) rather than on crop eradication, 3) encourage increased levels of Andean nation military involvement in counternarcotics operations, and 4) provide for enhanced U.S. military support to the counternarcotics forces of the host nation. Coordination of international drug efforts among U.S. agencies and with foreign counterpart agencies also receives greater policy emphasis under the ongoing U.S. strategy.

President Bush's strategy focuses on "high value" traffickers, operations, and shipments; calls for improved drug intelligence support; seeks an improved command, control, and communications system for antidrug operations; and calls for increased funding of U.S. Department of Defense antidrug operations, primarily to interdict the flow of drugs across the southern U.S. border.

Elements of the Andean Strategy

A major component of the administration's drug strategy is the Andean strategy, estimated to cost US$2.2 billion for fiscal years 1990-1994 (FY 1990-FY 1994). The initiative is designed to help the major coca-growing, processing, and shipping nations — Bolivia, Colombia, and Peru — to reduce illicit drug activities. The U.S. strategy includes enhanced economic, military, and law enforcement assistance, in addition to preferential trade treatment for these countries. A broad spectrum of multilateral initiatives is included in the strategy as well.

Short-term goals of the strategy may be summarized as follows:

1. To help these three nations strengthen political and economic conditions and institutional capabilities in order to take effective action against trafficking organizations;

2. To assist these nations in increasing the effectiveness of their military and law enforcement establishments against the cocaine trade by supporting efforts to a) isolate major growing areas, b) destroy labs, and c) block delivery of precursor chemicals;

3. To damage trafficking organizations significantly by seizing key traffickers and their assets (US-ONDCP 1990, 50); and

4. To strengthen and diversify the legitimate economies of the Andean nations to enable them to overcome the destabilizing effects of eliminating cocaine (US-ONDCP 1991, 79).[1]

U.S. assistance provided pursuant to the Andean strategy is conditioned on drug-control performance and the existence of sound economic policies in the host countries. In the case of Peru, meeting specific human rights criteria is an added factor.

To implement the strategy, the U.S. government has relied on resources from numerous agencies, together with a combination of foreign aid, trade benefits, and investment initiatives. Lead actors include the Department of State's Bureau of International Narcotics Matters (INM), the Drug Enforcement Administration (DEA), and the Department of Defense. Secondary roles have been assigned the Border Patrol, the Coast Guard, and the Customs Service. Increasingly active and important roles are being performed by the Justice Department, the Treasury Department, and the intelligence agencies. As regional economic stability becomes a more frequently emphasized element of the strategy, the roles of the Agency for International Development (AID), the Office of the United States Trade Representative (USTR), and the Department of Commerce can be expected to intensify.

The administration's FY 1993 request for Andean strategy narcotics-related assistance would provide US$176.6 million to Bolivia, US$163.5 million to Peru, and US$138.6 million to Colombia — a total of US$478.7 million.[2] Of the assistance requested for FY 1993, some US$109.6 million is for law enforcement assistance and DEA support; US$110.6 million, for military assistance; and US$258.5 million, for economic assistance. Broken down, the military assistance requested for the 1993 fiscal year is roughly equal to that allotted for law enforcement assistance, and the combined amounts for these two types of assistance come to slightly less than that requested for economic assistance (see Appendix I).

Key to the economic elements of the initiative is the Andean Trade Preference Act.[3] The Act, proposed by President Bush in November 1989 and eventually passed, in a somewhat scaled-back form, by the Congress in November 1991, would reduce U.S. tariffs on an estimated US$325 millions-worth of imports from the Andean nations. Items subject to reduced rates include cut flowers, leather handbags, luggage, and vegetables. Items excluded from the Act by congressional action include llama and alpaca wool goods and rum. As a result of the Act, according to some reports, the dollar value of Andean exports to the United States is expected to increase more than threefold over the next decade. Despite positive benefits offered, some critics complain that the Act excludes key Andean products like tuna, sugar, shoes, textiles (including llama and alpaca wool), and petroleum from preferential access to U.S. markets and that it is not likely to lead to any rapid diversification away from the export of coca to more legitimate trade (Thurston 1992).

The Enterprise for the Americas Initiative (EAI) is another vehicle to be used to implement the strategy's economic objectives. The Enterprise seeks to promote debt relief, trade, and investment opportunities in the region. Framework agreements on trade and investment have been signed with the three Andean strategy nations and Ecuador as well (US-AID 1992, 3-4).[4]

Multilateral initiatives are an integral part of the strategy that seeks support of the European Community (EC) in efforts to reduce production of illicit drugs in source countries and their distribution through transit countries. Multilateral cooperation aimed at curbing both the laundering of drug money and shipments of precursor chemicals is also stressed (US-AID 1992, 49-62).

The multilateral approach was dramatized by the first Andean drug summit meeting held in Cartagena (Colombia) on February 15, 1990. At that meeting, U.S. President Bush discussed drug cooperation efforts with the presidents of Bolivia, Colombia, and Peru. In a communiqué, all the presidents pledged to cooperate with one another in a concerted attack on every aspect of the drug trade and to exchange information on the flows of both precursor chemicals and drug money. In the "Document of Cartagena," the parties agreed 1) to work to reduce demand, 2) to act within a framework that respects human rights, and 3) to work together to increase trade, development, and the marketing of new exports. The United States pledged its willingness to finance activities that would foster sound economic policies, including programs for alternative development and crop substitution. The United States also agreed to facilitate private investment in areas where economic conditions are favorable. The parties reaffirmed their will to bring about a net reduction in the cultivation of coca. Participants also signed side agreements designed to promote cooperation in law enforcement and the enhancement of public awareness both during and following the summit meeting. A follow-up Andean summit meeting was then tentatively scheduled to be held in San Antonio (Texas) in late February 1992, with additional invitations to be extended to Ecuador, Mexico, and Venezuela.

Evaluation of Strategy Progress and Effectiveness

Administration and other groups evaluating Andean strategy programs have come to differing conclusions. Some are encouraged by results achieved to date and optimistic over prospects for ongoing success; others suggest "start-up" has been slow but, now that implementation is in full swing, prospects for success are promising; yet still others maintain that the strategy has so far proved to be a failure and will continue so into the future. Analysts generally recognize that evaluating program efficiency and strategy effectiveness are not simple tasks.

Administration's First-Year Assessment

Despite lack of ability to demonstrate short-term success in reducing the amount of cocaine entering the United States by 15 percent in the last two years,[5] administration officials are encouraged by the results of the strategy thus far. For example, DEA statistics reveal record levels of cocaine seizures and destruction of labs (see Appendix II). On October 10, 1990, Assistant Secretary of State for International Narcotics Matters Melvyn Levitsky reviewed the first fiscal year of the Andean strategy and noted both areas of success and problem. Areas of success cited included the following:

1. Successful start-up: Executive branch agencies were brought together to develop implementation plans.

2. Enhanced commitment of new democratic governments in the three Andean nations to cooperate with U.S. counternarcotics objectives.

3. More U.S.-Andean coordinated focus on high-level targets and better use of intelligence to support these efforts.

4. Enhanced seizures and pressures on the trafficking organizations.

5. Dispersion of trafficker activity brought about by enhanced detection and monitoring by the U.S. military.

6. Initiation of efforts to give those involved in coca production viable economic alternatives.

Potential problem areas implied or identified included the following:

1. Concern that Congress, by earmarking economic assistance funds to "high-priority" recipients, may leave less funding for presidential discretionary allocation to counternarcotics programs.

2. Need to tailor U.S. programs in such a way that they do not adversely affect fragile social, economic, and political institutions of sovereign countries.

3. Need to improve the pace of laboratory destruction and cocaine seizures in host nations.

4. Need to develop new international mechanisms to address money laundering and precursor chemical flows.

5. Need for better programs to use seized assets and to deny traffickers the ability to exploit judicial loopholes which may exist in host nations that enable them to regain such assets.

6. Need to develop cooperative programs to deal with allegations of human rights violations and corruption (Levitsky 1990, 1-3).

Subsequent Assessments by Administration and Other Sources

As the Andean strategy entered its third year, three reports identifying problems and challenging aspects of its implementation were released: 1) a State Department Inspector General's report on U.S. drug control efforts in Bolivia (US-DS 1991), 2) a General Accounting Office (GAO) report on U.S. drug programs in Peru (US-GAO 1991a), and 3) a GAO report on U.S. counternarcotics assistance to Colombia (US-GAO 1991b).

The GAO report on Peru concluded that it is unlikely that U.S. counternarcotics strategy would be effective in Peru unless significant progress is made in overcoming serious obstacles. Obstacles, noted to be primarily beyond U.S. ability to control, include 1) difficulties in implementing government control over military and police units involved in counternarcotics operations, 2) extensive corruption, 3) lack of coordination between the military and police agencies of the host nation, 4) lack of control over airports, 5) political instability caused by insurgent groups, 6) an economy heavily dependent on coca leaf production, and 7) human rights violations committed by the military and police (US GAO 1991a, 4-6).

The State Department Inspector General's report dealing with Bolivia noted that, although the quality and quantity of U.S. counternarcotics assistance had been enhanced, there had not been a corresponding reduction of Bolivia's illicit drug industry, which supplies 35 percent of the world's cocaine. The report suggested that progress in reducing Bolivia's drug trade was a long-term task, requiring at least ten years. It noted that to implement such a program productively, however, two concerns must be addressed: 1) the political will and economic ability of the host country to implement drug control programs effectively and 2) long-standing fragmentation of, and coordination among, U.S. government agencies involved, particularly at the field level. The report noted that, at strong U.S. urging, the host nation

> has taken a number of concrete steps to combat drugs and corruption. Nevertheless, Bolivia's political will is questionable, as demonstrated by some recent appointments of corrupt officials to key drug control positions (US-DS 1991, 1-11).

The GAO report dealing with Colombia focused on program management and supported the viewpoint that both legislation and policy permit Colombia to use U.S. aid against both drug traffickers and insurgents involved in the drug trade. However, the report went on to note, "the necessary management oversight of U.S. aid was not in place. Without such oversight, there is no assurance that the aid is being used effectively and as intended." The report further noted,

> U.S. officials have not finalized plans for 1) designating how the aid should be used by military units, 2) monitoring how the military aid is used, and 3) evaluating the effectiveness of the aid in achieving counternarcotics objectives (US-GAO 1991b, 1-5).

Responding to these three reports, Assistant Secretary of State Levitsky noted, in his October 1991 testimony, that the GAO report on Colombia acknowledged dramatic accomplishments made against the traffickers in Colombia but that the other reports questioned the slow pace of accomplishments in Peru and Bolivia (Levitsky 1991). He stated that the overall counternarcotics situation in Peru was much improved over three years ago and that the report made only passing references to Peru's deathbed economy, violent insurgencies, human rights abuses by security forces, and an unwieldy, demoralized government bureaucracy. Despite such dismal obstacles, he argued that the new Alberto Fujimori government had made a considerable effort to 1) involve the military to support counternarcotics operations, 2) correct human rights problems, and 3) set the stage to provide alternative sources of income for coca farmers.

Moreover, he noted that, for the first time, after many years of rapidly expanding coca cultivation in Peru, the amount of area farmed had leveled off.[6] Levitsky questioned whether it was realistic for Congress to expect an economic program, much less a counternarcotics program, to succeed in Peru, if Congress withholds US$10 million in narcotics-related foreign military financing from the Peruvian army because of their human rights abuses.

In addressing the subject of Bolivia, Levitsky noted that, in less than two years since the Andean strategy had begun, and with U.S. assistance, the Bolivians had 1) regained effective control over the Chapare coca-growing region; 2) reduced the number of trafficking organizations, including the arrest of one major kingpin; 3) taken custody of seven major traffickers, utilizing a controversial decree which allowed traffickers to turn themselves in in exchange for reduced sentences and exemption from extradition; 4) achieved a net reduction in 1990 coca cultivation; and 5) removed corrupt officials.

In addressing the subject of Colombia, Levitsky focused on management techniques and end-use, performance-monitoring techniques for U.S. programs. On the policy level, he addressed the concern expressed by the State Department Inspector General's report that the Colombian government may not be using all its resources — particularly its military force — to the best effect in fighting the drug traffic. Levitsky stressed that 1991 cocaine and lab seizures were up, and not without significant Colombian government casualties in the drug war. Moreover, he noted that engagement of the Colombian military in the drug war was relatively recent and that, despite minimal seizures, complex multi-service raids had been conducted.

Levitsky's October 1991 testimony came in the wake of two earlier GAO reports that examined the status of the U.S. Defense Department's support in countering the drug traffic and the effect of that Department's detection, and monitoring, of cocaine flows. The latter of these two reports concluded that, among other things, the efforts of the Defense Department had not reduced the supply of drugs in any significant way and that it was unlikely that interdiction alone could make a difference, regardless of how well the Defense Department carries out its mission (US-GAO 1991c and 1991d). Such findings are reportedly supported by conclusions reached in an internal Pentagon document obtained by *Newsweek* magazine. According to *Newsweek*, the author of the report concluded that 1) the Andean strategy so far has "only marginally impacted on the narcotraffickers"; 2) Peru is such "a quagmire of deceit and corruption, [that] attainment of U.S. objectives is impossible"; 3) the flow of cocaine from Colombian processing centers has not been slowed; and 4) generally, antidrug aid to Latin America has been held up by congressional micro-managing and bureaucratic inertia (*Newsweek* 1992, 4).

Issues for Decision Makers

The Andean strategy poses a number of important issues for policy makers, including 1) overall soundness of strategy, 2) effectiveness of U.S. drug policy leadership, 3) adequacy of resources, 4) need for host nation cooperation, 5) danger of a single-issue foreign policy, and 6) criteria for evaluation of effectiveness.

Overall Soundness of Strategy

A key question raised by policy makers is whether or not the strategy can work; that is, will President Bush's proposed increases in aid (military, economic, law enforcement) provide the Andean nations with sufficient assistance to combat drug production and traffic? And, if so, would this have a favorable impact in the sense of reducing illegal drug use and drug-related crime in the United States?

Interdiction/law enforcement activity and economic diversification are cornerstones of the current strategy. Such policies aim at reducing the supply of illicit drugs available to the U.S. market. Proponents of the strategy strongly maintain that providing economic alternatives to growers and raising risks and costs to refiners, traffickers, and consumers will reduce the supply and use of cocaine in the U.S. marketplace. Proponents of the interdiction component, in particular, maintain that there can be no effective interdiction without host nation cooperation and that the overall strategy package is promoting such results: seizures are up, trafficking organizations are being disrupted, and assets are being targeted. Moreover, many believe that the power wielded by the trafficking organizations — via corruption, intimidation, and violence — poses a threat to the United States and other nations of such a magnitude that it warrants disruption of their criminal activities, independent of any effect that action may have on illicit drug use in the United States. Proponents also argue that it is unrealistic to expect the Andean countries — particularly, the more coca-dependent countries of Peru and Bolivia — to commit economic suicide by destroying a major source of foreign currency without some assistance to overcome the destabilizing effects of such action. In this context, economic aid is viewed as part of the price that must be paid to obtain the cooperation of host nations in implementing policies whose components may well provoke economically and politically disruptive fallout.

On the other hand, critics not only see drug production as expanding but also see interdiction as costly and, at best, able to seize only a small percentage of the illicit drugs entering the United States. They suggest that, given a best-case scenario, one in which illicit drug supplies to the United States were severely curtailed, users would simply pay more for their drugs or switch to substitute drugs. For these analysts, the sole utility of interdiction is that it may hold the line against such time that policy makers can put efficient demand reduction programs into effect within the United States. Consequently, they suggest buying time is the best that could be expected from the Andean initiative.

Some question whether it is realistic to assume that economic stabilization and diversification programs in the Andean nations, even if implemented successfully, can make any real inroads in reducing drug production, traffic, and use to more tolerable levels. Given years of economic assistance, for example, Peru might achieve economic levels equal to today's Mexico — a major producing/transit nation for illicit drugs. Given even more years of economic assistance, so the argument goes, Peru might then possibly achieve an economic level comparable to that of California, a major center for the production of, and traffic in, marijuana. Still others go even further to suggest that, in terms of economic aid, any amount given to Peru is a waste of money from the standpoint of being able to produce economic results due to Peru's apparent inability to institute meaningful reform in a context of overwhelming debt, bureaucratic inefficiency, corruption, and insurgency.

Effectiveness of U.S. Drug Policy Leadership

A second, ongoing question that faces those who oversee the implementation of U.S. drug policy remains: how effective is leadership and coordination of overall U.S. drug policy, and how does this impact on the Andean strategy?

Critics have repeatedly charged that, in effect, the drug war does not have a leader. In response to such charges, the U.S. Congress created the Office of National Drug Control Policy (ONDCP). Yet despite this move, criticism lingers, and there is still a considerable body of opinion that views the ONDCP as largely ineffective in carrying out its mandate to guide and coordinate the agencies and activities of the U.S. counterdrug community. This view holds that the office was doomed to failure from the very beginning, since it was designed primarily as a body to coordinate policy but without any real authority to command or enforce its will. It has also been suggested that the effectiveness of the ONDCP has been further undermined by frequent turnovers in personnel and a failure both to recruit and retain first-rate professional talent. An additional weakness is the apparent perception, on the part of the U.S. drug control bureaucracy, that the ONDCP does not receive presidential backing in its disputes with other federal agencies, thus undercutting any efforts it makes to direct policy even more (Gordon 1992; Biskupic 1992, 314). As a result, the Office of National Drug Control Policy is frequently blamed for what its critics see as two "lost" years in getting the Andean strategy under way, years wasted in cajoling other government actors to join in a common game plan, in the midst of interagency squabbles and bureaucratic delays.

Supporters of the Office of National Drug Control Policy, its activities, and leadership exercised so far maintain that the ONDCP has used its limited authority effectively and to the maximum extent possible. An ongoing, national, drug control strategy has been formulated and updated; the existing labyrinth of government agencies engaged in some aspect of drug control has been brought together and is "on board," and resources are now marshalled more effectively and targeted toward desired results — all commendable accomplishments for a relatively new, and small, government entity with limited authority, staff, and resources. Many who work with the ONDCP on a daily basis laud the high quality and professionalism of its staff and recommend that, if its responsibilities are increased, its authority and operating budget should be as well.

Adequacy of Resources

A third issue facing policy makers is the adequacy of resources. Are funding levels, equipment levels, or levels of U.S. direct involvement adequate to enable the Andean nations to combat the drug traffic and production to any significant degree? And are these levels sufficient to overcome the destabilizing economic effects which the elimination of coca may (will) have on their respective economies? The Andean strategy calls for US$2.2 billion to be disbursed, over a five-year period, for various types of assistance: military, law enforcement, and economic. Dwarfing such projected levels of aid are estimates, from various sources, that the illegal drug trade generates, on a worldwide basis, something in excess of US$300 billion per year in gross total revenues to criminal elements engaged in this business. These amounts suggest a scale of "enemy" resources characteristic of nations rather than businesses. Given the scale of "enemy" resources, are U.S. expenditures sufficient to wage effective "battle" in the Andean region? U.S. law enforcement personnel often stress the need for additional funding and equipment, such as UH-60 helicopters to attack processing labs. Without additional commitment in funding and equipment, many such personnel argue that efforts at interdiction by air, in the Andean region, will be severely limited and, by implication, much less effective. This raises the question of how much additional funding might be needed to "win" such a "war" in the region. Given the enormous disparity between the tens of billions of dollars the Andean drug trade grosses annually vis-à-vis the US$2.2 billion — spread out over five years — of the Andean strategy, would another billion make a difference? A law enforcement response to such questions would be that parity of resources is not the issue here but, rather, how to concentrate limited resources on trafficker weak links.

Some analysts suggest that the expanding demand for cocaine in Europe, coupled with a stagnating market in the United States, will stimulate an expansion in both production and traffic in the nations that make up the Andean strategy. This is expected, in turn, to continue to raise the costs of the U.S.-Andean counterdrug programs in the region, a prospect that has prompted the suggestion that perhaps the time is ripe for U.S. policy makers to raise the issue of sharing the counterdrug burden with the European Community (EC) and its member states.

On the economic front, oft-cited conservative estimates suggest that the drug trade brings in at least US$600 million per year in foreign exchange for Peru, Bolivia, and Colombia. Given the increasing demand on the United States for foreign aid by states in Eastern Europe and the former Soviet republics, not to mention other emerging international needs, and given the growing pressure to meet domestic needs and fund programs within the United States, and given the possibility that opium-producing countries may also seek a greater share of U.S. economic assistance to enable them to overcome destabilizing effects of efforts to eliminate opium production, can the United States realistically be expected to fund an expanding Andean initiative? And, if other foreign funding partners are brought in, to what degree might this result in reducing U.S. control over the international antidrug policy agenda? Would it be possible to reach consensus on concerted action? If not, would this limit the ability of the United States to take independent action? And given the fact that increased levels of counternarcotics aid comes out of the existing budgets of other foreign policy programs, what trade-offs might occur by increasing Andean funding and cutting aid programs elsewhere?

Need for Host Nation Cooperation

A fourth issue facing policy makers is the need for the host nation to cooperate fully if a program is to succeed. The Andean strategy assumes the presence of willing partners. As partners, however, foreign nations are often willing to cooperate in differing degrees for differing reasons. Although nations may diverge in the priority assigned to various policies on their agenda, stability — both economic and political — usually ranks at the top. In the Andean nations, on one level, the drug trade contributes to the economy, and political stability may be undermined by attacking the traffickers head on in what some see as a U.S. "gangbusters" style. Moreover, countries, such as Peru, which experience domestic insurgencies are likely to give the highest priority to containing these threats to political stability and the status quo and prefer to devote their law enforcement efforts to that end first, relegating the fight against the drug trade to, at the very least, second place. Such differences over what takes priority may vary from country to country. It is often these differences in perception as to priorities which are largely responsible for the delays encountered in working out details of bilateral agreements to implement the Andean drug initiative.[7]

Other factors may also enter into the situation, even when host nations make every effort, in good faith, to cooperate with U.S. counternarcotics goals. Conditions endemic to the Andean region often present obstacles, among them widespread corruption, an inability (in countries such as Peru) to control areas where drugs are grown and traffickers operate, and fragile judicial institutions which operate under conditions that make it difficult to bring traffickers to trial. The decision — by Colombia and Bolivia — not to extradite major traffickers to the United States is widely viewed by law enforcement personnel as a major impediment to full implementation of the Andean strategy. This situation will likely continue until the Andean nations are able to establish institutions with the power to prosecute and jail major traffickers.

Danger of a Single-Issue Foreign Policy?

A fifth issue arises from the potential consequences of what many view as the emergence of a single-issue foreign policy for certain Latin American countries, i.e., a policy to counter the cocaine trade. Too concentrated a focus on drug-related issues may serve to obscure other, fundamental, long-term policy goals, such as maintaining stability, preserving democracy and respect for human rights, protecting the environment, and overcoming poverty. The United States, it is charged, by promoting involvement of the military in fighting the drug traffic in host nations, is inadvertently strengthening the power of the military at the expense of often fragile, civilian democratic institutions in the region. Moreover, where links prevail between traffickers and insurgents, as is true of some areas in Peru, analysts warn that U.S. personnel who are engaged in antidrug support functions may find themselves drawn, despite efforts to avoid it, into a counterinsurgency war.

Generally speaking, many in the Congress view providing counter-narcotics training to law enforcement and military agencies, particularly in the case of Peru, as problematic at best, since such agencies often have dismal histories of systematic violations of human rights. Another consideration is that if U.S. economic aid is focused primarily on countering the trade in cocaine, it may not be most effectively applied toward economic development but become skewed in the service of too single-minded an approach to its goal. And then there is the question of what would happen to all this antidrug assistance, now focused upon Andean coca and cocaine, if U.S. consumption of that drug were to subside and be replaced by a new drug of choice — heroin, for instance — emanating from a new venue?

Criteria for Evaluation of Effectiveness

A final, and key, question facing policy makers is how to evaluate the "success" of the strategy. An allied, but subsidiary, issue is this: given demonstrated trafficker ability to adapt quickly to policy changes and change course accordingly, a need may exist to modify policy, goals, and implementation methods. For this reason, many see the strategy as a changing or evolving document. In this context, quantitative goals — such as a drop in the amount of cocaine entering the United States — are viewed as important barometers of progress. However, failure to achieve such goals in the short run does not necessarily mean that the strategy will fail over the long run. Experts generally agree that, due to the clandestine nature of the business, it is impossible to know with any precision the exact amounts of coca leaf grown, cocaine produced, and cocaine shipped; in addition to which, important sectors of the trade are decentralized by the presence of many small suppliers.

Without access to such data, and without truly reliable base figures, it is difficult to gauge with any reliability whether, indeed, drug production and shipment to the United States is increasing or decreasing according to any specific percentage. Moreover, since the law enforcers can seize only a small percentage of the drugs on the market, any sustained increase in the amount seized may only indicate, on one level, that more drugs are entering the country and are available for seizure. A major weakness of the arguments that question the reliability of statistics, however, is that they are the only measure now available. No one has yet proposed a better guide or way to measure what is, by its very nature, a clandestine operation. Consequently, given these limitations, most analysts use such figures with caution and complement their evaluations with other, less tangible indicators.

Some of the indicators used in evaluating the effectiveness of the strategy include such tangible figures as number of aircraft seized or intercepted, amount of cocaine seized, number of arrests of major traffickers, dollar value of assets seized, quantities of chemicals seized, and hectares of drugs eradicated. For example, the GAO, in addressing the issue of developing criteria to measure counternarcotics program effectiveness in Colombia, noted that "to be most useful to U.S. decision makers, the performance criteria should include reliable indicators of changes in Colombia's production and shipments of cocaine" (US-GAO 1991b, 6). However, analysts suggest that less tangible indicators might include host government levels of cooperation and attitudes, host country public opinion on drug cooperation, host nation levels of corruption, changes in trafficking modes, increases in costs to traffickers, restructuring of trafficker organizations, and levels of coordination and cooperation among the U.S. government agencies that formulate, implement, fund, and oversee the strategy.

Since every strategy must undergo a certain initial start-up period, it may be premature to pass any definitive judgment as to the efficacy of the Andean strategy, only now gaining momentum. However, few disagree that implementation of the law enforcement side of the strategy depends, to a major extent, on sound intelligence data. It often takes time to develop, and put in place, intelligence sources that are reliable and trustworthy. The economic assistance component of the strategy is also relatively new, beginning only in FY 1991. Although a major economic element of the strategy, the Andean

Trade Preference Act, was proposed by President Bush in November 1989, it was not enacted until almost two years later, in November 1991. Finally, no objective evaluation of the strategy can be carried out in an intellectual vacuum but, necessarily, must consider either the consequences of no strategy at all or be compared to an alternative, competing strategy, thus far not available.

Notes

1. This goal was first added as a separate, and distinct, fourth item in the 1991 strategy.

2. See Appendix I. Note that Congress, as of February 5, 1992, has not passed a foreign operations appropriations act for FY 1992, and it is unclear whether it will fund programs of this size.

3. Andean Trade Preference Act, passed by Congress on November 26, 1991, was signed into law on December 4, 1991 (for text, see U.S. Congress 1991, H-10641).

4. For more on the Enterprise for the Americas Initiative, see Serafina and Cody (1990).

5. U.S. government statistics on the level of increased or decreased cocaine entry do not appear to be currently available.

6. This could be interpreted as implying that coca leaf production in Peru had leveled off as well. However, enhanced farming techniques could also have increased yields-per-hectare, resulting in increased production. Also, if planted areas and yields remained constant, but more potent strains of coca were planted, the potential for enhanced cocaine production would, nevertheless, increase.

7. For additional information on the U.S.-Peruvian relationship, see Cochrane (1991) and Taft-Morales (1990).

References

Biskupic, J. 1992. "Drug 'Czar' Meets Skepticism about His Clout, Success." *Congressional Quarterly* 50, 6 (February 8): 314.

Cochrane, N. 1991. "Peru-U.S. Relations Under the Fujimori Government." September 20 Congressional Research Service Report 91-689 F. Washington, D.C.: U.S. Government Printing Office.

Levitsky, M. 1991. Statement of Assistant Secretary of State Melvyn Levitsky before the House Government Operations Subcommittee, October 23. Washington, D.C.: Government Printing Office.

Levitsky, M. 1990. Statement of Assistant Secretary of State for International Narcotics Matters, Melvyn Levitsky before the House Foreign Affairs Committee Task Force on International Narcotics Control, October 10. Washington, D.C.: Government Printing Office.

Newsweek. 1992. "The Drug War: A Bad Report Card." (January 27): 4.

Serafino, N., and B. Cody. 1990. "The Enterprise for the Americas Initiative: Issues for Congress." Congressional Research Service CRS Issue Brief 90-130. Washington, D.C.: U.S. Government Printing Office.

Taft-Morales, M. 1990. "Peru: Country Background Report." May 10, Congressional Research Service Report 90-247 F. Washington, D.C.: U.S. Government Printing Office.

Thurston, C. 1992. "Andeans Hope to Match Caribbean Export Growth." *Journal of Commerce* (January 16): 1A, 3A.

United States Agency for International Development (US-AID). 1992. *Andean Counterdrug Initiative: Economic Cooperation*, April 1, 1991-March 31, 1992. Washington, D.C.: AID.

United States Congress. 1991. Congressional Record, House of Representatives (November 20): H-10641. Washington, D.C.: U.S. Government Printing Office.

United States General Accounting Office (US-GAO). 1991a. *The Drug War: U.S. Programs in Peru Face Serious Obstacles.* Report to Congressional requesters, GAO/NSIAD/92-36, October. Washington, D.C.: GAO.

US-GAO. 1991b. *Drug War: Observations on Counternarcotics Aid to Colombia.* GAO/NSIAD-91-296, September. Washington, D.C.: GAO.

US-GAO. 1991c. *Drug Control: Impact of Department of Defense Detection and Monitoring on Cocaine Flow.* GAO/NSIAD-91-297, September. Washington, D.C.: GAO.

US-GAO. 1991d. *Drug Control: Status Report on Department of Defense Support to Counternarcotics Activities.* GAO/NSIAD-91-117, June. Washington, D.C.: GAO.

United States Office of National Drug Control Policy (US-ONDCP). Executive Office of the President. 1992. *National Drug Control Strategy: A Nation Responds to Drug Use.* January. Washington, D.C.: Government Printing Office.

US-ONDCP. 1991. *National Drug Control Strategy.* February. Washington, D.C.: Government Printing Office.

US-ONDCP. 1990. *National Drug Control Strategy.* January. Washington, D.C.: Government Printing Office.

United States Department of State (US-DS). 1991. *Drug Control Activities in Bolivia: Audit Report* 1-CI-030. October. Office of the Inspector General. Washington, D.C.: Government Printing Office.

Witkin, G. 1992. "The Bad-News Drug Czar." *US News and World Report* (February 10): 33.

APPENDIX I

**U.S.-Andean Strategy Narcotics-Related Assistance
(itemized by account in millions of U.S. dollars)
Authorized Program by Fiscal Year — Budget Authority**

Country	FY 1990 Actual	FY 1991 Actual	FY 1992 Estimate	FY 1993 Request
Colombia:				
Military Assistance	71.2	37.1	30.3	44.8
Economic Assistance	3.9	50.0	50.0	50.0
Law Enforcement	22.0	32.5	30.1	37.4
DEA Support	4.9	6.2	6.4	6.4
Subtotal	**102.0**	**125.8**	**116.8**	**138.6**
Peru:				
Military Assistance	0.5	18.9	30.8	30.6
Economic Assistance	3.8	60.0	100.0	100.0
Law Enforcement	20.0	24.6	28.1	28.1
DEA Support	3.6	4.7	4.8	4.8
Subtotal	**27.8**	**108.2**	**163.7**	**163.5**
Bolivia:				
Military Assistance	38.8	30.9	35.2	35.2
Economic Assistance	42.0	87.9	124.5	108.5
Law Enforcement	16.7	20.7	21.4	22.7
DEA Support	8.4	10.1	10.2	10.2
Subtotal	**105.9**	**149.6**	**191.3**	**176.6**
Andean Narcotics Information System (ESF):	0.0	0.5	0.0	0.0
Total Assistance				
Military Assistance	110.5	86.9	96.3	110.6
Economic Assistance	49.6	198.5	274.5	258.5
Law Enforcement	58.7	77.8	79.6	88.2
DEA Support	16.9	21.0	21.4	21.4
Subtotal	**235.7**	**384.1**	**471.8**	**478.7**
DOD Section 506(a)(2)	27.8	0.0	0.0	0.0
Excess Defense Articles	0.0	3.1	0.0	0.0
Subtotal	**27.8**	**3.1**	**0.0**	**0.0**
Grand Total	263.5	387.2	471.8	478.7

Note: State Department accounts are operating under a Second Continuing Resolution until March 31, 1992. Therefore, FY 1992 estimates are subject to change. In addition, for both FY 1992 and FY 1993, no decisions have been made on an FMF split between military assistance and law enforcement. Therefore, the FY 1992 levels for these activities are estimates only.

Source: Office of National Drug Control Policy 1/31/92.

APPENDIX II

Drug Enforcement Administration
Drug Suppression Program (FY 1990 - FY 1991)

Source Country

Country/ Organization	FY 1990	FY 1991
SNOWCAP Peru/Bolivia	159 base labs destroyed 20 HCL labs destroyed 26 aircraft seized 3.5 metric tons cocaine base seized	160 base labs destroyed 21 HCL labs destroyed 47 aircraft seized 5.5 metric tons cocaine base seized

Transit Country

Country/ Organization	FY 1990	FY 1991
OP Bahamas, Turks and Caicos (OPBAT)	3.5 metric tons cocaine HCL seized No aircraft seized 3 vessels seized	6.6 metric tons cocaine HCL seized 4 aircraft seized 3 vessels seized
Northern Border Response Force (NBRF)	NA*	27 metric tons cocaine HCL seized 18 aircraft seized No vessels seized
Central America Drug Enforcement Centers (CADENCE)	NA*	8.2 metric tons cocaine HCL seized 3 aircraft seized (Guatamala) 2 vessels seized

* Programs not active in FY 1990.

Source: Drug Enforcement Administration, January 1992.

Chapter 3

The U.S. Military and the War on Drugs

Donald J. Mabry

Introduction

U.S. antinarcotics policy has failed so abysmally that the presidency and Congress dragged a reluctant military into the antidrug crusade even though three successive defense secretaries argued against such a move. Each argued that military personnel are not and should not be police, that utilizing military personnel for law enforcement activities would detract from military readiness, that the mission of the armed forces is to protect that nation from foreign armies not drug smugglers, and that civilian law enforcement agencies should be given the resources necessary to do the antidrug task. Moreover, military personnel warned Congress of the danger of military involvement; General Stephen Olmstead, then deputy assistant secretary for drug policy and enforcement, argued that the military is capable of doing the job but also argued that civilians would not like the way it would be done, for soldiers would use machine guns and not worry about Miranda rights. Merchants and tourists would not like the consequences of search techniques implemented at the borders or on the high seas.[1]

Unpersuaded, the federal government mandated and subsequently escalated military participation. After the 1981 amendment of the Posse Comitatus Act to allow the Department of Defense (DoD) to give some logistical support to civilian police, the military loaned equipment to civilian law enforcement agencies. In subsequent years, as civilian law enforcement personnel became less and less able to cope with the drug epidemic, the demand for military involvement increased, as did funding for military antidrug efforts. In 1982, in Operation BAT in the Bahamas, the U.S. military first started aiding the suppression of drug activities in the Caribbean and Latin America by loaning equipment and coordinating some of its activities with those of law enforcement officials. Four years later, U.S. military personnel played the major role in planning and conducting Operation Blast Furnace in Bolivia. As part of Operation Snowcap, created in 1987, DoD personnel began

43

teaching military skills to Drug Enforcement Administration (DEA) agents who were to be stationed in the Andes. In late 1988, the military was ordered to play a major role in helping interdict drug traffic into the United States, to create an integrated intelligence and communications network, and to train foreign military personnel and both U.S. and foreign police forces.[2] In essence, the Omnibus Drug and the Defense Authorization Acts of 1988 made the DoD an agency which spies on and polices civilians by putting the military in charge of interdiction and surveillance.[3]

In light of world events in 1988-1990, use of military resources for non-military purposes became more attractive to DoD officials. As late as October 1989, the Pentagon continued to argue that its traditional mission of defending the nation against foreign militaries and their weapons was still valid and would be compromised by using soldiers, sailors, and pilots as cops.[4] The military, in spite of pressure from civilians and Secretary of Defense Richard Cheney to increase its antidrug activity, moved slowly. The toppling of the Iron Curtain and Cheney's November 1989 announcement of plans to cut the DoD budget by $180 billion over five years sent shock waves through the military. Between the 1989-1990 collapse of the Soviet empire and the beginning of the Persian Gulf crisis in August 1990, many Americans believed that the U.S. military had little use for its multi-trillion-dollar installed capacity and sought a "peace dividend." Some believed that moving the military into the antidrug business was one way to collect. The decline in a military threat made the Pentagon and its supporters fear the possible loss of budgets, power, and influence; consequently, they became more interested in participating in the antidrug crusade in both its surveillance and Andean aspects. By February 1990, DoD offered to fund much of the proposed full surveillance system out of its existing budget. Preserving the budget became more important than preserving the integrity of the military mission.

Defense Department Surveillance

From a personnel and resource management perspective, the Defense Department seemed ideal to create a unified, well-coordinated Control, Command, Communications, and Intelligence (C3I) system. Years of wrestling with inter-service rivalries and, at times, of coordinating with foreign military commanders taught DoD executives how to lead disparate groups to achieve a common goal. Moreover, because the Coast Guard and state National Guard units would form an integral part of this anti-smuggling effort, DoD could easily reach into the civilian sector since both of these groups were also military units[5] and accustomed to working with DoD. Since DoD has an existing C3I structure for these units, its task under the new assignment would be to fold the intelligence-gathering and communications efforts of civilian law enforcement agents into a system directed against drug smuggling.

Another presumed advantage in making DoD the lead agency for detecting drug smugglers was its extraordinary technical capabilities developed from its long experience in monitoring the skies and the waters for incoming Soviet or other hostile military aircraft, warships, and missiles. As events in Operation Desert Storm demonstrated, the U.S. military's ability to use its integrated satellite, radar, and communications technology may be unsurpassed. Acquisition of the ability to react against suspected smugglers in "real time" (fast enough to intercept them before they crossed the U.S. border or escaped) is clearly desirable and comparable to the mission of such agencies as the North American Aerospace Defense Command (NORAD), whose goal is to detect hostile military acts against the United States quickly enough for the military to react. Thus, proponents of making DoD the lead agency envisioned simply adding the ability to alert law enforcement agencies to the presence of suspected drug smugglers to an existing detection system along the southern U.S. border and in the Caribbean Basin.

Because the new system would utilize many of the existing human and material resources of both DoD and civilian agencies, it appeared relatively inexpensive. Intelligence data collected by one agency would, henceforth, be shared automatically with all agencies involved in anti-smuggling via a common communications system rather than being gathered and used by one agency because it was unable or unwilling to share. In addition, routine military patrols in the basin could more easily be diverted to investigate suspicious craft and signal authorities closer to the United States. In sum, by putting DoD in charge, Washington envisioned an anti-smuggling net through which drug criminals would rarely pass. By the summer of 1991, DoD was extending its surveillance activities, providing coverage of the Caribbean Basin and much of the Andes. Part of Operation Support Justice, DoD and Latin American governments were trying to prevent cocaine smugglers from using northbound air corridors.[6]

Few believed, however, that this enhanced detection ability would do little more than harass drug smugglers and, thus, raise their and their customers' costs. The very high profit margin on cocaine meant that smugglers could sustain very heavy losses and still operate at a profit and that the effect on street prices inside the United States would be negligible. Aerial detection, although an essential component of any such interdiction strategy, succeeds when it forces smugglers to hide cocaine shipments inside commercial passenger aircraft or inside cargo ships, places where most of the deployed high technological military equipment cannot reach. Put another way, the military-led surveillance system exacerbates the problems faced by civilian law enforcement agencies. In a December 1991 report, the General Accounting Office raised serious concerns about when, if ever, the DoD interdiction communications systems would be effective and at what cost. Because interdiction has not stopped the flow of cocaine into the United States, the Inter-American Commission on Drug Policy recommended reducing funding for interdiction.[7]

Andean Drug Policy

In the Andes, Washington's drug foreign policy rests more on destroying crops and laboratories in Latin America in the belief that the cheapest and most efficient solution to the desire of Americans for illicit drugs was to eliminate their supply at the source. Washington officials understood such a policy, for they had been using it with varying degrees of success and failure for many years in various parts of the world.[8]

Throughout Latin America, the supply-reduction foreign policy has been difficult to achieve because Washington cannot control events abroad. Because no nation wants foreigners eradicating crops, destroying laboratories, and arresting traffickers on its own territory, Washington has pressured producing and transit nations to use their own personnel to accomplish these tasks.Further, DEA and other U.S. officials (including military personnel) were sent as advisors and proctors. In the Andes, the United States, in conjunction with host governments, created special drug police, hired coca eradication workers, and provided a wide range of other technical assistance. The Bureau of International Narcotics Matters of the State Department, for example, developed its own air wing for use in the antidrug campaigns in Bolivia and Peru. U.S. military personnel began advising local police and military on techniques to protect field workers against the inevitable violent reactions of those whose source of income was being destroyed. Often, host country security forces could not or would not protect antidrug agents. Regardless of what Washington might want, control of events rests in the hands of Andean governments and their security forces, those growing the coca or processing it, and the drug merchants. In Colombia and Peru, moreover, guerrilla movements sometimes control events. The issue of control is not limited to foreign actors, for Washington cannot coordinate its own forces in Bolivia and Peru.[9]

Nor can Washington stop the ability of drug traffickers to corrupt police and military officers.[10] One reason that Colombia has been unable to capture its principal traffickers has been their ability to buy intelligence information and protection from bureaucrats, cops, and soldiers. The same problem exists in Peru. Narcotics corruption in Bolivian official ranks is "pervasive" according to the U.S. Department of State. Washington is so cognizant of the ties between the former military dictatorship of General Luis García Meza (1980-1982) and international cocaine trafficking that it obtained the resignation of García Meza's former army intelligence chief Faustino Rico Toro almost immediately after Rico Toro was appointed in early 1991 to head the National Council Against Drug Abuse and Trafficking. Corruption permeates the Anti-Narcotics Special Forces (FELCN). In other words, Washington lacks a reliable security force in each of these nations, one uninfluenced by drug money and not intimidated by the threat of violent retribution.

Narcoterrorism

Colombian events in 1989 opened the door to a greater U.S. military role in Latin America, for the narcoterrorism argument provided the rationale for using military resources to stifle the drug business. Anti-guerrilla campaigns are a military specialty. Although guerrillas were not the protagonists in the drug terrorism campaigns of 1989-1990 and counterterrorism is a police specialty, few made these distinctions as bombs exploded and people were shot in Colombia. Confusing matters further was the fact that the Colombian National Police is a branch of the Colombian military, and, thus, army generals wrote the final shopping list when U.S. President George Bush promised the $65 million in emergency aid. By the time the Colombian crisis began, U.S. civilian agencies had begun to realize that they were stalemated, at best, and that only a more active DoD role might give them the resources necessary to break the impasse. Allying with DoD would guarantee consistently larger funding for the drug war. DoD could get whatever funding it wanted to support soldiers in the field, whereas cops could not, and civilian agencies could piggyback on patriotic sentiment.

Colombian reality, however, did not support the U.S. narcoterrorism thesis. Conservative businessmen used assassins to conduct highly publicized attacks against the law enforcement system of Colombia. In spite of some isolated instances of cooperation between one or more guerrilla movements, on the one hand, and drug gangsters, on the other, the two are not integrally related nor has the Colombian government treated them as such. Of the two, the Colombian government has viewed the guerrilla movements as the more serious threat. Guerrilla movements were active for many years before narcotrafficking and its violence became an issue. Colombian police fight criminals, be they *narcotraficantes* or more ordinary crooks, and account for 80 percent of drug busts. In fact, one of the most serious problems faced by the police was the military-narcotraficante cooperation to kill their common enemy, leftist guerrillas. Military officers sometimes compromised police raids in exchange for trafficker information on the location of guerrilla bands.

Peru provides a much better argument for the use of the military, for it is both the principal source of coca and a place where Sendero Luminoso guerrillas are involved in the drug enterprise, principally as protectors of farmers and lab technicians. U.S. personnel, sent when Peru did not eradicate crops quickly enough, came into harm's way because they risked confrontation with Sendero. Peruvian security forces proved unable or unwilling to protect these agents or the Peruvians they supervised. Exacerbating the security problem was the decision of farmers and lab owners to disperse their enterprises to reduce the chances that the United States would destroy them. In doing so, they made the antidrug forces more vulnerable, for the latter had to stretch their supply lines. If the crop eradication and lab destruction program was to succeed, the Upper Huallaga Valley (UHV) had to be made secure.[11]

Many UHV residents welcomed the arrival of Sendero in the valley. When coca growing and trafficking boomed in the lawless UHV and tensions were subsequently raised by the antidrug campaign, Sendero Luminoso moved into the valley and imposed order, something the Peruvian government had not done. Colombian traffickers, who had been abusing the growers, were disciplined and taxed; Sendero thus gained support from the growers and income with which to pursue its political ends. In a very real sense, Sendero became the government of the UHV. The Peruvian military could not dislodge them.

The Peruvian military failed largely because it was ordered to follow a contradictory policy. It could fight Sendero or engage in antidrug efforts but not both. Antidrug efforts drove people into the protective arms of Sendero, while attacks on Sendero gave the drug producers a free hand to pursue their business. Peruvian military leaders, by and large, preferred to concentrate on Sendero, believing that Sendero was a serious threat to national security and one that the military was trained to fight. The United States, however, more interested in destroying drugs and protecting antidrug workers, pressured Peru to focus on drugs.

By 1990, faced with the continued threat of Sendero to Peruvian antidrug efforts and the commensurate inability to eradicate crops, Washington unsuccessfully tried to up the ante through a proposed $35 million military aid package. DEA had reported in late 1989 that Peru was unlikely to militarize its antidrug campaign, but the new proposal called for the construction of a military training base near Santa Lucia to train six Peruvian strike battalions and a second base on the Tombo and Ene rivers. The United States would also supply more river patrol boats, refurbish ground-attack jets, and install more radar in the valley.[12] U.S. policy, in effect, has been to create an arms and use of technology race in the Andes, since both the traffickers and Washington buy the latest equipment. Andean governments cannot keep up and have become dependent upon Washington. Moreover, Washington has decided that more U.S.-style force would solve the problem. Some Americans began arguing that the Peruvian situation was low-intensity conflict (LIC), the current military euphemism for counterinsurgency warfare.

The newly elected government of Alberto Fujimori rejected the proposed aid in September 1990, arguing that Peru's problems could only be solved by political and economic, not military, means. Peruvian officials believed that combining the antidrug campaign and the anti-Sendero war was the road to disaster. Sendero has power in communities whose residents believe that they have been abused by the government, so the key to defeating Sendero lay in the Peruvian government regaining the confidence of its people. Military campaigns, especially if directed by U.S. soldiers, would have the opposite effect. When Fujimori balked, Washington threatened to cancel all aid to Peru.[13] In 1991, Fujimori began yielding to U.S. demands; Peru's severe economic crisis left him little choice.

Militarization of the Drug War

The U.S.-Bolivian decision to seek a military solution perhaps best illustrates the militarization of U.S. drug foreign policy in Latin America. One cannot make the narcoterrorism argument, in either of its forms, for, unlike Colombia and Peru, Bolivia does not have a guerrilla threat or substantial narcotraficante violence. Bolivia is very important to the suppression of the cocaine trade, however, because it is the second-largest coca producer. In the 1990-1991 agreement between Washington and La Paz, Bolivia agreed to accept $32.2 million in military aid in exchange for militarizing its antidrug efforts, supplanting UMOPAR, the antidrug police. This agreement, much of it made in secret by the Bolivian government and "sprung" on the congress and the citizenry, aroused a storm of protest in Bolivia and vows by coca farmers to resist military efforts. As one of the poorest nations in the hemisphere, Bolivia could not risk closing foreign aid. Moreover, to a nation historically controlled by its military, the offer of additional money and equipment for that military must have been irresistible. Although the Bolivian government has been democratically elected since 1981, civilian power is extraordinarily weak. Bolivians, as well as Colombians and Peruvians, understand that such a policy means that Washington has greater faith in Andean militaries than it does in Andean police.

The two wars fought by the Bush administration increased interest in a military solution, for both were short and successful. The success of the 1989 Panamanian war (Operation Just Cause) heightened interest in a military solution, for the military was successfully used as a civilian posse to capture a drug trafficker, General Manuel Noriega. By the summer of 1990, General Maxwell Thurman, commander of the Southern Command (SOUTHCOM) and architect of the Panamanian invasion, had begun planning a low-intensity conflict in Colombia, Bolivia, and Peru, one in which local military forces, aided by the U.S. military, would launch "simultaneous" strikes against drug traffickers.[14] By 1991, a version of that plan, Operation Support Justice, was under way in the Andes.[15] The DEA, the State Department, and the Office of National Drug Policy began advocating a more substantive military role in the Andes to condition Congress and the public to accept a military solution and then later testified in favor of the administration's 1990 proposal to increase military aid to Andean nations. Operation Desert Storm, conducted by the Central Command, generated tremendous popular support in the United States for its military, but it also undercut the Southern Command, which specializes in low-intensity conflict. Although LIC teams were used in Desert Storm, their work went largely unnoticed, and LIC commanders had to make a special effort to obtain any publicity. SOUTHCOM needs a role to justify its continued existence.

The apparent model for U.S. military policy in the Andes is a work of fiction. In Tom Clancy's best-selling novel, *Clear and Present Danger*,[16] U.S. Spanish-speaking light infantry soldiers were infiltrated into Colombia to destroy cocaine laboratories and kill enough drug traffickers in an effort to start a civil war within the ranks of the traffickers. The Bush administration planned to use Bolivian, Colombian, and Peruvian soldiers instead of Hispanic-Americans. Under U.S. supervision, these battalions would launch a simultaneous strike against drug traffickers. Since this would be centrally coordinated by the United States, the planners believed that the traffickers could be captured, killed, or forced to flee the Andes. These simultaneous attacks would so disrupt the trafficking organizations that coca leaf prices would drop so low that farmers would voluntarily quit growing coca.

This is the thread which explains why the United States has insisted that these nations allow the United States to create and deploy special light infantry battalions even though doing so creates great risks for those nations: Washington policy makers believe those LIC theorists who argue that special operations units and counterinsurgency techniques can be successfully applied against criminal organizations. The targets are not the gunmen or guerrillas in Colombia nor guerrillas and farmers in Peru nor farmers in Bolivia. Even by proxy, the United States does not want to go to war against the Andean civilian population. The targets are the higher echelons of the cocaine business and their labs.[17] Regardless of the intention of official policy, the likelihood is high that the result will be a "dirty war" against the more general population. "Surgical strikes" by ground forces are rarely surgical. In Bolivia, for example, these units are to be deployed not in the Chapare, the heart of illicit coca growing, but in the Beni and other lab locales in order to avoid conflict with farmers.

Although it is not possible to know exactly how these battalions will be used, for such information is classified, many important, obvious questions can be raised. How long will such forces exist? Will their existence create unwanted tensions within their own military establishments? Will these battalions attack fellow military personnel or police or politicians or businessmen who are involved in the drug trade? If they are successful in capturing or killing drug kingpins, will the lieutenants of the latter simply replace their bosses, as happened in the Clancy novel? As these battalions begin their campaigns, will the business headquarters and laboratories in these three nations move to safer haven in Ecuador, Chile, Paraguay, Argentina, Venezuela, and Brazil? Will the United States then try to pursue the same policies there? If the price of coca leaf drops sufficiently to drive farmers out of business, will they meekly acquiesce or will they fight back? If guerrilla movements are as dependent upon drug money as some suggest, will they fight to preserve their sources of income and weaponry? If, for example, Peruvian farmers and Sendero join forces to fight, how many soldiers will be necessary to defeat them? Will Bolivian coca farmers conduct armed resistance?

Regardless of the answers to these questions, the Bush strategy does represent a militarization of antidrug efforts in the Andes and a threat to democratic government there. Although proponents, using LIC doctrine, assert that the military will only be supporting civilian agencies, such is unlikely to be the case. To succeed, such campaigns must have a centralized command and control system, a role that each national military will insist upon playing, for no military will voluntarily subject itself to police control. Military officers will then be the chief law enforcement agents in the nation. In fact, the United States, by insisting that the civilian police forces in these nations are incompetent to destroy what the United States itself terms criminal organizations, has telegraphed the message that militaries are more important than civilian institutions. Militaries do not practice democracy within their own ranks and, in the Andes, they have consistently been the most powerful anti-democratic force. Enhancing their power, which this initiative does, diminishes democratic governments there. To the extent that U.S. soldiers coordinate the actions of these battalions, democracy is also diminished for they are not elected by these nations to be in control. If there is to be a multinational, simultaneous strike against traffickers, U.S. advisors, in direct and constant contact with SOUTHCOM, will have to coordinate the forces. If that occurs, then the important decision-making power will have passed from Bogotá, La Paz, and Lima to the United States.

LIC does not work against drug crime for a number of reasons. Too many people have a vested interest in the continuance of the trade. Besides the obvious examples of the criminals and the drug consumers, there are also the numerous persons who sell all kinds of goods or provide services to drug farmers, processors, transporters, bankers, and so forth. One tenet of LIC is "winning the hearts and minds" of the people in order to deny support to the opponent. Opposition to drug traffickers in Latin America emanates primarily from their use of violence, not from the fact that they are engaged in drug trafficking. Too many people have a vested interest in the continuance of the coca enterprise for LIC doctrine to work. The fact that coca-chewing is part of Andean culture makes gaining popular support even more unlikely. LIC units need other militaries to fight. The goons used by traffickers are not armies, even guerrilla armies. Although the United States has the physical capability to destroy coca fields in short order, the tactic could only be used if the United States also wanted mass uprisings against it. Destroying coca-processing labs is more difficult, for they are dispersed and relatively easy to replace. If, for example, all the Colombian and Peruvian labs were destroyed, would the United States then penetrate Brazil, Ecuador, and Chile, where some labs currently exist and more would be sure to follow? Colombia, Bolivia, and Peru are not small nations; combined, their land area equals one-third that of the United States, the area east of the Mississippi River. The number of troops required would be large. If the United States tried to use local troops, it would inevitably find operations compromised by the influence of nationalism, familial ties, and money. Finally, although drug trafficking is a serious political problem for Bolivia, Colombia, and Peru, the application of LIC doctrine by the United States would be even greater.

The strategy of using Andean militaries to suppress the drug business in Latin America is problematical at best. It assumes a mutuality of interest between the United States, on the one hand, and Andean militaries, on the other, which does not exist. Further, it incorrectly links drug traffickers and guerrillas and, by doing so, inadvertently aids both. Finally, it threatens democracy in Latin America, a long-term foreign policy goal of the United States.

Counterinsurgency warfare in Colombia and Peru, even with U.S. aid, will not end the drug trade, for leftist guerrillas and rightist businessmen are natural opponents who have only occasionally cooperated for mutual convenience. Traffickers want the guerrillas beaten; the guerrillas raise the cost of doing business and attract too much attention from the government, thus complicating normal business operations. The traffickers can reach accommodations with the military.

To varying degrees, the militaries of these nations are riddled with narcocorruption, as the 1991 *International Narcotics Control Strategy Report* points out. The Colombian armed forces have long been abusing the population. One report asserts that the military, in league with right-wing death squads, terrorizes and kills innocent people in the state of Uraba. The level of corruption can reach quite high; the Bolivian military government of 1981 was implicated in the cocaine trade. Military commanders in the Upper Huallaga Valley have been accused of being allies of the traffickers. Communication systems are insecure and fast helicopters and high-powered weapons are of marginal utility when someone picks up the telephone to warn traffickers that a raid is about to take place.[18]

Using militaries to arrest criminals and destroy crops and factories further institutionalizes militaries as the authority within those states, encouraging them to marginalize or replace civilian government. This is a serious concern. Bolivia was governed by a series of military dictatorships between 1964 and 1982. Civilian government is of recent vintage in Peru; the military ruled from 1968 to 1980. Colombia has not had a military dictatorship since that of General Gustavo Pinilla of 1954-1958. Colombia's military has only 60,000 members for an almost thirty-two million population, and Colombian civilians seek to keep it under their control. Nevertheless, the military often ignores its civilian commanders. Military dictatorship is a long-standing scourge in Latin America that the United States should not encourage through its antidrug policy.[19]

The solution of the insurgency problems in Peru and Colombia must come from those countries, not the United States. Both the Peruvian military and Sendero Luminoso are Peruvian, and the Peruvian government should be able to find Peruvian military leaders smart enough to outwit fellow countrymen. There is no evidence that Sendero has received outside aid; in fact, Sendero obtains its weaponry by buying or stealing it from the Peruvian military. Although Peruvian counterinsurgency measures attack the symptoms of Peru's problems, the civilian government has to deal with the causes of the insurgency, something the Fujimori administration wants to do. Colombia has begun using political accommodation as well as repression to solve its insurgency problem; it is too early to estimate its potential success, but the entry of M-19 into electoral politics suggests that other guerrilla movements might also be persuaded to make a similar move.

The Andean Initiative contains no inherent limits to how much the U.S. military will do in the Andes. The United States is not going to invade Bolivia, Colombia, Peru, or Mexico; that is not the issue in spite of the fears of some Latin Americans. Washington policy makers understand very well the adverse consequences of such an action. Latin Americans have made it clear that they do not want foreign troops, from the United States or elsewhere, on their soil. Many barely tolerate the presence of U.S. advisors. Neither civilians nor military personnel want to get bogged down in an unwinnable war in one or more large Latin America nations. But if the military aid sent for FY90 and FY91 is insufficient to make a significant dent in the drug trade, will the United States send more? What is the cutoff point or the point of diminishing returns?

Militaries are killing machines not police forces; they are trained to kill people in sufficient numbers to convince the survivors not to fight. Military personnel are not trained nor suited to nation building. Is there any evidence from any country that suggests that military units are successful economic entrepreneurs? Are these bureaucratic entities, dependent as they are upon convincing governmental leaders and the public that the latter should transfer some of their wealth into the military, people who know how to farm and market the resultant products or to start and foster business enterprises? In real wars, the military is unleashed like a pit bull and then rechained once the conflict is over, but the "drug war" is not a war and will not end quickly. The evolving antidrug strategy calls for a greatly enhanced military establishment performing a civilian function indefinitely. The anti-smuggling screens and the maritime-aerial patrols would have to be sustained else drug smuggling would resume if demand for foreign drugs continued or could be regenerated. If true military emergencies occur, either even more resources would have to be devoted to the Pentagon or the military's antidrug mission would have to be compromised. Moreover, the smuggling problem is not just a drug smuggling problem. The nation has little control over its borders. American enterprise is being undercut by smuggled goods. Terrorists and weapons can easily enter the country.[20] Should the military be given so much potential authority over civilian commerce?

The very fact that militaries are being used for civilian law enforcement is an admission of the failure of civilian government. This is particularly true for the United States with it historic tradition of keeping the military out of civilian affairs. Civilian law enforcement agencies such as the Coast Guard did not fail; they were never given the resources to do the job. Civilian government officials failed to resist the seductiveness of the popular image of the military and the personal political gains which come from supporting the military establishment. Dazzled by the glitter, glory, and gold of a possible military solution, these leaders fail to see that illicit drug use is a domestic, civilian problem, both in the United States and Latin America, one wherein free enterprise capitalists are servicing the American consumer market. Public concern over the spread of illicit drug use and the violence associated with crack prompted the U.S. government to call in the military. Using the military for the police function of illicit drug suppression emanates from anger not reason.

The Drug Problem and Social Control

Not surprisingly, many Americans think that the use of military force abroad will solve the nation's drug problem. The message that violence works permeates their films, athletic events, novels, television programs, and music. Many citizens believe that they have lost control of their lives and believe that the use of violence will enable them to reassert control. They want to use the police or the military to repress those they believe are "misbehaving." Within the United States, they have demanded and received more monies for police action and incarceration. In foreign policy, they have sent U.S. police and U.S. military advisors to Latin America to supervise the destruction of property and the arrest of malefactors and, in the case of the military, to help suppress leftist insurgencies in the name of drug control. Yet, illicit drug use and drug-related street violence persists.

The drug problem pales in comparison to other national problems even though it received an inordinate amount of attention in the 1980s. The drug issue was part of a much larger issue in U.S. society, that of social control. The Reagan administration represented, among other things, an effort to restore the controlling effects of more traditional values, for many Americans believed that life had gotten out of hand. Americans wanted their national government to fight those things which they believed threatened the "American way of life," whether those things were the intrusive role of the national government in the conduct of business and industry (hence, the demand for deregulation), threats from the "Evil Empire" (hence, the massive military buildup directed against the Soviet Union and intervention against leftists in Central America), international terrorism (hence, the bombing of Libya), or social issues such as sexual activity and drug usage (hence, the anti-abortion, anti-alcohol, and anti-cocaine/heroin/marijuana crusades). The election of George Bush in

1988 ratified popular satisfaction with the Reagan administration, even though many serious domestic problems had increased during the decade. In the 1990s, the nation must decide what, if anything, it will do about its educational system, persistent poverty, deterioration of its economic infrastructure, reduced clout in the international economy, urban decay, environmental pollution, budget deficits, and the U.S. role in international affairs.

The Bush administration appears intent on "militarizing" the drug crusade even more. Without access to the appropriate documents, my comments must be treated as speculative. Nevertheless, press reports certainly indicate that the United States plans a larger role for militaries. Thus, Laura Brooks reports that "Southcom says 'discussions are under way' to support unidentified antidrug forces in Central America with special forces military training."[21] Latin American militaries, through the Interamerican Defense Board and the Armies of the Americas program, both sponsored by the United States, may deeply involve themselves in the international antidrug crusade. This was one possibility seriously discussed at the March 1991 meeting of twenty-five Latin American military officers in Montevideo, Uruguay. The decline of military dictatorships has left these military establishments (except in a few cases) with little to do.[22]

The role of militaries is likely to grow because U.S. politicians, of both political parties, refuse to identify and tackle the causes of illicit drug use in the United States. Doing so risks giving bad news to the electorate, that they are both the cause and the solution to the problem. The electorate does not want bad news. It wants to believe that the national government is solving the problem. Conducting surveillance and paying for the training and deployment of Latin American military units against the drug business give the appearance of doing something. The amount spent is small by U.S. terms, making it easy to appropriate. It is very large in Latin American terms, giving the United States significant leverage in those nations. Finally, so many Washington agencies get a piece of the antidrug money pie that reallocating or reducing the size of the pie is probably impossible. Neither the DEA nor the State Department's Bureau of International Narcotics Matters, to take two examples, has a bureaucratic interest in reducing the international antidrug budget. Neither does the Department of Defense; its incentive is to preserve as much of its budget as possible.

Needed Research

Policy makers and scholars know too little about what the U.S. military is doing in the antidrug crusade in the Andes and the implications of such activity. Although some data are hidden from public view, much information is readily available for those who carefully read congressional reports and hearings and reports by agencies such as the General Accounting Office. Over time, administration officials testify many times about policy and inevitably reveal more than is intended. Court cases in the United States provide valuable data. Periodicals from affected nations provide rich sources of information. Personal interviews provide additional data as well as insights into what has been happening.

We need answers to many questions. What is actually happening in the nations receiving U.S. antidrug aid? How can the effectiveness of DoD efforts be measured (something which DoD has been avoiding)? What are the strategy and tactics of SOUTHCOM, and how appropriate are they? Have detection and interdiction efforts in the Caribbean Basin made any demonstrable difference and, if so, how? How appropriate and effective is the use of military high technology? This is a study which needs to be done by persons with technical expertise. How many of the billions being appropriated to the militaries actually are being used to counter narcotics? Inside Latin America, what are the effects of U.S. military aid and the use of Latin American militaries in counternarcotics work?

Notes

1. General Stephen Olmstead, USMC, makes this point in Congressional Research Service, *Narcotics Interdiction and the Use of the Military: Issues for Congress* (Washington: GPO, 1988), 15, 24. For a scholarly warning, see Morris J. Blachman and Kenneth Sharpe, "The War on Drugs: American Democracy Under Assault," *World Policy Journal* (Winter 1989-90), 135-163.

2. Donald J. Mabry, "Andean Drug Trafficking and the Military Option," *The Military Review* (March 1990). "The Possible Roles of the U.S. Military in the Andes," *The Andean Drug Strategy and the Role of the U.S. Military. Proceedings of a seminar held by the Congressional Research Service, (November 9, 1989)*. Report of the Defense Policy Panel and Investigations Subcommittee of the Committee on Armed Services, House of Representatives, 101st Cong., 1st Sess. Washington, D.C.: Government Printing Office, (January 1990). 39-41, "The U.S. Military and the War on Drugs in Latin America," *Journal of Interamerican Studies and World Affairs* 30:2 (Summer-Fall 1988).

3. David C. Morrison, "Police Action," *National Journal* (February 1, 1992), 267-70.

4. Stephen Duncan, Testimony to hearing of Subcommittees on Legislation and National Security and Government Information, Justice and Agriculture, U.S. House of Representatives, October 17, 1989, 101st Cong., 1st Sess. Mimeo.

5. In peacetime, the Coast Guard is civilian and under the jurisdiction of the Transportation Department, but it uses a military organization to facilitate its conversion to a military unit in wartime. State militia (National Guard) are military but are not impeded by the Posse Comitatus Act (1878) which forbids the national military from engaging in civilian law enforcement.

6. Charles Lane, et al., "The Newest War," *Newsweek*, January 6, 1992, 21.

7. U.S. General Accounting Office, *Drug Control: Communications Network Funding and Requirements Uncertain*, GA/NSIAD-92-29 (Washington, D.C.: GAO, December 1991); Inter-American Commission on Drug Policy, *Seizing Opportunities*. San Diego: Institute of the Americas, 1991, 9.

8. William O. Walker, III, *Drug Control in the Americas*, Rev. ed. (Albuquerque: University of New Mexico Press, 1989).

9. Office of the Inspector General, U.S. Department of State, *Reports of Audit: Drug Control Activities in Bolivia*, 12-CI-001 (Washington, D.C.: October 1991); General Accounting Office, *The Drug War: U.S. Programs in Perú Face Serious Obstacles*, GAO-NSIAD-92-36 (October 1991).

10. Bureau of International Narcotics Matters, U.S. Department of State, *International Drug Control Strategy Report* (Washington, D.C.: Government Printing Office, March 1991), 26, 80, 97, 99, 118-119.

11. For a more detailed examination of the coca enterprise and U.S. drug policy in Perú, see Rensselaer W. Lee, III, *The White Labyrinth: Cocaine and Political Power* (New Brunswick, N.J.: Transaction Publishers, 1989) and Edmundo Morales, *Cocaine: White Gold Rush in Perú* (Tucson: University of Arizona Press, 1989).

12. *New York Times*, April 22, 1990. On the DEA assessment of Perú's priorities, see *DEA Review* (December 1989), 60-61, as quoted in Government Operations, *Anti-Narcotics Activities*, 38.

13. Alex Emery, "Fujimori: Won't Sign U.S. Military Aid Agreement to Combat Drugs" Associated Press Dispatch, published by Perú @ATHENA.MIT.EDU, September 13, 1990. Emery quotes U.S. Ambassador Anthony Quainton as having said in an interview with the news magazine *Caretas* that if Perú "does not sign the agreement, the aid would go to other countries." See also Michael Isikoff, "Talks Between U.S., Perú on Military Aid Collapse," *Washington Post*, September 26, 1990. César Atala, Peruvian ambassador to the United States in 1989, argued that a better solution to the coca-growing problem in his country was for the United States to buy the entire crop; see his testimony in United States Senate Committee on Governmental Affairs Permanent Subcommittee on Investigations. *U.S. Government Anti-Narcotics Activities in the Andean Region of South America. Hearing before the Permanent Subcommittee on Investigations of the Committee on Governmental Affairs*, United States Senate, 101st Cong. 1st Sess. September 26, 27, 29, 1989. S. Hrg. 101-311 (Washington, D.C.: GPO, 1989), 74. Gustavo Gorriti testified in the same hearings, arguing that mixing drug eradication and counterinsurgency was akin to pouring fuel on a fire; see his testimony on pages 128-132.

14. "Risky Business," *Newsweek*, July 16, 1990, 16-19. Lane et al. "The Newest War," *Newsweek*, January 6, 1992, 18-23. Simultaneous was not carefully defined in the article.

15. Lane, "The Newest War," 18-23. The best book on U.S. military efforts in the Andes is Washington Office on Latin America, *Clear and Present Dangers: The U.S. Military and the War on Drugs in Latin America* (Washington, D.C.: October 1991).

16. Tom Clancy, *Clear and Present Danger*, New York: G. P. Putnam's Sons, 1989.

17. United States Departments of Defense and State, "Andean Drug Efforts: A Report to Congress," *Congressional Record* (March 7), 102nd Cong., 1st Sess.

18. The problem of drug-related corruption in public security forces in the United States or Latin America is well documented. For some examples, see Government Operations, *Anti-Narcotics Activities*, 40-43, and the quotation from the *DEA Review*, December 1989, on page 60 of the same report; Kevin Healy, "Coca, The State, and the Peasantry in Bolivia, 1982-1988," *Journal of Interamerican Studies and World Affairs* 30:2 & 3 (Summer 1988), 111; and Coletta Youngers, "Colombia Military's Link with Drug Dealers," *The Christian Science Monitor*, September 11, 1989.

19. Augusto Varas, ed., *Hemispheric Security and U.S. Policy in Latin America*, 2nd ed., rev. and expanded (Lincoln: University of Nebraska Press, 1989).

20. J. Dillin, "US Paying Stiff Price for Porous Borders." *The Christian Science Monitor* (October 10, 1989), 1-2.

21. Laura Brooks, "US Military Extends Drug War Into C. America," *Christian Science Monitor*, June 25, 1991, 1.

22. Samuel Blixen, "Southern Cone Militaries Find Common Ground: MERCOSUR Allows for Growing Military Autonomy," *Latin America Press*, 23:21 (June 6, 1991), 1.

References

Blachman, Morris J., and Kenneth Sharpe. 1989. "The War on Drugs: American Democracy Under Assault." *World Policy Journal.* (Winter): 135-193.

Blixen, Samuel. 1991. "Southern Cone Militaries Find Common Ground: MERCOSUR Allows for Growing Military Autonomy." *Latin America Press.* 23(21), June 6: 1.

Brooks, Laura. 1991. "U.S. Military Extends Drug War into Central America." *The Christian Science Monitor.* June 25: 1.

Bureau of International Narcotics Matters, U.S. Department of State. 1991. *International Drug Control Strategy Report.* Washington, D.C.: Government Printing Office.

Clancy, Tom. 1989. *Clear and Present Danger.* New York: G.P. Putnam's Sons.

Committee on Armed Services. U.S. House of Representatives. 1990. *Report of the Defense Policy Panel and Investigations Subcommittee.* Washington, D.C.: GPO.

DEA Review. 1989. December.

Dillin, J. 1989. "U.S. Paying Stiff Price for Porous Borders." *The Christian Science Monitor.* October 10: 1-2.

Duncan, Stephen. 1989. *Testimony to hearing of Subcommittees on Legislation and National Security and Government Information.* U.S. House of Representatives. October 17. Mimeo.

Emery, Alex. 1990. "Fujimori: Won't Sign U.S. Military Aid Agreement to Combat Drugs." Associated Press Dispatch. September 13.

General Accounting Office. 1991. *Drug Control: Communications Network Funding and Requirements Uncertain.* Washington, D.C.: GAO. December. GA/NSIAD-92-29.

General Accounting Office. 1991. *The Drug War: U.S. Programs in Peru Face Serious Obstacles.* October. GAO/NSIAD-92-36.

Government Operations. 1989. *Anti-Narcotics Activities.*

Healy, Kevin. 1988. "Coca, the State, and the Peasantry in Bolivia, 1982-1988." *Journal of Interamerican Studies and World Affairs* 30(2-3), Summer.

Inter-American Commission on Drug Policy. 1991. *Seizing Opportunities.* San Diego: Institute of the Americas.

Isikoff, Michael. 1990. "Talks Between U.S., Peru on Military Aid Collapse." *Washington Post.* September 26.

Lane, Charles, et al. 1992. "The Newest War." *Newsweek.* January 6: 21.

Lee, Rensselaer W., III. 1989. *The White Labyrinth: Cocaine and Political Power.* New Brunswick, N.J.: Transaction Publishers.

Mabry, Donald J. 1990. "Andean Drug Trafficking and the Military Option." *The Military Review.* March.

Mabry, Donald J. 1989. "The Possible Roles of the U.S. Military in the Andes." *Andean Drug Strategy and the Role of the U.S. Military.* Proceedings of a seminar held by the Congressional Research Service. November 9.

Mabry, Donald J. 1988. "The U.S. Military and the War on Drugs in Latin America." *Journal of Interamerican Studies and World Affairs* 30(2), Summer-Fall.

Morales, Edmundo. 1989. *Cocaine: White Gold Rush in Peru.* Tucson: University of Arizona Press.

Morrison, David C. 1992. "Police Action." *National Journal.* February 1: 267-270.

New York Times. 1990. April 22.

Newsweek. 1990. "Risky Business." July 16: 16-19.

Office of the Inspector General, U.S. Department of State. 1991. *Reports of Audit: Drug Control Activities in Bolivia.* Washington, D.C.: GAO, October. 12-CI-001.

Olmstead, Stephen. 1988. *Narcotics Interdiction and the Use of the Military: Issues for Congress.* Washington, D.C.: Government Printing Office.

U.S. Departments of Defense and State. 1990. "Andean Drug Efforts: A Report to Congress." *Congressional Record.* March.

U.S. Senate Committee on Governmental Affairs Permanent Subcommittee on Investigations. 1989. *U.S. Government Anti-Narcotics Activities in the Andean Region of South America.* Hearing. September 26-29. S. Hrg.101-311. Washington, D.C.: GPO.

Varas, Augusto, ed. 1989. *Hemispheric Security and U.S. Policy in Latin America.* Lincoln: University of Nebraska Press.

Walker, William O., III. 1989. *Drug Control in the Americas.* Rev. ed. Albuquerque: University of New Mexico Press.

Washington Office on Latin America. 1991. *Clear and Present Dangers: The U.S. Military and the War on Drugs in Latin America.* Washington, D.C.:WOLA.

Youngers, Coletta. 1989. "Colombia Military's Link with Drug Dealers." *The Christian Science Monitor.* September 11.

Chapter Four

After San Antonio

Bruce Michael Bagley

Introduction

In an effort to extend and accelerate regional cooperation and coordination in the "War on Drugs" in the Western Hemisphere, President George Bush hosted a widely publicized, regional, antidrug presidential summit in San Antonio (Texas) on February 26-27, 1992.[1] This *cumbre* was conceived as an expanded sequel to the first "Andean" drug summit held in Cartagena (Colombia) on February 15, 1990. In addition to the original four-country participants in Cartagena I — the United States, Colombia, Peru, and Bolivia — Ecuador, Venezuela, and Mexico attended Cartagena II as well.[2]

This chapter endeavors, first, to set the San Antonio summit in historical and policy context by briefly reviewing the Reagan and Bush administrations' execution of the "war" on drugs. In this area, special attention is focused on the 1990 Andean summit and its subsequent impact on regional drug trafficking during the 1990-1992 period. It then undertakes to identify and clarify the key points of consensus and conflict that emerged during the San Antonio summit. The following section advances some basic criteria or benchmarks to assess the relative success or failure of San Antonio in terms of effectiveness of drug control efforts in the hemisphere over the next two to four years. Finally, there is an examination of the transition from Bush to Clinton focusing on the initial efforts made by the Clinton administration to develop a coherent drug control policy.

From Reagan to Bush: An Overview of U.S. Drug Control Policies in Latin America (1981-1991)

Confronted with rising domestic pressure to do something about the burgeoning U.S. drug "epidemic" during his first year in office, in 1982 President Ronald Reagan dramatically declared "war" on drugs and unveiled his administration's plans to launch a "full-scale" attack against drug abuse and dealing at home and against production, processing, and trafficking abroad. Strongly backing Reagan's proclamation of "war," bipartisan majorities in the U.S. Congress, in 1982 and thereafter, enthusiastically enacted tougher domestic antidrug legislation, expanded federal drug enforcement budgets, widened the role of the U.S. military in drug control efforts both at home and abroad, stepped up interdiction programs at U.S. borders and overseas, and increased levels of U.S. assistance to Latin American and Caribbean source and transit countries, as requested by the Reagan administration.

Washington's progressively "tougher" antidrug campaign in the 1980s was paralleled by intensifying U.S. diplomatic pressures and economic sanctions against Latin American and Caribbean governments judged to be less than fully cooperative with the U.S.-sponsored war on drugs. As result of this rapid escalation, in the mid- and late 1980s, U.S. authorities could legitimately claim some victories had been won in the antidrug fight. Federal cocaine seizures, for example, rose from just 2 tons in 1981 to 27 tons in 1986 and to almost 100 tons by 1989. Local and state agency confiscations in the United States also increased steadily over the decade. Moreover, U.S. foreign assistance programs clearly contributed to a substantial reduction in the flow of marijuana and heroin smuggled into the United States from Mexico during the early 1980s.

Despite such certifiable advancement, however, overall the greatly expanded U.S. drug control and interdiction efforts during the 1980s proved ineffective in stemming the explosive growth of drug consumption and trafficking in the United States. Alternative sources of supply and transshipment quickly emerged to meet rising U.S. demand. The decline in Mexican marijuana production was, for example, quickly offset by a parallel boom in marijuana exports from Colombia, Belize, and Jamaica. Likewise, the "success" of the Reagan-sponsored South Florida Task Force (a federal interagency coordinating body headed by then-Vice President George Bush) in the mid-1980s' interdiction campaign against marijuana and cocaine trafficking from Colombia through the Caribbean was offset by a resurgence of Mexican marijuana smuggling and the proliferation of alternate cocaine transportation routes through Central America and Mexico during the latter half of the decade.

In late 1988, frustrated by the manifest ineffectiveness of the Reagan administration's supply-side antidrug strategy and tactics — and faced with increasingly shrill public demands for Washington to "do more" to curb the U.S. drug problem in advance of the November congressional and presidential elections — the U.S. Congress enacted the Anti-Drug Abuse Act of 1988. While this law continued to underwrite the Reagan administration's supply-side programs, which included expanded eradication and crop substitution, enhanced law enforcement, and intensified interdiction efforts in source countries, it also focused more explicitly on demand-side programs than previous U.S. antidrug legislation. In a highly symbolic move, 50 percent of the federal funding for fiscal year 1990 (FY 1990) was earmarked (out of a total federal drug budget of US$9.3773 billion) for domestic demand control and enforcement programs (versus the standard 30 percent of the Reagan years). This shift was not merely cosmetic nor simply a function of election year politicking. It reflected widespread disillusionment in the U.S. Congress with the ineffective, but increasingly costly, supply-side antidrug policies that had been pursued by the Reagan administration during its two terms in office. In short, the shift was driven by failure.

The heightened priority assigned to demand-side measures in the 1988 law and the accompanying FY 1989 budgetary authorizations hinted that a conceptual transition away from Washington's traditional supply-side myopia might be underway when President Bush took office in January 1989. Nonetheless, the transition was at best embryonic and tentative. The new legislation did not abandon existing U.S. supply-side programs abroad but, rather, expanded them while simultaneously opening a second front directed at reducing demand in the United States.

In practice, however, the Bush administration's budget proposals continued to emphasize controlling the supply through interdiction (70 percent) over reducing the demand (only 30 percent). Given the substantial increases for all aspects of the war on drugs during the Bush presidency, however, the total funding allocated to demand-side programs by the U.S. government rose substantially. The bulk of the increased federal resources for demand reduction during Bush's first term were dedicated primarily to domestic interdiction and law enforcement (70 percent), rather than to programs for prevention, education, and treatment (30 percent).

Militarization of the War on Drugs and the Andean Strategy

Despite high-level Pentagon resistance to broadening the U.S. military's role in the escalating war on drugs observable during the Reagan presidency, on September 19, 1989, Bush's new Secretary of Defense, former Congressman Richard Cheney (R-Wyoming), publicly proclaimed that detecting and countering the production and trafficking of illegal drugs was a "high-priority, national security mission" for the Pentagon. In effect, this dramatic policy statement presaged the Bush administration's rapid expansion of the U.S. military's involvement in drug control efforts at U.S. borders and abroad. The same policy logic also led the Bush administration to step up U.S. pressures on Latin American governments to expand the participation of their armed forces in the fight against drug production and trafficking region-wide. Between FY 1989 and FY 1990, funding for the U.S. military's antidrug activities almost doubled, rising to US$450 million. By FY 1992, it had reached US$1.2 billion.

The Bush administration's inclination to militarize the war on drugs in Latin America was reflected in the rapid expansion of drug-related military aid to cocaine producing nations: from some US$5 million in 1988 to US$150 million in 1991. It was also underscored by Washington's 1989 decision to construct Vietnam-style fire bases for operations of the U.S. Drug Enforcement Administration (DEA) in Peru's Alto Huallaga valley, in Drug Czar William Bennet's statements that U.S. Special Forces might be sent to the Andean coca producing countries if requested, in the deployment of sophisticated U.S. surveillance satellites over Mexican territory without Mexican authorization, in the administration's expressions of U.S. support for the creation of an international strike force despite objections from virtually all Latin American leaders, and in its emphasis on military aid in the highly publicized "Andean strategy" to combat cocaine trafficking, announced in September 1989.

The first phase of Bush's Andean strategy (the US$65 million aid package sent to Colombia in late September 1989 to support President Virgilio Barco's August 18 declaration of "total war" against Colombia's drug cartels) provided mostly conventional military arms, even though the Barco government had requested mainly police equipment, electronic intelligence-gathering devices, and technical assistance for Colombia's debilitated judicial system. The second phase (the FY 1990 budgetary request for US$261 million in antidrug assistance programs for Bolivia, Peru, and Colombia) funded Andean military and police activities almost exclusively. President Bush's unilateral decision (December 20, 1989) to send U.S. troops into Panama to topple the Noriega government and bring him to the United States for trial on drug trafficking and money-laundering charges similarly highlighted Bush's inclination to use U.S. military power to prosecute the war on drug trafficking in the hemisphere.

The Andean Summit

To defuse the widespread, albeit relatively short-lived, condemnations of the U.S. military intervention in Panama voiced by most Latin American governments in January 1990, the Bush administration proclaimed its commitment to greater multilateral regional cooperation on drug control issues in the hemisphere. To dramatize this commitment, President Bush reaffirmed his promise to attend the upcoming "Andean Drug Summit," in Cartagena (February 15) despite extensive media speculation regarding the potential security risks posed by Colombia's narcoterrorists and statements from Peru's Alán García that he would boycott the meeting to protest the U.S. "occupation" of Panama.

To persuade García to reconsider, President Bush announced that U.S. forces would begin a phased withdrawal from Panama prior to the Andean summit. To soften regional criticism of the U.S. Andean strategy's excessive emphasis on military tactics, the Bush administration publicized its plans to deliver US$2.2 billion in economic development funds to the Andean nations to ease their passage through a 1991-1995 "transition period" in which they would move away from coca cultivation and trafficking. Finally, to ensure a closing communiqué acceptable to the Andean presidents, in the weeks prior to the summit, U.S. and Andean negotiators painstakingly hammered out a compromise document that significantly modified the original U.S. proposals regarding the role of the Andean militaries in drug control operations and acceded to Andean demands that the United States give a higher priority to reducing its demand for drugs at home.

At the Cartagena I summit itself, President Bush did not publicly press the Andean leaders on the sensitive issues of foreign and domestic military involvement in their countries' antidrug campaigns. Moreover, he explicitly recognized that U.S. consumption was a key factor fueling the hemispheric drug trade, which had to be controlled, and he publicly pledged that his administration would step up demand-reduction programs in the United States. In short, President Bush went to considerable lengths, both before and during Cartagena I, to reassure the regional leaders that Washington sought cooperation, not conflict; that it was aware of the economic and social costs of Andean antidrug efforts; and that it would provide not only police and military assistance, but also development aid to help ameliorate the disruptive effects of suppressing the cocaine trade in the Andes.

Within weeks, however, the cordiality and cooperative spirit projected during the summit began to fade. The Colombians, for example, were deeply offended by the U.S. Navy's seizure of two Colombian freighters (March 1990) within the country's 200-mile maritime boundary without previous consultation. They also expressed resentment regarding the Bush administration's failure to heed its promise to help make up for the income lost by Colombia owing to the U.S.-driven dissolution of the International Coffee Agreement in mid-1989 and its decision to invoke additional countervailing duties on Colombian cut flower exports. In July 1989, Colombia's president-elect, César Gaviria, had sharply criticized Washington's "protectionist" trade policies vis-à-vis the Andean nations and pointed out that his country wanted expanded "trade, not aid" to underwrite its war against drug trafficking.

In August 1990, President Jaime Paz Zamora of Bolivia protested bitterly that Washington's Andean strategy aid for his country was inadequate and misguided. It was inadequate because the US$80-90 million promised was insufficient to promote alternative economic development opportunities for Bolivia's 200,000 peasant coca farmers. Paz Zamora set his country's needs at closer to US$1 billion annually. It was misguided because U.S. assistance was conditioned on his acceptance of an expanded role for the Bolivian armed forces in the drug fight. In his view, expanded military involvement could pose serious dangers to democratic stability. President Alberto Fujimori of Peru also decried Washington's aid program for his nation on similar grounds: it overemphasized military repression and short-changed development assistance. Although both Paz (in FY 1990) and Fujimori (in FY 1991) ultimately acceded to Washington's "conditionality," resentments and frictions concerning the insufficiency of development aid seriously constrained subsequent implementation of antidrug programs in both countries.

The effectiveness of U.S. drug control assistance in all three Andean countries was also undercut by the deep-seated, drug-related corruption that permeates their national political institutions, including military and police forces. U.S. military aid and training may have brought about some marginal improvement in the performance of the various Andean military and police forces involved in antidrug operations, but, absent fundamental economic, social, and political reforms within these countries, they have not engendered meaningful increases in the Andean governments' will or ability to control drug production, processing, and trafficking within either their respective national territories or the region as a whole. Indeed, realistic assessments of the situation suggest that the cost-effectiveness of U.S. military assistance programs in the Andean region will be very low.

In light of the higher priority that the Andean armed forces have traditionally accorded to the preservation of internal order and suppression of "communist" or revolutionary insurgencies, the likelihood that they will dedicate significant portions of their limited resources or manpower to drug control efforts is very small for the foreseeable future. In fact, U.S. military aid is far more likely to be used to combat rebel forces than drug traffickers. In the process, there is a real danger of heightened human rights abuses by the armed forces of the region (e.g., Peru) and of military threats to civilian authority and democratic political stability.

The San Antonio Summit

The draft proposal distributed by the Bush administration in January 1992 to the Latin American governments invited to the San Antonio summit contained no major shifts in the basic premises or priorities underlying Washington's approach to regional drug control.[3] Of the 30 points put forward in the U.S. draft, 14, or just under half, dealt with questions of interdiction and law enforcement, 9 focused on alternative development issues, 4 on demand reduction, and only 2 on multilateral cooperation. Overall, the document strongly suggested that the U.S. administration intended to press its Latin American counterparts at the San Antonio meeting to re-affirm and intensify their individual and collective interdiction and law enforcement activities.

The highest priority item on the U.S. agenda was a recommendation for the formal creation of regional mechanisms to coordinate antidrug policy. Two specific bodies were suggested: a Regional Examination Conference and a Regional Action Group. Both were to meet regularly every six months. Cartagena I had endorsed the idea of regular evaluations but failed to activate a workable system.

It was probable that the Latin Americans would agree to the formation of a new regional antidrug coordinating body, but most certainly would insist on the need for less unilateralism, or more multilateral mechanisms. It was also quite likely that some (e.g., Bolivia, Peru, and Ecuador) would seek increased economic and development aid from Washington. Most, if not all, pushed for expanded access to U.S. markets for their exports and for greater equity and reciprocity during the transition to free trade agreements (especially in areas like intellectual property, textiles, and agricultural quotas).

Due to the U.S. recession, surging protectionist sentiments in the U.S. Congress, and the exigencies of U.S. presidential campaigning, President Bush found it difficult to respond to these demands satisfactorily, for the potential for heightened friction and recriminations was considerable. The Latin American leaders also highlighted the necessity for further reduction of consumption in the United States. They sought to link their progress on the supply side to corresponding U.S. progress on the demand side.

Assessing Success and Failure

The Bush administration's attempts to elicit fuller and more effective cooperation from the Latin American governments after Cartagena I were largely unsuccessful. U.S. strategies and tactics need to be redirected, and the overall strategy must seek a better balance between demand- and supply-side priorities. Washington's tactics must move away from unilateral pressures and sanctions to multilateral cooperation.

The basic reason for Bush's disappointing failure is that the drug trade in the Americas epitomizes the type of issue (environmental problems are another) that simply cannot be resolved through unilateral or bilateral approaches alone. Indeed, rather than curtailing regional drug trafficking in the 1980s and early 1990s, U.S. unilateral, supply-side policies often exacerbated drug-related violence and instability and undermined multilateral cooperation on drug control issues.

To reverse the counterproductive aspects of past policies and develop more promising drug control efforts in the region, the potential pay-offs from a shift to multilateralism could be substantial. Such a shift would signal to the Latin American and Caribbean governments that their interests and needs will be taken into account. It would pave the way for the adoption of more rational and equitable formulas for cost-sharing and resource allocation in regional drug control programs. It would provide a mechanism for attracting and distributing support from extra-hemispheric governments (e.g., the Europeans and Japanese). Finally, it would allow for the design and implementation of more consensual, and thus workable, drug control efforts in the hemisphere.

There are, of course, limits to effective national and regional action in this issue area, whether such actions are undertaken unilaterally or collectively. It is unrealistic to expect, for example, that the hemisphere drug trade will be curbed in the short or even medium term, no matter what approach, or combination of approaches, is adopted. On the demand side, consumption reduction will unquestionably be a difficult, expensive, and time-consuming process under even the most optimistic scenario. On the supply side, given that even such advanced capitalist-country governments as the United States or Italy have proven unable to eliminate organized crime in their societies, despite repeated attempts to do so over the twentieth century, the less developed and institutionalized nation-states of Latin America and the Caribbean cannot realistically be expected to do so, especially against the immensely wealthy and well-armed international drug trafficking rings they presently face.

"Progress" in the realm of drug control need not imply complete fulfillment of utopian goals such as total victory or a "drug-free" society. Measurable movement toward the more modest and feasible objectives of effective containment and gradual reversal of the negative economic, social, and political ramifications of drug trafficking and consumption in the region would certainly constitute real "progress." From this perspective, rather than evaluating the effectiveness of Cartagena II in terms of its ability to "win" the "war on drugs" or to "end" the region's drug "scourge" once and for all, the criteria should be more pragmatic and realistic. Incremental progress constitutes a more realistic scale against which to measure the effectiveness of drug control efforts in the Western Hemisphere.

First, will Cartagena II allow political leaders in the hemisphere to move away from the counterproductive cycles of rhetorical denunciations and periodic tensions that characterized U.S.-Latin American narcodiplomacy during the 1980s? Second, will it contribute to the development of the policy coordination mechanisms necessary to address the hemisphere's multifaceted drug problems seriously? Third, will the U.S. government — still the regional hegemon — prove willing and able to mobilize the leadership and resources required to reduce U.S. drug consumption and attendant violence, to reduce U.S.-based money laundering, chemical exports, and arms trafficking? Fourth, will the Latin American and Caribbean governments in source and transit countries prove willing and able to strengthen their legal systems and law enforcement agencies, reduce their endemic institutional corruption, and lower their economic dependence on drug exports? Fifth, will the international community provide the levels of economic and technical assistance that the nation-states of Latin America and the Caribbean require to initiate and sustain economic and institutional reforms needed to control the powerful and corrosive effects of the region's illicit drug trade on their social and governmental structures?

From Bush to Clinton

Despite the nearly $100 billion spent by the Reagan and Bush administrations on the U.S. "War on Drugs" during the preceding twelve years, at the outset of the Clinton presidency in January 1993 the consensus among drug policy analysts both at home and abroad was that Washington's supply-side, law enforcement strategy had not worked and that a new "battle plan" was urgently needed. In the United States, disenchantment with existing policy derived from the dismaying evidence that illegal drugs (especially cocaine and heroin) were cheaper, more potent, and more readily available at the end of Bush's term in office than they had been in 1981 when President Ronald Reagan launched America's contemporary antidrug crusade. Indeed, U.S. hospital emergency room admissions for cocaine and heroin abuse in 1992 — Bush's final year in office — surpassed the previous record set in 1989 during his first year in the White House, revealing a distressing worsening of hard-core use in U.S. society.

In Latin America and the Caribbean, as well as in the U.S. Congress, disappointment with the U.S.-led war on drugs was similarly driven by failure. In spite of massive increases in U.S. international narcotics control assistance, especially under Bush, overall levels of illicit drug production, consumption, trafficking and related corruption, violence and terrorism in the hemisphere had continued to spiral upwards throughout the 1980s and early 1990s. Moreover, Washington's emphasis on supply reduction strategies and repressive tactics ("militarization") were heavily criticized for inflicting — however unintentionally — serious damage on the fragile democratic institutions of several regional allies. In short, U.S. drug policy in much of the hemisphere was viewed not merely as costly and ineffective, but as perversely counter-productive as well.

Reflecting this rising tide of complaints and disillusionment, during the 1992 U.S. presidential campaign the Democratic challenger, Bill Clinton, pledged that he would redirect Washington's antidrug policy away from the Reagan-Bush emphasis on supply-side strategies and tactics toward "a comprehensive national crusade against drug abuse" and related crime and violence at home. As a first step in the promised revamping of the drug war, in February 1993, Clinton and the Democrat-controlled U.S. Congress began to scale back the Bush administration's commitment of hundreds of millions of dollars annually for the fight against cocaine trafficking in the Andean region by capping the Fiscal Year (FY) 1994 authorization for the Andean strategy at US$174 million, a 35 percent reduction vis-à-vis Bush's FY 1993 budget. Following the completion in May 1993 of a classified review of U.S. overseas drug control programs by the National Security Council (NSC) — ordered by President Clinton in late January — which concluded that drug cultivation and trafficking in Latin America and Asia had continued essentially unaffected despite the massive infusion of U.S. equipment, training, and aid under Bush, total U.S. funding for international drug control for FY 1994 was reduced by 8 percent ($44 million less than Bush's FY 1993 high of $536 million for international antidrug operations).

The Clinton administration's determination to shift U.S. drug policy from supply-side to demand-side priorities was again underscored in early February 1993 when President Clinton announced that he would reduce the support personnel assigned to the U.S. drug czar from the total of 146 reached under Bush to just 25. According to Thomas F. McLarty, Clinton's Chief of Staff, the intention of this reorganization was to concentrate the U.S. government's antidrug effort on federal assistance for education, treatment, and local and state law enforcement in the United States, rather than on overseas programs or border control efforts. Although Clinton attempted to allay concerns that the down-sizing of the czar's staff signaled a de-emphasis of drug issues under his presidency by pledging to elevate the czar position to Cabinet status, many skeptics expressed doubts that the drug czar could operate effectively with such a small staff. Clinton's subsequent nomination as Director of the Office of National Drug Control Policy (ONDCP) of former New York Police Chief Lee Brown — whose expertise on drug issues was primarily domestic — provided further evidence of the new emphasis on demand- over supply-side policies. At his May 25, 1993, confirmation hearings before the Senate Judiciary Committee, nominee Brown vowed to develop "a comprehensive and balanced" U.S. drug strategy, while cautiously avoiding specifying how he would recommend dividing federal antidrug resources between supply-control and demand-reduction efforts. The Committee chairman, Senator Joseph Biden (D-Delaware), noting that Brown's Senate confirmation had come too late to allow him to influence the FY 1994 budgetary process, advised that the new czar should concentrate, instead, on designing new strategic priorities for the FY 1995 cycle.

In early May, a few weeks prior to Brown's hearing, Clinton's recently confirmed Attorney General, Janet Reno, in the most extensive comments on overall U.S. drug policy made by any high-level appointee of the new administration, expressed serious reservations about the cost-effectiveness of the multi-billion-dollar annual U.S. government expenditures to curb the production of illicit drugs abroad and to interdict drug smuggling into the United States. In her opinion, U.S. drug policy should focus on expanding domestic education, prevention, treatment, and rehabilitation programs and on devising alternatives to imprisonment for drug offenders rather than on expensive and ineffective supply-control initiatives abroad.

Although the new Clinton administration provided few details on exactly how it intended to approach the complex issues of drug use and abuse in U.S. society in its first six months in office, all the signals coming from the White House pointed unmistakably toward a major policy shift. In fiscal terms, Clinton's revised priorities raised expectations that he would propose to reduce the 70 percent share of federal drug funds routinely allocated to supply control and law enforcement under Reagan and Bush (versus the 30 percent share allotted for education and treatment) to a more equitable ratio — perhaps even a 50-50 percent split.

Belying its own rhetoric, however, the Clinton administration's FY 1994 drug budget of $13.04 billion, submitted to Congress in late March 1993, modified the ratio between supply- and demand-side funding typical of earlier Reagan and Bush budgets only marginally (64 versus 34 percent). Clinton's final budget proposal did reduce funding for U.S. international drug operations, particularly for the Andean strategy as announced previously, but increased domestic spending for demand reduction only modestly: e.g., treatment (6 percent) and law enforcement (7 percent). The overall impression was that the new budget contained no fundamental changes in U.S. policy or priorities.

Despite the decidedly incremental nature of the Clinton administration's final 1994 drug budget, the proposed cuts in U.S. antidrug aid for the Andean strategy, nevertheless, provoked sharp protests from government leaders throughout the Andean region. Despite their agreement that existing U.S. antidrug policy was not working and that alternative, less militaristic tactics were needed, they feared that the new U.S. administration might abandon international drug control programs altogether. The comments of Colombian President César Gaviria Trujillo reflected the Andean leaders' general uneasiness:

> We are not worried that it is not the first item on the agenda; we are
> not worried if the emphasis changes or has new components. But
> we are worried that the fight will be weakened or the political will
> be lost to fight drug trafficking.

Given the transition from a well-known, incumbent Republican to an unfamiliar Democrat in the White House, such doubts and concerns regarding future U.S. policy intentions and commitments on drug control issues were not surprising, especially in view of Clinton's explicit emphasis on U.S. domestic over international priorities. The contretemps that attended Clinton's search for an acceptable Attorney General, the urgency of other, often unanticipated foreign policy crises (e.g., Bosnia, Somalia, Haiti, and Russia), and the slow pace of nominations and confirmations of Clinton appointees responsible for drug policy and Latin American affairs unquestionably heightened the uncertainty in governing circles throughout the Andean region during Clinton's first eight months in the White House.

Transition-related glitches do not, however, fully explain the current confusion over the direction of U.S. international drug control efforts under Clinton still observable at the end of his first year in the presidency. Beyond these problems, the underlying reality was that the new administration, while publicly skeptical of past Reagan-Bush strategies and tactics abroad, had not put forward an alternative approach of its own. Basic questions regarding what should or would be the role of the United States, if any, in international drug control remained undefined.

To come up with appropriate alternatives to current policy, the Clinton administration will have to part from an accurate diagnosis of the specific roles played and dilemmas faced by each country in the regional political economy of drug trafficking and a realistic assessment of the nature and scope of the threats to U.S. interests posed by the trade in each individual country, subregion, and the hemisphere as a whole. It must then evaluate which policies have worked and which have not, which are cost-effective and which are not, and which can muster the necessary political support (both at home and abroad) and which can not. Only by proceeding in this fashion will it be feasible for the new administration to design and implement a revised international drug control strategy with any chance of success.

Notes

1. This summit was originally scheduled to be held in Miami (Florida) but was moved, at the request of the Bolivian and Mexican delegations, to San Antonio (Texas) in late January 1992 because of their fears of disruptive demonstrations by anti-Castro Cubans in that city.

2. U.S. President Bush and Bolivian President Jaime Paz Zamora had represented their respective countries at Cartagena I and did so again at Cartagena II. Peruvian President Alberto Fujimori had succeeded President Alan Garcia in July 1989 and thus had not attended Cartagena I. Neither Ecuador's Rodrigo Borja nor Mexico's Carlos Salinas de Gortari had been invited to the first conclave but did represent their nations at San Antonio. Venezuela's Carlos Andres Perez did not attend Cartagena I either, but he did receive an invitation to Cartagena II. After an attempted military coup nearly toppled his government early in February 1992, however, he decided not to attend personally but, rather, to send Foreign Minister Armando Duran to represent Venezuela.

3. In early January 1992, U.S. Under-Secretary of State Robert Gelbart visited the six Latin American participants in Cartagena II and distributed U.S. proposals for the summit's agenda, and a meeting to discuss the U.S. proposals was held in Quito (Ecuador) the first week in February.

Colombia

Chapter Five

The Size of the Illegal Drug Industry

Francisco E. Thoumi

Introduction

The growth of the illegal, psychoactive drug industry has had a dramatic impact on Colombia. Most studies of the financial effects of this industry — mainly, cocaine and its byproducts, but extending also to marijuana, quaaludes, other psychoactive substances, and, more recently, heroin — have focused upon trying to estimate its size and determining its impact on the national economy. On the whole, the conclusion of most observers has been that its effects on the economy have been more negative than positive (Kalmanovitz 1989; Reyes 1990; Sarmiento 1990; Urrutia 1990; Thoumi 1987). Among the more deleterious consequences of this trade, it has

- led to re-valuation of the currency which, in turn, contributed to the decline of some of Colombia's traditional industries;
- promoted speculative investments;
- created a climate of violence of such magnitude that it stimulated the flight of domestic capital and discouraged investment, both domestic and foreign, more generally;
- diverted much of the investment that did take place into socially unproductive, low-yielding enterprises, chosen more for their utility in laundering illegal profits than for profitability; and
- increased costs of the business sector by forcing business to invest heavily in security.

The few who have taken an opposite view argue that trade in illegal narcotics (mostly cocaine) has benefitted the country, particularly Medellín and the Antioquia department. Arango, for one, claims that growth of the cocaine trade 1) halted a process of social and political deterioration set in motion by de-industrialization, primarily in the Medellín area; 2) provided economic support to an economy in crisis; and 3) opened channels for upward mobility to frustrated social groups (Arango 1988, 183).

This research was part of a multi-country project funded by the United Nations Research Institute for Social Development (UNRISD).

The growth of the illegal drug industry in Colombia raises some interesting questions, many of which have received insufficient attention. For instance, why Colombia? Why was it Colombians who became so involved in this industry? Why do Colombians control the main cocaine marketing systems? Why are the principal manufacturing centers for cocaine and its derivatives (like *bazuco*) located in Colombia rather than in some other countries?

Answers to these questions are neither obvious nor trivial. After all, narcotics can be, and are, produced in many locations. In the specific instance of cocaine, for example, Colombia's dominant product in this industry, the country is neither a main producer of the raw material, coca, nor does it have a domestic market of sufficient size to support a large industry.

These questions gain cogency for several reasons. First, the international demand for cocaine and other narcotics is not likely to drop sharply in the near future. Second, the major consuming nations do not appear about to decriminalize, legalize, control, or regulate the industry. Given this situation, it is most probable that the profits to be derived from the international traffic in cocaine and allied drugs will remain at very high levels. Hence, the cocaine industry will continue to impact Colombia and its government, at least for the foreseeable future. Finding the answers to the above questions could help the Colombian government, if not others, to determine the most productive course to follow in dealing with the illegal drug industry.

Several attempts to answer these questions have been made. Since cocaine is the dominant drug in the Colombian pantheon, most of the literature on illegal drugs in Colombia focuses on cocaine.

Some prominent Colombian politicians have argued that the country's advantage in producing cocaine is simply due to its location: halfway between the main producing regions and the largest market.[1] Other authors share this view. MacDonald states,

> First and foremost, the South American country benefits from its geopolitical location. It is strategically located between the coca-producing nations of Peru and Bolivia and the routes through the Caribbean and Central America that lead to the lucrative North American and European markets (1988, 28).

However, MacDonald also felt that geography was not the only factor responsible for Colombia's critical role in the South American drug traffic. He cites three other important elements: 1) Colombia's vast forests, which lend themselves to easy concealment of laboratories and landing strips; 2) Colombians' entrepreneurial skills, which could be applied to develop a sophisticated refining and marketing system; and 3) the presence of a sizable Colombian community in the United States, providing the nucleus from which a distribution network could be recruited. He suggests that these factors were able to interact as a package, concluding that "other nations have some of these factors, but not all, the most important being the lack of geopolitical location. Only Mexico in Latin America may come close" (MacDonald 1988, 29). A similar point was made by Whynes when he stated that the geographical location of Colombia as a point of infiltration by air and sea into the United States was, and remains, ideal (Whynes 1992).

Still other analysts have pointed to a different set of factors, combining what might be called economic culture and environment. Both Arango (1988), as well as Arango and Child (1987), have suggested that Colombia's cocaine industry grew, in part, as a response by Antioqueño entrepreneurs to threatening economic change.[2] For this to happen, several factors had to coalesce. For many years, from the 1940s to the early 1970s, Medellín had supported a flourishing textile industry. In the mid-1970s, this industry, unable to compete with an increased level of contraband, began to decline, giving rise to increasing unemployment. Contraband trade had a long tradition in Antioquia but was not a disgrace; in Antioqueño society, one's social worth was weighed according to one's wealth, regardless of the source of that wealth. According to this argument, these factors combined to make Medellín and Antioquia particularly hospitable to a new item of contraband. Finally, the industry may have been spurred by a fortuitous mistake: the fact that many North Americans do not have a clear idea of South American geography, leading them to confuse one country with another (Colombia with Bolivia, for example). Colombian smugglers in Panama frequently found themselves fielding inquiries from U.S. dealers regarding sources of cocaine, thus prompting the Colombians to find ways to meet that demand themselves.[3]

Other analysts have added to this argument. In an early work, Craig argues that the Colombian environment was particularly conducive to the growth of the illegal drug industry because of the prevalence and social acceptance of contraband, the large growth of the underground economy during the 1970s, and the willingness of Colombian dealers in illegal drugs to use violence.[4] Craig sums up his assessment of the Colombian environment and entrepreneurial abilities this way:

> They (the Colombians) are, indeed, master smugglers. Yet even the greatest of talents requires a proper arena in which to perform. In this regard, Colombia constitutes a virtual amphitheater (1981, 246).

Dombois (1990) points out that the negligible presence of the state in many areas of the country, widespread corruption of the state's bureaucracies (promoted, at least partially, by a clientelist political system), and the existence of an active guerrilla movement created a very auspicious environment for the industry's growth. More recently, Sarmiento (1990, 33) has argued that Colombians developed a comparative advantage in the illegal drug trade by mastering the appropriate technology needed to break or circumvent the antinarcotics laws and/or to thwart the enforcement efforts of the governments of the producing and consuming countries. Sarmiento indicates that the main elements of this technology are "transportation, commercialization, the capacity to bribe and intimidate, and, above all, to mobilize the (economic) surplus."[5] This last point is important because the drug profits give the businessmen engaged in this illegal trade the ability to buy, or provide themselves with, sufficient protection to operate successfully.

The explanatory power of these analyses varies substantially. In general, although these arguments are plausible, they fail to provide a definitive explanation as to just why it was Colombia — rather than some other country — which came to occupy a primary, central position in the international *narcotráfico*.[6]

Let us take a closer look at some of the reasons advanced. First, given 1) the huge difference between the cost of production and the wholesale prices obtaining in the United States and 2) the fact that cocaine has a very high value per unit of volume and weight, neither physical distance between sources of supply and the end market nor transportation costs are major considerations in determining the locus of its manufacture. The geopolitical argument, while apparently reasonable, still does not adequately explain why the refining process was lodged mainly in Colombia since the relative simplicity of the cocaine refining process would have enabled it to be located just as easily (perhaps, even more so) near its raw material sources. Nor does this argument explain why it was Colombians who controlled the marketing and transportation of both coca paste and its finished product, cocaine. Colombia is not a primary point for transshipment of cocaine as is true of some of the countries in Central America and the Caribbean, whose geopolitical location is important. Cocaine differs from marijuana in this respect, since the latter is bulky to transport, making Colombia less suitable and other locations (in the Caribbean, Central America, and Mexico) more desirable for this purpose, providing, as they do, closer proximity and better access to the U.S. market.

Other causal factors mentioned — increased unemployment, state corruption, a tradition of smuggling — may, indeed, be important but can also be found in other countries (such as Peru) with a long history of coca production and consumption; they in no way single out Colombia as being in some way uniquely qualified to be the site for cocaine production and refining.

In fact, the relation between cause and effect could run just as easily in the opposite direction. One could argue, with equal cogency, that the decline of Medellín's manufacturing sector could just as well have been a result, at least in part, of the re-valuation of currency and other "dutch disease" effects of the lucrative export of illegal drugs.[7] Similarly, difficulties in the textile industry that are attributed to the increase in, and unfair competition from, the trade in contraband could just as easily be attributed to the increased export of illegal drugs, which earned the foreign exchange needed to purchase that contraband, thus acting as a stimulus to the latter.

Even conceding the sociological characterization, and relevance, of Antioqueño society and values, several factors are left unexplained: why, then, did other large drug cartels develop outside Antioquia? And why were some of the principal leaders of the Medellín cartel (like Carlos Lehder and Gonzalo Rodríguez-Gacha) not Antioqueños?

What about the argument of dealers confusing Bolivia with Colombia? Certainly the explanation is ingenious, but it is difficult to believe that people engaged in smuggling, which involves at least a minimum knowledge of geography to stay in business, would confuse the location of the countries so crucial to their success.[8]

While rising unemployment may stimulate the search for new sources of income, the cause-and-effect between Medellín unemployment and growth of a narco-industry remains to be demonstrated. Many cities in the Andean countries have had levels of unemployment equal to, or higher than, that of Medellín, particularly during the early 1980s, yet failed to become major players in the narcotraffic, much less players of like magnitude. Moreover, Colombia has witnessed a large degree of internal migration over the last 40 years. In this situation, Medellín has been a particularly strong magnet for domestic migrants for a variety of reasons, a fact which has resulted in a higher equilibrium level of unemployment.[9] Some of these attractive factors were 1) a larger protected manufacturing base than other Colombian cities, which gave its workers higher than average incomes, and 2) the best municipal public utilities in the country, with better service than was available elsewhere. Though Medellín's high unemployment and Antioqueño cultural idiosyncracies may have contributed to the growth of the *sicarios* (assassins-for-hire) industry, which is concentrated there, these factors do not explain the trafficking side of the business.

From an economist's point of view, there is a certain appeal in the argument that Colombians developed the appropriate "technology" for this business, made up of such elements as corruption, intimidation, and — above all — the ability of drug dealers to use their income for those purposes (Sarmiento 1990). This ability is treated as a "factor of production," an approach which is unsatisfactory on both theoretical and policy grounds.

On the theoretical level, two issues are involved. First, in order for us to accept Sarmiento's thesis of "comparative advantage," he must demonstrate that the ability to mobilize the economic surplus was greater in Colombia than in other countries. This he has not done. Indeed, the ability to mobilize the economic surplus to protect the industry is not necessarily greater in Colombia than in other countries. To give but one example, that ability could have been greater in Panama where there was no need to convert foreign exchange and where the secrecy of the financial system was so much greater since the very reason for its existence was to enable individuals to break, or circumvent, the laws of other countries.

Second, the production function of a firm is defined as the physical relationship between inputs and outputs, a relationship that is independent of the market structure and the institutional framework in which the firm operates. However, Sarmiento's approach makes the production function dependent upon those elements which he then treats as factors of production. From a policy viewpoint, treating the institutional environment as one of the firm's factors of production makes it possible to sweep institutional deficiencies and weaknesses (which underlie the growth of the illegal drug industry) under the rug instead of confronting them. Such elements as widespread corruption, intimidation, and the like are the result of a decaying institutional environment — a fact which is conveniently overlooked when they are treated as "factors of production." True factors of production carry a positive productive value and, presumably, should be encouraged since they make a positive contribution to the gross domestic product (GDP).

Though the psychoactive drug industry in Colombia covers several products, cocaine is the single drug responsible for the largest share of that industry, has the largest impact on the country, is the focus of the literature — and will be the focus of the remainder of this discussion.

The next section describes the cocaine production function and its characteristics and identifies the sources of the industry's value added. The third section discusses the basis of Colombia's international advantage in the cocaine industry. It is argued there that a set of factors, many of which were present in other countries, but which — as a package — are unique to Colombia, gave the country its cost advantage in cocaine production and distribution. The fourth, and concluding, section briefly raises possible policy alternatives for the Colombian government, given this package of factors.

The Cocaine Production Function and the Industry's Value Added

In order to determine the source of the cocaine industry's production and marketing advantages, it is necessary to understand how its production system functions and the characteristics of its marketing system. The process of raising coca and manufacturing cocaine is well known and has been discussed frequently in the recent literature (Arango and Child 1987). Coca is grown over a large area, including parts of Bolivia, Peru, Brazil, Colombia, and Ecuador. Although there are many varieties of the coca plant, four are the most prevalent. The alkaloid content of the leaves varies a great deal, with the Bolivian and Peruvian type, plus one grown in Colombia, yielding a substantially greater amount of cocaine than the rest. As farmers have become more proficient in cultivating coca in recent years, the yields obtained have increased accordingly.[10] The manufacturing process uses a very simple technology, is not capital-intensive, and does not have large economies of scale. The coca leaves are placed in a plastic sheet and then mixed with sodium carbonate to release the alkaloid content. The mix is subsequently transferred to a container to which gasoline and sulfuric acid dissolved in water are added. After about 12 hours, the contents of the container are passed through a press, producing coca paste, a product that is easy to transport. This paste is later converted into coca base through a process that requires ammonia, potassium permanganate, and some filters to remove impurities. Three more chemicals — chloridic acid, ether, and acetone — are applied to the base in a process that requires only some "cooking" to transform it into cocaine. This final step is not complicated, but it can be dangerous due to the ether's flammability.[11] *Bazuco*, a form of cocaine commonly used in Colombia, is made up of cocaine base mixed with tobacco. Because this mixture frequently has many impurities, it is particularly dangerous for the smoker.[12]

Coca cultivation is highly responsive to such factors as location and climate. Due to the bulk and volume of coca leaves, cocaine's raw material, it is more feasible to process the leaves into paste as close to the source as possible. However, once the paste is obtained, it is easy to transport and can be manufactured into the final product anywhere. Hence, the manufacturing stage takes on the characteristics of a footloose industry which is not tied to any particular location.

In the cocaine industry, the value added at each stage of manufacture bears no relation to the way such factors are computed in the manufacture of legal products. The value added to cocaine at each stage of its manufacturing process is in direct proportion to the amount of risk attendant upon that stage. Thus, the value added to cocaine increases rapidly at each stage of its manufacture commensurate with the risks involved in that stage and does not correspond to factor opportunity costs. In other words, the high value added in this industry is due to its illegal nature and the risks this imposes. Thus, peasants in Bolivia and Peru get a very small share of the final sales price because their risk is comparatively low; while most of the price increase takes place at the marketing and distribution end of the business, in the United States, where the risks are much greater.

Since the manufacturing process is relatively footloose and free of being tied to any one location and the product's high value added is a function of the risks involved in its manufacture and distribution, this stage of the industry tends to gravitate toward the location presenting the lowest risk. Consequently, to understand the Colombian advantage for this business, one should focus on those factors that lower the industry's risks. The following section will argue that, for a long time, Colombia offered a set of conditions which, together, 1) minimized the cocaine industry's risks, 2) attracted the refining of cocaine, 3) allowed Colombians to control the marketing of coca leaves in Bolivia and Peru, and 4) involved them in the U.S. cocaine market. In a way, it could even be argued that Colombia developed an "absolute advantage" in those aspects of the industry.

When the manufacturing function of other illegal drugs produced in Colombia is examined, many characteristics similar to those found in the production of cocaine become evident. Marijuana is another freeranging product in the sense that it can grow naturally almost everywhere; there are even varieties with a very high yield which are grown hydroponically (e.g., in liquid nutrients, without soil). Quaaludes can be manufactured very easily in chemical laboratories engaged in the production of other, legal drugs if the right chemical compounds are available. Neither of these products requires large capital investments; their production technologies are available in most countries, and their production costs are not significantly affected by the volume, or scale, of production. Consequently, production of these illegal substances can, and does, tend also to gravitate toward the location(s) of lowest risk.

Basis of the Colombian Advantage

Colombia's main advantage as locus for illegal drug production comes from a growing de-legitimation of its governmental system, particularly in the last 45 years, which has caused a weakening of the state and its institutions.

During the twentieth century, Colombian society experienced many dramatic changes. The country evolved from a traditional rural society, in which pre-capitalist institutions and productive relations prevailed on the haciendas, into an urban economy based on industry and services that required new institutions and a new system of labor relations in order to function without conflict. As often happens in such circumstances, society lagged in meeting the new demands being placed upon it and failed to develop the institutions needed fast enough to adjust to the changing conditions. The result was a profound institutional crisis.[13]

The traditional, closed political system — based on political parties controlled by agricultural economic elites, whose own power was based on political and economic control of the peasants working on their haciendas — failed to open sufficiently, or in time, to accommodate the new groups coming into existence. As the society modernized, the representatives of the "old order" struggled to hang onto power and maintain the status quo. They did manage to retain control, but at a very great social cost: the gradual de-legitimation of regime and a very high level of violence.

Colombia has a long history of political violence. Indeed, the period in Colombian history known as *La Violencia* (an undeclared civil war which extended from the late 1940s to the early 1960s) is infamous in Latin American history of this century due to its widespread violence, extreme cruelty, and wanton killings (estimated at 2 to 3 percent of the country's population).[14] During *La Violencia*, both political parties, the Liberals and Conservatives, supported their own guerrilla groups, although the Conservatives, who were in power, were able to augment their forces with both the police and the army in fighting the Liberal-supported guerrillas. The roots of this protracted conflict originated in differences among the ruling elites over the adoption, and implementation, of measures designed to introduce more progressive labor relations and reform land tenancy practices. These measures had been sponsored by the Liberal party, who controlled the government from 1930-1946, following a 30-year period of Conservative hegemony.

However, the period immediately following World War II saw many changes in Colombian society: growing urbanization, industrialization, and the development of accompanying infrastructure. These changes tended to undermine the power and strength of the traditional rural interests. It was in this climate that *La Violencia* erupted. However, the length and depth of the violence so exhausted the body politic that, in 1953, a military government was installed — with overwhelming popular support — with an implicit mandate to end *La Violencia*.

The weakening of the traditional rural interests also served to blur the differences between the two party elites, who also feared losing power to the military. By 1958, the changed environment and these fears led the parties to establish the "National Front," a power-sharing agreement between the two parties, which was to last 16 years. This agreement succeeded in eliminating the violence of the two traditional Liberal and Conservative parties, but, at the same time, it totally excluded all other parties and Colombians who held different political views.

During the military government of the mid-1950s, the guerrillas were granted amnesty in exchange for turning over their arms and returning to civilian life. However, the raised expectations of the guerrillas and the exclusionary political system led some guerrilla groups to continue their battle. By the mid-1960s, organized guerrilla organizations were in control of isolated regions of the country where they had established "independent republics," in which they 1) garnered contributions from peasants in the region, 2) collected protection payments from large landlords, and 3) provided health, education, and security to the peasantry. As time went by, these movements became more class-oriented, providing the base from which Marxist guerrillas emerged in the last two decades.

In the National Front arrangement, the leaders of the two "recognized" parties agreed to divide most government jobs between the two of them (including those of elected officials) and to alternate the presidency. In so doing, a sort of political "cartel" was established, which not only held a monopoly on power but, at the same time, foreclosed the entry of any new groups from either the extreme Left or Right. As excluded groups found more legitimate avenues to power blocked, they organized into guerrilla groups, usually locating in areas where the state had a very weak presence and frequently taking over many of the state's functions.

Not only was this political system exclusionary, but it also developed clientelistic practices in which politicians came to serve as intermediaries between the citizens and government, exchanging public services and public employment for votes. As the Colombian economy grew more complex, the government took on more and more functions; at the same time, it became less and less effective in fulfilling them. Inefficiency began to snowball. The law was increasingly disregarded. As government bureaucracies became more inefficient, they became less accountable, and less responsive, to the public they were supposed to serve. Corruption in both the private and public sectors increased. Most important of all, the state lost effective control over large areas of the country. Thus, the de-legitimation of the state was revealed by a widening gap between the written laws and socially acceptable behavior, i.e., between the *de jure* and *de facto* social norms. The underground economy expanded greatly.

Unfortunately, this process — of de-legitimizing and weakening the state — is not uncommon in Latin America and the Caribbean. Other states have also grown weaker and increasingly incapable of enforcing their own laws and controlling their territories. However, in comparing the Colombian experience with those other countries (particularly in the Andes, where there is a history of coca cultivation and use), one finds two important differences: 1) the de-legitimation process began earlier in Colombia and 2) has been characterized by a much higher level of violence than has been true of the other Andean countries.

Both *La Violencia* and the de-legitimation of government have left legacies which have worked to permit, if not encourage, the development of the cocaine industry. First, the government lost control of large areas of the country. Although the state had never had a strong presence in those areas, the guerrillas demonstrated that the government could not assert control in those areas even if it wished. Second, the experience of *La Violencia* was to place a low value on human life. One of its legacies is that Colombians are quick to resort to violence in dealing with conflict — a very useful attribute in a high-profit, high-risk, and conflict-prone business. The propensity of Colombian drug dealers to use violence to wipe out their Bolivian and Peruvian competitors, particularly during early stages of the industry's development in the 1970s, is notorious.

De-legitimation of the Colombian state has contributed to Colombia's advantage over other states vis-à-vis the narcotraffic in yet other ways. Smuggling, or the import of illegal goods, has a long history in many Latin American and Caribbean countries. Colombia has a long tradition in this area, with some characteristics that are peculiarly its own. In the mid-1950s, in fact, the import of many contraband consumer goods was institutionalized.[15] More recent developments, like the creation of free zones to set up export assembly plants and to store imports while import licensing and nationalization processes are concluded, have also facilitated contraband which can be brought into these zones and then smuggled out of them. The institutionalization of this contraband trade has lent it an aura of legitimacy which tended to destroy any social stigma that might once have been attached to it.

Of equal, if not more, importance is that Colombia is one of the few countries which also had a history of export contraband. It has consistently smuggled both manufactured products and livestock out of Colombia into Venezuela and Ecuador throughout time. Coffee is another commodity which has frequently been smuggled out in order to bypass the quotas imposed by the International Coffee Agreement. For a long time, Colombian emeralds have been smuggled out of the country: workers in government mines would steal the gems and sell them to smugglers. Also, the smugglers themselves developed illegal, wildcat mining organizations. This experience in smuggling the export of illegally obtained goods could then be applied to the export of narcotics, when that market developed, since it provided the know-how, as well, of selling in the international black markets. Thus, many emerald smugglers became involved in exporting marijuana in the mid-1970s and, later on, became cocaine exporters.

Not only did the contraband trade help to establish links between Colombian and foreign smugglers, but it enabled Colombians to gain experience in laundering money and other shady transactions involving international capital.

Colombia has been the only Andean country which has had exchange controls and tariff restrictions from 1931 right up to the middle of 1991. Controls on foreign exchange and import-licensing systems were tightened in 1967. Together with high tariffs on imports, these provided powerful incentives for the development of an active black market in foreign exchange, which had originally been supplied by the export of emeralds, worker remittances (from Venezuela and the United States), tourism, and other contraband exports. The foreign exchange obtained in this market was used mostly to underinvoice imports and to finance capital flight, tourism, and contraband imports. The active black market in foreign exchange provided both the expertise on how to launder money as well as the channels by which drug profits and capital could be brought into the country.

Colombia is not the only Andean state to experience a de-legitimation process. Whereas the crisis in the Colombian state was evident by the late 1940s, with the onset of *La Violencia*, it did not materialize in Perú and Bolivia until the 1970s and 1980s. In this respect, Colombians engaged in the illegal drug business gained a head start, and an advantage, over their neighbors in the same trade.

There is yet another factor, unrelated to the issue of regime legitimacy and weak state, which also facilitated Colombia's prominence in the narcotraffic. Because of the make-up of Colombia's internal geography, many regions are isolated and, given the weak presence of the national government, were forced to become fairly self-sufficient. These factors combined to make them good locations in which to set up facilities to manufacture and refine illegal psychoactive drugs. In addition, Colombia's large size, relative to the smaller Central American and Caribbean countries, made it attractive to entrepreneurs in the illegal drug business for two reasons: 1) the larger territory makes detection just that much more difficult, and 2) bribery, often an intrinsic part of illegal enterprise, is cheaper and easier. In small countries, it is usually necessary to bribe authorities at the highest level; in Colombia, it has only been necessary to bribe authorities, particularly in isolated regions, at the local level, a cheaper and less risky action altogether.[16]

Colombian capitalism has always operated on the expectation of very high, short-term profits. In the nineteenth century, successive economic booms plus major obstacles to internal transportation combined to produce extremely segmented markets with widely differentiated prices. These differences generated an entrepreneurial class based on "production speculation," that is, those who invested little in long-term capital equipment, focused activities on trade, and expected a quick turnover and high, short-term profits (Ocampo 1984, 61). After World War II, modernization and structural changes in the economy were accompanied by some changes in this area also, as some entrepreneurs began to invest with longer horizons in mind, and more stable economic activities and de-personalized markets evolved. Many, however, continued to pursue their traditional, rent-seeking path. During the 1970s, two developments reinforced the old "production speculation" mentality: 1) liberalization of the capital market, begun under the Pastrana administration (1970-1974) and strengthened by the López government (1974-1978); and 2) the coffee boom (1975-1978). Capital market liberalization led to a wave of financial speculation, high short-term returns, and a series of major bankruptcies in the early 1980s; the coffee boom again provided very high, windfall profits and the expectation of high gains.

A final, but no less important factor has been a large Colombian migration, both legal and illegal, to the United States. This emigrant group, with only weak loyalty to the host country, subsequently provided an excellent base from which to recruit, and organize, a network for the distribution of illegal exports from Colombia.[17] Again, the large emigration from Colombia preceded a similar emigration from the other Andean countries, contributing to the Colombian headstart and providing another international advantage.

In sum, the conjunction of these factors worked to give Colombia, and those of its citizens engaged in the cocaine trade, an overall advantage in the manufacture and international distribution of this illicit drug. The high level of violence in Colombian society had inured its members to this way of dealing with opponents; hence, Colombia's narco-businessmen were unusually quick to use force in dealing with (or eliminating) competitors, enabling them, early on, to control not only the purchase of the raw material (coca leaves) but also the channels for distribution of the end product in the United States. The fact that the national government maintained only a weak, or tenuous, presence in large portions of the country provided the illegal industry with areas proven to be outside of government control in which it was relatively safe to operate, safe havens for coca laboratories, landing strips, and the like. The existence of organized guerrilla groups, intent on weakening the state even further, also facilitated the safety of the cocaine manufacturing industry.[18] Indeed, in the late 1970s and early 1980s, guerrilla organizations "sold" protection to the cocaine businessmen.

Finally, the experience of the "production speculation" capitalist provided both precedent and rationale for the get-rich-quick mentality which underlay development of the narcotraffic, while the Colombian experience in smuggling exports out of the country contributed expertise in the practical aspects of the business. And the large Colombian community in the United States helped to lower the risks of illegal exporting as well.

As MacDonald (1988) has pointed out, no other Latin American or Caribbean country was able to assemble the entire "package" of factors which proved so conducive to development of the illegal psychoactive drug industry in Colombia. Nevertheless, the situation was even more complex than he reported. These factors have special relevance in the Colombian case because they all served to lower the risks in manufacturing and marketing of illegal drugs in general, and cocaine in particular. To the extent that other Andean countries (primarily coca-growing) replicated Colombian developments and processes (such as de-legitimation, guerrillas, and so on), they entered into these experiences significantly at a later point in time, enabling the Colombian narcotraffic to pioneer the manufacturing facilities, marketing systems, and use of violence which established their primacy in a cutthroat industry.

Conclusions and Perspectives

Colombia's advantage in the cocaine business does not rest primarily on its abundance of natural resources nor its location midway between the main areas of coca cultivation and the major market for cocaine. Its advantage is made up of a combination of factors which made Colombia the country of lowest risk for both the trade in coca leaves and the manufacture and export of the finished product — cocaine — to the United States. Its advantage also owes a great deal to certain domestic institutional, and some external, factors.

Given the nature of this Colombian advantage, one might ask: what policies could government adopt that would modify, or eliminate, this advantage? The answer lies in what the government can, and cannot, control. First, the Colombian government cannot change the extremely high profitability of the industry which derives, in part, from its illegality in the consuming countries, and from the abundance, and cheapness, of its raw material (grown mainly in countries other than Colombia). The high profitability reflects the conflicting policies, inspired mostly by the United States, that are aimed at making consumption of cocaine as expensive as possible and the price of its raw material (coca leaves) as low as possible. To achieve these two contradictory goals, the value added goes up drastically at each and every step of production, commensurate with the risk attendant upon that step, from coca leaf to the price paid by the cocaine consumer.

Second, the large Colombian network in the United States, which facilitates the Colombian export trade in cocaine, is an external factor over which the Colombian government has no control.

Third, given the industry's value-added characteristics, the most that the Colombian government could hope to do would be to displace the industry out of the country, induce it to move elsewhere, and, if possible, to push Colombian nationals out of the industry.

In the long run, these goals can be approached via institutional reforms to increase regime legitimacy and the government's ability to implement its policies. The current Gaviria administration has undertaken many reforms in that direction, including a new constitution, which aims to weaken clientelism and strengthen representative democracy, and a process designed to open the economy and eliminate economic privileges, among others. However, such policies bear fruit only over the long run.

Another policy, with a more short-term outcome, would be to negotiate with the drug traffickers to end their activities in exchange for some sort of quid pro quo, like legitimizing at least part of their capital, reducing sentences, or similar concessions. However, for such an arrangement to succeed, it would also be necessary to include on the agenda the requirement that the present traffickers help prevent new Colombian traffickers from taking their place. As long as the high profitability of the industry persists, it will provide an automatic incentive for newcomers to try to step in and replace those acquiescing in a negotiated withdrawal. It should be recognized that the business, as such, would likely continue. The most the Colombian government could hope to attain would be to ensure that such newcomers would not be Colombian nationals.

The possibility of replacing Colombian traffickers with non-Colombians may be helped along by some recent developments, like the increased de-legitimation of the Peruvian regime and the rise of non-Colombian "cartels" after 1989, when the "war on narcoterrorism" raised the stakes for Colombian traffickers. These circumstances may increase the odds of replacing Colombians with non-Colombians and, at least, make the possibility more likely. Nevertheless, it is difficult to negotiate successfully with drug traffickers, who do not share common goals and are notoriously unreliable. Some drug dealers want wealth and a high standard of living. Others want political power. Those with previous criminal records, often those most prone to violence, are also the most apt to continue in the business. On the other hand, many of the small dealers are addicts who are, or have become, psychologically disturbed and cannot be relied upon to respect an agreement.[19]

The government might also attempt to increase the risks of doing business in Colombia which, as we have seen, might increase the costs of doing business there and, thus, make the country less attractive as a location. However, even this strategy can expect but a limited success at best. Basically, increasing the risk of cocaine manufacturing and distribution in Colombia means increasing the risk of a higher level of violence within the country. It could stimulate cocaine manufacturing to move to other countries, where Colombian traffickers would have to find partners in order to operate safely. Loss of the Colombian base would make them more vulnerable to new competitors. Since Colombians control important cocaine distribution channels, however, one can predict that increasing the risks of operating in Colombia will not fully remove Colombian organizations from cocaine traffic but, rather, will force them to find allies in other countries. Though such a result might be considered a step in the right direction, it would not necessarily solve Colombia's main problems because its role in the illegal drug trade would remain. Another point to consider is that raising the level of risk involved would have to be a long-run strategy if it were to become an effective deterrent; this could well imply an increase in the militarization of an antidrug campaign — a situation that could be highly destabilizing.

This quick survey of policy alternatives indicates that the Colombian government, by itself, cannot do much to reduce the supply of illegal drugs. At best, it can only try to neutralize some of the negative effects that the industry has had on the country. However, it cannot produce a stable, long-run solution to the problems associated with the illegal psychoactive drug industry. Indeed, this is one of those cases in which the current generation might be paying for the sins of past governments.

Notes

1. For instance, the Colombian ambassador to the United States has argued, "Because of its location in the northwest corner of South America, Colombia has been chosen by the narcotrafficking gangs as one of the main crossroads from which cocaine is brought to the United States" (Mosquera Chaux 1989, 3).

2. Medellín is the capital of the Antioquia department, which has the reputation of producing the most entrepreneurial Colombians and which, during the first half of the twentieth century, became the cradle for Colombian industry. There is a well-known body of literature that has dealt with the reasons why Antioqueños developed those entrepreneurial skills (see, for example, López-Toro 1970 and Twinam 1980).

3. The belief that North Americans confuse the two countries was reinforced when President Reagan made this mistake during his visit to Colombia in the early 1980s. While this reason may appear trivial, it has been seriously advanced by Arango (1988) and Arango and Child (1987, 128), two influential Colombian journalists and academics, one of whom was the head of the economics department at the Universidad de Antioquia. For this reason, it should be mentioned, if only to dismiss it. Their statement was based on an interview with a former smuggler who, during the late 1960s, was supposed to have served as a link between Antioqueños and smugglers in the Colón Free Zone of Panama.

4. For example, Richard Craig cites an interview with an agent from the U.S. Drug Enforcement Administration (DEA), in which the latter reportedly said, "I've worked in narcotics for many years in several countries, but never have I seen anything like the Colombian trafficker. He is really one mean bastard" (1981, 248).

5. Author's translation.

6. I hesitate to call this a "comparative advantage" since comparative advantage theories explain the advantage in terms of the relative endowment of factors of production: natural resources, labor (skilled and unskilled), capital, and technology. As argued here, the Colombian advantage was not developed based on the proportion of reactive factors but on such institutional factors as corruption, lack of state legitimacy, and the state's inability to control large regions of the country.

7. The "Dutch disease" was a term coined by *The Economist* back in the late 1970s to refer to the adverse effects on Dutch manufacturing of the natural gas discoveries of the 1960s (a "booming" sector), essentially through the subsequent appreciation of the Dutch real exchange rate. It has since been generally applied to any natural resource "boom" which exercises a similar effect.

8. Even if a few U.S. buyers had confused the two countries, their confusion would have made for a good joke and would have been easily clarified. A simpler, more likely hypothesis is that, since the Colombian smugglers were supplying the Colón Free Zone from the south, they were either asked if they could bring in other products from that general direction or they themselves searched for those products.

9. Actually, Medellín's case is a very nice illustration of the migration and unemployment model: a region with better paying jobs and a higher than average standard of living attracts more migrants than other regions until higher unemployment discourages further migration (Todaro 1969). Thus, the higher unemployment level in Medellín is expected as a result of its better paying jobs, and it acts as a migration control mechanism.

10. The U.S. Bureau of International Narcotics Matters (INM) attributes some of its own underestimates of cocaine output during the 1980s to the fact that coca yields were higher than previously thought, as growers developed improved plant varieties and applied new growing techniques (US-DS/INM 1990).

11. It is clear that the technology to produce cocaine is relatively simple and well known today. Curiously, Arango and Child argue that the technology to produce cocaine was produced in the mid-1960s, by members of the U.S. Peace Corps. They state that the Peace Corps people, who enjoyed marijuana when they arrived in the early 1960s, soon discovered coca-chewing. In their search for better "trips," they developed the cocaine-refining technology in use today (Arango and Child 1987, 125-126).

12. Arango and Child argue that *bazuco* was introduced to the Colombian market in 1981 when the cocaine base produced in eastern Colombia failed to find an international market due to a drop in the price of cocaine. These authors claim that the base produced on the eastern prairies was of lower quality due to the fact that it was manufactured with less-than-pure chemicals, a fact that is hard to explain (Arango and Child 1987, 143).

13. The Colombian literature on this issue has grown substantially in the last few years; some relevant examples include Leal (1984 and 1989), Kalmanovitz (1989), and Leal and Zamosc (1990).

14. Kalmonovitz provides a very good discussion of the economic developments that led to *La Violencia* (1989, Chapter 6), while a detailed socio-political analysis is found in the classical work of Guzmán et al. (1962).

15. The government decided to promote the development of the 44 sq. km. islands of San Andrés and Providencia, making them into a free port area from which any Colombian tourist could bring back to the mainland a certain amount of tariff-free goods for personal use. This policy promoted the development of a group of entrepreneurs who specialized in bringing to the mainland small amounts of contraband goods for sale. This business grew substantially and eventually gained sufficient legitimacy that all efforts at concealment were abandoned. Most cities developed markets for contraband goods from San Andrés and Providencia which operated freely and openly. In these markets, goods can actually be ordered from many U.S. catalogs, and, indeed, today most of the contraband sold in these markets no longer comes from those islands.

16. Local authorities tend to be both poorer and much less in the limelight than are authorities on the national level. National authorities also have many more resources at their disposal, including more contacts with international and foreign law enforcement agents. It is worth noting that, in Colombia, most national authorities at the highest level have remained untainted by contact with the illegal drug industry, whereas some of their counterparts in the smaller Central American and Caribbean countries have been active participants.

17. Peter Reuter has argued that this is an important factor in accounting for Colombia's ability to export cocaine to the United States compared to its limited penetration of the European market, where the Brazilians appear to have an edge as a result of the number of Brazilian emigrants there (Reuter 1985); a similar point has been made by Krauthausen and Sarmiento as well (1991, Chapter 3). Arango points out that Colombians who returned to Medellín after organizing the marketing and distribution of cocaine in the United States enjoy a high status and are considered respected and influential members of the community (1988, 25).

18. Reyes (1990), Molano (1987), Jaramillo (1989), Mora (1989), and Cubides (1989) study various aspects of the relationship between the drug industry and the guerrilla organizations.

19. Arango reports the results of interviews with 20 "middle and high level" narco-businessmen from Medellín in which 25 percent stated that they would remain in this business even if their wealth is legitimized without penalties. While it is obvious that the sample is not "scientific," and that the answers might be biased, this outcome suggests the difficulties likely to arise should an agreement be reached with the narco-businessmen (Arango 1988, 123).

References

Arango, M. 1988. *Impacto del Narcotráfico en Antioquia.* 3rd ed. Medellín, Colombia: J. M. Arango.

Arango, M., and J. Child. 1987. *Narcotráfico: imperio de la cocaína.* México (DF), México: Editorial Diana.

Craig, R. 1981. "Colombian Narcotics and United States-Colombian Relations." *Journal of Interamerican Studies and World Affairs* 23, 3 (August): 243-270.

Cubides, F. 1989. "Estado y poder local (Organización Comunitaria y Política en el Medio y Bajo Caguán)." In *Colonización, coca y guerrilla,* 3rd ed., eds. J. E. Jaramillo, L. Mora, and F. Cubides. Bogotá, Colombia: Alianza Editorial Colombiana.

Dombois, R. 1990. "¿Por que florece la economía de la cocaína justamente en Colombia?" In *Economía y política del narcotráfico,* eds. J. Tokatlián and B. Bagley. Bogotá, Colombia: Ediciones Uniandes.

Guzman, G., O. Fals-Borda, and E. Umaña-Luna. 1962. *La violencia en Colombia: estudio de un proceso social,* 2nd ed. Bogotá, Colombia: Ediciones Tercer Mundo.

Jaramillo, J. 1989. "Historia y dimensiones socioculturales del proceso colonizador." In *Colonización, coca y guerrilla,* 3rd ed. eds. J. E. Jaramillo, L. Mora, and F. Cubides. Bogotá, Colombia: Alianza Editorial Colombiana.

Kalmanovitz, S. 1989. *Economía y nación: una breve historia de Colombia.* Bogotá, Colombia: Siglo XXI Editores.

Krauthausen, C., and L. Sarmiento. 1991. *Cocaína y co.: un mercado ilegal por dentro.* Bogotá, Colombia: Tercer Mundo Editores.

Leal, F. 1989. "El sistema político del clientelismo." *Análisis Político* 8 (September-December): 8-32.

Leal, F. 1984. *Estado y política en Colombia.* Bogotá, Colombia: Siglo Veintiuno Editores.

Leal, F., and L. Zamosc, eds. 1990. *Al filo del caos: crisis política en la Colombia de los Años 80.* Bogotá, Colombia: Tercer Mundo Editores.

Lopez-Toro, A. 1970. *Migración y cambio social en Antioquia durante el siglo diez y nueve.* Bogotá, Colombia: Universidad de Los Andes, Centro de Estudios sobre Desarrollo Económico.

MacDonald, S. 1988. *Dancing on a Volcano: The Latin American Drug Trade.* New York, N.Y.: Praeger Publishers.

Molano, A. 1987. *Selva adentro: una historia oral de la colonización del Guaviare.* Bogotá, Colombia: El Ancora Editores.

Mora, L. 1989. "Las condiciones económicas del medio y bajo Caguán." In *Colonización, coca y guerrilla,* 3rd ed., eds. J. E. Jaramillo, L. Mora, and F. Cubides. Bogotá, Colombia: Alianza Editorial Colombiana.

Mosquera Chaux, V. 1989. "Las relaciones entre Colombia y los Estados Unidos y el narcotráfico internacional de drogas." Paper presented at a Symposium on Colombia-U.S. Relations, School of Advanced International Studies (SAIS), Johns Hopkins University, Washington, D.C., March 6.

Ocampo, J. 1984. *Colombia y la economía mundial 1830-1910.* Bogotá, Colombia: Siglo Veintiuno Editores.

Reuter, P. 1985. "Eternal Hope: America's Quest for Narcotics Control." *The Public Interest* 79 (Spring): 79-95.

Reyes, A. 1990. "La violencia y la expansión territorial del narcotráfico." In *Economía y política del narcotráfico,* eds. Juan Tokatlián and Bruce Bagley. Bogotá, Colombia: Ediciones Uniandes.

Sarmiento, E. 1990. "Economía del Narcotráfico," In *Narcotráfico en Colombia: dimensiones políticas, económicas, jurídicas e internacionales,* eds. Carlos G. Arrieta et al. Bogotá, Colombia: Tercer Mundo Editores-Ediciones Uniandes.

Thoumi, F. 1987. "Some Implications of the Growth of the Underground Economy in Colombia." *Journal of Interamerican Studies and World Affairs* 29, 2 (Summer): 35-53.

Todaro, M. 1969. "A Model of Labor Migration and Urban Unemployment in Less Developed Countries." *American Economic Review* 59 (March): 138-148.

Twinam, A. 1980. "From Jew to Basque: Ethnic Myths and Antioqueño Entrepreneurship." *Journal of Interamerican Studies and World Affairs* 22, 1, (February): 81-107.

U.S. Department of State. Bureau of International Narcotics Matters (US-DS/INM). 1990. *International Narcotics Control Strategy Report* (March). Washington, D.C.: US-DS/INM.

Urrutia, M. 1990. "Análisis Costo-Beneficio del Tráfico de Drogas para la Economía Colombiana." *Coyuntura Económica* 20, 3 (October): 115-126.

Whynes, D. 1992. "The Colombian Cocaine Trade and the 'War on Drugs'." In *The Colombian Economy: Issues of Trade and Development,* eds. Alvin Cohen and Frank Gunter. Boulder, Colo.: Westview Press.

Chapter Six

Drug Trafficking and Society in Colombia

Alvaro Camacho Guizado

The production and distribution of cocaine have become key phenomena in shaping Colombian society in the last decade of the twentieth century. Albeit belatedly, Colombians have begun, in recent years, to understand its significance within their social milieu. The direction taken by the processes associated with drug trafficking will, no doubt, determine the future evolution of Colombian society; final outcomes of this dynamic, however, ultimately depend, to a great extent, on the alternative explanations formulated vis-à-vis basic causes, effects, and scope. Inexorably, the basic complexity of this phenomena is exacerbated by extranational dimensions of the trade which place the country at the epicenter of an international industry beyond internally designed Colombian control.

This chapter examines the various diagnoses that have been postulated to explain Colombia's central role in the hemisphere's cocaine trade via a review of the available social science literature analyzing the national and international dimensions of the issue. Then, it focuses on the major analyses that explore the effects of *narcotráfico* on Colombian society.[1] The chapter concludes with some key hypotheses regarding the significance of this historical conjuncture in the country's short- and mid-term future.

The International Problem

Colombia's international relations, particularly with the United States, experienced crucial changes in the late 1970s as the "drug problem" garnered great importance in Washington.[2] What had been historically defined initially as a criminal problem and subsequently as a health problem[3] gradually acquired the dimension of an external threat to national security.[4] This new perception precipitated a redefinition of the relationship with the producing countries in Latin America. By converting its internal laws into international principles, the U.S. government, despite public declarations to the contrary, did not exclude the possibility of direct intervention in the producing and exporting countries to eliminate the sources of supply and, therefore, ensure its national security, notwithstanding the opposition to that course of action expressed in the United States and in Latin America by government agencies involved in drug enforcement.[5]

In U.S. society, there have emerged inconsistencies and tensions among prohibitionists, liberals, and libertarians, among the CIA, the DEA, and other governmental agencies, between the legislative and executive branches, and over political/diplomatic and military options.[6] Even globally, there has been no fundamental consensus, as revealed by the difficulties in approving and executing the 1988 Vienna Convention, in forging a concerted European Community antidrug policy, and in the formation of an International Antiprohibitionist League.[7]

At the same time, various studies have indicated that producing countries can successfully undertake crop eradication while managing the socio-cultural contradictions between eradication and traditional coca consumption.[8]

The relationship between Colombia and the United States does not escape these ambiguities, and some authors have pointed out the discrepancies in terms of definitions as well as courses of action proposed by the governments of both countries. Thus, there are differences over the origin of the problem. The U.S. government locates it on the supply side and searches for unilateral or bilateral mechanisms to solve it, ties it to its internal health and security conditions, and relates it to a policy to control international enemies. The Colombian government, on the other hand, sees it as a question of the demand and searches for multilateral control mechanisms, relates it to its problems of social stability and democracy, examines the implications of the social violence unleashed in repressing it, and tries to separate the country's interests from the strategic concerns of the United States.[9]

This topic is one of the central theses of this presentation: for the United States, the problem is narcotraffic; for Colombia, it is the narcoviolence or narcoterrorism — a situation where narcotraffickers have, with the use of arms, imposed their point of view, vis-à-vis the state and popular movements.[10] In this context, the problem of exporting drugs becomes less crucial.

The debate on the economic impact of narcotrafficking is equally important. Consumer countries merge ideological economic reasoning and liberal policy, like the well-known arguments of Milton Friedman and *The Economist,* with the moral ideology of those who consider that the acquisition of drugs by addicts implies a rise in delinquency. Others move in the field of economic policy and calculate the positive and negative effects of the business, both for the United States and for the producing and exporting countries.[11]

The political effect of narcotraffic in the area of international relations has also been ambiguous. While the image of Colombia and Colombians has been stigmatized outside the country and the Colombian state has been placed in the spotlight by international organizations that defend human rights,[12] it has served to create a sense of solidarity geared toward unconditional support of the government. The internationalization of this global problem has had a paradoxical effect: by asserting that consumption is at the base of the chain, Colombia has sought to avoid isolation as a threat to the internal security of the United States, but, simultaneously by demanding reciprocity from the international community, it has lost its autonomy over the management of an internal problem.

One of the most notable efforts in the internationalization of the issue of narcotrafficking was the Cartagena meeting of 1990, where the United States, Colombia, Bolivia, and Peru signed a declaration of cooperation. So far, the results have been meaningless.[13] While the U.S. government finds obstacles to implementing the Andean Initiative that resulted from the meeting, it has adopted hostile measures in an attempt to establish aerial and naval blockades, violations of air space that have been denounced by the Minister of Foreign Relations in Colombia. The use of direct military actions has also been contemplated.[14] The aid offered by the United States has been minimal and inadequate because it encourages guerrilla warfare but not the necessary police operations, a fact confirmed by high-ranking officers of the Colombian police force.[15]

This shift of resources toward antiguerrilla struggle has also been denounced by officials involved in the appropriation process.[16] More recently, on the occasion of the debate of the Asamblea Nacional Constituyente on the terms of extradition, high-ranking U.S. officials exerted public pressure on the government of Colombia, and the voters, so that this measure would not be repealed.

On the other hand, there have been positive advances in terms of the liberalization of tariffs for Colombian, Peruvian, and Bolivian products by the European Economic Community. The EC is working toward the development of a policy of cooperation that is in direct contrast with U.S. policy.

The National Problem

In Colombia, the debates that deal with the analysis of narcotraffic have divided Colombian society, yet there is agreement in considering it one of most serious problems the country has ever faced.

General Studies

Colombian literature on this topic has grown almost parallel to the rising incidence of the phenomenon. One of the first works to address some aspects of coca trade in Colombia appeared in London in 1978. Its author, an anthropologist at Universidad del Cauca, had studied the significance of coca for the indigenous population of the region.[17] Parallel to the anthropological treatment, Anthony Henman analyzed some political dimensions of narcotrafficking. In his judgment, antidrug policy was nothing more than a smoke-screen to hide the process of corruption, generalized repression, and monopolization of the business by the same organizations that were in charge of combatting it, namely the military. To support his thesis, he offered a series of examples of members of the armed forces directly involved in illicit deals associated with narcotraffic.

At the same time that Henman's book was distributed, a series of analyses and reports, newspaper-style, started to circulate in Colombia, in which some of the affirmations made by Henman were ratified.[18] It has to be noted, however, that several of the statements made by the author of *Mama Coca* had come from some of these publications.

In 1979, at the annual symposium of the National Association of Financial Institutions (ANIF) titled "Marihuana, Mito-Realidad," the problem of marijuana was extensively discussed in Colombia for the first time.[19] The points of view presented at the meeting included the opinions of national and international experts on the medical, judiciary, international, and socioeconomic aspects of marijuana; it was also the first time that ANIF's president, Ernesto Samper Pizano, suggested the possibility of legalizing Cannabis. The debate on legalization continued,[20] and Samper Pizano repeated his arguments for the need to control an informal and subterranean economy that does not generate taxes while contributing to generalized corruption, to the take-over of businesses by capital of doubtful origin, and above all, to the crisis of values traditionally associated with honest labor and social respect in Colombia.

In 1981, Alvaro Camacho published a book in which he presented hypotheses related to the social dimensions of the production and distribution of marijuana and emphasized the development of a new social class that would threaten the traditional hegemony. The book described processes associated with corruption and repression and pointed to contradictions between the old dominating classes and new bourgeoisie in terms of economic and political dimensions.[21]

In 1984 and 1985, Mario Arango and Jorge Child wrote two books that dealt with many topics associated with cocaine.[22] Mixing historical facts with political analyses and well-founded affirmations with hearsay, the authors described the problem from a basic theory of imperialism. In the second book, they discussed the topic of extradition and specifically the problems of extradition of Colombians to the United States.

In 1988, Arango published another book in which he dealt with the creation and development of the narcotrafficking network in Antioquia, using the results of a poll administered to 20 entrepreneurs who smuggled drugs. After briefly studying traditional antioqueño values, Arango found that those old values were reproduced by the people interviewed. In that sense, the smugglers did not constitute a threat to the dominant cultural patterns but sought to fit within the framework of existing society. While it is true that the new financiers reproduce traditional values, the violence that they continuously display is not a part of the pattern inherent in the antioqueño prototypes. Furthermore, to consider that the mechanisms of wealth accumulation used by narcotraffickers have a parallel with the traditional methods used by the antioqueños is nothing less than a major mistake. More recently, Arango has published a new book where he tries to analyze the elements that are essential for the development of the ethical and traditional values of the antioqueños to explain how their decadence is at the root of the development of narcotraffic and urban violence in Medellín.[23]

But the book on narcotraffic that has had the widest editorial success in Colombia is one written by Fabio Castillo, *Los Jinetes de la Cocaína*.[24] The author gathered what is probably the most extensive factual information on narcotrafficking in Colombia. He wrote a detailed history of the development of the business and its different regional organizations, of the factors that played a role in the attempts to penetrate the institutional life of the country, and of the resulting actions of the government to control and/or eradicate the phenomenon. Castillo occasionally commits flagrant mistakes and attributes adventuresome imputations to people whose relationship with narcotraffickers has been, if not occasional, at best indirect and marginal, and his purifying zeal makes him see mafiosi everywhere, in all areas of national life. This bias reduces the value that could otherwise be assigned to his journalistic investigation.

In 1988, Camacho published a new work on this topic.[25] It is a more extensive re-edition of the previous book and attempts to carry the narration and analysis until the end of 1987. Three new considerations appear in this text: one section, dedicated to the examination of the history of prohibitions, seeks to find common elements; another examines the most important transformations resulting from the decline in production and export of marijuana and the rise of cocaine; and finally one of the most provocative topics is that of the narcoguerrilla. The author tries to show the weakness in the political arguments used to justify the term narcoguerrilla and block President Belisario Betancur's peace program.

In a text published originally in French in 1986 and then in Spanish in 1988, Alain Delpirou and Alain Labrousse dealt with the Colombian problem and described the international road map of the coca route.[26] The authors present, among other things, extensive documentation to illustrate how U.S. authorities devised the theory of the narcoguerrilla, clearly designed to involve the government of the FSLN in Nicaragua in drug-trafficking operations. The well-known episode of "Coca-gate," where the commerce of cocaine was used to raise funds to finance the Nicaraguan "contras," illustrates the type of policy used by the U.S. government and demonstrates the contradictions between the strategies of the CIA and the DEA.

Daniel Pecaut, as he followed the Colombian situation through the last two decades,[27] has systematically dealt with this issue. Pecaut hypothesizes that the complexity of Colombia's violence in recent years is explained by the economics and politics of drugs which are at the center of a growing controversy over what is and is not political. He proceeds to examine the development of drug activity and to show that what was originally conceived as a parallel economy started to acquire the dimensions that have made it the center of large areas of the country's political life. Independent of the political purposes narcotraffickers may have had, their actions started to undermine the base of the state of law and increased, to the level of paroxism, the institutionalized use of sicarios. The complex and changing relationship between narcotraffickers and guerrillas has contributed to the development of a dirty war, with the intervention of the military, paramilitary groups, sicarios, insurgent armed bands, and peasant movements. Pecaut thinks that the economics and politics of drugs are basic causes of Colombia's current crisis.

This review of the literature cannot end without mentioning other books that have been widely distributed in the streets of Colombian cities. Fabio Rincón is a journalist who has specialized in writing a book every time there is an important event in the life of the country. Among those works related to narcotraffic,[28] he has produced mixtures of factual information and high doses of fantasy and imagination in a disorderly, semibaroque rhetoric. Rincón has contributed notoriously to the banalization of the problem and to its transformation into a theme for best sellers, scarcely related to serious analysis or the search for the truth.

In 1988, Gustavo Veloza published a book on the war between the Colombian mafiosi organizations that had a high degree of editorial success.[29] It is a recompilation of information on the origins of the different cartels as well as the basis of their confrontation, and he uses information from national and international newspapers to make affirmations that cannot be supported. He deals with statements that, while acquainting the reader with intimate details of the lives of the so-called capos, do not contribute, in any way, in terms of analysis or credible sources. Veloza asserts that the struggle between the cartels began after members of the Medellín cartel decided to assassinate Minister Lara Bonilla in 1984. This decision was rejected by the members of the Cali organization, and there ensued a general confrontation in which the control of the international markets played an important role. According to the author, the high degree of violence in Medellín for which narcotraffickers are responsible and the relatively reduced violence in Cali correspond to the different tactical management of the trade by the members of the Cali cartel.

At the end of 1989, the Colombian public was surprised by the publication of a book with an explosive title.[30] The anonymous author defined himself as a narcotrafficker and proceeded to present a defense of his activity.

The book presents a mixture of candor and astuteness, and its fundamental value lies not so much in the factual information that it offers, but in the profile that it draws of the business and its main players. It is worthwhile to examine some of its assertions. The first one deals with the role that is played by U.S. narcotraffickers who keep a major portion of the profits from the business. The accusation of the Colombian government's hypocrisy for surrendering to U.S interests is remarkable; it is the central element in the narcotraffickers' self-definition as patriots who bring their money to the country to create sources of employment, while others export it or enjoy it only for themselves. His self-description is equally interesting:

> Despite the implacable persecution unleashed against narcotraffickers, the harassment to which we have been victims, and the violence that our families and our properties have endured, curiously enough, I still do not feel delinquent. I do not consider myself delinquent because I feel like a patriot: a good son, good husband, good father, and good friend. ... In truth, being a narcotrafficker, I do not feel delinquent or sinner: I have not killed anybody or ordered any killing. I have not stolen from anybody nor have I kidnapped, much less extorted or bribed. I have paid my debts. I have not cheated the government. I pay taxes. I do charity work. I attend mass. I fulfill my obligations to my family. I pay good salaries to my employees. I do social work. I collaborate in politics without demanding any retribution. I believe in the democratic system; I even admire U.S. society in many areas, except in its double moral standard and its discrimination toward latinos and Colombians. My family, which is aware of my activities, does not see me as a criminal. Nor do my "clean" friends. Nor do the persons with whom I do business. Nor the priest who receives my donations. Nor the politicians to whom I give my contributions. Nor the members of the police or the military who are my friends ... In one word, all those who know me, and that is a lot of people, do not treat me like a criminal. I think that a criminal, like a thief or a kidnapper, or an assassin, is a person socially repudiated. If I am not ... it is because I am not a criminal ... because of all of the above, I do not understand why am I being persecuted and wanted for extradition to the United States (39-40).

Then, he adds strong diatribes against the classist dimensions of the war against narcotraffickers. He reiterates the argument given by Gonzalo Rodriguez Gacha to a Colombian journalist in a radio interview when he emphasized that if the business had been controlled by the traditional oligarchy, there would have been no war. Therefore, according to the authors of the interview and the book, it is a class war against a layer of workers who have obtained some wealth and position in Colombian society.[31]

Many more assertions are contained in his confession; he recognizes, for example, that some narcotraffickers who are also landowners financed and strengthened paramilitary groups; that there are more than a million and a half narcotraffickers who, even if they have not yet become involved in the war on drugs, will not permit the government to win; that the case of the capture and extradition of Carlos Lehder will not be repeated, since sicarios have already been paid by narcotraffickers to take revenge for their eventual transferral to U.S. jails; that the narcotraffickers' violence is only defensive; and that the basis for all confrontations is the threat of extradition. Even though it is clear that for the author the activity is fundamentally commercial, he underlines the political nature of narcotraffic and insistently calls for dialogue and debate.

One work, published in 1990 with high academic standards, has been written by several authors from Universidad de los Andes.[32] Special attention should be given to the proposal presented by these authors because they are recognized authorities, some of whom have held positions of high political responsibility. The authors suggest the reduction of the comparative advantage that is enjoyed by the business of narcotraffic, the design of new formulas of repression that respond to real threats, the possibility of partially depenalizing the problem, the strengthening of the state with the goal of reducing violence, and the implementation of international autonomous policies that "de-narcotize" foreign relations and allow the country to assume, with more realism, the international as well as the local dimensions of the problem. In synthesis, the central proposal consists of a demand for a modern, strong, legalized state that will assume more successfully the task of designing policies and strategies that seek to resolve and go beyond the current improvised tactical responses determined by the actions of narcotraffickers.

In 1991, Ciro Krauthausen and Luis Fernando Sarmiento published a book[33] in which, inspired by Max Weber, they make a detailed description of the nature of narcotrafficking organizations and support the thesis that the entrepreneurs of the business manage real enterprises rationally oriented and that the high level of their profits is due to the clandestine nature of the operation which avoids the legal mechanisms of regulation. The authors describe the resources used in the business concerns (capital, violence, the sicario system, the corruption of the state's machinery) and the system of clandestine networks.

While the text systematically applies a sociological theory, the concern with Weber's orthodoxy distracts from the creative analysis: one of the points that should be emphasized is that not all the narcotrafficking organizations, as social organizations, act with the same patterns of rationality. It is known that there are strong differences between regional groups and that there are also substantial variations of social behavior from one organization to another. On the other hand, the rationality instrumental to the business of narcotrafficking contrasts with the cultural expressions of "overspending" and conspicuous consumption, with the violent practices of local domination, and with attitudes that blend the traditional values of landowners with the social "arribismo" of many traffickers.

The Impact on the Economy

In the area of economics, the main debates have dealt with the amount of income that has come into the country and its macroeconomic and sectoral effects. The most notorious fact about the economic debates is the wide-ranging discrepancy of the sources, figures, calculations, and analysis offered. This is paradoxical taking into consideration, as economists do, that their discipline has reached a level of precision and scientific method that the other social sciences are far from achieving.

The earliest calculations known in Colombia were presented by Roberto Junguito and Carlos Caballero in 1978; recently, the debate has focused mostly on the studies by Hernando José Gómez and Salomón Kalmanovitz. Works by Jesús Antonio Bejarano, Juan José Echavarría, Alicia Puyana, and Eduardo Sarmiento are also worthwhile mentioning.[34]

As a consequence of the discrepancy in the figures, the interpretation of global effects also differs. While some maintain that the net income from drug exports and its specific weight in the GNP is descending, others consider that both categories have increased. Some consider that Colombia is not a "narcoeconomy" and that the disappearance of the illicit drug business would not have major effects on the national economy. They feel that the impact of the business is more negative than positive because this type of income stimulates smuggling and the flight of capital, is concentrated in fewer hands, contaminates exports, and distorts the relative prices of the goods desired by traffickers as well as the assignation of resources in the global economy.

Others affirm that the "narcoeconomy" has been fundamental for the support of the national economy. Were it not for it, there would have been a currency crisis, and the measures to adjust it would have been as dramatic as those taken in other Latin American countries.[35] The first group argues that narcotraffic is a sort of curse over the country and its liquidation would result in beneficial effects for the national economy. Others believe that narcotraffic is inextricably linked to the country's economy and is, therefore, almost impossible to eliminate.

Echavarría is probably correct when he affirms that, "we are speaking of science fiction because the results of any study depend, fundamentally, on the price chosen for the calculations. The difference in sales figures is high as a consequence of the enormous price differentials along the chain. ... Nor is it possible to know how many dollars that get into the country are destined for contraband, for rural property purchases, or for other ends."[36]

Regardless of the real dimension of the macroeconomy associated with narcotrafficking, its regional and sectoral incidence should not be overlooked. The example of the agrarian issue illustrates this situation: while there is general consensus that agricultural and ranching economy has responded to variables of macroeconomic order, it is no less certain that the investments of narcotraffickers have played a counterreformist role.[37] Apparently, narcotraffickers control close to 4.3 percent of agricultural land in the country (3 percent of Colombia's total rural area). By using heavy capital investment and the organization of armed groups, they have eliminated the possibility that their land could ever be expropriated through agrarian reform.[38] It is presumed that many landowners have sold their land when faced with the impossibility of competing with narcotraffickers in investments that include the increased use of modern technology and methods, the monopoly of technicians from the surrounding areas, and wage-raising to increase their domination. Other landowners managed to keep this pace and to make their land less expropriatable while increasing their level of income. Furthermore, as a consequence of "cleansing" actions, there has been a reduction on demands for the land, and peasants who have survived migrated to more populated areas.

In terms of the building industry, the figures have also been very inconsistent. Oscar Borrero, for example, initially calculated that between 10 and 20 percent of the value of construction in Colombia corresponded to the business of narcotraffickers and stated that, between 1979 and 1988, the total value of real estate attributed to the subterranean activities reached a total of $5.455 million.[39] Nevertheless, Fabio Giraldo has stated that this figure would correspond to multiplying (times two) all the deposits accumulated in the Colombian Saving System of Constant Value (UPAC) in the 15 years since its inception.[40] It is Giraldo's argument that since the transactions of the drug barons are mainly for luxury housing, it would be possible to arrive at an estimate of approximately $123 million for 1988, a figure lower than the one presented by Borrero for the same year.

In synthesis, in spite of the difficulties in obtaining any agreement on the economic information available on the impact of narcotrafficking and the fact that figures do not provide realistic bases for precise conclusions, the previous comments can offer an approximate measure of its magnitude and importance. Furthermore, they can be better understood after an examination of the impact of narcotrafficking in other areas.

The Impact on Society and Culture

Even though there is agreement on concrete and specific figures, it seems clear that narcotraffickers have developed a certain tension between patterns of uncontrolled accumulation of capital and the cultural values that define those social sectors that have not been able to recognize fully the new wave of social change. The development of a new bourgeoisie, that simultaneously defies and defines a structure of global class domination, seems to be based on this contradiction between economics and culture. Side by side with the ambiguous policy of attraction and repulsion apparent in some of the traditional dominant sectors,[41] some narcotraffickers have tried to create an image of themselves that brings them closer to traditional values to demonstrate the benefits of a system that allows for ascending social mobility.[42]

This vertical mobility also refers to those who have increased their income through the business and services demanded or offered by narcotraffickers. These suppliers have experienced the same social process, and, in the eyes of the general population, can be confused with those who made their fortune in activities independent of the illicit drug business. The country's global historical encounter of limitations in social mobility is interpreted so that all those who experience more or less drastic ascending changes in their life-styles become stigmatized for being mafiosi.

Vertical mobility is also tied to a horizontal displacement that affects peasants uprooted from their land, old landowners transformed into tenants, fortune hunters who roam areas of coca cultivation, and officers and ex-officers of the armed forces who make their living off the business of violence and protection.

This double mobility has generated appetites and resentments, created additional difficulties and wider resistance and condemnation in the face of the existing social barriers. The previously used descriptions of an "emerging class" and a "submerging class" still describe a complex process of social change that has not ceased to have contradictory effects. And there has been a revival of a deep ethical ambiguity in Colombian society. The new values associated with success, daring, and death have been accepted while acts of machismo seem to be out of control;[43] the old conceptions of the hierarchical order of society, the religious beliefs and the sempiternal truths that deny the social existence of the differences and the different, all those values that guided the configuration of Colombia as a nation and set up a particular structure of domination seek to ratify their validity, in spite of many symptoms of obsolescence.

Narcotraffickers have been socially accepted or rejected because they represent the values, aspirations, hates, fears and envies of large segments of the population. To stop being poor in one coup de grace or with one audacious move; to be able to ride the city streets in shiny, expensive automobiles; to parade with current or former beauty queens; to be able to hand out favors to members of the intelligentsia, the church, the worlds of politics, show business, and finance; all these actions contrast with the arrogance, the arbitrariness, and the efficiency in ordering assassinations and terrorist acts.

Narcotraffickers seem to move in a modern society and contribute toward its development, but at the same time, they maintain a predilection for traditional values such as the desire to possess land and the admiration of horses and other symbols of landed gentry. At the same time, their methods of business and competition and their survival as entrepreneurs are characterized fundamentally by the violence and savagery in the means they choose to solve their conflicts and overcome the obstacles that confront them. Nora Segura is correct when, in her study about drugs and women in Colombia, she concludes by highlighting the profoundly conservative effects of narcotraffic.[44]

The Impact on Politics and Future Perspectives

The shadow of narcotraffic, particularly its terrorist version, was at the core of Colombia's past general elections. Even though its responsibility for the death of three presidential candidates has not been proven, the fact is that one of them had spent a considerable portion of his political career rejecting the corrupt and criminal practices of narcotrafficking. Whether or not some narcotraffickers may have been the intellectual authors of the assassinations, the fact is that they became a direct threat to the political establishment, although they did not seem to be interested in overthrowing the government.

There is no doubt that the increase in violence has been the main political effect of narcotraffic,[45] and three types of violence have been identified: one is exercised at the heart of narcotrafficking organizations, as punishment for the violations of codes that are innate to the business; another, directed against officers, state institutions, and journalists who have voiced opposition to the behavior of narcotraffickers, included terrorism with indiscriminate effects on the general population; and the third one had as its objective popular leaders and organizations, specifically peasants and unions.[46] In order to execute their actions, narcotraffickers have established alliance networks that may eventually contradict each other, a fact that ostensibly confuses the scene and complicates the political and judicial treatment and solution.

The mechanisms unleashed against the violence of narcotrafficking are not less worrisome. In effect, when the level of confrontation increased as a consequence of the additional number of assassinations, what started as initial tolerance on the part of the nation's security organisms turned into a policy that gave privilege to the use of responses so violent that they surpassed the framework of their own legality. Massacres, tortures and purges have been enforced in the struggle against narcotraffic, and, frequently, excesses by the authorities have resulted in the escalation of a "dirty" war in which the victims have been innocent people.

National policies have not shown any continuity. During the Virgilio Barco administration, measures to facilitate the repatriation of narcotraffickers' capital through an official fiscal amnesty were approved, yet the possibilities for their acceptance as members of Colombian society were reduced because they were still considered enemies of humanity. While radical condemnations were being issued, new spaces were opened, albeit surreptitiously, for negotiations that responded to the purely personal interests of high government officials.

Parallel to the expression of democratic ideas, there was evidence of official tolerance and complicity with the excesses of the military, even though their jurisdiction over the civilian population had been canceled. President Barco's policy, then, was contradictory, ambiguous, and paradoxical and resulted, finally, in an inevitable polarization of forces.

With the Cesar Gaviria administration, there has been a complete shake-up in the response to narcotraffic. It started with the affirmation that narcoterrorism was the country's main problem and that it was not possible to reduce its activities merely by political or military measures. The government, then, transformed its policy of direct confrontation and frontal war into one of appeasement, and new legal measures were implemented, through which some of the important narcotraffickers surrendered to the judicial system[47] in exchange for guarantees that they would not be extradited and that their human rights would be respected. These decrees coincided with the formal prohibition to extradite Colombians that was legislated by the new constitution.

In the specific area of trafficking, Gaviria has continued to insist on the internationality of the problem, has ratified that consumer demand is at the root of the business, and has insisted that Colombia has not received the reciprocity it deserves for its strong efforts in interdiction and prosecution of narcotraffickers. In contrast to Barco, who never emphasized the distinction between demand and supply as he sought international aid, Gaviria has, as a priority, asked for an international policy of tariff reduction and commercial trade balance that will reward the country for its efforts. This summary of the official position of the Gaviria government was formally expressed at the Cartagena meeting of 1990.

While the policy against terrorism has, no doubt, been successful, the same statement can not be applied to the policy that deals with drug trafficking. The surrender of some of Medellín's capos did not reduce exports but resulted in the fragmentation of exporting organizations, although it had been postulated that the cartels were organizations that exercised a high degree of control in their internal affairs as well as in setting product prices in the international market. Nevertheless, when the heads of narcotrafficking were toppled and jailed, not only did the business not contract but, on the contrary, it began to expand. This fact confirmed the suspicion of some analysts that the cartels were not rigid and fixed operations but rather lax organizations that permitted the incorporation of new exporters.[48] More recent information reports on the diversity in size and importance of narcotrafficking organizations in several regions of Colombia and supports this affirmation.

Moreover, the recent development of poppy cultivation opens new sources of uncertainty. It is not fully known whether coca exporters have diversified or substituted their sources or if new actors, independent of existing organizations, have appeared. However, it is presumed that if the poppy business develops, there will be a new organizational framework that would deal with the internal production of raw materials, without having to depend on a considerable number of Bolivian or Peruvian producers and complex technologies as was the case with cocaine.

It would be, then, an independent business; But it would have against it not only the official Colombian experience in drug persecution, but it would also involve a group of countries, specifically European, pursuing more extreme and radical actions in the fight against heroin, a more threatening problem than cocaine. Colombia would find itself immersed in a new international context where it would be difficult to involve other countries like Bolivia and Peru, which are part of the current cocaine chain.

In the short term, one of the central problems for Colombia consists of designing strategic policies to confront narcotraffic and implementing them in ways that contemplate not only the violence directed at the political system but the additional manifestations associated with non-political victims. Even though they are relatively obscured by lack of information, the frequent deaths of citizens in some regions of the country, rumored to be caused by the internal strife of traffickers, do not cease to have an effect on Colombian society. In fact, it can be said that the internal measures that tend to minimize the levels of political confrontation have been effective, and this is necessary for future actions that will reduce even more the level of conflict. It is also clear that the absence of a global strategy against the business of narcotraffic facilitates the continuation of other types of violence.

This lack of a global strategy will result in the dissatisfaction of the U.S. government with partial internal Colombian solutions and the use of pressure so that state actions are extended to the eradication of production and export of cocaine and heroin in Colombia. To do this, the United States will promote the opinions of large segments of its population who consider that the problem of drugs is Number One, "more important than unemployment, failures in the welfare and national educational systems, or the threat of communism at the international level."[49]

Additionally, whether a new situation of violence generates effects that are as harmful or dangerous as the present ones will depend on the strategy that is adopted, on the type of pressure the United States and other countries apply to Colombia, and on Colombia's response. It is not possible to continue to believe that narcotraffickers with a "low political profile" are less likely to unleash a level of violence equal or stronger than that displayed by members of the Medellín cartel. Those traffickers, whose alliance with members of the armed forces or with security institutions make them less vulnerable to the state's judicial action and who use corruption as a means to hide their interests while they display their violence more efficiently, can not be judged with less severity by Colombian society and its crumbling democracy.

If the option of the reduction of political violence can be foreseen in the near future, there remains the need to find solutions to the forms of violence previously mentioned. What to do, for instance, to end the violence used to liquidate competitors? What about the violence against peasants or popular organizations? If those kinds of violence are different from political violence, does this imply that the judicial treatment of the perpetrators should also be different? If this is the case, what kind of punishment should be given to those who are guilty of more than one kind of violence? And if the answer is negative, can the same treatment be administered to all those who are guilty, regardless of the qualifications and circumstances?

Furthermore, the maximum prison term that the Extraditables who are already in jail would receive is, according to some jurists, somewhat more than three years; by 1995, at the latest, they would be free and supposedly reintegrated into Colombian society. This instance presents an element of judicial absurdity, because their punishment would not be determined on the basis of the crimes committed but on the willingness and pragmatism of the state to negotiate. In effect, any common citizen could be condemned to harsher sentences for crimes of lesser magnitude than those attributed to the Extraditables. There is no doubt that this kind of argument, used with the ability and persuasiveness that characterizes some of Colombia's judicial experts, will be taken into consideration by a large segment of the population. The situation, then, can potentially become a great "narcissistic" injury that harms the judicial system of a country immersed in legality.

The fact that some narcotraffickers have surrendered does not imply that the current executioners of violence who have been associated with them will also surrender. The loss of income, as well as the process of social violence that has become deeply ingrained, will, no doubt, convert the sicarios, pandilleros, and paramilitary groups into uncontrollable forces capable of generating a new, disorganized violence that can produce complex and dangerous effects.

If the judiciary problem is ever resolved, the reinsertion into society of the Extraditables and those who surrender will not be a simple process, and it will depend on multiple circumstances. Is it logical to think that narcotraffickers will be accepted as legal businesspeople, using their accumulated wealth as a starting point? This option will depend on whether or not the social class into which they aspire to insert themselves has the capacity and willingness to receive them. Experiences with delinquent entrepreneurs are recent, so they can not be used as the basis for speculation in this respect, but it is expected that the criminal violence displayed and the political and social offenses inflicted upon society and the state by their actions of terrorism and assassination will not make them easily accepted.[50]

To forgive and to forget might serve to oxygenate the government's future democratic programs and projects; for many Colombians, however, this is a suicidal policy, and they will not cease in their attempt to increase the forces of retaliation and intolerance. While there are manifestations of the inability to accept the past in order to build a future that is less threatening; while the Colombian state continues to show weakness in the protection of its citizens; while the economic and legal fragility of some and the strength of others allow arms to be a source of privilege; while peasants are ignored and become so vulnerable that they can be induced to grow coca or poppies; while the corruption of the armed forces and the intimidation or bribery of judges continue to sustain criminal activities; while   anticommunism serves to legitimize alliances that intend to clear consciences and embrace the belief that it is acceptable to annihilate the opposition; while all of the above still rule, the conditions for the use of violence, not less lethal for not being political, will continue.

Beyond the strictly judiciary response is the necessary demand that the solution given to the problem can achieve the end of all forms of narcoviolence and narcotraffic without threatening the legitimacy of the state and the political regime. To achieve this, it is fundamental that any option utilized limits itself, with severity, to the explicit margins of a state of law so that it can be differentiated from the violent practices of the narcotraffickers. Otherwise, the remedy can prove to be more deadly than the disease.

Notes

1. See the bibliography on this topic presented by Alejandro Reyes and Ana Maria Bejarano, "Producción y tráfico de drogas", *Análisis Político*, #7, mayo-aogosto, 1989; and Luis Fernando Sarmiento and Ciro Krauthausen, "Bibliografía sobre el mercado ilegal de la cocaína," *Análisis Político*, #12, enero-abril, 1991.

2. Whatever the explanations, the facts are that if Colombia has had to receive warnings along with Peru and Bolivia, it has also received special attention due to the fact that its participation as a wholesale distributor of the product places it at the top of the chain. See Guy Gugliotta and Jeff Leen, *Kings of Cocaine*, New York: Harper, 1990; Rensselaer W. Lee III, "Tráfico de drogas y países en desarrollo"; Ethan A. Nadelman, "Latinoamérica: economía política del comercio de cocaína"; Richard B. Craig, "El tráfico de drogas: implicaciones para los países suramericanos"; Bruce Michael Bagley, "Colombia y la guerra contra las drogas" and "Nueva guerra de los cien años?", in Juan Tokatlián and Bruce Bagley (eds.), *Economía y política del narcotráfico*, Bogotá: CEI-Cerec, 1990; Jonathan Marshall, "Drugs and United States Foreign Policy" and Thomas Szasz, "The Morality of Drugs Control," both in Ronald Hamowy (ed.), *Dealing with Drugs*, Lexington: Lexington Books, 1987.

3. D.F. Musto, "The History of Legislative Control over Opium, Cocaine and their Derivatives," in Hamowy, *Dealing with Drugs*; Alvaro Camacho, *Droga y Sociedad en Colombia: El Poder y el Estigma*, Cali-Bogota: Cidse-Cerec, 1988, 38-49; Lester Grinspoon and James Bakalar, *Cocaine: A Drug and its Social Evolution*, New York: Basic Books, 1985; Rosa del Olmo, "Drogas, distorsiones y realidades" and Luis Suárez Salazar, "Conflictos sociales y políticos generados por la droga," both in *Nueva Sociedad*, #102, July-August 1989.

4. Government of the United States, "Estrategia para el Control de las Drogas en 1989," cited by Michael Reid, "El Plan Bush en América Latina", in Diego García-Sayán (ed.), *Narcotráfico: Realidades y Alternativas*, Lima: Comisión Andina de Juristas, 1990; Luis Alberto Restrepo, "Estrategia norteamericana de seguridad y tráfico de drogas; lectura de un informe al congreso de los Estados Unidos", in *Análisis Político*, No. 13, May-August, 1991.

5. Coletta Youngers and John Walsh, "La guerra contra las drogas en los Andes: una política mal encaminada" and Augusto Maxwell, "Una ley contradictoria", in Diego García-Sayán (ed.), *Coca, cocaína y narcotráfico: laberinto en los Andes*, Lima: Comisión Andina de Juristas, 1989; Reid, "El Plan Bush...." See the debates on the Bush Plan (Bennett) and the "Informe de la Comisión de Política y Relaciones Internacionales" in García-Sayán, *Narcotráfico...*, 153-224 and 241-44.

6. Gugliotta and Leen, *Kings of Cocaine*; Penny Lernoux, *In Banks We Trust*, Garden City, New York: Doubleday-Anchor, 1984; Gustavo Gorritti, "Perú y el Plan Bush", and García-Sayán, *Narcotráfico* ...; Randy E. Barnett, "Curing the Drug-Law Addiction: The Harmful Side Effects of Legal Prohibition," in Hamowy, *Dealing with Drugs*; Ethan Nadelman, "Víctimas involuntarias: Consecuencias de las políticas de prohibición de drogas." Debate Agrario, #7, Lima, July-December, 1989; Jose Steinsleger, "Los paraísos financieros. El Caso de Panamá," in García-Sayán, *Coca, cocaína....*

7. See the comments on the Vienna Convention by Rosa del Olmo, Raphael Perl, Marcela López Bravo de Ruiz, and Baldomero Cacéres in García-Sayán, *Narcotráfico...*, 07-152; Ligue Internationale Antiprohibitioniste, "L'Antiprohibitioniste," #1, Brussels, 1989.

8. Peter A. Lupsha, "El tráfico de drogas: México y Colombia, una perspectiva comparada"; Richard B. Craig, "El tráfico de drogas: implicaciones para los países suramericanos", both in Tokatlián and Bagley, *Economía y política...*; Alejandro Camino, "Coca: del uso tradicional al narcotráfico"; Henry Oporto Castro, "Bolivia: El complejo coca-cocaína"; Anthony Richard Henman, "Tradición y represión: dos experiencias en América del Sur"; Humberto Campodónico, "La Política del Avestruz", all in García-Sayán, *Coca, cocaína....*

9. Juan Gabriel Tokatlián, "Seguridad y drogas: su significado en las relaciones entre Colombia y los Estados Unidos"; from the same author, "Reflexiones en torno a las drogas y la seguridad nacional: la amenaza de la intervención?" both in Tokatlián and Bagley, *Economía y política....*

10. Alvaro Camacho, "Cinco tesis para una sociología política del narcotráfico en Colombia." Paper presented to the International Seminar on Narcotraffic and Human Rights, Saint Anthony's College, Oxford, June 1990.

11. Nicholas H. Hardinghaus, "Droga y crecimiento económico. El Narcotráfico en las cuentas nacionales", in *Nueva Sociedad*; Rensselaer W. Lee III, Richard B. Craig, and Ethan A. Nadelman, *Nueva Sociedad.*

12. It is clear that this is not the only reason for concern on the part of those organizations. The continuous violation of human rights in Colombia is not exclusive to narcotraffic. The Colombian government has had a high share of responsibility in this area.

13. Comisión Andina de Juristas, Conferencia Internacional " A un año de Cartagena". Final declaration, Lima, March, 1991.

14. See *Newsweek*, July 16, 1990. In fact, U.S. military forces have completed operations Hatrick I, II, and II.

15. See *La Prensa*, September 13 and November 23, 1989.

16. *El Espectador*, October 24, 1990; United States General Accounting Office, Report to Congressional Requestors, *Drug War Observations on Counternarcotics Aid to Colombia*, Washington, D.C., September 1991.

17. Antonil, *Mama Coca*, London: Hassle Free Press, 1978. This book was later published in Colombia by Editorial Oveja Negra with the same title but under the author's real name, Anthony Henman.

18. *Alternativa*, several issues.

19. ANIF, *Marihuana: legalización o represión*, Bogotá: Biblioteca ANIF de Economía, 1979.

20. ANIF, *La Legalización de la marihuana*, Bogotá: Biblioteca ANIF de Economía, 1980.

21. Alvaro Camacho, *Droga, corrupción y poder. Marihuana y cocaína en la sociedad colombiana*, Cali: Cidse, Universidad del Valle, 1981. A similar presentation appears in Mylene Sauloy, "Historia del narcotráfico colombiano a través de sus relaciones con el poder", in *Memoria del V Congreso de Historia de Colombia*, Bogotá: Icfes, 1986.

22. Mario Arango and Jorge Child, *Narcotráfico: imperio de la cocaína*, Medellín: Editorial Percepción, 1984; *Los condenados de la coca*, Medellín: Editorial J.M. Arango, 1985.

23. Mario Arango, *Los Funerales de Antioquia la grande*, Medellín: Editorial J.M. Arango, 1990.

24. Bogotá: Editorial Documentos Periodísticos, 1987.

25. Alvaro Camacho, *Droga y Sociedad en Colombia: el poder y el estigma*, Cali-Bogotá, Cidse-Cerec, 1988.

26. Alain Delpirou and Alain Labrousse, *El sendero de la cocaína*, Barcelona: Editorial Laia, 1988.

27. Daniel Pecaut, *Crónica de dos décadas de política colombiana*, Bogotá: Siglo XXI, 1989.

28. See Fabio Rincón, among others, *Ochoa, Colombia sin mafia, La Extradición, Los recitales del 'Cartel', Lehder el hombre, Leyenda y verdad de El Mexicano*.

29. Gustavo Veloza, *La guarra de los carteles de la cocaína*, G.S. Editores, n.p., 1988.

30. Anonymous, *Un narco se confiesa y acusa: carta abierta al pueblo colombiano*, Bogotá: Editorial Colombia Nuestra, 1989.

31. This characterization of narcotraffickers as neoliberal, democratic, and anti-imperialist fighters had been emphasized by Diana Duque, *Colombia, una guerra irregular entre dos ideologías*, Bogotá: Intermedio Editores, 1991. The author considers that Gonzalo Rodríguez Gacha's anticommunist attitudes and his actions handing out weapons to arm paramilitary groups in their fight against the guerrilla and the peasant movement turned him into a patriot.

32. Carlos G. Arrieta, Luis J. Orjuela, Eduardo Sarmiento, Juan G. Tokatlián, *Narcotráfico en Colombia: Dimensiones políticas, económicas, jurídicas e internacionales*, Bogotá: Coediciones Tercer Mundo-Ediciones Uniandes, 1991.

33. *Cocaína & Co.*, Bogotá: Coediciones IEPRI-Tercer Mundo, 1991.

34. Roberto Junguito y Carlos Caballero, "La otra economía", *Coyuntura Económica*, V, VIII, #4, December 1978; Hernando José Gómez, "El tamaño del narcotráfico y su impacto económico"; Salomón Kalmanovitz, "La economía del narcotráfico en Colombia", both in *Economía Colombiana*, #226-227, February-March 1990; Jesús Antonio Bejarano, "Implicaciones económicas del narcotráfico: el estado del debate"; Juan José Echavarría, "Exportaciones de droga y crecimiento industrial", and Alicia Puyana, "Algunas consideraciones sobre aspectos de la economía del

narcotráfico", presented at the International Seminar on Narcotraffic and Human Rights, Saint Anthony's College, Oxford, June 1990; Eduardo Sarmiento, "Economía del Narcotráfico" in Arrieta, et.al., *Narcotráfico*....

35. Salomón Kalmanovitz, "La economía del tráfico de cocaína," in *Cien días vistos por Cinep*, No. 6, June 1989.

36. Echavarría, "Exportaciones de droga...," 5.

37. Hernando Gómez Buendía, Eduardo Sarmiento Anzola, and Carlos Moreno Ospina, "Impacto del conflicto armado y del narcotráfico sobre la producción agropecuaria en Colombia. 1980-1988," Bogotá: Instituto de Estudios Liberales-Misión de Estudios del Sector Agropecuario, February 1989; Eduardo Sarmiento and Carlos Ospina, "Narcotráfico y Sector Agropecuario en Colombia", *Economía Colombiana*, #226-227, February-March 1990; Alejandro Reyes, "La violencia y la expansión territorial del narcotráfico."

38. Sarmiento and Ospina, "Narcotráfico y Sector...."

39. Oscar Borrero, "La finca raíz y la economía subterránea", Camacol Seminar "Economía ilegal, café y construcción", Bogotá, November 8, 1989. Cited by Kalmanovitz, "La economía del narcotráfico en Colombia", *Economía Colombiana*, #226-227, February-March 1990.

40. Fabio Giraldo Isaza, "Narcotráfico y construcción", *Economía Colombiana*, #226-227, February-March 1989.

41. Camacho, *Droga y sociedad en Colombia*.

42. Mario Arango, El impacto del narcotráfico.... See the letter from the Rodríguez Orejuela brothers to the mayor of Cali in *Semana*, #440, October 9-16, 1990, 20.

43. The implications of this new economic sector — so large, dynamic, and profitable — for the Colombian society are enormous: They continue to hold old-fashioned values that attribute success in life to daring and luck. Machismo has gotten out of hand. Corporate crime has destroyed the already-damaged institutions that administer civil justice: the mafia has bribed politicians, police, and military forces, customs agents, and prison wardens. It has joined extreme rightist groups to liquidate hundreds of activists, sindicalists, teachers and university professors, judges, journalists, and public officials. At the same time, on the dangerous struggle that has evolved between, on the one hand, political-military movements, legalized leftist parties and civic groups and, on the other hand, a government reluctant to negotiate with the opposition but willing to use violence to defeat it, narcotraffickers have joined ranks with the right in spite of their specific nationalistic, anti-United States position which has occasionally led it to tactical alliances with some political-military groups from the left. Salomón Kalmanovitz, "Colombia en la encrucijada de la sinrazón", in *La encrucijada de la sinrazón y otros ensayos*, Bogotá: Tercer Mundo, 1989, 23-24.

44. Nora Segura "Mujer y droga: consideraciones sobre un problema no considerado", presented at the International Conference on Narcotraffic and Human Rights, Oxford, June 11-14, 1990 (for future publication).

45. See, among others, Hernando Gómez Buendía, "Cuál es la guerra? Colombia, EEUU y la droga", *Nueva Sociedad*, #106, March-April 1990; Alvaro Camacho, "Cinco tesis para una sociología política del narcotráfico y la violencia en Colombia";

Alejandro Reyes, "La violencia y la expansión territorial del narcotráfico"; Iván Orozco Abad, "Los diálogos con el narcotráfico: historia de la transformación fallida de un delincuente común en un delincuente político"; Carlos Eduardo Jaramillo, "El asesinato colectivo en Colombia". All of the above presented at the International Seminar on Narcotraffic and Human Rights, St. Anthony's College, Oxford University, June 1990; Estanislao Zuleta, "La violencia política en Colombia," *Revista Foro*, #12, June 1990. A revealing example of the exaggerations produced by the statistical treatment of the violence of narcotraffic and its relation to other violent conflicts in the country is found in the analysis of *Coyuntura Social*, in effect, it offers the figure of 11,254 deaths caused by drug activity in 1989, which represents 48 percent of the total number of homicides. It does not seem very credible that narcotraffic could be responsible for the deaths of so many people in one year, but most significant is that the statistical procedure has a clause of *caeteris paribus* so large as to make it unacceptable. What appears there as a supposition is really a hypothesis that not only requires proof but the elaboration of more specific figures. For a critique of these figures, see Alvaro Camacho, "El ayer y el hoy de la violencia en Colombia: continuidades y discontinuidades", in *Analisis Político*, No. 12, 1991; Rodrigo Uprimny, "La violencia de los números: una crítica de las interpretaciones del Ser-Fedesarrollo", in *Coyuntura Social*, No. 4, 1991; and Rodrigo Losada Lora, "Respuesta a 'La violencia de los números'."

46. Alejandro Reyes Posada, "La violencia y la expansión territorial del narcotráfico"; Carlos Medina Gallego, *Autodefensa, Paramilitares y Narcotráfico en Colombia*, Bogotá: Editorial Documentos Periodísticos, 1990.

47. Decrees 3030, 303, and 2054 of 1990.

48. Alvaro Camacho, "Cinco tesis ...".

49. David Scott Palmer, "Política exterior norteamericana y el plan Bush", en Comisión Andina de Juristas, *Narcotráfico: Realidades y Alternativas*, 171.

50. In this respect, it would be very constructive to study some experiences such as those of Italy and the United States. In the first one, one can get lessons of the highly successful insertion of ex-members of the Red brigades as well as of the most involved Sicilian mafia. The first instance seems to have been well controlled, while the second was especially important in one region of the country. In the United States, the conversion of some mafiosi to legal businesspeople and the new entrepreneurial organization of the mafia could also offer basis for comparison. The major difference with the Colombian case, however, lies in the fact that the Italian and U.S. mafias have not had the centrality that narcotrafficking has assumed in Colombia.

References

ANIF. 1979. *Marihuana: Legalización o Represión*. Bogotá: Biblioteca ANIF de Economía.

ANIF. 1980. *La Legalización de la Marihuana*. Bogotá: Biblioteca ANIF de Economía.

Arango, Mario. 1988. *Impacto del Narcotráfico en Antioquia.* 3rd ed. Medellín: Editorial J.M. Arango.

Arango, Mario. 1990. *Los Funerales de Antioquia la Grande*. Medellín: Editorial J.M. Arango.

Arango, Mario, and Jorge Child. 1984. *Narcotráfico: Imperio de la Cocaína*. Medellín: Editorial Percepción.

Arango, Mario, and Jorge Child. 1985. *Los Condenados de la Coca*. Medellín: Editorial J.M. Arango.

Arrieta, Carlos G., Luis J. Orjuela, Eduardo Sarmiento, and Juan G. Tokatlián. 1991. *Narcotráfico en Colombia: Dimensiones Políticas, Económicas, Jurídicas e Internacionales*. Bogotá: Coediciones Tercer Mundo-Ediciones Uniandes.

Camacho, Alvaro. 1988. *Droga y Sociedad en Colombia: El Poder y el Estigma*. Cali-Bogotá: Cidse-Cerec.

Camacho, Alvaro. 1990. "Cinco Tesis para una Sociología Política del Narcotráfico en Colombia." Paper presented to the International Seminar on Narcotraffic and Human Rights. Saint Anthony's College, Oxford.

Camacho, Alvaro. 1981. *Droga, Corrupción y Poder. Marihuana y Cocaína en la Sociedad Colombiana*. Cali: Cidse, Universidad del Valle.

Camacho, Alvaro. 1991. "El Ayer y el hoy de la Violencia en Colombia: Continuidades y Discontinuidades." *Análisis Político*. No. 12.

Castillo, Fabio. 1987. *Los Jinetes de la Cocaína*. Bogotá: Editorial Documentos Periodísticos.

Comisión Andina de Juristas, Conferencia Internacional. 1991. "A un Año de Cartagena." Final Declaration. Lima. March.

Delpirou, Alain, and Alain Labrousse. 1988. *El Sendero de la Cocaína*. Barcelona: Editorial Laia.

Duque, Diana. 1991. *Colombia, una guerra Irregular entre Dos Ideologías*. Bogotá: Intermedio Editores.

Echavarría, Juan José. 1990. "Exportaciones de Droga y Crecimiento Industrial." Presented at Saint Anthony's College, Oxford.

El Espectador. 1990. October 24.

García-Sayan, Diego, ed. 1990. *Narcotráfico: Realidades y Alternativas*. Lima: Comisión Andina de Juristas.

García-Sayan, Diego. 1989. *Coca, Cocaína y Narcotráfico: Laberinto en los Andes*. Lima: Comisión Andina de Juristas.

Gómez, Hernando José. 1990. "El Tamaño del Narcotráfico y Su Impacto Económico." *Economía Colombiana*. No. 226-227. February-March.

Gómez Buendía, Hernando, Eduardo Sarmiento Anzola, and Carlos Moreno Ospina. 1989. "Impacto del Conflicto Armado y Del Narcotráfico sobre la Proucción Agropecuaria en Colombia. 1980-1988." Bogotá: Instituto de Estudios Liberales-Misión de Estudios del Sector Agropecuario.

Gómez Buendía, Hernando, Eduardo Sarmiento Anzola, and Carlos Moreno Ospina. 1990. "Cuál es la Guerra? Colombia, EEUU y la Droga." *Nueva Sociedad*. No. 106. March-April.

Grinspoon, Lester, and James Bakalar. 1985. *Cocaine: A Drug and Its Social Evolution*. New York: Basic Books.

Gugliotta, Guy, and Jeff Leen. 1990. *Kings of Cocaine*. New York: Harpers.

Hamowy, Ronald. 1987. *Dealing with Drugs*. Lexington: Lexington Books.

Hardinghaus, Nicholas H. 1989. "Droga y Creciemiento Económico. El Narcotráfico en las Cuentas Nacionales." *Nueva Sociedad*. No. 102. July-August.

Henman, Anthony. 1978. *Mama Coca*. London: Hassle Free Press.

Isaza, Fabio Giraldo. 1989. "Narcotráfico y Construcción." *Economía Colombiana*. No. 226-227. February-March.

Jaramillo, Carlos Eduardo. 1990. "El Asesinato Colectivo en Colombia." Presented at Saint Anthony's College, Oxford. June.

Junguito, Roberto, and Carlos Caballero. 1978. "La Otra Economía." *Coyuntura Económica*. 7(5) December.

Kalmanovitz, Salomón. 1990. "La Economía del Narcotráfico en Colombia." *Economía Colombiana*. No. 226-227. February-March.

Kalmanovitz, Salomón. 1989a. "La Economía del Tráfico de Cocaína." *Cien Días Vistos por Cinep*. No. 6, June.

Kalmanovitz, Salomón. 1989b. *La Encrucijada de la Sinrazón y Otros Ensayos*. Bogotá: Tercer Mundo.

Krauthausen, Ciro, and Luis Fernando Sarmiento. 1991. *Cocaína & Co*. Bogotá: Coediciones IEPRI-Tercer Mundo.

Lernoux, Penny. 1984. *In Banks We Trust*. Garden City, N.Y.: Doubleday-Anchor.

Ligue Internationale Antiprohibitioniste. 1989. "L-Antiprohibitioniste." No. 1. Brussels.

Losada Lora, Rodrigo. 1991. "Respuesta a 'La Violencia de los Números'." *Coyuntura Social*. No. 4.

Medina Gallego, Carlos. 1990. *Autodefensa, Paramilitares y Narcotráfico en Colombia*. Bogotá: Editorial Documentos Periodísticos.

Nadelman, Ethan. 1989. "Víctimas Involuntarias: Consecuencias de las Políticas de Prohibición de Drogas." *Debate Agrario*. No. 7. July-December.

Un Narco se Confiesa y Acusa: Carta Abierta al Pueblo Colombiano. Bogotá: Editorial Colombia Nuestra.

Newsweek. 1990. July 16.

del Olmo, Rosa. 1989. "Drogas, Distorsiones y Realidades." *Nueva Sociedad*. No. 102. July-August.

Orozco Abad, Iván. 1990. "Los Diálogos con el Narcotráfico: Historia de la Transformación Fallida de un Delincuente Común en un Delincuente Político." Presented at Saint Anthony's College, Oxford.

Pecaut, Daniel. 1989. *Crónica de dos Décades de Política Colombiana.* Bogotá: Siglo XXI.

La Prensa. 1989. September 13 and November 23.

Puyana, Alicia. 1990. "Algunas Consideraciónes sobre Aspectos de la Economía del Narcotráfico." Presented at Saint Anthony's College, Oxford.

Restrepo, Luis Alberto. 1991. "Estrategia Norteamericana de Seguridad y Tráfico de Drogas, Lectura de un Informe al Congreso de Los Estados Unidos." *Análisis Político.* No. 13. May August.

Reyes, Alejandro, and Ana María Bejarano. 1989. "Producción y Tráfico de Drogas." *Análisis Político.* No. 7. May-August.

Reyes, Alejandro, and Ana María Bejarano. 1990. "La Violencia y la Expansión Territorial del Narcotráfico." Presented at Saint Anthony's College, Oxford.

Sarmiento, Eduardo, and Carlos Ospina. 1990. "Narcotráfico y Sector Agropecuario en Colombia." *Economía Colombiana.* No. 226-227. February-March.

Sarmiento, Luis Fernando, and Ciro Krauthausen. 1991. "Bibliografía sobre el Mercado Ilegal de la Cocaína." *Análisis Político.* No. 12. January-April.

Suárez Salazar, Luis. 1989. "Conflictos Sociales y Políticos Generados por la Droga." *Nueva Sociedad.* No. 102. July-August.

Tokatlián, Juan G., and Bruce M. Bagley. 1990. *Economía y Política del Narcotráfico.* Bogotá: CEI-Cerec.

Uprimny, Rodrigo. 1991. "La violencia de los Números: Una Crítica de las Interpretaciones del Ser-Fedesarrollo." *Coyuntura Social.* No. 4.

U.S. General Accounting Office. 1991. *Drug War: Observations on Counternarcotics Aid to Colombia.* Washington, D.C.: GAO, September.

Veloza, Gustavo. 1988. *La Guerra de los Carteles de la Cocaína.* G.S. Editores.

Zuleta, Estanslao. 1990. "La Violencia Política en Colombia." *Revista Foro.* No. 12. June.

Chapter Seven

Drug Trafficking and the Guerrilla Movement in Colombia

Alejandro Reyes

The most common justifications for combating international drug trafficking emphasize the violence and moral decomposition, the risks to public health, and the loss of labor productivity associated with drug consumption in advanced capitalist countries. Drug producing and transit countries are usually perceived, in this "North-centric" analysis, as accomplices and beneficiaries of the business, ready to poison the youth of the more developed countries in exchange for drug dollars. Drug control policy has consequently been oriented toward encouraging the producer countries to undertake crop eradication programs and to step up local enforcement designed to disrupt and dismantle trafficking networks operating within their borders. To guarantee cooperation from source and transit nations in the "war" against narcotraffic, the major consuming countries have sought to pressure them by tying aid, trade concessions, and external credits to compliance. The recourse, if a country failed to comply, has included anything from militarization of anti-drug campaigns and armed intervention to the arrest and imprisonment of a head of state (e.g., the U.S. invasion of Panama and capture of General Manuel Noriega in December 1989-January 1990).

World narcotraffic does not function within a model, despite the vision and policy of the U.S. government, of countries operating as international, autonomous, and responsible actors. The real actors of the business are illegal enterprises that create and develop networks which can penetrate the societies and the states where they operate and which escape, with a greater or lesser degree of success, official control. Those enterprises behave as closed mafias, and their impact in the country where they are established varies according to the size and stability of each society and its political regime.

The United States is a segmented society that is recognized throughout the world for its ability to incorporate mafias without affecting national equilibrium: each new sect or interest group adds a new segment, which competes with others without altering the relative situation of the whole. This same appraisal does not apply to countries torn by internal strife, such as Colombia or Peru, where governments threatened by guerrillas and social protest defend their legitimacy while attempting to reform their economic and administrative structures to integrate themselves into a global economy. In those countries — more so in Colombia than in Peru — the appearance of mafias that control the economy of drugs has generated substantial political and social change, bringing them dangerously close to a major national crisis.

In Colombia, the government has done more than Peru to achieve a negotiated solution with the guerrilla forces. It has signed peace pacts with four of the six guerrilla groups that existed three years ago, and it has held peace talks, in Caracas, Venezuela, with the Fuerzas Armadas Revolucionarias de Colombia (FARC) and the Ejército de Liberación Nacional (ELN). Moreover, in 1991, the Colombian government defined a new framework for the internal application of justice which excluded extradition for narcotraffickers but strengthened the technical and human resources to prosecute them legally. In that way, it lessened the possibility of terrorist attacks with explosives in public places, the main weapon of narcotraffickers who had faced President Virgilio Barco's "war against narcotraffic" at the end of 1989.

The use of violence by narcos to pressure the government was, nonetheless, only one dimension of the problem facing Colombia. Another was the violence accompanying social disorganization in areas where traffickers and guerrillas fought for control of territory. The violence associated with the activities of narcotraffickers has made far more difficult the pacification of regions affected by the guerrilla war. For several years, armed confrontations between narcotraffickers and guerrillas dominated areas of cultivation, processing, and traffic. In those regions where the narcotraffickers acquired large properties, they created death squads that not only displaced the guerrillas but also terrorized the local population and neutralized justice and the application of law on the part of the government. The social reorganization process enforced by some narcotraffickers had two objectives: 1) elimination of leaders and followers of the previous social organization which had grown under the influence of the guerrillas; and 2) creation of its own social base, organized as self-defense groups which received better salaries and benefits if they joined the local drug business but, even if they did not, could enjoy the relative prosperity brought about by the new drug-based economy.

As narcotraffickers have altered so markedly the course of violence, the attitude of the government toward their behavior was determined by developments in the peace processes. In other words, one of the implicit factors that has intervened in the peace talks between guerrillas and government was the government's policy vis-à-vis narcotraffickers who still possess the largest accumulation of capital in the national economy; who have acquired over one-third of the country's best livestock land; and who have participated, as regional powers, in the social conflict and armed struggle in some of the largest areas of Colombia.

Narcotraffic and Its Impact on Violence

The behavior of narcotraffickers as members of local elites combined their role as criminal dealers with their role as dynamic entrepreneurs who aspired to attain legitimate social recognition. In either case, they brought the use of violence from their business transactions to conflicts, inherited or created by their own activity, with social or political adversaries. Narcotraffickers have emerged as local powers in a setting previously defined by the social conflict and armed struggle that shaped a dynamic, and unpredictable, political system. This violent clash brought about new relationships, created by narcotraffickers through the use of money and arms, that affected the entire nation and its population, including the guerrilla groups.

Two modalities of violence, used by narcotraffickers interested in territorial domination when facing their real or potential adversaries, can be identified. In the first one, they organized local wars with private armies against guerrilla groups; such was the case when Fidel Castaño went against the Ejército Popular de Liberación (EPL) in Córdoba and Urabá and when Gonzalo Rodríguez Gacha fought against the FARC in Ariari, Guaviare, the plains of Yari, and Putumayo.

In the second modality, the selective assassination of opponents using hired guns (*sicarios*) as an instrument prevails. This has occurred in the cities of Medellín and Cali and surrounding areas of influence. In other regions, both forms of violence have been utilized, as happened in the Magdalena Medio and in wide areas of the Atlantic Coast like Cesar and Magdalena where armed groups financed and led by narcotraffickers and bands of sicarios hired for selective actions operated simultaneously.

The most anonymous form of violence used by the narcotraffickers has consisted of offering rewards, with preestablished payment rates, to liquidate opponents who are generically defined. This happened in the case of Pablo Escobar against the Medellín police or the case of many others against the Unión Patriótica, the political leftist movements, or the social base of the guerrilla groups. This type of violence created a spontaneous supply of assassins who chose their victims arbitrarily without any need for the traffickers to decide upon each individual death.

The most intimidating, and basically terrorist, form of violence practiced by some narcotraffickers has been the use of explosives in public places. Hundreds of innocent victims were sacrificed in an attempt to intimidate the population and, thus, to counteract the offensive that followed the August 1989 decree by the Barco government against the most important leaders of the illegal drug business.

Narcotraffic and Regional Powers

The relationship between elite groups and the state has long determined the power structure prevalent in each region, but this structure was transformed with the appearance of territorial domination by narcotraffickers. In those areas where the power of the state has been more privatized in the hands of political-patrimonial elites (as is the case in some regions of the Atlantic Coast), the penetration of narcotraffickers was easier and resistance by the state was weaker. The main source of traditional power, which rested on the monopolistic ownership of the land, changed hands when new narco-landowners emerged in many areas of the country.

In those regions with more complex political and economic structures, like Medellín and Cali and their environs, narcotrafficking enterprises achieved serious transformations in the composition of urban elites and their social relation with popular groups. The traditional entrepreneurial elites were faced with unequal competition from narcotraffickers and, in both cities, a group of narcos invested their capital and pooled their resources to take advantage of the profit-making associated with narcotraffic. In some of the larger and medium-sized cities, narcotrafficking companies have been created, and similar social transformations have occurred.

In Medellín and Cali, the generous irrigation of money, employed to buy existing criminal manpower, generalized the practice of hiring professionals to settle accounts or eliminate obstacles to the drug business by police or judges. Criminal bands multiplied and the rate of homicides shot up in the two cities during the 1980s. In Medellín, the greatest number of victims lived in an urban zone that has been stigmatized as the birthplace of the sicarios, an area where conflicts between youth gangs has resulted in an average life expectancy of less than twenty years of age.

Narcotraffic and Social Conflict

In many regions of the country toward the end of the 1970s, power based on land tenure and the financial capability of the narcotraffickers redefined the conflicts faced by traditional elites and popular groups. In that decade, the main problem was the struggle over ownership of unused latifundios (large estates). It was followed by the peasants' struggles for property titles and by state support of rural modernization programs to prevent the formation of new latifundios as well as the further impoverishment of the population.

Until the middle of the 1970s, the conflict over unworked land was resolved politically in favor of the large property. In the 1980s, the armed protection of the haciendas, prevalent in areas where peasants were exercising pressure, was reinforced and generalized by narcotraffickers, so that in the middle of that decade almost all the struggle for land had been eliminated through a combination of military harassment and paramilitary terrorism. The first loser in the conquest of territories and regional power by narcotraffickers was the mass of peasants who had wanted the land. In 1989, the Congress of Peasant Organizations, meeting in Arauca, declared that, for fear of the consequences, they would desist in their reclamation of land in areas where narcotraffickers exercised territorial control. Thus, the conflict inherent in colonization was replaced by the conflicts initiated with an increase in the areas under coca cultivation, a process that integrated large regions of agricultural land to a monetary economy that, in turn, created ephemeral bounties for farmers and attracted workers in search of fortune.

The new sources of revenue in areas of colonization economically strengthened the guerrilla groups, while they also transformed their attitudes and their roles toward the rural population; the relationship became a pragmatic arrangement where the guerrillas exacted tribute in exchange for the regulation of public order and the protection of the market. These social functions of the guerrilla took priority over the socio-political dimension of the armed struggle. In this way, it is possible to explain the pragmatism with which the population accommodated and submitted itself to all those using force, whether guerrillas, the armed forces, or the paramilitary groups.

During the 1980s, the dominant conflicts were the civic mobilizations, urban as well as rural; these conditions demanded that the state increase its coverage and efficacy in attending to basic needs and enhancing democracy in order to liberate the people who had become victims of conflicts between armed groups.

Adjustment and Conflict between Narcotraffic and Guerrillas

The relationship between narcotraffickers and guerrillas changes from region to region, but two common models can be described. When the guerrillas have exercised wide control over peasant coca growers, the growers and the narcotraffickers pay a tariff in exchange for the guerrillas keeping order. This is the case in areas such as Caquetá, Guaviare, and some parts of Meta.

The second model is one that prevails in regions where narcotraffickers have acquired vast amounts of territory that are dominated by armed groups under their control and where they have fought and defeated the guerrillas and intimidated the population. The armed conflict between narcotraffickers and guerrillas originated by the guerrillas' pretension to apply to the narcotraffickers the same regimen of forced contributions that they had imposed on the other landowners; these attempts were answered with the creation of armed squadrons for antiguerrilla struggle. The three best-known cases of the narcotraffickers' victory were those of Córdoba, the south of Magdalena Medio, and the region of the Ariari river in Meta.

When one of the two models clearly prevails, the situation is relatively stable because one group controls the means of violence and the rest of the population submits to its power. There are regions, however, where, in reality, there is an unstable equilibrium of mixed forms of domination, where neither guerrillas nor groups armed by narcotraffickers and other entrepreneurs exercise complete supremacy in the region, and yet, both have influence over the population. This has been the case in the northern region of Magdalena Medio, the north of Valle and, for several years, in Putumayo, until guerrillas defeated the paramilitary units of Rodríguez Gacha.

Narcotraffic and the Counterinsurgency Struggle of the State

Since 1981, the armed forces have defined their strategy of stimulating the organization of private support groups for the task of counterinsurgency. This shift was a response of the armed branches to the peace initiative of President Belisario Betancur. The policy started as a reaction against the political demise of the highly repressive tactics that characterized the previous administration. Under the Turbay Ayala government, the guarantees and freedom of citizens were compromised while the army and the police lost prestige and were rejected by wide sectors of public opinion. At the same time, a policy of dialogue and ceasefire with the guerrillas was advanced by the Betancur government, and in opposition to that policy, the armed forces requested the financial support of the landowners threatened by the guerrillas, offered them official weapons and military instruction, and organized the first self-defense groups in the region of south Magdalena Medio between 1982 and 1985.

This strategy coincided with a time when many narcotraffickers began to invest in large haciendas in those regions where property was concentrated and where there was frequent guerrilla harassment of the landowners. As a consequence, what was expected to be a way to defend the traditional social order against subversion opened a political and legal space for some narcotraffickers to join the task of counterinsurgency for their own benefit, as allies of the armed forces.

For several years, between 1981 and 1989, there was an ambiguous attitude toward the self-defense groups or paramilitary groups as they were called by the public. In 1984, as a reaction to the assassination of Minister of Justice Rodrigo Lara Bonilla, the government revived the Treaty of Extradition, signed with the United States in 1979, and attempted to prosecute major narcotraffickers. The traffickers had, however, already created linkages with officers of the armed forces and had rewarded some of them monetarily. These ties weakened substantially the repressive capacity of the government against them.

Only gradually, due to the impulse generated by the assassinations of political figures of more importance, did the government harden its position. In August 1989, when narcotraffickers from Medellín were accused of assassinating the favored presidential candidate Luis Carlos Galán Sarmiento, President Barco declared "war" against narcotraffic. The official hostility gave an advantage to those members of the armed forces who were not a part of the network of infiltration by narcotraffic. It also allowed the government to advance a process of internal purification to remove the officials involved. Nonetheless, the severity of the purge was decreased vis-à-vis those who had been compromised in cooperating with paramilitary groups, and almost none of the officers accused of human rights violations were affected.

The war of 1989 and 1990 placed the most important narcotraffickers on the defensive but, except for the death of Gonzalo Rodríguez Gacha, it did not achieve the capture of the majority of them nor did it reach its objective of neutralizing the terrorist offensive that was unleashed with the use of explosives in public places. The government did advance in the deactivation of the bands of sicarios who served narcotraffickers in Medellín, but it did so at the cost of violating the human rights of youngsters from the poorest neighborhoods of the city. This urban warfare took the lives of perhaps 250 members of the police and of hundreds of adolescents from the communes, many of whom were assassinated by the police in retaliation for their suspected actions.

In response to these actions, groups of inhabitants in the affected neighborhoods created armed organizations, known as popular militias, to control internal order, attack delinquency, and defend themselves from the police. After the campaigns started in 1985 and 1986, some such militias in Medellín evolved to create urban commandos for the revolutionary groups M-19, the EPL, the FARC, and the ELN.

The central coordination sustaining paramilitarism was, to a large degree, deactivated in the last two years. Many of Pablo Escobar's partners did not want to join him in the terrorist campaign he led against the government. The death of Rodríguez Gacha allowed the Departamento Administrativo de Seguridad (DAS) to dismantle the paramilitary groups that he had financed in the emerald zone, in Ariari, and in areas of Caquetá. The decision of Fidel Castaño to demobilize his paramilitary army in September 1990, after the ceasefire with the EPL, also contributed notably to the end of tensions in Córdoba, Urabá, and the Lower Cauca in Antioquia.

The paramilitary groups, however, have not disappeared. Even today, there are groups organized by lesser known narcotraffickers and groups formed by large landowners and those in the business of extracting emeralds that have the veiled support of regional politicians. Moreover, some members of the armed forces continue to take advantage of paramilitary actions as a fighting weapon in the zones influenced by the guerrillas.

The Policy of Submission to Justice

In June 1991, the new policy of the Cesar Gaviria government, defined as the submission of narcotraffickers to justice, induced the voluntary surrender of Pablo Escobar and the Ochoa Vásquez brothers, together with some of their partners and collaborators. This policy is basically sound because it shifts the war against narcotraffic toward the procedural controversies that the judicial system must address. Moreover, it is a realistic policy that helps the country avoid the wear-and-tear to its military capability in a conflict against adversaries capable of paying very high prices, or of extracting very high dues, for silence and complicity; in short, a conflict exists that is impossible to win.

The submission of narcotraffickers to the law is a challenge to the state and forces the state to limit its inspection of their actions to penal investigation, the search for evidence, and due process of law. It, therefore, demands that the state strengthen its capacity to investigate and control organized crime by legal means. The constitutional prohibition against extraditing Colombians, established in the reform of 1991, seeks in the future to prevent justice against Colombian narcotraffickers from being administered by U.S. judges.

Another aspect of this policy is no less important. It consists, basically, of guaranteeing each and every citizen, including narcotraffickers, the right to presumption of innocence until proven guilty. It implies that the state renounces the use of weapons appropriate for war, such as confiscation, or more controversial tactics, such as torture or assassination, in its struggle against narcotraffic.

In this way, indiscriminate criminalization and "witch hunting" are suspended. At the same time, the door is opened to allow narcotraffickers whose crimes have not been proven to legitimize their ties to society through the judicial system. This new situation can become an incentive so that those who have acquired large fortunes in the business of illegal drugs, and have not been discovered, can desist from narcotrafficking and assume the status of legitimate financiers — surrounded by the guarantees offered by a system in search of stable capital for the country's development. Should the traffickers be those who have already invested in land ownership or legal businesses, they can fully assume their role as new partners with the regional elites.

Those who continue in the drug market will still encounter operations like police interdiction, a practice whose efficiency, with the best of results, accounts for only one-fifth of all drug shipments. Since President Barco's war against drugs has extended throughout Latin America, this "lottery," in which four out of five bets can win, continues to be played but has become increasingly more dangerous for Colombian narcotraffickers.

The policy of submission to justice also provides an exit gate from criminal activity for the members of paramilitary bands, because it exonerates them from punishment for the crime of bearing arms and helps to legalize their status before the nation's authorities. The inability of the judicial establishment to identify the individuals responsible for drug-related war crimes also works, in this case, legally to reintegrate members of paramilitary groups into society.

This policy, however, remains insufficient. The advance toward progressive internal pacification of the country demands that the Colombian state confront and neutralize the death squads and the hiring of sicarios by narcotraffickers and other powerful, extralegal actors in national politics. In addition, the internal moralization campaign in the armed forces should continue until all existing ties of clandestine collaboration with the narcotraffickers are severed.

Conclusion: Synthesis of the Changes that Narcotraffic Introduced to the Problem of Pacification in Colombia

The control of one of the largest sources of capital accumulation currently existing in Colombia, through their participation in the multinational drug market, resides in the hands of a relatively small group of illegal entrepreneurs. The partial investment of that capital has been concentrated in land tenure. It has also destroyed most of the ability of the judicial system to confront organized crime. It has allowed an absentee and generally unstable group of major narcotraffickers to occupy the role of war lords, which they assumed with the cooperation of many members of the armed forces and the agreement of numerous landowners who sought to expel the guerrillas from extensive sections of the country. These "services," as well as the reception accorded their economic capability, have permitted some narcotraffickers to enter and become a part of the social and political elite of those regions where they have concentrated their investments. In that way, public attention is not focused as much on the depradations of the narcotraffickers. And the Colombian public views in a different light the problem of the democratization of the political regime.

The problem that the country will face in the near future is how to apply the national law to these gangster elites without increasing the number in their ranks. That is, how can the government in Bogotá protect the nation's political, judicial, and administrative system from bribery and intimidation, disband organized paramilitary groups and sicarios, and force the narcos to fulfill their obligations as holders of a major portion of the collective wealth for the general benefit of the population? For each social sector and for each region, this problem can be assessed in a different form, according to its own local situation and to the degree of penetration of narcotraffic.

Narcotraffic has affected most deeply, by imposing its own kind of legality, those institutions and human groupings that face the most severe crisis in Colombia. The harm caused to each one of these sectors is only a reflection of the nation's internal weakness. Narcotraffickers have come to replace the punitive action of the state in those areas where the state had essentially a nominal presence; skillfully, they joined with the state when the same public force called for the collaboration of private capital in the struggle against guerrillas.

The political system of clientelism was infiltrated more easily in those places where electoral outcomes depended more on money and where the exercise of public administration was incompetent. Local territorial elites were joined or partially replaced by narco-interests in those areas where they had been weakened either by their own inefficiency or by a potent threat from guerrillas. The narcos attacked the guerrillas, in part, by means of either extortion or the imposition of fear. They also developed a criminal work force that hired members of groups abandoned by society in the slums where unemployment is highly concentrated. Finally, some narcotraffickers are on the road to achieving legitimation as citizens and investors without criminal proceedings pending under the law. This new, complex situation generates the framework for understanding the power relationships within which the demobilization and reinsertion of guerrillas in society and future social conflicts will be fought in Colombia.

Chapter Eight

Drug Summitry:
A Colombian Perspective

Juan Gabriel Tokatlián

This chapter will attempt to evaluate the so-called "war on drugs" in terms of U.S.-Colombian relations, considering the framework agreed upon at the Cartagena summit of February 1990 and during the period from this gathering up to the San Antonio summit of February 1992.[1] Taking as a point of reference the agreements contained in the Cartagena Declaration of February 15, 1990, a balance will be made of the results of the fight against narcotics.[2] Cartagena I epitomized the opportunity to concentrate government efforts in controlling consumption, distribution, trafficking, processing, and production of drugs. It also implied the possibility of forming the basis for an international regime for narcotics.

Three underlying elements characterize this document: a sort of quid pro quo logic (if the Andean countries satisfactorily achieve the stated goals, Washington will respond with support and assistance); an anti-conflictual rhetoric (recognizing that both demand and supply generate the drug business); and a highly repressive rationality (if the parties were "tough enough," they will almost certainly win).

The Magic of the Market and Economic Promises

The first commitment emerging from Cartagena I was U.S. economic assistance for antidrug efforts in Andean countries. Governments in the area were to establish extensive reforms as well as liberalize their respective economies. If this was achieved, the U.S. administration — with internal legislative backing — would, by means of financial aid and trade promotion, provide the resources to alleviate the socio-economic impacts of internal repression in the region.

In the case of Colombia and the United States, achievements can be summarized as follows:

1. Colombia, from the end of the government of President Virgilio Barco (1986-1990) to the beginning of President César Gaviria's administration (1990-1994), promoted and implemented several programs for economic structural change. Legal conditions were improved for investment of foreign capital; fiscal austerity was preserved, reducing social investments; the dismantling of inefficient state enterprises was expedited; the privatization process was encouraged; the national economy was opened up and its internationalization was provided with incentives.[3]

However, this opening process did not increase exports, create more employment, or encourage substantial growth. Even more, monetary reevaluation, high interest rates, the elimination of a number of foreign exchange controls, and a new capital amnesty have acted as catalyst for the transfer of vast amounts of dollars to Colombia.[4] More than the so-called "sinister window" that operated since the mid-1970s, the neoliberal aperture of the early 1990s created a kind of "perverse door" that allowed for a large influx of narcodollars.[5]

Parallel to this process, it is worth mentioning that U.S. private investment in Colombia continued its declining path begun in 1987. The expectations originated by Cartagena I and President Gaviria's impulse toward greater and faster economic opening did not materialize. U.S. investment in Colombia as a percentage of total U.S. investment abroad declined from 0.99 percent in 1987, to 0.67 percent in 1988, to 0.45 percent in 1989, to 0.41 percent in 1990, to 0.30 percent in 1991. In absolute numbers, the fall was from US$3.10 billion in 1987 to US$1.75 billion in 1991, while overall U.S. investment in the world moved from US$314 billion to US$450 billion.[6]

Simultaneously, Colombian exports to the United States were US$2.343 billion in 1989, increased to US$2.793 billion in 1990, and contracted to US$2.561 billion in 1991. The participation of the U.S. market within Colombian exports was 40.8 percent in 1989, grew to 41.2 percent in 1990, and fell to 35.2 percent in 1991.[7] A more protectionist attitude on the part of Washington was obviously inconsistent with the "spirit" of the Declaration of Cartagena of 1990. In that sense, it was difficult, if not impossible, for Washington to encourage U.S. private sector investment in Colombia.

2. As can be observed in Table 1, the extent of U.S. economic assistance to Colombia was of little significance when compared to the amounts given to the armed forces and for law enforcement. Between 1989 and 1991, direct military aid — US$218.3 million — and funds for law enforcement — US$50 million — exceeded significantly (a total of US$268.3 million) the economic contribution of only US$54.7 million. If the fact that the U.S. Anti-Drug Abuse Act of 1988 authorized the United States to back the provision up with US$200 million in credit

to Colombia through the Export-Import Bank for the acquisition of military material to be used to combat the dual problem of drugs and guerrillas is also taken into consideration, then the dimension of economic assistance becomes even smaller.[8] Attention should be drawn also to the point that the military forces (army, navy, air force) have received 82 percent of the assistance, while the antinarcotics police got the remaining 18 percent.[9] Table 2 shows how the Colombian Antinarcotics Police carried out the bulk of the operations against drugs and were responsible for 88 percent of the captures, seizures, destructions, and confiscations performed in the country during 1991.

3. Undoubtedly, approval in December of 1991 by the U.S. Congress of the Andean Trade Preference Act (ATPA) was a positive achievement that established a tariff reduction for ten years for products originating in Colombia, Perú, Bolivia, and Ecuador. As indicated by the U.S. legislative debate, the total number of Andean imports from the United States for 1990 was US$5.4 billion. Forty-three percent of this amount now enters without duties under the classification of most-favored-nation or the General System of Preferences. In reality, only US$324 million in additional Andean goods (6 percent of the total of imports) could currently enter the U.S. market tariff-free.[10] According to the Colombian Institute for Foreign Trade (INCOMEX), approximately US$250 millions' worth (8.3 percent of total exports to the United States in 1990) of Colombia's exports will benefit from the lowering of duties, mostly in merchandise such as flowers, fruit, vegetables, gelatin and fungicides, and, to a lesser degree, leather manufactures.[11]

Expectations for additional income for Colombia derived from ATPA through new exports equals US$10 million per year. In short, more than the creation of a greater bilateral exchange, what results from the optimum use of ATPA is mere compensation for damages caused to Colombia by the downslide in coffee prices since the fall of the International Coffee Agreement in July 1989 stimulated by Washington. As a consequence, ATPA was politically meritorious and economically cheap, not only from the viewpoint of the executive but also from that of the U.S. Congress. For Colombia, it did not mean the generation of more overall trade but the substitution of one type of export for another.

Distorted Simultaneousness and Multiple Tensions

The second major commitment stated in the 1990 Cartagena Declaration was a dual and parallel emphasis on controlling supply and demand of narcotics, complemented by an active collaboration on several fronts of the "war on drugs." In the case of Colombia and the United States, the results obtained were the following:

1. As seen in Table 3, improvement in the capacity for cocaine interdiction by Colombian authorities was notable. In the two-year period before the February 1990 summit, 49 tons of cocaine were confiscated in the country. In the two years following the meeting and prior to the San Antonio summit, the amount of cocaine confiscated reached 114.5 tons, that is, more than twice as much as the previous 1988-1989 period. Concomitantly, efficiency in terms of interdiction was enhanced, increasing the number of cocaine seizures from 5.13 percent of the total amount produced in 1989 to 10.51 percent of the total in 1991. Additionally, while 10.6 tons of cocaine base were seized in 1988-1989, 17.1 tons of cocaine base were confiscated during 1990-1991. Furthermore, 7.7 tons of cocaine were interdicted abroad (mainly in the United States) in 1991, due to intelligence information provided by Colombia. Parallel to this, 613 coca processing labs were destroyed between 1990 and 1991.[12]

It is important to mention that there was also progress in terms of eradication. Marijuana production, which in 1988 covered 9,200 hectares, dropped to 2,000 hectares in 1991. At the same time, coca production, which had occupied 43,000 hectares in 1989, decreased to 38,400 in 1991.[13] Finally, of the 2,500 hectares of opium poppy discovered by 1991, 1,406 hectares were eradicated manually in that same year.[14] By January 1992, the Colombian government decided to apply the herbicide glyphosate to eliminate 2,900 hectares of amapola.[15] To sum up, Colombia's "big stick" policy was felt in the all-out "war on drugs".

2. By mid-1990 with the inauguration of President Gaviria's tenure, Colombia devised a new strategy to cope with domestic drug-related violence. The government instituted a "plea bargain" system in order to confront narcoterrorism — a Colombian problem — while expanding international cooperation to fight drug trafficking — a global problem.[16] By mid-1991 and as a result of the Barco-Gaviria commitment against the narcotics phenomenon, Carlos Ledher was extradited to and sentenced in the United States, José Gonzalo Rodríguez Gacha was dead, and Pablo Escobar together with the Ochoa family was imprisoned. In brief, the recognized upper echelons of the Medellín cartel were thought to be placed out of business. This, in turn, helped the administration to devote more resources and manpower to combat narcotrafficking, a cornerstone of the rationale underlying Cartagena I.

Not surprisingly then, three reports on Colombia, Perú, and Bolivia appearing in the United States between September and October of 1991 clearly pointed out that Colombian collaboration in the antinarcotics war was the most outstanding and active.[17] Comments made by the U.S. Bureau of International Narcotics Matters of the Department of State, in its 1992 report, indicated that there was no doubt that Bogotá cooperated decisively with Washington in the area of reducing drug trafficking.[18]

3. In Table 4, it becomes evident that the "rationality" reflected in the U.S. antinarcotics budget was an indication that, even after the Cartagena summit, Washington's perception and understanding of the nature of the drug phenomenon had not changed, despite grandiloquent rhetoric concerning the "joint responsibility" of the factors of demand and supply in the generation and expansion of the business. Resources for antidrug activities increased, multiplying funds for programs against supply while "simultaneously opening up a second front directed at the reduction of demand in the United States."[19] However, in light of the San Antonio meeting, the Bush administration insisted that supply continued to be the main problem.[20] In effect, there was no real transformation of the overall U.S. strategy to cope with the drug issue in the last two years. The Republican discourse and policy were still overwhelmingly supply-oriented.

4. Beyond the budgetary topic, it was expected that the reduction of drug use in the United States would be effective. The quantity of heavy users of cocaine decreased significantly after the mid-1980s. According to U.S. surveys, in 1988 the number of monthly consumers of cocaine reached 2.9 million. In 1990 — the year of the Cartagena summit — it dropped even more to 1.6 million. The total of weekly users of cocaine fell from 862,000 in 1988 to 662,000 in 1990. Parallel to this, in the past decade, heroin use in the United States remained stable at approximately 490,000 consumers. At no time did U.S. authorities state that the reduction of cocaine users was due, in part or completely, to the antidrug efforts of the Andean countries. Nonetheless, at the beginning of the 1990s, tendencies toward a decrease in cocaine use and stability in heroin demand appeared to change. In effect, the number of monthly users of cocaine rose to 1.9 million, while the total of weekly consumers grew up to 855,000. At the same time, heroin consumption increased by 75 percent in 1991.[21]

The "part" corresponding to the United States in terms of curtailing drug demand did not seem to have been satisfactorily fulfilled. The fact that the 1989 U.S. antinarcotics strategy outlined by President Bush had been surprisingly changing in the next three years had not gone unnoticed. As Raphael Perl reported, "An important goal of the strategy was to reduce the amount of illicit drugs illegally entering the United States by 15 percent within two years and by 60 percent in ten years. The President refined the strategy and forwarded it to Congress on January 25, 1990. The following year, in February 1991, policy makers modified goals to a 20 percent reduction by the year 2001. In January 1992, predetermined fixed percentage reductions were eliminated...."[22] This U.S. uncommitted position partially explains why President Gaviria insisted upon a 50 percent réduction of demand and supply of drugs by the year 2000 and 70 percent by 2005 at the 1992 San Antonio gathering.

    5. Colombian expectations in relation to U.S. collaboration on several fronts of the antinarcotics war as an outcome of the Cartagena I agreements were not fully met. In fact, contrary to what had been suggested and presumed, incidents and inconsistencies have multiplied. For example, in March 1989, after complex diplomatic negotiations, the display of a complex radar system in the north and south of the country was agreed on. At that time, President Barco paid a heavy political cost and was accused of ceding the nation's sovereignty and "Vietnamizing" Colombia.[23] Two years later, in the midst of a crisis caused by Iraq's invasion of Kuwait, the United States decided to ask for one of the mobile radars located on the border with Perú, to dismantle it, and transfer it to the Persian Gulf for "national security" reasons.

Despite having signed a bilateral memorandum agreeing to provide legal evidence to judge traffickers in Colombia, Washington has been slow, if not hindered, with its compliance. Even though the White House expressed acceptance and support of President Gaviria's policy of "plea bargain," there were periodic "unintentional" flights by U.S. aircraft over prisons where well-known drug traffickers were located.[24] In spite of the fact that the U.S. government recognized the efficiency and professionalism of the Colombian Antinarcotics Police, some U.S. federal agencies insist on involving the Colombian armed forces more actively in the "war of drugs." Hence, the Gaviria administration had to reject — after much pressure — US$2.8 million in U.S. assistance to create an antidrug unit at the level of the Colombian army.[25] And the list of frictions and difficulties can be widened.

Elusive Cooperation and Lack of Convergence

A third crucial commitment that emerged from Cartagena I emphasized the importance and urgency for extensive diplomatic cooperation between the parties involved. This was to be accompanied by joint action in international fora and mutual efforts in favor of making the world community aware of the relevance and necessity to combat the problem of drugs.

Findings in this area can be summarized as follows:

    1. In the time that elapsed between Cartagena and San Antonio, the fight against narcotics was "cocainized," "Andeanized," and "militarized."

Cocaine (more than marijuana, heroin and other synthetic drugs) occupied the core of official concern in the hemisphere. The struggle against illegal drugs was concentrated almost exclusively in the Andean region. And the strategy that was promoted by the U.S. administration was that of increasing military involvement and repression.[26] Practically none of the programs implemented from 1990 to 1992 helped to improve bilateral cooperation (in U.S.-Colombian relations), multilateral agreements (between the United States and the Andean governments), and international coordination (at the level of the United Nations). The militarization of the "drug war" also contributed to a major deterioration of the already poor state of human rights in the Andean region in general and in Colombia in particular.[27]

2. The tendency, encouraged by Washington during the 1980s and crystallized since 1990 in Cartagena I, toward the establishment of an antidrug, national security regime at the hemispheric level reduced credibility, legitimacy, and symmetry regarding concerted regional efforts to contain and mitigate the phenomenon of drugs.[28]

3. At the end of two years of "commitments" of a general nature, more friction than cooperation, more conflict than agreement, and more dissociation than articulation had resulted. This was due, in great measure, to the diplomatic mistakes on the part of the United States and to the conceptual blindness of most U.S. policy makers in charge of the international antinarcotics policy of Washington who continued to operate during 1990-1992 under the dogmatic supply-side perspective in the approach and treatment of such a complex and multifaceted phenomenon as drugs. Within this context, at San Antonio there were no joint policies against drugs, but only pragmatic and unilateral attitudes, in a sort of "everyone for himself" when facing each country's drug problem. Obviously, this was the antithesis of hemispheric collaboration and collective action.

A Brief Conclusion

Paraphrasing the title of a well-known novel by Gabriel García Marquez, to write about a future presidential antidrug summit will mean describing, with some certainty and great misfortune, the *Crónica de un fracaso anunciado* (Chronicle of an Announced Failure). After San Antonio, it will be very hard to achieve what Cartagena was not able to accomplish: the generation of a legitimate, credible, and symmetrical "non-securitized" regime on drugs. "Only by modifying U.S. conceptual premises (toward an international political economy approach), strategies (focusing on demand as well as supply), and tactics (from pressure and unilateral sanctions to incentives and multilateral cooperation) will it be possible for the nations of the continent, North and South, to attain authentic progress in the control of drug trafficking and abuse."[29]

For Colombia, in particular, the amazing growth of amapola cultivation and Pablo Escobar's bizarre escape from prison during 1992 provoked the concentration of resources and manpower on confronting heroin production (more than cocaine processing and export), narcoviolence (more than drug trafficking), and the Medellín cartel (more than other groupings).[30] This unwanted reality — together with expanding corruption at home and abroad — produced an additional limit to the improbable achievements of the new "commitments" derived from the San Antonio summit.

Table 1
U.S. Antinarcotics Assistance to Colombia, 1989-1991
(in millions of dollars)

	1989	1990	1991
Military Aid*	73.1	93.2	52.0
Law Enforcement**	10.0	20.0	20.0
Economic Assistance***	2.8	2.1	49.8

*   Includes Foreign Military Financing (F.M.F.), International Military Education and Training (I.M.E.T.), and special emergency assistance.
**   Corresponds to funds for law enforcement provided by the U.S. Department of State, Bureau of International Narcotics Matters.
***   Refers to Economic Support Funds (E.S.F.).

SOURCE: Compiled personally with data from the U.S. House of Representatives Foreign Affairs Committee, 1991, and the Office of National Drug Control Policy, 1992.

Table 2
Colombian Antinarcotics Activities 1991

Type of Activities		Army	Navy	Air Force	Police	D.A.S.*	Total
Drug Traffickers Captured							
Colombians		215	24	2	1153	113	1507
Foreigners				2	21	3	26
Drugs Confiscated							
Cocaine	KLS	10485	154		57975	52	68666
Base of Cocaine	KLS	2480	193		8622	43	11338
Basuco-Crack	KLS	216	1		1014	4	1235
Coca Leaves	KLS	2259	2988		147101		152348
Marijuana	KLS	11344	351		360763	863	373321
Morphine	KLS				17		17
Opium Paste	KLS	1			10		30
Crop Eradication							
Coca	HTS	100	196		129	1	426
Marijuana	HTS				6		6
Poppy Seeds	HTS	147			1097	162	1406
Arms-Vehicles-Others Confiscated							
Arms		29	30		254	11	324
Radios		10	2		98		110
Vehicles		8			102	5	115
Boats and Crafts		1	14		29		44
Airplanes		1		1	25		27
Ammunition		7146	161		17075	229	24611
Grenades		8			92		100
Dynamite	KLS		115		43	75	233
Labs Destroyed							
Labs		30	43		219	1	293
Electric Plants		3	5		50		58
Presses		8	8		64		80
Scales		12	13		160	5	190

Continued next page

Table 2 (Continued)
Colombian Antinarcotics Activities 1991

Type of Activities		Army	Navy	Air Force	Police	D.A.S.*	Total
Labs Destroyed (Continued)							
Gasoline	GLS	16258	4375		202069		222702
Ether	GLS	35423	1563		240078		277064
Acetone	GLS	28397	315		194225	3	222940
Liquid Ammonia	GLS	44660	737		18836		64233
Sulphuric Acid	GLS	5221	738		27558		33517
Hydrochloric Acid	GLS	14165			61059	1	75225
M E C	GLS				70079		70079
Butane and Ethane	GLS				903		903
Thinner	GLS				207		207
Hexane	GLS				9085		9085
Solvent	GLS				8580		8580
Light Carbonate	KLS	2300	910		89331		92541
Caustic Soda	KLS	10524	610		84069		95203
Permanganate Potassium	KLS	126	230		13756		14112
Sodium Sulphate	KLS	742	3850		30		4622
Quicklime	KLS	4306	600		20346		25252
Light Salt	KLS	3150	400		5871		9421
Cement	KLS	250	1930		194850		197030
Airstrips Destroyed					90		90

* Departamento Administrativo de Seguridad, D.A.S.

Source: Policía Antinarcóticos, *Balance Actividades 1991*.

Table 3
Interdiction of Cocaine in Colombia, 1988-1991
(in tons)

	1988	1989	1990	1991
World Production of Cocaine*	587.40	596.10	611.90	662.20
Seizures in Colombia	18.70	30.30	44.90	69.60
Percentage Confiscated in Colombia from Total World Production	3.18	5.13	7.33	10.51

* The total world production of cocaine resulted from applying the coefficient 500: 1 (used by the U.S. Department of State) to calculate the transformation of coca into cocaine. The metric tons of coca leaves were the following: 293.700 (1988); 298.070 (1989); 305.970 (1990); and 331.140 (1991)

Source: Compiled personally with data from U.S. Department of State Bureau of International Narcotics Matters, *International Narcotics Control Strategy Report*, 1992 and Policía Antinarcóticos, *Balance Actividades 1991*.

Table 4
Total Federal Budget of the United States
for the Control of Drugs, 1988-1992
(in percentages)

	1988	1989	1990	1991	1992
For Supply	70.3	71.2	69.9	67.9	68.6
For Demand	25.9	5.2	26.6	28.0	27.2
For Research	3.8	3.6	3.5	4.1	4.2
Total	100.0	100.0	100.0	100.0	100.0

Source: WOLA, *Clear and Present Dangers. The U.S. Military and the War on Drugs in the Andes*, 1991.

Notes

1. The presidents of the United States, Colombia, Perú, and Bolivia attended the Cartagena, Colombia, summit of February 15, 1990. The presidents of the United States, Colombia, Perú, Bolivia, Ecuador, and México and the foreign minister of Venezuela attended the San Antonio, Texas, summit of February 26-27, 1992.

2. The Declaration of Cartagena appears in *Colombia Internacional*, No. 9, January-March 1990. An analysis of its content is found in Bayardo Ramírez, K. Zambrano, S. Ochoa, A. Lovera and L. Millán, "Análisis geopolítico-estratégico de la declaración de Cartagena," in Various Authors, *La cuestión de las drogas en América Latina*. Caracas: Monte Avila Editores, 1991. On the San Antonio summit, see Douglas Jehl, "Drug Summit Leads to Only a Vague Pact," *The Los Angeles Times*, February 28, 1992, and Joseph Treaster, "On Dais of Drug Summit, U.S. Seemed Cornered," *The New York Times*, February 29, 1992.

3. See, among others, Libardo Botero et al., *Neoliberalismo y subdesarrollo*. Bogotá: El Ancora Editores, 1992.

4. See, in particular, Eduardo Sarmiento, "Tres años de Apertura," in *Economía Colombiana*, No. 241, January-February 1993 and Libardo Sarmiento and Alvaro Zerda, "Ajuste estructural, desarrollo económico y social. Dos años de revolución pacífica," in *Economía Colombiana*, No. 241, January-February 1993.

5. The *ventanilla siniestra* was a mechanism that authorized the Banco de la República (Colombia Central Bank) to receive hard currency without investigation of its origin or purpose, thus condoning, at least implicitly, the repatriation and laundering of the profits of Colombian drug traffickers.

6. See Alvaro Montenegro, "La inversión de E.U. en Colombia," *El Tiempo*, February 1, 1993.

7. See Departamento Administrativo Nacional de Estadística, DANE, "Estadísticas de comercio exterior," 1992.

8. See *El Espectador*, July 15, 1989, and *El Tiempo*, July 22, 1989. Ann Frey, spokeswoman for the Eximbank, indicated that it was the first time that a bank guarantee was granted for this type of operation; it was somewhat unusual because the Export-Import Bank only provided credit support for exports.

9. See U.S. General Accounting Office, *Drug War. Observations to Counternarcotics Aid to Colombia*. Washington, D.C.: U.S. GAO, September 1991.

10. See U.S. House of Representatives, "H.R. 661, The Andean Trade Preference Act, as Amended. Background and Purposes," November 1991, and Ministerio de Desarrollo, "Análisis del impacto sobre la economía Colombiana del proyecto de ley de comercio preferencial para el área andina," September 1991.

11. See INCOMEX, "Proyecto de ley sobre preferencias comerciales andinas," December 1991 and Martín Gustavo Ibarra, "El A.T.P.A., desafío a capacidad empresarial," *La República*, August 19, 1992.

12. See Policía Antinarcóticos, *Balance actividades 1991*. Bogotá: Policía Nacional de Colombia, December 1991.

13. See U.S. Department of State, Bureau of International Narcotics Matters, *International Narcotics Control Strategy Report*. Washington, D.C.: U.S. Government Printing Office, March 1992.

14. See Policía Antinarcóticos, *Balance actividades....*

15. See Juan G. Tokatlián, "Glifosato y política: Razones internas o presiones externas?" *Colombia Internacional*, No. 18, April-June 1992.

16. See Rodrigo Pardo, "Los intereses nacionales de Colombia y la cooperación internacional frente al narcotráfico," *Revista Cancilleria de San Carlos*, No. 6, March 1991, and Juan Gabriel Tokatlián, "Cambio de estrategia," *Semana*, No. 418, May 8-15, 1990.

17. See U.S. General Accounting Office, *Drug War. Observations...*; U.S. General Accounting Office, *The Drug War: U.S. Programs in Peru Face Serious Obstacles*. Washington, D.C.: U.S. GAO, October 1991; and U.S. Department of State, Office of the Inspector General, *Drug Control Activities in Bolivia*. Washington, D.C.: U.S. Government Printing Office, October 1991.

18. See U.S. Department of State, Bureau of International Narcotics Matters, *International Narcotics....*

19. Bruce M. Bagley and Juan G. Tokatlián, "Droga y dogma: La narcodiplomacia entre Estados Unidos y América Latina en la década de los ochenta y su proyección para los noventa," *Documentos Ocasionales C.E.I.*, No. 23, September-October 1991.

20. See Frank J. Murray, "Supply is Focus of Drug Summit," *The Washington Times*, February 27, 1992, and Douglas Farah, "Drug Summit to Convene as Supply Surges," *The Washington Post*, February 25, 1992.

21. See, among others, Joseph Treaster, "Use of Cocaine and Heroin Rises Among Urban Youth," *The New York Times*, December 19, 1991, and Joseph Treaster, "War on Drugs Shifts Its Focus to Heavy Users," *The New York Times*, December 20, 1991.

22. Raphael F. Perl, "The Andean Drug Initiative: Background and Issues for Congress," *C.R.S. Report for Congress*, February 13, 1992.

23. On the U.S.-Colombian radar system negotiations during the Barco government, see Ana Mercedes Botero and Juan G. Tokatlián, "La administracion Bush y America Latina: Una Perspectiva desde Colombia," *Colombia Internacional*, No. 6, April-June 1989. On the U.S. priority over Iraq vis-à-vis the drug issue, see Douglas Farah, "U.S. Anti-Drug Initiative Lagging, Say Colombians: Gulf War Takes Priority Over War on Cocaine," *The Washington Post*, January 21, 1991.

24. See Juan Gabriel Tokatlián, "Prólogo. De Drogas y dinosaurios." In *Cocaina & Co.*, Ciro Krauthausen and Luis Fernando Sarmiento. Bogotá: Tercer Mundo

Editores/Instituto de Estudios Políticos y Relaciones Internacionales de la Universidad Nacional, 1991.

25. The communique of the Ministry of Defense rejecting the conditionality of U.S. military aid can be seen in *El Espectador*, February 28, 1992.

26. See Bruce M. Bagley, "Myths of Militarization: The Role of the Military in the War on Drugs in the Americas," *University of Miami/North-South Center Drug Trafficking in the Americas Series*, 1991; Bruce M. Bagley, "Myths of Militarization: Enlisting Armed Forces in the War on Drugs," in *Drug Policy in the Americas*, ed. Peter H. Smith. Boulder, Colo.: Westview Press, 1992; Washington Office on Latin America, *Clear and Present Dangers: The U.S. Military and the War on Drugs in Latin America*. Washington, D.C.: WOLA, 1991; Mark P. Hertling, "Narcoterrorism: The New Unconventional War," *Military Review*, Vol. LXX, No. 3, March 1990; Donald J. Mabry, "Andean Drug Trafficking and the Military Option," in *Military Review*, Vol. LXX, No. 3, March 1990; and U.S. General Accounting Office. *Drug War*. Washington, D.C.: U.S. GAO, June 1991.

27. See, among others, Americas Watch, *The Drug War in Colombia: The Neglected Tragedy of Political Violence*. New York: Americas Watch, 1990; Alexander Laats and Kevin O'Flaherty, "Colombia: Human Rights Implications of U.S. Drug Control Policy," *Harvard Human Rights Journal*, Spring 1990; and "Is U.S. Antinarcotics Assistance Promoting Human Rights Abuse in Colombia?" *Human Rights Working Paper*, Vol. 1, No. 1, March 1991.

28. See Bruce M. Bagley and Juan G. Tokatlián, "Droga y dogma...." On the limits and shortcomings of the "war on drugs," see Peter R. Andreas, Eva C. Bertram, Morris J. Blachman, and Kenneth E. Sharpe, "Dead-End Drug Wars," *Foreign Policy*, No. 85, Winter 1991-1992.

29. See Bruce M. Bagley and Juan G. Tokatlián, "Droga y dogma...."

30. During 1992, Colombian authorities concentrated their efforts to contain the expansion of the heroin business: 12,716 hectares of poppy seeds were eradicated, while 36.1 kilograms of heroin, 9.1 kilograms of morphine, and 107.6 kilograms of opium paste were confiscated. Only 30.8 tons of cocaine and 5.9 tons of cocaine paste were seized. See Policía Antinarcóticos, *Balance actividades 1992*. Bogotá: Policía Nacional de Colombia, December 1992. Again coping with narcoterrorism became a priority; controlling drug trafficking was less crucial.

References

Americas Watch. 1990. *The Drug War in Colombia: The Neglected Tragedy of Political Violence*. New York: Americas Watch.

Andreas, Peter R., Eva C. Bertram, Morris J. Blachman, and Kenneth E. Sharpe. 1991-1992. "Dead-End Drug Wars." *Foreign Policy*. No. 85, Winter.

Bagley, Bruce M., and Juan G. Tokatlián. 1991. "Droga y dogma: La narcodiplomacia entre Estados Unidos y América en la década do los ochenta y su proyección para los noventa." *Documentos Ocasionales C.E.I*. No. 23, September-October.

Bagley, Bruce M. 1991. "Myths of Militarization: The Role of the Military in the War on Drugs in the Americas." *Drug Trafficking in the Americas Series*. Miami: University of Miami North-South Center.

Bagley, Bruce M. 1992. "Myths of Militarization: Enlisting Armed Forces in the War on Drugs." In *Drug Policy in the Americas,* ed. Peter Smith. Boulder, Colo.: Westview Press.

Botero, Ana Mercedes, and Juan G. Tokatlián. 1989. "La administración Bush y América Latina: Una perspectiva desde Colombia." *Colombia Internacional*. No. 6, April-June.

Botero, Libardo. 1992. *Neoliberalismo y subdesarrollo*. Bogotá: El Ancora Editores.

Cárdenas, Mauricio, and Luis Jorge Garay. 1993. *Macroeconomia de los flujos de capital en Colombia y América Latina*. Santafé de Bogotá: Tercer Mundo Editores/ Fedesarrollo/Fescol.

Colombia Internacional. 1990. "Declaration of Cartagena." No. 9, January-March.

El Espectador. 1989. July 15.

El Espectador. 1992. February 28.

Departamento Administrativo Nacional de Estadística. 1992. "Estadísticas de comercio exterior." Bogotá.

Farah, Douglas. 1992. "Drug Summit to Convene as Supply Surges." *The Washington Post*. February 25.

Farah, Douglas. 1991. "U.S. Anti-Drug Initiative Lagging, Say Colombians: Gulf War Takes Priority over War on Cocaine. *The Washington Post.* January 21.

Hertling, Mark P. 1991. "Narcoterrorism: The New Unconventional War." *Military Review*. LXX(3), March.

INCOMEX. 1991. "Proyecto de ley sobre preferencias comerciales andinas." December.

Ibarra, Martín Gustavo. 1992. "El A.T.P.A. Desafío a capacidad empresarial." *La República*. August 19.

Jehl, Douglas. 1992. "Drug Summit Leads to Only a Vague Pact." *The Los Angeles Times*. February 28.

Krauthausen, Ciro, and Luis Fernando Sarmiento. 1991. *Cocaína & Co*. Bogotá: Tercer Mundo Editores/Instituto de Estudios Políticos y Relaciones Internacionales de la Universidad Nacional.

Laats, Alexander, and Kevin O'Flaherty. 1990. "Colombia: Human Rights Implications of U.S. Drug Control Policy." *Harvard Human Rights Journal*. Spring.

Laats, Alexander, and Kevin O'Flaherty. 1991. "Is U.S. Antinarcotics Assistance Promoting Human Rights Abuse in Colombia?" *Human Rights Working Paper*. 1, March.

Mabry, Donald J. 1990. "Andean Drug Trafficking and the Military Option." *Military Review*. LXX, March.

Ministerio de Desarrollo. 1991. "Análisis del impacto sobre la economía colombiana del proyecto de ley de comercio preferencial para el área andina." September.

Montenegro, Alvaro. 1993. "La inversión de E.U. en Colombia." *El Tiempo*. February 1.

Murray, Frank J. 1992. "Supply is Focus of Drug Summit." *The Washington Times*. February 27.

Pardo, Rodrigo. 1991. "Los intereses nacionales de Colombia y la cooperación internacional frente al narcotráfico." *Revista Cancillería de San Carlos*. No. 6, March.

Perl, Raphael F. 1992. "The Andean Drug Initiative: Background and Issues for Congress." *C.R.S. Report for Congress*. February 13.

Policía Antinarcóticos. 1991. *Balance actividades 1991*. Bogotá: Policía Nacional de Colombia. December.

Policía Antinarcóticos. 1992. *Balance actividades 1992*. Bogotá: Policía Nacional de Colombia. December.

Ramírez, Bayardo, K. Zambrano, S. Ochoa, A. Lovera, and L. Millán. 1991. "Análisis geopolítico-estratégio de la declaración de Cartagena." *La cuestión de las drogas en América Latina*. Caracas: Monte Avila Editores.

Sarmiento, Eduardo. 1993. "Tres años de apertura." *Economía Colombiana*. No. 241, January-February.

Sarmiento, Libardo, and Alvaro Zerda. 1993. "Ajuste estructural, desarrollo económico y social. Dos años de revolución pacífica." *Economía Colombiana*. No. 241, January-February.

El Tiempo. 1989. July 22.

Tokatlián, Juan G. 1992. "Glifosato y politíca: Razones internas o presiones externas?" *Colombia Internacional*. No. 18, April-June.

Tokatlián, Juan G. 1990. "Cambio de estrategia." *Semana*. No. 418, May 8-15.

Treaster, Joseph. 1992. "On Dais of Drug Summit, U.S. Seemed Cornered." *The New York Times*. February 29.

Treaster, Joseph. 1991a. "Use of Cocaine and Heroin Rises Among Urban Youth." *The New York Times*. December 19.

Treaster, Joseph. 1991b. "War on Drugs Shifts Its Focus to Heavy Users." *The New York Times*. December 20.

U.S. Department of State, Bureau of International Narcotics Matters. 1992. *International Narcotics Control Strategy Report*. Washington, D.C.: U.S. Government Printing Office, March.

U.S. Department of State, Office of the Inspector General. 1991. *Drug Control Activities in Bolivia*. Washington, D.C.: U.S. Government Printing Office, October.

U.S. General Accounting Office. 1991a. *Drug War: Observations to Counternarcotics Aid to Colombia.* Washington, D.C.: GAO, September.

U.S. General Accounting Office. 1991b. *The Drug War: U.S. Programs in Peru Face Serious Obstacles.* Washington, D.C.: GAO, October.

U.S. General Accounting Office. 1991c. *Drug War.* Washington, D.C.: GAO, June.

U.S. House of Representatives. 1991. "H.R. 661. The Andean Trade Preference Act, as Amended. Background and Purposes." November.

Washington Office on Latin America. 1991. *Clear and Present Dangers: The U.S. Military and the War on Drugs in Latin America.* Washington, D.C.: WOLA.

Chapter Nine

Glyphosate and Drug Control Policy in Colombia

Juan Gabriel Tokatlián

At the end of January 1992, the Colombian National Council of Dangerous Drugs (Consejo Nacional de Estupefacientes — CNE) publicized its decision to fumigate manually and by air opium poppy crops with the herbicide glyphosate and stated that the eradication process would be supervised by "environmental auditing."[1] Eight years before, on May 14, 1984, the administration of President Belisario Betancur (1982-1986) supported the destruction of marijuana crops with chemical products and recommended that final approval of this decision be made by the Council of Ministers — a full cabinet session. On May 22, the Council ratified the procedure for spraying with glyphosate. On June 1, the Ministry of Justice, led by Enrique Parejo González, gave the order to the Director of the National Police, General Victor Delgado Mallarino, to fumigate marijuana plantations. On July 4, the CNE authorized the "experimental" fumigation of two hectares. However, between July and September 1984, "massive" chemical eradication of marijuana production was begun.[2]

The valuable experience of the last decade seems to have been forgotten. Today, glyphosate is being discussed "technically" again, and the debate surrounding the use of this herbicide is being "depoliticized." A large number of scientists from different government agencies agree on the low-level toxicity of glyphosate but admit their ignorance about its long-term effects on humans, fauna, flora, and waters. Nevertheless, since glyphosate — industrially manufactured under the names Roundup, Rodeo, Shackle, Vision, Accord, or Polado — is being applied to legal cash crops without dramatic consequences for people and the environment, its use in eradication of opium poppy is seen as legitimate.[3]

Since "conspiratorial theories of history" are useless to explain this kind of decision, President César Gaviria's (1990-1994) decision to utilize herbicidal fumigation of amapola should be better scrutinized. It does not seem plausible that the Colombian government would have decided to spray glyphosate one month before the presidential antidrug summit of San Antonio expecting high diplomatic or economic dividends in return.[4]

On the one hand, the United States did not give priority to economic assistance in its collaboration with Colombia: in the three-year period, between fiscal years 1989 and 1991, direct military assistance (US$73.1 million for 1989, US$93.2 million for 1990, and US$52 million for 1991) and assistance for law enforcement (US$50 million during these same three years) significantly exceeded — with a total of US$268.3 million — economic contributions — US$54.7 million.[5] On the other hand, U.S. trade benefits to Colombia as a consequence of Bogota's commitment and performance in the antinarcotics war has had ambiguous results. The U.S. Congress, at the insistence of the executive, approved in December 1991 the Andean Trade Preference Act (ATPA) which lowers duties on a variety of products coming from Colombia (8.3 percent of the country's total exports), Peru, Bolivia, and Ecuador and generates new annual exports from Colombia to the United States totalling approximately US$600 million in ten years.[6] However, this amount of tentative future "earnings" is almost the same as what the country has been "losing" since the collapse of the International Coffee Pact in July 1989 up to 1992, provoked by the intransigent attitude of Washington. In summary, rather than increase bilateral exchange, what results is merely compensation for losses caused by the drop in coffee prices.

In addition, in terms of its own internal achievements, the White House did not have much to show in order to place more unilateral pressure on Bogota. While the number of heavy cocaine users fell from 2.9 million in 1989 to 1.6 million in 1990, it rose to 1.9 million in 1991. The total number of heroin consumers grew by 75 percent from 490,000 in 1990 to approximately 900,000 in 1992.[7] The percentages of U.S. antinarcotics budget allocations in the drug war to control supply, to curb demand, and to improve research did not change despite the advocacy for more emphasis on stopping consumption: 70.3 percent, 25.9 percent, and 3.8 percent, respectively, in 1988; 69.9 percent, 26.6 percent, and 3.5 percent in 1990; 68.6 percent, 27.2 percent, and 4.2 percent for 1992.[8]

Opium Poppy: A Growing Problem for Colombia

Thus, poppy eradication was not part of an "imperial design" or a by-product of a "clandestine" trade-off between Washington and Bogota. In reality, President César Gavíria and his government were surprised by the real and potential dimensions of the heroin business in Colombia and, therefore, decided "not to lose time" in preparing a repressive policy as their key alternative. Conceptual blindness and creative paralysis combined to initiate a renewal of the old antidrug "big stick" policy. Social communication, exchange of opinions, and balance of options were left behind.

And if it meant acting forcefully, Gavíria's administration apparently knew what to do: directly attack the less decisive level of the drug network, the cultivation aspect. However, this tended to have negative social effects on the peasantry and the indigenous population while doing little to stop the drug lords and the narcobusiness. Instead of designing a strategy directed at "reducing harm" and avoiding additional problems, the executive devised its antinarcotics policy "against someone" and put forward tactics that have been injurious to the peasants' part in the illegal phenomenon. The government opted for vigorous enforcement over harm minimization.[9] In other words: Drug traffickers undoubtedly contribute to environmental degradation in that they pay the peasants to cultivate opium poppy crops. As a result, forests are cut down, mountain resources are destroyed, and rivers are degraded through chemical spills. However, the government cannot stimulate this practice further by implementing a policy that only serves to encourage the geographical transfer of crops. Its responsibility is to contain and reduce the ecological and social costs derived from drugs, while trying to avoid the perverse logic of increasing — by its actions — the territorial and trade expansion of this multifaceted illicit business.[10]

Within this context, national and international examples must be considered in a realistic and non-dogmatic way. During 1984-1985, 5.546 hectares (1 hectare = 2.47 acres) of marijuana were eradicated in Colombia with 11,418 gallons of glyphosate.[11] This "major victory" against marijuana was short-lived. The crop was transferred from the Sierra Nevada and the Perijá mountain ranges to the state of Cauca. With this transfer, productivity per hectare increased from 1.1 metric tons to 3.5 metric tons per hectare, and the alkaloid component of tetra-hydro-cannabinol (THC) of Colombian marijuana rose. Between 1986 and 1987, during the administration of President Virgilio Barco (1986-1990), an additional 22,368 hectares of marijuana were eradicated with nearly 50,000 gallons of glyphosate.[12] Nevertheless, in 1988 Colombia once again became the main exporter of marijuana to the United States, with an estimated production of 8,000 metric tons.[13] Even though the supply of Colombian marijuana to the U.S. market decreased afterwards, it was due more to the fact that the United States developed its own high-quality *sin semilla* variety, five times more potent than the Colombian marijuana and thus more attractive to North American consumers, than to the chemical fumigation in Colombia. Fumigation, for all practical purposes, ended around 1989-1990.

As for opium poppy in Colombia, something similar has occurred. In 1991, the Administrative Security Department (Departamento Administrativo de Seguridad — DAS) announced that there were 2,500 hectares under cultivation.[14] In their evaluation of that year's activities, the Colombian Antinarcotics Police reported that they had destroyed manually, without herbicides, 1,406 hectares of amapola; confiscated 17 kilograms of morphine and 30 kilograms of opium; and dismantled five heroin processing labs.[15] Notwithstanding this "great triumph," in January 1992 the CNE authorized the fumigation with glyphosate of 2,900 hectares, the total discovered up to that point. However, in March 1992, the Director of the Antinarcotics Police,

Brigadier General Rosso José Serrano Cadena, pointed out that nationwide opium poppy production had increased to 10,000 hectares.[16] By April 1992, new data demonstrated the existence of 20,000 hectares located in thirteen Colombian states (departments). Therefore, if manual eradication had not prevented the expansion of the business, how would chemical fumigation do so?[17]

At the international level, Guatemala has had "success" in using glyphosate in eliminating opium poppy crops and has been cited as a good example to emulate.[18] This is, however, doubtful to say the least. In 1990, Guatemala had a net production (after fumigating with herbicides) of 845 hectares of opium poppy, while in 1991 net production (after applying more glyphosate) grew to 1,145 hectares. The total amount of heroin produced in Guatemala increased in the following manner: in 1988, 8 metric tons; in 1989, 12 metric tons; in 1990, 13 metric tons; and in 1991, 17 metric tons.[19]

As pointed out by Peter Reuter, the effect of tougher measures against the illegal drug industry did not seem to accomplish its stated goals. Instead, it resulted in an increase in violence linked to the phenomenon, additional incentives for corruption, growing income for traffickers, and more social and health risks for consumers.[20]

Conclusion

In no way should the seriousness of the problem of amapola cultivation and heroin production in Colombia be ignored. As was alluded to, the number of heroin users in the United States (and also in Europe) is growing; the wholesale price of a kilo of heroin in the United States ranges from between US$80,000 to US$240,000 (four to ten times more than the kilo of cocaine).[21] Furthermore, there is a strong probability of contracting AIDS among those who inject heroin. In New York alone, 65 percent of heavy users that take drugs intravenously are HIV positive.[22] Finally, the mafias that control the international network of heroin are violent organizations with proven contacts with Colombian traffickers.[23] The prospect of additional drug (heroin)-related violence in the country is high.

As one specialist has said, heroin has the ability to "wipe out all painful aspects of psychic life. It creates a perception of the world wherein all worries are absent. For this reason, it is the perfect girlfriend who satisfies our deepest desires and draws us into a progressive passivity."[24] This does not mean that we should become inactive spectators, as though we were under the influence of heroin. The problem is so serious that to neglect it through a misguided strategy is to open the doors to the establishment of regional *narcocracias* around the country — a form of mafia-governed authoritarian sanctuaries at the local level. The solution, however, will not come from spraying the country with herbicides.

Notes

1. According to Article 90 of the 1986 National Statute of Dangerous Drugs, the ministries of Justice, Health, Education, and Agriculture were represented at the CNE. The state of siege decree 944 of May 25, 1987, combined the ministries of Defense and Communication into the National Council of Dangerous Drugs. Concerning the use of glyphosate in illicit crop eradication in Colombia, see Juan Gabriel Tokatlián, "La política exterior de Colombia hacia Estados Unidos, 1978-1990. El asunto de las drogas y su lugar en las relaciones entre Bogotá y Washington." in *Narcotráfico en Colombia,* eds. Carlos Gustavo Arrieta, Luis Javier Orjuela, Eduardo Sarmiento, and Juan Gabriel Tokatlián. (Bogotá: Ediciones Uniandes/Tercer Mundo Editores, 1990). On the 1992 CNE decision to apply glyphosate, see "Comunicado del CNE a la opinión pública," Santafé de Bogotá, January 31, 1992. A critical appraisal of this determination can be found in Fernando Cortés, "El glifosato, opio ecológico," *La Prensa,* February 9, 1992.

2. The 1984 decision to eradicate marijuana plantations with glyphosate was announced to the media at the end of June. See *El Espectador,* June 28, 1984. The order to begin eradication was given by the ministry of Justice through a special directive (D.M. No. 1048) to the National Police. The subsequent disputes over the scope and the limits of the process of eradication were due to a "semantic" (nonetheless, significant) question. According to reports by the Colombian Attorney General's office, the CNE approved "experimental" fumigation. Supporting this argument, the Secretary of the Council of Ministers — the full cabinet meeting — registered that "massive eradication" was not authorized. However, Minister Parejo proceeded to initiate "massive" glyphosate spraying. Although Enrique Parejo may have acted precipitously and even without the full support of the Council, his action was never discouraged publicly by President Betancur and was highly praised by the U.S. government.

3. On the commercial varieties of glyphosate, see Caroline Cox, "Glyphosate." *Journal of Pesticide Reform,* Summer 1991. The Antinarcotics Police reported the virtues of using glyphosate in amapola eradication. See Policía Antinarcóticos, *El glifosato en la erradicación de cultivos ilícitos* (Bogotá: Policía Nacional de Colombia, 1992).

4. On the San Antonio summit that convened the presidents of Colombia, México, Perú, Ecuador, Bolivia, and the United States and the minister of Foreign Affairs of Venezuela, on February 26-27, 1992, see "Cartagena II: Whiter the War on Drugs in the Americas." *North-South Issues,* February 1992. A very coherent but not too persuasive analysis linking U.S. official demands to combat drugs to the Colombian decision to apply glyphosate can be found in Alfredo Molano, "La amapola, a Caracas," *El Espectador,* February 9, 1992.

5. See U.S. Agency for International Development, "Fiscal Year 1993: Summary Tables," Washington, D.C., March 1992.

6. On the effects of ATPA for Colombia, see Marta Lucia Ramirez de Rincon, "Colombia frente a la ley de preferencias comerciales para el área andina," *Revista Camara de Comercio de Bogota,* No. 83, June 1992; Luis Fernando Rodriguez Naranjo, "La ley de preferencia para el área andina: Una oportunidad de aprovechamiento inmediato," *Revista Camara de Comercio de Bogotá;* and Gabriel Martinez, Alvaro

Uribe, and Marta Carreño, "Las iniciativas andinas de la C.E.E. y EE.UU. y las perspectivas de las exportaciones agropecuarias," *Revista Nacional de Agricultura*, No. 893, December 1990.

7. See, among others, the editorial "The New Heroin Bargain," *The New York Times*, February 10, 1992; Richard White, "Drugs: The Forgotten Debate," *The Christian Science Monitor*, March 20, 1992; Michael Isikoff, "International Opium Production Up 8% Last Year," *The Washington Post*, March 1, 1992; Joseph Treaster, "Smuggling and Use of Illicit Drugs are Growing, U.N. Survey Finds," *The New York Times*, January 13, 1992; Joseph Treaster, "Use of Cocaine and Heroin Rises among Urban Youth," *The New York Times*, December 19, 1991; David Lyons, "Heroin Traffic Tailgating Cocaine," *The Miami Herald*, October 12, 1992; "The Curse of China White," *Newsweek*, October 14, 1991; Michael Isikoff, "Cocaine Use on the Upswing," *The Washington Post*, December 19, 1991; Joseph Treaster, "Emergency Rooms Cocaine Cases Rise," *The New York Times*, October 24, 1992; and Clara Germani, "Drug Abuse in U.S. Continues to Decline, But Cocaine Use Up," *The Christian Science Monitor*, December 20, 1991.

8. See U.S. Government, The White House, Office of National Drug Control Policy. *National Drug Control Strategy*. Washington, D.C.: U.S. Government Printing Office, 1992.

9. On harm minimization, see Geoffrey Pearson, "Drug Policy and Problems in Britain: Continuity and Change," in *Crime and Justice: A Review of Research*, eds. Norval Morris and Michael Tonry. (Chicago: University of Chicago Press, 1991) and Stephen K. Mugford and Pat O'Malley, "Politics Unfit for Heroin? A Critique of Dorn and South," *International Journal of Drug Policy*, Vol. 2, No.1, July-August 1990.

10. See Juan G. Tokatlián, "La narcocracia no le teme al glifosato," *Ecológica*, No. 11-12, May-August 1992.

11. See *La lucha contra el narcotráfico en Colombia* (Bogotá: Presidencia de la República, October 1988).

12. See *Informe del Presidente de la República, Virgilio Barco al Congreso Nacional*. (Bogotá: Presidencia de la República, July 20, 1989).

13. See U.S. Department of State, Bureau of International Narcotics Matters, *International Narcotics Control Strategy Report* (Washington, D.C.: U.S. Government Printing Office, March 1989).

14. Departamento Administrativo de Seguridad, Dirección, "Aspectos de interés sobre el cultivo de amapola," Bogotá, November 1991.

15. See Policía Antinarcóticos, *Balance Actividades 1991* (Bogotá: Policía Nacional de Colombia, December 1991).

16. This statement was made during a seminar on "Glyphosate" organized by the Universidad de los Andes. Previously, in December 1991, General Serrano Cadena pointed out in answering a question about whether amapola could be stopped on time: "I say that we are on time because, in reality, there are no more than 2,500 hectares cultivated with poppy seeds; any other figure is exaggerated." See *El Tiempo*, December 22, 1991.

17. See Edgar Torres, "Amapola: se disparan las cifras," *El Tiempo*, April 19, 1992, and Precidencia de la República, "La amapola en Colombia," October 1992.

18. See the study on glyphosate in Guatemala done by Labat-Anderson Inc. of Arlington, Virginia, for the U.S. Department of State's Bureau of International Narcotics Matters and disseminated in Colombia in 1992: "Estudio conciso del medio ambiente para la erradicación de la amapola y la marihuana en Guatemala," March 31, 1987.

19. See U.S. Department of State, Bureau of International Narcotics Matters, *International Narcotics Control Strategy Report* (Washington, D.C.: U.S. Government Printing Office, March 1992).

20. See Peter Reuter, "On the Consequences of Toughness," in *Drug Policy in the Americas: The Search for Alternatives*, eds. Melvyn Krauss and Edward Lazear. Stanford, Calif.: Hoover Institution Press, 1991.

21. See Drug Enforcement Administration, Office of Intelligence, "Illegal Drug Price/Purity Report," November 1991.

22. See Mathea Falco, "Introduction," in *Toward a National Policy on Drug and AIDS Testing*, eds. Mathea Falco and Warren I. Cikins (Washington, D.C.: The Brookings Institution, 1988).

23. See, among others, Joseph Treaster, "Colombia's Drug Lords Add New Line: Heroin for the U.S.," *The New York Times*, January 13, 1992; William Drozdiak, "Europe Finds Colombian Cartels Well Ensconced," *The Washington Post*, April 11, 1991; William Drozdiak, "World Crime Groups Expand Cooperation, Sphere of Influence," *The Washington Post*, October 5, 1992; and David Ames, "Cocaine Demand in Europe Draws Interest of Mafia," *The Miami Herald*, December 23, 1992.

24. See Luis Schnitman, *Crack, droga, adicción y cultura* (Bogotá: Catálogo Científico, 1987), 147.

References

Ames, David. 1992. "Cocaine Demand in Europe Draws Interest of Mafia." *The Miami Herald*, December 23.

Bagley, Bruce M. 1992. "Cartagena II: Whither the War on Drugs in the Americas." *North-South Issues*. Miami: North-South Center.

"Comunicado del C.N.E. a la opinión pública." 1992. Santafé de Bogotá. January 31.

Cox, Caroline. 1991. "Glyphosate." *Journal of Pesticide Reform*. Summer.

Newsweek. 1991. "The Curse of China White." October 14.

Departamento Administrativo de Seguridad. Dirección. 1991. "Aspectos de interés sobre el cultivo de amapola." Bogotá. November.

Drozdiak, William. 1991. "Europe Finds Colombian Cartels Well Ensconced." *The Washington Post,* October 5.

Drug Enforcement Administration, Office of Intelligence. 1991. "Illegal Drug Price/ Purity Report." November.

El Espectador. 1984. June 28.

Falco, Mathea, and Warren I. Cikins, eds. 1988. *Toward a National Policy on Drug and AIDS Testing.* Washington, D.C.: The Brookings Institute.

Germani, Clara. 1991. "Drug Abuse in U.S. Continues to Decline, But Cocaine Use Up." *The Christian Science Monitor.* December 20.

Informe del Presidente de la República, Virgilio Barco al Congreso Nacional. 1989. Bogotá: Presidencia de la República. July 20.

Isikoff, Michael. 1992. "International Opium Production Up 8 percent Last Year." *The Washington Post.* March 1.

Isikoff, Michael. 1991. "Cocaine Use on the Upswing." *Washington Post.* December 19.

La lucha contra el narcotráfico en Colombia. 1988. Bogotá: Presidencia de la República. October.

Lyons, David. 1992. "Heroin Traffic Tailgating Cocaine." *The Miami Herald,* October 12.

Martínez, Gabriel, Alvaro Uribe, and Marta Carreño. 1990. "Las iniciatives andinas de la C.E.E. y EE.UU. y las perspectivas de las exportaciones agropecuarias." *Revista Nacional de Agricultura,* No. 893, December.

Molano, Alfredo. 1992. "La amapola, a Caracas." *El Espectador,* February 9.

Mugford, Stephen K., and Pat O'Malley. 1990. "Politics Unfit for Heroin? A Critique of Dorn and South." *International Journal of Drug Policy* 2(1), July-August.

The New York Times. 1992. "The New Heroin Bargain." February 10.

Office of National Drug Control Policy. 1992. *National Drug Control Strategy.* Washington, D.C.: Government Printing Office.

Pearson, Geoffrey. 1991. "Drug Policy and Problems in Britain: Continuity and Change." In *Crime and Justice: A Review of Research,* eds. Norval Morris and Michael Tonry. Chicago: University of Chicago Press.

Policía Antinarcóticos. 1992. *El glifosato en la erradicación de cultivos ilícitos*. Bogotá: Policía Nacional de Colombia.

Policía Antinarcóticos. 1991. *Balance Actividades 1991*. Bogotá: Policía Nacional de Colombia. December.

La Prensa. 1992. "El glifosato, opio ecológico." February 9.

Presidencia de la República. 1992. "La Amapola en Colombia." October.

Ramírez de Rincón, Marta Lucia. 1992. "Colombia frente a la ley de preferencia comerciales para el área andina: Una oportunidad de aprovechamiento inmediato." *Revista Camara de Comercio de Bogotá*, No. 83, June.

Reuter, Peter. 1991. "On Consequences of Toughness." In *Drug Policy in America: The Search for Alternatives*, eds. Melvyn Krauss and Edward Lazear. Stanford, Calif.: Hoover Institution Press.

Rodríguez Naranjo, Luis Fernando. 1992. "La ley de preferencias para el área andina: Una oportunidad de aprovechamiento inmediato." *Revista Camara de Comercio de Bogotá*, No. 83, June.

Schnitman, Luis. 1987. *Crack, droga, adicción y cultura*. Bogotá: Catálogo Científico.

El Tiempo. 1991. December 22.

Tokatlián, Juan Gabriel. 1990. "La politica exterior de Colombia hacia Estados Unidos, 1978-1990. El asunto de las drogas y su lugar en las relaciones entre Bogotá y Washington." In *Narcotráfico en Colombia*, ed. Carlos Gustavo Arrieta. Bogotá: Ediciones Uniandes/Tercer Mundo Editores.

Tokatlián, Juan Gabriel. 1990. "La narcocracia no le teme al glifosato." *Ecológica*. No. 11-12, May-August.

Torres, Edgar. 1992. "Amapola: Se disparan las cifras." *El Tiempo*. April 19.

Treaster, Joseph. 1991. "Use of Cocaine and Heroin Rises Among Urban Youth." *The New York Times*. December 19.

Treaster, Joseph. 1992a. "Emergency Rooms Cocaine Cases Rise." *The New York Times*. October 24.

Treaster, Joseph. 1992b. "Colombia's Drug Lords Add New Line: Heroin for the U.S." *The New York Times*. January 13.

U.S. Agency for International Development. 1992. "Fiscal Year 1993: Summary Tables." Washington, D.C., March.

U.S. Department of State. Bureau of International Narcotics Matters. 1989-1992. *International Narcotics Control Strategy Report*. Washington, D.C.: Government Printing Office.

U.S. Department of State. 1987. "Estudio Conciso del Medio Ambiente para la Erradicación de la Amapola y la Marihuana en Guatemala." March 31.

White, Richard. 1992. "Drugs: The Forgotten Debate." *The Christian Science Monitor*. March 20.

Peru

Chapter 10

The Andean Cocaine Dilemma

Edmundo Morales

Introduction

The ancient shrub, coca (Erythroxylon coca) has grown into a much-politicized sphinx in the Andes of South America. Indications are that in Bolivia and Peru nearly 1.5 million people are employed in the underground activities (Gorriti 1989,71) involving the growth of coca and the production of cocaine.[1] Lawmakers have become aware of the need to invest in economic development in the Andes in order to counter and replace the economic dependence of Indians and peasants there on the illicit coca-cocaine economy (*El Peruano* 1991). Coca production is increasing from 20 percent (INM 1988) to 35 percent (Lee 1988,504) per year in Bolivia and Peru, respectively. Estimates are that cocaine accounts for $1 billion of Colombia's legal export, $700 million of Peru's, and $450 million of Bolivia's (Lee 1989,3). Allegations are that the infiltration of cocaine money into radical political movements makes Peru the country with the most fragile democracy in the Americas. Due to outside pressure, the Peruvian and Bolivian governments are faced with fighting against those things that become the economic livelihood of thousands of people. In the United States, on the other hand, official statistics indicate that the number of cocaine users has declined from 12 million in 1985 to 8 million in 1988 (Rosenbaum 1990,7). But in reality cocaine in the inner cities is more readily available than ever. Waiting lists for treatment of addiction to cocaine are long, and drug-related crime in the inner cities is increasing (Purdy 1990).

In light of the failure of current policies to control and eradicate coca and cocaine, a new model of anticocaine economic development is needed that would lead, in the long run, to an effective integration of the former coca-producing groups into the international market economy, consequently bringing about relatively adequate subsistence economies and political stability in the region. I suggest in this chapter removing the criminal language that creates animosity and hatred toward policy-making groups and launching multisectoral projects for development that would involve the private sector, specialized government agencies, research institutions, and indigenous populations. These suggestions are elaborations on policy recommendations presented in other works (Gorriti 1989 and 1991; Morales 1986, 1989, 1990, and 1991) and are more extensively discussed in the last section of this chapter.

The Dilemma

Studies on the social and anthropological aspects of coca in the Andean culture abound (Arango and Child 1987; Bolton 1976; Burchard 1974; Gade 1979; Hanna 1974; Mayer 1986; Mortimer 1975; Plowman 1986) and recently, many books and articles have documented the influence of the illicit coca and cocaine economy on Latin American countries, especially Bolivia, Colombia, and Peru (Andreas and Youngers 1989; Bagley 1986; Gamarra 1990; Healy 1990; Lee 1989; MacDonald 1988; Morales 1989).

Three conspicuous social and political consequences arise directly from dependence on illicit coca economy, however effective it is as a means of income for the dispossessed peasants and Indians. They are 1) pervasive corruption of Andean society at every level, 2) emergence of nouveaux riches and deepening of social cleavages, and 3) the rise of substance abuse among urban and rural populations of the world. In the traditional coca economy, corruption was limited to small numbers of bureaucrats, legal coca growers, local merchants, and coca traders. Government employees who oversaw the production and marketing of the coca leaf demanded bribes from coca farmers and traders on the grounds of existing, or hypothetical, violations of coca production and marketing regulations. The threat of corrupt officers was that they would imprison the peasant if the bribes were not paid. Bribes were in cash or in kind. In kind bribes ranged from many days' labor performed by coca traders to a few arrobas (one arroba equals 25 pounds) of coca from farmers, traders, or coca retailers. In exchange for the bribe, corrupt officers would either drop charges or underreport production.

During the seventies, the town of Tingo María was the center of the cocaine boom in Peru. (Tingo María is the capital town of the province of Leoncio Prado in Huánuco.) The Ministry of Agriculture reports that the size of coca in the department of Huánuco increased from 4,600 hectares in 1975 to 15,000 hectares in 1980. For the same period, the production of coca is reported to have been 3,496 metric tons (MT) for 1975 and 18,000 MT for 1980 (Jerí 1985,39). Assuming that soil, the age of the plants, and the maturity of the leaves were ideal, the average yield of leaves should have been about 10,000 MT for 1975 and 30,000 MT for 1980. Today, the lucrativeness of the "white gold rush" entices judges, politicians, civil servants, and military and law enforcement bodies alike. Farmers and drug traffickers pool cash to bribe police who, in their turn, may collude in delaying raids or in the smuggling of chemicals needed for the production of cocaine. In fact, it is reasonable to argue that in Bolivia and Peru it is impossible to tell who in the government is not involved in cocaine trafficking (Lee 1989,194).

At different points in their history, Andean countries, including Ecuador, have experienced booms in the exploitation of their natural resources. Mining during colonial times, guano in the nineteenth century, cacao in the twentieth century, and fishing in the early sixties of this century all represent economic drives that have attracted people in the same fashion that the gold rush had in North America. As in all economic booms, the mass exploitation of the coca leaf as a natural resource benefits some groups more than others because coca farming is subject to the basic principle of the capitalist economy; that is, those who create the commodity are less rewarded than those who control the capital (cash, chemicals, transportation infrastructure) and marketing of the final product. The rise of a new middle class, the nouveaux riches, and the social cleavages fostered by the inflow of coca dollars abound in Latin America (Lee 1989; Arango and Child 1987; Castillo 1987; *Caretas* 1982, 1984, 1985; and Morales 1989). To illustrate the rise of a new middle class, I present the case of one family who migrated from a mining city in the Bolivian Altiplano to the lowlands. I collected data on this case during fieldwork in the summer of 1990.

In the Santa Cruz Department of Bolivia, an area comparable in drug trafficking to Tingo Maria in the Huallaga Valley of Peru, I made friends with the receptionist of one of the many bus companies. Knowing that I was a photographer, she asked me to go to her house to photograph her family. Initially, I was surprised that no one in the family asked any personal questions. At the end of the photo session, while drinking expensive liquors and spirits, the father of the Soza family (the name is fictitious) asked me questions about my address in Bolivia, my birthplace, and where I had visited in South America. Having faced similar situations during my fieldwork in Peru, I was cautious in discussing some social, economic, and political issues that in Bolivia are more intertwined with the production of cocaine than in Peru. When I stated that I was a naturalized U.S. citizen, the oldest brother turned to his sister making a face as if he were saying "I smell a rat in the house." Then he asked me whether my visit to Bolivia had anything to "contribute to the good cause of drug law enforcement." He supported his position of honest citizen with the statement that "one member of the family was an antidrug police (UMOPAR)."[2] This cunning move to try "to catch a spy" was not that much different from the local drug lords' business propositions I had dealt with back in Peru. Later, the receptionist candidly articulated her family's position regarding foreigners, especially American citizens of distinct national origins who come under many diverse disguises. Her apology when she realized my interest was academic stemmed from the fact that "I never asked questions about the prices of cocaine, places where cocaine is made, or the names of dealers." "Not even indirectly," she added.

In the case of the Sozas, there was no need to ask indirect questions nor was it necessary to search for direct evidence of the presence of the "white business in the family." It was evident at once in their lifestyle as consumers, which did not correlate with the family's status before moving to the lowlands. The father is a retired government employee with a social security check of $25 a month; the eldest son is a bank employee who earns about $180 a month; the UMOPAR brother, whom I did not meet, makes about $75, and the receptionist about $50 a month. This $420 total monthly income of the Soza family is an enviable amount by Bolivian standards but not enough to buy a big house in a middle-class neighborhood, four cars (two had been bought in cash on the Brazilian border), send two sons to a private university, and have two housekeepers with a combined salary of about $120 a month. The receptionist laughed at my question of why she worked for a salary less than that of one of her housekeeper's salary. When I left for Cochabamba, she asked me to deliver a note containing a business message to someone. I asked her not to put it in an envelope, to which she agreed.[3] The brief friendly note concluded with the sentence, "The big order for my relative's pharmacy will follow this communication."

In Bolivia and Peru, most of the people who participate at different stages in the underground economy are migrants from different parts of the country, including the coast. These people are dislodged from their native homelands to areas where they encounter physical dysadaptation and social alienation. They are exposed to new behaviors and health hazards. Oftentimes, the dream of earning a better living in the "green mines" exacerbates frustration or ends in diseases or leads to deviant behaviors, such as prostitution and drug abuse. Although it benefits hundreds of thousands of people, the cocaine industry has also brought into Latin America substance abuse of endemic proportions. In rural and urban areas of Bolivia and Peru, thousands of addicts smoke at least 500 kilos of coca paste each year (Flores-Agreda 1986,33) and hundreds of entertainment users snort an unknown amount of cocaine hydrochloride.[4] Many times, non-coca chewing migrant workers smoke coca paste to get extra strength they need, while consuming minimal food in order to save money. In many ways, the use of the coca leaf in forced labor imposed upon Andean populations during the Spanish domination has been replicated almost two hundred years after independence.

In Latin America, the relationship between the illicit economy and vulnerable underdeveloped governments is similar to the relationship between the United States and Latin American countries and international organizations.[5] The economic strength (*el poderoso señor don dinero*) of coca-dollars ultimately wields power over politicians, government employees, law enforcement officers, and bank executives. It even corrupts Catholic priests. In the mid-1970s, during the beginning of the cocaine boom in the Huallaga

Valley, one of the first traffickers in a remote village was a European Catholic priest who had two local peasants manufacture coca paste for him. The priest would take monthly "business trips" to Lima and one or two trips per year to Europe. (Customs officers at the airport would bow to the priest and let him board the plane without even checking his briefcase.) After many years in operation, the coca-paste pit was raided because of its conspicuousness in the barren mountains where it was set up. The two peasants who worked for the priest were sent to prison for almost ten years. The priest left the area and feigned insult when confronted by the allegations of the two "cretin Indians" ("Indios sucios," a pejorative term often used in the Andes).

Mistreatment and abuse by government officials, law enforcement agents, and some drug traffickers are making Indians and peasants aware of their conditions. For almost half a millennia, these Indians have remained behind the scenes of national life and have been isolated from one another. The expansion of coca agriculture and the publicity that has been given to cocaine trafficking have, to a great extent, been the catalysts for changes being experienced in the Andes today. Dependency on the coca-dollar has bridged communication between regions and tens of different groups clustered throughout the cordilleras. Before the boom of cocaine, for instance, entire communities in Peru were isolated from the rest of the country. Any manufactured product coming out of the community was thought to be imported. (The term *extranjero* was used to describe commodities and notions transported to local communities without regard to their national origin.) Indians and peasants knew very little of the existence of provinces and cities other than Lima. Even the coca-producing rain forests were only alluded to as mysterious lands that only brave, experienced montañeros[6] could dare to travel.

The conquest of the Amazon and the concomitant emergence of a widespread informal economy around coca and cocaine have brought tremendous economic, social, and political consequences both in Bolivia and Peru. The fragile soil of the rain forests has been used as an alternative to pacify groups and populations whose economies have been devastated by international market factors or by failed reformist policies, such as the mining industry in Bolivia and land reform in Peru. Today, many Indians know of the plights of their counterparts and, more important, they are becoming more conscious of their position in national life. The U.S.' drive to eradicate the most effective source of cash and the increasing political awareness among natives are creating preconditions for the development of organized social protests and political movements in which many marginal groups are beginning to participate. This may be one of the reasons why the Shining Path in the Huallaga Valley has gained support from some groups and tolerance from others.

The political economy of cocaine production has bypassed legal channels between the metropolis and the periphery. In this new North-South arena, national elites have lost control of their brokerage role between capital exporting groups and labor power. This can be observed by following the cocaine industry upstream. Because of its higher cash yields, farmers and petty traffickers produce and supply a commodity that connects them to international markets. However, the producer-consumer bond is rather complex and equally disadvantageous for those who comprise the base of the underground social structure. The international cocaine elite find every possible excuse and rationale to exploit farmers, "cooks," long-haul transporters, and law enforcers. National elites and emerging power groups also benefit from this economy. They take advantage of loans and tax breaks available to investors to engage in development projects, and they use their political influence and economic power to augment their capital assets. For instance, bankers and industrial investors in Peru use their small airplanes and helicopters to exchange Soles (national currency) for coca dollars directly from cocaine towns.

Economic Development or Political Dissension

All economic booms that have exploited natural resources in Latin America have benefited foreign investors, old Spanish families who controlled all aspects of national life, and a limited number of the new rich. National dominant groups, because of their ancillary position in the international political economy, have contrived to maintain Indians and peasants in a status quo. Agriculture and marketing of coca and its derivatives was part of this stationary economy. Bolivia and Peru, as the backbone of the Andean society and culture and as the two largest suppliers of coca to the cocaine industry, must learn from their past experience to develop their national peripheries. The new policies of coca must help shape a more equitable society. However, this is an extremely difficult political task for governments whose dependency on the international metropolis makes them managers of meager funds. Their social and political survival is contingent on how they please and absorb capricious policies dictated by powerful governments whose demands are based on sheer power rather than on knowledge and reason.

It is clear that the alternative to reducing drug abuse in the United States is the reduction of demands. Otherwise, the flow of cocaine from South America will continue for the foreseeable future. In light of the failure of both meager crop substitution projects and law enforcement programs implemented by cooperation and collaboration (umbrella terms for political pressure) between supply and demand governments, here I further elaborate what I suggested in an earlier work (Morales 1989, 169). Anticocaine economic development in the Andes is not as simple as many would like to think. The main reason for the failure of crop substitution projects is the lack of a holistic conception of coca as well as underestimation of the significance of the cocaine economy for the region. Scientific and technical assessments of the region were not effected, nor were evaluations of the Andean populations' economic needs considered in the equation of the anticoca and cocaine programs. If the alternative to solving this problem is reduction of supply, the only viable choice is comprehensive economic development. For a sensible definition and implementation of economic development of the Andean subregions, three important considerations come to the foreground: the political context of funding, the geographical and ecological differences of the Andes, and the U.S. government's paranoid inclusion of drugs in the definition of national security.

An understanding of the demographic characteristics of the Andes must also be incorporated in the planning of any economic solution to the coca dilemma. So far, Andean governments have centered their developmentalist efforts on land reform, education, and road penetration. These three major moves to change the countryside, however laudable, have failed. Neither the state-controlled cooperatives nor the *minifundios* have revived the Andean people's agricultural nature. Production of food has been neglected or abandoned to the point that sometimes foodstuffs are imported from other parts of the world. Education and road penetration as cosmetic development approaches (Morales 1989, 144) have, in their turn, created needs and expectations that neither local nor national economies can satisfy. These development programs were implemented without assessing the needs of highland populations or estimating the potentiality of local economies in the world market. Another important variable in the modern Andean dilemma, ignored by policy makers for obvious ideological and religious reasons, is the disparity between population growth and natural resources available. If economic development is the answer to solving the current Andean dilemma, then it is about time for national governments to contemplate family planning and birth control methods to avoid the population explosion which would be the result of regional economic growth.[7] However, any educational campaign that aims at controlling population increase in the Andes will be rigidly opposed by the Catholic Church.

The U.S. government's paranoid inclusion of drugs in the definition of national security is a sign of frustration because its military and law enforcement approaches to the problem have failed.[8] It is inevitable that, as national citizens, some cocaine traffickers take part in political struggles that their countries may be facing. The alleged narco-guerrilla connection (Lee 1989,155) in the minds of policy makers deters forays and, at the same time, is a justification for arms aid and possible military intervention, such as Operation Blast Furnace in Bolivia in the summer of 1986. In its desperation to eradicate coca in its upstream stages, the U.S. Central Intelligence Agency (CIA) may have devised the narco-guerrilla theory. As Lee (1989,156) suggests, "interpretation of the narco-guerrilla connection, such as it is, depends less on hard evidence than on the vagaries of politics and the motives of the different institutional actors."[9] In essence, the war on drugs is an effective political artifice in the eyes of average citizens to legitimize the linkages between national security, communist conspiracy, and drug trafficking (Morales 1989,167). To U.S. politicians, whether radical ideological movements and drug trafficking are a threat to national security is irrelevant, for their arguments are rooted in the satisfaction of group interest rather than solving the drug problem and other social problems.

There have been reports that the guerrilla insurgents' presence in the coca-producing regions has been consolidated, driving away local government authorities and neutralizing U.S.-sponsored eradication forces (Gonzalez 1989). These reports confirm that the guerrillas are not operating in league with international drug traffickers. On the contrary, their political and military influence is based upon the protection and organization they have provided the thousands of coca-producing peasants. The guerrillas have prevailed in the region because they successfully defend poor producers from abuses of government officials, law enforcement agents, and some drug traffickers. In the event there exists an alliance between the radical political movements and narco-traffickers, the cocaine underground economy's support for the armed insurgents would not be that much different from the Reagan administration's secret arms deals with Iran to support the anti-Sandinistas in Nicaragua. In principle, they both support anti-government forces to fight ideological adversaries.

Eradicating coca to reduce cocaine supply and effectively controlling cocaine trafficking are more complex than is understood by policy makers whose exclusive law-enforcement orientation distorts and narrows the nature and scope of the problem. The convoluted logic of supply and demand, whereby supplier and consumer governments blame each other for their indirect support of the cocaine underground, makes cocaine production and trafficking more a political issue than it merits. Current drug policies indicate an unwillingness to face up to the issues of supply and demand. While it is true that an effective eradication program may lead to less cocaine supply, the U.S. approach to the problem of cocaine production in South America is unrealistic and inconsistent. Its policies and programs of reduction of supply and demand do not coincide with its strength in the international political arena.

The Republican government's simplistic approach to the problem of cocaine in the Andes is the same as its symptomatic approach to the problem of drug abuse in the United States. That is, the roots of the problem of drug abuse in the United States are part and parcel of the structural problems, which drug control policies on the whole do not address. Policies blueprinted to favor some sectors of the U.S. government bureaucracy, imposed upon the weak governments of Bolivia and Peru and used as political bandwagons, will not be sufficient to stop the constant increase of coca and cocaine production in the Andes. The U.S. government should recognize and admit that current policies for reducing the supply of coca in the Andes are not working. Instead, a comprehensive plan for economic development must be implemented. If this holistic approach is not taken, the United States will be left to concentrate its efforts solely on demand reduction at home, a more costly and more difficult, well-nigh impossible, undertaking, given the existing social, economic, and political conditions.

The blame for the existence of the cocaine sphinx (drug production, trafficking, and abuse) must be integrated in the international arena, especially in the North-South continental arena. The first step in the integration of this blame must be the removal of language that labels activities related to coca farming and initial steps of cocaine manufacture as illicit farmers, traffickers, smugglers, narcos, and so forth. The negative connotation of such labels leads to feelings of animosity and hatred and may, though unconsciously, motivate physical aggression. The negative labels attached to the different roles that people play in the industry, on the other hand, may indirectly encourage people to take higher risks for higher economic rewards. It should be understood that contraband and banditry are a heritage of the Spanish domination and are rooted in the Andean folk culture. Today, many traditions and rites in the Andes, especially along the eastern and western ranges, have been subverted or eradicated totally. It is not rare to see children playing "pichicatero" (slang for drug trafficker) where the roles of successful traffickers, carriers, addicts, and law enforcers are clearly defined.

Recent political events suggest that peace in the world may be breaking out. But, to the urban homeless, the landless peasant, and hunger-stricken populations who live in infrahuman conditions and are condemned to die slowly, peace may be a mere abstraction and a euphemism for the modern version of group supremacy. If advanced, industrial societies want to boast a long-lasting peace, they must turn their eyes to the rest of the world to try to make living conditions more viable than they are today. To give a new meaning to peace and to fight many social and political maladies, multisectoral projects and programs of economic development need to be launched. Economic development must be a collective endeavor that includes and involves investment by public and private sectors, dissemination of grounded scientific knowledge by practical academics housed at research institutions, and participation of indigenous populations in decision making and diffusion of innovative knowledge.

The visit of the Peruvian president to the United States may have convinced some representatives in the U.S. Congress to release aid of $94.9 million (Treaster 1991). If released, 63 percent ($60 million) of this economic aid would be used to meet Peru's payments of its $23 billion foreign debt and 37 percent ($34.9 million) will go to military aid (Treaster 1991; Gorriti 1991).

That is, the only aid that Peru will receive will be military, for the $60 million barely covers the interest of Peru's sizable debt (payment of which helps the country's status in international financial circles). To use a metaphorical explanation, this is something like a pawn shop operation in which the U.S. government is the pawnbroker, the Peruvian government is the debtor, and Peru's willingness to accept U.S. military definition of the cocaine industry and improvement in human rights is the security. This approach does not get at any grass roots economic development.

In light of the magnitude of the problem and in light of the fiscal crisis of U.S. investment by the private sector in the countryside, it is a viable alternative to right the increasing dependency of thousands of people on illicit and informal economies. Investment in the countryside must necessarily be in agriculture, for the modern Andean man has neglected to maintain his agricultural nature. It is estimated that today Andean populations, including those on the coast, use 40 percent less land than both the pre-Incas and Incas used hundreds of years ago. Long before the rise of the powerful Incas, Mochicas and Chimus built sophisticated aqueducts to bring water from inter-Andean valleys tens of miles away to irrigate the desert land of the northern Peruvian coast (Cardish 1987,30; Hyslop 1984,248; Fung-Pineda 1986,89). Any development move in the Andes must attempt to revive the agricultural nature of the Andean people. Otherwise, populations will always seek activities that best satisfy their essential needs, for hunger and misery make people overlook values and morals.

The stagnant economy of Peru and the limited resources of Bolivia cannot finance any economic development that would offset the hard cash yield of coca and cocaine.[10] Foreign aid is the only way of funding extensive economic development. It has been suggested that populations in Bolivia and Peru that depend on the new coca economy require aid of at least $5 billion (Gorriti 1989; Morales 1989) in addition to other economic opportunities and favorable tariffs. Unquestionably, funding must come from governments who are interested in "eradicating" the coca leaf from the Andean culture to reduce (not to solve) their problem of drug abuse. It is also certain that economic development is the most cost effective and viable approach to wean the Andean peasantry from its direct and indirect dependence on coca-dollars. Two logical concerns arise in the event that funding from industrial societies is secured: management and allocation of funds.

The current aid-sponsored projects support a sizable bureaucracy and indirectly encourage further dependency on coca-dollars. If anti-coca development funds are pumped into these projects, aid will not reach coca farmers, regardless of the amount invested. These funds would further exacerbate the problem of those who remain at the base of both national and underground economies. Investment in the coca producing areas must discourage production of crops for which world markets are saturated. For instance, how could pineapples and citrus fruits from Chapare, Bolivia, possibly compete with pineapples from Hawaii or citrus fruits from Florida?

So far the U.S. government has been allied only with politicians and small, national dominant groups whose interests do not coincide with the interest of the majority. The question is not to maintain and improve the legal, diplomatic channels that have proven ineffective in gaining the heart of the Andean people, but to change this alliance and make the majority of people participate in an all-out war against social maladies including drug production and trafficking and radical ideological movements. People in Latin America, especially in the Andes, are no longer passive and static as they were three decades ago. The Inca domination, the Spanish invasions, the capitalist colonial economy, the failed reforms put forth by revengeful leaders have taught the people a hard lesson. Andeans never had the opportunity to forge their own destiny because they have always lacked knowledge and technology to exploit their scarce natural resources rationally. Products such as potatoes and tree tomatoes, which are indigenous to the Andes, have flourished in countries that are technologically more advanced than the Andean countries (NRC 1989).

To gain a strong, long-lasting political alliance with the region, aid to develop Andean groups must be aimed at bringing change from within rather than imposing change from outside. One should not assume that bandaid quasiphilanthropic programs, such as sending surplus food and politically tagged economic packages, are the best strategies for maintaining peace in the region. This strategy may have proven effective decades ago, but today the Aristotelian philosophic approach of assuming that some groups must comply with the imposition of the ruling groups is no longer the case. For better or worse, Indians and peasants are becoming aware of their reality, and the ideological influence of radical political movements plays an important role in this germinal awareness. Before this awareness takes deep roots that would alienate people from the rest of the Americas, the industrial world must consider attracting the Andean indigenous rather than dominant groups. The question then becomes how to persuade the industrial world to change its attitude toward the Andes: a lengthy and painful process both for groups providing and receiving aid.

Reorientation of the misadventures in the Amazon and the use of a new language in the coca sophistry (Gorriti 1991) will not suffice to decipher the cocaine sphinx's riddle: regional economic development and continental political harmony. Since the Andes is a complex region, a sensible and relevant assessment of both geographical and ecological differences, as well as human resources, must be effected before implementing or making a commitment to invest in any economic development. Given the complexity of the Andean reality, imposition of standardized aid packages conceived by neophytes whose expertise is not grounded on empirical knowledge creates anything but self-sustaining economies. The irony of the policies of development by national groups, who are as ignorant of the countryside's reality as are their foreign counterparts, is the lack of interest to find suitable seeds of development with potential to satisfy the basic human needs, to promote change, and to create other needs that could make the Andean people part of the increasingly interdependent world.

Interdependency, however, cannot be conceived of unless the dependent local, regional economies participate in the national market. The growth and expansion of markets for commodities, or products manufactured or produced by microeconomies, must result from long-term dependent and independent projects and programs. The implementation of economic development funded, again, by multisectoral action would lead progressively to many independent microeconomies, which could then become part of the national and international interdependent economy. Collaborative research could be used to launch projects that could attract indigenous people to participate in the process. The last phase of the dependent-independent model of economic development would be the progressive transfer to local populations of technological and innovative knowledge, management of existing projects and programs, and decision making. Needless to say, anticocaine investments in economic development would involve long-term commitments, which may not agree with the U.S. government's propensity for quick fixes whose value is short-lived.

Notes

1. Ethan Nadelman (in Gorriti 1989) calculates that, in 1986, for every 300 cocaine exporters, there were 222,000 coca farmers, 74,000 paste processors, 7,400 transporters, and 1,333 refiners. However, it should be emphasized that, in the cocaine underground economy at large, it is practically impossible to make calculations.

2. Unidad Movil de Patrullaje Rural (UMOPAR) is a special unit of the Bolivian and Peruvian government police whose exclusive task is to control the increasing production of coca and manufacture of cocaine in the mountainous jungles.

3. Nowadays in cocaine producing countries (Bolivia, Colombia, and Peru), one has to be extremely cautious when transporting any small package or envelope. Traffickers and vicious law enforcers take advantage of some naive nationals and tourists to send cash, checks, and small amounts of cocaine, or they simply plant drugs on someone they want to harm. During my last field trip in 1990, although there was nothing to be afraid of, the fear of the common practice among Bolivian drug traffickers of planting cocaine on foreigners and/or enemies haunted my mind for many days.

4. Coca paste, also known as cocaine paste or cocaine sulphate or simply paste, is an intermediate substance in the production of cocaine hydrochloride, a crystalline powder which usually shows an acid reaction to the pH indicators and is soluble in water. In Bolivia and Peru, it is difficult to estimate the total consumption of cocaine, for the bulk of entertainment users are middle-class people whose attitudes and behavior in reporting drug abuse are deceptive.

5. International organizations, such as the OAS and the United Nations, cannot stand against the U.S. government's pressure. For example, compare the recent U.N. resolution against Iraq with that of its position during the war for the Falkland Islands (*quien paga manda*).

6. Men from the highlands who go to the jungle to bring coca and other products, such as dried fruits, coffee, and tea back to the highlands. For more details on the role of coca in the highlands, see Bolton (1976), Burchard (1974), Hanna (1974), Mayer (1986), Morales (1989), Mortimer (1975), and Plowman (1986).

7. In twenty years, the population of Peru increased by about 70 percent from ten million in 1961 to seventeen million in 1981 (INE, XXIII). Economic growth has declined constantly since the military reformist government took office in 1969.

8. Due to its frustration in fighting cocaine at the source, the U.S. government has even begun to develop voracious caterpillars to kill coca plants. Bolivia and Peru rejected this plan for a biological war on cocaine.

9. Peruvian President Alberto Fujimori and other Latin American officials have complained that too much of the Andean plan was slated for military purposes instead of development aid that could offer peasants an alternative to growing coca (Isikoff 1990).

10. Despite the unpredictable changes in the prices of the coca leaf because of law enforcement, a peasant is still better off growing coca than shifting to a legal cash crop (Lee 1989,91) for which there is neither financial aid nor technical support nor competitive markets.

References

Andreas, Peter, and Coletta Youngers. 1989. "U.S. Drug Policy and the Andean Cocaine Industry." *World Policy Journal.* Summer: 529-562.

Arango, Mario, and Jorge Child. 1987. *Narcotrafico: Imperio de la Cocaina.* Bogota, Colombia: Editorial Diana.

Bagley, Bruce M. 1991. "Drugs, Political Violence, and Democracy in Colombia." Paper presented at the 40th Annual Conference at the University of Florida, Gainesville.

Bolton, Ralph. 1976. "Andean Coca Chewing: A Metabolic Perspective." *American Anthropologist.* 78 (3): 630-633.

Burchard, Roderick E. 1974. "Coca y trueque de alimentos." In *Reciciprocidad e intercambio en los Andes peruanos,* eds. Giorgio Alberti and Enrique Mayer. Lima, Peru: Instituto de Estudios Peruanos, 209-251.

Cardish, Augusto. 1987. "Native Agriculture in the Highlands of the Andes." *National Geographic Research.* 3 (1): 22-39.

Caretas. 1982. "Si, La Villa Mercedes es de Landberg." Lima, Peru. No. 685. February 15.

Caretas. 1984. "Entrevista en la Maison de Sante." Lima, Peru. No. 811. August 6.

Caretas. 1985. "Las Amistades de Don Reinaldo." Lima, Peru. No. 863. August 12.

Castillo, Fabio. 1987. *Las Jinetes de la Cocaina.* Bogota: Editorial Documentos Periodisticas.

Flores-Agreda, R. 1986. "Drug Abuse Problems in Countries of the Andean Subregion." *Bulletin on Narcotics.* 37 (1&2): 27-36.

Fung-Pineda, Rosa. 1986. "The Late Pre-Ceramic and Initial Period." In *Peruvian Prehistory,* ed. Richard W. Keatinge. New York: Cambridge University Press, 67-96.

Gade, Daniel W. 1979. "Inca and Colonial Settlements, Coca Cultivation, and Endemic Disease in the Tropical Forest." *Journal of Historical Geography.* 5 (3): 263-279.

Gamarra, Eduardo E. 1990. "Bolivia's Perestroika?" *Hemisphere.* 2 (2): 16-19.

Gonzales, Raul. 1989. "Coca's Shining Path." *NACLA Report on the Americas* 22 (March): 22-24.

Gorriti, Gustavo. 1989. "How to Fight the Drug War." *The Atlantic.* July: 70-76.

Gorriti, Gustavo. 1991. "Misadventures in the Amazon." *The New York Times.* September 8.

Hanna, Joel. 1974. "Coca Leaf Use in Southern Peru: Some Biosocial Aspects." *American Anthropologist.* 76 (2): 282-96.

Healy, Kevin. 1986. "The Boom Within the Crisis: Some Recent Effects of Foreign Cocaine Markets on Bolivian Rural Society and Economy." In *Coca and Cocaine: Effects on People and Policy in Latin America,* eds. Deborah Pacini and Christine Franquemont. Cambridge, Mass.: Cultural Survival, 101-143.

Healy, Kevin. 1990. "The Coca-Cocaine Issue in Bolivia: A Political Resource for All Seasons." Paper presented at the 89th Annual Meeting of the American Anthropological Association, New Orleans. December.

Hyslop, John. 1984. *The Inka Road System.* New York: Academic Press.

International Narcotics Matters (INM). 1988. *International Narcotics Control Strategy Report.* Washington, D.C.: U.S. Department of State, Bureau of International Narcotics Matters.

Instituto Nacional de Estadistica (INE). 1981. *Censos Nacionales VIII de Poblacion y III de Vivienda.* Lima: INE.

Isikoff, Michael. 1990. "Talks Between U.S. and Peru on Military Aid Collapse." *The Washington Post.* September 20.

Jerí, Raul. 1985. "Los Problemas médicos y sociales generados por el abuso de drogas en el Peru." *Revista de la Sanidad de las Fuerzas Policiales.* Lima, Peru. 46:36-44.

LaFuente, Basilia. 1967. *Peru Before the Incas.* Englewood Cliffs, N.J.: Prentice-Hall.

Lee, Rensselaer W., III. 1988. "Why the U.S. Cannot Stop South American Cocaine." *Orbis.* 32 (Fall): 499-519.

Lee, Rensselaer W., III. 1989. *The White Labyrinth: Cocaine and Political Power.* New Brunswick, N.J.: Transaction Books.

MacDonald, Scott B. 1988. *Dancing on a Volcano: The Latin American Drug Trade.* New York: Praeger Publishers.

Malamud-Goti, Jaime. 1992. *Smoke and Mirrors: The Paradox of Drug Wars.* Boulder, Colo.: Westview Press.

Mayer, Enrique. 1986. "Coca Use in the Andes." *Studies in Third World Societies.* Williamsburg, Va.: College of William and Mary, Department of Anthropology.

Morales, Edmundo. 1986. "Coca and Coaine and Economy and in the Andes of Peru." *Economic Development and Social Change.* 35 (1): 143-161.

Morales, Edmundo. 1989. *Cocaine: White Gold Rush in Peru.* Tucson: University of Arizona Press.

Morales, Edmundo. 1990. "The Political Economy of Cocaine Production: An Analysis of the Peruvian Case." *Latin American Perspectives.* 67 (Fall): 91-109.

Morales, Edmundo. 1991. "Coca and Cocaine in Peru: An International Policy Assessment." *International Journal of Addictions.* 25 (3): 295-316.

Mortimer, William G. 1975. "The Divine Plant of the Incas." In *The Coca Leaf and Cocaine Papers,* eds. George Andrews and David Solomon. New York: Harcourt Brace Jovanovich, 50-242.

National Research Council (NRC). 1989. *Lost Crop of the Incas: Little Known Plants of the Andes with Promise for Worldwide Cultivation.* Washington, D.C.: National Academy Press.

El Peruano. 1991. "Convenio Antidroga." Lima, May 16.

Plowman, Timothy. 1986. "Coca Chewing and the Botanical Origins of Coca (Erythroxylon spp.) in South America." In *Coca and Cocaine: Effects on People and Policy in Latin America,* eds. Deborah Pacini and Christine Franquemont. Cambridge, Mass.: Cultural Survival, 5-33.

Purdy, Matthew. 1990. "Cocaine use still heavy, experts say." *The Philadelphia Inquirer.* December 30, A1.

Rosenbaum, Marsha. 1990. *Just Say What?: An Alternative View on Solving America's Drug Problem.* San Francisco: National Council on Crime and Delinquency.

Treaster, Joseph B. 1991. "Peru Chief's Visit Helps Aid Changes." *The New York Times.* September 24, A3.

Chapter Eleven

Peru, Drugs, and Shining Path

David Scott Palmer

Introduction

In just twenty years, Peru has shifted from beacon of hope to basket case. As late as the mid-1970s, Peru's reformist military government (1968-1980) appeared to offer significant possibilities for economic and political development (defined as improved distribution of income and greater participation by the citizenry).[1] From 1940 to 1975, economic growth and low inflation had been the norm. A major agrarian reform during the military *docenio* (12-year rule) created production cooperatives nationwide; the industrial community gave workers a meaningful management role in the operation of their firms. Both stirred the imagination of many Peruvians and the academic community alike.[2] However, since 1980, a succession of elected civilian governments — Fernando Belaúnde Terry (1980-1985), Alán García Pérez (1985-1990), and Alberto Fujimori (1990-) — have failed to deal effectively with the military regime's legacy of reform, on the one hand, and severe overextension on the other.[3]

Even though the vast majority of the Peruvian population continued to support democracy over its alternatives right up to President Alberto Fujimori's autogolpe in the spring of 1992 (April 5), the democratic process had failed to improve the well-being of the average citizen in the 1980-1992 period. In fact, it had just the opposite effect, as Peru's gross national product (GNP) declined by over 30 percent during this time. Unprecedented triple-digit inflation early in the decade was followed by staggering four-digit levels, which rose to a peak of 7,650 percent in 1990. Estimates of unemployment

The author wishes to express his appreciation to the Instituto de Estudios Internacionales, Universidad de Chile (Santiago) for its support in preparation of this article. In particular, he wishes to thank Institute Director Dr. Maria Teresa Infante for inviting the author to serve as Visiting Scholar-in-Residence (June-July 1992) and the Institute staff for invaluable assistance.

An early draft of this article was presented at the North-South Center Conference on Drug Trafficking Research in the Americas (directed by Bruce Bagley) held in Miami (FL), March 11-14, 1992.

and underemployment went from a 50 percent level in the early 1980s to over 80 percent in the early 1990s. Over fourteen million of Peru's twenty-two million citizens were believed to live below a very conservatively drawn poverty line.[4] Many survived by working in the burgeoning informal sector, with low wages and no benefits but also no taxes, which, by the mid-1980s, was estimated to account for at least 40 percent of all economic activity in Peru (de Soto 1986). The population of Lima, Peru's coastal capital, grew from five to eight million as rural and provincial town dwellers flocked to that city to find some employment opportunities or to escape the spreading political violence. Between 1980 and 1992, this violence claimed over 25,000 lives, most from civilians rather than combatants, and was responsible for well over $20 billion in property damage (Bernales Commission 1992).

Thus, by the time of President Fujimori's surprise suspension of the constitution, congress, and the judiciary, the majority of the Peruvian population was clearly worse off — in terms of economic well-being and personal safety — than it had been in 1980. Civilian, democratic business-as-usual government, worthy of support in the abstract, simply had not done the job. This popular frustration may help explain the overwhelming support (about 80 percent) for the April autogolpe, even though it included no specific measures to deal with citizen problems (Peru 1992; *Resumen Semanal* 1992).

This is the lugubrious context, then, in which to present and analyze Peru's drug production and trafficking and the insurgency of the Shining Path (Sendero Luminoso). No country in the hemisphere has the multitude of problems Peru faces: debt, recession, drugs, and insurgency. Before the autogolpe, however, one could discern in the Fujimori government (which took office July 28, 1990) a plan and a certain amount of progress.

The Economic Problem

In the economic arena, inflation was brought down to 139 percent (in 1991) through application of a drastic shock program. In that year, Peru experienced some very modest (2 percent) economic growth for the first time in four years. Late in 1990 and at great initial sacrifice, the Fujimori government began to resume payments (from $20 to $30 million per month) on the huge arrears (about $5 billion) which Peru owed to international financial institutions, an accumulation which had developed after President García suspended payments on the country's foreign debt in 1987. These token payments symbolized the Fujimori government's commitment to re-insert Peru into the international financial community, as part of its strategy to stabilize the economy and restore economic growth.

In September and October 1991, this commitment bore fruit when the government was able to negotiate a major financial package, totalling some $2.1 billion, with the International Monetary Fund (IMF), the World Bank, the

Inter-American Development Bank (IDB), and a special support group made up of developed countries that included, among others, the United States, Japan, Spain, and Germany. At about the same time, several governments, including the United States and Japan, worked out substantially expanded bilateral assistance programs with Peru that totalled several hundred million dollars. Economic stabilization and re-insertion during President Fujimori's first 15 months in office contributed to a steady improvement in his approval ratings, as registered in public opinion polls, from lows of 33 percent (January 1991) to almost 70 percent by October of the same year (Resumen Semanal 1991a-1991d).

The Drug Problem

The drug production and trafficking problem posed a different, but equally complex, set of issues for Peru. Since Peru is the world's largest producer of coca leaf (about 65 percent of all produced), that country has long been the focus of substantial U.S. government attention via the latter's antidrug strategy. Although Peruvian-U.S. relations were beset by numerous policy differences, particularly during the García administration, cooperation on programs designed to reduce the production of, and traffic in, coca and cocaine paste not only remained high but also gradually expanded, though total resources were modest on the whole: from about $4 million (1985) to some $10 million (in 1989).[5] However, the problems faced were daunting indeed. Despite the injection of additional resources and new payments, and even after the presidents of Colombia, Bolivia, Peru, and the United States joined together, at Cartagena (Colombia), to formulate the Andean strategy in February 1990, estimates of Peru's coca production still continued to increase (US-DS/INM 1992, 167).

One basic problem was that coca production was the major, often the sole, source of income for almost all of the approximately 300,000 farmers in the Upper Huallaga Valley (UHV).[6] Buyers usually paid for the crop in cash right at the farm or nearby. The UHV has a climate and soils almost ideally suited for the growing of the two varieties of coca plant highest in alkaloid content for processing into cocaine (Gonzáles 1992, 106). A 1988 survey concluded that coca prices ranged anywhere from 4 to 34 times higher than leading alternative crops — cacao and corn, respectively (Alvarez 1989). Furthermore, transporting other products to markets outside the UHV was increasingly problematical due to the dramatic deterioration of the single access highway.[7] Peasants, as rational actors, simply grew what would bring the highest return at the least risk.

U.S. antidrug legislation has emphasized eradication of the coca plant and has made its continued funding contingent upon certification, required annually, that progress is being made in this direction. However, local eradication teams have faced widespread hostility from growers and in 1989 were forced to suspend operations after a number of their members were killed. Furthermore, a potential chemical substitute, tebuthieron (or Spike), which was designed to kill the coca plant without damaging other crops, provoked both a strong protest against its use by the Peruvian government in 1988 and an initial decision by its U.S. manufacturer not to sell the product to the U.S. government for this purpose. Even though small test plots in the UHV were eventually authorized in 1989, with results apparently uniformly positive, neither the Peruvian nor the U.S. governments thought it prudent to proceed to large-scale applications (Bigler 1990). After 1989, attention shifted to seizures of the coca leaf and eradication of seed beds, which in 1991 resulted in a very modest reduction, of 500 hectares, in the total area cultivated: from 121,300 hectares to 120,800 hectares, according to U.S. government surveys (US-DS/INM 1992, 107).[8] Nevertheless, total production of the coca leaf continued to increase, up an estimated 3 percent (US-DS/INM 1992,107).

The Guerrilla Problem

An additional factor, and major impediment, complicating Peru's efforts to mount an effective antidrug campaign, particularly in the Upper Huallaga Valley, has been the significant presence there of two guerrilla forces: the Shining Path (Sendero Luminoso), also known as the Communist Party of Peru (PCP), and the Tupac Amaru Revolutionary Movement (Movimiento Revolucionario de Tupac Amaru or MRTA). This presence stands in sharp distinction to Bolivia, the other major coca producing country in the Andes, which accounts for about 30 percent of total production, second only to Peru. Both Sendero and the MRTA have been competing, off and on, for control of the Upper Huallaga ever since 1984-1985, with the Sendero forces gaining decisive advantage in 1989 and again in 1991-1992. For the Shining Path, which is the major force of the two and believed responsible for over 80 percent of all guerrilla incidents, the Upper Huallaga Valley has proved to be a significant target of opportunity.[9]

By protecting the coca-growing peasants there from joint Peruvian-U.S. government efforts to combat the drug trade, Sendero believes it can gain additional support bases for its proposed New Democracy in Peru. And by controlling as many of the estimated 120 landing strips in the Huallaga as possible, Sendero is able to collect the sums (estimated at anywhere from $6,000 to $15,000 per flight) paid by traffickers, mostly Colombians, to protect their cocaine paste pick-up operations. The estimates of annual revenues received by Sendero from its activities in the UHV range all the way from $10 to $100 million (US-GAO 1991, 24). It is widely believed, though not definitely proven, that this income is used primarily to fund the organization's domestic operations throughout Peru, from salaries for its militants to financial support for families of "fallen heroes" to fees for sympathetic lawyers to try Sendero cases in the courts (Palmer 1992b; *Caretas* 1992a). The very efforts of the Peruvian army to pursue the Shining Path only make it easier for the drug business in the UHV to operate. By the same token, when the police step up their action against the drug traffickers, it only serves to heighten the opposition of coca-growing peasants and drives them further into the arms of Sendero. To date, no systematic, coordinated approach has even been attempted, much less succeeded.

The Enforcement Problem

Rivalry between Peru's army and its police is one reason for the lack of coordination between the two forces in the Upper Huallaga. Each is dependent upon a different government ministry (the police come under the Minister of the Interior; the army is the reponsibility of the Minister of Defense) and each has a different mission: law enforcement for the police; counterinsurgency for the army. As the economic crisis became increasingly acute in the late 1980s, largely due to the maladroit policies of the García administration, revenues dropped and budgets were slashed. The budget for the armed forces was cut by over 50 percent in 1989-1990. Salaries dropped precipitously: to less than $200 per month for top generals and to about $10 monthly for enlisted personnel (Palmer 1992c). Resources to support field operations were severely curtailed as well. However, because police forces in the Upper Huallaga Valley were part of the joint U.S.-Peruvian antidrug effort, they received supplementary funding (as part of the assistance package) as well as special training by U.S. Drug Enforcement Administration (DEA) personnel (US-GAO 1991, 20).

U.S. funds also contributed to the construction, in 1989, of a new antidrug operations base in the UHV, at Santa Lucía, complete with equipment, including loaned helicopters and pilots. However, U.S. antidrug legislation does not permit the funding of counterinsurgency operations carried out by the Peruvian army. The dramatic difference in their levels of support only exacerbates the tension between the army and the police in the region.

These inter-service rivalries were dramatically, and tragically, exposed in March 1989. The Sendero Luminoso launched a large-scale night attack on the police station in Uchiza, the major population center of the mid-UHV (Gonzáles 1992, 112-113). Although the Uchiza police commander pleaded desperately for reinforcements and Minister of the Interior Armando Villanueva specifically requested aid from military units located only minutes away by helicopter, no order was issued and no assistance was sent. The Uchiza post fell by morning; Sendero forces killed every surviving officer, and the town came under the complete control of Sendero.

The following month, a new army commander, General Alberto Arciniega, was appointed to head up the Huallaga emergency zone and immediately launched an aggressive counterinsurgency attack against Sendero (Gonzales 1992, 112-118). By keeping up a constant military pressure, and by specifically eschewing any interference in the peasants' coca-growing activities, General Arciniega succeeded in pushing their forces out of most of the UHV within seven months. By November 1989, he was able to conduct an Armed Forces Day ceremony, attended by thousands of Valley residents, in the same Uchiza square which had been the scene of Sendero's triumph over the police the preceding March.

However, because the government's economic crisis had forced General Arciniega to rely, to a significant extent, on local resources (i.e., drug money) to finance his military operations, he was the target of significant opposition by Peruvian police and the U.S. government (Levitsky 1989, 170). Before the year was out, he was reassigned to Lima. Because a succession of replacements failed to be effective, within a year the Shining Path had regained, if not strengthened, its position in the Upper Huallaga Valley.

President Fujimori appeared to grasp, early in his administration, the complexities of dealing with the multiple challenges, from both drugs and the insurgents, in the UHV. Under the Andean strategy, the United States was fully prepared to support his antidrug efforts and expected him to accept the $35.9 million in U.S. military assistance which had been authorized in fiscal year 1990 (FY 1990). However, Peru's president turned the aid down in late September folowing repeated conversations between the two governments in which U.S. officials tried, but failed, to meet Peru's concerns (US-DS, Office of Andean Affairs 1990). Fujimori based his rejection on what he saw as the U.S. preoccupation with a military focus for its antidrug strategy in Peru to the exclusion of all else. The Peruvian president felt that aid should also deal with the economic side of the problem, more specifically, with alternative development assistance for the coca-growing campesino. The practical consequence of this difference of opinion was that Peru forfeited any new resources, under the Andean strategy's first full year of funding, because the imminent end of the U.S. government's fiscal year (September 30, 1990) precluded time for further negotiations. The allocation for Peru went primarily to Colombia instead.

Eventually, President Fujimori's insistence on both an economic and a military response to the twin challenges of drugs and insurgency in Peru paid off. This occurred even though his bargaining power vis-à-vis the United States was minimal, and even though the two countries had different priorities on their respective agendas (Palmer 1992a). For the United States, the major problem in Peru centered on drugs; for Peru, the major problems were, first, the economy, and then the insurgency. Months of discussions led to Peru submitting an alternative proposal in January 1991 which, after more extensive talks, became the basis for an umbrella agreement that was finally signed by the two countries in May 1991. This agreement addressed the different priorities of each country in ways acceptable to both governments.

The accord emphasizes the continuing importance of the drug issue for both countries and the need for their close cooperation in dealing with the problem (US-DS, Office of Andean Affairs 1991). However, Peru's economic concerns also receive prominent mention, including specific reference to "micro-economic structural adjustment ... directed at ... the disadvantaged," the role of the Enterprise for the Americas, and a pledge by the United States to lend its active support to Peru in international economic arenas. The agreement also recognizes the need to provide security in the coca-growing and cocaine paste producing areas as a sine qua non for reducing drug production in those areas and enabling economic development programs to advance. To ensure and achieve this security objective, the United States specifically connects its military assistance to helping the Peruvian armed forces deal with subversion by recognizing

. . . the need to feed, equip, train, provide with uniforms, and adequately support the armed and police forces who will be fighting against narcotrafficking *and those who support and encourage it* (US-DS, Office of Andean Affairs 1991, 7-section 25a).

Many of the specific details concerning economic assistance, including President Fujimori's proposed Alternative Development Program, which had been a part of Peru's original proposal (January 1991), were omitted from the final agreement. These were left as the subject for subsequent discussions and possible supplementary accords at some time in the future. Nevertheless, the May 1991 document clearly responds to Peru's desire for an agreement in which the United States clearly recognizes, and prominently addresses, its economic and security needs in addition to the drug issue. President Fujimori's patience and pragmatism eventually produced an accord which responded more fully to Peru's own definition of its needs than the original U.S. proposal of July 1990. The agreement also demonstrated that Peru very much wanted a military assistance component to help its army deal more effectively with the insurgency.

Statements by the executive branch of the U.S. government, as well as sentiments expressed by the Congress, clearly reflect the emphasis upon countering drug production and traffic in its relations with Peru. However, Peru's insistence on including economic and social issues was not incompatible with U.S. foreign policy concerns, given not only the dramatic shifts in East-West issues but also those initiatives of the Bush administration which relate to North-South concerns such as the North American Free Trade Agreement (NAFTA), the Enterprise for the Americas Initiative (EAI), and the Brady Plan.

U.S. officials were also increasingly worried about Peru's severe domestic problems. As a result, the Peruvian government was able to advance its economic goal of international reinsertion, its social goal of new resources to alleviate rising poverty, and its security goal of military assistance against the insurgency by responding to the U.S. foreign policy priority of the "Drug War." U.S. government authorities wanted a counterdrug agreement badly enough to be willing to incorporate the economic and security needs of the Peruvian government into the overall accord.

Once again, in September 1991, the U.S. Congress debated the assistance proposed for Peru in the umbrella agreement under an end-of-fiscal-year deadline. At almost the last possible moment, it voted to acquiesce in the Bush administration's request for narcotics-related aid. However, in the process, the Congress expressed its concern over military assistance due to the checkered human rights record of Peru's armed forces and police. Even though the Bush administration had certified in July that Peru was making sufficient progress in human rights matters to be eligible for continued U.S. assistance, various human rights organizations disputed that finding (Americas Watch 1991; Youngers 1992; Amnesty International 1991). Nevertheless, and despite any misgivings, the Congress appropriated most of the aid requested ($111 million out of $133.8 million). It did reduce the amount requested for military assistance from $39.9 million to $24.5 million, and it also subjected the disbursement of those monies to a series of conditions and controls.[10]

Congressional concern over Peru's security situation, particularly among those who follow Latin American matters, heightened in the months that followed. In March 1992, the Subcommittee on Hemispheric Affairs of the Committee on Foreign Affairs (in the House of Representatives) held hearings on whether or not the U.S. government should provide military aid for the specific purpose of combating the guerrillas and independent of the programs designed to counter and reduce the growing of, and traffic in, coca and cocaine. The testimony covered a wide range of divergent views, ranging from full support for counterinsurgency aid (both military and economic aid), through opposition on human rights grounds, to — at the other end of the spectrum — opposition based on the view that the situation was already out of control and that the United States had no vital interest in Peru.[11] However, the Congress had taken no further action prior to President Fujimori's autogolpe (April 5, 1992). At that point, the Congress joined with the Bush administration in expressing U.S. opposition to the Fujimori action and supported the immediate suspension of U.S. aid.[12]

The growing congressional concern over the insurgency in Peru was shared by Bush administration officials as well. Any specific new steps which might have been forthcoming, however, would now have to await the restoration of democracy there or, at the very least, clear signs that the Fujimori government was moving in that direction.[13] The momentum to help Peru, which had been mounting in U.S. government circles, now halted abruptly (and possibly was even reversed) by news of the autogolpe. This was bad news for President Fujimori, who had repeatedly stated that his government's first priority, after stabilization and reinsertion into the international economic community, was "the fight against terrorism."

As of mid-1992, the best estimates of guerrilla strength in Peru were that the Shining Path had from 5,000 to 6,000 armed militants and an active support network of about 50,000. Although the MRTA was thought to number between 700 and 1,000 armed cadres, it had been badly hurt both by the capture of key leaders in July 1992, including the head of the organization, Victor Polay Campos, and by internal divisions (*Caretas* 1992b). Sendero operated in large swaths of the largely Indian highlands, in the Upper Huallaga Valley and east into the neighboring jungle, and — increasingly — in Lima. The MRTA's main areas of activity were also the Valley, nearby jungle, and Lima. The Shining Path was by far the greater threat: it was more militant, better organized, and had been operating for a much longer period of time.[14] In Peru, incidents attributed to the insurgents and deaths resulting from political violence had ebbed and flowed since their onset in 1980. From 12 deaths in 1980, to 3,587 in 1984, the total had peaked at 3,708 in 1990, before declining (by 14 percent) to 3,181 in 1991.[15]

The Shining Path, also known as the Communist Party of Peru (PCP), has a number of distinctive features which set it apart from most revolutionary movements.[16]

1. It began in a small, isolated provincial university, in Ayacucho, not in the capital.

2. This university, San Cristóbal de Huamanga, had a specific extension-to-the-countryside mission in all of its academic programs from the outset of its re-establishment in 1959 (and no law school), very unusual in Latin American universities at the time.

3. Abimael Guzmán Reynoso, professor of the University of Huamanga education program, director of the teacher training school, and founder/head of the PCP, adopted, and defended, a cult of personality right from the beginning, unique in revolutionary movements prior to taking power (Gorriti 1992, 149-150).

4. The movement we now call Shining Path developed and organized over a 17-year period before Guzmán launched the people's war.

5. A number of Sendero officials, including Guzmán, not only made extended visits to China at the height of the Cultural Revolution there (1966-1976) but also adhered to the radical "permanent revolution" approach espoused by China's Gang of Four, and which subsequently lost out to Deng Xiaoping and the "bureaucratic revisionists."

6. The PCP launched its people's war just as Peru was returning to electoral democracy following the 1979 Constitutional Convention, in which the Marxist Left (which had captured 34 percent of the vote) had been actively involved — and thus was not a time of political restrictions or repression.

7. Sendero has insisted from the outset that it would develop its guerrilla struggle on its own terms and without any outside material support.

8. Sendero's attacks on all Communist countries — especially the Soviet Union, China, Cuba, and Albania — have been consistent, vicious, and unrelenting.

9. The PCP relishes the current crisis of world communism, which it views as only confirming President Gonzalo's (Guzmán's nom de guerre) vision of his party as the vanguard of a new, and ideologically correct, communist movement.

10. Shining Path's symbiotic relationship with the coca growers and producers and traffickers of cocaine has been remarkably profitable and has been used primarily to strengthen the movement internally.[17]

11. Sendero focuses on the periphery of Peru's social, economic, and political systems rather than in their center and systematically works to sever the connections of the central government (e.g., teachers, mayors, birth records, development workers) with the country's rural and urban grass roots.

12. Sendero normally uses force very selectively and for political ends, not indiscriminately and for military ends, in order to cut key ties or to make an example of a particularly courageous local opponent; the goal is to neutralize and intimidate at the base of society as a step toward gaining local support (Marks 1992).

These distinctive features have made Shining Path a formidable opponent. Shifting to a more urban-oriented strategy, as presaged by Guzmán's one published interview (in 1988), has heightened a sense of insecurity among those who comprise Peru's social, political, and economic center, who are concentrated in Lima (Arce Borja and Talavera-Sánchez 1988). Over the years the government, while experiencing some successes, has often been ineffective, even incompetent, in dealing with Sendero.[18] Several examples include the following:

1. The release of Guzmán after his capture in 1979;

2. The delay by the Belaúnde government in recognizing and responding to the Sendero challenge in the early 1980s;

3. The almost exclusive reliance on military force rather than a judicious combination of military and economic assistance actions;[19]

4. Retention of most military forces on the borders with Ecuador and Chile rather than greater dispersal to the areas of greatest conflict with the insurgents;[20]

5. Ineffective administration of the prisons, allowing Sendero almost complete control over its own inmates;

6. Delayed and incomplete legal reforms and judicial system revisions to respond to terrorist incidents and to prosecute suspects effectively;

7. Overly rapid rotation of military personnel in emergency zones and affected areas, discouragement of incorporation into the military of local recruits for service in their home areas, and disincentives for senior military officers to take imaginative initiatives to carry out their assignments in areas of conflict;

8. The embarrassing episode in which the entire contingent of MRTA inmates (47 in all) escaped from the Canto Grande prison in Lima in June 1990;

9. Recourse to an autogolpe rather than continuing to negotiate the political process between the executive and congress.

While the assumption of extra-constitutional emergency powers may have boosted President Fujimori's popularity in the short run, it also worked to impede his self-proclaimed goal of "finishing off" Sendero before the end of his term, scheduled for 1995.[21] First, from $200 to $300 million of foreign economic assistance was suspended. Second, the process of reinsertion into the international economic community was significantly delayed, by the postponement of some $500 million in credits promised by the support group. Both actions seriously upset Peru's domestic timetable for economic recovery. U.S. military assistance, which would have strengthened the ability of the Peruvian army to push back the Shining Path in the UHV, was suspended as well, and the 30 U.S. military advisers were withdrawn. Even though Peru-U.S. relations suffered a further shock when the Peruvian air force mounted an attack on a U.S. C-130 on a reconnaisance flight (April 24, 1992), the counterdrug program and humanitarian aid continued. However, local political organizations and nongovernmental entities in the urban shantytowns and rural communities lost their ties to political party counterparts and advocates in Congress.

The democratic political process in Peru, however imperfect, had provided the government with a foundation of legitimacy which was swept away by the autogolpe. Taken together, these effects of the "April surprise" undo much of the work of the Fujimori government during its first 20 months in office and play into the hands of Sendero. Even if democracy is restored sooner rather than later and international economic support flows, from all sources, are normalized, additional months will be lost before the pre-April

5 momentum can be restored. The extraordinary diversity and complexity of Peruvian society and the quiet courage of millions of its citizens provide an ongoing bulwark against any imminent victory by the Shining Path. The Peruvian government has often been its own worst enemy; Fujimori's autogolpe provides but one more example.

What is to be done? One can do much more than wring one's hands. Several concrete initiatives are very much in order. These include the following:

- Restore democracy rapidly and fully.

- Implement the Alternative Development Program to get resources to society's periphery or grass roots.

- Combine pursuit of a military shield cum civic action with protection of Peruvian and foreign development workers.

- Implement initiatives to decentralize resources in tandem with formal political decentralization.

- Strengthen ties of political parties with their bases of support, especially those who receive aid from the foundations of foreign political parties.

- Emphasize interdiction of the drug traffic in order to reduce the resources that now flow to the Shining Path.

- Encourage, and protect where necessary, nongovernmental organizations (NGOs) and church programs at the grass roots.

- Enhance military aid and training to improve troop and unit responses to the insurgency and to help reduce human rights abuses.

- Consider seriously giving assistance in specialized intelligence techniques in order to help Peruvian authorities locate key Sendero figures.

The overall goal is to improve the well-being and security of Peru's large and diverse periphery, to strengthen the institutional structure at the local level, to rebuild local ties to the center (to parties that have political input and to government organizations that can deliver), and to increase the efficiency and the effectiveness of military action. Such a package would have a good chance of turning the tables on the insurgency. The government, rather than Shining Path, would then appear more like the proverbial phoenix, rising from the ashes of its multiple crises. Sendero, rather than the government, would then become the Peruvian Achilles, with its ideological orthodoxy converted into its fatal flaw. To continue the mythological metaphor: Peru would finally resolve its dilemma of being caught between the Scylla of the insurgency and the Charybdis of politico-economic chaos, to break the stalemate that has been its fate since the mid-1970s.

[**Editor's note:** Peruvian police arrested founder of Sendero Luminoso Abimael Guzmán in Lima on September 12, 1992. Charged with high treason by Peru's Supreme Council of Military Justice, he was sentenced to life in prison at an island navy base and fined, along with two others, a largely symbolic $25 billion.]

Notes

1. See, for example, Lowenthal (1975) for an early, and generally positive, assessment.

2. As reflected in an impressive number of books and articles during the 1970s and early 1980s on Peru, the military regime, and its reforms.

3. There are many fewer treatments of Peru's post-1980 civilian governments than of its 1968-1980 military governments. However, developments in Peru have been covered in detail in articles that have appeared in the *Latin American and Caribbean Contemporary Record* (which is published annually by Holmes and Meier), most frequently by Cynthia McClintock (1985); as well as articles that have appeared in *Current History*, most years since 1980, in the issue devoted to Latin America or South America, most frequently by David Werlich (1991). See also recent works by Crabtree (1992), Graham (1992), and Rudolph (1992).

4. The above figures are from various issues of *Resumen Semanal*, which are published in Lima weekly by the Centro de Estudios y Promoción del Desarrollo (DESCO).

5. For one analysis, see David Scott Palmer (1992a); for another discussion, both broader and more critical, see Andreas and Sharpe (1992).

6. This is an estimate by the U.S. government (US-DS/INM 1992); others are lower.

7. Reports of 15-day minimums to traverse the Valley by truck to get to the major markets of Huancayo or Lima were common (US-DOD 1991; U.S. Embassy, Peru 1992a).

8. Other estimates of the number of hectares under coca cultivation are much higher, up to 315,000 hectares according to estimates of the Peruvian government (U.S. Embassy 1992c).

9. See Gonzáles (1992, 106-112) for a discussion of drug production and trafficking and connections to the insurgency in the Upper Huallaga Valley. Also see this article for further details on the discussion which follows (105-125).

10. These conditions on U.S. military aid to Peru may have been a factor in a significant drop in Peruvian military and police violations of human rights. Peru's *Coordinadora Nacional de Derechos Humanos* reported sharp declines in disappearances attributed to government forces between October 1991 through February 1992, compared with a similar five-month period prior to the approval of aid (May-September 1991). These dropped from 181 in the May-September period to 60 in the October-February period (U.S. Embassy, Peru 1992b).

11. Those invited to testify (March 11-12, 1992) were Bernard Aronson, Assistant Secretary of State for American Republics Affairs; Alexander Wilde, Washington Office on Latin America; Gabriela Tarazona-Sevillano, a Peruvian lawyer at Davidson College; Gordon McCormick of the RAND Corporation; and the author. Aronson, Tarazona-

Sevillano, and Palmer presented the case for full, if conditioned, support. Wilde opposed on the grounds of human rights abuses; McCormick felt that any aid would be wasted on a lost cause.

12. Humanitarian aid was not affected nor was counterdrug assistance. However, on April 24, 1992, Peruvian air force fighter planes strafed a U.S. C-130 transport plane as it returned from a mission in Peru, even though the flight had been approved in advance, and cleared, by Peruvian authorities. The C-130 was severely damaged, and a U.S. serviceman was killed. After this incident, U.S.-Peruvian relations were strained, but neither humanitarian nor counterdrug aid was suspended as a result.

13. Fujimori's ambivalence was demonstrated by a list of 19 contradictory statements he had made between April 9 and June 19, 1992, concerning the arrangements for restoring democracy to Peru (*Caretas* 1992c).

14. For a graphic illustration of the disparity between Sendero and the MRTA, the Bernales Commission attributed 1,314 of the 3,181 deaths in 1991 due to political violence in Peru to attacks by Sendero (48 percent), as opposed to 139 (4 percent) it attributed to the MRTA.

15. Deaths due to political violence in Peru, by year since 1980, are as follows:

1980 . . . 12

1981 . . . 82

1982 . . . 193

1983 . . . 1,977

1984 . . . 3,587

1985 . . . 1,476

1986 . . . 1,451

1987 . . . 1,115

1988 . . . 1,451

1989 . . . 2,881

1990 . . . 3,708

1991 . . . 3,181

These figures do not include an estimated 3,000 disappearances from 1980-1991, which were believed to be related to the political violence. Figures for 1980-1990 were compiled by DESCO and published in *Resumen Semanal* (as corrected and recompiled by Sandra Woy-Hazleton 1990); 1991 figures are from the Bernales Commission, which uses different sources and counting criteria (up through 1990, Bernales Commission figures tended to be 10 to 15 percent higher than those compiled by DESCO).

16. This summary relies on a wide range of studies by scholars and journalists, both Peruvian and non-Peruvian. Three books which, together, provide a full overview of the Shining Path, from its origins through 1991, are those by Gustavo Gorriti (1990); Carlos Iván DeGregori (1990); and David Scott Palmer (ed., 1992d).

17. There is also an alternative formulation that a good portion of the estimated $250 million earned by the PCP over the years from its taxes on the drug trade may have gone to foreign bank accounts in the name of Guzmán and those of several top officials in Sendero (*Caretas* 1992a).

18. Examples of government successes include the Arciniega campaign in the Upper Huallaga Valley, the capture of important leaders of Sendero and most of the top leadership of the MRTA, the recovery of important guerrilla documents and film in raids on safe houses, and an effective military/civic action program in the urban shantytown of Ate-Vitarte. The government's failures and limitations are amply described by Gordon McCormick in two studies done for the U.S. Department of Defense (McCormick 1987 and 1992).

19. An exception which seems to prove the point was the combination of military strategy and economic incentives which was followed during the first half of the García administration. The result (as shown by figures in note 15) was a drop in casualties from a total of 6,487 for the years 1983 and 1984 and the first seven months of 1985 to a total of just 3,120 for the balance of 1985 and all of 1986 and 1987 (representing a drop of almost 52 percent). The number of terrorist incidents and human rights violations declined substantially as well, and return rural migration increased. For a case study, see Isbell (1992).

20. One authoritative 1991 estimate was that over 80 percent of all Peruvian military were positioned on or near the country's borders; by mid-1992, the same estimator put the figure at about 70 percent (US-DOD 1991 and 1992). Additional information and analysis may be found in Palmer (1992c).

21. Several reasons have been advanced to explain why President Fujimori carried out his autogolpe. One plausible motive put forward is his lack of political experience and consequent frustration with the need to negotiate with a congress controlled by opposition parties. Another is that he was pressured by the military, though this is less plausible because he had successfully juggled promotions to ensure top commanders loyal to him. A third, right out of the notorious Lima rumor mill, is that his wife, frustrated at not being allowed to accompany the president to Japan in late March, accused Fujimori family members of selling used clothing donated by Japan to Peru's needy, so the president pulled off the coup to impede an investigation. (Peru's equivalent of the General Accounting Office, which would have been responsible for any review, was among the institutions suspended.) Yet another, also quite plausible, is that Fujimori was incensed that former president Alán García, whom he blamed for creating the mess which he inherited in Peru, had not only escaped being charged with corruption because the Supreme Court, made up largely of García appointees, refused to hear charges but was also beginning to challenge Fujimori after being elected, once again, to head the American Popular Revolutionary Alliance (APRA) party. It is also believed that President Fujimori did not fully anticipate how negative the international reaction would be.

References

Alvarez, E. 1989. "Coca Production and Crop Alternatives in the Upper Huallaga Valley." Paper presented to the annual meeting of the New England Council of Latin American Studies, University of Connecticut, Storrs (October).

Americas Watch. 1991. *Into the Quagmire: Human Rights and U.S. Policy in Peru* (September; Americas Watch Report). New York, N.Y.: Americas Watch.

Amnesty International. 1991. *Peru: Human Rights in Crisis, A Time for Action* (AMR 46/ 68/91). London, England: Amnesty International.

Andreas, P., and K. Sharpe. 1992. "Cocaine Politics in the Andes." *Current History* 91, 562 (February): 74-79.

Arce Borja, L., and J. Talavera-Sanchez. 1988. "La entrevista del siglo: el Presidente Gonzalo rompe el silencio." *El Diario* (July 24): 2-73.

Bernales Commission. 1992. *Report of the Comité Especial sobre las Causas de la Violencia y las Alternativas de Pacificación en el Perú*. Lima, Peru: Congreso Nacional.

Bigler, G. 1990. Author conversation with Information Officer, U.S. Embassy, Lima (Peru), February 6.

Caretas (Lima). 1992a. "Abimael y las drogas." No. 1218 (July 6): 34-36.

Caretas. 1992b. "MRTA contra MRTA." No. 1218 (July 6): 24.

Caretas. 1992c. "Cronología." No. 1216 (June 22): 13.

Crabtree, J. 1992. *Peru under García: An Opportunity Lost*. Pittsburgh, Pa.: University of Pittsburgh Press.

DeGregori, C. 1990. *Ayacucho 1969-1979: el surgimiento de Sendero Luminoso, del movimiento por la gratuidad de la enseñanza al inicio de la lucha armada*. Lima, Peru: Instituto de Estudios Peruanos.

De Soto, H. 1986. *El otro sendero*. Lima, Peru: Instituto Libertad y Democracia.

Gamarra, Eduardo, and James Malloy, eds. 1992. *Latin American and Caribbean Contemporary Record: 1989-1990*. Vol. 9. New York: Holmes and Meier.

Garcia Sayan, D., ed. 1989. *Coca, cocaína y narcotráfico: Laberinto en los Andes*. Lima, Peru: Comisión Andina de Juristas.

Gonzales, J. 1992. "Guerrillas and Coca in the Upper Huallaga Valley." In *The Shining Path of Peru*, ed. David Scott Palmer. New York, N.Y.: St. Martin's Press.

Gorriti, G. 1992. "Shining Path's Stalin and Trotsky," In *The Shining Path of Peru*, ed. David Scott Palmer. New York, N.Y.: St. Martin's Press.

Gorriti, G. 1990. *Sendero: historia de la guerra milenaria en el Peru, I*. Lima, Peru: Apoyo.

Graham, C. 1992. *Peru's APRA: Parties, Politics, and the Elusive Quest for Democracy*. Boulder, Colo.: Lynne Rienner Publishers.

Isbell, B. J. 1992. "Shining Path and Peasant Responses in Rural Ayacucho." In *The Shining Path of Peru*, ed. David Scott Palmer. New York, N.Y.: St. Martin's Press.

Levitsky, M. 1989. Testimony of the Director of the Bureau of International Narcotics Matters, U.S. State Department. Hearings of U.S. Senate, Committee on Governmental Affairs, Permanent Subcommittee on Investigation, September 26-29. 101st Cong., 1st sess. Washington, D.C.: U.S. Government Printing Office.

Lowenthal, A., ed. 1975. *The Peruvian Experiment*. Princeton, N.J.: Princeton University Press.

McClintock, C. 1985. "Peru." In *Latin America and Caribbean Contemporary Record: 1984-85,* Vol. 4, ed. Jack Hopkins. New York, N.Y.: Holmes and Meier.

McCormick, G. 1992. *From the Sierra to the Cities: The Urban Campaign of the Shining Path* (report for U.S. Department of Defense). Santa Monica, Calif.: RAND Corporation.

McCormick, G. 1987. *The Shining Path and Peruvian Terrorism* (report for the U.S. Department of Defense). Santa Monica, Calif.: RAND Corporation.

Marks, T. 1992. "Making Revolution with Shining Path," In *The Shining Path of Peru,* ed. David Scott Palmer. New York, N.Y.: St. Martin's Press.

Palmer, D. 1992a. "United States-Peru Relations in the 1990s: Asymmetry and its Consequences." In *Latin America and Caribbean Contemporary Record: 1989-1990,* Vol. 9, eds. Eduardo Gamarra and James Malloy. New York, N.Y.: Holmes and Meier.

Palmer, D. 1992b. "The Shining Path in Peru: Insurgency and the Drug Problem." In *Low Intensity Conflict: Old Threats in a New World,* eds. Edwin G. Corr and Stephen Sloan. Boulder, Colo.: Westview Press.

Palmer, D. 1992c. "National Security." In *Peru: A Country Study,* ed. Rex Hudson. Washington, D.C.: U.S. Government Printing Office (for Library of Congress, Federal Research Division).

Palmer, D., ed. 1992d. *The Shining Path of Peru.* New York, N.Y.: St. Martin's Press.

Peru Mission to the Organization of American States (OAS). 1992. "Manifiesto a la nación del señor Presidente de la República" (April 5, Lima). Washington, D.C.: Peru Mission to OAS.

Resumen Semanal. 1992. "Popularidad del gobierno." Vol. 15, No. 666 (April 15-23): 1.

Resumen Semanal. 1991a. "Popularidad del gobierno." Vol. 14, No. 648: 2.

Resumen Semanal. 1991b. "New York Times." Vol. 14, No. 627 (July 5-11): 1.

Resumen Semanal. 1991c. "Popularidad." Vol. 14, No. 623 (June 7-13): 1-2.

Resumen Semanal. 1991d. "Inflación del año." Vol. 14, No. 601 (December 21, 1990-January 3, 1991): 1.

Rudolph, J. 1992. *Peru: The Evolution of a Crisis.* Westport, Conn.: Praeger.

U.S. Department of Defense (US-DOD). 1992. Author interview with DOD analyst, Carlyle (Pa.), June 11.

U.S. Department of Defense (US-DOD). 1991. Author interview with DOD analyst, Washington, D.C., September 15.

U.S. Embassy, Peru. 1992a. Author interview with U.S. political officer, Lima, June 29.

U.S. Embassy, Peru. 1992b. Compilation of disappearances attributed to Peruvian government forces before and after approval of U.S. aid to Peru; made available to author by Embassy staff; April 22.

U.S. Embassy, Peru. 1992c. Interview with the Director of the Drug Enforcement Administration in Peru, July 13.

U.S. Government Accounting Office (US-GAO). 1991. *The Drug War: U.S. Programs in Peru Face Serious Obstacles* (report to Congressional requesters; GAO/NS/ AD 92-36; October). Washington, D.C.: US-GAO.

U.S. Department of State, Bureau of International Narcotics Matters (US-DS/INM). 1992. *International Narcotics Control Strategy Report* (March). Washington, D.C.: U.S. Department of State.

U.S. Department of State, Office of Andean Affairs. 1991. "An Agreement between the United States of America and Peru on Drug Control and Alternative Development Policy" (May). English language text provided to author by US-DS Office of Andean Affairs; also available in *Appendix of Latin America and Caribbean Contemporary Record: 1989-1990,* Vol. 9, edited by Eduardo Gamarra and James Malloy. New York, N.Y.: Holmes and Meier.

U.S. Department of State, Office of Andean Affairs. 1990. Author conversations with officials, Office of Andean Affairs, U.S. State Department, Washington, D.C., September 21.

Werlich, D. 1991. "Fujimori and the 'Disaster' in Peru." *Current History* (February): 61-64, 81-83.

Woy-Hazelton, S. 1990. "Actos terroristas y número de víctimas" (unpublished tables from *Resumen Semanal* 13 (March 2-8): 559). Lima, Peru: Centro de Estudios y Promoción del Desarrollo (DESCO).

Youngers, C. 1992. *Peru Under Scrutiny: Human Rights and U.S. Drug Policy* (WOLA Issue Brief 5: Issues in International Drug Policy). Washington, D.C.: Washington Office on Latin America (WOLA).

Bolivia

Chapter Twelve

Recent Literature on Drugs in Bolivia

Kevin Healy

There has been a proliferation of research in diverse publications stimulated by the increasingly high profile and importance of the drug issue for Bolivian national life. In this chapter, this growing body of literature has been organized into four general categories. The areas of literature cover coca leaf consumption, coca leaf production, the illegal cocaine industry, and the role of the state.

Coca Leaf Consumption Literature

There have been several studies conducted over the past two decades on the coca leaf consumption patterns of the Bolivian population. William Carter and Mauricio Mamani (1978) conducted the seminal study in the mid-1970s on the uses of coca leaf in Bolivia (Carter 1983). The centerpiece of the study was a national survey which focused on the rural communities, mining districts, and small towns where coca leaf usage was most common. Their study demonstrated the vibrant, widespread use of the coca leaf for chewing, medicinal purposes, ritual practices, and various other uses. The research results served to disprove the sponsoring U.S. government's hypothesis that consumption was on the wane throughout the country. The Carter and Mamani study demonstrated the central place of the coca leaf in the traditional life-style of the Andean people by arguing that the society would be socially and culturally impoverished without it. Carter's research program also incorporated work from other international scientists who examined the coca leaf's positive nutritional value and its role in regulating body temperature (Carter 1983). More recent surveys also have shown widespread support for the coca leaf in the capital city of La Paz (Roth and Bohrt 1987).

Coca Production Literature

The coca leaf production literature consists of studies in the Yungas and Chapare coca growing regions in Bolivia. The value of this body of research is its contribution to a sophisticated understanding of peasant production systems. The literature, for the most part, tends to place the coca-cocaine industry itself in the background rather than front and center. Moreover, various of these studies took place before the coca-cocaine boom of the late 1970s and 1980s.

These detailed studies commonly use the peasant household as the key unit of analysis (Albo 1978; J. Weil 1980 and 1986; C. Weil 1989; Blanes 1983; Henkel 1982; Flores and Blanes 1983; M. Painter and Bedoya 1991; Sanabria 1986; M. Painter 1991a; CIDRE 1990). Some studies have focused on the adaptation of a household to a new frontier tropical settlement area. Research works include articles and books from doctoral dissertations by U.S. and British scholars in anthropology and geography as well as large surveys conducted by Bolivian social research centers and nongovernmental organizations. Social researchers have employed household surveys, family histories, secondary data, official sources, key informants, and participant observer techniques to obtain their data.

Since the latter half of the 1980s when social science field work in the Chapare became more dangerous, studies of this ethnographic genre by individual researchers in communities became extremely difficult (J. Weil 1990). However, the Dirrecion de Reconversion Agricola (DIRECO), the government agency heading voluntary coca leaf eradication programs, stepped in to fill part of this gap. Although DIRECO's survey data should be treated with caution given peasant farmers' heightened fears against coercive coca eradication, the data is extensive and useful. This is especially true because The Institute for Developmental Anthropology (IDA) was able to use its privileged access to the data (via USAID) to produce high quality academic publications of peasant production strategies, community demography, and related topics. CIDRE, a Cochabamba-based nongovernmental organization with close relations with the peasant sidicatos in the Chapare, also carried out in the late 1980s a household survey among coca producers in the Chapare (CIDRE 1990). Equal caution should be used with this data, given similar biases as mentioned with DIRECO, although CIDRE enjoyed the trust of the leaders of peasant sindicato federations.

Fortunately, there exists important research at various time intervals for understanding changing production patterns in response to international markets. For both the Chapare and Yungas, we have socio-economic studies for the consecutive decades of the 1960s, 1970s, and 1980s. This "peasant studies" literature has advanced our understanding about cropping systems, land and labor utilization, socio-cultural practices, market integration, farm technology, environmental changes, wealth, income and consumption levels, access to basic services, gender factors, and the stages of peasant colonization and process of resettlement.

This literature along with the broader socio-economic research on peasant communities in Bolivia has also contributed greatly to our knowledge about "push" factors behind permanent and temporary highland peasant migration to the Chapare colonization zone for coca leaf production. Socio-economic factors, such as land degradation, demographic changes, declining terms of trade for highland crops, natural disasters, discriminatory national agricultural and other macro-economic policies, have accelerated highland migration to these coca growing zones in recent decades (Painter 1991a; Perez-Crespo 1991; Urioste 1989; Healy 1986 and 1992; Flores and Blanes 1983; Jones 1991). Sanabria's work has given a detailed view over time of families who migrate frequently to the Chapare from nearby highland communities combining a detailed perspective on economic behavior in both highland and lowland environments (Sanabria 1986 and 1992).

There also exists historical work on some aspects of Yungas coca leaf production during the colonial period and the nineteenth century patterns of production and consumption as well as several decades during the first half of the twentieth century (Saignes and Bourliaud 1992; Klein 1986; Canelas Orellana and Canelas Zannier 1982). This material has helped to shed light on coca's role as an important commercial crop in generating revenues for both Republican and colonial governments and harnessing the labor supply for Bolivia's key mining activities (Klein 1986; Pando, Mercado, Roth, Mamani, and Mancilla 1989; Parkerson 1989). Indeed, coca was Bolivia's main agricultural export during the nineteenth century and a critical source of state revenues during long intervals. Historical research shows how coca leaf farming has passed through various institutional arrangements. During the eighteenth and nineteenth centuries, the expanding hacienda system wrested the major share of coca leaf production from the style, the traditional Andean unit of social and political organization (Klein 1986). The hacienda dominance of coca production subsequently ended with the 1953 agrarian reform which carved up these landed estates into small plots under the ownership and management of a new peasant free-holder class.

Contemporary peasant studies also underscore the economic importance of coca in the local economy prior to the cocaine boom of the late 1970s. Field research in the mid-1970s in the Chapare demonstrated that coca leaf sales represented two-thirds of the farm family income (J. Weil 1980), and in the Yungas during the late 1960s and first half of the 1970s coca leaf production expanded at twice the rate of population increase (Albo 1978). Despite its continual economic importance, peasant farmers prefer to incorporate it into diversified production systems.

The literature also has touched on the environmental effects from coca leaf production (Blanes 1983). Coca is labor-intensive (Henkel 1982; M. Painter and Bedoya 1991; Parkerson 1989), which as a shrub is better for the ecology than annual crops grown in the tropical Chapare. The expansion for coca leaf production through accelerated migration has involved the destruction of rain forest areas which represents a loss in soil and biodiversity and causes unpredictable adverse environmental and climatic changes. The size of the coca-related rain forest destruction in Bolivia, however, relative to that caused by commercial logging operations, is still a matter of debate (J. Painter 1992).

Henkel's recent work, however, challenges this negative picture of coca leaf production in the Chapare. He points out that one hectare of coca can support a peasant family in the rain forest, whereas combinations of other tropical crops require much more land (Henkel 1993). His reasoning is that much less rain forest is destroyed as a result of coca than crops such as rice, bananas, and citrus. Also since the coca boom of the early 1980s increased peasant migration to the Chapare, the effect has been to reduce the utilization of marginal agricultural lands in the highlands for a net benefit to the environment (Henkel 1993). In the Yungas region, the environmental role of coca leaf production yields mixed results. Although the spread of coca production to marginal agricultural lands has been harmful to the environment (Debate Agrario 1988,37), the production technology of terrace construction on steep hillsides is effective soil conservation practice for high mountain valleys (Lieberman 1990).

During the first half of the 1980s, findings from the Chapare showed a broad distribution among the peasantry of impressive economic benefits (e.g., income and wages) suggesting that coca leaf expansion was remarkable for combining rapid agro-economic growth with social equity (Flores and Blanes 1983; Blanes 1983; Healy 1986; Pando, Mercado, Roth, Mamani, Mancilla 1989). However, more recent findings suggest that producer wealth differences are leading to a process of social differentiation similar to characteristic patterns of capitalist farmer expansion in Latin America. The basis for this social differentiation is a social strata of producer families, perhaps colonists who migrated to the Chapare in the 1960s, with coca holdings in production whose size ranges between 20 and 40 hectares (Rivera 1990b), an amount much higher than the averages found by DIRECO in recent surveys (Painter and Bedoya 1991).

Over time, it has become clear that the apparent transition underway from "peasant" to "farmer" (Blanes and Flores 1983; Blanes 1983) ended with the fall in coca leaf prices during the second half of the 1980s. Under this lower price structure, Chapare coca leaf production once again represented a variant of peasant "survival strategies" rather than profitable entrepreneurship.

Cocaine Industry Literature

There is a growing literature on the coca-cocaine industry and its role in the national economy. However, the main obstacle to accurate data and better analysis is the illicit nature of the business itself. As Painter points out, "Cocaine traffickers are yet to publish quarterly bulletins of statistics of their activities." Moreover, different methods for attaining raw data, differing yield figures, prices and conversion factors work to prevent agreement on values (J. Painter 1992; see also de Franco and Godoy 1992).

Despite the difficulties, Bolivian and foreign economists have engaged in data collection and analysis to determine the illegal sector's relative and absolute size, economic growth, impact on employment and other variables and multiplier effects in the rest of the economy (de Franco and Godoy 1992; Lee 1989; Sage 1987; Quiroga 1990; Franks 1991). Economists with the Bolivian government's national planning unit attempted to quantify the size of its coca-cocaine economy as a basis for making new foreign aid requests at the 1990 Cartagena Drug Summit.

In this literature, numerous discrepancies have appeared on the size of the industry in terms of percentage of GDP and export value, and impact on employment. However, recent efforts have attempted to sort out and explain the differences through careful examination of methodologies and assumptions behind the numbers and economic analysis (J. Painter 1992; de Franco and Godoy 1992). These recent publications help to piece together the outlines of an expanding coca-cocaine industry based upon the best available material (J. Painter 1992). It shows that 60,000 peasant families grow 52,000 hectares of coca leaf to supply some 80,000 tons of coca leaf for approximately 4,500 small, rustic coca paste laboratories managed by peasant and other commercial entrepreneurs (J. Painter 1992, 57). Under the control of some 30 to 40 Bolivian drug trafficking organizations, the paste then moves downstream to well-protected and hidden installations for processing into cocaine base and hydrochloride products (in both Bolivia and Colombia). Law enforcement agencies are able to interdict only 1 to 2 percent of these illicit products whose sales pump between $200 and $370 million into the Bolivian economy (J. Painter 1992, 59; Franks 1991). The illegal industry provides some 181,000 part- or full-time jobs to the relatively small and second poorest economies in our hemisphere.

However, in order to appreciate the magnitude of these figures within the Bolivian context, several other aspects must be taken into account. Note that the coca-cocaine economy's total number of jobholders represents about 10 percent of the Bolivian labor force and coca-cocaine earnings represent 12 percent of GNP, which is comparable to the manufacturing and trade sectors and surpassed only by the agricultural sector. Between 1986 and 1990, the total value of the diverse coca-cocaine products averaged 43 percent of Bolivian exports (J. Painter 1992, 58).

In recent years, the Bolivian traffickers themselves have tried to increase national drug earnings through vertically integrating the industry for greater hydrochloride production. In so doing, they have competed with Colombian organizations to gain more control over the final value established for their illicit South American products. They initially appeared to be successful in opening up more high-priced markets in Western Europe and in establishing increased vertical integration for about 25 percent of the industry's raw material. However, recent findings suggest that the Bolivian traffickers' early successes have been reversed and Colombian organizations have reasserted their dominant role in processing and trafficking Bolivian cocaine (J. Painter 1992).

Related political economy literature has provided a view of this economic expansion through the interplay of national political, economic, social, cultural, and historical factors (Henkel 1990; Sage 1987; Healy 1986; Lee 1989; Pando, Mercade, Roth, Mamani, Mancilla 1989; Flores and Blanes 1983; J. Painter 1992; Malamud-Gotti 1992; Oporto 1989). These works have presented a kind of national map of the industry by indicating its spatial distribution and its social division of labor.

The literature shows, for example, that the spatial organization of production and trafficking has changed from its original geographic locations of the 1970s and early 1980s. During the 1980s, a shift occurred to move the first stages of the industry (coca paste production) from the commercial farmers of the Norte de Santa Cruz area to the Chapare's peasant producers which produced in smaller, less easily detected installations. In a parallel way, the industry moved its paste-making operations from eastern areas to the Yungas coca growing provinces. However, in the Yungas area, which is easier to police than the Chapare, the industry in the early 1990s relocated its paste production operations back to remote areas of eastern Bolivia (Leons 1993).

The Bolivian drug literature has been informative about production infrastructure, transportation arteries, and a labor force composition incorporating members from the top to the bottom of society's social pyramid (Henkel 1990; Lee 1989; Malamud-Gotti 1992; Healy 1986; Pando, Mercado, Roth, Mamani, and Mancilla 1989; Franks 1991; Aguilo 1988). Some of this literature also informs about the sources of supply, smuggling methods, and transport routes of precursor chemicals (i.e., kerosene, sodium bicarbonate, ether).

The industry also has floating labor in the Chapare comprising mostly young migrants from thousands of rural mountain communities and marginal urban occupation in search of income-earning opportunities (Jones 1991; Healy 1986). Many from this population belong to the group of "pisadores" or "pisacocas" (coca leaf stompers), which during the first half of the 1980s was one of the fastest growing occupational categories in Bolivia.

However, the captains of the industry, the drug traffickers themselves, perhaps for obvious reasons, have been given much less scrutiny by social scientists than peasant producers. Their wealth, earnings, criminal organizations, and economic behavior are only dimly perceived in the existing drug literature. The main sources of data for social researchers are from the DEA, the U.S. State Department, and Bolivian and international newspaper accounts related to antinarcotics operations and political scandals.

Some of the most imformative works on the identities and social backgrounds of the traffickers were published over a decade ago (Bascope 1979; LAB-Tepala 1982), which show the participation of members of the agricultural, ranching, political, and military elite from the Beni and Santa Cruz regions. Not surprisingly, recently published testimonies of traffickers surfaced in response to the Bolivian "repentance" policy appear to be self-serving and unreliable sources about the industry's operations (Irusta 1992).

James Painter presents an updated picture on Bolivian traffickers and their organizations from the fragmentary ad hoc information available. He uses the DEA and Bolivian government sources to show the industry's leaders managing some 30 to 40 drug trafficking organizations in the country, 13 of which control 75 to 80 percent of the total volume of trafficking (J. Painter 1992). Unlike the "cartel style" organizations of Colombia, this top echelon of the Bolivian drug trade hierarchy comprises tightly knit, clan-like family units from the Santa Cruz and Beni regions (Painter 1992; Gamarra 1992). Buyers from the trafficking organizations even conduct an annual meeting to establish prices in Bolivia for the coca leaf and coca paste (J. Painter 1992).

Another area of inquiry about the cocaine industry refers to the economic networks for product distribution within the drug trafficking chain. These smuggling networks involve both the blackmarket activities in the supply of precursor chemicals and other materials to the coca paste and cocaine production refining areas and also the transportation and distribution of cocaine for national and international trafficking (Aguilo 1988; Malamud-Gotti 1992; Healy 1986).

The literature describes, for example, groups such as "zepes," "boleros," and "mulas" for their role in transportation of coca, coca paste, and cocaine. It also gives a glimpse of how drug traffickers from the Santa Cruz and Beni regions organize their buying operations with their own agents and maintain a communications network to facilitate and protect their operations in the Chapare (Malamud-Gotti 1992, 14).

By contrast, there is surprisingly little in-depth research in recent years about the backward and forward linkages of the coca-cocaine economy with business and tertiary sectors both regionally and nationally (an exception is the work of de Franco and Godoy 1992). The transport, entertainment, and construction industries and mushrooming informal sectors would be logical places for examining the drug economy's multiplier effects (Henkel 1990; de Franco and Godoy 1992). Despite the apparent large influx of automobiles and electro-domestic items into the country, there has been no systematic, imaginative research on the dollar-laundering activities for importing or smuggling goods.

The Bolivian drug literature also lacks solid, extensive studies about the market size for the consumption of pitillos (cocaine mixed with tobacco) and other cocaine products as a result of the industry's expansion in Bolivia (Painter 1992). The few studies which have been done show a very small (1 to 2 percent) but growing market of national consumers (J. Painter 1992).

What might the general balance sheet of gains and losses be from Bolivia's largest agro-industry for the country's economic development? Various authors have shown that in terms of jobs, income, and foreign exchange, perhaps the impact is unparalleled in its importance for a Third World economy (Healy 1986 and 1988; Henkel 1987; Lee 1989; J. Painter 1992). In addition, the coca-cocaine industry has had a welfare function by becoming a social cushion for peasant families suffering from negative effects of hyper-inflation and a structural adjustment program along with the natural disasters of drought, floods, and frost in the mountain areas. Henkel argues that coca has been kind to the rain forest in allowing a peasant family to survive on one hectare of production and in siphoning away peasant producers from marginal highland areas (Henkel 1993). The coca-cocaine dollars also have helped to stabilize Bolivia's economy after periods of severe economic crisis (J. Painter 1992). Moreover, the laundering of drug dollars has brought economic benefits to Bolivian consumers by lowering prices for various imported products (Henkel 1990).

On the other side of the ledger, there are distortionary effects known as the "Dutch disease," (de Franco and Godoy 1992) such as the overvalued exchange rate that stimulates imports and damages national light industry and undermines exports which are a key part of the structural adjustment strategy (J. Painter 1992). The negative environmental impact in the Chapare can be seen from the amount of rain forest destroyed, increased use of pesticides, and the dumping of precursor chemicals into rivers and streams which kills various species and contaminates water supplies.

The impact of the industry on Bolivian food production at first appeared to have been negative during the boom years of the first half of the 1980s (Healy 1986, Tullis 1987), and yet more recently analysts have argued that increased coca producer income has led to a higher demand for food, thereby cancelling out the negative effects of reduction of acreage for food (de Franco and Godoy 1992). The little research available on the topic of drug trafficker investments has indicated that they are more interested in luxury consumption with their profits than productive investments (J. Painter 1992) and that significant capital investments tend to go for speculative purposes (Blanes 1989).

The literature also makes clear that the industry in terms of benefits to peasants and other low-income groups enjoyed a boom period during the first half of the 1980s and then went into decline with a fall in coca leaf and paste prices. This economic change also was manifest in the declining wage levels for the industry's labor groups, such as "pisadores" and farm workers, and consequently reduced migration. Peasant coca growers during the earlier boom period were netting from a production hectare of the leaf $7,000 to $8,000, while in the latter period earnings fell to between $1,000 and $1,500.

Even though short-run economic benefits accrue to the peasant sector, Bolivian analysts such as Roberto Laserna have called attention to Bolivia's inability to take advantage of this impressive income flow into the Chapare for purposes of broad-based, lasting, social and economic development (ILDIS, CERES 1990, 55).

The Literature on the Role of the State in Relation to Coca-Cocaine Issues

Studies on the coca-cocaine issues in Bolivia focus on the role of the state in a variety of ways. The drug literature demonstrates the multiple roles of the state in law enforcement and economic development and as a political actor which responds to the actions of various interest groups in Bolivian society and abroad. The role of the state in relation to the coca-cocaine issue signifies complex, conflict-ridden political and social relationships in a variety of changing scenarios. This political research invariably enters into the international area to address the impact of U.S. counternarcotics policy in Bolivia.

This literature commonly depicts the Bolivian state as a highly dependent actor, both politically and economically, especially with respect to the U.S. government (Gamarra 1991; J. Painter 1992; Barrios 1992; Canelas Orellena and Canelas Zannier 1982). According to this perspective on U.S. relations and foreign policy, a number of measures have been imposed on Bolivia which have threatened its national sovereignty and democracy. The most serious threat has been the attempts documented in the literature to "militarize" the drug war by involving the Bolivian army, the trainers from U.S. Special Forces units and other new programs (Gamarra 1991; Malamud-Gotti 1992; Barrios 1992; WOLA 1990; Youngers 1991). The "militarization" of drug trafficking itself came to the fore under the regime of General Garcia Mesa in 1981 (Dunkerley 1984; Canelas Orellana and Canelas Zannier 1982), and now is appearing under another form.

However, threats to the rights of innocent citizens through excessive antinarcotics law enforcement are not new phenomena in Bolivia's drug war. Even prior to the "militarization" issue, the Unidad Movil de Patrullaje Rural (UMOPAR), the specialized antidrug police force, had created a repressive environment in the Chapare leading to numerous abuses of civil liberties among peasant coca producers and a corresponding negative image of the associated DEA agents who supervise them (Healy 1986; Lee 1989; Rasnake and M. Painter 1989; Malamud-Gotti 1992; J. Painter 1992). This scattered picture of excessive military and police activities suggests that the stated U.S. policy objectives of fostering democracy and curbing drug trafficking are working at cross-purposes. However, the biggest paradox for antinarcotics policy is that while objectives are not being met and become less attainable for the next round, the implementation leaves new social and political problems in its wake (Malamud-Gotti 1992).

The existing literature on the role of the state has been very informative and consistent in its depiction of the poor coordination between U.S. and Bolivian agencies, bureaucratic infighting within agencies of both countries, extensive corruption in law enforcement and military units, and linkages between political actors and the cocaine industry (Gamarra 1991; Malamud-Gotti 1992; Lee 1982; J. Painter 1992).

The U.S. government has set up various signposts of progress — coca hectares eradicated, maceration pits and seedling nurseries destroyed, light planes confiscated, the passage of tough antinarcotics laws, and police drug seizures — to measure the Bolivian state's performance in waging the drug war. The "certification process," which involves the withdrawal of foreign aid for unsatisfactory Bolivian government performance in coca leaf production, has been a form of public chastisement and a constant source of tension between the two unequal partners. Yet within this policy scenario, gains are both elusive and illusory, seldom true to their surface meaning (Malamud-Gotti 1992).

For example, the record-setting coca leaf eradication in the Chapare of 1990 is a case in point. On the surface, it appeared that the $2,000 per hectare compensation was an effective reward for the coca growers and led to new milestones in crop eradication figures. However, closer examination shows that many peasants multiplied this amount by depositing their payments in FINSA, a savings bank in Cochabamba, which buoyed by its own narco dollars provided exorbitantly high interest earnings (J. Painter 1992). When the financial intermediary collapsed, many peasant farmers turned their backs on the crop eradication programs.

Similarly, research findings suggest that such crop eradication efforts inadvertently may be facilitating the elimination of old coca bushes at the end of their production cycle or opening new coca leaf fields (Sanabria 1992; Lee 1989; Institute of the Americas 1991). In this case, an ostensible coca eradication worked to subsidize the replacement of old fields with new ones, thereby expanding rather than reducing production in the Chapare.

This literature shows how the major policy initiative in the region of the late 1980s, the "Andean strategy," attempted to escalate drug war efforts against strong opposition from the media, political parties, and unions (Gamarra 1988-1989 and 1991; Youngers 1989). The researchers have documented the mostly negative and counterproductive effects of this strategy and challenge official claims of success for other activities such as Operation Blast Furnace, Operation Snowcap, the raids on isolated towns of the Beni serving as havens for the traffickers, and the DEA's work on the front lines of the drug war. The attempts to reform the court system to deal with the increased drug trade also appear to be counterproductive and contradictory (Salas 1992).

Critical Bolivian accounts and analysis of the combined U.S.-Bolivian drug policy impact and related political and social conflicts also exist for the late 1970s and early 1980s (Canelas Orelana and Canelas Zannier 1982) and for the government of the Unidad Democratica Popular (1982-1985) period (*Narcotrafico y Politica* 1985).

Drug-related research has also shown the internal political pressures on the state to resist the antinarcotics policies advocated by the U.S. government. One of the most outspoken and visible opposition groups has been the peasant sindicato federations from the Chapare which relentlessly have defended the coca leaf grower interests. The sindicato federations have achieved considerable political mobilizations and have elicited a number of concessions by means of negotiated agreements with the state (Healy 1988 and 1990).

The recent change in state policy from the "coca por desarrollo" thesis to promoting the export of "mate de coca" and other coca leaf derivatives through "industrialization" suggests that the sindicato federations have scored points in their campaigns to revalorize the coca leaf and promote a concept of "coca con desarrollo" (Comite Civico 1988).

However, in light of this political pressure and the mentioned economic benefits from this illegal industry, the state's "political will" to pursue vigorously the antinarcotics goals has been called into question (Andreas, Betram, Blackman, Sharpe 1991-1992; J. Painter 1992). Drug traffickers have continued to demonstrate their influence over the state from the national level down to the local arenas during the past decade even in the face of escalating law enforcement activity.

Another place where one might question the state's political will is in the Chapare's so-called "alternative development programs" whose ineffective implementation has been stopped and started by USAID and the Bolivian Ministry of Agriculture and Peasant Affairs at various times since the late 1970s. The increasing impoverishment of peasant households over the past decade in both highland and lowland rural communities itself raises questions about the state and its foreign aid backers' social commitment to the peasant sector. The foreign resources and political pressures on the state to increase peasant development in the Chapare have not enabled it to overcome its characteristic antipeasant bias in national agricultural policy. This is true, in part, because of the inherent conflict between peasant-based agricultural development programs and structural adjustment policies (Healy 1993).

Explanations in the drug literature for their failure in rural development in the Chapare include the relatively low external financing (J. Painter 1992), USAID and state agencies' institutional foibles and rivalries (M. Painter and Rasnake 1989), narrow political and personal interests (Jones 1991), the lack of peasant farmer participation in project decision making and national policy (Healy 1993), negative impact on peasant agriculture from structural adjust-ment programs (Healy 1993; J. Painter 1992), and the futility of competing with illicit crops in implementing rural development programs (Lee 1989). Henkel also suggests — at least, implicitly — that alternative development programs will fail because of the limited capacity of the rain forest to absorb peasant production systems with alternative crops (Henkel 1993).

There also have been important policy and development program debates by Bolivian independent analysts and government officials in relation to coca reduction and alternative development in both the Yungas and Chapare (Debate Agrario 1987 and 1988; ILDIS, CERES 1990a).

Despite the poor record of state-led rural development for peasant populations, the literature does suggest that progress on this front is possible through a different approach to rural development based upon grass roots participation and consensus together with higher levels of financing (Healy 1993; J. Painter 1992). The rural development framework must incorporate both the highland Cochabamba Valleys and the Chapare, given the latter's limited carrying capacity and related rural development potential as a rain forest zone. Available financial and economic resources could be diverted from many counterproductive law enforcement activities and combined with other new investments for Bolivia's peasant sector to shape a genuine alternative development path.

References

Albo, Xavier. 1978. "El Mundo de Coca en Coripata, Bolivia." *American Indigena*, Vol. 38, #4, October-December.

Andreas, Peter, Eva Betram, and Kenneth Sharpe Blachman. 1991-1992. "Dead End Drug Wars," *Foreign Policy*, Number 85, Winter.

Barrios, Moron Raul. 1992. "La Guerra Contra Las Drogas En Bolivia: Algunas Consecuencias Politicas." Paper presented at the XVII International Congress of the Latin American Studies Association (LASA), Los Angeles.

Blanes, Jose. 1983. *De Los Valles al Chapare, Estrategies Familiares En Un Contexto de Cambios*. Cochabamba: CERES.

Canelas Orellana, Amado, and Juan Carlos Canelas Zannier. 1982. *Bolivia: Coca Cocaina*. Cochabamba: Los Amigos del Libro.

Caro Deborah, Riordan, and Melissa Cable. 1992. *The Cochabamba Rural Household Survey: Preliminary Findings*. Washington, D.C.: Genesys Lactech.

Caro Deborah, Riordan, and Melissa Cable. 1989. "Cocaine, Informality and the Urban Economy in La Paz, Bolivia." In *The Informal Economy: Studies in Advanced and Less Developed Countries*. eds. Manuel Castells Portes and Laura Benton. Baltimore: The Johns Hopkins University Press.

Carter, William. 1983. *Ensayos Cientificos Sobre La Coca*. La Paz: Editorial Juventud.

Carter, William, and Mauricio Mamani. 1978. "Patrones Del Uso de la Coca en Bolivia." *America Indigena*, Vol. XXXVIII, No. 4.

CEDIB. 1988. "Todo Sobre la Coca Cocaine." *Realidad Nacional*. Cochabamba: Centro de Documentacion Informacion y Biblioteca.

CIDRE. 1990. *Monografia del Tropico: Departamento de Cochabamba*. Cochabamba.

Comite Civico Pro Cochabamba. 1988. *Coca, Foro Nacional Sobre La Problematica Coca-Cocaina*. Cochabamba.

Debate Agrario. 1988. *La Campesina y Cultivo de la Coca*. La Paz: Edobal.

de Franco, Mario, and Ricardo Godoy. 1992. "The Economic Consequences of Cocaine Production in Bolivia: Historical, Loca and Macroeconomic Perspectives." *Journal of Latin American Studies*, 24, Great Britain.

Dunkerley, James. 1984. *Rebellion in the Veins*. London: Verso.

Flores, Gonzalo, and Jose Blanes. 1983. *Donde Va El Chapare*. Cochabamba: CERES.

Franks, Jeffrey. 1991. "La Economica de la Coca en Bolivia: Plaga o Salvacion." Muller & Asociadados Informe Confidencial No. 64. La Paz.

Gamarra, Eduardo. 1988-1989. "The United States, the 'War on Drugs' and Bolivian Democracy," *Latin American and Caribbean Contemporary Record*, Vol. 8. New York: Holmes and Meier.

Gamarra, Eduardo. 1992. "U.S. Military Assistance, the Militarization of the War on Drugs, and the Prospects for the Consolidation of Democracy in Bolivia." Presented at the XVI Congress of the Latin American Studies Association, Washington, D.C.

Gill, Lesley. 1987. *Peasants, Entrepreneurs, and Social Change: Frontier Development in Lowland Bolivia.* Boulder, Colo.: Westview Press.

Healy, Kevin. 1986. "The Boom Within the Crisis: Some Recent Effects of Foreign Cocaine Markets on Bolivian Rural Society and Economy." In *Coca and Cocaine, Effects on People and Policy in Latin America,* eds. Deborah Pacini and Christine Franquemont. Cambridge, Mass.: Cultural Survival Report 23.

Healy, Kevin. 1988a. "Coca, the State, and the Peasantry in Bolivia, 1982-1988." *Journal of Interamerican Studies and World Affairs,* Vol. 30, No. 2-3(Spring).

Healy, Kevin. 1988b. "Bolivia and Cocaine: A Developing Country's Dilemmas." *British Journal of Addiction,* 83.

Healy, Kevin. 1991. "Political Ascent of Bolivia's Coca Leaf Producers." *Journal of Interamerican Studies and World Affairs,* Vol. 33, No. 1(Spring).

Healy, Kevin. Forthcoming. "Public Policies in Conflict: Structural Adjustment and Alternative Development for Crop Reduction.' In *Privatization Amidst Poverty: Contemporary Challenges in Latin American Political Economy,* ed. Jorge A. Lawton. Coral Gables, Fla.: North-South Center, University of Miami.

Healy, Kevin. 1994. "The Role of Economic Development: A Focus on Peasant Development Prospects in Peru and Bolivia." In *Drugs and Foreign Policy: A Criticall Review,* ed. Raphael Perl. Boulder, Colo.: Westview Press.

Henkel, Ray. 1988. "The Bolivian Cocaine Industry." *Studies in Third World Societies,* 37:53-81.

Henkel, Ray. 1982. "The Move to the Oriente: Colonization and Environmental Impact." In *Modern Day Bolivia: Legacy of the Revolution and Prospects for the Future,* ed. J.R. Ladman. Tempe: Arizona State University Press.

Henkel, Ray. 1990. "The Cocaine Problem." Unpublished mimeo. Tempe: Arizona State University.

Henkel, Ray. 1993. "Environment and Cocaine in Chapare." Paper presented at the Symposium at the New York Botanical Garden, June.

Henman, Anthony. 1985. "Cocaine Futures." In *Big Deal, the Politics of the Illicit Drug Business.* London: Pluto Press.

ILDIS and CERES. 1990. *Debate Regional, El Chapare Actual, Sindicatos, ONG's en la Region.* Cochabamba: ILDIS and CERES.

Institute of the Americas. 1991. *Seizing Opportunities: Report of the Inter-American Commission on Drug Policy.* San Diego, Calif.: Centre for Iberian and Latin American Studies, University of California.

Irusta, Gerardo. 1992. *Narcotrafico: Hablan Los Arrepentidos, Personajes y Hechos Reales.* La Paz.

Jones, James C. 1991. "Farmer Perspectives on the Economics and Sociology of Coca Production in the Chapare." Institute for Development Anthropology Working Paper No. 77.

Jordan Pando, Roberto, Jose Mercado Ortiz, Eric Roth, Mauricio Mamani, and Ivan Mancilla Arze Quiroga. "Coca, Cocaismo y Cocainismo en Bolivia." In *La Coca..Tradicion, Rito, Identidad.* Mexico: Instituto Indigenista Interamericano.

Larsen, Brooke. 1989. *Colonialism and Agrarian Transformation.* Princeton, N.J.: Princeton University Press.

Lee, Rensselaer. 1989. *The White Labyrinth, Cocaine and Political Power*. London: Transaction Publishers.

Leons, Madeline Barbara. 1992. "After the boom: Adaptation to Decline in Coca Prices and Processing in the Bolivian Yungas." Presented at the Latin American Studies Association Meetings, Los Angeles.

Leons, Madeline Barbara. 1993. "Risk and Opportunity in the Coca/Cocaine Economy of the Yungas." *Journal of Latin American Studies*, Vol. 25, 121-157.

Lieberman, Max et al. 1990. *Evaluacion Ecologica del Cultivo de la Coca e los Yungas de La Paz, Estudio del Impacto Ambiental*. La Paz: CEED-LIDEMA.

MacDonald, Scott B. 1988. *Dancing on a Volcano: The Latin American Drug Trade*. New York: Praeger.

Malamud-Gotti, Jaime. 1992. *Smoke and Mirrors, The Paradox of the Drug Wars*. San Francisco: Westview Press.

Narcotrafico y Politica II, Bolivia 1982-85. 1985. Cochabamba. (no author cited)

Oporto, Henry Castro. 1989. "Bolivia: El Complejo Coca Cocaina." In *Coca, Cocaina y Narcotrafico*, ed. Diego Sayan. Lima: Comision Andina de Juristas.

Painter, James. 1992. *Bolivia and Coca: A Study in Dependency*. Geneva: United Nations Research Institute for Social Development (UNRISD).

Painter, Michael. 1991a. "Upland-Lowland Production Linkages and Land Degradation in Bolivia." Institute for Development Anthropology, IDA Working Paper No. 81.

Painter, Michael. 1991b. "Cocaine Export Policy and Development Policy." *Bulletin of the Institute for Development Anthropology*, Vol. 9, No. 1(Spring).

Painter, Michael, and Eduardo Bedoya. 1991. "Socio-Economic Issues in Agricultural Settlement and Production in Bolivia's Chapare Region." Institute for Development Anthropology, IDA Working Paper No. 70.

Painter, Michael. 1990. "Institutional Analysis of the Chapare Regional Development Project (CRDP)." Institute for Development Anthropology, IDA Working Paper.

Parkerson, P.T. 1989. "Neither Green Gold nor the Devil's Leaf: Coca Farming in Bolivia." In *State, Capital and Rural Society: Anthropolitical Perspectives on Political Economy in Mexico and the Andes*, eds. B.S. Orlove, M.W. Foley, and T.F. Love. Boulder, Colo.: Westview Press.

Perez-Crespo, Carlos. 1991. "Why Do People Migrate? Internal Migration and the Pattern of Capital Accumulation in Bolivia." Institute for Development Anthropology, IDA Working Paper No. 74.

Rasnake, Roger, and Michael Painter. 1989. "Rural Development and Crop Substitution in Bolivia: USAID and the Chapare Regional Development Project." Institute for Development Anthropology, IDA Working Paper No. 45.

Quiroga, Jose Antonio. 1990a. *Cultivo de Coca y Trafico de Cocaina*. La Paz: CEDLA.

Quiroga, Jose Antonio. 1990b. *Coca/Cocaina, Una Vision Boliviana*. La Paz: AIPE-PROCOM/CEDIA/CID.

Rivera, Alberto. 1990a. *El Chapare Actual: Sindicatos y ONG's En La Region*. Cochabamba: ILDIS, CERES.

Rivera, Alberto. 1990b. *Diagnostico Socio-economico de la Poblacion del Chapare.* Cochabamba: PDAR (Programa de Desarrollo Alternativo Regional).

Roth, Erick, and Raul Bohrt. 1987. *Actitudes de la Poplacion La Paz hacia la Produccion y Consumo de la Hoja de Coca.* La Paz: Centro Interdisciplinario de Estudios Comunitarios.

Sage, Colin. 1987. "The Cocaine Economy in Bolivia: Its Development and Current Importance." *Corruption and Reform,* 2:99-109, Netherlands.

Salas, Luis. 1992. "The Impact of the Drug War on the Administration of Justice in Bolivia." Paper presented at the State of the Art Conference on Drug Trafficking Research, Miami, Fla.

Sanabria, Harry. 1986. "Coca, Migration, and Social Differentiation in the Bolivian Lowlands." In *Drugs in Latin America,* ed. Edmundo Morales. Studies in Third World Societies Publication No. 37. Williamsburg, Va.: Dept. of Anthropology, College of William and Mary.

Sanabria, Harry. 1992. "Holding Their Ground: Crop Eradication, Repression, and Peasant Rersistance in the Chapare of Bolivia." Presented in the XVII International Congress of the Latin American Studies Association, Los Angeles.

Sanabria, Harry. Forthcoming. *The Coca Boom and Rural Social Change in Bolivia.* Ann Arbor: University of Michigan Press.

Stearman, Alynn MacLean. 1985. *Camba and Kolla, Migration and Development in Santa Cruz, Bolivia.* Orlando: University of Central Florida Press.

Tullis, Lamond. 1987. "Cocaine and Food: Likely Effects of a Burgeoning Transnational Industry on Food Production in Bolivia and Peru." In *Pursuing Food Security: Strategies and Obstacles in Africa, Asia, Latin America and the Middle East,* eds. Lamond Tullis and Ladd Holist. Boulder, Colo.: Lynne Reinner.

Weil, Connie. 1989. "Differential Economic Success Among Spontaneous Colonists in the Chapare, Bolivia." In *The Human Ecology of Tropical Land Settlement in Latin America,* eds. Deborah Schuman and William Partridge. Boulder, Colo.: Westview.

Weil, Jim. 1980. "Coca and Tropical Colonization: The Adaptiveness of a Cash Crop." *Central Issues in Anthropology,* 2(1).

Weil, Jim. 1986. "Cooperative Labor as an Adaptive Strategy Among Homesteaders in a Tropical Colonization Zone: Chapare, Bolivia." In *The Human Ecology of Tropical Land Settlement in Latin America,* eds. Deborah Schuman and William Partridge. Boulder, Colo.: Westview.

Weil, Jim. 1990. "Through a Darkening Glass: Fifteen Years of Research Concerning the Lives of Bolivian Coca Cultivators" Presented at the American Anthropological Association annual meeting, New Orleans.

WOLA. 1991. *Clear and Present Dangers: The U.S. Military and the War on Drugs in the Andes.* Washington, D.C.: Washington Office on Latin America (WOLA).

Youngers, Coletta. 1991. "A Fundamentally Flawed Strategy: U.S. War on Drugs in Bolivia." In the series Issues in International Drug Policy, Issue Brief No. 4, Washington Office on Latin America, September 18.

Chapter Thirteen

U.S.-Bolivia Counternarcotics Efforts During the Paz Zamora Administration: 1989-1992

Eduardo A. Gamarra

Introduction

B olivia's importance as a major producer of coca leaves and as the world's second largest exporter of cocaine base and hydrochloride has produced few works on the making of Bolivian counternarcotics foreign policy. Only a select number of books focus exclusively on U.S.-Bolivia relations.[1] For the most part, analyses of Bolivian counternarcotics policy have been limited to loose collections of press accounts, which document only significant events or crises that make Bolivia newsworthy, and chapters in edited books and conference papers.[2]

Rather than summarizing the findings of these works, this chapter analyzes counternarcotics policies as the principal component of U.S.-Bolivia relations during the government of Jaime Paz Zamora. These preliminary notes present a descriptive analysis of the forces, actors, and processes which have shaped the foreign policy of the government of Jaime Paz Zamora (1989-1992).

Bolivian counternarcotics policy is a reflection of external forces and pressures, especially from the United States. In this chapter I argue that Bolivia's extreme dependence, the magnitude of its economic crisis in the mid-1980s, and the difficulties of consolidating a democratic government are at the heart of its vulnerability to external pressures.

The context which gave rise to U.S. counternarcotics policies has been analyzed in detail elsewhere.[3] With the declaration by President Ronald Reagan in 1986 that drug trafficking constituted a threat to U.S. national security, counternarcotics policies became the most significant aspect of U.S. policy toward the Andean ridge. Owing largely to domestic factors, such as rising consumption, crime, and drug-related deaths, Washington policy makers demanded effective and prompt solutions to drug trafficking. Democrats and Republicans alike called for harsher sentences, greater interdiction efforts, and, to a lesser extent, more prevention programs.[4]

The end of the Cold War, which minimized the possibility of a nuclear confrontation, paradoxically boosted the rationale for a "drug war" in the Andes. Books like Tom Clancy's *Clear and Present Danger* and sensationalistic accounts in the U.S. media gave credence to the belief that Andean drug lords indeed constituted a threat to U.S. national security.

George Bush's administration came into office and presided over a continuation of the greatest escalation in counternarcotics policies in history. Within eight months of his inauguration, Bush's counternarcotics team headed by the newly created office of the "Drug Czar" had crafted a so-called Andean strategy. Four months later and in the name of furthering the antidrug cause, U.S. troops invaded Panama. Antidrug zealots in Congress and in the administration continued to push each other in the direction of harsher policies aimed at ending the flow of cocaine from the Andes.[5]

This context explains the magnitude of U.S. pressure on the Andean countries to impose more stringent counternarcotics measures. As a result, Bolivian policy makers had little autonomy in foreign policy decision making. Autonomous decisions were limited by parameters imposed by an international environment which declared the manufacturing of drugs and the growing of coca a threat to the national security of nations throughout the Americas. This does not mean that Bolivian policy makers were incapable of crafting relatively autonomous foreign and domestic counternarcotics policies; however, their decisions were demarcated by rigid external parameters which gave them little room for negotiation and compromise.

While successive Bolivian governments faced international pressures, they also faced intense domestic demands from myriad social forces and actors affected not only by counternarcotics policies but also by a troubled transition to democratic governance in the context of the country's gravest economic crisis in history. The presence of active social groups, which attempt to influence the course of policy, led some analysts to conclude that the major factors leading to the formation policies are "intermestic," i.e., a combination of international and domestic pressures and an interaction of state and international and domestic non-state actors. While this concept is useful as an analytical tool, it assumes equality in bargaining positions among governments and gives excessive weight to the "pluralistic" character of the political process in Bolivia and the rest of Latin America.[6]

Bolivia's weak, elected civilian governments of the 1980s and early 1990s were trapped not only by external demands for greater efficiency in fighting drug lords and reducing the size of coca crops but also by intense domestic pressures. Organized labor, political institutions, such as parties and legislatures, peasant coca growers unions, and regional organizations which faced severe economic hardship stemming from both reduced profits from the drug industry and harsh austerity measures imposed by democratic governments rallied against government programs.

Bolivian governments were only able to postpone or defuse conflictive situations with particular social groups. Although Bolivian governments attempted the same strategy with U.S. demands, they were less successful. As a result, Bolivian governments responded first to U.S. and other international pressures and bypassed, repressed, or simply ignored domestic groups.

Domestic actors and forces were often neglected even on issues which directly affected them, as the battle for militarization of the drug war discussed in this chapter illustrates. Once policies were in place, the Bolivian government faced the task of negotiating separate deals with each social group. Agreements reached with these groups, in turn, were respected only to the extent that they did not conflict with external demands. This has been the general pattern of foreign policy making during the Paz Zamora government.

Joint U.S.-Bolivia counternarcotics policies have also been plagued by numerous problems and contradictions, such as the lack of coordination between U.S. and Bolivian agencies, bureaucratic infighting within agencies of both governments, pervasive corruption in law enforcement and military units, and linkages between political actors and the cocaine industry.[7]

The narrative presented below ratifies and highlights previous conclusions regarding the overall futility of interdiction and repressive strategies but also notes the very serious problems of focusing solely on alternative development strategies. This chapter is divided into two broad sections. Section one provides a brief background of joint U.S.-Bolivia counternarcotics policies. The second section traces the ups and downs of U.S.-Bolivian relations during the Paz Zamora government noting a pattern of recurrent progress and failure, advancement and retreat.

Section One

U.S. Policy and Bolivian Responses in the 1980s

When Jaime Paz Zamora took office in August 1989, he faced the difficult task of continuing the economic policies of Victor Paz Estenssoro whose government had been credited with ending hyperinflation in 1985 and renewing a process of growth after an entire decade of economic decline. Moreover, Paz Estenssoro established a pattern of governance which enabled his government to bring under control domestic political and social unrest resulting from the imposition of austerity measures.[8] This strategy consisted primarily of the formation of a political pact, dubbed Pacto por la Democracia, between the ruling Movimiento Nacionalista Revolucionario (MNR) and Accion Democratica y Nacionalista (ADN), the principal opposition party headed by General Hugo Banzer Suarez. By virtue of this pact, the

government of Paz Estenssoro controlled the National Congress and organized labor and pressed ahead with most of its policy initiatives, including
counternarcotics strategies.

The Paz Estenssoro administration was responsible for the implementation of a set of counternarcotics policies which, during Operation Blast
Furnace (July-November 1986), included the use of U.S. military troops. A
landmark bilateral agreement signed in February 1987 produced even greater
Bolivian reliance on U.S. assistance and ushered in a period of significant U.S.
military presence, with and without the knowledge and/or congressional
authorization. The signing of two annexes to the agreement (1988 and 1989)
tied U.S. assistance to progress on crop substitution and legitimized the
Bolivian government's alternative development proposal. Simultaneously,
however, under extensive U.S. pressure, the Paz Estenssoro government
signed Law 1008, a more stringent version of zero tolerance ordinances in use
throughout the United States.

Beginning in 1987 under the name Operation Snow Cap, DEA officers
became directly involved in drug seizures and arrests throughout Bolivia. U.S.
military personnel engaged in "good will" civic action programs tied to
counternarcotics throughout Bolivia; the Pact for Democracy allowed the
government to secure congressional approval for the arrival of U.S. troops to
work on airports and other facilities. U.S. border patrol members guarded
roads into and out of the Bolivian Yungas and Chapare Valleys. Members of
the U.S. Navy Seals and Coast Guard officers trained their Bolivian counterparts in Bolivia's vast network of Amazon tributaries. Finally, the elite rural
counternarcotics police (UMOPAR) received extensive U.S. special forces
training, and the Bolivian navy and air force became engaged in support
activities throughout the Beni department.[9] By any measure, this was the
largest buildup of counternarcotics efforts in Bolivian history.

Between 1985 and 1989, the Paz Estenssoro government convinced two
successive Republican administrations of its commitment to fighting drugs.
Although it faced a constant uphill battle with the U.S. Congress, in the end,
even the most recalcitrant U.S. legislators were convinced that Bolivia's
octogenarian president, who had presided over a remarkable transformation of
the Bolivian economy, would press ahead with U.S. initiatives. In retrospect, it
is evident that the MNR government ushered in policies which would inevitably
increase U.S. and Bolivian military presence in counternarcotics policies.

Like Blast Furnace, Snow Cap yielded few long-term results. A few drug
lords were captured, tons of cocaine were seized, and coca crops were
eradicated. Yet cocaine continued to flow out of Bolivia as the Andean country
became the world's second producer of cocaine hydrochloride. Moreover,
corruption eroded the integrity of all institutions charged with fighting the drug
war, especially UMOPAR. The usual accusations of connections by leading
politicians to the drug trade surfaced daily.[10] The policy also created inter- and

intra-bureaucratic feuding as competition escalated between branches of the police and the armed forces to enter into the drug war. On the U.S. side, similar bureaucratic "turf" disputes among the numerous agencies involved in Bolivia undermined any and all counternarcotics efforts.[11]

Washington stressed positive outcomes despite the obvious signs of failure; for the United States the Paz Estenssoro government was, after all, a showcase of sound economic policies and democratic principles. Pushing ahead too quickly on counternarcotics matters could undermine the progress made in terms of bilateral agreements but could also threaten the progress on economic reform. When Paz Estenssoro left office in August 1989, the New Economic Policy was still considered one of the most significant structural reform programs in Latin America.

Section Two

Touch and Feel: Paz Zamora and the Activist Ambassador

Paz Zamora and the MIR campaigned in the 1989 elections on a promise of restoring some national dignity and sovereignty to Bolivia's counternarcotics efforts. As the narrative below will illustrate, this objective was never achieved. To the contrary, Bolivia's counternarcotics strategy now lacks any local input in either design or implementation. While much of this can be attributed to the failure of the Paz Zamora government to negotiate, this was largely a result of the pattern of bilateral counternarcotics relations already underway since 1985.

Upon his inauguration on August 6, 1989, Paz Zamora was faced with the task of implementing the Bush administration's Andean strategy, a plan unveiled in September 1989, and standing by the commitments made to the United States by the outgoing Paz Estenssoro administration. Primarily because of the absence of guerrilla groups and few visible violent drug lords, Bolivia became a critical player in the implementation of the strategy. U.S. aid nearly doubled, a multi-agency task force consolidated its activities throughout Bolivia, and the U.S. mission became the second largest in Latin America.

Paz Zamora attempted to replicate the pattern of governance imposed by the MNR and his uncle, Paz Estenssoro. Like the MNR, his party, the Movimiento de Izquierda Revolucionaria (MIR), entered into an alliance, labelled Acuerdo Patriotico (AP), with ADN to govern the country. Owning a majority in Congress, the AP government sought to distance itself from the counternarcotics policies of the previous government. Paz Zamora initiated a so-called "direct line diplomacy," which carried him around the globe in the three years since his inauguration. Paz Zamora initially believed he could substitute U.S. counternarcotics assistance with Western European aid for alternative development and other noninterdiction programs. He also erroneously believed that he could "decocainize" relations with the United States.

At the time Paz Zamora reached the presidency, no other issue but cocaine mattered in U.S.-Bolivia relations. Bolivia's importance to the Andean strategy was highlighted by the presence of Robert Gelbard, the highest ranking State Department official ever to serve as ambassador in La Paz. When Gelbard arrived in Bolivia in October 1988, Operation Snow Cap was netting poor results and the Bolivian side of the war on drugs showed few gains. Shortly after Gelbard's arrival, for example, DEA and UMOPAR members were held at gunpoint by the Bolivian navy, which was responsible for patrolling key rivers in the Beni department. Moreover, the flow of cocaine paste from Bolivia continued to increase unabated.

From Bolivia Gelbard was a key player in designing and implementing the Bush administration's counternarcotics policy. In some measure, Bolivia became a laboratory for policies. Bolivia's strategic location offered a geographic setting from which radar and other equipment could monitor the entire region. Between 1989 and 1992, a dramatic increase in U.S. funded and supervised counternarcotics operations took place.

Shortly after his arrival, Gelbard's activist high profile style became visible. Having served as a Peace Corps volunteer in Cochabamba during the 1960s, he felt a particular empathy with Bolivia. Many charged his empathy for Bolivia got in the way of his ambassadorial functions.[12] Indeed, Gelbard opined on every major and minor development in the country, often in off-the-cuff remarks which made headlines and embarrassed other embassy officials. On the other hand, Gelbard's empathy allowed him to develop bonds of friendship with important political and business sectors which enhanced his effectiveness. For most of his three-year tenure, Gelbard's activist style won him many allies. This style, however, also bred many enemies. Many of Gelbard's critics have claimed that his style led to a growing anti-American sentiment.

In the Bolivian context, any U.S. ambassador commands a great deal of influence. All U.S. ambassadors have been powerful domestic actors, shaping and influencing the course of many events in Bolivia; in the case of Robert Gelbard, this role was greatly magnified. Several reasons account for the new ambassadorial role which occurred with the arrival of Robert Gelbard. First, because U.S. policy made Bolivia a key component of the Andean strategy, Gelbard became a prominent actor beyond La Paz. Second, Gelbard's belief that he and the embassy could resolve the bulk of Bolivia's development problems, coupled with his personal interest for the country, changed the manner in which the ambassadorial role was conducted. Third, Gelbard maintained powerful contacts inside the Bush administration and in the U.S. private sector which allowed him to deliver promises no previous ambassador had been able to produce in the past.

Gelbard's temperament was an important ingredient that set the tone of U.S.-Bolivia relations. On more than one occasion, for example, Gelbard wrote angry letters to journalists, academics, and others who disagreed with his policy views. Some even charged him with attempting to censor press and academic reports on his role and U.S. policy.[13] For Gelbard, controlling all information about U.S.-Bolivia relations, specifically about his role and actions, was crucial. This same style of confrontation became visible in Gelbard's dealings with political actors in Bolivia. Often this style was counterproductive, and the ambassador was forced to apologize to those whom he attacked.

Gelbard became a domestic actor in every sense. He involved himself in partisan disputes, negotiated solutions to political impasses, delivered speeches recommending policy to the Bolivian government, and publicly accused former and current government officials of maintaining links to the cocaine industry. Seldom, however, was Gelbard able to present evidence to support his charges. While other Latin American countries have hosted ambassadors from the United States who intervened in domestic politics, few coveted the public attention and controversy that came with the role as did Gelbard.

Under Gelbard's direction, U.S. economic assistance to Bolivia became the largest in South America. Assistance included the building of roads, bridges, electric systems, potable water and sewer systems, soil and conservation programs, health and education programs, the strengthening of the agricultural sector, and the promotion of new products for both domestic and export markets. At the same time, however, military assistance to Bolivia increased eightfold, and the U.S. embassy insisted on a greater role for the Bolivian military in counternarcotics activities.

Gelbard's power transcended Bolivia. His sight was targeted on Washington; as a career diplomat with political ambitions, Gelbard's actions in Bolivia were as much oriented to foster change in Bolivia as they were aimed at influencing the bureaucracy at the State Department and the Washington establishment. The ambassador was well-connected with academic and political circles commonly described as neo-conservative. Having served under Elliott Abrams, the controversial Undersecretary of State for Latin American Affairs recently convicted in connection with the Iran-Contra scandal, Gelbard maintained significant ties with prominent members of the U.S. right.

It was not surprising when Gelbard turned his attention to the Bolivian mission in Washington. Specifically, he fought an intense battle with Jorge Crespo, the Paz Zamora government's envoy to the United States who initially opposed efforts to militarize the drug war in Bolivia. When Crespo attempted to mobilize resources available to him in Washington, such as promoting congressional hearings on the matter, Gelbard's attention focused on getting rid of the ambassador. In an interesting and ironic twist of events, Gelbard reportedly accused Crespo of intervening in U.S. domestic affairs.[14]

However one analyzes Gelbard's ambassadorship, it is clear that his activism contributed to the implementation of a policy which satisfied the interests of the Bush administration in the region. In the long run, however, Gelbard's activism was counterproductive to U.S. interests. His activist style — especially the zeal with which he carried out counternarcotics policy — intimidated Bolivian leaders who were often forced to accept conditions not called for by the State Department or the U.S. Congress but were added by the ambassador in La Paz.[15] In retrospect, it is clear that Gelbard's leverage over Bolivian policy makers, which included economic aid promises, influence over international financial institutions, and perhaps most important, information linking prominent political sectors to narcotics activities, determined the achievement of the ambassador's short-term goals. In the process, however, the long-term objectives of U.S. counternarcotics policies may have been undermined. This is particularly true with respect to the amount of anti-American sentiment which Gelbard's abrasive style generated.[16]

This was the ambassador Jaime Paz Zamora faced upon taking office. Immediately following the new president's inauguration, the U.S. embassy demanded proof of the government's commitment to continue the counternarcotics policies of the outgoing Paz Estenssoro government. From the outset, the embassy and the Drug Enforcement Agency (DEA) had strong suspicions that prominent members of the MIR were linked to drug trafficking.[17]

According to U.S embassy officials, these concerns were presented to President Paz Zamora, who appeared more concerned over maintaining party unity within the ruling MIR than pursuing the alleged ties to the drug industry.[18] Paz Zamora's refusal to pursue these accusations established the tone of relations during the early months of the Acuerdo Patriotico's rule. Citing an internal Bureau of International Narcotics Matters (INM) memo, the *Washington Post* captured the U.S. frustration about the Bolivian government well:

> In almost every area [the government's performance] indicates a total lack of commitment to the antidrug war.... Eradication of coca fields has lagged far behind U.S. goals . . . [Paz Zamora appointed] a number of corrupt officials to key antinarcotics roles and when confronted by the U.S. ambassador, responded that "since most police were corrupt it didn't matter anyway."[19]

In the early months of the Paz Zamora administration, relations with the United States cooled down considerably. Paz Zamora, a long-time friend of European social democracy, attempted to establish closer relations with Western European nations whom he believed better understood Bolivia's coca-cocaine problem. The key moment came when Paz Zamora addressed the United Nations in September 1989 where he unveiled his now-famous "coca for development thesis." The Bolivian president appeared to challenge the thrust of U.S. counternarcotics strategies which had begun to call for a prominent military role in interdiction activities.[20] Perceived by the Bush administration as the Bolivian response to the highly publicized antidrug document known as the Bennett Plan, U.S. officials were not pleased with the speech or with Paz Zamora's antics with the international press. During a visit to Washington in October 1989, for example, Gelbard publicly complained about the alleged ties between Bolivian government officials and drug traffickers.

Paz Zamora's strategy of multilateralizing the drug issue paid off by forcing the Bush administration to implement a regional strategy to supplement bilateral accords. Paz Zamora's discussions with outgoing Peruvian president Alan Garcia and with Colombia's Virgilio Barco also nudged President Bush to agree to attend a summit with the leaders of Bolivia, Colombia, and Peru in February 1990. In accepting the notion of joint responsibility for the drug problem, the United States agreed to modify its previous bilateral strategy and pursue a more regional focus. The Bolivian government believed it had scored a unique victory by earning the privilege of hosting the preparatory sessions in the eastern city of Santa Cruz.

In this context, Ambassador Gelbard controlled many levers. With information linking government officials to drug-related corruption, his word determined the release of U.S. economic support which was critical to the implementation of Bolivia's economic recovery plans. Not surprisingly, the Bolivian government gave in to U.S. pressures. In November 1989, a joint raid on drug traffickers in the town of San Ramon in the Beni department loosened tensions between the U.S. embassy and the Bolivian government and opened the door to greater interdiction activities.[21]

Equally significant, however, was Paz Zamora's inability to live up to the previous government's promises regarding coca eradication programs. In the final months of his administration, President Paz Estenssoro had been able to buy time by signing Annexes I and II to a 1987 U.S.-Bolivia antidrug agreement. Under the terms of these annexes, Bolivia agreed to reduce coca paste and leaf production through a strategy of reducing the price for coca leaf. Based on the experience of Operation Blast Furnace, officials argued that if the price for the coca leaf could be depressed significantly, peasants would move to other more profitable cash crops. In theory, they claimed that repressing the trafficker (or middleman) would reduce demand for coca leaves, thus depressing its market price. A critical aspect of this strategy involved the continuation of Operation Snow Cap.[22]

The United States and Bolivia agreed that alternative crops and markets had to be identified for roughly 300 thousand Bolivians who depend on the coca-cocaine economy. Bolivia agreed to the eradication of five thousand hectares of coca leaf cultivated land during 1989 in return for $23.5 million distributed to peasants who voluntarily eradicated their coca crops. As stipulated in Bolivia's Law 1008, forced eradication was to take place only in areas where coca is grown for the production of cocaine. All other areas, classified as transitional, were subject to the voluntary eradication program outlined in

Annex II. In 1989, four $5.8 million quotas were to be disbursed if Bolivia met the eradication targets. Failure to reach the five thousand hectare target by December 31, 1989, would result in the automatic imposition of sanctions called for by the U.S. Foreign Assistance Act and the terms of Annex II.

Throughout 1989, however, crop eradication reached a standstill; the final figures demonstrated the failure of voluntary eradication programs which were at the core of Bolivia's alternative development strategies.[23] Facing U.S. sanctions, the Bolivian government diverted attention from the eradication campaign by agreeing to expel former Colonel Luis Arce Gómez, the Minister of Interior under the cocaine-tainted dictatorship of General Luis Garcia Meza, to the United States. Arce Gómez was tried, convicted, and sentenced to 30 years in jail by a federal court in Miami, Florida.[24] U.S. assistance flowed once again despite the poor eradication performance of 1989 and the violation of the terms of Annex II.

Underlying the apparent U.S. good will, the fundamental intent was to coerce Bolivia into fighting the drug war on Washington's terms. Robert Gelbard reiterated that the United States was mainly interested in consolidating democracy, reactivating the Bolivian economy, and only as a third objective, fighting the war on drugs. But U.S. actions revealed a different order of priorities. The U.S. ambassador insisted that Bolivia's elite police force (UMOPAR) was incapable of fighting the drug war on its own and proposed several alternatives. The most controversial was a proposal to establish a multinational or regional strike force that may have included a U.S. military contingent. While this proposal was never made public in Bolivia, it was discussed in great detail in the U.S. Congress, the United Nations, and finally in a meeting between U.S. State Department and Bolivian government officials.[25] Although the deployment of U.S. troops was unlikely, it is worth recalling that advisers to the Bolivian UMOPAR, Navy, and Air Force had been active in Bolivia since at least 1986. From the perspective of the Bolivian government and members of the opposition, greater concern existed about the dangers of ordering the armed forces, especially the army, into coca growing regions.

Throughout 1989 Ambassador Gelbard undermined his own efforts at convincing Bolivians that no U.S. troops would be employed. In March 1989, for example, the *Washington Times* reported on Gelbard's request for troops to replace DEA and UMOPAR forces. In Bolivia the outcry was fueled by nationalistic banners raised in the heat of the campaign for the May general elections. Even after the Bolivian Congress approved a "civic action" mission of 300 Southern Command troops, questions persisted about possible military objectives behind expanding runways in Bolivia's airports.[26] With the arrival of civic action programs, the door was opened for escalating the role of the U.S. armed forces.

The Cartagena Summit, Bolivia's New Commitment to the Drug War, and the Gelbard-Paz Zamora Romance

The Cartagena Declaration of February 16, 1990, became the most significant agreement ever signed between Andean presidents and the United States. U.S. officials counted on the signing of an extradition treaty and a commitment on the part of the Bolivian government that the army would be ordered to fight the drug war. Bolivia, in turn, believed that it would finally obtain U.S. endorsement of its alternative development plans. Under the terms of the Declaration of Cartagena, Bolivia and the United States agreed to implement interdiction, eradication, and alternative development strategies through bilateral agreements.

The commitments signed by Presidents Bush and Paz Zamora at the Cartagena Summit in other areas are worth reiterating:

> In the short term, there is a need to create and to strengthen social emergency programs and balance-of-payments support to mitigate the social and economic costs stemming from [crop] substitution. In the medium and long term, investment programs and measures will be needed to create the economic conditions for definitive substitution of the economy in those countries where it exists or that sector of the economy affected by narcotics trafficking (*Cartagena Accord*, 3).

U.S. satisfaction with what it termed Paz Zamora's new-found commitment to the drug war was demonstrated by the Bush administration's prompt recommendation to Congress in March 1990 that Bolivia be certified as having fully cooperated with the United States in antidrug efforts in 1989. This recommendation contradicted earlier views in Washington about the Bolivian government; U.S government officials, including Ambassador Gelbard in La Paz, praised the Bolivian government's willingness to fight the drug war.

The paradox of the Cartagena Declaration and the U.S. government's Andean strategy was that while their principal objective was to strengthen democracy, the implementation of the policy in Bolivia was anything but democratic; in fact, the policies pursued by the Paz Zamora government were carried out without consultation with broader sectors of Bolivian society. The U.S. Andean strategy was negotiated and implemented only with the knowledge of a few members of the ruling parties.

The implementation of this policy illustrates the general pattern of policy making in Bolivia and says a great deal about the reality of dependence. Bolivia's extreme dependence on U.S. aid had the effect of reducing the space available to its policy makers to pursue policy alternatives. In counternarcotics, as in broader economic policy, the autonomy of the government to design its own policies was restricted by the U.S. government and international financial institutions. Thus, while the Bolivian government may want to pursue a less repressive policy, to receive aid and other benefits, it must follow U.S. initiatives.

This pattern of decision making rarely takes into consideration the domestic political consequences of pursuing these policies. The ruling Acuerdo Patriótico controlled Congress and jealously guarded information about counternarcotics policy; however, this has only served to postpone the political costs associated with implementing U.S.-conceived counternarcotics strategies.

The impact on democracy of this essentially authoritarian style of policy making was negative. Public confidence in the Paz Zamora government dropped considerably, and social tension stemming from the resulting political fallout coincided with an even graver issue: the increase in terrorist activities and concern that ties could develop between narcotics traffickers and emerging insurgent groups such as the Ejercito de Liberacion Nacional's Comision Nestor Paz Zamora (ELN-CNPZ) and the more recent Ejercito Guerrillero Tupac Katari (EGTK). The Paz Zamora government appears to have forestalled the growth of these groups and reduced fears that they could hook up with peasants opposed to the government's counternarcotics policies.

Paz Zamora's Shifting Priorities: Responses to Annex III

During a visit to Washington, D.C., in May 1990, President Paz Zamora, after vainly resisting pressures from the U.S. State Department, signed Annex III to the 1987 U.S.-Bolivia antidrug agreement in return for $33.2 million in U.S. military assistance and promises that economic aid would also be disbursed.[27] Under the terms of Annex III, the Paz Zamora government agreed to order the Bolivian armed forces into counternarcotics missions only if police forces were overrun by narcotics traffickers. According to high-ranking U.S. embassy officials, Paz Zamora also agreed to sign an extradition treaty which would allow Bolivian drug traffickers to be sent to the United States for prosecution.[28]

Even as Paz Zamora denied the "militarization" of the drug war, he ordered two regiments to initiate antidrug operations.[29] The government insisted that it was only requesting the "participacion ampliada" (expanded participation) of the army. Already a large antimilitarization effort had been mounted by opposition political parties, labor, and campesino groups who feared the consequences of such a policy. Paz Zamora's response to the protesters is worth noting:

> When I arrived in Bolivia after my trip to the United States and announced the victory of dignity and the negotiating capacity [of our government], I was surprised [to find] that every day militarization is spoken about. This has obstructed the dignified way in which Bolivia has achieved these results without realizing that militarization had not been achieved and that the training and equipping of our armed forces is an inseparable part of the global strategy of alternative development. He who continues to speak about [militarization] is

either stupid or anti-Bolivian, because, without a doubt, it is a way of damaging the dignity of the nation and its armed forces.[30]

In July, August, and November 1990, campesino unions carried out road blockades and strikes, announced the establishment of armed campesino defense committees, and called on campesinos in general to dodge compulsory military service. In August, after signing an agreement with campesino unions not to militarize its antidrug efforts, the government announced that instead of ordering troops into the Chapare where confrontation with peasants was inevitable, U.S. military aid would be used to deploy army units which were to monitor and prevent ecological damage caused by the processing of coca paste in the Bolivian jungles.[31]

Throughout 1990, official Bolivian claims that the solution to the drug war requires more than guns, radar, and helicopters enraged many in the U.S. State Department's Bureau of International Narcotics Matters, who believed that Bolivians had gone back on previous commitments. Gelbard, the outspoken U.S. ambassador, publicly reprimanded the Bolivian government and warned the armed forces that aid would be disbursed only if the army military entered the drug war. According to Bolivian embassy officials, Gelbard also headed efforts to hold up the signing of trade and investment agreements as a way to pressure the Bolivian government into signing an extradition agreement.[32] Faced with a no-win situation, Paz Zamora's government engaged in a contradictory policy: he complied with U.S. requirements but also attempted to convince Bolivians that his government was not giving in to the Americans.

The formulation of antinarcotics policy in Bolivia led to intolerant actions on the part of the government. Egged on by the U.S. embassy, the Bolivian government labelled any opposition to the militarization policy as cooperation with narcotics traffickers. Leaders of the Coca Grower's Federation, for example, were accused of trafficking in cocaine or providing traffickers with protection.[33] Members of political parties who opposed the policy suffered the same fate.

In vain, the Paz Zamora government delayed the decision to order the armed forces into counternarcotics operations. A contradictory strategy of keeping secret the terms of Annex III and denying that extradition was part of any agreement served only to undermine the credibility of the government. As a result, the political costs to the Acuerdo Patriótico of following through with promises made to Washington were high. Calls for peasant armed defense committees, draft resistance movements, and road blockades and the like to prevent the entry of the armed forces into coca growing regions strengthened. Moreover, the government came under intense pressure from the opposition, which utilized the issue to reprimand the Paz Zamora administration publicly for giving in to U.S. designs.

Although embassy officials claimed that all the United States demanded was for the government to follow through with the terms of agreements signed in Washington, it was clear that economic assistance depended on continued progress regarding eradication of coca leaves and, at least according to Bolivian government officials, compliance with military involvement in drug interdiction efforts.[34] U.S. embassy officials, however, denied that economic aid depended on the entry of the armed forces into counternarcotics operations.

A careful reading of Annex III reveals that U.S. assistance to the Bolivian armed forces was conditioned on their entry into the drug war. Specifically, $14 million in U.S. aid to the army, the most controversial portion of Annex III, was tied to its entering into counternarcotics operations. As noted elsewhere, while conditioned aid may not be the correct description, the result was the same. In fact, it may be more accurate to argue that U.S. embassy officials manipulated inter-institutional rivalries within the armed forces to nudge the army into the drug war.[35]

Conditioned aid has characterized U.S. assistance to Bolivia since at least the 1950s. From the perspective of the United States, positive results were obtained. In 1986 when U.S. aid was suspended, for example, the Bolivian government chose to enter into Blast Furnace, the controversial joint military operation. In 1987 the U.S. Congress decertified Bolivia and threatened to impose new aid sanctions under the terms of the 1985 Foreign Assistance Act. This led to the February 1987 U.S.-Bolivia bilateral agreement which outlined joint efforts to combat coca leaf and cocaine paste production. Faced with decertification in 1988, Bolivia agreed to implement Law 1008, approved by the Bolivian Congress in July 1988 and signed into law by President Paz Estenssoro in December. Recent charges by U.S. government officials based on DEA estimates that Bolivia has become the world's second largest producer of cocaine have justified demands for an escalation of interdiction activities.

Symbols of Bolivian Cooperation

In December 1990, the Bolivian government proudly informed Washington it had not only met the eradication target of five thousand hectares for 1990 but had surpassed it by nearly one thousand hectares.[36] While this achievement reflected a temporary restructuring of the cocaine industry following the major crackdown in Colombia, Bolivia's eradication efforts were noteworthy and gave a great stimulus to its alternative development proposals.[37]

Another symbol of Bolivian cooperation was the September 1990 arrest of Carmelo "Meco" Dominguez, a trafficker who allegedly was responsible for shipping large quantities of cocaine to Mexico. The DEA classified Dominguez's operation "as the most lucrative of Bolivia's 35 major traffickers."[38] According to Ambassador Gelbard, the operation which netted Dominguez was the most significant single counternarcotics operation in Bolivian history because it demonstrated that simultaneous strikes could be carried out against the subsidiaries of the nationwide drug organizations.[39]

Another major blow to Bolivia's drug trafficking organizations was achieved in December 1991 with the arrest in San Diego, California, of Jorge "Techo de Paja" Roca Suarez. According to the indictment, Roca Suarez lived in the United States for 30 years and returned to Bolivia in 1981 to work with his uncle, Roberto Suarez Gomez, as a cocaine paste buyer in the Chapare. When Suarez Gomez was arrested in 1988, Techo de Paja became the head of a new trafficking organization referred to as "el cartel de los techos" which developed its own links into Colombia, Panama, Mexico, and the United States. U.S. authorities also charged him with membership in another trafficking cartel known as "la corporación" or the "Cartel de Santa Ana." The United States also demanded that the Bolivian government extradite Techo de Paja's mother, Blanca Suarez, and sister, Asunta Roca, who, according to the indictment, were important players in the Bolivian cartel. As shall be seen, this request tested the Bolivian government's private promise to the United States that an extradition agreement would be signed.

Jaime Paz's Perplexing Decisions

The good will generated by the surpassing of eradication targets and the arrests of "Meco" Dominguez and Techo de Paja, however, was shattered less than two months later. The Bolivian government's resolve to combat narcotics trafficking came under intense scrutiny in late February 1991 when President Paz Zamora named retired Colonel Faustino Rico Toro to head the National Council Against Drug Abuse and Trafficking (FELCN). Rico Toro, who had headed the infamous G-2 army intelligence unit under the drug-tainted government of General Luis García Meza, was widely suspected of providing protection to narcotics traffickers and was reportedly linked to Klaus Barbie, the infamous "Butcher of Lyon," who served as adviser to the Bolivian military. When the United States announced its intention to cut off $100 million in economic and military assistance, Rico Toro quickly resigned. Under suspicion from the United States, Guillermo Capobianco, the minister of interior, and Colonel Felipe Carvajal, the chief of police, were also forced to step down before U.S. aid was restored.[40]

The reasons for the nomination of Rico Toro are still difficult to comprehend. Throughout the two years of the Paz Zamora government (and since at least 1985), all nominees to head counternarcotics agencies were submitted to the DEA for screening of possible drug connections.[41] Given the drug war success, Paz Zamora's decision to name Rico Toro was unwise at best.

While the nomination may have had something to do with the patronage requirements of the ruling Acuerdo Patriotico alliance (Rico Toro was an important political player in Cochabamba), the United States charged it was part of an elaborate conspiracy to place persons with contacts to the drug industry in key positions.[42] That Capobianco and Carvajal were involved in a conspiracy to name persons who would protect traffickers in high government positions, however, is speculation; in fact, no formal charges against these two individuals could be substantiated. It is worth noting, however, that every minister of interior since 1980 has been accused of providing protection to drug lords.

The paradoxes of this situation are even more remarkable when one notes that Capobianco was involved in the December 1989 expulsion of former Minister of Interior Colonel Luis Arce Gómez to the United States where he was tried and convicted in January 1991. In any case, the Rico Toro affair undermined the credibility of the government and damaged relations between the United States and Bolivia.

Not coincidentally in April 1991, the Bolivian National Congress, which is controlled by the ruling Acuerdo Patriótico, voted to allow the entry into Bolivia of 110 U.S. military advisers to train two army battalions in counternarcotics techniques. Critics charged that the training had more to do with counterinsurgency than with counternarcotics operations. By admitting that Bolivia had become part of a "low-intensity conflict scenario," U.S. officials recognized that the differences are few. In fact, throughout coca growing regions, the Bolivian army has already initiated LIC-type psychological operations aimed at convincing the peasantry that its intentions are to help them build a "better tomorrow."[43]

Less than a few hours after the National Congress voted to allow U.S. advisers into Bolivian territory, a huge Galaxy airplane arrived carrying personnel and equipment. U.S. military personnel had already been active in Bolivia under the banner of DEA Snow Cap operations; in fact, a multi-agency task force which included the U.S. Coast Guard, Navy, DEA, and Border Patrol, among others, had been active in Bolivia since at least 1987. A two-part article in the June and July 1991 editions of *Soldier of Fortune* traced the path of a group of elite Navy seals patrolling the rivers of the Beni department.[44] These operations were unknown to most Bolivians, including their elected representative in the National Congress.[45]

The arrival of 56 U.S. advisers on April 23, 1991, set off a wave of protests and a very serious confrontation between the Bolivian government and peasant unions from the Chapare and Yungas regions where coca leaves are produced. Peasant unions threatened to march and block roads if the government did not rescind Annex III and expel the American advisers. A confrontation was avoided in May 1991 when the government agreed to hold discussions with peasant unions; but, in mid-June 1991, all talks broke down and the marches and road blockades were initiated. The government responded with force, arresting dozens of peasant leaders and breaking up the marches. In late June the government claimed absolute victory after sensing that the peasant unions lacked any real power. Nevertheless, the incident revealed the potential for a serious confrontation with peasants.

The image of Paz Zamora's government was shattered once again in May 1991 when Carmelo "Meco" Dominguez allegedly escaped from the Panoptico jail in La Paz. Meco's escape came on the eve of the arrival of Robert Martinez, the newly appointed U.S. drug czar. When Dominguez showed up in a Santa Cruz hospital less than twenty-four hours later, Bolivian government officials claimed a resounding law enforcement victory. They were hard-pressed to explain, however, how one of the highest ranking members of the Bolivian drug mafia was able to secure a medical pass. Nevertheless, Bob Martinez declared that the drug war was being won in Bolivia.

From Operation Safehaven to Repentance Decrees

The most important joint U.S.-Bolivia counternarcotics operation, dubbed Safehaven, was initiated in March 1991 and culminated in late June 1991 when approximately 640 UMOPAR troops, supported by the air force and the navy, swept down on the town of Santa Ana del Yacuma in the Beni department. Working under the direction of DEA intelligence and personnel, the Bolivian armed forces surrounded the town and in house-to-house searches by the UMOPAR police attempted to round up Bolivia's principal drug traffickers.[46] The joint U.S.-Bolivia raid specifically targeted Hugo Rivero Villavicencio, presumably one of Latin America's most wanted drug lords. According to the government, Rivero Villavicencio was Bolivia's link to the Medellín cartel and had replaced Techo de Paja as the head of the Santa Ana cartel. According to U.S. and Bolivian government officials, Santa Ana del Yacuma had become Bolivia's Medellín. Reports claimed that nearly 60 Colombian traffickers resided in the town and worked closely with Hugo Rivero Villavicencio.

It became increasingly clear that Operation Safehaven in Santa Ana was to be Ambassador Gelbard's final good-bye, the culmination of a successful tour. The Santa Ana experiment was the largest military counternarcotics operation ever to take place in Bolivia or anywhere else. Despite all the hoopla, however, the operation's success was arguable. Not a single major or minor drug lord was arrested. Moreover, charges accumulated about civil rights violations by both U.S. and Bolivian personnel. Independent reports clashed with the official version of the Bolivian government and the U.S. embassy which claimed that the operation had been a huge success. In fact, several airplanes belonging to persons suspected of drug trafficking were confiscated. The most arguable claim was that the operation had restored Bolivian sovereignty to Santa Ana, which had presumably fallen under the control of the drug traffickers.

As the story unfolded, it became clear that the operation was a staged media event for U.S.-based journalists. Foreign correspondents were invited by embassy officials and allowed to go along to observe the operations. Bolivian reporters were conspicuously excluded. To add insult to injury, most Bolivian newspapers were forced to translate *Miami Herald* coverage to inform their readers about events taking place in national territory.[47]

In the aftermath of Santa Ana, Ambassador Gelbard accused Santa Ana's naval garrison commander, Navy Lieutenant Carlos Revollo, and members of the Beni prefecture of warning the traffickers of the impending operation. Bolivian military officers, including the commander-in-chief of the armed forces, charged the DEA with violating the rules of engagement and of beating the Navy officer. These events highlighted Ambassador Gelbard's departure from Bolivia in early July 1991.[48]

U.S. discomfort was especially evident when it was revealed that traffickers negotiated an amnesty or repentance decree (decreto de arrepentimiento) with the Bolivian government. On July 29, the Bolivian government announced a decree which granted drug traffickers 120 days to surrender to authorities to avoid extradition to the United States. Traffickers were also expected to surrender their assets and collaborate with Bolivian authorities in capturing other traffickers. The Bolivian government argued that this would minimize a Colombian-style wave of violence.[49] U.S. displeasure, however, was rooted in the Bolivian government's refusal to live up to its promise to sign an extradition treaty. With the amnesty decree, the possibility of extraditing the major drug kingpins appeared remote.

On September 15, Hugo Rivero Villavicencio, Operation Safehaven's principal target, turned himself in to DEA and UMOPAR agents under the mediation and protection of Santa Ana del Yacuma's Catholic parish.[50] From the perspective of the Bolivian government, this provided evidence of the success of nonviolent ways of dealing with the drug lords. Government officials claimed that the surrender of four drug lords broke the links between the Medellín cartel and Bolivia.

General Lucio Añez, the retired commander of the FELCN who had enjoyed DEA trust until he was removed from his post under questionable circumstances, claimed that at least six drug trafficking groups existed in Bolivia with international connections. He claimed these were still up and running despite the amnesty repentance decree and the positive results it had had.

Information about the structure of the Bolivian narcotics industry and the manner in which the drug lords decided to turn themselves in became available as each trafficker entered a plea in Bolivian courts. It was evident that the drug traffickers had met to arrange the terms of their surrender and agreed to turn themselves in to avoid extradition.

The stories told by the traffickers illustrate at least one reality about the Bolivian drug lords: they are mainly family men with close family ties to each other and to many in the Bolivian political class. Unlike their Colombian counterparts, they are less prone to violence and, in general, opted for the amnesty decree because of family pressures.

The stories of Erwin Guzmán and Winston Rodriguez are worth noting. Guzman declared, at a hearing before the Judicial Police on September 24, that he turned himself in because he feared extradition to the United States. After entering a guilty plea, he noted that if he committed any crimes, they were only in Bolivia. Guzmán also denied the existence of a Santa Ana cartel. He claimed his net worth was $350,000, 1,500 head of cattle, and real estate property. Guzmán also denied knowing Guillermo Betancur, a Colombian trafficker arrested by Bolivian authorities, who accused him of having linkages with the Medellín cartel.[51] A similar story came from Winston Rodríguez Daza, who claimed he was innocent of drug trafficking and promised not to commit any more crimes "if I committed any." He did admit, however, that he rented a hacienda with the knowledge that it would be used for making drugs. His net worth was said to be $250,000. By Colombian standards, Bolivia's drug kingpins were paupers.

Given the success of the amnesty decree, the Paz Zamora government argued that an extradition treaty with the United States would not be signed. Moreover, the government claimed that because a 1900 extradition agreement and the 1988 Vienna Convention Accords on narcotics trafficking already established mechanisms for extradition, another law was unnecessary. Upset by another delay on extradition, U.S. embassy officials sent up another trial balloon. If no other legislation was necessary, then the U.S. embassy could formally request the Supreme Court to rule on the extradition of Techo de Paja's mother and sister. The Supreme Court delayed ruling on the matter in 1991 but reached decision in July 1992.[52]

U.S. embassy officials demanded that the Bolivian government extradite arrested traffickers once their sentences in Bolivia had been completed.[53] Members of the ruling ADN warned against the perils of the decree; if it does not become a law, the U.S. embassy could demand the extradition of all those who turned themselves in if those individuals are accused of crimes outside of Bolivia. Deputies in Congress noted that traffickers could turn to violence if the government allowed their extradition.

When the deadline expired on November 29, seven of the top ten traffickers had turned themselves in to Bolivian authorities. On December 5, the government confirmed that Rafael Rivero Villavicencio, the brother of Hugo Rivero Villavicencio, also turned himself in despite having missed the November 29 deadline. Their surrender gave credence to the government's claim that the drug war could be waged without a significant escalation of violence. Skeptics of the plan point out that the strategy has done little to reduce the flow of cocaine out of Bolivia and that some may continue to traffic drugs from their prison cells.

In the year since the deadline, the so-called arrepentidos have lobbied the government for leniency. On February 5, 1992, in a public letter to the president, the seven accused and convicted drug barons demanded minimum sentences because of their collaboration with Bolivian authorities. In late February 1992, Erwin Guzmán received a five-year sentence.

Missed Eradication Targets and U.S. Sanctions

On August 20, 1991, Carlos Iturralde, the minister of foreign affairs, announced that the Bush/Paz Zamora accords had been renewed. As far as Annex I was concerned, economic assistance would increase from $91 million to $132 million for 1991. Annex II's so-called Emergency Fund for Alternative Development (Fondo de Emergencia para el Desarrollo Alternativo) would be financed through U.S. balance of payments supports. The minister announced that Annex III would provide about $35 million in aid for the armed forces, provided the armed forces entered into the drug war.

This announcement, however, did not conceal the growing concern on the part of the Bolivian government that it would not meet its 7,000 hectares eradication target for 1992 and would face a $22 million penalty. Members of CONALID, the coordinating counternarcotics agency, publicly denied that the government would embark on a forceful eradication campaign; however, in private they noted that without forceful eradication programs not only would the target be missed but the government's claims about alternative development would be dealt a serious blow. Achieving eradication targets has always been problematic. In 1989 only 2,450 hectares of 5,000 were eradicated. The remarkably high figures for 1990 would not be repeated in 1991. Government officials claimed that the dramatic slowdown in eradication figures was the result of a continued high demand for cocaine in the United States and problems with interdiction in Bolivia. Nevertheless, the Bolivian government eradicated 5,486 hectares of coca in 1991, a respectable figure relative to pre-1990.

In theory, interdiction is meant to upset the commercialization process by lowering the price of coca leaf. When interdiction is sustained and carried out properly, the price of coca leaf drops, forcing peasants to seek other crops.[54] Bolivian government officials noted in private that the main reason for the eradication failure in 1991, however, was corruption within the FELCN which prevented the interdiction programs from being carried out in a sustained fashion. Clearly, the naming of Col. Rico Toro disturbed a sustained interdiction process. The resignation of Rico Toro's successor (also accused of ties to the drug industry) in September produced another setback for interdiction. Accusations of corruption within UMOPAR also had a widespread impact on the police forces. A member of CONALID argued:

In the last semester, the FELCN has not operated in regular fashion and for that reason the price of coca leaf has risen. At the moment the price is about $B150. It went up at one point to nearly $B180.

U.S. embassy officials claimed, nevertheless, that the price for coca leaves dropped dramatically as a result of Operation Safehaven (Santa Ana). The fact remained that eradication targets would not be met by the government.

On September 15, government officials admitted that a greater number of campesinos had turned toward the manufacturing of cocaine and that others were boycotting crop substitution programs. While expressing their concern over the presence of explosives and arms in the Chapare region, they noted that the production of base and cocaine hydrochloride continued apace. Government officials also claimed that the boycott of crop substitution programs was directed at fomenting armed violence.[55]

In October 1991, the ministry of foreign affairs admitted that the United States had frozen $22 million until Bolivia met its 7,000 hectare target. Novel proposals surfaced in the Bolivian National Congress. Deputy Gregorio Lanza, for example, proposed that the government raise the payment per hectare to campesinos from $2,000 to $3,500. Lanza argued that this would motivate campesinos to eradicate the 7,000 hectares the Bolivian government promised to meet by December 31, 1991. In fact, to meet the December 31 deadline, Bolivia would have had to eradicate 44 hectares per day between November 12 and the end of the year to meet the 7,000 hectare limit. Richard Bowers, the new U.S. ambassador, had his own proposal. During a press conference where he announced that the United States would not extend the December 31 deadline for eradication, Bowers stated:

I have my own machete and I'm ready to help you [eradicate coca] if you need assistance.[56]

Bowers' "machete en mano" statement stirred a wave of criticism in the National Congress and in labor organizations. Filemon Escobar, a deputy with the United Left party, called the ambassador's declaration

an incitement to violence because his underlying proposal is the forceful eradication of coca which will be rejected by [coca growers.][57]

Escobar's statement was not too far-fetched. Tensions between the government and coca growers were already high in Cochabamba's Chapare owing to an August 11 decision by the Dirección de Reconversion Agricola (DIRECO) to use UMOPAR officers to protect the mobile eradication brigades which began forcefully eradicating coca in a last ditch attempt to meet the 1991 target. Coca producers, in turn, announced that their self-defense committees would be put into operation. Clashes appeared inevitable.

On August 22, a communique from the ministry of information confirmed that a coca grower died of gunshot wounds. According to the communique, UMOPAR troops fired a round as they attempted to defend DIRECO officials who had initiated the forceful eradication of coca in the Chapare. The communique claimed that campesinos destroyed nine trucks and that UMOPAR fired off a warning round which unfortunately struck the campesino who subsequently died. The government claimed that the confrontation was the result of the actions of "agitators who oppose the government's concerted actions." On August 25, the undersecretary for Social Defense contradicted the official communique arguing that no one really knows who killed the peasant. He claimed that it might have even been one of the campesinos who killed the man.

The U.S. embassy's initial refusal to consider granting Bolivia an extension to meet the 7,000 hectare goal was replaced at year's end by a three-week extension. Government officials admitted that the 7,000 hectare target would not be met even with the new extension granted by the U.S. government. When the official figures were released on January 6, 1992, only 5,487 hectares had been eradicated by December 31. Bolivia still risked losing the $22 million because no new extensions were likely.

The Thrust Toward Militarization

Ambassador Richard Bowers pledged to carry on with the basic thrust of U.S. policy initiated by his predecessor. Unlike Gelbard, Ambassador Bowers initially adopted a lower profile. Bowers' few public statements, however, ratified U.S. intentions to carry on with assistance to the Bolivian military.[58] The new ambassador ratified that the army would be ordered into the drug war only when President Paz Zamora gave his authorization.

On September 6, the Paz Zamora government was caught off guard when Bowers informed the press that the Bolivian army would enter into the drug war shortly. At the time of Bowers' announcement, the military high command had already made a decision. The ambassador's declaration set off another round of rumors and counter-rumors. On September 9, for example, the U.S. embassy denied allegations by a government minister who claimed that the U.S. military advisers would also train Bolivian troops in counterinsurgency strategies. Embassy officials claimed that the advisers only trained the Bolivians in counternarcotics efforts. According to military strategists, little difference exists between counternarcotics and counterinsurgency training. In fact, the whole thrust of counternarcotics strategies in Bolivia involves low-intensity conflict training.

From the perspective of the coca growers, Bowers' revelation only confirmed their view that the militarization strategy aimed to convert the coca producing regions into occupied zones similar to the occupied mining centers of the 1960s and 1970s. Bolivian government officials, however, argued that the army would not enter into drug producing zones.

On October 3, 1991, Admiral Alberto Sainz Klinsky, the new commander-in-chief of the Bolivian armed forces, announced that two U.S.-trained army battalions initiated Operation "Definite Notice" in the remote border Angel Sandoval province in the department of Santa Cruz. According to Carlos Saavedra, the minister of interior, the mission of the Bolivian army troops was to destroy cocaine laboratories.

The government had a difficult time explaining the rationale for sending in the troops. Saavedra argued the FELCN had not been overrun and that the entry of the army was meant to make counternarcotics efforts more efficient. This explanation contradicted previous government statements and the policy guidelines of both the Cartagena agreement and Annex III, which noted specifically that the army would be ordered into the drug war only if and when police forces were overrun by drug lords. In October 1991, nothing indicated that this was the case.

Even members of the ruling MIR reacted negatively to the entry of the army. Gastón Encinas, the president of the Chamber of Deputies, for example, accused the government of giving in to U.S. pressures. On October 4, 1991, the Confederacion Sindical Unica de Trabajadores Campesinos de Bolivia (CSUTCB) declared a state of emergency and demanded that the government reconsider the decision to order the U.S.-trained battalions into the drug war. The campesino union warned that any resulting violence would be the government's responsibility.

Some observers noted that the militarization (or the euphemistic "participacíon ampliada" of the army, as the government officials prefer to call it) had been accepted by the Bolivian government to avoid the suspension of U.S. economic assistance because the government had failed to meet the eradication targets for 1991.[59] Again the claims of success by the U.S. embassy and the Bolivian government exceeded the evidence. According to the State Department's INM measures, the success of Definite Notice included the "arrest of traffickers; destruction of cocaine processing laboratories; seizure of trafficker properties, aircraft, and narcotics; and temporary depression in coca prices."[60]

The entry of the army represented the latest escalation in a long campaign which started with civic action programs, U.S. special forces advisers, the establishment of a so-called Centro de Instrucciones de Operaciones en la Selva (CIOS), and rural psychological operations in coca growing regions. According to some critics, Bolivians were still bracing for two more U.S. demands: the signing of an extradition treaty and the construction of a permanent military base somewhere in the Beni or Pando.[61]

The high profile of the army campaign led to skeptical reactions. A Santa Cruz daily, for example, noted that the drug traffickers were already moving elsewhere to avoid detection. According to military chiefs, however, the army's Ranger regiment dismantled sophisticated communications equipment and arrested six drug traffickers during its first operation. On October 11, the ministry of information announced that the Ranger regiment destroyed a cocaine factory southeast of the town of San Matías which had a capacity to produce 110 kg. of the drug per week. Press reports, however, contradicted the official optimism. Most noted the lack of success of the army operations.

The inevitable political fallout of ordering the military into the drug war was immediate. On October 7, 1991, in a letter to the Bolivian vice president, the Movimiento Bolivia Libre (MBL) demanded the convocation of a special session of Congress to hear charges of violation of the constitution by the ministers of defense, foreign affairs, and interior, the cabinet officials charged with the decision to militarize the counternarcotics war. Nevertheless, the government continued with its plans. On the same date in Riberalta-Beni, the training of the four hundred CIOS regiment troops by U.S. advisers was initiated.[62]

As joint U.S.-Bolivia counternarcotics policy reached a climax with the entry of the army into the drug war, the Office of the Inspector General (OIG) released the results of an audit conducted in early 1991 of the State Department's programs in Bolivia. The OIG's main concern was as follows:

> although both the quality and the quantity of our assistance have been enhanced across the board, there has not been a corresponding reduction in Bolivia's illicit drug industry which supplies 35 percent of the world's cocaine.[63]

The report argued that, to achieve any measure of success, two issues would have to be resolved. First, the political will and economic ability of Bolivia to carry out drug control activities would have to be assured. Second, the fragmentation and lack of coordination between agencies, both U.S. and Bolivian, would have to be improved. The most critical aspect of the audit, however, was directed at every aspect of U.S. military assistance. A single paragraph illustrates the general tone of the report:

> U.S. counternarcotics assistance to the Bolivian military has increased significantly under the Andean strategy. However, we found that the Bureau for International Narcotics Matters (INM) Air Wing's rotary wing assets are underused, raising questions about plans to acquire even more INM aircraft; several questions remain unresolved regarding DOD's fixed wing program; and the lack of permanent leadership coupled with inadequate program support limited the progress of the riverine program. Further, the role, mission, and operating locale of the Bolivian army units are unclear.[64]

The Bolivian government claimed the report was unimportant; instead, it claimed that real success had been achieved in counternarcotics operations. Furthermore, Paz Zamora questioned why no such investigations were made of the U.S. mafia.

Just as quickly as it began, the participation of the army in counternarcotics efforts ended. On October 14, the minister of interior announced that the participation of the army in counternarcotics efforts had ended for the year. No plans were made for any future army incursions. Plans for other military roles abounded, especially the use of the military to combat terrorism.[65]

President Paz Zamora went to great lengths to justify the significance of the Bolivian armed forces for the consolidation of Bolivian democracy. In the final months of 1991, and in the wake of reports that the Bush administration had proposed the elimination of the Latin American armed forces, Paz Zamora argued that it was possible to "speak only of the modernization of the armed forces, certainly not its disappearance."

The controversy generated by the army's entry into the drug war, coupled with the futile campaign the two U.S.-trained battalions carried out, indefinitely postponed plans for an increased role of the Bolivian armed forces. As early as December 1991, U.S. officials had decided that the political costs of involving the army were too high and canceled plans to press ahead with future training operations.

This decision did not sit well with the Bolivian armed forces. In February 1992, an anonymous communique sent to the Bolivian National Congress by a group calling itself "Movimiento Militar Boliviariano" claimed that because 80 percent of all U.S. military assistance benefitted U.S. interests, the government should design an economic recovery plan for the armed forces. The communique demanded a greater role for the military in alternative development and civic action programs. Moreover, it called on the National Congress to examine how U.S. military assistance had been disbursed.[66]

On February 10, 1992, the Constitutional Affairs Committee of the Chamber of Deputies announced it would initiate a trial (Juicio de Responsabilidades) against the ministers of defense, interior, and foreign affairs for allowing the participation of the army in counternarcotics affairs without the approval of the National Congress. Members of the opposition in Congress were eager to embrace the complaints by the anonymous faction of the armed forces. While this congressional maneuver was unlikely to prosper given the Acuerdo Patriotico's control over the legislature, for only the second time since the beginning of joint U.S.-Bolivia counternarcotics efforts, the National Congress engaged in oversight. Not surprisingly, members of Congress lacked adequate information and engaged more in political posturing than in serious inquiries into the foreign policy activities of the Paz Zamora executive.

The timing of the congressional inquiry into foreign policy matters coincided with another congressional investigation into the sale of military real estate (land) by members of the cabinet to a retired officer without proper authorization from the legislative body. The political fallout was tremendous: the minister of defense, the commanders of each branch of the armed forces, and the commander-in-chief were all forced to resign. Once again, the image of the armed forces was tarnished by the corrupt actions of a few officers and their civilian co-conspirators. For all practical purposes, this was the final straw that determined the army's withdrawal from the drug war.

Old Conflicts and New Investigations: the Huanchaca Affair

In February 1992, political tensions intensified dramatically when a congressional committee agreed to reopen an investigation into the September 6, 1986, assassination of Noel Kempff Mercado, a Bolivian scientist, and his collaborators by drug traffickers in Huanchaca, a remote zone in the department of Santa Cruz. Owing largely to the stalling tactics of members of the then-ruling Pacto por la Democracia coalition, the first congressional inquiry in 1986 cleared all members of the MNR government. Even the assassination of Edmundo Salazar Terceros, the deputy who chaired the congressional committee, did little to sway the investigation. A second congressional inquiry in 1987 pointed an accusatory finger at former Minister of Interior Fernando Barthelemy; however, no indictments were handed down.

In February 1992, a new inquiry was initiated despite charges by members of the MNR that the investigation was politically motivated. As the commission conducted its search, charges and counter-charges surfaced. In the end, the country's three principal parties, ADN, MIR, and MNR, were accused of involvement in activities ranging from murder to protecting drug traffickers. The MNR was accused of protecting traffickers in the Chapare during the time Minister of Interior Barthelemy was in office. Barthelemy was also accused of ordering the murder of Deputy Salazar. Charges of linkages to Roberto Suarez again hounded ADN and General Banzer. The MIR, in turn, relived charges which surfaced during the Rico Toro affair. Even the DEA ended up on the butcher's block.

Facing either the complete collapse of the political class or the indictment of many prominent militants of the principal parties, several proposals were put forth. The MNR suggested calling on the United Nations to look into allegations against all political parties. Members of the political parties even traveled to Washington to request the mediation of former Ambassador Gelbard.[67]

In the end, the Chamber of Deputies voted to dismiss Deputy Barthelemy from Congress and lifted his parliamentary immunity. Moreover, the majority in the Chamber voted to allow the Huanchaca affair to be investigated by the judicial branch. Accusations of a "pact of silence" between the principal political parties surfaced immediately. Even the threat of a malfeasance trial against Barthelemy was averted when the left was unable to hold a quorum to hear the charges. The final congressional report, however, revealed a byzantine underworld and its connections with the highest levels of the Bolivian political system. It also condemned the DEA for not reporting the activities of the Huanchaca cocaine lab despite aerial reconnaissance photos and prior knowledge of its activities. In a final note, the congressional committee demanded the extradition of Jesus Gutiérrez, the DEA agent in charge in 1986. Claiming that agents enjoy diplomatic immunity, Ambassador Bowers and Richard Bonner, the head of the DEA, refused the congressional committee's request.

Extradition, Civic Action, and Double Standards

U.S. counternarcotics operations in Bolivia have included civic action programs since at least 1988. Broadly conceived as part of a psychological operations campaign aimed at securing "grass roots" approval for the presence of the U.S. military, civic actions became one more controversial component of the drug war. No other country in South America has allowed as many U.S. civic action activities; in fact, nearly everywhere they have been accompanied by controversy. With the sole exception of a 1989 authorization by the National Congress allowing U.S. troops to level a hill at the end of an airport runway in the city of Potosí, no civic action activity obtained the required congressional permission. The presence of U.S. civic action teams became so prevalent that few bothered to note that congressional authorization is required each and every time U.S. or any other foreign troops enter Bolivian territory.

Civic action activities in 1992 were no exception; however, the magnitude of the program was such that it became the final straw. In late June U.S. troops from the 18th Airborne out of South Carolina began arriving in Santa Ana del Yacuma, the town where just a year earlier Operation Safehaven was staged. Presumably arriving on a mission to build a small school for the town, 120 or so troops (the number ranges from 120 to 150) swept into town in C-127 aircraft. Too large to land in Santa Ana, four huge Galaxy planes landed in Santa Cruz.

As more troops and equipment were disembarked, suspicion soon captured the imagination of the occasional visiting journalist. Soon the La Paz dailies were flooded with stories ranging from troops dumping nuclear waste to building a base for an invasion of the Amazon basin.[68] A congressional mission was assembled and departed for Santa Ana to investigate the activities of the American soldiers.[69]

To understand the controversy, it is important to delve into the logic of civic action from the perspective of the U.S. military. According to U.S. military planners at U.S. Army South Headquarters in Panama, civic action activities are part and parcel of a routine training mission. In the new international context of the end of the Cold War, reductions in defense spending, and even the closing of bases around the world, the principal training mission for U.S. troops will be rapid deployment exercises. Thus, civic action allows U.S. troops to combine both goodwill missions with these training exercises.[70] Bolivia proved to be an ideal location for rapid deployment exercises and civic action. Plans for U.S. troops to parachute into Santa Ana del Yacuma, however, had to be scrapped when the controversy flared up in the Bolivian press.

The Bolivian government, however, could not explain why U.S. troops were spending so much time, effort, and money to build a very small school.[71] When U.S. embassy officials confirmed that besides civic action U.S. troops were indeed carrying out military exercises, the controversy deepened. Government officials were also short an explanation about why no congressional approval for the operation had been secured.

The congressional commission which visited Santa Ana concluded that only 10 of the 120 U.S. troops were certified engineers. Its visit to the jungle town was a prelude to the launching of a full-blown round of congressional interrogations of members of the cabinet. A sad and ludicrous note was added when all Ronald Maclean, the foreign minister, could utter was "you don't look a gift horse in the mouth."

The exercises were approved before Ronald Maclean took office and his predecessor was responsible for the failure to secure congressional approval.[72] His statement to the press, however, sealed his reputation as a generally ineffective minister with no capacity to negotiate with the United States.[73] Again, the failure to prepare the political groundwork before the arrival of the U.S. troops ratified the general pattern that dominated the Paz Zamora administration's relations with the United States. Counternarcotics activities were planned by the United States with little or no Bolivian input. The Bolivian government agreed to implement policies in secret to avoid political costs. All "secret" initiatives inevitably became public, revealing that most were unconstitutional.

Despite the controversy, the civic action exercises of 1992 went on as scheduled and the U.S. soldiers built the Santa Ana school. In a ludicrous turn of events, a day before their return to the United States, the government used its Acuerdo Patriótico majority in Congress to secure ex-post facto approval for the visiting troops. This action was reminiscent of the actions of the Paz Estenssoro government in 1986, when it obtained congressional support for Blast Furnace one month after the arrival of U.S. troops.

Two additional incidents illustrate the deteriorating climate surrounding U.S.-Bolivia counternarcotics policy. The first involved two American citizens serving as priests in Bolivia. According to an American priest who was boating down a river in the department of Pando, he was intercepted by members of the U.S. Navy and Coast Guard sometime in late June 1992. Noting that no Bolivians were on board the U.S. vessel, the priest told the story to Archbishop Casey of Pando, another American resident of the region. Casey called a press conference and denounced the incident as a violation of Bolivian sovereignty and the terms of engagement for U.S. Navy and Coast Guard personnel. Ambassador Bowers denied the story; instead, he accused Archbishop Casey of lying and claimed that, in a private phone conversation, the priest had denied the veracity of the story.[74] In public, however, the Archbishop stood by the priest's account and repeated his charges against U.S. policy. The incident generated enough international attention to warrant an editorial in the *Miami Herald.*

A second incident in July 1992 concerned extradition and the future of a U.S.-Bolivia extradition treaty. The accumulation of foreign policy crises climaxed with the decision by the Bolivian Supreme Court to allow the extradition of Asunta Roca Suarez. As "Techo de Paja's" sister was spirited out of the country on a DEA plane, the political fallout hit the government head on. Accusations that the government had bribed the members of the court surfaced.[75] U.S. praise for the Supreme Court's decision was immediate. After all, the U.S. embassy had waited since May 1990 for the Bolivian government to give in to something resembling a legal process to extradite Bolivians accused of drug trafficking. With a new procedure in place, embassy officials now demanded the extradition of several other alleged traffickers.

The extradition of Bolivian nationals to the United States through a legal mechanism became a preferable option to the likelihood of another kidnapping. As in other Latin American countries, the U.S. Supreme Court's ruling in June that U.S. agents did not violate an extradition treaty by kidnapping a foreign national stirred a prolonged debate in Bolivia. Politicians argued that the Bolivian Supreme Court ruled in the Roca Suarez case to prevent the kidnapping of several Bolivians who face drug charges in the United States.

The Roca Suarez ruling, however, indefinitely postponed a decision by the Bolivian government on the signing of a new extradition treaty explicitly covering drug-related crimes. U.S. embassy officials have argued that the United States will still demand a new treaty. Bolivian officials are confident that all future extradition requests will be processed under the terms of the 1900 treaty and the Vienna Convention accords of 1988.

The final straw which ratified the Bolivian perception that double standards were being applied in U.S. policy also occurred in July 1992. An off-duty DEA officer shot and wounded a Bolivian national at a bar in the city of

Santa Cruz. The details of the incident were never released, but speculation was that both were intoxicated and were arguing over a woman. In any event, the DEA officer was arrested; however, following a visit by a U.S. consular agent, he was released, charges were dropped, and he was promptly flown out of the country and back to the United States.[76] Again the Bolivian government could not provide an explanation of the incident and why the DEA officer was allowed to leave the country. Only after pressure from numerous quarters, including political parties, the National Congress, and organized labor did the government formally request the extradition of the DEA agent. As of this writing, the U.S. embassy has not responded to the request.

Conclusion

U.S.-Bolivia counternarcotics efforts since 1989 have been characterized by false starts, promises, and disappointing results. Over the past three years, the Bolivian government has pursued interdiction policies designed in the United States — either by executive branch agencies or congressionally sanctioned oversight — and has little success in pushing forward its "coca for development" or alternative development program. Since 1985, Bolivia has signed two major bilateral counternarcotics agreements (1987 and 1992); in addition, more than any other country in South America, the last two democratic governments of Bolivia have agreed to allow overt and covert U.S. military and law enforcement activities.

The Paz Zamora administration has opted to play along with the Americans for several reasons: European contacts not coming through with promises of greater aid for noninterdiction programs, relentless pressure from an "activist" ambassador, U.S. accusations of involvement against prominent members of the government undermining its ability to negotiate with the United States, U.S. threats to withdraw conditioned assistance, U.S. leverage over international financial institutions, and the lack of an acceptable Bolivian alternative to U.S. policy.

Why has the United States pursued potentially destabilizing policies for the past seven years? Conventional wisdom about U.S. counternarcotics policy suggests that foreign policy is largely the work of intermestic forces. In the United States, numerous groups ranging from mothers against drunk drivers to congresspersons seeking reelection have influenced the course of policy; in fact, their pressure has made U.S. policy harsher. Bolivian pressure groups and democratic institutions, however, have had little influence over the direction, tone, and substance of counternarcotics policy. They have been systematically excluded to avoid damaging political costs.

The consequences of this pattern of bilateral relations has been illustrated. U.S.-Bolivia counternarcotics policies encourage Bolivian governments to behave unconstitutionally. Whenever policies can avoid the potentially troublesome obstacles of democratic politics, such as the Santa Ana del Yacuma civic action exercises, U.S. and Bolivian planners skirt the process. In fact, Bolivian counternarcotics planning has become the absolute patrimony of a few bureaucrats in the key ministries and police organizations. Congress, which has a constitutional role in foreign policy making, has virtually no input. Neither does the Bolivian public.

In 1992, the results of U.S.-Bolivia counternarcotics efforts are very clear. Progress is measured exclusively in terms of bureaucratic goals, as Malamud-Gotti points out.[77] Unreliable statistics on coca hectarage eradicated, tonnage of cocaine seized, traffickers arrested, airplanes confiscated, and the like provide legitimacy to the actions of both the multiple U.S. agencies and the Bolivian civilian, police, and military units involved. It is also clear that more cocaine is leaving Bolivia than in 1989 when Paz Zamora took office despite claims from the bureaucracies involved. This situation speaks clearly to the futility of interdiction-based efforts as well as alternative development programs.

Anti-Americanism spawned by this pattern of foreign policy making is the most obvious and potentially troubling consequence. The perception by Bolivians that their sovereignty has been lost is the product of overzealous counternarcotics efforts which occasionally violate the rules of engagement. In fact, U.S. actions in Bolivia lack accountability. U.S. congressional oversight is rare and ineffective. Thus, the perception that Americans are acting with impunity may not be incorrect. Why does the United States pursue the policy anyway? Perhaps the answer lies in a quote from a U.S. military planner at the Southern Command in Panama. Noting the new unchallenged status of military power, he boldly stated, "Why do we invade nations and carry out bully policies? Because we can."

Notes

1. The most significant works in Spanish on U.S.-Bolivia relations are Raúl Barrios Morón, *Bolivia y Estados Unidos: Democracia, Derechos Humanos, y Narcotrafico* (La Paz: FLACSO, 1989), which focuses solely on the García Meza period (1980-1982); and Carlos Navia Ribera, *Los Estados Unidos y la Revolucion Nacional* (Cochabamba: CIDRE, 1984). In English, consult Claire Hargraves, *Snow Fields* (New York: Holmes and Meier, 1992); and Jaime Malamud-Gotti, *Smoke and Mirrors* (Boulder: Westview Press, 1992). A less academic treatment of joint counternarcotics efforts is provided by Michael Levine, *Deep Cover* (Delacorte Press, 1990.)

2. See, for example, Gamarra, "Bolivia ante la Estrategia de Estados Unidos", in *Cuarto Intermedio* Number 20 (August 1991) and "U.S. Military Assistance, the Militarization of the War on Drugs, and the Prospects for Democracy in Bolivia," paper presented at the XVI Congress of the Latin American Studies Association, Washington, D.C., April 1991.

3. Consult, for example, Bruce Bagley, "The Myths of Militarization", (Miami: North-South Center 1991).

4. This became especially pronounced during the 1988 election when drugs were considered the principal problem facing Americans.

5. U.S. policy makers faced pressures from numerous interest groups which emerged in the midst of the great drug scare of the mid-1980s. This was reflected especially by the intensity with which "liberal" members of Congress pushed for tougher sanctions against drug producing nations. Note, for example, that on several occasions, the Bush administration served as an advocate for nations, such as Bolivia, which had been decertified by the Democratic majority to receive economic and military assistance.

6. See, for example, Abraham Lowenthal, *Exporting Democracy* (Johns Hopkins University Press, 1991).

7. See Malamud-Gotti, *Smoke and Mirrors*, and Gamarra, "U.S. Military Assistance...".

8. This process has been analyzed in detail. Consult James Malloy and Eduardo A. Gamarra, "The Patrimonial Dynamics of Party Politics in Bolivia," in Scott Mainwaring and Timothy Scully, eds., *Party Politics in Latin America* (Stanford University Press, 1993) and E. Gamarra, "Hybrid Presidentialism and Democratization in Bolivia," in Scott Mainwaring and Matthew Shugart, eds., *Presidentialism in Latin America* (University of North Carolina Press, 1993).

9. For a brief history of the Paz Estenssoro government's counternarcotics strategy, Eduardo A. Gamarra, "Militarization, the War on Drugs, and the Prospects for Bolivian Democracy," paper presented at the XVI Congress of the Latin American Studies Association. U.S. counternarcotics strategies also dominated programs administered by U.S. AID, especially those aimed at strengthening political institutions. Assistance to the judiciary, for example, was tied to counternarcotics strategies. Consult E. Gamarra, *The Administration of Justice in Bolivia: An Institutional Analysis* (Miami, FIU, Center for the Administration of Justice, 1991).

10. None were more problematic to the Paz Estenssoro government than charges against Fernando Barthelemy, the minister of interior during Operation Blast Furnace, of links to the narcotics industry. Barthelemy's role in the investigation of the September 1986 murder of Noel Kempff Mercado, a prominent scientist, in the Huanchaca region of eastern Bolivia became the main issue.

11. For an in-depth examination of these disputes, consult Jorge Malamud-Gotti, *Smoke and Mirrors.* See also "U.S. Congress . . . 1990."

12. Gelbard claimed he had initially opposed his assignment to Bolivia fearing he would be unable to maintain a detached and objective perspective. In retrospect, Gelbard believes his mission was successful because he was able to serve both U.S. and Bolivian national interests. Interview, Washington, D.C., September 20, 1991.

13. Interview with Ana María Campero, director of *Presencia,* a leading La Paz daily who was often the target of Ambassador Gelbard's wrath.

14. Interview with Ambassador Jorge Crespo, Washington, D.C., June 5, 1990. Crespo spearheaded efforts in Washington to counter the momentum toward full-scale militarization. Bolivian embassy officials noted in several interviews that the ambassador's efforts in Washington proved costly. In an ironic twist of events, Ambassador Gelbard reportedly accused Crespo of "involvement in the internal affairs of the United States" and allegedly exerted pressure on the Paz Zamora government to secure his resignation. Gelbard denied these allegations in an interview with the author on September 26, 1991, and accused Crespo of promoting disinformation about U.S. policy objectives.

15. Ambassador Crespo interview, June 5, 1990.

16. This is not to say that the policies would have worked with a less activist ambassador. The policies of the Andean strategy, in my view, are conceptually flawed.

17. Interviews with officials at the Bureau of International Narcotics Matters in Washington, D.C., April 1991, and embassy officials in La Paz, July 1991, confirmed that the United States suspected Guillermo Capobianco, the minister of interior, and Colonel Carvajal, the newly appointed commander of the police. Ambassador Gelbard in my September 26, 1991, interview claimed that these specific linkages were discovered much later.

18. In several interviews with members of the MIR, the embassy's accusations against Capobianco were dismissed. Most argued that the embassy never presented evidence to support their accusations.

19. Michael Isikoff, "Blunt Assessment of Bolivia Ignored," *Washington Post,* March 1, 1990. This assessment was confirmed in several interviews with high-ranking members of the U.S. embassy in La Paz in July 1991.

20. For an analysis of the Bush administration's National Drug Control Strategy and the role of the military, consult Bruce Bagley, "The Myths of Militarization" (Miami: North-South Center, 1991). For Bolivia's response, see E. Gamarra, "U.S. Military Assistance, the War on Drugs, and Democratization in Bolivia." It is worth noting that the Bolivian government developed a long-term strategy to replace the coca-cocaine economy which included plans to create jobs and to substitute coca income and crops.

21. Nevertheless, U.S. government officials were dismayed by the failure of the raid. According to an internal INM memo quoted by the *Washington Post*, the raid failed to achieve even minimal success and cost the U.S. government over $100,000. Moreover, U.S. government officials believed Bolivian officials tipped off Colombian traffickers who fled the scene long before the raid took place.

22. For a review of Snow Cap, consult U.S. Congress, 1990, Committee on Government Operations, *Stopping the Flood of Cocaine with Operation Snow Cap: Is It Working?* 101st Cong., 2nd sess. House Report: 101-673.

23. The State Department's INM, however, was clearly disappointed by 1989 eradication figures. Despite a commitment of $200 million, "the Bolivians have eradicated only about half their own legal target of 12,350 acres of coca, while new plantings by farmers caused overall production to increase for the year by 9.2 percent." Quoted in Isikoff, "Blunt Assessment of Bolivia Ignored."

24. U.S. embassy officials argued that the Arce Gómez expulsion was not so much to get U.S. pressure off the government's back but because Paz Zamora did not know how to deal with him in Bolivia. In short, the best way was to expel him to eliminate a potentially embarrassing domestic problem. The expulsion of Arce Gómez, however, violated the Bolivan constitution and set off a long-lasting confrontation between the Paz Zamora government and the Supreme Court.

25. See, for example, Mark Dion, Testimony Before the Select Committee on Narcotics Abuse and Control, House of Representatives, June 7, 1989.

26. U.S. troops arrived in Potosí in May 1989 to level the Pati Pati hill that obstructed the runway in that city's airport. This "civic action" mission was supported by Potosí's local civic committees. Other localities around the country requested similar programs; however, controversy continued to surround the program as some groups claimed it was part of a covert effort to build a U.S. military base in Bolivia.

27. While most of the aid was to go toward equipping and training, Annex III claims that a substantial, but unspecified, portion of this amount will go to civic action programs. The army was to obtain training and equipment for two infantry battlions for countermarcotics operations, training and equipment for two engineering battalions for civic action programs, training and equipment for a transport battalion, and training and equipment for a supply and services section. The air force was scheduled to receive helicopter and airplane parts, six new UH-1H helicopters, and maintenance and repairs for its entire air fleet. Additionally, the air military police was to receive training and equipment. The navy obtained up to eight Piraña patrol boats and four additional 36-foot patrol boats. Navy personnel received training and equipment.

28. Interview, July 1991.

29. See "Paz Zamora anuncia ingreso de FF. AA. a la lucha antidroga," *Ultima Hora*, May 19, 1990, 20.

30. *Ultima Hora*, May 19, 1990.

31. See Christopher Marquis, "Bolivia to Use U.S. Drug Aid For Environment," *Miami Herald*, September 11, 1990.

32. Interviews with members of the Ministry of Industry and Trade and with members of the Bolivian embassy staff in Washington confirmed this view. Former Ambassador Gelbard, however, claimed that this was also part of the disinformation

campaign orchestrated by the Bolivian embassy in Washington. Interview, Washington, D.C., September 26, 1991.

33. Government officials argued that union leaders were receiving payments from drug traffickers and that these leaders were the ones who opposed the eradication of coca crops. In a resolution dated September 27, 1991, the XII Coca Growers Union Ampliado gave the minister of interior 72 hours to arrest union leaders linked to drug trafficking or the CSUTCB would sue for defamation. As of this writing, the government has not charged or arrested any peasant leaders.

34. Interview with Ambassador Jorge Crespo, June 5, 1990, and Bolivian government officials in July 1991.

35. Interviews with high-ranking members of the army who were present during the Annex III negotiations and claimed that U.S. embassy officials told them that if they chose not to accept the $14 million, it would be given to the navy and air force. In the context of an economically austere national budget, $14 million was difficult to pass up. Army officers were also misled perhaps into believing that the $14 million would provide benefits to the entire institution and not only to two regiments that were to be trained by the United States.

36. The figures for 1990 were remarkable: 7,865 hectares were eradicated although the target was only 6,000.

37. The escalation of counternarcotics operations in Colombia interrupted the aerial link between the Colombian cartels and the paste factories in Bolivia. An oversupply of coca leaf in the Bolivian market contributed to a considerable drop (to about $10 per 100-lb. weight) in prices.

38. Meco Dominguez's drug-related businesses included a car dealership and a posh nightclub in Santa Cruz and several airplanes. Police also seized $337,000 in cash at the time of his arrest.

39. For an English account of the event, consult Sam Dillon, "Bolivian Cocaine Ring Decimated, U.S. Says," *Miami Herald*, September 29, 1990. On May 14, 1991, "Meco" escaped from the La Paz prison where he was being held but was "recaptured" when the government realized his disappearance would not be seen as something positive when Robert Martinez, the U.S. drug czar, arrived to check on Bolivian progress in the drug war. It was later revealed that "Meco" had a special pass to visit his personal physician in Santa Cruz.

40. For a fascinating journalist's account of the incident, consult Clare Hargraves, *Snowfields* (New York: Holmes and Meier, 1992).

41. DEA screening goes beyond counternarcotics agencies. Leaders of the major political parties revealed in interviews that their lists of candidates for Congress and other political offices are also screened by the DEA. Interviews with embassy officials confirmed these accounts. Ambassador Gelbard noted proudly after the inauguration of Paz Zamora that he had forced "corrupt congressmen out of the legislature."

42. For an extensive discussion of the conspiracy alluded to by the embassy, consult Claire Hargraves, *Snowfields* (New York: Holmes and Meier, 1992) and *Inmobiliarias: la estafa del siglo!* (La Paz: CEDOIN, Informe Especial, December 1991).

43. See Raúl Barrios Morón, "Drug War Psychology," in *Hemisphere* (1991).

44. See "Piranha Patrol," *Soldier of Fortune* (June 1991) and "Death to the Tyrant Cocaine," *Soldier of Fortune* (July 1991).

45. Interviews with members of the Bolivian National Congress over the past year and a half demonstrated the absolute lack of information that the legislature has in matters related to foreign affairs, especially the conduct of the drug war.

46. Significantly, the army was not part of the operations because the two battalions had not completed their training in Santa Cruz.

47. See, for example, "Bolivian Hub of Drug Trade is Shut Down," *Miami Herald*, June 30, 1991, and Sam Dillon, "Bolivia to Cut U.S. Role in Drug War," *Miami Herald*, July 16, 1991.

48. The charges made by Gelbard against the navy officer were corroborated subsequently. From the point of view of Carlos Iturralde, the minister of foreign affairs, however, Gelbard chose a most inopportune time to make the charges public. The outgoing ambassador chose to inform the press moments after accepting the "Condor of the Andes," Bolivia's highest award. The confrontation which followed was punctuated by the minister's boycott of a Fourth of July reception at the U.S. embassy and Gelbard's initial refusal to sign an economic assistance package. Moments later, Gelbard departed Bolivia. A few days later, Paz Zamora told a Spanish newspaper that he had breathed a sigh of relief when the U.S. ambassador left the country.

49. On September 13, 1991, Gastón Encinas, the president of the chamber of deputies, argued that because of the success of the repentance decree, the militarization of the drug war was no longer necessary. A coca union leader offered a more realistic view. He claimed that despite the repentance decree, by October 15, the armed forces would enter counternarcotics operations, including a forced eradication campaign. He argued that the government believed that with the repentance decree, the price of coca would drop; however, this was not the case. In late September, the "carga" of coca (100 lbs.) sold for 250-280 bolivianos and showed no signs of a decline. Even the commander of the army manifested his hope that the amnesty or repentance decree would produce enough "arrepentidos" so that the militarization of counternarcotics efforts could be avoided.

50. According to the DEA and UMOPAR, the organization led by Hugo and his brother Rafael Rivero Villavicencio was capable of providing 1,000 kg. of cocaine per month to Colombian drug lords.

51. Betancur, allegedly the principal intermediary between the Santa Ana and Medellín cartels, died in a La Paz jail. The official report was that he died of tuberculosis; however, following complaints from the Colombian embassy, it became clear that Betancur died because of a lack of adequate medical attention.

52. U.S. embassy officials doubted that the Supreme Court would allow the extradition of Roca's relatives and insisted that sooner or later the Bolivian government would have to sign a new treaty.

53. In a press communique on September 25, the U.S. embassy reiterated that it reserved itself the right to request the extradition of any Bolivian who violated U.S. antidrug laws. However, the communique also supported the repentance decree. On September 27, responding to the backlash produced by the embassy communique, the Catholic Church (Archbishop Luis Sainz) asked the government to keep its promise to the drug traffickers who turned themselves in.

54. Interview with Javier Lupo Gamarra, Director General, CONALID, La Paz, Bolivia, July 7, 1991.

55. On September 26, for example, Gonzalo Torrico, the undersecretary for social defense, told a group of campesinos in the Chapare that the government was worried by evidence of greater narcotrafficking activity despite the surrender of six traffickers. He noted that in Chapare alone, 300 kg. of cocaine had been confiscated in two months. Torrico warned that the government would continue to apply repression and alternative development policies.

56. "Embajador Bowers listo para erradicar cocales con machete en mano," *Hoy Internacional*, November 11-17, 1991, 7.

57. "Embajador de EE. UU. recibe dura crítica parlamentaria por su oferta de 'machete'." *Hoy Internacional*, November 11-17, 1991, 7.

58. Like Gelbard, Bowers has a flare for controversial statements. In May 1992, for example, responding to Bolivian government efforts to promote the industrialization of coca leaf, he argued that the coca leaf was not a "sacred leaf" as the Bolivians believed, but the leaf of slavery, which had facilitated the conquest of the Andean region by the Spanish.

59. Erick Torrico, "Coercion, el refugio del gobierno," in *Informe* Año XI, number 228 (October 1991).

60. Bureau of International Narcotics Matters, *International Narcotics Control Strategy Report* (March 1992), 93.

61. This charge was ratified in a personal interview with members of the principal opposition force. My interviewee claimed to have spoken off the record with members of the U.S. embassy (February 1992) who argued that a U.S. base was in the works. In my view, however, given the current mood in the United States and the plans to close numerous bases around the globe, no such plan is likely.

62. At the inauguration of the CIOS, U.S. Ambassador Bowers argued that military operations were aimed at destroying the communication nets of the traffickers and would not target or arrest any individuals. Bowers' statement intended to differentiate the mission of the army from that of UMOPAR.

63. Office of the Inspector General, "Drug Control Activities in Bolivia," (United States State Department, October 1991), 1.

64. Office of the Inspector General, "Drug Control...," 2-3.

65. On October 16, 1991, for example, the Commander of the Navy, Vice Admiral Rolando Herrera, announced that the counternarcotics war could be expanded to include counterterrorism. On October 17, the Commander of the Army, Guido Sandoval, and Mario Rueda Peña, the minister of information, agreed that the military could be tapped to take on a counterterrorism role. These declarations came in the wake of increased terrorist activity on the part of the so-called Ejercito Guerrillero Tupac Katari.

66. This group expressed solidarity with the attempted coup leaders in Venezuela, charging Bolivian politicians with corruption and selling out to the Americans.

67. Personal communication from R. Gelbard to author, April 24, 1992.

68. See, for example, "Tropas de EE. UU. entrenan en Bolivia para ocupar Amazonia," *La Razón,* July 15, 1992, A1 and 7.

69. At the same time, the U.S. ambassador prepared a trip to Santa Ana to show the residents an HBO video on the impact of crack cocaine on the streets of Miami.

70. Interview with senior army officer, Panama City, Panama, July 27, 1992. It is noteworthy, however, that while the U.S. military is open to discuss the nature of most of its activities in South America, anything related to counternarcotics is classified.

71. According to a senior U.S. army officer, a Galaxy costs between $20,000 to $30,000 per flight hour. Perplexed Bolivians could not understand why the United States would spend so much to build a school that cost under $50,000. In interviews with the commanders of the armed forces, they noted that the Bolivian military could build the same school for one-tenth the cost.

72. I am also suggesting that it is the responsibility of U.S. officials, who are presumably promoting the development of democratic values in Bolivia, to insure the legality and constitutionality of any U.S. or joint U.S.-Bolivia action. In this instance, the U.S. ambassador and the commander of the U.S. military group in Bolivia failed to prepare the political groundwork before the 18th Airborne arrived. Not only were U.S. interests not served, but the Bolivian government's already tarnished image was severely compromised.

73. Maclean's difficult position was illustrated to me in an interview on July 15, 1992. Despite repeated requests to the U.S. embassy, the ministry of foreign affairs has been unable to obtain an accurate count of the number of U.S. personnel in Bolivia. In short, the government bows to U.S. pressures, and the minister takes all the public heat.

74. Interview with Ambassador Bowers, La Paz, July 9, 1992.

75. Roca Suarez's lawyer claimed that the Supreme Court magistrates demanded $500,000 to secure a favorable judgment. The defense team suggested that a higher payment may have been made by the government to satisfy U.S. demands.

76. According to embassy officials, the DEA agent had just arrived in Bolivia and lacked a permit to carry a weapon. For a slanted and belated version of the incident and the general mood in Bolivia in August about U.S.-Bolivia relations, consult Nathaniel Cash, "Anti-American Feeling in Bolivia Could Reverse Progress in Drug War," *Miami Herald,* September 20, 1992. Cash adopts the U.S. official version that the DEA officer "accidently" shot and wounded the Bolivian man.

77. Malamud-Gotti, *Smoke and Mirrors.*

References

Bagley, Bruce M. 1991. *The Myths of Militarization*. Miami: North-South Center.

Barrios Morón, Raúl. 1989. *Bolivia y Estados Unidos: Democracia, Derechos Humanos, y Narcotráfico*. La Paz: FLACSO.

Barrios Morón, Raúl. 1991. "Drug War Psychology." *Hemisphere*.

Bureau of International Narcotics Matters. 1992. *International Narcotics Control Report*. Washington, D.C.: U.S. Department of State.

Dillon, Sam. 1990. "Bolivian Cocaine Ring Decimated, U.S. Says." *Miami Herald*. September 29.

Dillon, Sam. 1991. "Bolivia to Cut U.S. Role in War on Drugs." *Miami Herald*. July 16.

Gamarra, Eduardo. 1991a. "Bolivia ante de la Estrategia de Estados Unidos." *Cuarto Intermedio*. No. 20. August.

Gamarra, Eduardo. 1991b. "U.S. Military Assistance, the Militarization of the War on Drugs, and the Prospects for Democracy in Bolivia." Presented at the XVI Conference of the Latin American Studies Association, Washington, D.C., Spring.

Gamarra, Eduardo. 1991c. *The Administration of Justice in Bolivia: An Institutional Analysis*. Miami: Florida International University, Center for the Administration of Justice.

Gamarra, Eduardo. 1993a. "The Patrimonial Dynamics of Party Politics in Bolivia." In *Party Politics in Latin America*, eds. Scott Mainwaring and Timothy Scully. Palo Alto: Stanford University Press.

Gamarra, Eduardo. 1993b. "Hybrid Presidentialism and Democratization in Bolivia." In *Presidentialism in Latin America*, eds. Scott Mainwaring and Matthew Shugart. Chapel Hill: University of North Carolina Press.

Hargraves, Clare. 1992. *Snowfields*. New York: Holmes and Meier.

Hoy Internacional. 1991a. "Embajador Bowers Listo Para Erradicar Cocales con 'Machete' en Mano." November 11-17:7.

Hoy Internacional. 1991b. "Embajador de EE. UU. Recibe Dura Critica Parlamentaria por su Oferto de 'Machete'." November 11-17: 7.

Isikoff, Michael. 1990. "Blunt Assessment of Bolivia Ignored." *Washington Post*. March 1.

Levine, Michael. 1990. *Deep Cover*. New York: Delacorte Press.

Lowenthal, Abraham. 1991. *Exploring Democracy*. Washington, D.C.: Johns Hopkins University Press.

Malamud-Gotti, Jaime. 1992. *Smoke and Mirrors*. Boulder, Colo.: Westview Press.

Marquis, Christopher. 1990. "Bolivia to Use U.S. Drug Aid for Environment." *Miami Herald*. September 11.

Miami Herald. 1991. "Bolivian Hub of Drug Trade is Shut Down." June 30.

Navia Ribera, Carlos. 1984. *Los Estados Unidos y la Revolución Nacional*. Cochabamba: CIDRE.

La Razón. 1992. "Tropas en Estados Unidos Entrenan en Bolivia para Ocupar Amazonia." July 15: A1,7.

Torrico, Erick. 1991. "Coerción, el Refugio del Gobierno." *Informe R.* 11(228), October.

Ultima Hora. 1990. "Paz Zamora Anuncia Ingreso de FF.AA. a la Lucha Antidroga." May 19.

U.S. Congress. Committee on Government Operations. 1990. *Stopping the Flood of Cocaine with Operation Snowcap: Is it Working?* Washington, D.C.: U.S. Government Printing Office.

Ecuador

Chapter Fourteen

Ecuador and the War on Drugs

X. Adrian Bonilla

Introduction

This chapter condenses a series of previous studies — among them, theoretical approaches — with the objective of producing contemporary reflections sustained by present empirical data. First, U.S. policy will be analyzed concerning the problem of drugs and specific considerations developed in the case of Ecuador. The topic of Ecuadoran international policy with its motivations and relative measures that directly affect society will then be discussed.

The chapter will then look at a series of international treaties and agreements in order to locate corresponding dynamic policies. These elements are the framework from which to systematize existing information on state structural reforms and their social effect as pertains to interdiction policies. Finally, the international context surrounding considerations of money laundering in Ecuador will be discussed.

The conclusions will deal with a critical explanation of Ecuadoran policy, as well as the U.S. policy nurturing it, introducing them to the process of drug trafficking and its problems that have grown in Ecuador despite the introduction of an orthodox approach based on the U.S. Department of State's Andean strategy.

U.S. Policy: Intrepid Persistence

Up to the 1990s, Ecuador's involvement in the War on Drugs was conceptualized as peripheral in relation to complexities in the production of coca-cocaine and other illegal drugs. Although it was recognized that money laundering operations were taking place in Ecuador, as well as the refining of raw materials and the commercialization of chemical bases, and that Ecuador was being used as a transit station, there existed no data that outlined the dimensions of the conflict.[1] None of these characteristics of Ecuadoran participation seem to have changed; the role the country plays cannot, however, be considered secondary if one takes into consideration those indicators that have created what the North American government believes is reality and which have sustained the so-called "success" of the war on drugs, that is, the seizure of shipments, the imprisonment of suspects, and the destruction of laboratories.[2]

The latter cannot be explained merely by the efforts carried out by Ecuador directed at strengthening control and repressive measures that have been orthodox in the application of an antidrug strategy, and which have brought about structural legal reform in the country's penal system and in certain legislation directed at the financial system. The explanation involves a reality with an international character that meets with the will of Ecuadoran decision makers — in the event that they have determined alternatives — and places the political process in the hands of actors they have no control over, such as traffickers themselves and the U.S. government.

Besides contributing to rhetoric that legitimizes antidrug policies and generally participates with procedural observations, the Ecuadoran government has not, as far as state international fora organized to combat drug trafficking, presented autonomous initiatives; on the contrary, they have repeatedly followed the general antidrug strategy designed by the Department of State of the United States which has been the policy that has held the initiative and imposed its hegemony.[3]

Washington's policy has caused reactions varying from expert opinion to ideological opposition. In the academic area, one can mention two general criticisms. First, that the realist perception of the world[4] has neglected to consider the presence of multiple transnational and subnational actors, as well as the difficulty of Latin American states involved in the conflict in controlling their own territories, to such an extent that the concept of national security has come to mean a partial approach. In the very proposal of principle of the war on drugs lies the incapacity to stop drug trafficking.[5]

On the other hand, an analysis that refers to the production of hegemony as a relevant variable may propose that the antidrug war has been operative in the production of discourse that interpolates U.S. society in order to generate legitimacy for a concrete sector of power represented by the Republican party. Its policy has had international dimensions in a world characterized by a universalized economy, where the political dimension of the state, society, and world order have levels of interrelationship.[6]

This can be proven empirically by the rigid tenacity of U.S. policy in implementing a strategy that favors interdiction, repression, and, today, militarization of the war on drugs (despite the fact that throughout the three past presidential administrations there has been no reduction in production or flow of narcotics nor the social and political conflict derived from it), and because an aggressive intolerance developed since 1986 coincides with indicators showing a slow decline in North American drug use prior to this policy. With this data, it is possible to build the hypothesis that the problem is an ideological creation of politicians whose battle horse was precisely to use the opposite argument: that is, that in the mid-1980s, there was an uncontrollable growth in demand that verged on a social epidemic.[7]

It is clear then that the problem of drug trafficking has received a political treatment that prevails over the criteria of public health. This is how President Ronald Reagan had considered it since 1982, and this perception has not changed. It is also the same status granted it in the present analysis.

One point of reference seems to summarize U.S. antidrug policy in the Andean region and that is militarization of the conflict. It is expressed in budgetary terms where more than 50 percent of resources allocated to the antidrug fight in source countries is used on military assistance.[8] In addition to increasing its presence in the area, the U.S. government insists on transforming a problem that could have been social into a true war for producer nations by a series of programs on the articulation of the armed forces of Latin American countries.[9]

The realist perception in the war on drugs has failed. The prohibitionist policy has increased drug earnings; it has complicated the political picture and has challenged the fragile institutionality of source countries. Production has been internationalized, spreading the conflict into various geographical and social areas.[10]

In Latin America, this type of strategy faces a series of contradictions. First, given that the objective is to eliminate drug trafficking, the strategy does not assume that the answer to the problem cannot be possible unless nation states represent society as a whole or at least partially. This objective is difficult to achieve within a context characterized by a precarious institutionality wherein instruments for this type of activity lack support or legitimacy. The first case involves, for example, local governments and the system of justice, those eluded by the strategy of militarization. The second case alludes to the role of the armed forces and the police in contexts where arbitrariness has been common — indexes of human rights violations in the entire area are not, precisely, indicators of legitimacy. But there is still more and it has to do with the use of troops —medium strength commands and even top staff — into networks of informal reproduction of societies living in the midst of structural poverty, which supposes logical conditions so that corruption defeats the original plans for control.

An alternative policy, therefore, would entail the consolidation of state presence in the region by means of its institutionality, which cannot occur if mechanisms to promote development in those countries affected by trafficking are not taken into consideration.[11] Procedures such as those mentioned which imply structural reforms that will create more space for civilian participation (and representation), that is, for democratic expansion, cannot take place under conditions of aggression where the imposition of force causes social reactions that will subvert order. On the other hand, for North American policy, this can imply a nationalistic feeling of rejection without the benefit of a strategy that is limited by the affluence of U.S. funds which isolate other regions of the world involved in trafficking.[12]

In Ecuador, where frictions between the armed forces and drug traffickers as well as with Colombian guerrilla groups have been rather sporadic, the government has backed a military decision to participate in the conflict, using their own resources.[13] There, participation in the war on drugs has been conceived as a sort of extension of the Enterprise for the Americas Initiative because of the eventual commercial advantages of export products. Hence, the economic elite, who normally have used the argument of national sovereignty as a mechanism of political pressure,[14] have not denounced North American participation in decision making related to national security.

The Andean antidrug strategy in regards to transit countries has given the greatest priority to Ecuador, Brazil, and Venezuela. This is a major provision if one takes into account that the "balloon" effect, that is, the expansion of drug trafficking into areas in which there were no previous operations, is precisely an old result of repressive policies that did not include social processes. Such was the case of the transport of Mexican marijuana into other countries and more profitable drugs such as Colombian cocaine, or presently, the growing of opium poppy. The total amount asked on behalf of Ecuador in 1992 in the fiscal budget, $3 million, doubles that of 1990 and is to be used to improve intelligence services, search for and capture traffickers, and destroy laboratories.[15]

In light of this, the Texas conference has not produced any change for Ecuador, except the development of preexisting policies. Although agreements were reached for the stabilization of penal and financial legislation, in the area of military escalation the objective of forming a mutual military force was far from being achieved. On this occasion, thanks to a preparatory meeting in Quito, the Ecuadoran government assumed an Andean position on the drug war.

North American evaluation of the Ecuadoran drug policy is generally positive.[16] The problem is that the Department of State uses basic parameters in its strategic design for the Andean region, those that elude the dimension of the problem in Ecuador because it is not a producer country. Despite this, there is no counterproposal from the Ecuadoran government toward this policy; its indicators are the same.

Ecuadoran Foreign Policy: Cooperation and Acceptance

In addition to data on captures and trials, as well as the budget that the Ecuadoran government allocates to its antidrug policy, there is a generalized consensual attitude regarding the drug war in Ecuador which has been revealed in the unanimous position of the press and political parties. As far as U.S. cooperation, there have been few discrepancies.

The general attitude of Ecuadoran society, in comparison with other Andean countries involved in the drug problem, seems to favor the policy of control and repression. Effectively, after a survey of companies carried out in Colombia, Ecuador, Peru, and Bolivia by USIA,[17] it was found that Ecuadorans grant the least value to alternative development as an option to narcotics production. At the same time, they are the most favorable to greater military or police intervention, controls on money laundering, the confiscation of properties linked to trafficking; they are slightly second to Peruvians in their willingness to work closely with the United States in favor of extradition.[18]

Similar positions are demonstrated regarding the policy of seizures and repression of drug traffickers. Nor is there any variation on the issue of herbicides as environmentally dangerous. Ecuadorans choose what, in their opinion, is the lesser evil, that is, contamination. Additional data along these lines indicates repugnance in the Andean world toward legalization.

How can we interpret these attitudes? First of all, we should mention that, despite the role Ecuador plays in the circuit of illegal drug production, it has not suffered with any immediacy the impact of physical violence related to drugs. Ecuador does not have a rural guerrilla organization that maintains ties of protection for cultivators. There are no peasants dedicated to the business. At present, trafficking networks operating in the country are a function of Colombian illegal operations; therefore, there is no challenge to state institutionality; there is no narco-bourgeoisie that tries to be part of the political system nor one that directly challenges the power of the state.

One can say that the publicity campaign against the consequences of the use of drugs has been extremely strong and effective, above all in a society where the problem of use has been so small that there has essentially been no one to fight against. Discretion used in handling U.S. presence has been notable. The image of being a victim of neighboring countries has alienated the problem of popular perception and has even been assimilated outside of the country.[19] All of these elements have created a favorable climate, one that can also be explained by Ecuador's economic needs in an economy that is forced to export and which could not do so under circumstances in which neighboring countries enjoy preferences Ecuador does not. Hence, the national objective in the war on drugs, apart from financial assistance, has always been mediated by inclusion in the Andean system of preferences which grants certain advantages in the North American market to those products exported from the region.

Violence related to drugs is interpreted erroneously by society. Youth gangs have been the object of concern of the media in the main cities of Ecuador. By reproducing crimes attributed to them, a semblance has been attempted that is remotely similar to U.S. street violence seen on television. With the exception of conflicts over land and urban property, this is probably recognized as the greatest problem of social violence in Ecuador. However, approaches of an anthropological nature with on-site field research have proven that the criminal activity of youth gangs is normally carried out within contexts made possible by the use of illegal drugs, such as alcohol, while illegal activities operate within the framework of socialization and the daily lives of these people.[20]

In conjunction with the fact that Ecuadoran society is generally ignorant of the direct repercussions of the war on drugs, this picture explains the support given this strategy, and even more so when military participation in Ecuador's contemporary political life has not implied anything but the eventual implementation of policies of exclusion or generalized repression. On the subject of extradition, it is fitting to note, however, that despite the popular support this survey has shown, virtually all political sectors of the country are opposed to the possibility of including this legal mechanism in the new antidrug law, as suggested by the president of the republic; it was immediately withdrawn. Bolivia, who has suffered several acts with the direct participation of the United States, is the nation that is more opposed to working with the United States; or Colombia, who, under pressure, applied extradition treaties against nationals, is a country that openly indicates rejection of this instrument.

Because there are no crop problems in Ecuador and that only a fraction of the population survives by this means, there is no notion of the social problem nor are there conditions for the formation of ideas related to alternatives for development, which frankly occurs in a majority of the other three countries. During the survey, the Ecuadoran people in most cases were asked about the problem they are not experiencing at present, but which affects them because of the legitimization of policies that have caused the elimination of these very problems.

Consensus based on error, publicity, and the country's structural needs, in addition to inconsistencies in incredibly abundant resources directed at prevention and repression legitimize other paradoxes of a technical nature. One of the most outstanding is that while the national police and the military customs police are the agencies that made the greatest number of drug seizures while simultaneously incarcerating the greatest number of people, their budgets are less symbolic when compared to that of the armed forces. This leads to the conjecture that efficiency in the war on drugs is not the object as much as the social legitimization and implementation of the motivation that helps to generate policies, as well as their ideological profitability.

In his state of the union address of March 1991, President George Bush mentioned that Ecuador was receiving $15 million for development, $3 million for expenditures on the war on drugs, and $5 million for military assistance, figures that do not always coincide with data. In the same address, President Bush praised the decision of Andean countries to become involved in this struggle, mentioning — something unusual — Ecuador.[21]

Ecuadoran resources for antidrug activities in 1991 came mainly from the United States. Although not all of it was used in control and repressive activities, most was invested in this line. According to the U.S. embassy, approximately $40 million, from which $36 million comes from the armed forces, are the estimates of cooperation in joint projects, as well as by U.S. agencies that work autonomously with links to joint activities, such as USAID and USIS. For the fiscal year 1992, the United States will only invest US$9,328,926, while the Ecuadoran state will invest a figure close to $2.5 million.[22]

Data on U.S. assistance, however, is subject to different interpretations. For the Ecuadoran foreign ministry, which has complained that they are not being considered in the Andean strategy on drugs, North American assistance in 1990 reached US$4,965,000 and in 1991 it did not exceed $5 million.[23]

A brief analysis of the budget mentioned by CONSEP as well as the foreign ministry proposes the greatest lines assigned for activities against drug trafficking in repression and control. Even more, tendency toward militarization is clear. While in 1990, the foreign ministry confirmed that the national police received $910,000 and the customs police, $170,000, the armed forces in training, support, and munitions received US$3,585,000.[24] In 1991, for police activities (customs, national police, and INTERPOL), planned assistance by the Department of State reached US$2,546,000, a figure that should be compared to the $36 million in support and training of the armed forces contributed by their counterparts in the United States. There were $2 million for training and $300,000 for the evaluation of the Ecuadoran penal system, both granted by USAID.

This data speaks for itself and suggests a contradiction in antidrug policy, at least in the case of Ecuador. If legitimization of activities is sustained in an address that attacks the use of drugs and defends itself with preventive rhetoric, expenditures for state and international cooperation to achieve this objective are, undoubtedly, small. In this fashion, legitimacy covers objectives that differ from those proposed publicly and which, given the large amount of interest in this conflict which is sustained in U.S. policy, would have to be concerned instead with the capacity of the North American government, the most influential actor, in imposing its concept of the world and its specific objectives through consensus as well as potential pressures, above all through Ecuador's vulnerability in economic matters in its relationship with the United States.

This does not mean, however, that the system of values and perceptions related to the war on drugs which is undertaken by the United States is not shared as much by Ecuadoran decision makers as by a majority of social sectors. Political needs constitute specific decisions. Also the objective of destroying a concrete cultural perception[25] entails a series of strategies for the use of propaganda strategies which work on the collective social image creating values and perceptions of problems related to official and dominant ones and, thus, the consensus that clothes antidrug policies.

Within this spirit, the activity of Ecuadoran international policy has evolved, carried out by an overwhelming majority of lawyers and expressed in a series of treaties throughout the past two years. Only a few of these will be mentioned in order to illustrate how political motivation grows. It is fitting to note that since the First Convention on Opium in 1925, Ecuador has not excluded itself from any legal international instrument regarding the issue. Even the Geneva Convention of 1988 was ratified by the country in March of 1990, despite the resentment it caused in most Andean governments. It legitimized the eventual possibility that a country could be pressured from outside over the issue of extradition, since despite the fact that the Ecuadoran Constitution expressly prohibits this recourse, relevancy of ratification is political — it may permit the exercise of coercive mechanisms by a state more interested in extradition than in the constitution.[26]

From 1990 until the beginning of 1992, several bilateral agreements were signed with the United States as well as with Guatemala, Peru, Brazil, Bolivia, Mexico, Colombia, and Argentina to combat drug trafficking. Ideological justification normally repeats the considerations of the Vienna Convention and the Declaration of Guadalajara of 1991. Besides those signed with the United States, in this chain of treaties it is relevant to mention a Memorandum of Understanding for Judicial Cooperation[27] with Colombia, in which it is agreed to exchange information, supply evidence that could be proof in a penal cause, receive inquiries and testimonies, as well as leave open other forms of cooperation.

The only limit to cooperation is left to the discretion of the central judicial authority in each of the states, which for the effects of this convention openly in opposition to the constitutional traditions of both states, is no longer the president of the court or supreme justice tribunal, but the General Prosecutor of theNation, who also is president of CONSEP in Ecuador, and the secretary general of the presidency in Colombia. Judicial management is placed in the hands of the executive power and is subject to political variables that are inevitably tied to international dynamics, which include other actors. Procedures, on the other hand, are direct and more fluid.

The memorandum of cooperation with Colombia contains social aspects that could well have been the object of a treaty; however, they were not necessary. This memorandum exemplifies a practice that is not exceptional, above all, in those societies where political institutionality and popular participation in the decision-making process are uncommon.

The month of September 1990 was productive in Ecuadoran cooperation with the United States; several agreements were reached. The first of
these, one of cooperation in the control of narcotics with the national police
and INTERPOL,[28] signed by the minister of the Ecuadoran government and the
U.S. ambassador, proposed the allocation of US$910,000 to train Ecuadoran
personnel in the destruction of crops, interdiction, and the dismantling of
domestic and international organizations involved in drug trafficking. The
goals were an increase in interdiction by blocking highways, waterway
operations that are specific to the project, and air operations and establish five
integrated control centers. The United States donated vehicles, radio
equipment, and boats, and they paid for the use of airplanes and other
operational costs. Ecuador supplied, among other expenses, the salaries of
572 officers and policemen who would carry out the objectives of the
agreement, which was almost the total number of men in normal work in the
city of Quito, a city with more than a million inhabitants.

For the control of narcotics by the customs military police, a similar
agreement was reached on September 19, 1990, between the minister of finance
of Ecuador and the U.S. ambassador. US$170 million was donated for the
control of airports and highways, as well as to increase maritime patrol.[29] It is
interesting to note that the customs military police was a state instrument used
to avoid the loss of fiscal revenues because it controlled the smuggling of
merchandise, foods, appliances, and fuels. Hence, its commander is the
minister of finance. The sign of the times has practically converted it into a
combat unit whose original purpose (although forgotten) is confused with other
tasks, which essentially have nothing to do with fiscal loss due to tax evasion.

The agreement for technical cooperation with the armed forces, signed
September 20, 1990,[30] confirmed the donation of US$100,000 to finance
intelligence activities and carry out border control in those provinces
bordering on Peru and Colombia. As in previous cases, resources would not
vary according to their field of application: patrolling, detection of laboratories, arrests, training, and all the rest of the emotional activities involved in the
war on drugs.

Given the date of expiration of obligations in 1992, out of these three
agreements, the agreement signed with the national police has been renewed.[31] On this occasion, the budget is increased to $1,065,000 and,
contrasting with the former project, American personnel advisers are included
with an additional US$135,000. This is probably evidence of an important
change in dealing with the problem.

The same political resource used for judicial cooperation with Colombia
served in the preparation of a Memorandum of Understanding for the
Prevention of Deviation of Chemical Substances,[32] a concept which has not
yet been defined in the same memorandum. At any rate, there exists a direct

relationship with the DEA and CONSEP to observe transactions underway and, with the use of a series of control mechanisms, keep the quantities that are being sold from being unusually suspicious.

Despite the fact that the problem has gotten worse, it is possible to say that Ecuadoran foreign policy — at least, in regards to the treaties that have been signed and ratified at the San Jose conference where no revision was made of general considerations — has not developed an autonomous profile.

Consideration of interdiction and the idea of "doing more of the same" have been faithfully applied from 1990 to 1992 despite the fact that the number of arrests, the prison population, and those suspected of money laundering are constantly increasing. If this analysis is proposed in the area of hegemony, thinking this category in the international arena as a historical and social process wherein a coalition of actors (or actor) has the capacity to provide subordinates with its concepts of the world to others, there is consensus that ideologically reports to the Ecuadoran government by means of perceptions that do not directly elude to the actual intended reality.

In keeping with the former reasoning, Ecuador does not have drug abuse as its primary social problem—that is, in comparable amounts. It is not a country that produces coca leaves; its peasantry is not linked to these processes. The organized crime of drug traffickers, still invisible, does not currently present a challenge for governmental authorities, although there is an apparent risk for the political system. Where does it come from? The answer can be found in the fact that the Andean antidrug strategy, in some fashion or other, has met with decisions that place priority to sets of interests maintained in interdiction, prohibition, repression, and control. This is the perspective of the U.S. government which interprets the moral environment of the nation and legitimizes a bloc in power.

The war on drugs is based upon the defense of U.S. values.[33] Without the moral aspect, the political leadership's call to all of society involves a process of internal legitimization which is expressed internationally by the dimension of U.S. hegemonic power. Independent from the fact that the drug policy is efficient in the drug war — captures, imprisonment, and destruction of laboratories and crops — it is not efficient because it has not been able to stop the flow of narcotics or paralyze production which has, on the other hand, increased.

Ecuadoran collaboration in the war on drugs is undeniable despite the fact that the problem has worsened in the country. National objectives in the conflict have been mediated by the need for international collaboration, basically with the United States. It has meant accepting the interests of the United States as our own. There is no evidence of an autonomous policy in official declarations or in those decisions that have been adopted. The fact is that within this reality, the causes of penetration of narcotics into Ecuador can be attributed to the general design of the antidrug strategy and to the reactions of cartels. This is basically illustrated by the expansion of the phenomenon, processes in which the political decisions of the Ecuadoran government have been marked by the absence of an identity that is translated into cooperative will.

Interdiction: Growth's Relationship

Although Ecuador still does not grow coca and other illegal drugs in sufficient amounts for export, the policies that control the activities of the agencies in charge of the control and repression have not kept these agencies from participating in captures and arrests. A series of events related to Ecuador's role in the cycle of production and commercialization of illegal drugs illustrates the qualitative change it has suffered in the past two years, and which has also been the main source of legitimization of decision-making processes and institutional state modification in approaching this phenomenon.

One change is the discrete publicity concerning the participation of North American advisers in the war on drugs which was always handled carefully, above all after the extremely negative political cost it meant for former president Leon Febres Cordero (1984-1988) who admitted units of the U.S. army to train in Ecuadoran territory in 1986.[34] It was a May 1991 visit of Adjunct Secretary for Narcotics Affairs of the Department of State, Melvyn Levitsky, which allowed for the dissemination of information on the presence of advisers, with the peculiarity that there was no protest by any politician, above all from those on the left who normally protested North American presence in Ecuador.

In order to combat trafficking, a special police was formed comprised of 40 people trained by foreign experts to control borders and participate in special operations.[35] It seems that the most vulnerable geographic region of Ecuador is the so-called Amazon triangle or ECUPECO, the mutual region between Colombia, Ecuador, and Peru. Repression has been carried out in this region, but the subsistence economy of the local peasants is permeated by the presence of drug traffickers who develop institutional means of survival parallel to the state, assuming some of the services, maintaining networks for trade in basic products, and providing occasional work for residents.[36]

Despite this, Ecuador has not become a country that grows coca. In 1991, theDepartment of State did not attempt to form estimates of the dimension of the crop as it has practically been insignificant in 1990 — 120 hectars of coca that could be harvested, in comparison to 40,100 in Colombia and 121,300 in Peru, Ecuador's neighbors.[37] From the North American perspective, the pillars of this situation —that is, that there had not been any crop activities since the 1980s — can be attributed to the strengthening of

Ecuadoran penal law, U.S. collaboration, and the political determination of Ecuadoran governments (according to statements made by Bernard Aronson, Adjunct Secretary of State for Latin American Affairs).[38] The reality, however, is that Ecuador was never a producer, because crops for ritual and traditional use, which were later operational in Andean countries for export to the U.S. and European cocaine markets, were eradicated in the sixteenth century during the Royal Sessions of Quito, due to reasons of a structural nature related to organization in the production in the colony.[39] Thus, the Andean strategy in the war on drugs in Ecuador has obtained a major victory which can be explained, among various reasons, by the fact that it has met with an enemy who died four centuries ago.

As for seizures, since 1991 the greatest numbers yet have been achieved which have an important legitimizing effect on Ecuadoran society unaccustomed to this type of data. US$350 million estimated in 360 kilos of cocaine were abandoned on a street in Quito in what seems to have been a disagreement between illegal organizations.[40] In February 1992, a shipment of 300 kilos of pure cocaine was discovered (valued at $300 million) on the northern border with Colombia.[41]

This last incident concerned government officials since it was thought that the drug might have been refined in Ecuador, dramatically changing Ecuador's role in the drug circuit and implying the presence of consolidated drug trafficking organizations with important networks inside the country. It also represented the possibility that favorable conditions are being created internally for gaining profit from coca. Fortunately, after an investigation, it was found that the shipment was Colombian.[42] However, the authorities in charge of the control and repression now began to operate from the hypothesis of the refining country on a major scale, a possibility that has never been officially analyzed and which most political decision makers, as well as social actors, remain isolated from, despite the dramatic influence it would have on an economically vulnerable society with a precarious political institutionality and an environment characterized in past years by a tendency toward polarization and informality in political competition.

An additional element in this analysis deals with diversification of points of destiny and with the fact that Ecuador is at present one of the most important export centers of the product, a reality that was not yet evident at the end of the 1980s. The picture of four nuns with surprised expressions on their sincere faces, each with a package of two kilos in their hands, arrested in the Quito airport in mid-April 1991, stunned the world and in some way helped to reveal Ecuador's present situation. Small and large shipments have been confiscated in Spain, Portugal, Italy, Japan, Great Britain, Holland, and other countries. Ships bearing the Ecuadoran flag, planes, and an almost entire range of Ecuadoran exports have appeared in the red chronicle of newspapers linked to export operations.[43]

Ecuadoran policy in past years has been characterized by a progressive toughness. Cocaine seizures have doubled in four years, while marijuana seizures during the same period have been reduced by half.[44] This could indicate that Ecuador is orienting its antidrug activity according to the demands of the international market, and that cocaine is the object of interdiction, while marijuana, whose relevance for Ecuador is basically the internal market, may be evidence that it does not profile state policy — it is difficult to say that the number of marijuana users has decreased, a negative hypothesis made by a majority of agencies dedicated to prevention.

It also shows that the greatest cause of imprisonment in a country with an oversaturated prison population is related to narcotrafficking. Between 1990 and 1991, there were 3,643 penal trials from this cause,[45] which takes into consideration a greater number of arrests from presumptions or violations, as well as cases that never materialized because of the intervention of informal factors or corruption. All of this draws an incredible picture. If the United States were a transit country subject to Ecuador's antidrug policies, the approximate populational relationship would be nearly 100,000 cases in the past two years.

Despite the majority consensus by the people and political decision makers, as well as the economic elite in combating the phenomenon, Ecuadoran participation is building up within the circuit of production of illegal drugs. There has not existed an autonomous Ecuadoran policy with its own identity regarding the drug trafficking phenomenon. Its foreign policy has been flexible, and political debates have even been proposed on the legal realities that deviate from Ecuadoran traditions. Borja has even suggested extradition in a legislative bill, as well as uncommon penal measures.

State discourse speaks of a society faced with the dangers of use; that is, U.S. antidrug discourse is assumed without the benefit of inventory. For Ecuadoran decision makers, the country's social problems are subsumed under the "universal" categorization surrounding the prohibitionist perception. U.S. problems are, thus, nothing less than Ecuadoran problems.[46] These are the premises that legitimize policies of prohibition, control, and repression. The agency in charge of developing and carrying out combat strategies is the central agency, CONSEP (National Council for the Control of Illegal Drug Substances), comprised of six ministries and directed by the General Prosecutor of the nation.

Armed with the rhetoric of the Cartagena declaration and every other international instrument for combatting drug trafficking that Ecuador has signed, CONSEP (the Ecuadorian nemesis of organizations directed by Bob Martinez) intends with its policies to protect Ecuadorans from the undue use of illegal drugs, increase mechanisms for prevention in order to preserve the country's health, participate in Andean organizations against drug trafficking, concentrate existing information, and periodically evaluate activities.[47]

The Ubiquitous Ghost of Money Laundering

One of the main points of political motivation in antidrug decision making has been that of money laundering. Because of the scarcity of data as well as the abundance of suspicions, it has been the touchstone of all Ecuadoran society with political access or influence. The economic elite, the armed forces, government officials, and all of those who have at some time discussed drug trafficking, have referred to the phenomenon of money laundering as the most difficult trap for Ecuadoran society.

Data comes from North American sources. The *Miami Herald* in September 1989 suggested that the dollar amount laundered in the Ecuadoran financial system was approximately $400 million.[48] Since then, this amount has been confirmed despite proof. It has been mentioned in academic works and has been officially accepted by the U.S. government, which is as if reality itself were produced by the effect of debate in Ecuador;[49] however, banks, both public and private, have denied this version again and again.

Arguments by the financial sector through its Association of Private Banks are based on the fact that the total amount of dollars negotiated in Ecuador in 1990 did not exceed $317 million, from which several illegal activities must be taken into consideration, as well as the flow of dollars from abroad through transfers made by immigrants.[50] Even by admitting that dollars coming from drug trafficking operations will be laundered, the problem is not limited to this source. In Ecuador, conflicts related to smuggling — inevitable in an economy of subsidies and protection — have been traditional, as well as speculation by the same private company in order to evade taxes, by overinvoicing imports and underinvoicing exports.

Versions which have become more and more exaggerated always remain within the context of ideological production which creates a fear of the uncontrollable. In March 1991, for example, it was claimed that in just one operation, Colombian cartels had tried to launder $250 million in Ecuador,[51] which, within the dimensions of the Ecuadoran economy, is an extremely disproportionate figure. Any legislative measure or initiative, although peripheral, affects or influences the economy or financial system.[52] The ghost of money laundering has become a conventional weapon for participation in turbulent Ecuadoran politics.

Starting with the U.S. policy of applying the 1970 legislation of the Treasury Department in the war on drugs which demands reports of any transactions of amounts greater than $10,000, Andean countries, and in this case Ecuador, have had to develop similar legislation so that U.S. control can be effective. In September 1991, a bilateral agreement with the United States was reported with the objective of applying controls and transmitting information of "monetary transactions" in Ecuadoran financial and banking institutions, in amounts exceeding $10,000.[53] In practice, this instrument implemented by the Treasury Department in the United States and by the Superintendency of Banks in Ecuador, given the discrepancies in computer resources used by both countries and their institutions, means giving the control of this type of transaction carried out in Ecuador to North American authorities who can then initiate an investigation and suggest appropriate actions.

The most outstanding case uncovered in money laundering involved the exchange house C&F, whose owner was married to a sister of the president of the republic. The U.S. accounts of this company were frozen by the courts because a postal inspector detected massive transfers, some of which ended up in Cali. The businessman was arrested and tried in Miami and the exchange house was liquidated in Ecuador. A national debate followed to reform banking law in order to control "whitening," a still-to-be-implemented policy.[54]

On the other hand, the ghost of money laundering revolved around a special parliamentary commission formed to study related denunciations. The president of the commission, Fernando Larrea, is a leader of the People's party. Its coastal base, PRE, is led by the controversial figure Abdala Bucaram who was charged with drug trafficking in Panama by Noriega, apparently in a plot organized by the Febres Cordero government, according to a claim by the accused. The case is, however, that Larrea's principal adviser was a former presidential candidate who has also been publicly accused of financing his campaign with drug money.[55]

Independent of the stories which are nothing but manifestations of political practices, the activities of the commission ended with a terrifying report that proved the absolute vulnerability of the Ecuadoran financial system and which accused certain institutions. However, within Ecuadoran institutionality, such a report had a rather propagandistic effect. It did not take into account the framework of financial independence legislation leaves; for example, there is no law placing a limit on the amount of money a bank can acquire nor controls to determine if a transaction made by a foreign or Ecuadoran banking institution is of doubtful source.[56]

The report was never translated into any judicial measure, and it never achieved the objective of concentrating political solidarities. There was no political party to speak out officially, but instead, in vague and rhetorical terms; private banks as well as state financial institutions abstained from complying with the conclusions, and the U.S. embassy has not even used the document as a means of legitimization of its policy.[57] In addition to the fact that technical details brought out mainly by banks can discredit its conclusions, the reason this has happened could be because of the limited summons capacity of institutional political power to which Larrea belongs, whose common practice has been inscribed in an appeal for the mobilization of resources based on opportunity and verbal violence.

In summary, there is still insufficient information concerning the amount of money assumed to be laundered in the Ecuadoran financial system. This has not kept the issue from being approached ideologically as a way to sustain and generate antidrug consensus as well as to participate in the turbulent Ecuadoran policy announcing an unknown danger that causes fear. Nevertheless, given the dimensions of the country's economy as well as the institutional fragility of mechanisms for representation that continue to recur to clientelistic and patrimonial practices, the Ecuadoran political system is highly vulnerable to the influence of drug trafficking.

Final Reflection

The dimensions of the drug conflict have expanded in Ecuador from 1989 to the beginning of 1992, despite the fact that since the mid-1980s, Ecuadoran governments have involved themselves almost unconditionally in antidrug efforts based on U.S. initiatives. There are reasons that explain the failure in stopping the phenomenon as well as the persistence of the United States in its particular policy.

First, in detaining the growing drug traffic, Ecuador does not depend on a reality limited by borders. The circuit of coca-cocaine production, the clearest motivation of this war, is an international phenomenon that involves several countries as well as a series of heterogeneous factors. Historical and structural conditions have determined a situation of poverty in all of the Andean region which necessitates the adaptation of strategies for survival, one of which is cultivation in neighboring countries. While Ecuador is fulfilling its duty in the complex production of illegal drugs, the problem cannot be resolved by local policies exclusively.

Because it lacks its own initiative and there exists no common Andean policy — the situations of producer countries are not identical and there exists competition in the U.S. legal export market — Ecuador has borrowed U.S. antidrug discourse and strategy. This has had social impacts ranging from the reform of important legislative acts to the redefinition of security policies as well as the role of the police and the armed forces.

The repressive emphasis of North American-Ecuadoran strategy has gained the general consensus of society, mainly because certain consequences of the conflict are unknown to the population, for example, the violence that accompanies productive processes in Colombia, Peru, and Bolivia. Another element is the fact that Ecuador assumes for itself those problems that legitimize such a strategy in U.S. society, for example, drug use and the street violence linked to it. However, both variables are empirically smaller in Ecuador; therefore, an ideological and propagandistic platform is being built around them capable of general support.

A similar conclusion is derived from an analysis of the money laundering process, a topic that has become a problem for the Ecuadoran economy, given its relatively small dimensions. However, given the absence of econometric research, there exist multiple versions and contradictions which have resulted in political consideration of the problem in order to legitimize antidrug measures as well as to generate the electoral potential for certain party forces.

U.S. refusal to radicalize a strategy that has had no positive results and which has created problems and conflict in the Andean region can be understood in the development of a discourse that condenses a series of additional social and political practices. One of the functions is to use North American values which legitimize the means for political direction and a power bloc, within an international context where the dimensions of the policies of nation states transcend the limits of borders, because productive processes have been internationalized and because political actors, their interests, and dynamics, are processed within a setting characterized by interdependence as a framework of power and hegemonic relations.

Notes

1. See Adrian Bonilla, "Ecuador. International Actor in the War on Drugs," in Bruce Bagley, et al., eds. *The Political Economy of Drug Trafficking. The Case of Ecuador*, 36-40.

2. See data under the subtitle, "Interdiction" in this same chapter.

3. For the purposes of international relations, we will use the term "hegemony" to define a complex relationship of consensus and coercion, based on which an international actor or international group of actors who function in a common social area imposes upon others his or their way of thinking about problems as well as a set of policies that become decisions.

See Robert Cox, "Social Forces, States and World Orders," in Robert Keohane, ed., *Neorealism and Its Critics*, Columbia University Press, New York, 1986, 230-234; and Adrian Bonilla, "The Unsuspected Virtues of the Perverse. Theory of International Relations as Political Discourse. The Case of the War on Drugs." Paper presented at the opening session at the North-South Center, Miami, 1991.

4. The same that supposes a Hobbesian idea that anarchy in the international system causes self-assistance for national survival to place security at the top of the agenda, and considers nation state to be the exclusive and rational actors of international politics.

See John A. Vazquez, "Coloring It Morgenthau: New Evidence for an Old Thesis on Quantitative International Politics," in *British Journal of International Studies*, No. 5, 1979, 211; and Robert Keohane, "Theory of World Politics, Structural Realism and Beyond," in Keohane, *Neorealism ....*

5. See Bruce Bagley, "U.S. Foreign Policy and the War on Drugs. Analysis of a Policy Failure," in *Journal of Interamerican Studies and World Affairs*, Vol. 30, Nos. 2-3, Miami, 188-211.

6. See Adrian Bonilla, "The Unsuspected Virtues...," Miami, 1991.

7. A detailed analysis of drug use indicators, the shift in North American public policy, and the role of the media can be found in the anthropological focus prepared by Eric L. Jensen, Jurg Gerber, and Ginna Babcock, "The New War on Drugs. Grass Roots Movement or Political Construction," *The Journal of Drug Issues*, Vol. 21, No. 3, 651-667.

8. For the fiscal year 1991, expenditures were

US$142.3 million in military assistance,

US$1.87 million in efforts toward reducing demand,

US$72.5 million in police activities, and

US$49.7 million in economic assistance.

Source: Inter-American Commission on Drug Policy, *Seizing Opportunities*, Institute of The Americas and University of San Diego, La Jolla, 1991.

9. See Washington Office on Latin America, *Clear and Present Dangers: The U.S. Military and the War on Drugs in the Andes,* WOLA, Washington, 1991, 12-20.

10. Juan Gabriel Tokatlían, "Reflections on Drugs and National Security: The Threat of Intervention," in Bruce Bagley and Juan Gabriel Tokatlían, eds., *Political Economy of Drug Trafficking,* CEI-Uniandes, Bogota, 1990, 353-360.

11. See Bruce Bagley, "The Myth of Militarization: An Evaluation of the Role of the Military in the War on Drugs in the Americas," University of Miami (Mimeograph), 1991, 30+.

12. See Bruce Bagley, "The Myth of Militarization."

13. President Borja announced in Texas that Ecuador has maintained radar, air, and maritime operations on its own.

14. Prior to the visit of Peruvian President Alberto Fujimori at the beginning of 1991, the Guayaquil political leadership, traditionally articulated in agroexport interests, carried out a nationalist campaign which was denounced by the Andean Pact as an attempt against Ecuadoran interests.

15. Department of State, *International Narcotics Control Foreign Assistance Appropriation Act. Fiscal Year 1992 Budget Congressional Submission,* Washington, D.C., 1991, 11.

16. Department of State, *International Narcotics Control Strategy Report,* Washington, D.C., March 1991, 105-108.

17. USIA, *Research Memorandum, Andean Public Opinion on the Drug War: Attitudes toward Counter-Narcotics Actions,* Washington, October 1991. The survey in Ecuador was taken by the company INMAVER GALLUP, with headquarters in Colombia.

18. Sixty-three percent of Ecuadorans support extradition, as do 60 percent in Peru, 43 percent in Bolivia, and 11 in Colombia. Eighty-eight percent of Ecuadorans approve of greater military presence, as do 72 percent in Peru, 67 percent in Bolivia, and 66 percent in Colombia. Eighty percent in Ecuador believe that ties must be extended with the United States, as do 81 percent in Peru, 47 percent in Bolivia, and 53 percent in Colombia. Sixteen percent in Ecuador agree with legalization, as do 18 percent in Peru, 18 percent in Bolivia, and 27 percent in Colombia.

19. Melvyn Levitsky, Adjunct Secretary of State for Latin American Narcotics Affairs, was referring specifically in those terms to Ecuador. See "New Measures against Drug Trafficking," *El Comercio,* March 20, 1991, Quito, A3.

20. See Xavier Andrade, "Behind the Perverse," Degree Thesis in Anthropology, Catholic University, Quito, February 1992.

21. "Bush Praises Andean Support against Drugs," Report by the Agency EFE published by *El Universo,* March 3, 1991, 10.

22. National Council for Narcotic Substances, *The Problem of Drugs in Ecuador,* CONSEP, January 1992, 23.

23. "U.S. Is Not Helping Ecuador in the War on Drugs," in *El Universo,* October 27, 1992, Guayaquil, 1.

24. CONSEP, "The Problem of Drugs . . . "

25. That of "the culture of drug use," according to Melvyn Levitsky, in an interview granted via satellite with the Ecuadoran, Venezuelan, and Mexican press, February 21, 1992.

26. A more thorough study of international drug legislation with Ecuadoran participation can be found in Adrian Bonilla, "Ecuador, International Actor in the War on Drugs," in Bruce Bagley, Adrian Bonilla, and Alexei Paez, eds., *The Political Economy of Drug Trafficking: The Case of Ecuador*, FLACSO/North-South Center, Quito, 1991.

27. Signed by Colombia and Ecuador in Guayaquil, August 20, 1992. RE: Original Document. Office of Treaties, Ministry of Foreign Relations, Quito.

28. The obligation was agreed to until February 3, 1992. See original document, Project No. 311801-0102, General Treaty Office, Ministry of Foreign Relations, Quito.

29. The obligation was until February 28, 1992. See original document, Project No. 311801-0103, General Treaty Office, Ministry of Foreign Relations, Quito.

30. The obligation was until March 31, 1992. See original document, Project No. 311801-0105, General Treaty Office, Ministry of Foreign Relations, Quito.

31. Agreement for the control of narcotics. National Police-INTERPOL, date of expiration of obligation: February 25, 1993. See original document, Project No. 311801-0102, General Treaty Office, Ministry of Foreign Relations, Quito.

32. Signed by the governments of Ecuador and the United States on June 17, 1991. See original document in the General Treaty Office, Ministry of Foreign Relations, Quito.

33. "Americanism," based on the values of private property, individual freedoms, and market economies, supposes a vision of the world, a discourse that functions for those sectors that need such a social environment in order to be economically productive and politically advanced. See Enrico Augelli and Craig Murphy, *America's Quest for Supremacy and The Third World. An Essay in Gramscian Analysis*, Pinter Publishers, London, 1988, 59-60.

34. Following an unorthodox practice in carrying out Ecuadoran foreign policy, Febres Cordero, right-wing businessman, tried to build a "special" bilateral relationship with the United States. It permitted the presence of North American troops (with a negative final balance of operations); it broke relations with Nicaragua and assumed unconditionally Reaganite discourse on "narcoterrorism." However, none of these attitudes seriously interested the U.S. government, and although the relationship between both states did not deteriorate, neither did it improve. Ecuador received no extensions, above all in the area of investments where its interests lay. See Adrian Bonilla, in Bagley, *La Economia politica del narcotrafico. el case ecuatoriano*, 1991.

35. The General Prosecutor of the Nation, Gustavo Medina, has emphasized that he recognizes the presence of foreign experts, that the problem is in demand. See "DEA Support in the War on Drug Trafficking Is Confirmed," *El Universo*, August 8, 1991, 9.

36. See Nelson Romero, "Narcochemistry in Ecuador," in Laufer, et al., *The Plagues of America*, CAAP, 1990. This researcher, in a study for the IDB, proposes a series of data that would transform the region into a sort of Ecuadoran coca paradise. However, despite the fact that it contributes certain references, the type of analysis tends to exaggerate progress.

37. Department of State, Bureau of International Narcotics Matters, *International Narcotics Control Strategy Report*, March 1991, 101-110.

38. Statements compiled in "Ecuador Is No Longer a Potential Coca Producer," *El Universo*, Guayaquil, August 2, 1991.

39. See Adrian Bonilla, 1991, in Bagley, *La economia politica....*

40. "Narcotrafficker Conflict," *Hoy*, October 15, 1991, Quito, 8B.

41. "Cocaine Valued at 300 Million Dollars Is Confiscated," *El Universo*, Guayaquil, February 12, 1992, 12.

42. "Those Arrested with 4 Tons Are All Colombian. The Drug Came from Cali," *Hoy*, February 14, 1991, Quito.

43. See "Ecuador Is Now a Center of Operations for the Drug," *Hoy*, February 15, 1992, Quito.

44. CONSEP, *The Problem of Drugs...*, Appendix 1.

45. CONSEP, *The Problem of Drugs...*, Appendix 3.

46. The philosophical principles that promote the Ecuadoran drug was use the term "internationalization" to relate it to the idea of modernity. This inspires present policy which supposes Ecuador's lack of specification conceived as a function of this world crusade. See CONSEP, *The Problem of Drugs...*, 2-5.

47. CONSEP, *The Problem of Drugs...*, 14-17.

48. See A. Paez, *La economia politica del narcotrafico*, 1991.

49. This figure appears in the document of the antinarcotics budget requested of the U.S. Congress, *Foreign Assistance Appropriation Act*, 261. Melvyn Levitsky has also confirmed that the amount laundered in Ecuador is $500 million. See *El Universo*, April 21, 1991, Guayaquil.

50. See "Daya Admits that Dollars Are Being Laundered in the Country," *Hoy*, December 12, 1990, Quito. The argument of dollars derived from migrants is fairly solid and even more so since the southern part of the country — that is the provinces of Azuay and Cañar — are those with indicators of positive growth notwithstanding the crisis; they owe their growth to dollars coming from abroad, among other causes.

51. "A Connection with Narcodollars May Have Been Interrupted," in *Meridiano*, March 14, 1991, 1.

52. Thus, for example, former vice-president Leon Roldos maintains that a legislative bill to regulate mining activity can be a mechanism of dollar laundering as it favors the immediate concession of zones of exploration. See *El Comercio*, April 18, 1991, Quito, 12C. Many politicians have made statements similar to this.

53. See "Agreement between Ecuador and the United States against dollar laundering," *El Universo*, Guayaquil, September 9, 1991, 9.

54. A complete account of the case appears in *Weekly Analysis*, No. 18, May 6, 1991, Guayaquil.

55. See "Narcotrafficker Advisers and Prosecutors," paid announcement in *El Comercio*, September 5, 1991, Quito, 6A.

56. See Paul Bonilla, "Dollar Laundering in Ecuador," in Bagley, *La economia politica...*, 125-148.

57. See an evaluation of the parliamentary report in *Weekly Analysis*, Vol. 21, No. 27, June 1991.

References

El Universo. 1991. "Agreement Between Ecuador and the United States Against Dollar Laundering." September 9, 6A.

Andrade, Xavier. 1992. "Behind the Perverse." Degree Thesis in Anthropology, Catholic University. Quito. February.

Bagley, Bruce. 1988. "U.S. Foreign Policy and the War on Drugs: Analysis of a Policy Failure." *Journal of Interamerican Studies and World Affairs*. 30(2-3): 188-211.

Bagley, Bruce. 1991. "Myths of Militarization: An Evolution of the Role of the Military in the War on Drugs in the Americas." University of Miami. Mimeo.

Bagley, Bruce, and Juan Gabriel Tokatlián. 1990. *Political Economy of Drug Trafficking*. Bogota: CEU-Uniandes.

Bagley, Bruce, Adrian Bonilla, and Alexei Paez. eds. 1991. *La Economia Politica del narcotrafico: el caso ecuatoriano*. Quito: FLACSO/North-South Center.

Bonilla, Adrian. 1991. "The Unsuspected Virtues of the Perverse. Theory of International Relations as Political Discourse. The Case of the War on Drugs." Presented at North-South Center's Opening Session. Miami.

El Universo. 1991. "Bush Praises Andean Support Against Drugs." March 3, 10.

El Universo. 1992. "Cocaine Valued at 300 Million Dollars Is Confiscated." February 12, 12.

El Comercio. 1991. April 18, 12C.

Meridiano. 1991. "A Connection with Narcodollars May Have Been Interrupted." March 14, 1.

Hoy. 1990. "Daza Admits That Dollars Are Being Laundered in the Country." December 12.

El Universo. 1991. "DEA Support in the War on Drug Trafficking Is Confirmed." August 8, 9.

El Universo. 1991. "Ecuador Is No Longer a Potential Coca Producer." August 2.

Hoy. 1992. "Ecuador Is Now a Center of Operations for the Drug." February 15.

Inter-American Commission on Drug Policy. 1991. *Seizing Opportunities*. La Jolla: Institute of the Americas and University of San Diego.

Jensen, Eric L., Jurg Gerber, and Ginna Babcock. 1992. "The New War on Drugs: Grass Roots Movement or Political Construction?" *The Journal of Drug Issues*. 21(3): 651-667.

Keohane, Robert. ed. 1986. *Neorealism and Its Critics*. New York: Columbia University Press.

Hoy. 1991. "Narcotrafficker Conflict." October 15, 8B.

El Comercio. 1991. "Narcotrafficker Advisers and Prosecutors." September 5, 9.

National Council for Narcotic Substances. 1992. *The Problem of Drugs in Ecuador*. Quito: CONSEP. January.

El Comercio. 1991. "New Measures Against Drug Trafficking." March 20, A3.

Romero, Nelson. 1990. "Narcochemistry in Ecuador," in *The Plagues of America.* Quito: Centro Andino de Accion Popular, CAAP.

Hoy. 1991. "Those Arrested with 4 Tons Are All Colombian. The Drug Came from Cali." February 14.

El Universo. 1991. April 21.

El Universo. 1992. "U.S. Is Not Helping Ecuador in the War on Drugs." October 27, 1.

U.S. Department of State. 1991. *International Narcotics Control Foreign Assistance Appropriation Act. Fiscal Year 1992. Budget Congressional Submission.* Washington, D.C.

U.S. Department of State, Bureau of International Narcotics Matters. 1991. *International Narcotics Control Strategy Report.* Washington, D.C.

USIA. 1991. *Research Memorandum, Andean Public Opinion on the Drug War: Attitudes toward Counter-narcotics Actions.* Washington, D.C.

Vazquez, John A. 1979. "Coloring it Morganthau: New Evidence for an Old Thesis on Quantitative International Politics." *British Journal of International Studies.* No. 5.

Washington Office on Latin America. 1991. *Clear and Present Dangers: The U.S. Military and the War on Drugs in the Andes.* Washington, D.C.: WOLA.

Weekly Analysis. 1991. 21(18) May 6. Guayaquil.

Weekly Analysis. 1991. 21(27) June. Guayaquil.

Chapter Fifteen

Drug Trafficking, Drug Consumption, and Violence in Ecuador

Xavier Andrade

Introduction

The tendency toward a repressive viewpoint in the war on drugs in the Andean area is not just the product of policies based on unilateral solutions which are directed by the United States toward our countries. In this war, multiple internal actors, who handle the problem in accordance with diverse interests in the short and long term, join forces.

In Ecuador, toward the mid-1980s, discourse from positions of power that have recognized the country as an "island of peace" in comparison to the social and political violence of the rest of the Andes is reinforced and the existence of growing lines of articulation are accepted in terms of the political economy of narcotrafficking. As a result of this paradox, official evaluation — widely shared by the media — exalts the progress made in the war in restraining the phenomenon while advocating greater international "assistance," which will double by 1992, according to North American sources (USDS 1991a, 11).

Contrary to Peru, Bolivia, and Colombia, Ecuador is mainly defined as an area that serves as a "bridge" for a considerable part of the cocaine destined for export and chemical "bases" headed for processing zones. Another relatively important link seems to be in its role as a money laundering station, especially in the spheres of circulation of financial capital and also apparently in the area of real estate. However, information on this topic — though academic — is still unclear.[1]

From this perspective — marked in general terms by a triumphant discourse in combating the problem — changes in internal legislation appear to respond to a demand to absorb recent developments as well as to radicalize

283

repressive policies that sustain the arguments of political decision makers. Thus, from September 1990, the country has had a "modern" law on drugs. In the process of its preparation and subsequent promulgation, the attitude of President Rodrigo Borja (Social Democrat, 1988-1992) was interesting in that he replaced his systematic silence concerning the ultrarepressive content of the original legislative bill with a public defense of his agreement to end the problem based on the application of the most violent measures contained in that document which, once edited, was approved by Congress.[2]

Such a position can be understood as a continuation of the discourse of his greatest political opponent, former president Febres Cordero (Conservative, 1984-1988). During his administration, President Cordero had exalted among his successes the annihilation of the "narcoguerrilla" — which turned out to be fiction — and the destruction of coca crops. These achievements had been loaded with so much political imagery that Cordero was considered by North Americans and his most recalcitrant political opponents to be a leader in the war and a model of behavior for other Andean governors.

The new law explicitly maintains a dominant repressive position in the tradition of Ecuadoran legislation on the problem since 1916, a tradition that can be understood as a reflection of international agreements on drugs.[3] Present juncture includes a new ingredient marked by the emergence of a limited critical attitude on the part of public opinion of the institutional apparatus linked to control and repression, especially directed toward the National Police, given public awareness of the level of corruption that affected even the highest spheres of such institutions. This fact even promoted the restructuring of certain police agencies. Nevertheless, one institutional reaction has been to exalt the importance of the police function in the war on drugs and other criminal activities, with which the debate has been displaced little by little from the political picture.

In this work an approach will be sought for certain social effects related to the war on drugs in Ecuador. We will center our interest accordingly on those social factors that are linked to drug use. Such an approach becomes so important in the case of Ecuador that repressive activities have traditionally been directed at consumers and small-time traffickers. Coercion against such actors has been part of an important parameter of success in the war on drugs for its internal justification.

For the purposes of this work, I will begin with an evaluation of studies on drugs in this country and then follow with a discussion of the limitations and possibilities implicit in studies on social effects, particularly emphasizing present discussion regarding the progress of internal use and, second, one of the groups of consumers considered the most problematic from society's point of view because of its involvement in promoting violence.

An Evaluation of Drug Studies

If we consider academic works on the topic of drugs within the international context and specifically the Andean region, it can be stated that social sciences in Ecuador have barely begun to take the first steps toward needed reflection. In 1988, the first social research projects were begun on certain contemporary dimensions associated with the problem of drugs. The positive consequence of such an attempt has been to expand discussion to include different topics beyond medical and legal concerns which predominated previously in the approach to drugs.[4]

Thus, we have witnessed recent studies on the macroeconomic process involving illegal money operations. These are brief and isolated studies that still lack adequate methodologies which allow them to include different sectors that have had an impact on the economy (Acosta and Little 1990; Luna 1991). Wilson Mino (1991) has developed an interesting methodological proposal on money laundering, one that is, however, limited in its operativeness in the study of money circulating in black markets. Along this same line, the work of Nelson Romero (1990) approaches the problem of "narcochemistry," which provides the patterns for seeing Ecuador as a "narcotized society," that is, intersected in its different dimensions by drugs; however, since information on the chemical base industry is contradictory, what is needed is a rigorous review of quantitative data.

Another element of interesting analysis is that of political science. Studies such as those carried out by Alexei Paez (1988, 1991) and Adrian Bonilla (1991) have helped to clarify the relationship between the war on drugs as an international policy and its repercussions for the country and the Andean region. Criticism is implicit in all of these studies about the absence of a proposal and — in a strict sense — of a national and regional policy that can have a global impact on the phenomenon and readdress the problem in terms of its multilateral scope. Such studies also contribute the initial elements which can clarify the decision-making processes in antidrug policy.

From a legal standpoint, the work of Hernan Salgado and Ernesto Alban (1989) presents an interesting review of Ecuadoran legislation concerning the drug issue, beginning with the Law on Opium Trade (1916) and then a law in effect at the time of publication of the study which discussed the many legal frameworks with resolutions taken at the international level. A study by Paul Bonilla (1991) has centered on the problem of the potential permeability of the present legal framework and the processes of economic investments tied to "narcodollars." Finally, a study by Cesar Banda and Pablo Andrade (1991) is concerned with the permeability of the judicial system as a whole to corruption in judicial practices related to drug trafficking cases.

A work by Pilar Nunez (1990), which deals with the drug problem in the media, deserves particular attention. Although theoretically it is maintained with traditionally interpretative limits in the apprehension of the media as an apparatus of cultural control, its value lies in illustrating the manipulation of information on "drugs" by revealing abstract and universalist discourse which includes the preparation of messages by the media, certain opinion leaders, and determined communication expressions.

Studies of Social Effects

In the area of the social effects of drug use, the research effort developed by Pablo Andrade and Paul Bonilla (1990) on the first "epidemiological survey" carried out in the country in 1988 is outstanding. In reality, previous research has been carried out with a similar purpose but with marked methodological deficiencies; they are restricted to certain popular sectors defined a priori as "consumers." The Andrade and Bonilla study is the first rigorous quantitative study that presents a relatively reliable picture of the phenomenon in Ecuador while helping to draw lines of comparison with Andean reality.

Within this perspective, the approach to an Andean model of use of drug substances in terms of the more prevalent legal and illegal drugs is important. Indexes — for illegal drugs — in the Ecuadoran case are the lowest in the region. Nevertheless, in this same work, one must notice an insistence on maintaining a bias which, in light of the survey's data, seems to exaggerate the extent of use of certain (illegal) drug substances in comparison to those that are the most prevalent, both annually and monthly, that is, alcoholic beverages, tobacco, and other drugs.

In these works, this particular aspect barely holds any relevancy when faced with the problem of the prevention of drug use (P. Andrade 1990). In a more recent study, still in its preliminary stages, research on drug use is directly limited to more widely used drugs, that is, marijuana, cocaine sulfate, and cocaine hydrochloride, without discussing such a theoretical-methodological slant (P. Andrade and Herrera 1990).

There is also a similar study (in preparation) that attempts to present an explanatory model of drug use in Ecuador based on a systemic theoretical framework (Laufer 1990). In the measure by which the process of forming models, as defined by the theory of systems, requires a strong grasp of practically nonexistent quantitative data, the business seems to be condemned to failure, but not without having contributed interesting data on the many variables involved — the theoretical bias of this interpretative movement that permeates all analysis of an approach to the problem as a "deviation."

Another interesting contribution has been developed around the spontaneous discontinuation of illegal drug use (P. Andrade and Villacis

1990). It entails an eminently qualitative study, of psychological interest, that utilizes the experiences of informants-drug users and the motivations they have had in voluntarily quitting drugs, that is, without participating formally in rehabilitation. Certain elements are emphasized but not developed, such as, for example, the problem of the cultural model of drug use and the contexts and expectations linked to such models.

Finally, the use of drugs has been studied with attention to determined social actors, basically street children (Tenorio 1989) and youth gangs (X. Andrade 1990b). Both are qualitative studies that are concerned with rescuing the discourse and daily life of informants but with a different focus: the first settles on the problem of drug use from a theoretical framework ascribed to Lacanian psychology, while the second is an ethnology in the classical sense of the term as it is used in anthropology. Both must be understood as initial attempts whose principal contribution, in my view, is that of drawing attention to an awareness "from within" of the problem of drugs, as experienced by specific groups of "problematic" users, beyond merely rhetorical consider-ations and abstract criticisms which define them as examples of "extreme situations" caused by drug use.

As for anthropology's contributions, which is the field of study we are interested in, the picture is very weak. On the other hand, regarding the study in its "modern" usages, it is fitting to mention two timely contributions. The first, by Jose Sanchez Parga (1990), which studies coca in Andean societies, analyzes use from an historical perspective in contrast to drugs in today's world. Despite the fact that such a study places such a substance within the framework of a cultural "social-logic" of use, it explicitly echoes antidrug discourse — which it questions in principle — by directly associating the use of drugs in contemporary societies to some form of "social delinquency" while defining our societies as "illicit cultures."[5]

Another anthropological study is dedicated to an analysis of illegal drug trade on a small scale. It constitutes the first ethnographic approach to the dynamics implicit in illegal drug trafficking by small traffickers (X. Andrade 1990a). Such an approach realizes a dynamic that contrasts with official discourse, according to which the multiplicity of relations and strategies for survival (reciprocity, redistribution, market restriction, internal trade to client networks) discredit the picture of "amoral businessmen," while placing traffickers on the point of connection between offer and demand and not in the direct control of markets. Thus, it is understood that the existence of marginal, not hierarchical, trade structures makes possible the movement of the trade, independent of its ties to the allegedly machiavellian structure of "drug trafficking" viewed as a whole.[6] From this perspective, myths about the quality of these actors as "support" for repressive actions, that is, "articulation" of the drug trade with society, are removed or, at least, made more relative.

Once this initial picture of studies on drugs and narcotrafficking in Ecuador is clarified and the limitations on the academic debate surrounding the issue are brought to light, it will be necessary to consider the repercussions of the war on drugs in our country in order to direct the need for reinforcement of research efforts on the different dimensions of the problem, particularly related to the social effects and social formations affected by such efforts.

The Number of Repression

Official data regarding the prison population support the fact that crimes related to illegal drugs were the most prevalent in 1990, when they then represented 35.30 percent of the total number of inmates nationally, and displaced — for the first time — crime against property and against people which had traditionally been the most relevant throughout the decade. On the other hand, in 1990, the female prison population at the national level was formed by a little more than 72 percent of drug cases.

In 1992 — the first period for which there exists official figures — in contrast, this phenomenon represented only 18.46 percent, that is, almost half of the present number of prisoners. In the two years immediately following, it occupied second place, and thereafter, it decreased. However, the tendency shows drug trafficking as the third greatest cause of imprisonments during the first half of the 1980s, while in the second half its ascending curve is well known.[7] Up until now, one would think in terms of success in the crusade if such figures are verified as indicators of advances in defeating the problem. Nonetheless, these data must be framed within a concrete context, which is one we will provide in detail.

Ecuador is a paradigmatic case that illustrates certain contradictions implicit in antidrug discourse which are resolved in practice under the common denominator of punitive treatment of the problem. One can understand that in the various legal frameworks, prosecution and coercion are strengthened against drug dealers faced with the "pious assistance" claimed by consumers. Law varies from a "tough" focus toward dealers and the "soft" treatment (prevention and rehabilitation) of users. Such premises operate at the level of public opinion.

In practice, however, if data related to the expansion of the antidrug war in Ecuador is analyzed, what is outstanding is that prison overpopulation is due in good measure to the imprisonment of drug users, as revealed by the number of annual arrests. According to the Department of State of the United States, the following data have been reported regarding arrests — for cases related to drugs — carried out by national institutions of control and repression in past years.[8]

1985: 2,120 arrests

1986: 1,900 arrests

1987: 2,730 arrests

1988: 2,173 arrests

1989: 2,550 arrests

1990: 3,367 arrests

Although 1987 reported the greatest relative increase, an ascending tendency prevails in the years corresponding to the present administration. To these figures must be added official data from INTERPOL from their annual reports (1985-1989), which confirm such tendencies, but, at the same time, reveal a high percentage of people who, within the category of "arrests," correspond to consumers. In order to give us a good idea of those who are mostly affected, to these could be added those arrested for mere possession:

	For Use	For Possession	For Trafficking
1985:	63.2%	9.6%	31.3%
1986:	65.3%	6.2%	28.4%
1987:	66.1%	8.3%	25.5%
1988:	59.9%	8.1%	32.1%
1989:	57.1%	19.3%	23.5%

Two paradoxes stand out: The first is that Ecuadoran legislation — including existing legislation — does not in a strict sense penalize the use of drugs; it does not distinguish it as a legal element. The second is that in 1987, considered one of the most successful years, the number of "narcotraffickers" represents only one-fourth of the total number of arrests, while that of drug users constitutes two-thirds.

Drug Use

In Ecuador, there is no quantitative data on the evolution of illegal drug use. There are temporary figures corresponding to 1988 which are the only ones that try to reflect national reality (P. Andrade and P. Bonilla 1990). The results of that survey were published when there existed only two documents corresponding to different stages of progress in the only thorough research on internal demand that exists. [9]

This research was initially developed in the largest cities of Ecuador, that is, Guayaquil and Quito; subsequently, Quito was concentrated on, following clear methodological criteria and using the 1988 national survey as a frame of reference. In the first phase, the survey was populational, while in the second phase it was restricted to a population of drug users that was statistically representative while adding a qualitative study.[10]

In the first study, quantitative data regarding the evolution of drug use in the interim period tends to gather variables — grouped under the notion of "field of action" — that had not initially been considered in the epidemiological survey.[11] Comparative references were sought between the user population and the nonuser population, and the study did not dedicate itself to the study of vital prevalence. Hence, the quantitative data presented throughout the study is not intended to offer elements that can measure the evolution of the phenomenon since, in fact, the report made its own contributions.[12]

The main contributions from our perspective lie in the presentation of certain information related to the opinions and the social representations regarding drugs. Perceptions of the differential treatment which drug users deserve in relation to drug dealers, for example, stand out. In the first case, the population is clearly inclined to favor a "humanitarian" treatment (that is, that they especially prefer prevention) in addition to control in the educational area and support in the form of some type of counseling; a little more than 10 percent consider police repression to be the alternative to treatment for drug abuse.

In contrast, opinions related to the trade in illegal drugs in reference to drug dealers indicate society's open tendency to favor repression of the problem; a majority of people — two-thirds — were in favor of more repressive solutions such as the death penalty, life imprisonment, an increase in sentences, or more police control, while approximately 22 percent in Quito and 16 percent in Guayaquil were in favor of solutions such as the integration of offenders into society and offering them alternative employment.

It is interesting to point out how society as a whole reproduces the basic dichotomy we had discussed previously between mild treatment for drug users and a tough treatment for drug dealers. This brings to light the permeability of hegemonic discourse on the problem of drugs. One can understand the marked rejection in both cities to a hypothetical legalization of illegal drugs. One cannot, however, go without mentioning that the percentages of consensus — partial or total — are also important; 12 percent in the case of Quito and 9 percent Guayaquil elected this measure.

This report also discusses how such permeability affects all of society, including the user population itself, which could in the future bring light on the problem of the impact of hegemonic policies in determining the character of user groups as well as the phenomenon of drug use. Undoubtedly, this is a call for a political and historical approach; the problem involves studying the processes by means of which "official representations of the 'problem' of drugs have been assimilated into real representations that drug users carry out by themselves and with their habits, helping to affect alarmist 'precautions' as well as to satisfy their own tendencies" (Henman, 10).

It is meaningful when making a comparison of the representations between drug users and nonusers that in the prosecution of the drug business and legalization, the authors underline as a general tendency the coincidence between those two groups. There exist no relevant differences, and existing aspects indicate a slight decline in punitive attitudes by the drug users themselves; from this perspective, "it can be observed that social discourse determines the opinion of the user group" (Henman, 26).

A study by Herrera (1992) is of particular interest because of its "approach to offer from demand."[13] It is the first such study to contribute data on the extension of the internal market upon the basis of quantitative estimates of a diverse nature and the priority given information gathered from a survey of the population that uses illegal drugs.[14] Although the data is preliminary, the study details procedures used in gathering the information. Undoubtedly, this effort deserves a meticulous methodological critique which for the purposes of this study is not important. In this consideration, it is fitting to note certain interesting indicators.

The extent of internal use of illegal drugs at the national level in 1991 corresponds to an estimated average of $29,694,450 annually (Herrera 1992, 3,5), most of which is spent on marijuana; it is the most popular drug and is the cheapest according to average monthly expenses in comparison with sulfate or hydrochloride of cocaine.[15] Finally, national Ecuadoran demand is for approximately 50 metric tons of marijuana, a little more than 7 tons of base, and something more than a ton of cocaine. There is other data regarding market behavior which helps to outline relevant research (P. Andrade 1990).

Finally, a study by Perez (1992) is the first attempt at qualitative research on heterogeneous groups of users of illegal drugs. It is an ethnographic approach which emphasizes the "emic" focus — that is, the interpretation of informers themselves. This is interesting given the capacity to interpret "drugs" — an object and a symbolic form — as a cultural creation. Culture provides it with its value in daily life as well as the logic implicit in practices of drug use according to the type of drug used.

One of the relevant aspects of this study is the indication of an alternative concept of hegemonic discourse on drugs by means of the demystification of the articulating elements contained in such discourse. Thus, for example, one can interpret reflection on the "initiation" of drug users as a break with the idea that the small trafficker is a supplier of demand. Such research confirms the role of the user group as a catalyst of drug use not only when initiating new users but also as agents of the continuation of trade in substances, imposing extramonetary dynamics such as redistribution — part of user networks — to modify the internal characteristics of the market as a whole. User networks present in time a stable operation; that is, they are exemplified in the cases mentioned in the manner in which users are recruited and maintain similarities with the group throughout the decade.

A common problem in research on drug use found in the study comes from the influence of the discourse of antidrug policy on preferred data. Special attention is given to "problematic" cases, and although the differences in user groups is recognized, this view is not adequately explored in order to understand them not as disruptors of social life, but, on the contrary, as catalyzers of productivity.

While it is a preliminary study, it is hoped that in the future these and other aspects such as cultural drug use models will be developed further. Despite the fact that the main methodological approach is concerned with the typology of the drugs used, the information presented does not realize the differences within such groups; hypotheses are usually stated based on ideological creations of the type of drugs and models of use rather than on ethnographic studies. One contribution for discussion in this area is provided by this work, which will follow with a consideration of youth gang activities.

Drug Use and Violence

One of the user groups that has suffered open repression is that of youth gangs established mainly in Guayaquil.[16] We will look at the ethnographic experiences related to such social formations, given that such a phenomenon has been permanently indicated as the clearest expression of the articulation between drugs and social violence, therefore legitimizing repressive activities. From this perspective, one can understand that the war on drugs is an ideological exercise;[17] it defines the profiles and practices of determined groups and social actors as "perverse." The case of youth gang members is paradigmatic in the case of Ecuador because as a social phenomenon it has, especially since the mid-1980s, become the most violent.[18]

In 1987, the year with the greatest amount of youth gang activity, "according to the Chief of Police of Guayaquil, there are more than 1,000 gangs located in suburban neighborhoods" (Vistazo, October 2, 1987). In the same year, Guayaquil police formed a special repressive organization called the G.E.A. (Special Anti-Gang Group) in order to combat gangs. Gangs came to be considered pathological social groups, a perception that helps to corroborate apocalyptic versions of official discourse — now based on the articulation between trafficking and use given criminal and violent expressions which transcend society and make them victims and, in the same measure, the assassins of "drug trafficking."

In the same year, a conflict developed between "authorities and gangs" (La Segunda, September 1, 1987, 60). It spread geographically into the area of influence of the port[19] and became problematic in that schools were affected.[20] Both tendencies have gotten worse. The most serious indication of gang violence is ten homicides per month.[21]

In 1988, when gangs began to affect the middle class, the official position remained convinced that political determination would suffice to eliminate the problem — now social and not just youth related.[22] Obviously, mere intentions and repressive measures were not enough to overcome the problem. In 1989, official figures varied between 1,200 and 1,500 gangs.[23] Although this data illustrates a manipulation of information since the only reports reveal figures that are way below these, in the last instance they indicate a growing tendency which transcends the existence of the original group of gang members, thereby providing continuity to the phenomenon.[24] During this year, gang activity intensified between August and September, although throughout the period the media continued to alert public opinion that violence was a recurring practice.[25] On this occasion, again official reaction — expressed by the Police Superintendent of Guayaquil — was apocalyptic: "War to the Death against Gang Members" (*La Segunda*, August 8, 1989). The Social Front of the national government declared an "Anti-Gang Campaign" (*Expreso*, September 13, 1989, 1A).

During the most recent period, the press has reported on the gang phenomenon from a criminal standpoint. They have returned to sensationalist journalism where violence is mechanically associated with drug use. The main contribution of this work is that, by a consideration of the typology of drug use, its model of use, and its function in the daily lives of gang members, such an association can be reproposed.

Given that the emphasis of the research was on violence, drugs were studied in three specific contexts: preparatory rites for confrontation between gangs, armed conflicts, and the preparation for carrying out criminal acts. Daily practices were also considered. The use of unprescribed medical drugs (principally stimulants) is highlighted in association with alcohol as substances used as catalyzers of violent practices of any type (from fights between gangs to homicides and crimes against property and people). Over-the-counter drugs, in this context, constitute social drugs; that is, they are used on a wide scale. In fact, motivations for their use are explicitly perceived in order to carry out their group work: war. As for the ritual perparation of such events, they are considered a virtually omnipresent element. It is evident that if one is talking about how youth groups cause the most problems for society (participation in "serious" monthly confrontations and daily delinquency), the use of pills without prescription acquires a new dimension. From our perspective, its use lies in the area of the contemporary problems of drugs in Ecuador, given the specificities of behavior of this group of social actors who form part of the larger group of national users.

Under a similar model, we find alcohol use which is related to the daily activities of gangs. This does not mean that its members get drunk every day, but that such a drug is used in any context as a mere socializer, creative and festive, as well as violent rituals. Mixing with pills serves as the perfect catalyzer of the values and attitudes needed to carry out violent acts effectively. For criminal practices, on the other hand, alcohol is used in the same fashion as it would be used daily for socialization. That is, it is used in considerably smaller doses, not enough to cause drunkenness but enough to stimulate the individual to carry out activities that can be very dangerous.[26]

Contrary to beliefs, the cultural model of use of illegal drugs corresponds to patterns that extend into heterogeneous social formations. Only cocaine sulfate promotes certain forms of criminal action in seeking larger amounts of the required drug. In these last cases, those who participate are not gangs as a whole, but isolated individuals who maintain their membership and were involved in a drug session. Thus, it should be emphasized that in comparison to such drugs as those legal ones mentioned above, the base is used marginally and eventually in criminal practices, while marijuana practices are reduced to socialization as in other groups not necessarily linked to delinquency or violence. In comparison with other illegal drugs preferred by gangs, "basuco" is significantly cheaper and has not been known to cause violence. Given the pharmacological nature of the drug which causes marked lethargic side effects, what it does is make individuals sleepy, not violent.

From this perspective, gang members lose their position as a "support" for repressive practices that include the widest sectors of society, and, of "articulation" between "the drug — subtly handled abstractly by the mass media — and social violence." Thus, we insist on an expansion of social bases of justified perversity by a reinforcement of repressive policies.

Conclusions

It is important to highlight certain critical elements regarding progress, primarily in studies of social effects. One of the main problems that must be taken into consideration is the isolated character of different studies. In fields such as political science, as well as economic studies and quantitative, sociological, and anthropological approaches, studies that have been conducted to date are efforts with no coordination among them; this reflects the absence of dialogue and, therefore, of academic debate regarding social problems. It is necessary to add that this is related to the absence of any institutional support for this type of study.

The studies begin in 1988 with two different efforts — that appear to be institutional — and with different interests. One has had an academic character, not under an articulated proposal but instead upon the basis of studies that correspond to the particular interests of those who carried them out in the institution (FLACSO). In this sense, the topics mainly utilized secondary sources because there has been no institutional support except that of the North-South Center of the University of Miami, the only academic center that has brought together Ecuadoran researchers to study the problem of drugs; a coordinated project — for the moment — has not been developed. One must understand that the acquisition of first-hand data has certainly been marginal in this research, which brings to the table discussion of the character and validity of data which researchers must attempt.

Nevertheless, the greatest contribution of this first group of works is that they have raised direct questions of the policies that — in terms of international relations — can only be understood as an uncritical and often quaint reproduction of discourse that has been unilaterally held. Since Ecuador is a country where hegemonic discourse has an effect on society, a fact that is expressed in the absence of internal debate on problems implicit in the official approach to drugs, it must be pointed out that such a contribution has already been recognized, although circumstantially, by the communications media.

It is exactly at the level of the need to look at alternative discourse in relation to official positions where there is a stalemate between the first group of works and those that were financed by an institution whose existence is justified by preventive works, the Our Youth Foundation. Let us begin with contributions in order to point out certain critical elements concerning these works. On the one hand, the most important thing is that valuable quantitative data in some measure helps to present a global picture of the phenomenon of internal demand in Ecuador as well as relative collateral aspects. This in itself constitutes a contribution, despite all the criticism that can be raised regarding the value of this type of approach to stigmatized phenomenon; the only thing that existed previously was a completely arbitrary manipulation of information acquired from heterogeneous and imprecise sources.

The challenge, therefore, is to maintain theoretical and methodological precision in this type of measure and maintain objective control of the information; a common trait in this type of work until now has been the lack of specification of a series of suppositions that characterize such approaches which are most of the time of institutional interests whose proximity to exaggeration of the size of the phenomenon is a requirement for its very existence. In this sense can be understood the echo of a good part of media's information.

Finally, it is fitting to highlight that qualitative research financed by this same institutional means allows for first-hand access to the reality of populational groups involved in drug use defined as "problematic," as was illustrated in this work with a comparison of drugs and violence. It serves to find the relationship of certain elements of hegemonic discourse which, while they can be treated more systematically and with greater dialog with the types of approaches that allow for the previously mentioned perspectives, could allow for a review of certain punitive policies as well as criticism of the opportunistic approach to the problem of drugs from positions of power.

Notes

1. The figure used in official and academic circles is $400 million, without questioning its validity (see USDS 1991a, 360-1; Paez 1992, 150). There is an initial study on money laundering that reveals figures that are far below this, but which are restricted to money used in free market transactions (see Mino 1991).

2. Those aspects defended by Borja to support his position of "all-out war" are summarized as follows: limitation on the resource of habeas corpus, the accumulation of sentences and an increase in them up to 25 years, and extradition in cases linked to drug trafficking, among others.

3. An interesting work which looks at the evolution of antidrug legislation in Ecuador is by Salgado and Alban (1989), although it is strictly restricted to the legal aspects of the problem. From the same viewpoint, on the present situation and perspectives, see Paul Bonilla (1991).

4. For a criticism of these initial works, see Paez (1988).

5. For a criticism of this type of dichotomy on drugs as cultural occurrences and the forms by which anthropological discourse functions as an echo of antidrug policy, see Andrade (1991b).

6. Del Olmo (1991) has reflected on the literature which provides alternatives for this picture and which realizes a multiplicity of forms and channels of market operations, distinct from those of "monopoly" or "cartels."

7. Information on the prison population has been collected in different statistical reports prepared by the National Office of Social Rehabilitation. Data contained in the Report "Statistics of the Ecuadoran Penitentiary System, 1990," the most recent, is particularly useful. For a comparative reference for 1990, 2,546 drug arrests were reported out of a total population of 7,679. At the beginning of 1982, on the other hand, there were 1,039 arrests for drugs out of a total of 5,628 (see Lopez, 163).

8. Data, taken from USDS reports of 1990 and 1991, vary for certain years despite coming from the same source. As for 1988, 1989, and 1990, they are taken more from the year 1991, as it was more up-to-date. This source contains no estimates or projections for the past year (see USDS 1990, 140; 1991a, 109).

9. I am referring to "Users of Illegal Drugs, Report from Research on the Populational Survey" by P. Andrade and Herrera, corresponding to October 1990, and a more recent study by Herrera. The data that we have collected from the first report corresponds to the month of August 1990.

10. In order to refer to the qualitative component, we have utilized a preliminary research report, summarized in the document entitled, "Users of Illegal Drugs: A Qualitative Interpretation" (Perez 1992).

11. Unfortunately, this idea is not discussed theoretically in the report. On the other hand, its conclusions are obvious (see P. Andrade and Herrera, 23-4).

12. The authors warn that different questionnaires were used, that is, incomparable in a strict sense. This is of particular importance regarding data on drug use. For example, in the greatest amount of data, that is, on the vital prevalence of marijuana use, base, and cocaine, based on male users — the majority — a comparative increase is contemplated between 1988 and 1990 for Quito, from 5.2 percent to 17 percent. In the case of Guayaquil, it was around 14 percent for male users. Nonetheless, as is indicated in the same text regarding the increase, "The first reason would be because there exists a real increase in use, but this increase is too large for such a short period of time. The second reason would be in the incorporation of old drug users who denied using drugs and who today say they did use drugs: and, finally, there are errors in this type of research, etc."

13. Herrera's report has three parts: "The Tale and Users," "Law and Users," and "An Approach to Offer from Demand." Here we have discussed the last paragraph because it seems to be the most pertinent for this study. The author warns that it is just an initial endeavor, and, therefore, the figures presented are subject to future review.

14. Data taken from censuses are also used: the Epidemiological Survey of 1988 and the population survey of 1991, already referred to.

15. Monthly estimates of expenditures by an average drug user correspond to approximately $8 for a marijuana user, $16 for a sulfate user, and $32 for hydrochloride.

16. In this paragraph, we make use of the systematized information contained in the research report "Youth Gangs: An Ethnographic Approach to the Problem of Drugs and Social Violence" and a subsequent work developed also by the author: "Violent Frontiers in the City: Youth Gang Activity in Guayaquil," a monograph prepared for FLACSO-Ecuador, 1991.

17. Henman has developed this point in "Cognitive Aspects of the Effects of Drugs: Towards a Genealogy of Representations."

18. Although there is no quantitative data to measure the evolution of this specific phenomenon, arrests can serve as an indicator of the growth in violence attributed to youth. In 1979, this number reached 1,704, while four years later 3,034 youths were arrested. That is to say that in that period, corresponding to the first half of the 1980s, the number of youth delinquents had doubled (*Vistazo*, "Youth Violence Increases," June 6, 1984, 9). An interesting situation is that in 1986, the area of operation of a majority of new gangs was limited to certain "red zones" of the port, where violence by these gangs was on a daily basis (*Vistazo*, "Green Light in the Red Zone," May 6, 1986, 78-82).

19. We are speaking specifically of the city of Machala (see *La Segunda*, "They Are Growing Like Bugs," November 11, 1987, 23), the Eloy Alfaro district (see *La Segunda*, "First Youth Encounter Turned Out Great," November 30, 1987, 17), the Naranjito district (see *La Segunda*, "Youth Gangs in Naranjito," March 4, 1988, 22), and the community of Duran (see *La Segunda*, "Gangs Have Their Way in Duran," November 26, 1988, 22).

20. See, among other articles, "Pirates Spread Terror in Olmedo High School" (*La Segunda*, July 15, 1987); "Gangs Attack Students" (*La Segunda*, August 29, 1987, 5); "High School Gangsterism" (*La Segunda*, January 4, 1989, 7); "High School Assailants" (*La Segunda*, January 19, 1989, 8).

21. Note "With This One There Have Been 20 in One Month: Assassin Gangs Took Another Victim," in *La Segunda*, August 31, 1987.

22. Thus, "...the Chief of the Guayas Regiment #2 has publicly stated that youth gangs will be eliminated, since their presence disturbs the tranquility of Guayaquil residents." See "Youth Gangs" in *La Segunda*, September 27, 1988, 7.

23. The first figure is cited in "Criminal Life" (*Comercio*, May 28, 1989, 4a); the second in "1,500 youth gangs" (*Expreso*, June 25, 1989, 1). It is difficult to measure the truthfulness of such statistics although the second source is said to have used data from a census prepared by the special unit of the GEA police. (Also see *Expreso*, "New Laws against Narcotrafficking," September 29, 1989, 8).

24. In September 1988, according to the Provincial Headquarters for Criminal Investigation, Fourth District, Guayaquil Plaza, there were 75 gangs in existence. Data for the year 1990 presented by an officer in charge of the repression of gang members reveals the existence of approximately 150 gangs (personal interview).

25. For an evaluation of the first trimester, see "Criminal Apogee: Red Alert!" *Vistazo*, April 20, 1989, 5.

26. The decisiveness, speed, and courage required to function in similar situations are conditions that must be maintained; therefore, informal social controls act to limit more explicitly the use of alcohol.

References

Acosta, Alberto, and Paul Little. 1990. "Drug Trafficking and the External Debt." In *Drug Trafficking and the External Debt: The Plagues of America*. Quito: Working Group on External Debt and Development.

Andrade, Pablo. 1990. "Use and Abuse of Drugs in the Andean Region." In *Society, Youth and Drugs*. Quito: Our Youth Foundation, No. 3.

Andrade, Pablo, and Cesar Banda. 1991. *Evaluation and Requirements of the Ecuadoran Judicial System*. Quito: ILANUD.

Andrade, Pablo, and Paul Bonilla. 1990. "Drug Use in Ecuador: A Quantitative Approach." In *Society, Youth and Drugs*. Quito: Our Youth Foundation, No. 3.

Andrade, Pablo, and Carlós Herrera. 1990. "Users of Illegal Drugs, Research Report from the Populational Survey," Preliminary Research Report. Quito: Our Youth Foundation.

Andrade, Pablo, and Lucia Villacis. 1990. "Why Drugs Were Abandoned: A Study on Former Habitual Users of Marijuana and Cocaine," Research Report, Mimeograph. Quito: FNJ.

Andrade, Xavier. 1990a. *Small Traffickers, an Anthropological Study on the Illegal Drug Trade on a Small Scale*. Quito: Our Youth Foundation.

Andrade, Xavier. 1990b. "Youth Gangs: An Ethnographic Approach to the Problem of Drugs and Violence." Research Report, s.e. Quito: Our Youth Foundation.

Andrade, Xavier. 1991a. "Violent Frontiers in the City: Youth Gang Activity in Guayaquil." Quito: FLACSO monograph.

Andrade, Xavier. 1991b. "Anthropologists as Moral Businessmen: An Irony Out of Drugs and the Use of Time." Quito: FLACSO monograph.

Bagley, Bruce, Adrian Bonilla, and Alexei Paez, eds. 1991. *La Economia del Narcotrafico: el caso Ecuatoriano*. Quito: FLACSO.

Bonilla, Adrian. 1991. "Ecuador: International Actor in the War on Drugs." In *La Economia del Narcotrafico*, eds. B. Bagley, A. Bonilla, and A. Paez. Quito: FLACSO.

Bonilla, Paul. 1991. "Dollar Laundering in Ecuador: A Legal Perspective." In *La Economia del Narcotrafico*, eds. B. Bagley, A. Bonilla, and A. Paez. Quito: FLACSO.

Del Olmo, Rosa. 1991. "The Geopolitics of Drug Trafficking." Paper presented at the International Seminar on the Impact of the Financial Capital of Drug Trafficking in the Development of Latin American and Caribbean Countries, La Paz.

Henman, Anthony. "Cognitive Aspects of the Human Mind: Towards a Genealogy of Representations," s.e., s.f.

Herrera, Carlos. 1992. "Users of Illegal Drugs: Report on the User Survey," preliminary research report, mimeograph. Quito: Our Youth Foundation.

INTERPOL. 1985-1989. "Statistics from the Work of the Drug Service and Interpol of the National Police."

Laufer, Jacques. 1990. "Drug Use in Ecuador: An Explanatory Model." Working Document, mimeograph. Quito: Our Youth Foundation.

Luna, Jorge. 1991. "Cocaine and Society." In *Society, Youth and Drugs*. Quito: Our Youth Foundation, No. 4.

Miño, Wilson. 1991. "Dollar Laundering and the Narcoeconomy in Ecuador." In *La Economia del Narcotrafico*, eds. B. Bagley, A. Bonilla, and A. Paez. Quito: FLACSO.

National Office of Social Rehabilitation. 1991. "Statistics of the Ecuadoran Penitentiary System." Annual Report, Quito.

Nuñez, Pilar. 1990. "The Communication Media and Drugs." Research Report, mimeograph. Quito: Our Youth Foundation.

Paez, Alexei. 1988. "Bibliography: Drugs in Ecuador and a Brief Preliminary Analysis." Quito: FLACSO-Ecuador document.

Paez, Alexei. 1991. "Ecuadoran Introduction into the Andean Dynamics of Drug Trafficking." In *La Economia del Narcotrafico*, eds. B. Bagley, A. Bonilla, and A. Paez. Quito: FLACSO.

Perez, Santiago. 1992. "Users of Illegal Drugs: An Ethnographic Approach," preliminary research report, mimeograph. Quito: Our Youth Foundation.

Romero Simancas, Nelson. 1990. "Ecuadoran Narcochemistry in the 1980s." In *Drug Trafficking and the External Debt: The Plagues of America*. Quito: Working Group on the External Debt and Development.

Sanchez Parga, Jose. 1990. "The Use of Drugs in Traditional Andean Societies, a Lesson for History." In *Drug Trafficking and the External Debt: The Plagues of America*. Quito: Working Group on the External Debt and Development.

Salgado, Hernan, and Ernesto Alban. 1989. "Legal Research: Analysis and Evaluation of Ecuadoran Legislation. Basic Premises for Legal Reform." In *Society, Youth and Drugs*. Quito: Our Youth Foundation, No. 1.

Tenorio, Rodrigo. 1989. *Children on the Streets and Drug Use*. Quito: Our Youth Foundation.

U.S. Department of State (USDS). 1990. International Narcotics Control Strategy Report. March.

USDS. 1991a. International Narcotics Control Strategy Report. March.

USDS. 1991b. International Narcotics Control Foreign Assistance Appropriation Act. Fiscal Year 1992 Budget Congressional Submission.

The magazine *Vistazo*— as well as *La Segunda, Expreso*, and *El Comercio*—was used in its issues corresponding to the 1980s.

Chapter Sixteen

The Impact of Drug Trafficking on Ecuadoran Politics: 1989-1992

Alexei Páez Cordero

Introduction

The drug trafficking problem in the case of Ecuador is much less visible than in the case of its Andean neighbors, Colombia, Peru, and Bolivia. The reasons why Ecuador has been singled out in such a way have been explored in recent editions of books (Bagley et al. 1991). However, the dynamic of drug trafficking on the Andean scale has transformed — significantly, in some cases — the level and kind of linking that keeps Ecuador in the Andean division of work related to the coca-cocaine production complex.

One of the reasons that these changes have such impact is that the international context of the struggle against drug trafficking can displace the illegal activities from the Andean part of the region to the Amazonic part (the so-called "balloon effect") and policies of interdiction are consistently practiced; on the other hand, the legal limits of the various countries — individually considered — also general adaptive tendencies in the drug trafficking structure, simultaneously producing social effects that were not originally calculated (Paez 1991b).

Finally, it can be argued that the measures taken by the drug traffickers not only fulfill a "reactive" need in the state's national and international policies but also follow an autonomous design that interacts with the latter, and that carries its own weight when it comes to explaining the evolution of drug trafficking in the last few years.

This chapter attempts to provide a global vision of the drug trafficking problem in the Ecuadoran case, departing from an analysis of the current position of the country in the coca-cocaine production complex. It will then describe and analyze public state policies in different areas that affect the internal dynamic of drug trafficking and, along these lines in the last section of the chapter, ponder the possible evolutions (implications) that these kinds of policies will have in the next few years, in order to be able to make projections in the Ecuadoran case.

Toward a Diagnosis

The role of Ecuador as an in-transit country for part of the cocaine that goes to the North American market has been known since the late 1980s. Reports from the Bureau of International Narcotics Matters (1989, 1990, and 1991; Bagley et al. 1991, 227-240) depart from this diagnosis. In the last one of these reports, it is pointed out that about 30 to 50 metric tons of chlorhydrate will have passed through Ecuador on the way to the United States.[1] The disbanding of the Medellin cartel led to a change in the routes; what is sustained has allowed for the possibility of substantial growth in the quantity of chlorhydrate of cocaine that is found to be passing through the country, as acknowledged by the authorities in charge of control.[2]

These functions of transporting the psychoactive material could be considered important, but the elective organization that makes them possible operates very silently.[3] The need to increase border controls has allowed for the unveiling of a policy that is intended to create new police units, with better equipment, at the advice and through economic aid from North America and the United Nations.[4]

Military participation, including the marines patrolling the rivers bordering the Amazon as well as the air force and the national army working to control the shipment of cocaine throughout the country, has been increased substantially. President Rodrigo Borja, at the San Antonio meeting, proposed that operating costs of the Ecuadoran Air Force involved in these kinds of missions be included in the financial assistance provided by the Andean Initiative (*El Comercio*, February 26-27, 1992).

The evolution of the Ecuadoran insertion into the dynamic of money laundering has already been discussed by others (particularly in Paez 1991a, 149). The figures that were originally used came from North American sources and statements from unknown state functionaries (*Miami Herald*, September 29, 1989) and rose to about $400 million annually. The Adjunct Secretary of State for Narcotics confirmed those figures[5] but without presenting how these calculations were reached.[6]

Even though the system of bank controls of foreign currency transactions in the country is one of the strictest in Latin America, according to ex-superintendent of Patricio Avila Banks and the Association of Private Banks (*El Universo*, November 27, 1991), since the transaction of more than $2,000 requires that written reports be made out to the Superintendent of Banks; reforms have been proposed that would tighten these controls even more. This is due, in part, to the scandal that occurred during 1991 and at the beginning of 1992 as a result of the Investigations of the Special Parliamentary Commission regarding money laundering, presided by the Deputy of the PRE (Partido Roldosista), Fernando Larrea, who proposed the aforementioned reforms.

The Legislative Commission presented its first report in December 1990, which received much criticism from bankers as well as from Executive authorities because of its poor factual argument and the lack of evidence or clues that would definitely link public figures, mentioned in the report, to the business of money laundering. Nevertheless, from this first report,[7] the following papers of the Special Commission revealed a list of 178 people that had transacted a global sum of US$680 million from March 1990 to February 1991[8] (*Analisis Semanal*, Ano XXI, #27, July 15, 1991). Larrea utilized two entities, one for money exchange and one bank, in the business of money laundering.[9]

However, the most spectacular case of money laundering in which an Ecuadoran money exchange was involved broke out at the end of April 1991, when the funds of the C & F money exchange were investigated by North American authorities, because of suspicions of money laundering that were later confirmed. This case had some special connotations: Jose Ribadeneira Icaza, brother-in-law to President Rodrigo Borja,[10] was found to be involved; it resulted in the resignation of the superintendent in charge of banks, because of pressure from President Borja for the immediate liquidation of the exchange, and it revealed a functioning system of money laundering that could evade North American controls.[11]

The constraints to the financial system — in legal terms — have produced a negative reaction by the banker's guild: this constraint substantially alters the income flows of dividends to a capital market that is in the process of liberalization and that is seriously limited by the increase in controls to the incoming capital[12] in the country; as indeed confirmed by the state authorities and the financial groups, in Ecuador there exist increasing restrictions and controls of foreign capital. The possibility of Ecuador accommodating itself to the current economic process — that implies the possibility of open capital flows in the transnational plan — seems limited, and in the meantime, the country would be facing a disadvantageous legal-normative situation as opposed to other countries with fewer controls and which are more integrated in neoliberal terms.[13]

In spite of what has already occurred, which implies a relatively positive evolution, that the points of entry of drug money are being defined and the institutionalized mechanisms of control are being perfected, there exist aspects of drug money laundering that are still not being investigated. One of those that is probably central is investment in real estate property, that could serve as a disturbance to owners of land in the whole country, but with a very special potential impact in an area of growing conflict such as the Ecuadoran Sierra.[14]

The visibility of the financial system blurs other types of investment by the drug traffickers, and as a result, it does not allow some relevant aspects to be seen in the long term: control of drug money laundering is given emphasis in terms of bank accounts before control in terms of changes of property,[15] even when these changes have deeper global repercussions in the medium and long term, before being expressed immediately as the investment rates and the capital in circulation in banking institutions.[16]

The third mode of the insertion of Ecuador into the coca-cocaine production complex has been that of trafficking in chemical precursors. According to data stated in an article published in 1990 (Romero 1990), this activity would mobilize large quantities of resources.[17] However, the quantitative bases from which these figures are derived are unknown, beyond the calculations that grossly try to provide information — possibly, in an alarming way — about this matter and that are proven in the same work cited.

Trafficking of precursors has been the object of attention of the state and also of bilateral and multilateral agreements. In the first aspect, trafficking of precursors has been perceived as a violation of the Law of Narcotics issued in September 1990. However, since long-term agreements — which would imply concerted interstate actions — have not been reached, trafficking that used to be legal could be potentially transformed into a purely illegal practice (in other words, it does not disappear but is out of state control) and, in this manner, could increase conflict in the country.[18] Moreover, control of precursor trafficking is done by interdiction and police actions, instead of controlling the productive sectors that feed off these consumptions,[19] which could be a more viable option for control with repercussions in other aspects of social life, such as conservation of the environment.

Trafficking of precursors continues to be an important activity in the country: since the new law that penalizes it was issued, significant seizures continue to be made. The same agreements with the United States concerning the adaptation of special forces of border police take on as one of their major objectives that of controlling precursor trafficking that still exists in spite of the implementation of laws and normative controls that penalize it.

A chapter of special importance in the Ecuadoran case is related to the social logic which evolves along the frontier, above the state decision, especially in Amazonia. Although the integration processes in the Andean region have been drawn looking toward relaxation of border controls to allow for fluid intraregional commerce by means of specific state decisions, some social processes — impelled by the commercial dynamic of the coca-cocaine complex — that have been occurring since the mid-1980s, provoke autonomous integrating dynamic processes on the social and economic level.

These processes allude to a sort of "perverse integration" of the Amazonic Ecuadoran zones with the adjacent ones of Colombia and Peru: the so-called

Amazonic triangle or ECUPECO triangle (Ecuador-Peru-Colombia) in the Ecuadoran province of Sucumbios, contiguous with the Colombian Putumayo. In the Amazonic triangle zone, the controlling commercial axis, in spite of its illegality, is coca production and cocaine refining. There exists a migration of labor force and commercial connection — networks of consumption — controlled by the groups that are in charge of coca production in the area[20] which poses major challenges for the state and Ecuadoran society in the future.

The Evolution of Public Policies

E cuador has had a very particular margin of operation as to the problem of drugs; although all the national legislation relating to the problem has initially proceeded from adaptations of international agreements previously signed concerning the matter (A. Bonilla 1991, 18-27), this plainly reactive and nonautonomous attitude has been transformed into a sort of political virtue in the context facing the Andes in the 1990s.

Despite the alarmist versions that tried to envision the country as a base for narcoguerrillas and coca production,[21] these are not sustained according to the existing information. As has been said before, it would mean a post-factum rhetorical justification to the extremely repressive actions of the administration of President Febres Cordero toward the incipient endogenous guerrillas (Paez 1991a).

State policy has, however, suffered qualitative transformations in the past two years that are worthy of mention: the issuance of the new law against drugs is one of the most important instances of institution transformation taking the problem into account. This law has been questioned by the same judges that execute it,[22] in a study developed in 1991 about the Ecuadoran Judicial System.[23] Aside from this, the overload of the country's penal system resulting from the implementation of a judicial framework that places an emphasis on repressive aspects causes the challenge posed by the law not only to be within the context of its procedural questioning but also in its social effects.[24]

Moreover, the high degree of involvement by the police in antidrug policy is confronted by the total loss of prestige of the institution, as a result of the continuous cases of corruption and violation of human rights.[25] Aside from this, the judicial system is in a permanent crisis (it has had more than five shutdowns in the last three years for a lack of resources), to which is added historical internal corruption. In any case, the largest number of prisoners arrested for drug trafficking corresponds overwhelmingly to consumers (57 to 65 percent) and small traffickers (20 to 25 percent) (X. Andrade 1991, 66-67); that the law punishes the smaller linkings first prior to the unlawful organizations is overloading the penal system and worsening certain aspects of the social crisis.[26]

To the increase in police measures and perspectives, the Ecuadoran state has added the growing involvement of military elements in the context of interdiction activities, faithfully following along with it North American policies (WOLA 1991, 6-21), for which the country has deserved to be qualified as an example in the war against drugs during the past two administrations.[27] Ecuadoran military activity in this aspect includes permanent patrols in the border areas and aerial interdiction of drug shipments, which have not been integrated into the aid programs, but instead have been accomplished autonomously, for the moment; President Borja has proposed that these kinds of activities be included in the budgets being contemplated by the Andean Initiative for the effect.

Taking into account the very particular profile of the Ecuadoran army in the Andean context,[28] the dangers of militarization of the struggle against drug trafficking seem even worse than in the neighboring countries. Since the Ecuadoran armed forces have developed an astounding level of presence and economic autonomy, and since they do not have to struggle against any important armed groups within the country, this turn in direction could acquire an intensity and depth that may consequently serve to escape from the grasp of civil politicians. The law governing narcotics and psychotropic substances proclaimed in 1990[29] contemplates the creation of the National Council of Control of Narcotics and Psychotropic Substances (CONSEP), which is the organization that should concentrate on all of the activities of control in the area. As has been observed in previous publications (Nadelman 1987), the inter-institutional conflict that originated in the superimposition of jurisdiction between various public bodies in the field of control of illicit trafficking of drugs produced more than one problem for the efficient administration of state policies.[30]

In actuality, CONSEP would have under its authority the global coordination of the activities of control of narcotics, but the institutional structure continues to have several interconnections: INTERPOL is dependent on the National Police; the Customs Police is part of the Armed Forces; while CONSEP has still not been able to set up a global system that would order and integrate the activities of the fragmented institutions of control.[31]

Conclusions: Toward a Perspective

Ecuadoran state policies toward drug trafficking have suffered a rapid evolution, with a tendency toward a toughening of police, military, and repressive attitudes during the last three years. This evolution has been guaranteed by an acritical consensus between the political class in long-term attitudes that fuel the drug trafficking problem and the war against drugs. The possibility of generating and implementing stricter legislation in the Andes, that strongly punishes cultivators and collectors,[32] takes root precisely in the particular Ecuadoran insertion into the Andean drug trafficking dynamic, a dynamic that results in the nonexistence of large social groups linked with the sowing.

Ecuador has proven itself to be highly sensitive to the drug trafficking dynamic. From the rhetorical and justificatory use of the matter, initially attempting to tie it to the problem of armed struggle, in the form of "narcoguerrillas" (nonexistent in the country) during the Febres Cordero administration, it moved into a kind of state silence toward the problem that lasted until the latter part of 1989. The proposals of an increase in sentences and tough regulations were heard and approved by political decision makers, in the hopes of demonstrating that Ecuador was an "island of peace" in the Andes, not contaminated by the phenomenon. (Although refining operations do exist in Ecuador, they are small compared to others in the Andes.)

The insertion of the country into the production complex, without the existence of an ample peasantry involved in coca cultivation, permits the most radical proposals of "attack" by the penal system. The social effects of this punitive policy, on the other hand, leave plenty of room to generate potential conflicts in the future. The conditions that drive small-scale traffickers are of a structural nature more than they are of unlawful intent. State policies for the Ecuadoran penal system, which is historically corrupt, and the national penitentiary system, which is totally overloaded, could generate catastrophic results in the medium term.

With respect to the problem of money laundering, the Ecuadoran economy also faces severe conditions of a structural nature. Lacking possibilities for an efficient integration into the world economy, the increase of control over free movement of capital — if it is not accompanied by compensatory measures at the macro level[33] — could produce an even greater decrease in the economic profile of the country in the next decade.

The controls over the financial system, in actuality, are only one of the boundaries to a global policy which should also pay attention to the real estate and construction activities in determined zones of the country. If current policies continue, the social effects accumulated over property and class structure will reach unforeseeable parameters during the next decade.

The poor social visibility of the drug trafficking phenomenon serves to conceal and has caused its political effects to disappear from sight. The scandalous use of incriminations for functionalizing them to the political conflict[34] is one of these; the other is the penetration of drug dollars in electoral campaigns and the presence of political figures in local power who are linked to mafias, especially in border areas.

In these same areas, the drug trafficking dynamic exceeds the capacity of state and national control. If it is true that in the Amazonic triangle the generation of networks and commercial circuits is aided on the basis of the coca-cocaine dynamic, these processes will be transformed into real and growing challenges to the state in the next decade. Thinking that a purely repressive police attitude can control economic and social processes in the long term reveals the worst political near-sightedness. The political decision makers seem to believe that in spite of the high sensitivity of Ecuador, there exists a low vulnerability of the country with respect to the problem of drug trafficking.

Yet, the drug trafficking dynamic does not only occur in reactive terms, but instead is a process whose nature and evolution depend on strategic decisions of diverse actors and not only on immediate effects of complacent and short-term policies. The high sensitivity happens in vulnerability sooner than later. If state policies continue to be guided by perceptions of acritical adaptation to repressive diagnoses, the consequences for Ecuador in the 1990s could be serious.

Notes

1. It is to be noted that these calculations are based (generally) on the extrapolation of the quantity seized — the same in the country as that which has been seized abroad and that is known to have come from Ecuador — multiplied by a factor that oscillates between 8 and 10. The limited reliability of these calculations is seen when large shipments are seized, which extraordinarily increases the extrapolation, as in the case of the recent seizure of about 3 tons of chlorhydrate (February 1992) which was to be brought into the country in a shipping truck.

2. Author interview with the "Police Commissioner" Guillermo Jijon, ex-director of the now-defunct DINACONTES (National Department against Drug Trafficking) and current Secretary General of the Attorney General for the State, central body of CONSEP (National Council of Narcotics and Psychotropic Substances).

3. The practically null visibility that the drug trafficking organizations have in Ecuador permits the entry of the country into the coca-cocaine production complex: with the lack of plantations and regions controlled directly by the heads of the trade. For the most part, the Ecuadoran mafias that are involved in drug trafficking try to maintain a familiar kind of profile (i.e., the Reyes de Loja Group). In the Ecuadoran case, drug trafficking is not related to social processes of breadth nor to main political problems, as in the case of other Andean countries.

4. A government spokesman, who wished not to be identified, confirmed to the foreign press that, in fact, 8 U.S. soldiers and coast guards currently provide technical assistance and manpower to the Marines and the Police of Ecuador in the struggle against drugs. Statements confirmed later by Melvin Levitsky, adjunct secretary of the North American Bureau of Narcotics. North American aid led to the formation of a group of 40 men with "modern armament, patrol boats, and communications equipment to confront the trafficking of drugs and chemical products" (*El Universo*, April 22, 1991; emphasis added). Regarding cooperation with the UN, on June 7, 1991, an agreement was signed calling for the strengthening of the operating capacity of the national specialized forces, the qualification and the equipping of customs and police forces, within the confines of a financing plan of $3.9 million, which comes from UNDCP (MRE 1992, 2).

5. Levitsky indicated, cautiously, that "if a concrete amount does not exist of the sum total of laundering of narcodollars in Ecuador, the amount could be between $300 and $500 million a year" (*El Comercio*, April 20, 1991).

6. For a critical analysis of the amount of US$400 million, see Paez (1991, 150 and s.s.).

7. The report of the Commission on Drug Money Laundering consists of two parts: one documental that includes accounts of movement of money of the country's banks and newspaper articles, plus the diverse reports of state functionaries to the Commission and the other, the actual report, that includes conclusions and recommendations. The adjective treatment (which attempts to link opposing politicians) of the drug money laundering problem and the fact that the Commission found itself

confronted with embryonic material that was not elaborate were the elements that stand out most in this first report. (See Report of the Special Commission of the Congress on the Investigation of Money Laundering in Ecuador, 1990.)

8. Evidently, not all of these transactions can be attributed to money laundering. Some of them, once submitted to investigations, have been found very unclear, and therefore could be attributed to illegal matters. It is not known what kind of concrete operations they could be, including overbilling and underbilling, contraband, and also legitimate income by legal transfer.

9. Serious presumptions exist about Ecuadoran Exchange and The Bank of the Andes being mechanisms utilized to launder drug money because they do not require any identification from their clients. Those who were alluded to replied by questioning the report. Ecuadoran Exchange would handle 56 percent of the buy-sell transactions of dollars (at the level of money exchanges), inasmuch as The Bank of the Andes would do it with 15 percent of the total (*Analisis Semanal*, #27: 302-303).

10. It should be noted that Ribadeneira Icaza had been separated from his wife for 17 years and that he did not have any contact with his former in-laws.

11. C & F was founded in 1982, as a continuation of "Comercial y Fiduciaria" that was operating since 1978. In 1989, (in Ecuador) it transacted US$60 million, and in the first six months of 1990, it transacted US$36 million, 20 percent more than in the same period of 1989. In the first semester of 1990, it had accounted for 4.3 percent of the exchange market, that is to say about 1 percent of the total exchange market. It negotiated money orders at values inferior to US$1,000, through which money was laundered, buying for less than $US10,000 and sending them back to accounts in the United States. In this manner, close to $70 million has been laundered since 1989. Ribadeneira was convicted at the beginning of February 1992.

12. Currently a law exists that hinders the processes of buying and selling bank shares, in the name of the control of possible income of illegal capital, more than the previous law and in a liberalizing context. Now, with the atmosphere of threats that exists in the financial groups, there would also be an attempt to control the free exchange market. This puts into question the free flow of capital, an essential element of any economic liberalization, perceived in the Ecuadoran case as a fundamental economic matter, in the hopes of achieving subregional integration and the efficient insertion of Ecuador into the new emerging international order.

13. For example, it suffices to make comparisons to the Chilean case where "Chile is also one of the easiest countries in which to launder money. The laws permit foreigners to enter the country with millions of dollars in cash, declare it to customs officials, and the next day make huge bank deposits without further investigations" (*New York Times*, January 23, 1992).

14. According to the Police Commissioner, already cited, Guillermo Jijon, "In our country, in the past ten years, there have been instances of very suspicious business dealings related to land ownership and the elevated costs of it in strategic points of the Coast and Amazonia, places where there have been proven to be large pieces of Ecuadoran land in the possession of Colombians and Peruvians, whose activities raise serious doubts in the Ecuadoran INTERPOL," as stated in a conference presented to the IAEN (Institute of Higher National Studies, specialized body of the Ecuadoran Armed Forces) (*El Comercio*, December 15, 1991). Melvyn Levitsky, in the same interview already cited, says, discussing the same subject, "Foreign drug traffickers try

to bring their money into Ecuador by buying buildings and property" (*El Comercio*, April 20, 1991). The investments found have been in areas of agriculture and cattle (Santo Domingo, Quevedo) on the coast, but in the mountainous region also; in particular, in the area of Cayambe (Mino 1991 and Paez 1991a). In June 1990, the so-called "Indigenous Uprising" occurred, through which a political actor with an ethnic disposition emerged on the scene, the CONAIE (Confederation of Indigenous Nationalities of Ecuador), who had as one of its main demands the redistribution of land, reform of the current agrarian structure which could potentially be in conflict with the changes in the property structure (that lean toward concentration), motivated by incoming drug capital in the acquisition of land. In this manner, a stage of violence of a different kind could be launched in the country (Paez 1991b).

15. According to Levitsky, agreements were signed to intervene in accounts "in specific cases," between the United States and Ecuador, as a central point of control of drug money laundering (*El Universo*, April 24, 1991).

16. As for the rest, it is related with the process already mentioned of free circulation of capital: the money that passes through the financial system as "laundered" circulates, for the most part, toward the international capital market, before being productively reverted to the national economy. For the country, the changes in the regulation and the concentration of property (probably) are more important in the long term than the circumstantial alterations of the movement of capital through the economy and the financial system.

17. "Drug chemistry (narcochemistry), whether illicitly or underground, at the level of laboratories that process cocaine, commercializes each Kg of chemical precursor at an average of *$20*, which would mean that the *7 Ecuadoran networks of drug chemistry*, composed of 30 cartels (?) would be mobilizing approximately *$212 million annually...*" (Romero 1990, 184; emphasis from the original). The drug chemistry networks are 1) the Loja-Cuenca-El Oro-Tumbez network; 2) the Imbambura-Carchi-Narino network; 3) the port network of Portoviejo-Manta-Guayaquil; 4) the Amazonic network of Pichincha-Sucumbios-Napo-Putamayo; 5) the Pichincha-Esmeraldas-Tucuman-Narino network; 6) the Pichincha-Tungurahua-Napo-Sucumbios-Putumayo network; and finally 7) the network of *institutional narcochemists*, controlled by members of the Military Customs Police. According to police sources, there are about 10 million Kgs of chemicals trafficked per year in Ecuador (Romero 1990, 180-181).

18. The simple declaration of the illegality of trafficking chemical products could result in a transfer to plainly illegal circuits (by reason of the high economic productivity of this activity) that would create supplementary challenges to the state in policies of drug traffic control. Because of this, international instruments are required that would allow for the control of the flow of chemicals from and to the providing and consuming countries; this implies an international cooperation (pattern?) that newly limits aspects of the free flow of merchandise, in this case, chemicals. Levitsky, in the same interview already cited (*El Comercio* and *El Universo*, April 20-24, 1991), points out that another one of the objectives of the agreements consists of implementing an efficient and bilateral system of control of chemicals. Since the United States is not the only provider of these substances, more global actions would need to be conceived, such as multilateral agreements with countries like Mexico and Germany as well.

19. For example, the tanneries (leather industries) require a large quantity of consumptions similar or compatible to those necessary for the refining of PBC and chlorhydrate; in this sense, greater control of the activities of the tannery would probably revert to controls also for the derivation of precursors from those industries to drug trafficking, which would bring about more sensible global administration of the ecology.

20. At the meeting in Cuenca of the Latin American Council of Churches (CLAI), held in April 1990, in preparation for the meeting of Latin American Pastors and Bishops to discuss drug trafficking and external debt (Kingston, June 1990), sociologist Nelson Romero examined the details of how "national" societies integrate in relation to the same economic process: coca production and cocaine refining. Romero based his data on an on-going study financed by the OAS, concerning the eastern portion of the border and the Colombian-Ecuadoran integration process. The merchandise — not only the luxuries but also for daily consumption (such as nourishment) — would depend on commercial networks developed by drug trafficking in the region, according to Romero, in this sort of "perverse integration" or "internationalization from below" (Paez 1992) that would be lived out in the zone.

21. In reference to coca production, Ecuador was always totally marginalized (Bagley et al. 1991), although in the same interview already cited, General Jijon states that "the country slowly has become production" (El Comercio, December 1991). On the other hand, he also said that Alfaro Vive Carajo and the "Ruminahui Movement" were similar to Shining Path, the MRTA, and M-19, since (textually) "they have seized entire populations ... to force the farmers, in some cases, to plant coca...." One serious criticism of the narcoguerrillas notion, used also in MacDonald (1990) for the Ecuadoran case, can also be seen in the book previously cited (Bagley et al. 1991).

22. ". . . between 60 percent and 80 percent of the judges surveyed oppose the law as inapplicable, antijuridical, unscientific, and because it affects the principle of presumed innocence, solely punitive..." (El Universo, July 31, 1991).

23. The study "Diagnosis and Requirements of the Ecuadoran Judicial System" was directed under the sponsorship of an organ of the UN, ILANUD, by Dr. Cesar Banda Batallas and psychologist Pablo Andrade Andrade. As the last phase of this study, a workshop for evaluation of the new Ecuadoran antidrug law was carried out, with the penal judges from the whole country and members of the Superior and Supreme Courts, from which the data in the previous note were extracted.

24. Of 13,961 cases pending of interest to the public sector (Meridiano, January 2, 1991), 4,195 were for drug trafficking. In 1991 there were 2,274 cases admitted for negotiation, of which 615 were for drug trafficking — in other words, the greatest percentage. Statements made by Dr. Gustavo Medina Lopez, Attorney General of the State.

25. The case of the Restrepo brothers, Colombian teenagers who disappeared within the context of police impunity, the continuous report of torture and corruption by policemen led the institution to demand the resignation of over 15 officers — some high ranking — that were involved. The soiling of the institutional image within the police force could be followed by the same reaction in public opinion, that came to less than 10 percent support by the population in the most chilling moments of the Restrepo scandal (Confidential Report, August-November, 1991).

26. It can be argued that trafficking on a small scale is no more than one of the many informal activities but is fully found in the context of illegality. Its solution depends, then, not on arbitrating police measures, but instead on applying social policies in the long term (X. Andrade 1991).

27. With respect to the actions against drug trafficking during Febres Cordero's term, see Paez (1991a); in actuality, Levitsky's statements maintain that Ecuadoran-North American cooperation is "very good" (*El Comercio*, April 21, 1991).

28. The Ecuadoran army — in general, the armed forces — redesigned their relationship with the national society since the latter part of the 1970s: growing investments in land and productive aspects; the installation of an autonomous financial system, and a large and expansive presence in the Ecuadoran economy are some of the elements of this new relationship. The increase in their functions in the war against drugs (militarized version) adds weight to the already large military apparatus in the face of the Ecuadoran society and state.

29. Official Register of Ecuador, Year III, Quito, Monday, September 17, 1990, No. 523.

30. With this kind of problem, there exists an extremely tense relationship between INTERPOL (part of the National Police) and the ex-DINACTIE, previously DINACONTES, part of the institutional structure of the Attorney General of the State, (discussed extensively in Nadelman 1987, 23). This competition between agencies of control remains: the discovery of a shipment of three tons of cocaine in February 1992 has been the object of competition since the National Police as well as the Customs Police take credit for it. The accomplishment of greater seizures increases the possibilities of participation in the international budgets allocated for interdiction and control.

31. Interview with General Guillermo Jijon, Secretary General of the Attorney General of the State.

32. Article 59 of the Antidrug Law declares sentences of 12 to 16 years for cultivators and 8 to 12 years for collectors (Bagley et al. 1991, 215).

33. For example, guarantees of foreign flows of investment and soft credits and in the long term, settlements of the external debt, greater expansion in tariff advantages, and substantial increase of commerce and legal exports with guarantees of stable markets.

34. In the current electoral process, subliminal messages are used to link lists of certain candidates with drug trafficking. Previously, an attempt was made to link an advisor of the Special Commission on Drug Money Laundering with trafficking because one of his relatives had been arrested. The same commission, in its report (1990), tried to link members of Borja's administration, who belong to the financial community, with money laundering.

References

Andrade, Pablo, and Cesar Banda. 1991. *Diagnostico y requerimientos del Sistema Judicial Ecuatoriano.* Quito: ILANUD.

Andrade, Xavier. 1991. "Actores sociales y politica antidrogas: los 1991 pequenos traficantes." In *La Economia Politica del Narcotrafico,* eds. Bruce Bagley, Adrian Bonilla, and Alexei Paez. Quito: FLACSO Sede Ecuador and North-South Center, University of Miami.

Bagley, Bruce, Adrian Bonilla, and Alexei Paez, eds. 1991. *La Economia Politica del narcotrafico: el caso ecuatoriano.* Quito: FLACSO Sede Ecuador and North-South Center, University of Miami.

Bonilla, Paul. 1991. "El lavado de dolares en el Ecuador: la perspectiva juridica." In *La Economia Politica del Narcotrafico: el caso ecuatoriano,* eds. Bruce Bagley, Adrian Bonilla, and Alexei Paez. Quito: FLACSO Sede Ecuador and North-South Center, University of Miami.

Informe de la Comision Especial Parlamentaria sobre Lavado de Dolares en Ecuador. 1990. Quito.

Mino, Wilson. 1991. "Lavado de dolares y narcoeconomia en el Ecuador." In *La Economia Politica del Narcotrafico,* eds. B. Bagley, A. Bonilla, and A. Paez. Quito: FLACSO Sede Ecuador and North-South Center, University of Miami.

Nadelman, Ethan. 1987. "The DEA in Latin America: Dealing with Institutionalized Corruption" *Journal of International Studies and World Affairs,* Vol. 29, No. 4.

MacDonald, Scott. 1990. "Cocaina y poder: Venezuela, Ecuador, y Chile." *Revista occidental.* Vol. 7, No. 3.

Paez, Alexei. 1991a. "La insercion ecuatoriana en la dinamica Andina del narcotrafico." In *La Economia Politica del Narcotrafico,* eds. B. Bagley, A. Bonilla, and A. Paez. Quito: FLACSO Sede Ecuador and North-South Center, University of Miami.

Paez, Alexei. 1991b. "Narcotrafico y Amazonia: el desarrollo y la violencia." In *Amazonia Nuestra: una vision alternativa,* ed. Lucy Ruiz. Quito: ABYA-YALA-CEDIME-ILDIS.

Romero, Nelson. 1990. "La narcoquimica ecuatoriana en la decada de los ochenta." In *Narcotrafico y Dueda Externa: las plagas de America.* Quito: CAAP-CECCA-CERG.

WOLA. 1991. *Clear and Present Dangers: The U.S. Military and the War on Drugs in the Andes.* Washington, D.C.: WOLA.

Paraguay

Chapter Seventeen

Drug Trafficking and Drug Abuse in Paraguay

José Luis Simón

Introduction

P araguay and its closest neighbors, the Río Plata Basin and the Southern Cone, have experienced an increasing challenge from the drug traffic in recent years. Initially, everything linked to drug use and traffic was considered — in general, much oversimplified terms — mainly as the social problem of a rich society, primarily that of the United States. The South American countries, preoccupied with surviving the blows of the "lost decade" while trying, simultaneously, to throw off authoritarian regimes in terminal crisis and to negotiate transitions to democracy, assumed this problem could not affect them. In any event, that aspect of the drug trade which concerned the countries of South America above all was the growing tragedy of Colombia, which was just beginning to make headlines in the world press.

However, when the United States converted the narcotraffic issue into a top national security priority, South America discovered that it too was involved in the problem. This was a result of Washington's "narco-diplomacy," as Bagley and Tokatlián would say (1991, 37), which served to complicate inter-American relations as it redounded throughout the hemisphere. It was also due to the fact that the Latin American societies themselves were experiencing an increase in the consumption of illegal drugs, with all of the domestic repercussions — crime, violence, corruption — which that implies as threats to the newly restored and vulnerable democracies.

This chapter will focus primarily on the situation in Paraguay, particularly how the change in political regime has affected Paraguay's approach to dealing with the problem, by 1) clarifying the nation's perception of its domestic drug problem and 2) exerting positive repercussions on the way in which the country makes, and acts upon, its policy-making decisions.

This is not to say that Paraguay's transition to democracy has, ipso facto, eliminated the challenge from international narcotraffic. Far from it. However, Paraguay's transition to democracy has undoubtedly had (and is still having) a positive influence on everything connected with the way in which the country deals with drug use and traffic since, thanks to the present climate of democratic freedom, the state has become much more responsive to society.

Another aspect of the Paraguayan situation which has been gradually gaining in importance since the transition began is that the initial focus on the international and politico-economic side of the narcotraffic is gradually giving way to (though it does not eliminate) a more "clinical" approach which focuses upon the consumer-addict. This "model" takes the individual as the center of study in attempting to ascertain the underlying reasons behind the pervasive, uncontrolled consumption of illegal drugs. Certainly, during the dictatorship, it was very dangerous, not to say impossible, to research the "drug problem" from the standpoint of the psyche or needs of the individual because those sectors of the powerful elite with the most influence were either actively involved in the drug traffic or were engaged in protecting it.

However, General Alfredo Stroessner's authoritarian political regime (1954-1989) does not offer sufficient explanation as to why the "clinical" approach has come to predominate in Paraguay, nor, apparently, are there numerous examples in the neighboring countries (such as Argentina, Chile, and Uruguay, to which we will refer briefly later on) of placing emphasis on the "interdependent political economy of the transnational drug business" (Bagley and Tokatlián 1991, 2).

Drugs and Narcotraffic in Stroessner's Paraguay

Not only is the link between Paraguay and the drug traffic not new, as the present situation might lead us to believe, but it actually provides one of the first cases of conflict in the hemisphere between the U.S. superpower and a South American country over an issue destined to climb, as we have seen in the past few years, to the head of the U.S. State Department agenda and, thus, to that of the international system on every level (Russell 1990, 30-33; Pérez-Llana 1991, 142; Tomassini, Moneta, and Varas 1991, 302).

Paraguay became involved with the international drug mafia during the Stroessner dictatorship, one of the more questionable angles of that authoritarian government which was justified as the "price of peace," which is to say that it purchased stability by being co-opted, paying the price by means of a national moral vacuum or generalized public corruption.[1] This being said, let us begin our discussion of Paraguay's links to the narcotraffic by stating that the country has experienced two distinct "cycles" in its relationship with the criminal organizations engaged in this lucrative business: the first involving heroin and, later, that of cocaine and marijuana.

The Heroin Cycle

The greatest corruption, which encouraged Stroessner and benefitted him and his entourage above all, would end by not only leaving a profound impression upon the society but by seriously prejudicing the foreign relations of the state. By the time the situation came to an end, the image of Paraguay projected to the outside world, and which still endures (with good reason), is one of serving as the "heart" of South America's illegal and smuggling activities.[2]

But Paraguay had to pay a "price," and not just in terms of its international image. Between the end of the 1960s and the beginning of the 1970s, which corresponds to the heroin cycle, the illegal entry of that drug into the United States, from Paraguay and with the protection of officials at the highest level, would bring the Stroessner regime into its first serious confrontation with a U.S. administration, that of Richard Nixon.

A journalistic view (one might almost say the official U.S. view) of the "*stronista* connection" with the thriving drug trade at this time was accidentally leaked to the press, as a form of indirect pressure on the López Palace, in a story by Nathan Adams that appeared in *Selecciones del Reader's Digest* (Adams 1973). In the Paraguay of that era, the local press was controlled, and the publication was silenced. Authorities confiscated the issue, which was then circulated clandestinely and at great risk to its possessors because it accused, on the basis of investigative journalism, high civil and military officials in the Stroessner administration of "protecting" those engaged in the drug traffic. Among the names mentioned was then-commander of the powerful First Cavalry Division, General Andrés Rodríguez, who subsequently became president of the Republic in the wake of the 1989 *golpe* which ushered in the transition.

The leader of the *Partido Liberal Radical Auténtico* (PLRA), for many decades the country's main opposition force, is Senator Domingo Laíno, who was a young deputy in the 1970s. In his book, *Paraguay: represión, etafa y anticomunismo,* he relies on secondary sources to reveal the grave crisis that engulfed Asunción-Washington relations as a result of the involvement of Paraguayan authorities with the drug traffickers (Laíno 1979). From reading this work, one learns how the United States finally succeeded, by applying strong diplomatic and economic pressure, in obtaining the extradition of a foreign leader of the drug mafia (a French citizen, Augusto José Ricord) despite the "judicial" maneuvers with which the *stronista* regime vainly tried to keep him in Paraguay (Mora 1990, 82-83).

After the extradition of Ricord, White House-López Palace relations returned to their usual Cold War level: i.e., the United States openly supported the Stroessner dictatorship. This arrangement would be disrupted — politically and diplomatically, due to the *stronista* regime's systematic violation of human rights and its refusal to concede even the smallest democratic reform or effort to modernize — with the coming of the Carter administration, only to be restored as part of the Latin American policies of the second Reagan administration. By then, the mid-1980s, the political and physical senility of the dictator had aggravated the recurring friction with Washington, in addition to the persistent involvement of the *stronista* governing elite in the illegal, international drug traffic.

The Cocaine and Marijuana Cycle

Following the above-mentioned crisis with the Nixon administration, Stroessner's Paraguay entered a period of great tension with the United States during Jimmy Carter's tenure in the White House. But in this stage, the main source of tension, rather than centering on the narcotraffic, concerned two different issues: human rights and democracy. Never before had relations between Asunción and Washington sunk so low (Abente 1990, 277-321, especially 302-303; M. Yopo H. 1991, 63-68).

It was for this reason that, when Ronald Reagan came to the White House, Stroessner breathed more freely in the López Palace in Asunción. Nevertheless, even though U.S.-Paraguayan relations had apparently been "normalized" during the first Reagan administration, the U.S. State Department implemented a kind of "silent diplomacy" that continued the basic Carter administration themes of democracy and human rights, but to which it added a third: drugs. It was at that point, at the end of 1985, that the White House abandoned silent diplomacy toward the López Palace by naming a former Assistant Secretary of State from the Office of International Narcotics, Clyde Taylor, as its ambassador to Asunción (Mora 1990, 84-88).

By the end of the 1980s, not only had Stroessner refused to modernize his authoritarian political regime, but he had also failed to comprehend the strategic importance which the United States assigned to the entire narcotraffic problem. In 1988, no less than Under-Secretary of State for Latin American Affairs Elliot Abrams and Ambassador Taylor publicly announced that the whole civil and military *stronista* hierarchy protected, and derived lucrative material benefits from, the drug traffic. Despite this allegation and considerable opposition from the Congress, the Reagan administration — in compliance with the anti-drug law of 1986, which was based on protecting "vital national security interests" — certified (in 1988) that Paraguay had cooperated with the United States in its war on drugs, although it also maintained that Paraguay (one of the U.S. "close friends and allies") "needed to do more to cooperate" in this area. It was in that context that the Drug Enforcement Administration (DEA) re-opened its office in Asunción and began to organize a Paraguayan antinarcotics police force financed by aid from the United States. As a result, the government was finally obliged to institute some repressive measures of intervention which, understandably, never endangered any members of the ruling elite who profited from the narcotraffic in Paraguay (Mora 1990, 84-88).

The Narcotraffic Challenge During and After the Transition

In discussing this subject, it is useful to pause briefly to describe the nature of the military coup that resulted in the overthrow of Stroessner. This will enable us to explore both the possibilities and the limits of the Paraguayan transition "in search of democracy," as one analyst defined it (Neild 1991), and will also enable us to consider how it has changed — if, indeed, it has — Paraguay's relationship with the narcotraffic and in what sense.

The overthrow of General Alfredo Stroessner *via* a bloody *golpe* (February 2-3, 1989) offers a typical example of a transition initiated *from above*, provoked by the internal disintegration of a traditional tyranny, toward which the authoritarian regime, after almost 35 years in power, had been drifting for some time.[3] As Stepan would say, the February 1989 event is an example of "political liberalization granted" by an important faction derived from the regime it deposed (specifically, here, by an influential sector of the armed forces), thus ushering in a process by which it is perfectly possible, if not inevitable, to arrive at democracy.[4]

In any event, since the inception of the transition in 1989, the López Palace has overseen a drastic change in Paraguay's international position (Simón 1989; Fernández E. 1990; Masi 1991). The overthrow of Latin America's oldest dictatorship created a worldwide stir, probably rivalling, on the international level, only that made by the totalitarian regime of Kim Il Sung of the People's Democratic Republic of Korea. Once the new Paraguayan leaders announced their plans for the country, including a liberalization of domestic politics as well as changes in the area of foreign affairs, the international community, at every level (governments, international governmental and nongovernmental organizations, communications media, and world public opinion) responded in a positive way, throwing caution to the wind and, almost immediately, giving General Rodríguez the benefit of the doubt regarding his declared intention to take the first steps that would lead toward the "democratization" of Paraguay (Labra 1990).

The transition has been going on ever since that moment, post-Stroessner, when Paraguay's foreign relations entered a new stage which basically required that the state overcome the dangerous (for its interests) situation of international political isolation which had overtaken it during the last years of the dictatorship. In other words, the López Palace had to negotiate Paraguay's positive reincorporation into a world system that

> was in the throes of a major crisis as a result of the major changes which were taking place in every area — economic, scientific-technological, military-strategic, political and cultural — and which impacted the positions of its members (ILET 1989, 4).

Various indications and documented sources would suggest that the new Rodríguez government has generally succeeded in this effort. This is due, in large part, to its interest (and a certain capability) in bringing its policy into line with that of the New International Order now in the process of creation. This effort has not been that easy to sustain, given the difficulties of operating *via* a foreign policy establishment which itself has been in crisis, a legacy of the dictatorship which has only been aggravated during the transition (Simón 1990a).

In order to understand the subject under discussion, it is important to keep in mind that every transition to democracy is a process in which present forces co-exist with those of the past as well as of the future to produce what is, in essence, a "problem of political realism," which is, in a definitive sense, nothing but a question of time. In other words, it must deal with the problem of "remodeling the authoritarian past," recognizing "the present effectiveness of the past," which is different from ignoring it or assuming that it is merely inert.[5]

Society in the Last Years of Stroessner

Paraguayan society at large began to recognize addiction (to legal as well as illegal drugs) as a contemporary problem of major concern long before it was so perceived by the state. This concern began to surface almost a decade ago (1981-1982), at a time when the possible end of the *stronista* dictatorship, which still ruled Paraguay without major problems and enjoyed relatively good international relations, was yet in view.

Certainly, at the beginning of the 1980s, the Paraguayan dictatorship still held the country in an iron grip, using the apparatus of the state as a personal fief or booty of war and placing every obstacle in the path of civilians who tried to organize to deal with social problems. Nevertheless, despite the political difficulties and lack of resources, various nongovernmental organizations (NGOs) initiated efforts at prevention and education, primarily to call the attention of the population and the state to the situation posed by "dangerous" drugs, including more traditional, and less-censured, addictive products like tobacco, alcohol, tranquilizers, and the like, in addition to illegal mind-altering substances.

The work of the nongovernmental organizations in the area of prevention was basically voluntary and mobilized primarily by professionals in the health field, in particular, psychiatrists, psychoanalysts, psychologists, social workers, university students, and a few other categories in the liberal helping professions (Retamar 1991). As for the rest, the drug problem, already of serious concern to Washington, had not yet been translated into a strategic issue on the international agenda nor, as a consequence, was it broadly reflected throughout the world since neither the international governmental organizations (IGOs) nor the NGOs had begun to grant either the attention or the massive resources which they were later to direct toward this complex problem in the latter half of the 1980s. The precariousness of means, then, affected the nascent Paraguayan NGOs in this area, whose predominant focus was, in most cases, a "clinical" one (biologist, psychologist, i.e., essentially with reference to the individual).

In general, the hard-line political situation that obtained under Stroessner prevented the communications media from being able to deal seriously with the drug problem nor, in particular, with any aspect of the drug traffic touching Paraguay's domestic scene. However, given the gravity of the problem and its increasing importance worldwide, during the last years of the dictatorship, it was impossible to keep the Paraguayan press from learning about both the problems of addiction and the narcotraffic in their various aspects. As a result, the numerous serious differences between Asunción and Washington that erupted during that time were inevitably reflected in the local press (*El Diario* 1988; *Hoy* 1988a and 1988b; *Patria* 1988a, 1988b, 1988c, and 1988d; *La Tarde* 1988a, 1988b, and 1988c; *Ultima Hora* 1988a, 1988b, and 1988c).

In addition, an "alternative press" had begun to emerge wherever this was possible, which was concerned to inform the general public of the international "costs," then becoming manifest, that resulted from the links between Paraguayan officials and the drug-trafficking *mafia*, thus involving both the dictatorship and the state itself. It was these campaigns by marginal journalists which were the first to point out that it was but a small step from being a "country for the transit of illegal drugs to a country which consumed them," thus adding to the risks for the population at large. Finally, this dimension — socio-economic, political, and international — connecting the various aspects of addiction to the larger, worldwide traffic revealed the close relationship that existed between the authoritarian/dictatorial model of government (repression, increased corruption, major party support) and the lucrative narcotraffic, without necessarily inferring that this link was of a mechanistic, cause-and-effect nature (Simón 1987 and 1988; PARPRESS 1987).[6]

Toward the end of 1988, those NGOs and their work teams that had been most concerned with prevention not only began to receive more international support but also began to receive, systematically, more publicity about their activities in the print, radio and television media which served to raise the awareness of the general public, though with a focus on the clinical aspects, particularly of a psycho-social or socio-cultural kind (PRE-VER 1992). At the same time, in a separate but related development, some of the above-mentioned NGOs organized programs of seminars and field trips for professionals and public officials.

Once the transition was underway, these activities increased enormously, including work on prevention in those parts of the state to which access had been all but impossible during the time of the dictatorship. Consequently, on February 3, 1989, and thereafter, the NGOs that were most actively engaged in prevention were able to hold their seminars, which were almost always under the auspices of the U.S. Embassy, for various audiences without too much inconvenience. For example, they were able to do this for members of the Commission on the Fight against the Narcotraffic of the Chamber of Deputies, of the judiciary (in this case, the multidisciplinary seminar-workshop on the "National Judicial Framework of the Drug Problem" organized by GESA, PRE-VER, CIDSEP/Catholic University, and sponsored by the U.S. Embassy and the National Plan for the Prevention of Drug Abuse, which was held in Asunción, June 21-22, 1991), as well as of the armed forces, thus achieving something impossible during the *stronismo*: a gradual melding of civil society and government.

It is worth recalling here that the "model" for analyzing the drug problem was slowly undergoing a process of refinement in which the international ramifications were gradually being incorporated. So far as we know, the first time that a program focussed on prevention was expanded to include the political and economic aspects was in a seminar for youth leaders, organized by GESA and PRE-VER and held in San Bernardino in the latter half of 1989.[7]

This does not mean that every doctor, psychiatrist, psychoanalyst, psychologist, or expert on prevention, not to mention therapists engaged in rehabilitation of patient-addicts, took a narrow approach to the problem — which can be true of some health professionals in this field. One good example of a psychoanalytical approach to the addiction problem, especially among adolescents, has been that of Arias, who joined the team of Paraguayan Red Cross professionals engaged in prevention (Arias 1990a and 1990b). Another professional in the field of mental health, Fresco of PRE-VER, has been engaged in gradually refining, through successive stages, his own model of analysis. He was finally fortunate enough to develop (alongside the other models already mentioned) a "geopolitical-structural" model, utilizing a concept developed by Venezuelan government experts in which the "drug system" combines all those aspects that relate to the subject (i.e., the biological, psychological, and social) on the demand/consumption side with everything that relates to narcotics production and traffic (including the financial aspects of profit and money laundering) on the supply side (Fresco 1991).

This multidisciplinary approach has certainly helped to enrich the study of the whole drug phenomenon, which was originally confined only to the international drug trade and its effects, by showing how the political-economic side interacts with local power structures and by introducing different views on the threats of drug addiction — though such a macro perspective is still relatively underdeveloped in Paraguay.

Another example in the same vein is that, up until now, every suggestion originally made by the nongovernmental organizations regarding prevention and rehabilitation to reform Law 1340/88 (*Reprime el Tráfico Ilícito de Estupefacientes y Drogas Peligrosas y Otros Delitos Afines*) [which the transition team once assumed would be effected by the Mental Health Department of the Ministry of Public Health and Social Welfare] were based on the already-mentioned models (ethical-judicial, medical-health, psycho-social, and socio-cultural) but omitted the so-called "geopolitical-structural" model, which included all those complex aspects — political and economic, domestic and foreign — associated with drug addiction and the drug traffic (Fresco 1991).[8] The same could be said of the *Programa de prevención, apercibimiento y asistencia a la drogadicción* of the Mental Health Department of the Ministry of Education and Culture, to which we shall refer later. This is still in effect and is one of the forerunners of the National Anti-Drug Secretariat (*Secretaría Nacional Anti-Droga* or SENAD), another subject to which we will refer later.[9]

This "clinical" approach is not only necessary from a logical standpoint but also reveals a clear evolutionary pattern, as was demonstrated by a recent epimediological study conducted by Miguez and Pecci "on the use and abuse of alcohol and drugs in ten cities of Paraguay." Carried out with methodological rigor, this empirical research concludes by noting an alarming increase in all kinds of addiction, to legal as well as illegal drugs, aggravated by the fact that an ever-younger population of addicts is involved. The study is important because it also reveals a corresponding increase in the cooperation of national NGOs with international agencies that are similarly involved and which, understandably, have influenced their present work. This study was financed (and will now be published) by external resources channeled through the Paraguay-Kansas Committee, a nongovernmental organization which supports a variety of development plans and projects in Paraguay and which was originally founded to enable the state of Kansas, in the United States, to direct assistance to, and facilitate cooperation with, Paraguay (Miguez and Pecci 1991).[10]

However, there were only a few within the field of psychiatry who presented the broader world view of drug addiction. One of these was Rolón, who published (in 1986) a book entitled *Narcotics and Dangerous Drugs*, which opened by giving a history of drugs, followed by an account of the international dimensions of this phenomenon and the processes which gave rise to it (the first part); legal aspects (the second part); and a final section (the third) which the author devoted to the "concept of narcotics and mind-altering drugs" (Rolón 1986).

Altogether, Paraguay began to develop studies on drug addiction and the narcotraffic in recent years from the international standpoint, and touching on all the various aspects that linked those two facets and which had, as we have seen, reaped the widest publicity, particularly during the 1980s.[11] One of these studies, which is still underway and will be published once it is completed, investigates the drug traffic in Paraguay from the perspective of its conditioning factors, both internal and external, and of its national as well as international repercussions.[12] Another analyst is Olmedo, who has written a paper on the subject of "Comparative Legislation, Doctrine and Jurisprudence Regarding Drugs and Money-laundering" (Olmedo 1991). The issue of "narcodollars" has received much unfavorable publicity in Paraguay recently, one indication of which is the frequency with which the press covers the subject (Aquino 1991, 11-13; *Acción* 1991).[13]

The Post-Stroessner State

Starting with the overthrow of Stroessner, the issue of the narcotraffic gradually, and with ever-stronger rhetoric, took its place on Paraguay's official agenda. This trend became apparent early in 1989, immediately after his departure, and has continued up until the present time (1992). It has been manifest in multilateral forums and organizations at every level (subregional, regional, hemispheric, and world, governmental and nongovernmental), in Paraguay's bilateral relations with other governments (such as with the United States), in the official government pronouncements (such as Rodríguez's annual addresses to the Congress, speeches to international bodies, and statements to the press), as well as in domestic policy decisions, of which the most conspicuous was Congress' approval of the law (immediately promulgated, in December 1991, by executive decree) which created the SENAD (*Secretaría Nacional Anti-Droga*), the antidrug agency designed to serve as the government's institutional arm in carrying out national drug policy, including coordinating civilian activities with those of the state, as we shall later show (Estigarribia 1990).

Public Policies on Drugs and Narcotics

International Aspects

First, it is important to note that the Foreign Ministry still lacks an undersecretary or general directorate of foreign policy or an internal agency specifically devoted to following world policies on the drug traffic, something particularly serious if we take current international relations into account.

Despite these limitations, the Republic of Paraguay is a signatory to a substantial number of international agreements (both multilateral and bilateral) created to deal with drug addiction and the narcotraffic. As a result, the López Palace is a party to the following multilateral and regional examples:

United Nations: International Committee on Narcotics Control and allied agencies within the UN organization;

Inter-American System: Inter-American Union for the Control of Drug Abuse (*Unión Interamericana para el Control del Abuso de Drogas* or CICAD);

South America: South American Accord on Narcotics and Mind-Altering Drugs; and

Plata Basin region: Joint actions of cooperation with bordering countries, particularly in the area of control, plus the Act of Buenos Aires of the Ministers of Public Health in the Plata Basin.[14]

As a result of the above arrangements, at the present time, the Asunción government will sign and ratify the following conventions, accords, and multilateral protocols:

- Single Convention on Narcotics (New York, 1961), ratified by Law 338, of December 10, 1971;

- Convention on Mind-Altering Substances (Vienna, 1971), ratified by Law 339, of December 10, 1971;

- Protocol to Modify the Narcotics Convention (Geneva, 1972), ratified October 27, 1972;

- South American Accord on Narcotics and Mind-Altering Drugs (Buenos Aires, 1973), and two additional protocols, all ratified by Paraguay; and the

- Convention against the Illicit Traffic in Narcotics and Mind-altering Substances (Vienna, 1989), ratified by Law No. 6/90 (July 19,1990) and that instrument deposited in New York on August 3, 1990.

We ought also to mention that Paraguay received help from the United Nations, within the framework of the UN Fund for Drug Abuse Control (UNFDAC) [known in Spanish as *Fondo de las Naciones Unidas para la Fiscalización del Uso Indebido de las Drogas* (FNUFUID)], on two occasions: the first of the accords was signed May 20, 1982 (Project ACK-60-382), for "Analysis of Drug Dependency in Paraguay," carried out by the Pan American Health Organization; and the second, subscribed to on June 28, 1984 (Project AD/PAR/84/383), also for the "Analysis of Drug Dependency in Paraguay," was for a study undertaken by the Paraguayan government, apparently through the Institute for Prevention, Treatment, and Rehabilitation of Drug Addicts, an agency of the National Department of Narcotics and Dangerous Drugs, which itself came under the jurisdiction of the Ministry of the Interior (*Perspectiva Internacional Paraguaya,* 1990).

On the other hand, and equally deserving of mention, Paraguay entered into bilateral agreements with a variety of countries in the region, particularly with the United States:

- Convention on Public Health with the Federated Republic of Brazil (July 1971);

- Accord with the United States "to combat the unauthorized use and illicit traffic in narcotics and other dangerous drugs" (ratified by Law 379/72);

- Treaty of extradition with the United States (ratified by Law 399/73); and

- Agreement of Joint Cooperation between the Government of the Republic of Paraguay and the Government of the United States of America to Reduce the Demand, Halt Illicit Consumption, and Combat the Illicit Production and Traffic of Drugs, September 1988 (Estigarribia 1990).

More recently, the López Palace has entered into the following bilateral agreements:

- Agreement between the Republic of Paraguay and the Federated Republic of Brazil on the Prevention, Control, Prosecution, and Repression of the Unauthorized Use and Illicit Traffic in Narcotics and Mind-Altering Substances (Brasilia, March 29, 1988);

- Convention on the Prevention of Unauthorized Use and Repression of, and Illicit Traffic in, Narcotics and Mind-Altering Substances (Asunción, November 28, 1989, and ratified by Law 18/90);

- Convention between the Republic of Paraguay and the Republic of Chile on the Prevention of Unauthorized Use of, and Repression of Illicit Traffic in, Narcotics and Mind-Altering Substances (Santiago de Chile, September 1990);

- Accord between the Government of the Republic of Paraguay and the Government of the Eastern Republic of Uruguay on the Prevention, Control, Prosecution, and Repression of Illegal Consumption and Illicit Traffic of Narcotics and Mind-Altering Substances and Its Specific Precursors and Chemical Products (Asunción, May 1991).[15]

Finally, it is necessary to pause briefly to review Washington's cooperation with Asunción on matters relating to drugs and the narcotraffic (Simón 1991, 28-32). The last accord negotiated, in 1991, was for a total sum of $390,000

> to improve the available database for the U.S. Embassy and Paraguayan antinarcotics forces; to increase the operating capacity of the Paraguayan government (for DINAR as well as for the joint special military and police forces); and to promote public awareness of the narcotics threat.

This U.S. allotment to Paraguay had its origins in a Letter of Agreement, dated June 30, 1987, which stipulated that certain sums were to be allocated annually (which does not necessarily mean that they have been disbursed) in the following amounts: $200,000 (1987), $350,000 (1988), $400,000 (1989), and $300,000 (1990) (Paraguay Ministerio de las Relaciones Exteriores 1991).

Since the advent of Rodríguez, collaboration between the López Palace and the White House on the subject of dangerous drugs and the narcotraffic, clearly a sensitive issue for the latter, has increased, and this has been publicly recognized by the special agencies in Washington. However, the United States continues to be concerned about Latin American cocaine mafias using Paraguay as a transit country for their "exports" from South America to the industrialized north, as well as as a site for money laundering, only a small part of which takes place in Latin America.[16]

National Aspects

General Rodríguez had scarcely assumed his position as president *de facto* of Paraguay when, at his first press conference in the López Palace, reporters raised the question of his alleged ties to the international drug mafias who had operated, and were operating, from Paraguay thanks to high government officials, both civil and military, as mentioned.[17] As might be supposed, the new head of state and commander-in-chief of the armed forces roundly denied the allegations of the international press in which he was characterized as a kind of "Noriega of the Plata Basin" (*Hoy* 1989; *El Diario Noticias* 1989, 4-5).

Nevertheless, world public opinion has never totally discounted the various rumors and reports that Rodríguez amassed a considerable personal fortune derived in some way from "narcodollars," though so far no one has ever been able to produce any convincing evidence regarding his participation, past or present, in that lucrative "business."[18] Furthermore, as repeated here, his domestic political actions, of a predominantly democratic nature, have ended the international isolation which Paraguay experienced during the final stage of the *stronista* dictatorship, repairing the relations between Asunción and Washington, among others.[19]

Consequently, it is important to note that, in his official statements, Rodríguez has frequently demonstrated the political will of his government to pursue the so-called "war on drugs" (Rodríguez 1991, 9). For the rest, since the present "war" has taken on a worldwide dimension, particularly over the past decade, Rodríguez's antidrug rhetoric and policies could be said to take on some of the "common sense" attitude which began to color the international view. At least, this has been true of the American states in the Western Hemisphere, as was demonstrated at the Cartagena II summit meeting held in San Antonio (Texas), February 27, 1992, at which the United States had little other recourse but to agree to a certain "consensus for continental action" toward the drug problem with the Latin American states (AFP 1992a and 1992b; Aspiazú 1992a, 1992b, and 1992c; Granovsky 1992a and 1992b; Rodrigo 1992; DPA 1992a and 1992b; Roque Bacarreza 1992; EFE 1992a and 1992b; Pajares 1992; Taillandier 1992).

Thus, right now in Paraguay the legal-judicial framework on drugs, narcotraffic, and drug dependency is in the process of revision, and it is very probable that, during the course of the present year (1992), the current Law 1340 will undergo major reform to modify and update date Law No. 357/72, which

> represses the illicit traffic in narcotics and dangerous drugs and other related crimes and establishes means for prevention and rehabilitation of drug dependency.

That law (1340/88) was approved shortly before the overthrow of Stroessner — with the sole objective of reducing Washington's criticism of Asunción which by then was both frequent and increasingly severe due to the local boom in narcotraffic — and certainly was not discussed in democratic fashion, as its development was supervised by lawyers and representatives of the authoritarian regime who added articles, divided into ten chapters, which were taken, piecemeal, from the laws of other countries (Paraguay Ministry of the Interior 1988).

Furthermore, between the two laws, i.e, Laws 357/72 and 1340/88, Paraguay also incorporated other drug-related provisions into its body of law on the subject:

- Decree No. 25587 (September 21, 1976) "by which is established the denomination, organization, and jurisdiction of the department for the repression of illicit traffic in narcotics, dangerous drugs and other related crimes," to be called the National Department of Narcotics and Dangerous Drugs, under the Ministry of the Interior; and

- Law No. 836, also known as the Health Code (December 25, 1980), whose articles are concerned with "narcotic substances and other dangerous drugs of drug dependency."[20]

Before referring to the steps taken by General Rodríguez's transition regime to give the country a modern, functional institutional framework which would give legal organization to the fight against drugs, let us recall some little-known decisions of the Stroessner dictatorship taken during its final five-year period. It is worth mentioning this period because it was during that time that the UNFDAC (or FNUFUID in Spanish) served as the only intermediary with Paraguayan government agencies. Most significantly, these domestic agencies, even those overseeing national programs for prevention and rehabilitation, were managed by that arm of the executive which is, by definition, the most repressive: the Ministry of the Interior.

What is certain is that, at the time, the person who called together the various public institutions and some of the private agencies which had done little or no specialized work on drugs and the narcotraffic to discuss both a "Preliminary Document Oriented to the Establishment of a National Plan for the Prevention of Drug Addiction" and a "Working Paper on Strategies,

Objectives, Programs and Institutional Framework of the National Plan for the Prevention of Drug Addictions" was a high police official, Comisario General Inocencio Montiel C., who served as Director General of the National Department of Narcotics and Dangerous Drugs and also, surprisingly, as National Director of the United Nations Project: AD/PAR/84/383 (FNUFUID).[21]

Of the "Preliminary Document," it appears important to us above all to take into account its short second chapter ("Basic Considerations on Production, Traffic, and Consumption of Drugs in Paraguay"), which is significant because it summarizes the Stroessner regime's self-interest in concealing the true magnitude of Paraguay's narcotraffic in which it was involved (extending official protection at the highest level), which precluded limiting either national production of its excellent marijuana in any way or the cocaine already "in transit" to the rich northern markets, in addition to expanding domestic consumption — all of which would prompt the arrival of U.S. Ambassador Clyde Taylor in Asunción, whose professional qualifications were mentioned earlier.

After these two above-mentioned documents (*Preliminar* and *Trabajo*) and various meetings led by the team of Comisario Montiel, in his double role as Director of the National Department of Narcotics and Dangerous Drugs, a repressive agency *par excellence*, as well as Director of the United Nations Project, a National Council for the Prevention of Drug Addiction was established, which was tied to the National Plan for the Prevention of Drug Addiction (1985-1988), under the joint and exclusive sponsorship of the public sector: the Ministries of the Interior, Public Health and Social Welfare, Education and Culture, Justice and Work, Agriculture and Livestock, Treasury, and the Technical Secretary for Planning (a dependency of the Presidency of the Republic).[22] In the same package, we ought also to include "Investigation into the Use and Abuse of Drugs," under the aegis of the Ministry of the Interior, through the National Institute on Prevention, Treatment, and Rehabilitation of Drug Addicts, an agency of the National Department of Narcotics and Dangerous Drugs.[23]

Before concluding our review of these antecedents of the antidrug policies of the last years of the dictatorship, we ought to add that, despite all the bureaucratic-institutional pompousness which flowed from the so-called National Plan for the Prevention of Drug Addiction, supported by FNUFUID, it contained a serious flaw which prevented it from being put into practice: the absence of political will on the part of the *stronista* regime to make any real effort to discourage the narcotraffic on Paraguayan territory, as the result of which drug addiction also expanded within the country (not to mention aggravating problems of drug consumption in other countries).[24] During the latter half of 1987, U.S. Ambassador Taylor took advantage of the First National *Jornada* for Journalists on the Prevention of Drug Addiction and used the print media to refer precisely to this problem: the absence of official Paraguay's will to combat the drug traffic. His language bordered on the undiplomatic, reflecting State Department concern over the self-serving inefficiency of the López Palace in this area (Taylor 1987a and 1987b).

From January 22, 1989, when Law 1340/88 went into effect, just shortly before the successful *golpe* against Stroessner, the Dirección Nacional de Narcóticos (DINAR) governed all responses, public or private, to the challenge of drug addiction and the narcotraffic in Paraguay, displaying an almost "imperialistic" view of the goals and responsibilities defined in Article 59.[25] Conceived within the repressive apparatus of the dictatorship, it is logical to assume that, given its origins, DINAR could not help but be contaminated by all the negative characteristics of *stronista* security forces.

Probably for this reason, one of the first steps taken by the incoming Rodríguez administration was to remove Comisario Inocencio Montiel Cabrera as head of the DINAR, appointing in his place a new Director-General — Fulvio Ramón Aldama — as Comisario Principal (DAEP). The change served to isolate the old DINAR leadership in every way (Comisario Aldama would also be removed from his post in the first months of 1992), for otherwise no real restructuring of that organization would have taken place.[26] Reading the DINAR's annual reports (*Anuarios*) for 1990 and 1991, numerous questions arise regarding its real ability to attain its goals and perform its legal functions (Paraguay Ministry of Interior [DINAR] 1990 and 1991a). For example, in those two years, no repressive measures of importance were reported which shed even the slightest ray of light on the true structure of the narcotraffic operating from Paraguay. At the same time, and taking into account the national situation, the Prevention Education Team of the DINAR reported many millions in expenses in 1990, as well as in 1991 (January-November, in the latter case), respectively: 181,242,240 guaraníes, on an annual budget (voted by the Congress) which rose during the year just past (1991) to 809,646,450 guaraníes — representing an increase of 55 percent over that allotted by the Congress for 1990 (Paraguay Ministry of Interior [DINAR] 1990, 32; and 1991a, 14, 25).

The next decision of the López Palace was to subscribe (May 16, 1991), through the Ministry of the Interior, to Decree No. 9528 "which creates the National Antidrug Secretariat (*Secretaría Nacional Antidroga* or SENAD) with the following resolution:

> **Article 10**: Create the *Secretaría Nacional Antidroga* (SENAD), which will govern and coordinate all government and nongovernment bodies that work in the prevention, rehabilitation, and repression of drugs; **Article 20**: The Secretariat mentioned in Article 10 will come under the direction of an Executive Secretary and a Deputy Secretary appointed by executive decree; and **Article 30**: Communicate, publish, and place in the Official Register.[27]

Almost immediately (May 20, 1991), the executive branch also issued Decree No. 9554 "which names the Executive Secretary and Deputy Secretary of the SENAD," such responsibilities falling, respectively, to Brigadier General Marcial Samaniego, and on Mayor (DEM) Luis Alberto Ocampos Vass.[28] Thus, with its leadership team in place, SENAD was converted into the nation's highest agency responsible for the fight against drugs, which meant that DINAR left the jurisdiction of the Ministry of the Interior — and not without some protest which the state soon overcame — to become a body institutionally subordinated to a new chain of command.

All indications suggest that the creation of the SENAD, as an executive and coordinating agency reporting directly to the President of the Republic, and similar to other agencies in neighboring countries (such as the Secretary of State for the Prevention of Illicit Traffic and Drug Addiction in the Argentine Republic), follows recommendations of the U.S. State Department and Drug Enforcement Administration (DEA). On the other hand, as responsible sources at a high level of the Paraguayan government commented when the appointment of General Samaniego to the sensitive post of SENAD Executive Secretary became known, the appointment was influenced by the fact that, besides his impeccable professional credentials of service in the Paraguayan military and as a graduate of West Point, he enjoyed the confidence of the U.S. State Department and the Pentagon.[29]

Initiating the transition process in Paraguay meant that the state became more open to society. In short, the democratic opening is one of the primary reasons why the legislative branch was able to hold the Round Table on Narcotraffic and Drug Addiction (June 1990) organized by the Chamber of Deputies' Commission on the Fight against the Narcotraffic, together with experts and representatives from both govermental and nongovernmental organizations.[30]

That experience of full, pluralistic parliamentary debate in Paraguay constituted an authentic, and positive, innovation which was repeated and deepened the following year (in 1991) when the new Chamber of Deputies hosted the above-mentioned *Primera Jornada sobre la Ley 1340: Análisis y Propuestas de Modificación*, which finally took place with the full participation of both public and private organizations.[31] On that occasion, over and above analyzing Law 1340/88 (which was postponed until 1992 by unanimous vote), and after various commentaries by specialists and experts, both national and international, the participants engaged in a thorough, extensive debate on the law which the executive had sent to the Congress, so that the SENAD would no longer function merely as the result of a presidential decree (according to contemporary Paraguay's authoritarian and "constitutional" tradition) but would acquire birth by virtue of a law voted upon in true parliamentary fashion. This democratic discussion enabled improvements to be made in the text submitted by the executive branch, especially regarding a guarantee of autonomy for nongovernmental organizations, which had not been included in the original (Decree 9528/91, which created the SENAD) but which emerged as the product of open debate — including input from General Samaniego — and was sanctioned by the Congress, *ex post facto*, as "Law No. 108/91 which creates the SENAD."[32]

Contrast, then, this attitude of open-mindedness and respect by the leader and officials of SENAD toward civilian organizations with that of DINAR bureaucrats, who always maintained an attitude of suspicion even after the transition was well advanced. The latter were never able to conceal their strange distrust of the nongovernmental organizations (NGOs) to the point that its authorities, instead of worrying about the risks of internal infiltration and corruption, stated in one of that "repressive-preventive-therapeutic" institution's official documents, and without any evidence whatsoever, that

> [we] have currently detected a maneuver by the traffickers to infiltrate public, private, and other institutions for the purpose of continuing to change the laws to suppress the drug traffic, especially in reduction of penalties and recovery of drugs seized. It is important to take this fact into account in order to forestall the implications of this discovery (Paraguay Ministry of Interior [DINAR] 1991b).

Before leaving discussion of the SENAD, we should also mention an aspect whose origins may be open to criticism. This has to do with the Special Forces in the Fight against the Narcotraffic and how it was born. The Special Forces were created by decree of the executive branch, based on an *ad hoc* Task Force made up of the military and police. First of all, up to the present time, this force, specially trained and armed for the purpose named, is not based on the legal structure of the armed forces since neither the Constitution in force, nor Law No. 74/91 (*De Organización General de las Fuerzas Armadas de la Nación*) contemplated the "war on drugs" as a type of conflict suitable for mobilization and military intervention (Paraguay Poder Legislativo 1991).

For the rest, the budding doctrine of "militarization," recently introduced by U.S. agencies as a world strategy to deal with the drug problem and fight criminals engaged in the narcotraffic — criminals, particularly in this hemisphere — has just been made relative by the Cartagena II summit meeting held in San Antonio (Texas) at the end of February, as its final statement showed (*Hoy* 1992a).

Despite the above, it is not the intention here to give the impression that the presence of military officers at the highest level of SENAD leadership necessarily suggests the inevitable militarization of Paraguay's drug policy. In reality, though we may run that risk (as do other countries), the SENAD leadership, headed by General Samaniego, is consonant with the national political reality. That is to say that, at the present time and given our recent history, it would have been practically impossible for the Paraguayan military to have accepted "civilian" directives from the SENAD and disciplined itself under its present institutional policy of "zero tolerance" of the narcotraffic, above all because the corruption inherited from *stronismo* also affected (as is obvious) members of the armed forces, some of whom have finally been separated from important military positions under suspicion that they were linked to drug-related crimes.[33] As soon as the occasion allowed, General Samaniego himself gave assurance on this point, emphasizing that no high-level "godfathers" existed to protect those who might be tempted by the narcotraffic (*Ultima Hora* 1992a).

Finally, and always in order to spell out the precise role of the Paraguayan military in national drug policy, it is important to remember that, under the institutional auspices of the SENAD, the first seminar-workshop on drug addiction and the narcotraffic was held for members of the armed forces (December 1991), organized by NGOs and with characteristics similar to other activities of this kind, such as the *jornadas* designed for members of the judiciary.[34] In brief, in contrast to the typical "bunker" attitude of the DINAR leadership, influential sectors of the armed forces, including those who make up the SENAD, are taking advantage of the transition process to make themselves more open to, and to forge links with, civil society. This shift in attitude is worth emphasizing in a country like Paraguay, where the Cold War helped to encourage and facilitate military intervention in politics, which wasn't hard given the authoritarian tradition which has predominated throughout the national history.[35]

It is also worth pointing out that, with the transition and despite efforts to the contrary by DINAR, the Department of Mental Health, under the Ministry of Public Health and Social Welfare (to which a psychiatrist, Agustín Carrizosa, was appointed head), began to assume a leading role, as shown by two documents that were developed at public request: the fore-mentioned *Programa de prevención, apercibimiento y asistencia a la drogadicción* (Paraguay Ministerio de Salud Pública y Bienestar Social 1990), and that entitled *Reordenamiento institucional en la lucha contra el narcotráfico y el use indebido de drogas* (Paraguay Ministerio de Salud Pública y Bienestar Social 1991). Considered as provisional by their authors, both documents could also be considered as forerunners for the creation of SENAD, and their concepts form the base of important proposals for change in Law 1340/88.

Reflections on Southern Cone Democracies and the Drug Problem

According to Bagley and Tokatlián, the conceptions surrounding the so-called "drug problem" underwent a dramatic change in the United States and a great part of South America and the Caribbean during the 1980s. At the beginning of the decade, U.S. politicians considered the traffic in, and consumption of, drugs as matters of civilian security and public health. For their part, Latin American and Caribbean authorities were either ignorant about drug-related issues or basically viewed them as North American problems which ought to be resolved in the United States by its own leaders. Nevertheless, by 1990 an apparent consensus existed in Washington and other regional capitals about drug production, smuggling, and abuse as constituting threats to national security and social welfare throughout the continent (Bagley and Tokatlián 1991, 1).

Despite this latter statement, one could say that in the Southern Cone of Latin America (excluding, in this case, Brazil), the studies and academic research on drugs and the narcotraffic, from the standpoint of political economy, did not attain the level of development which, for obvious reasons, was reached in the United States and the Andean countries.

An attempt to explain this situation as it applied to Paraguay has already been presented briefly in the introduction to this chapter. In addition, we ought to add that Paraguay is one of those countries in the region that is less developed in the area of the social sciences, particularly international studies. But that is not the case in Argentina, Chile, and Uruguay, neighboring countries in which the study of the social sciences and international relations are more advanced and which, as happened in Paraguay, have seen themselves affected by drugs, the narcotraffic, and the "narcodiplomacy" of the United States.

Certainly, Chile ought to be mentioned among these countries since it produces a bibliography of considerable magnitude on the subject under discussion, primarily through academic publications, such as those emanating from the prestigious School of International Studies of the University of Chile, or even more timely magazines on the order of *Cono Sur*, which is edited bimonthly by the international relations sector of the *Facultad Latinoamericana de Ciencias Sociales* (FLACSO) in Santiago (Bustamante 1990b; Nuñez Reyes 1988; B. Yopo 1989). In Argentina, on the other hand, and probably linked to its great psychoanalytic tradition, psychological and psychosocial approaches apparently predominate, those which we lumped under the heading of "clinical focus" in discussing the Paraguayan situation (Bulacio et al. 1988; Kalina 1988; Miguez 1989). However, neither drug addiction nor the narcotraffic has been given any significant attention by the communications media in that region even though there is no doubt that this issue has been increasing in importance in the print media of the countries that make up the Southern Cone.[36]

For example, it should also be noted that the most important bibliographic collection on Latin American international relations, that of the Grupo Editor Latinoamericano, who generally publish the volumes issued by the Joint Studies Program of *Relaciones Internacionales de América Latina* (RIAL) have not, up to now, published a book that can compare to those edited by, to name a few, Tokatlián and Bagley (1990); Bagley, Bonilla, and Páez (1991); Lee (1992); and García Sayán (1990). Moreover, the first RIAL *Anuario* to carry an in-depth article on the political economy of drugs and narcotraffic was that edited by Russell for the year 1990 (Bustamante 1990a). Before that, the *Anuario de Políticas Exteriores Latinoamericanas 1988-89* published an article by Bagley in its section entitled "Regional and Functional Issues" (Bagley 1989). It also happened that Tokatlián chaired a working group session on the narcotraffic not too long ago, at the XIII Annual Meeting of RIAL Center Members held in November 1991.[37]

Perhaps, one should not call attention to research and bibliographic orphanhood in Latin America when it is also true that an academic publication as important as *Pensamiento Iberoamericano*, in Madrid, just published its first article on drugs and the narcotraffic (Number 19, 1991). Apart from that, it is significant, to say the least, that the Inter-American Dialogue devoted its 1989 Report to everything related to the drug problem but neglected that subject entirely the following year (IAD Report 1989 and 1990). Consequently, one can only conclude that it was only at the beginning of the 1990s, and slowly at that, that the subject of drugs and narcotraffic figured as an object of study among the cognitive interests of the social scientists in the Southern Cone. It is now left to probe the deeper reasons for this state of affairs since, within the present framework of regional integration, the contracting parties (the states) are already advancing into the areas of defining policy and drawing up multilateral agreements on this subject.[38]

Conclusions

When the 1990s first began, one could say that the drug problem (addiction to psycho-active substances considered illegal, besides its illicit international trade) had definitely ended by imposing itself on the present international post-Cold War agenda; and together with other global concerns like the environment, the latter perhaps with more dramatic timeliness, upon occasion would seem to take up the space which, until a short time ago, was monopolized by the East-West conflict.

If this is so, it not only becomes essential but also urgent for specialists from Latin America's Southern Cone countries to explore, in a systematic way, more lines of investigation in order to arrive at a more precise understanding of the challenges that consumption of, and traffic in, illegal drugs pose for their respective states and societies so that they do not fall behind other parts of the continent. Throughout the world, this is a particularly timely and pressing issue which is demanding that public policies be rapidly adopted — both at home and abroad — to meet the problem. How can we make correct, or at least reasonable, decisions if we continue to lack knowledge about the problem? As has been said before, whether we like it or not, disruptions produced by the narcotraffic and drug consumption are impacting our present societies, always in a dramatic way.

Within the regional context of experiencing a deficit in knowledge of, and policies on, dangerous drugs and their illegal trade, the situation in Paraguay is not necessarily much different, although, as we have seen, the transition to democracy has helped to bring these issues to the surface of social and state concerns, in an association in which their respective representatives have entered into a phase of unusual cooperation and interaction, and not just regarding drugs and the narcotraffic.

Of course, one cannot posit that there is a direct relationship between a democratic political regime and waging an effective war on drugs and narcotraffic since, if this were so, just living in a democracy would solve the problem. But that does not happen as we sadly, and certainly, know. In any event, the present situation in Paraguay offers some evidence that the functioning of democratic institutions permits greater transparency in discussing public policies and influencing the decision-making process. The issue of what measures are effective in meeting the drug problem is linked, inextricably, to how much we know about the whole narcotraffic situation — economically as well as from the standpoint of policy, both national and international. In Paraguay, this whole process is only in a very embryonic stage, but at least it has already begun. Perhaps this initial work, with all its limitations, will provide some proof of that affirmation and offer evidence that interest does exist in continuing to investigate the subject.

Notes

1. Owing to the public corruption which pervaded Paraguay during the Stroessner dictatorship, the bishops of the country published a pastoral letter in 1979 entitled "The moral indemnity of the nation" (CEP 1979). A brief analysis of the public corruption, with the transition already under way, can be found in Simón and Mora (1991).

2. A typical depiction of the Paraguayan dictatorship and its vices is that given by Vinocur (1984).

3. This section analyzing the Paraguayan transition is based upon concepts regarding the transition to democracy put forth by Garretón (1987), particularly the introductory chapter entitled "Democracy, transition, and consolidation: a general outline" (25-88), but excluding his considerations on "democratic consolidation and its factors" (50-55).

4. For a view of "liberalization" from the top, see Stepan (1988a, 22, and 1988b).

5. The reference to the time and policy is taken from Lechner (1989, 127-28).

6. More recently, and since the advent of the transition, J.L. Simón has continued to be concerned with Paraguay's relationship with drugs and narcotics; see, for example, his series of ten successive articles in the daily newspaper *ABC Color* (Simón 1990b-1990k).

7. A seminar-workshop with the suggestive title of "Drugs and Their National and International Implications" was organized by Centro de Investigación y Reinserción Psicosocial (CIRPSI) and PRE-VER and took place October 28-29, 1989, at the Hotel de Lago in San Bernardino, 40 kilometers from Asunción.

8. See "Proposals to Modify Articles of Law 1340/88" (1990, Asunción, 9 pp.). A similar situation occurred before (in 1988) when the Paraguayan Medical Association went to Stroessner's "parliament" to make suggestions to change and implement Law 357/72, which 1340/88 would replace; on this point, see the letter signed by Aníbal Filártiga, president of the association, and by a representative to the committee of the "parliament," Manuel Fresco (h).

9. The document to which we refer is signed by the Director of the Department of Mental Health (Ministry of Health), Agustín Carrizosa.

10. This study also gives the methodology in an appendix. The "use and abuse" of both legal and illegal drugs in the country offers further evidence of the expansion of drug addiction, including a literature of testimony such as that of Hugo Duarte Manzoni (1989).

11. The increase in the international drug problem is given a very critical examination by Escohotado (1989). Another critical examination of this issue, only focusing exclusively on the legal area, is that of del Olmo (1991). See also, as other manifestations of the growing importance of drugs as an international issue, the Report of the Inter-American Dialogue (1989); or even, among numerous other examples, the

special issue of the *Journal of Interamerican Studies and World Affairs* (1988), published by the Institute of Interamerican Studies of the University of Miami (Coral Gables, FL).

12. In reality, the author of this work, at the beginning of his research on the subject, found himself writing a book on *The narcotraffic in Paraguay: External and internal conditioners, and their repercussions locally and for the country's international relations* (International Relations Program, Paraguayan Center of Sociological Studies (CPES), Asunción, forthcoming).

13. On laundering of drug money in the world, different views are given by Ziegler (1990), as well as Crawley (1990).

14. This information provided by Lic. Sandoval Fernández, General Secretary of the Ministry of Foreign Relations, Asunción, 1991.

15. Documentation provided by the Secretary-General of the Ministry of Foreign Relations, Asunción, 1991.

16. On the possible existence of "narcodollars" in Paraguay, see Amarilla (1992) and *Ultima Hora* (1992b). The United States is trying to get Paraguay to pass legislation that fully incorporates the recommendations of the Financial Action Working Group (Grupo de Trabajo de Acción Financiera or GTAF), and there are frequent references in the local press to the work, in Asunción, of Ambassador Jon Glassman to that effect; for example, see *ABC Color* (1992a). For the rest, up until now, the only instrument that exists in Paraguay for auditing or checking money laundering is totally ineffective for that purpose: this is Resolución No. 9, Acta No. 28 of the Central Bank of Paraguay (DOPI/Circular No. 9/89 of 28/II/89, and DOPI/Circular No. 12/89 of 9/III/89) and Executive Decree No. 216 of 27/II/89, which establishes the "Foreign regime for imports and exports of goods and services and the movement of capital." In this way, the obligation is established for banks, financial institutions, and agencies of foreign exchange to register information on all foreign exchange transactions of US$10,000, a requirement with which they certainly will not comply.

17. Here we refer to the early reports on Rodríguez and his connection to the narcotraffic mentioned in the second section of this article, headed "Drugs and Narcotraffic in Stroessner's Paraguay."

18. Some recent examples of the poor international image of Paraguay and its ruling elite is reported by Blixen (1991). Basically, this curious reporting is based on a rehash of statements by U.S. officials, the majority of which derive from supposed DEA informants whom the author never interviewed, but compiled from various local journalistic sources; a summary of this material, signed by Amorin and Blixen (1991) appeared in the prestigious Spanish-language weekly *Cambio 16*, whose editors regrettably failed to check the sensational aspects of the article originally published by the Left-wing Uruguayan publication.

19. U.S. Ambassador Jon D. Glassman described the relations between the White House and the López Palace as "excellent" in a speech given to the Paraguay-American Chamber of Commerce (September 1991) shortly after he presented his credentials there, according to a press release of that date given out by the U.S. Information Service (USIS) in Asunción.

20. Taken from a compilation of "national laws on the fight against the narcotraffic and drug dependency" made by the project AD/PAR/84/383.

21. The "Working Document..." is divided into 1) General considerations; 2) Justification for, and description of, the plan; 3) Plan strategies; 4) Plan objectives; 5) Plan programs; and 6) Institutional framework. On the other hand, the "Preliminary Document..." includes the following: 1) General antecedents; 2) Basic considerations (on production, traffic, and consumption of drugs in Paraguay); 3) Legal and institutional framework; 4) Technical assistance by FNUFID; 5) Considerations on a national plan for the prevention of drug addiction; and 6) Methodology for the formulation of the plan.

22. From a 71-page, typewritten manuscript, dated August 16, 1985, Asunción, in the possession of the author.

23. From an 8-page, typed paper giving the outline of the research ("On the use and abuse...") in the files of the author.

24. See "Results (first stage," de la *Encuesta nacional sobre uso y abuso de drogas* and the *Informe epidemiológico* . . . of Miguez and Pecci (1991).

25. Law 1340/88, Chapter VIII (of the DINAR): "Article 59: By DINAR will be understood to mean the *Dirección Nacional de Narcóticos,* whose aims are a) To plan and carry out the fight against the illegal traffic in, and control consumption of, the substances to which this law refers; b) To develop, qualify, and train its civil servants for the fight against the illicit traffic in, and control the consumption of, the substances to which this law refers and other related crimes; c) To implement public relations and information campaigns on the dangers of drug addiction and the serious individual and social consequences which these incur; d) To cooperate with the Judicial branch, the Minister of Public Health and Social Welfare, and other national institutions in coordinating activities that will best comply with the mandates of this law; e) To maintain relations and exchange information with similar foreign institutions or international bodies for the purpose of coordination and cooperation and on seizure of narcotic substances, dangerous drugs, or products containing same."

26. See Decree No. 4555, January 25, 1990, by which Fulvio Ramón Aldama is named to the post of Comisario Principal (DAEP) as director of the DINAR, replacing Comisario General Inocencio Montiel Cabrera; and Decree No. 12697, March 2, 1992, by which Juan Angel Aguero Ocampos is named Comisario Mayor as director of the DINAR, replacing Comisario General Fulvio Ramón Aldama.

27. In this executive decree, the verb "to rule" is used to indicate what, beginning then, would be the relations of the SENAD with respect to the nongovernmental organizations. That error in the text of the decree was later corrected, when the law was voted upon in the Parliament. Decree 9528 does not yet specify that the DINAR will leave the aegis of the Ministry of the Interior in order to be bodily incorporated into the SENAD, as its enforcement arm, after approval of the applicable law by the Congress.

28. With the designation of a general to the position of national secretary of the SENAD, accompanied by staff of officials from the armed forces, it remains clear that the fight against the narcotraffic leaves the authority of the Ministry of Interior policy. This coincides with a stage in the region in which the United States attempted to militarize the antidrug effort and could have influenced such a tendency in Paraguay. But in order to understand the appointment of General Samaniego, one must also take

into account the Paraguayan reality, in which a national antidrug strategy, to be truly effective, must rely on the cooperation of military institutions at every level, something which it would be very difficult for a civilian "national secretary" to obtain, at least at the present.

29. We consider as reliable and well founded the reports that General Samaniego enjoys the confidence of influential sections of the U.S. administration, particularly given the sensitive position he holds; on the other hand, there exists a civil consensus regarding this high military officer that, in his professional capacity, he was not linked to any instances of public corruption or violation of human rights under the Stroessner dictatorship.

30. On that occasion, the workshop was divided into two subgroups: 1) one of these on "drug addiction" (definition, causes, situation in Paraguay, formal and preventive education, NGO activities, and control of the prescription and sale by pharmacies); and 2) the other on the "narcotraffic" (Paraguay and its policies against drugs, enforcement activity, narcotraffic and international relations, and narcotraffic and the democratic transition). It was opened by the president of the Chamber of Deputies, José Antonio Moreno Rufinelli, and by chairman of the Chamber's Committee on the Fight Against the Narcotraffic, Nelson Villate.

31. A news analysis of this important parliamentary debate can be found in *ñe-engatú* (1991). A transcript of the text of the speeches and discussions that took place during that congressional workshop was compiled into a 68-page volume entitled *Mesa redonda sobre el narcotráfico* put out by the sponsoring committee (Paraguay Cámara de Deputados 1991).

32. A short history of the SENAD can be found in the speech made by its national secretary, General Marcial D. Samaniego, during the Mesa Redonda sponsored by the Chamber of Deputies in November 1991, the complete text of which is in the files of the author. The complete text of Law 108/91, which creates the *Secretaría Nacional Antidroga (SENAD)*, is as follows: "The Congress of the Paraguayan Nation Gives the Force of Law: Article 1: Establish the SENAD which will coordinate activities among governmental and nongovernmental bodies that work in programs fighting the narcotraffic; Article 2) The *Secretaría* mentioned in Article 1 will report directly to the President of the Republic and will be in the charge of an Executive Secretary and a Deputy Secretary, appointed by the executive branch; Article 3) Modify Article 58 of Law No. 1340/88 which is edited in the following manner 'To the effect of the application of that law, create the *Dirección Nacional de Narcóticos* (DINAR), an agency of the SENAD'; Article 4) Communicate with the executive branch. Approved by the Honorable Cámara de Deputados on the 28th day of the month of November of the year one thousand nine hundred and ninety-one, and by the Honorable Chamber of Senators, sanctioning the law, on the 30th day of the month of December of the year one thousand nine hundred and ninety-one." Subscribed by the Congress, the president of the Senate Chamber, Gustavo Díaz de Vivar, and of the Chamber of Deputies, José A. Moreno Rufinelli, and the respective parlimentary secretaries. On December 27, 1991, the President of the Republic ordered the step "Have the Law of the Republic, publish or insert in the Official Register, and subscribed to the proclamation, accompanied by two of his ministers, that of the Interior, Orlando Muchaca Vargas, and of Public Health and Social Welfare, María Cynthia Prieto Conti."

33. In 1990, Division General Otello Carpinelli, commander of the III Army Corps, in the Paraguayan Chaco, was removed from his position and actually tried by military tribunal for reasons which were never made clear; however, there were many rumors circulating about this event, including the discovery of an airplane abandoned in that area with a large cargo of high-quality cocaine, which was seized by authorities when they were notified (see *Análisis del Mes* [1990, 7] for the bare facts). Apart from corruption with no direct relation to the narcotraffic (see the series of articles on "Corruption in Ciudad del Este," on the Brazilian-Paraguayan border, which were published throughout 1991 by the newspaper *ABC Color)*, the print media has recently published information, commentaries, and analysis which relates the widespread corruption, both public and private, that is linked to the traffic in drugs, arms, as well as the risks of increasing criminal violence in the country; see, for example, *Hoy* (1992b and 1992c) and *ABC Color* (1991, 1992b, 1992c).

34. In December 1992, organized by GESA, PRE-VER, and the International Relations Program of CPES, and under the auspices of the SENAD, a seminar-workshop was held on drug addiction and the narcotraffic for high-level and junior officers of the armed forces, the first one of its kind in the country. In June 1991, as mentioned before, GESA, PRE-VER, and CIDSEP/UC had joined together to sponsor a seminar-workshop for judges on "The National Legal Framework on Drugs."

35. Slowly and despite a few stumbling blocks, the institutionalization of the armed forces has been going forward ever since the transition began. One very recent example of this is that the National War College has invited leaders of various disciplines, independent scholars, and professionals from a variety of specialized fields — many of whom lead organizations in the political opposition — to teach at its 1992 Lecture Course, which was just inaugurated.

36. See, for example, *Paz/Prensa*, a clipping service of articles that appear in the Latin American press on the subjects of peace, security, armaments, and regional cooperation policy of the South American Peace Commission in Santiago (see issue numbers 45, 47, 49, and 50 in 1990).

37. This Working Group was scheduled to return to meet again in Asunción during the first half of 1992.

38. For example, the meeting of the Ministers of the Interior of the Southern Cone countries met in Santiago de Chile in 1991 in order to establish measures for legal and police cooperation in the fight against delinquency, terrorism, and the narcotraffic; and the First Conference of South American Forces Operating against the Illegal Drug Traffic was held in Asunción in November 1991.

References

Abente, D. 1990. "Límites y posibilidades: el contexto internacional y las perspectivas de democratización en el Paraguay," In *Política exterior y relaciones internacionales del Paraguay contemporáneo*, ed. Jose Luis Simón. Asunción, Paraguay: Centro Paraguayo de Estudios Sociológicos (CPES), 277-321.

ABC Color Television (Asunción). 1992a. "Lucharán contra narcodólares." (February 25): 11.

ABC Color Television. 1992b. "Armas: Habría conexión entre Pedro Juan y Salto." (February 24): 76.

ABC Color Television. 1992c. "Aseguran que armas son traficadas a Brasil desde Miami, vía Asunción." (February 24): 76.

ABC Color Television. 1991. "Hay que impedir la 'cartelización' de nuestras fronteras." (March 31): 10.

Acción (Asunción). 1991. "¿Lavado de dólares en el Paraguay?," 117 (August): 14-17.

Adams, N. 1973. "Tráfico de heroína en Iberoamérica." *Selecciones del Reader's Digest* (San Pablo) 5, 29 (June): 133-168.

Agencia Francesa de Noticias (AFP) (San Antonio). 1992a."Amplio y preciso programa de cooperación en la lucha antidrogas." (February 27).

Agencia Francesa de Noticias (AFP). 1992b. "Bush dispuesto a revitalizar esfuerzo antidrogas." (February 26).

Amarilla, J. 1992. "Comercio y finanzas: la nueva cultura económica." *Hoy* (Asunción) (February 8): 18-19.

Amorin, C., and S. Blixen. 1991. "[resumen]." *Cambio 16*, 1049 (December 30).

Análisis del Mes (Asunción). 1990. (September): 7.

Arias, J. 1990a. "La drogadicción en los adolescentes," In *La familia del adicto y otros temas*, eds. J. Arias, R. Fernández Labriola, E. Kalina, and C. Pierini. Buenos Aires, Argentina: Nueva Visión, 141-168.

Arias, J. 1990b. "La drogadicción como fracaso en la individuación (la dependencia sujetando al sujeto)," In *La familia del adicto y otros temas*, eds. J. Arias, R. Fernández Labriola, E. Kalina, and C. Pierini. Buenos Aires: Nueva Visión, 169-182.

Aquino, M. 1991. "Claves sobre el lavado del narcodinero." *Acción* 117 (August): 11-13.

Aspiazu, M. 1992a. "América buscará colaboración en Europa y Asia para lucha contra drogas." *Agencia Española de Noticias* (EFE) (February 27).

Aspiazu, M. 1992b. "Bush pide dinero a latinoamérica porqué no tiene dinero." *Agencia Española de Noticias* (EFE) (February 26).

Aspiazu, M. 1992c. "San Antonio: todos iguales contra la droga," and "Presidentes vuelven sin dinero pero con un 'buen pacto.'" *Agencia Española de Noticias* (EFE) (February 28).

Bagley, B. 1989. "Tráfico de drogas y relaciones entre América Latina y Estados Unidos," In *A la espera de una nueva etapa. Anuario de políticas exteriores latinoamericanas 1988-1989,* ed. Heraldo Muñoz. Caracas, Venezuela: Programa de Seguimiento de las Políticas Exteriores Latinoamericanas (PROSPEL)/Nueva Sociedad, 365-383.

Bagley, B., A. Bonilla, and A. Paez, eds. 1991. *La economía política del narcotrafico: El caso ecuatoriano.* Miami: North-South Center, University of Miami.

Bagley, B., and J. Tokatlián. 1991. "Droga y dogma: La 'narcodiplomacia' entre Estados Unidos y América Latina en la década de los ochenta y su proyección para los noventa" (mimeo).

Blixen, S. 1991. "En Paraguay y con socios uruguayos, el presidente Rodríguez lava narcodólares." *Brecha* (Montevideo) (November 6): 1-5.

Bulacio, B., et al. 1988. *El problema de la drogadiccion: Enfoque interdisciplinario.* Buenos Aires, Argentina: Paidos.

Bustamante, F. 1990a. In *El sistema internacional y america latina. La agenda internacional en los años noventa,* ed. Roberto Russell. Buenos Aires, Argentina: Relaciones Internacionales de América Latina/Grupo Editorial Latinoamericano (RIAL/GEL).

Bustamante, F. 1990b. "La política de Estados Unidos contra el narcotrafico y su impacto en América Latina." *Estudios Internacionales* (Santiago) 23 (April-June): 240-271.

Centro Paraguayo de Estudios Sociológicos (CPES). Forthcoming. *El narcotrafico en el Paraguay: Condicionantes externos e internos, y sus repercusiones locales y para las relaciones internacionales del país.* Asunción, Paraguay: CPES/Programa de Relaciones Internacionales.

Conferencia Episcopal Paraguaya (CEP). 1979. "El saneamiento moral de la nación." *Cuadernos de Sendero.* Asunción, Paraguay: CEP.

Crawley, E. 1990. "Informe confidencial: Tráfico de drogas en América Latina." London, England: Latin American Newsletters Ltd.

(El) Diario (Asunción). 1988. "Taylor afirma: altos funcionarios protegen a narcotraficantes; Saldívar replica: 'Que dé nombres.'" (March 12): 8.

(El) Diario Noticias (Asunción). 1989. Special supplement: "Narcotráfico: uno de los peores flagelos; Así lo calificó el presidente Rodríguez, anunciando que abogará por leyes más severas." (February 7).

DPA. 1992a. "Cumbre antidrogas ratifica compromisos comunes interamericanos." (February 27).

DPA. 1992b. "Bush señala limitaciones financieras para combate antidrogas." (February 27).

Duarte Manzoni, H. 1989. *Drogas en Asunción: más allá del miedo.* Asunción, Paraguay: Editorial Arte Nuevo.

Agencia Española de Noticias (EFE). 1992a. "Presidentes vuelven sin dinero pero con un 'buen pacto'." (February 28).

Agencia Española de Noticias. 1992b. "Cumbre antidroga consagra cooperación y economía alternativa." (February 27).

Escohotado, A. 1989. *Historia de las drogas* (Vols. 1-3). Madrid, Spain: Alianza Editorial.

Estigarribia, H. 1990."Acciones emprendidas por el gobierno paraguayo contra la producción, el tráfico ilícito y el consumo indebido de las drogas." Presentation to the Cámara de Deputados de la Nación, Round-table on Narcotraffic and Drug Addiction, Asunción, June 13-14.

Fernandez, E.J. 1990. "Perspectiva de cambio de la política exterior paraguaya." *Sintesis* (Madrid) 10 (January-April): 325-334.

Fresco, M. 1991. "Las drogas y sus abordajes." Presentation to the "Primera Jornada sobre la Ley 1340: Análisis y propuestas de modificación" en la Camara de Deputados de la Nación, Asunción, Paraguay, November 16.

Garcia Sayan, D., ed. 1990. *Coca, cocaina y narcotrafico: Laterinto en los andes*, 2nd ed. Lima, Peru: Comisión Andina de Juristas.

Garreton, M. 1987. *Reconstruir la politica, transicion y consolidacion democratica en Chile*. Santiago, Chile: Editorial Anadante.

Granovsky, L. 1992a. "Perú forzó a eliminar plazos en la cumbre antidrogas." *AFP*, (February 27).

Granovsky, L. 1992b. "Latinoamérica exigió planes concretos en lucha antidrogas." *AFP* (February 27).

Hoy. 1992a. "La Declaración de San Antonio. Exhortación a cooperar contra el narcotráfico. Texto completo del manifiesto de siete presidentes de la región." *Hoy* (Asunción) March 4: 18-19.

Hoy. 1992b. "Bandas criminales de Brasil reciben armas vía Asunción." (February 24): 55.

Hoy. 1992c. "Existen cerca de 1500 pistas de aviación." (February 11): 23.

Hoy. 1989. "Rodríguez informó sobre los objetivos de su nuevo gobierno." (February 7): 8-9.

Hoy. 1988a. "Sobre supuesta protección al narcotráfico expresada por Taylor: terminante rechazo de la Cancillería." (March 12): 8.

Hoy. 1988b. "Drogas: Embajador Taylor dice que hay 'protectores'." (March 11): 1, 11.

Instituto Latinoamericano de Estudios Transnacionales (ILET). 1989. *La politica internacional de Chile en la decada de los noventa. Documento de Sintesis-Texto Provisional*. Santiago, Chile: ILET.

Inter-American Dialogue (IAD). 1990. *Report of the Inter-American Dialogue: The Americas in a New World*. Washington, D.C.: The Aspen Institute.

Inter-American Dialogue (IAD). 1989. *The Americas in 1989: Consensus for Action*. Washington, D.C.: The Aspen Institute.

Journal of Interamerican Studies and World Affairs. 1988. *Assessing the Americas' War on Drugs*. 30, 2/3 (Summer/Fall): whole issue.

Kalina, E. 1988. *Adolescencia y drogadicción*. Buenos Aires, Argentina: Ediciones Nueva Visión.

Labra, F. 1990. "Paraguay: nuevo perfil internacional." *Perspective Internacional Paraguaya* (Asunción) 2, 4 (July-December): 7-33.

Laino, D. 1979. *Paraguay: represion, estafa y anticomunismo*. Asunción, Paraguay: Ediciones Cerro Corá.

Lechner, N. 1989. "El realismo político, una cuestión de tiempo." *Leviatan* (Madrid) 35, 2 (Spring): 127-128.

Lee, R. 1992. *El laberinto blanco. Cocaina y poder politico*. Bogotá, Colombia: Centro de Estudios de la Realidad Colombiana (CEREC).

Masi, F. 1991. *Relaciones internacionales del Paraguay con Stroessner y sin Stroessner*. IDIAL Working Paper (March).

Miguez, H. 1989. *Uso indebido de susancias sicoactivas en el medio de trabajo: aportes de una metodologia participativa*. Buenos Aires, Argentina.

Miguez, H., and M. Pecci. 1991. *Estudio nacional sobre salud mental y habitos toxicos en el Paraguay: Informe epidemiologico sobre el uso y abuso del alcohol y las drogas en diez ciudades del Paraguay*. Asunción, Paraguay: Comité Paraguay-Kansas (November).

Mora, F. 1990. "Relaciones Estados Unidos-Paraguay: conflicto y cooperación." *Perspectiva Internacional Paraguaya* (Asunción) 2, 3 (January-June): 79-94.

ñe-engatú (Asunción). 1991. "Narcotráfico y addicción a drogas ilegales." IX, 53 (December): 17-18.

Neild, R. 1991. *Paraguay: una transicion en busca de la democracia*. Asunción, Paraguay: Ediciones ñandutí Vive-Intercontinental Editora, 90 pages.

Nuñez Reyes, G. 1988. "El tema de las drogas en la campaña electoral norteamericana." *Cono Sur* (Santiago) 7, 5 (September-October): 20-23.

Olmedo, G. 1991. "La legislación, doctrina y jurisprudencia comparada en materia de drogas y el lavado de dinero." Paper presented to the "Primera jornada sobre Ley 1340: Análisis y propuestas de modificación," organized by the Commission de lucha contra el narcotráfico de la Cámara de Deputados, Grupo de Estudio sobre Alcoholismo y Otras Adicciones (GESA), and Pevención de Adicciones (PRE-VER), and held at the National Congress, Asunción (Paraguay), November 16.

del Olmo, R. 1991. "La internacionalización jurídica de la droga." *Nueva Sociedad* 112 (March-April): 102-114.

Pajares, F. 1992. "San Antonio: la lucha con más acento latinoamericano." *Agencia Española de Noticias* (EFE) (February 27).

Paraguay Cámara de Deputados. 1991. *Mesa Redonda sobre el narcotrafico* (November). Asunción, Paraguay: Comisión de Lucha contra el Narcotráfico, 68 pages.

Paraguay Ministerio del Interior. 1991a. *Anuario de Direccion Nacional de Narcoticos* (DINAR). Asunción, Paraguay: Ministerio del Interior, República de Paraguay.

Paraguay Ministerio del Interior. 1991b. *DINAR: Reseña historica*. Asunción, Paraguay: DINAR.

Paraguay Ministerio del Interior. 1990. *Anuario de Direccion Nacional de Narcoticos* (DINAR). Asunción, Paraguay: Ministerio del Interior.

Paraguay Ministerio del Interior. 1988. Ley 1340/88, Edición oficial. Asunción, Paraguay: DINAR, Ministerio del Interior, 10 pages.

Paraguay Poder Legislativo. 1991. Ley No 74/91 de Organización de las Fuerzas Armadas de la Nación (November). Asunción, Paraguay: República de Paraguay.

Paraguay Ministerio de Relaciones Exteriores. 1991. *Boletin de Informaciones* (BDI) (Asunción), Nos. 11-20 (May-September): 14-15.

Paraguay Ministerio de Salud Publica y Bienestar Social. 1991. *Reordenamiento institucional en la lucha contra el narcotrafico y el uso indebido de drogas* (February). Asunción, Paraguay: Department of Mental Health (Dir: Agustín Carrizosa).

Paraguay Ministerio de Salud Publica y Bienestar Social. 1990. *Programa de prevencion, apercibimiento/concientizacion y asistencia a la drogadiccion*. Asunción, Paraguay: Department of Mental Health (Dir: Agustín Carrizosa).

PARPRESS (Asunción). 1987. "Embajador norteamericano reclama 'voluntad política' para combatir al narcotráfico." (December 29).

Patria (Asunción). 1988a. "Con el mismo razonamiento de Mr. Taylor." (March 15): 6.

Patria. 1988b. "Relaciones con luces y sombras." (March 14): 7.

Patria. 1988c. "Narcotráfico, Reagan y cooperación." (March 11): 7.

Patria. 1988d. "Reagan y el Paraguay." (March 4): 7.

Perez-Llana, C. 1991. *De la guerra del golfo al nuevo orden*. Buenos Aires, Argentina: Grupo Editorial Latinoamericano (GEL).

Perspectiva Internacional Paraguaya (Asunción). 1990. "Documentos." 2, 4 (July-December): 283-289.

Prevención de Addiciones (PRE-VER). 1992. *Informe de articulos de divulgacion en periodicos capitalinos*. Asunción, Paraguay: PRE-VER.

Retamar, M. 1991. *Las ONG de prevencion en Paraguay*. Asunción, Paraguay: Grupo de Estudio sobre Alcoholismo y Otras Adicciones (GESA).

Rodrigo, A. 1992. "A la búsqueda del consenso." ANSA (February 27).

Rodriguez, A. 1991. "Mensaje del Excelentísimo Señor Presidente de la República, General de Ejército Andrés Rodríguez, Al Honorable Congreso Nacional" (Asunción, April 10, 1991). Edición de la Presidencia de la República.

Rolon, A. 1986. *Estupefacientes y drogas peligrosas. La enfermedad y el delito*. Asunción, Paraguay: Edición del Autor-Imprenta Omega.

Roque Bacarreza, F. 1992. "Informe final sin plazos para la guerra contra narcotráfico." (February 27).

Russell, R. 1990. "La agenda global en los años 90: antiguos y nuevos temas." In *El sistema internacional y America Latina: La agenda internacional en los años 90*, ed. Roberto Russell. Buenos Aires, Argentina: Relaciones Internacionales de América Latina/Grupo Editorial Latinoamericano (RIAL/GEL).

Simon, J. 1991. *La politica exterior paraguaya en 1991. Modernizacion insuficiente, carencia de una vision global y condicionamientos de un estado prebendario en crisis*. Asunción, Paraguay: Centro Paraguayo de Estudios Sociológicos (CPES).

Simon, J. 1990a. "Introducción: algunas reflexiones sobre la política exterior y las relaciones internacionales del Paraguay contemporáneo." In *Politica exterior y relaciones internacionales del Paraguay contemporaneo*, ed. J. Simon. Asunción, Paraguay: Centro Paraguayo de Estudios Sociológicos (CPES).

Simon, J. 1990b. "Hacia una política nacional." *ABC Color Television* (Asunción) (July 25): 21.

Simon, J. 1990c. "El Paraguay y el narcotráfico." *ABC Color* (Asunción) (July 24): 26.

Simon, J. 1990d. "Despenalizar el consumo?" *ABC Color* (Asunción) (July 23): 21.

Simon, J. 1990e. "Las estrategia penalizadoras." *ABC Color* (Asunción) (July 22): 22.

Simon, J. 1990f. "Discutible política de EEUU." *ABC Color* (Asunción) (July 21): 9.

Simon, J. 1990g. "La violencia de la droga." *ABC Color* (Asunción) (July 20): 7.

Simon, J. 1990h. "El lado de la oferta." *ABC Color* (Asunción) (July 19): 7.

Simon, J. 1990i. "EEUU, la cara de la demanda." *ABC Color* (Asunción) (July 18): 7.

Simon, J. 1990j. "Una economía negra." *ABC Color* (Asunción) (July 17): 8.

Simon, J. 1990k. "Adicción y narcotráfico: una amenaza para nosotros?" *ABC Color* (Asunción) (July 16): 6.

Simon, J. 1989. "Del aislamiento a la reincorporación internacional: el Paraguay de la inmediata transición post-stronista." *Perspectiva Internacional Paraguaya* (Asunción) 1, 1/2 (January/June and July/December): 163-200.

Simon, J. 1988. "Narcotráfico vía Paraguay irrita a Washington." *Sendero* (Asunción) (January 15): 15.

Simon, J. 1987. "El narcotráfico afecta a nuestras relaciones internacionales." *Sendero* (Asunción) (October 16): 15.

Simon, J., and F. Mora. 1991. "Letting Go: Paraguay's Struggle to Bury its Stronist Past." *North-South Magazine of the Americas* 1, 3 (October-November): 34-38.

Stepan, A. 1988a. *Repensando a los militares en política; Cono sur: un analisis comparado.* Buenos Aires, Argentina: Planeta.

Stepan, A. 1988b. "Introducão." In *Democratizando o Brazil,* ed. A. Stepan. São Paulo, Brazil: Paz e Terra.

Taillandier, P. 1992. "'Problemas' para la adopción de un plan contra la droga." *AFP* (February 27).

(La) Tarde (Asunción). 1988a. "Opositores también piden nombres a Taylor." (March 12): 7.

(La) Tarde. 1988b. "'Que Taylor se atenga a las consecuencias.'" (March 11): 9.

(La) Tarde. 1988c. "Altos funcionarios protegen al narcotráfico, según Taylor." (March 11): 11.

Taylor, C. 1987a. "Entrevista con el embajador Clyde Taylor para el semanario 'Sendero'," *Conferencia Episcopal Paraguaya,* Asunción, August 24 (U.S. Information Service press release).

Taylor, C. 1987b. "Discurso pronunciado por el embajador Clyde Taylor, en ocasión de la conferencia sobre drogas para periodistas." Asunción, December 18 (U.S. Information Service press release).

Tokatlián, J., and B. Bagley, eds. 1990. *Economia y politica del narcotrafico.* Bogotá, Colombia: Centro de Estudios Internacionales/Universidad de los Andes/ Centro de Estudios de la Realidad Colombiana (CEI/UNIANDES/CEREC) .

Tomassini, L., C. Moneta, and A. Varas. 1991. *El sistema internacional y America Latina: La politica internacional en un mundo postmoderno.* Santiago, Chile: Relaciones Internacionales de América Latina (RIAL).

Ultima Hora (Asunción). 1992a. "'No habrá padrinos que protejan a narcotraficantes.'" (February 12): 8.

Ultima Hora. 1992b. "En operaciones de compra de divisas: los bancos y las casas de cambios movilizaron US$10,800 milliones." (February 11): 20.

Ultima Hora. 1988a. "'Investigaciones sobre las drogas están en su inicio.'" (March 12): 12.

Ultima Hora. 1988b. "Según el embajador norteamericano: narcotráfico, 'el Paraguay es fuente significativa.'" (March 11): 13.

Ultima Hora. 1988c. "Reagan certificó la cooperación latinoamericana en narcotráfico." (March 2): 2.

Vinocur, J. 1984. "The Republic of Fear: Thirty Years of Stroessner in Paraguay." *New York Times Magazine* (September 24): 21-25.

Yopo H., B. 1989. "Cuba y el narcotráfico." *Cono Sur* 8, 5 (September-October): 22-24.

Yopo H., M. 1991. *Paraguay-Stroessner: la politica exterior del regimen autoritario (1954-1989).* Santiago, Chile: Programa de Seguimientos de las Políticas Exteriores Latinoamericanas (PROSPEL).

Ziegler, J. 1990. *Suiza lava mas blanco. El escandalo de los narcodolares.* Buenos Aires, Argentina: Atlántida.

Chapter Eighteen

Paraguay and International Drug Trafficking

Frank O. Mora

Introduction

In international relations, small states such as Paraguay have been tradition-ally isolated, not only from world political and economic developments but also from the literature of international relations and Latin American studies. The reason for Paraguay's exclusion and marginal status is quite simple: it lies between two rival giants that determined its political, economic, and diplomatic makeup. Before 1989 much of the literature on Paraguay's foreign relations was usually part of a larger study of either Argentina or Brazil's foreign relations.[1]

This geopolitical and scholarly marginalization of Paraguay was also due to the basic configuration of the Cold War world that regarded small states as being inconsequential in world affairs. However, the transnationalization of world affairs and issues — such as the environment, trade, immigration, and drug trafficking — and the end of the Cold War has magnified the importance of studying these small states who are becoming important actors in an increasingly interdependent world system.[2] Further study of small states in relation to these transnational issues is imperative for analyzing the new dynamics of international relations.

In the case of Paraguay, the end of the Cold War and the collapse of the 35-year dictatorship of President Alfredo Stroessner in 1989 resulted in an impressive growth of published works on Paraguay's role in regional and world affairs.[3] In fact, the democratization of Paraguayan society has also led to the growth of researchers and journalists willing and able to investigate areas that would have been inconceivable to discuss and explore during the Stroessner regime. Consequently, the purpose of this chapter is to continue filling this scholarly void by analyzing the history and reviewing the literature and methodology employed in studying a transnational issue of utmost concern to Paraguay — international drug trafficking.

351

During the height of the Cold War, "global" issues such as the environment, immigration, and drug trafficking were secondary to the security parameters that dominated the East-West conflict. In fact, during the 1970s, outside of newspaper articles and government reports that denied a problem, little in-depth research was conducted on the causes and effects of international drug trafficking. However, when the drug trade became a top priority of U.S. national security, nations in Latin America were in many ways forced to address a problem that not only affects foreign relations but also their socio-economic condition. In terms of hemispheric relations, U.S. policy begins to change the agenda of interamerican relations. One analyst has referred to recent U.S.-Latin American relations as "narco-diplomacy" (Bagley 1989).

Despite the expansion of research on this important transnational issue since the mid-1980s, there is still much to be done in areas such as the role of transit countries, impact on the governability of the state, economic dimensions and repercussions, and its socio-psychological effects. In short, there are a number of issue-areas and dimensions of the problem that are placing special emphasis on the need to analyze the interdependent political economy of the transnational drug trade (Tokatlián and Bagley 1990). Because of a need for further research and methodological tools in analyzing the impact of the drug trade in these societies, this chapter will not only attempt to examine the role of Paraguay, a producing and important transit country, in the international drug trafficking trade, but also to offer some methodological suggestions for further study of countries in Latin America that play a similar role to that of Paraguay.

Despite Paraguay's detachment from the literature on foreign policy and relations, it is interesting to note that since the late 1960s research and reporting has been published by scholars and journalists alike on Paraguay's vast and popular contraband trade of which a sizable part included narcotics. The link between Paraguay and drug trafficking is nothing new; in fact, it constitutes one of the first cases of conflict in the Western Hemisphere between the United States and a South American country on the issue of international drug trafficking (Simon 1992).

Paraguay's relationship with the drug mafia begins in the 1960s under the corrupt and immoral dictatorship of President Alfredo Stroessner. The dictatorship allowed for the military, government officials, and members of the ruling Colorado party to take part in the contraband trade as the regime's legitimate "price for peace" in Paraguay (Simon and Mora 1991, 37). Generalized corruption in Paraguay is a lingering problem for the democratic transition government. This review of the literature on Paraguay's links to the international drug mafia and industry will divide the history of Paraguay's involvement into two distinct periods: 1) heroin (1967-1973) and 2) cocaine and marijuana (1985-1991).

Andre Ricord and the Heroin Connection (1967-1973)

Much of the debate on Paraguay's links to international drug traffic is addressed within the larger framework of U.S.- Paraguayan relations. The generalized corruption that was sanctioned by Stroessner and his cronies in the government and military not only destroyed the fabric of Paraguayan society but also seriously damaged Paraguay's relations with the world community, especially and most importantly with the United States. This corruption led to Paraguay's well-deserved reputation during the late 1960s of being the heart of contraband in South America (Clark and Horrock 1973; Vinocur 1984; Rosenberg 1987). It was also at this time that Paraguay's notoriety as an emerging drug entrepot began to undermine its relations with the United States.

In 1967 August (Andre) Ricord, member of the "French Connection," arrived in Paraguay to coordinate the transport of heroin from Marseille, France, to the United States via Paraguay (Roett 1989, 133; Mora 1990, 82; Roett and Sacks 1991, 149). Ricord used Paraguay as a privileged haven and transit point for running a lucrative heroin-smuggling business worth an estimated US $2.5 million (Laino 1979, 16; Roett and Sacks 1991, 149). According to U.S. federal agents, Ricord's organization was responsible for between 50 and 75 percent of all the heroin smuggled into the United States (Adams 1973, 235). It has been documented that Ricord received protection and was offered airplane landing strips by high military and police officers (Adams 1973; Clark and Horrock 1973; Lewis 1980, 131-139; Roett and Sacks 1991, 134).[4]

The protection the Paraguayan government offered to one of the largest drug smuggling rings in Latin America caused the first friction between two Cold War warriors: President Richard Nixon and General Alfredo Stroessner. The communist threat was less of a major preoccupation for the United States in a world characterized by detente. Drugs had become an important domestic issue and President Nixon in a July 1971 speech called on all friendly governments to cooperate with the United States in countering this new threat (*Latin American Report*, October 1971, 330). Paraguay was seen as a major player whose government did not heed Nixon's call for cooperation. The Nixon administration accused Asuncion of allowing Paraguay to be used as a transit point for drugs destined for the United States from Europe and requested that Ricord, after being arrested by the Paraguayan government, be extradited to the United States; the Stroessner regime vetoed the extradition request. (*Newsweek* 1972; Hoyer 1975, 299; Lewis 1980, 137; Mora 1988, 264). Soon after, bilateral relations deteriorated to their lowest point.

In 1972 President Nixon threatened to cut off U.S. aid if Stroessner did not agree to extradite Ricord. The United States cut off Paraguay's sugar quota, and Congress passed the 1971 Foreign Assistance Act which empowered the U.S. president to suspend economic aid to any nation that failed to cooperate in solving the drug problem. In the spring of 1972, nearly US$5 million in credit lines to Paraguay as well as military aid were suspended. The United States also threatened to suspend US$11 million in additional aid if Paraguay did not cooperate (Adams 1973, 273; Lewis 1980, 137). Finally, after the death in 1972 of General Patricio Colman (one of Ricord's chief backers) and increasing U.S. pressures, Stroessner gave in and extradited Ricord (*Latin American Report*, August 1974, 270).[5] Once Ricord was extradited, the smuggling of "hard" drugs from Paraguay declined and U.S.-Paraguayan relations returned to the days when Washington gave its unrelenting support to the Stroessner dictatorship, at least until 1977 (Latin American Bureau 1980, 54; Roett and Sacks 1991, 149; Simon 1992).[6]

Restricted and Limited Research and News Reporting

Because of Paraguay's relative international isolation and Stroessner's strict censorship of the national press, there are few primary sources available on Paraguay's role in the heroin trade. In the United States, *Newsweek* (January 24, 1972), the *New York Times*, and the *Washington Post* published a few articles on heroin smuggling in Paraguay, Ricord's role in the operation, and his extradition. A comprehensive journalistic portrayal on the Stroessner regime's ties to the heroin drug mafia was authored by Nathan Adams ("The Hunt for Andre," *Reader's Digest*, March 1973); it is suspected that this piece was "officially sanctioned and promoted" by the U.S. government as a means of pressuring and exposing corruption within the Paraguayan government (Simon 1992). This article, published in Spanish by *Selecciones del Reader's Digest* in June 1973, was confiscated by the Paraguayan government and banned from entering the country; however, the piece was secretly circulated in the country.

Adams' investigative article denounced prominent civil and military authorities for protecting drug traffickers in Paraguay,[7] and one of those implicated for having links to Ricord and the "French Connection" was General Andrés Rodríguez, then commander of the powerful First Army Corps and current president of Paraguay since February 1989.

In 1979 Domingo Laino, then a young legislator, authored a book that examined the corruption and repression that permeated all levels of Paraguayan government and society. Laino provided newspaper source documents reporting on the serious crisis in relations between Washington and Asuncion over the protection offered to drug traffickers by Paraguayan authorities (Laino 1979, 141-154). Laino's research reveals strong political-diplomatic and economic pressures which finally led to Ricord's imprisonment and extradition.

Press and self-imposed censorship in Paraguay led to limited newspaper reporting of these events by Paraguayan dailies. In fact, as Laino's bibliography confirms, most of the reporting was conducted by *abc color* and *La Tribuna* who were, at the time, sympathetic to the regime. In sum, most of the research on Paraguay's role as a transit point for heroin destined to the U.S. comes from secondary sources that were published after 1975.

Cocaine and Marijuana (1985-1991)

The inauguration of Jimmy Carter in January 1977 produced new frictions between Washington and Asuncion. The basis of U.S.-Paraguayan relations changed dramatically — no longer was the U.S. going to ignore human rights violations and the lack of political democracy in Paraguay. Carter's emphasis on human rights and democracy and the decision by Congress to cut off military hardware deliveries in 1977 ended decades of Washington's silence on Stroessner's dictatorship (Abente 1988, 90; Simon 1988, 28; Mora 1990, 83-84; Roett and Sacks 1991, 149; Yopo 1991, 61-69).[8] This conflict between the Carter administration and the Stroessner regime led to a decline in bilateral economic and commercial ties. Relations reached their lowest point ever. However, the drug trade and Paraguay's possible role in it never became an issue in the relationship. In fact, "the smuggling of 'hard drugs' from Paraguay apparently declined so much after the Ricord affair that the United States closed its Drug Enforcement Agency (DEA) office in Asuncion in 1981" (Roett and Sacks 1991, 149). There are no known primary or secondary sources available on Paraguay's possible involvement in the drug trade from 1975-1984.

When Ronald Reagan was elected in 1980, many in Asuncion rejoiced at seeing a Cold War warrior enter the White House. The Stroessner regime believed that Reagan's Cold War rhetoric meant that the United States and Paraguay could once again be partners in the war against international communism; however, Asuncion would soon be sadly disappointed. Despite an initial normalization of relations, especially during Reagan's first term, "the changes introduced by the Carter administration proved irreversible," and so the Reagan administration had no choice but to continue the cause of democracy and human rights in Paraguay (Abente 1988, 90).

During this time an additional issue of contention between both countries came to the forefront. By 1984, the U.S. government began once again to express concern over the involvement of the "Stronist" government elite in the illegal traffic of drugs (Burr 1988). Drug trafficking had once again become a vital international and domestic issue of concern for the United States and the world community. As the Cold War abated, the drug trade became the principal point of friction in U.S.-Latin American relations, especially in the case of Paraguay since evidence had surfaced that government and military officials were involved in the trafficking of precursor chemicals used to manufacture cocaine (*Latin American Weekly Report* 1985;

Goshko 1985; Brinkley 1985b; Bird and Holland 1985; *Latin American Regional Report* 1985; Bouvier 1988). The U.S. perception was that Paraguay had once again "joined the big leagues" in smuggling hard drugs like cocaine (Burr 1988; Roett and Sacks 1991, 150).

By the mid-1980s Paraguay was also being used by the Andean drug barons as an important transit point for cocaine shipped from processing laboratories in Bolivia to Europe and the United States. (OAS 1986, 51). One of the reasons for the flourishing role of Paraguay in the international drug trade in the late 1980s was the stepped-up enforcement operations by the United States and Latin American nations, particularly in the Andean region, which drove the drug barons to find cheaper and safer areas and routes for laundering drug money and transporting narcotics to the principal markets in the United States and Europe (Lee 1987; Surret 1988; Bagley 1989, 77).[9] Roett and Sacks (1991) attribute Paraguay's involvement in the drug trade to

> increased pressure on Bolivian drug traffickers as a result of U.S. efforts to destroy drug laboratories [there] had a spillover effect on Paraguay. ... drug dealers had identified Paraguay as a less hostile and less vigilant place to ply their trade. Third, although coca is not grown or processed within the country, Paraguay's vast Chaco, a virtually unpatrolled wilderness with over 900 airstrips, provided an ideal base for planes to land and take off. Fourth, Paraguayan law enforcement were poorly equipped to deal with sophisticated drug traffickers.... Fifth, Paraguayan sentencing of drug traffickers was notoriously lax. Sixth, money that passed through Paraguay's exchange houses was impossible to trace (151).

Furthermore, Paraguay, for the first time, became a major world producer of marijuana in the late 1980s (U.S. Department of State 1988 and 1989; Simon 1992). By 1985 the Reagan administration became so concerned that it abandoned its "silent diplomacy" approach of pressuring the regime to reform and appointed Clyde Taylor, former assistant secretary of state in the Bureau of International Narcotics Matters, as ambassador to Asuncion (Mora 1990, 85).

U.S. congressional and government officials let it be known to the Stroessner regime that publicized seizures of cocaine and precursor chemicals that implicated Paraguayan authorities would not be tolerated by the U.S. government (Boveda 1985, 41; Goshko 1985; *Atlanta Constitution* 1988b; Simon 1987 and 1992).[10] In the period between 1987-1988, Elliot Abrams, assistant secretary of state for inter-American affairs, and Ambassador Taylor made public declarations inculpating Paraguayan authorities of protecting and profiting from the illegal traffic of precursor chemicals and cocaine (*Sendero* 1987; Simon 1988; *Ultima Hora* 1988c; *Latinamerica Press* 1988, 1; *Ultima Hora* 1988b, 13; the *Washington Post* 1988c, A28; *Hoy* 1988b, 11;

Cohen 1988, A8; Simon 1988b; *La Tarde* 1988, 9).[11] By 1988 the Reagan administration had made the issue of drug trafficking in Paraguay a central theme in bilateral relations. The friction between both countries was widely covered in the Paraguayan press (*Patria* 1988, 2; additional references are mentioned above).

By 1988 Paraguay began to cooperate with U.S. drug control efforts.[12] In order to satisfy U.S. demands, Paraguay made important strides in combating the drug problem by improving its cooperation with U.S. Drug Enforcement officials (the DEA reopened its office in Asuncion in early 1988) and by conducting successful drug seizures (Mora 1990, 87).[13] Despite threats from Congress to decertify Paraguay as a candidate for U.S. aid under the provisions of the Anti-Drug Abuse Act of 1986, the Reagan administration supported full certification on the grounds of "vital national security interests" (Gelbard 1988a, 1988b; Wrobleski 1988a, 1988b). Nonetheless, the administration termed Paraguay one of a group of "close friends and allies that needs to do more to cooperate with the United States" (U.S. Department of State 1989; Roett 1989, 132). The Paraguayan government reciprocated by redrafting an antidrug penal code (Law 1340/88), and Paraguayan drug enforcement officers received training from U.S. instructors (Roett and Sacks 1991, 151).

The February 3, 1989, coup that overthrew the 35-year dictatorship of President Alfredo Stroessner meant not only the beginning of the democratic process in Paraguay but the complete normalization of relations between Washington and Asuncion. President Andrés Rodríguez attempted to dismiss any rumors that he was linked to the drug trade by affirming that his government "will wage a firm and intransigent struggle against drug traffickers, and will make the laws even stricter and stronger in order to repress it" (U.S. Department of State 1989, 81; Riding 1989; *Sun Sentinel* 1989, 17A; *Diario de Noticias* 1989f).[14]

The Rodríguez regime began courting the Bush administration when, on the day after U.S. recognition, Foreign Minister Luis Maria Argana promised the U.S. ambassador that all marijuana fields would be eradicated and that Asuncion would end Paraguay's role as a transshipment point for drugs destined for Europe and the United States (*Hoy* 1989, 6). It was clear to President Rodríguez that if he was to dismiss allegations of his previous involvement in the drug trade, he not only had to come out strongly against drug trafficking but also in full support of President George Bush's "New World Order" (*Diario de Noticias* 1989f).[15] By March, U.S. and Paraguayan antinarcotics forces began working together in Operation Roundup which consisted of spraying 'glifosato' on large marijuana fields (*abc color* 1989, 44). In short, as Roett and Sacks (1991) state, "Since the coup, Rodríguez has said and done everything in relation to drugs and democracy that Washington and Western Europe expected of him. So far, Rodríguez has cooperated fully with the U.S. government requests to intensify pressures on drug traffickers in Paraguay" (134; see also *Patria* 1990, 9; *Diario de Noticias* 1990a, 49; *Diario de Noticias* 1989c, 2; *Diario de Noticias* 1989a, 35).

It is important to note that the Rodríguez government, since the reincorporation of Paraguay into the regional and world system after years of isolation (Simon 1989; Labra 1990), has signed agreements and cooperated with its neighbors in several areas in the fight against drugs.[16] For example, the Caracas Declaration not only incorporated Paraguay into the Rio Group but also compelled it to sign an agreement requiring Paraguay to cooperate in the fight against drugs in Latin America (see, for example, *Diario de Noticias* 1989d, 32; *abc color* 1990a, 28; *Universal* 1990, 13; *abc color* 1991, 22).[17]

The Burgeoning and Proliferation of Literature and Research

The repressive political conditions that existed in Paraguay during the dictatorship impeded serious study by scholars and the press of the problems of drug trafficking. This was particularly the case during the last years of the Stroessner regime when it felt vulnerable in the face of internal and external pressures. However, because of the seriousness of the problem and the growing concern by democratic regimes in the Southern Cone over this important transnational issue, the Paraguayan press could not possibly ignore informing the public about the diverse effects of drug abuse and trafficking (Simon 1992). Furthermore, frictions between the United States and Paraguay, partly due to Washington's perception that Asuncion was not doing enough to stop the drug trade in Paraguay, inescapably led to full coverage of the conflict by the Paraguayan press.[18] Nonetheless, the Paraguayan government maintained strict censorship and prohibited any discussion of possible government involvement in the drug trade.

Starting in 1985, there was a "marginalized" press that provided a more comprehensive analysis of the drug problem in Paraguay. Much of this press was not censored or closed due to the protection given by the Catholic Church and international organizations; some of these periodicals were illegal but were either distributed or smuggled into the country clandestinely. Some of these "marginalized" periodicals included *Sendero, Nuestro Tiempo*, and *Ne-engantu*. This alternative press focused on informing the public of the international costs of Paraguay's links to the drug mafia in terms of the country's international image (Boveda 1985; Simon 1987 and 1988b). Nongovernmental organizations (NGOs) also played an important part in discussing and analyzing drug abuse, prevention, and trafficking in Paraguay (Simon 1992).

As drug trafficking became a more portentous issue in U.S. domestic and international affairs, the U.S. press gave greater coverage to the topic. Furthermore, the attenuation of the Cold War in the 1980s, allowed the press to report on transnational issues such as drug trafficking. In the case of Paraguay, the U.S. press was vociferously critical of Paraguay's links to the Andean drug barons (see citations mentioned above and in the references). This coverage was an added pressure on the U.S. government to give greater attention to the drug problem in Paraguay. Consequently, the U.S. government published several reports examining Paraguay's links to the drug trade (Burr 1988; U.S. House Foreign Affairs Committee Hearing 1988).[19]

When General Andrés Rodríguez came to power on February 3, 1989, his government took significant steps toward democratization; these included greater popular participation, respect for human rights, elections, and freedom of the press. This meant that dailies like *abc color*, that had been silenced since 1984, (and other news sources) were allowed to publish freely without pressure or intimidation from the government. There has been a truly impressive, dramatic change in which the press has been allowed to investigate and report on issues, such as drug trafficking, that would have been inconceivable during the Stroessner dictatorship (see, for example, Martínez 1990; Simon *abc color* series 1990). In many ways, this is due to an attempt by the Rodríguez administration not only to reinstate friendly relations with the United States, but also to confirm the reinsertion of Paraguay into the international community (Simon 1989; Masi 1990 and 1991).[20]

There has also been an open and frank debate about drug abuse and trafficking in political, academic, and government circles. Daily newspapers, such as *abc color* and *Diario de Noticias*, have given wide coverage to the impact of international drug trafficking on Paraguay (Martínez 1990; Simon 1990b, 26). In particular, *abc color* has been extremely active in publishing a series of articles concerning corruption in Paraguay (Simon and Mora 1991, 37).[21] Open discussion of drug abuse and trafficking has reached such a surprising point that Jose Luis Simon, an expert on international drug trafficking and an exiled opponent of the previous regime, has testified before the Committee on the Fight Against Narcotics of the Paraguayan Chamber of Deputies (Simon 1990). Two years before, such a milestone would have been unthinkable.[22]

Despite open reporting on the issue, Paraguayan journalists still practice self-censorship to the extent that they will not investigate or report in detail the possible involvement of high government officials in the drug trade.[23] In terms of the United States, since February-May 1989 when articles were published on the alleged involvement of President Rodríguez in the drug trade, the press has not continued its reporting as it did during the Stroessner regime. This is probably due to the Paraguayan government's decision to follow Washington's lead in the struggle against international drug trafficking.[24]

Conclusions and Future Research and Methodology Proposals

The development of social science research, especially in the area of international relations, has been overly underdeveloped in Paraguay, more than in any other country in South America. However, the multidisciplinary research that has been conducted in Paraguay since February 1989 has contributed to the enrichment of the political-economic dimension of international relations, one of whose objectives is to study drug trafficking and its global effects. This is due not only to the democratization of Paraguayan society but to the dramatic changes that are revolutionizing the study of international relations. Paraguay has entered a new regional system where security priorities are no longer defined militarily but by economic, commercial, and social determinants. Therefore, a more profound analysis of transnational issues, which oftentimes do not recognize formal borders, is needed to enhance the countries' ability to confront common problems.

Recognizing the importance of integration in the Southern Cone, research on Paraguay's role in the international drug trafficking trade must shift away from the context of U.S.- Paraguayan relations and toward a more regional framework. This will give greater import to Paraguay's immediate national interests that are increasingly being defined by its economic and commercial relations with its Southern Cone neighbors. Part of the discussion on free trade and economic integration must include drug trafficking. For example, the effects that the liberalization of trade and economy will have on the flow of drugs and illicit drug money in the Southern Cone is an important question that must be addressed within this larger discussion of economic integration.

It is, therefore, important to elaborate on the need to study further how international drug trafficking is becoming a prominent transnational issue that is changing not only the dynamics of the international system but also the social, economic, and political structure of these national societies.

Notes

1. Some of the few works dedicated to the study of Paraguayan foreign relations before 1989 include Luis Benítez, *Historia diplomática del Paraguay*. Asuncion: El Gráfico S.R.L., 1972; Carlos Calvo, *La República del Paraguay y sus relaciones exteriores*. Asuncion: Editorial Aravera, 1985; *Carlos Plate, Diplomacia y política exterior*. Asuncion: Cuadernos Republicanos Editorial, 1988; Mladen Yopo, "La política exterior del Paraguay: Continuidad y cambio en el aislamiento." In *América Latina y el Caribe: Políticas exteriores para sobrevivir*. Edited by Heraldo Muñoz. PROSPEL-CERC. Buenos Aires: Grupo Editor Latinoamericano, 1985: 447-467.

2. For a review of the transnationalization of world politics and issues, see, for example, Robert Keohane and Joseph Nye, *Power and Interdependence: World Politics in Transition*, Boston: Little, Brown and Company, 1977; James Rosenau, *The Study of Global Interdependence: Essays on the Transnationalization of World Affairs*. New York: Nichols, 1980; and Joseph Nye, "The Changing Nature of World Power." *Political Science Quarterly*, vol. 105, no. 2 (Summer 1990): 177-192;

3. Some of these works include José Luis Simon, ed. *Política exterior y relaciones exteriores del Paraguay contemporáneo*. Asuncion: Centro Paraguayo de Estudios Sociológicos, 1990; Mladen Yopo, *Paraguay Stroessner: La política exterior del régimen autoritario (1954-1989)*. Santiago de Chile: PROSPEL, 1991; and Frank O. Mora, *Enclaustramiento, hegemonía, dependencia, interdependencia, y aislamiento: Relaciones internacionales del Paraguay: 1811-1981*. Asuncion: Centro Paraguayo de Estudios Sociológicos, 1992.

4. Lewis and Adams identified General Andrés Rodríguez, former commander of the First Army Corps and then president of Paraguay, and Stroessner's chief of police General Patricio Colman of protecting Ricord. Rodríguez had purportedly turned his ranches into airstrips where planes would haul their cargos of narcotics (see also Lewis 1980, 136-137; Mora 1988, 99).

5. During this time, Paraguay signed two bilateral agreements with the United States dealing with drug trafficking and extradition. In 1972 Paraguay signed an accord with the United States to "combat the illicit use and trafficking of narcotics and other dangerous drugs." In 1973 an extradition treaty was signed which led to the extradition of Ricord. Under U.S. pressure, Paraguay also signed several multilateral conventions, accords, and protocols such as the 1961 Sole Convention on Narcotics (ratified by Paraguay in December 1971), the Convention on Psychotropic Substances (Vienna, 1971), and the South American Accord on Drugs and Psychotropic Substances (Buenos Aires, 1973) (Simon 1992).

6. It is important to note that Paraguay also signed a number of bilateral agreements with Brazil and other Southern Cone countries during this period (Simon 1992).

7. It is important to note that Adams provided no documental evidence proving or even backing allegations that government and military officials provided safe haven to heroin smugglers in Paraguay.

8. See also Mora, *Enclaustramiento, hegemonía...*, 1992.

9. This has been known as the "balloon effect" which means that as pressure is applied in one area, the flow moves into other areas of the sphere.

10. When members of the U.S. Congress visited Paraguay in 1985, the Paraguayan government promised that it would destroy nearly 50,000 gallons of chemicals that were believed to have been intended for the manufacture of cocaine. With that much chemical precursor in hand, it is thought that drug traffickers could make about 8 tons of cocaine — about 10 percent of U.S. supply for a year (Brinkley 1985a, A4). The Paraguayan government agreed to destroy the chemicals after having earlier refused a U.S. solicitation to destroy them (*Narcotics Control Digest* 1985).

11. The Paraguayan government resisted pressures from the United States until 1988. Government officials accused Ambassador Taylor of interfering in Paraguay's internal affairs and threatened to declare him "persona non grata" (the conflict had also much to do with U.S. pressures for democracy in Paraguay). See the *Washington Post* 1988b, A33.

12. In September 1988 Paraguay and the United States signed the "Accord on Mutual Cooperation between the Government of the Republic of Paraguay and the Government of the United States of America for the Reduction of Demand and Illicit Consumption, and to Combat the Production and Illicit Traffic of Drugs" (Simon 1992).

13. Despite growing cooperation from the Stroessner regime, the United States expressed some concern over allegations made by Senator Augusto Cáceres Carisimo that the Department of Narcotics of the Interior Ministry (DNDP) was "the largest drug trafficker in the country" (*Nuestro Tiempo* 1988).

14. Evidence exists that suggests that Rodríguez was deeply involved in trading illicit drugs in the early 1970s, mainly heroin, which may have produced his biggest profits; "however, evidence of Rodríguez's involvement is fragmentary, incomplete and often circumstantial" (Roett and Sacks 1991, 134). For further evidence, see Oppenheimer 1989, A19; and Brooke 1989, A3.

15. President Andrés Rodríguez also strongly supported Bush's "Enterprise for the Americas Initiative" and Operation Desert Storm.

16. Since 1989 Paraguay has signed the following multilateral and bilateral agreements: 1) Convention against the Illicit Traffic of Narcotics and Psychotropic Substances (Vienna, 1989), 2) Convention on the Prevention of the Illegal Use and Repression of Illicit Traffic of Narcotics and Psychotropic Substances (Asuncion, November 1989), 3) Convention between the Republic of Paraguay and the Republic of Chile on the Prevention of Illegal Use and Repression of Illicit Traffic of Narcotics and Psychotropic Substances (Santiago, September 1990), 4) Accord between the Governments of Paraguay and Uruguay on the Prevention, Control, Fiscalization, and Repression of the Illegal Consumption and Illicit Traffic of Narcotics and Psychotropic Substances and their Precursor and Chemical Products (Asuncion, May 1991) — see Simon 1992.

17. It is also important to note here that Paraguay had been cooperating with its neighbors since 1985 (Cagliotti 1985 and 1987).

18. See, for example, Paraguayan newspaper articles cited above or in the references that deal with frictions between Paraguayan government officials and U.S. Ambassador Clyde Taylor concerning allegations by Taylor that government authorities were involved in the drug trade.

19. Roett and Sacks (1991) also cite a 1989 Department of Justice report that reveals the amount of cocaine travelling through Paraguay and how the country was being used by the drug barons to export cocaine to Europe and the United States (165).

20. In the face of allegations concerning Rodríguez's past involvement in the drug trade, it was a top priority of his administration to clean his image and to dismiss any suggestion of his or his government's involvement in drug trafficking.

21. *Abc color* and other media sources have stated that former officials of the Stroessner regime, who until recently held high political positions in eastern Paraguay, have been operating clandestine airports used in the transport of all types of contraband, including drugs. *Abc color* has reported that Ciudad del Este is in the hands of a Paraguayan "Medellin Cartel" (Simon and Mora 1991, 37).

22. The debate on the creation of the Secretaría Nacional Antidroga (SENAD) and on reforming Law 1340/88 has been impressively frank and open (*Ne-engatu* 1991, 17-18). After an open debate, the creation of SENAD, which had been decreed by President Rodríguez on May 16, 1991, was approved by the legislature in December 1991 (Simon 1992).

23. One recent article that alleges that President Rodríguez is laundering drug money was published by an Uruguayan newspaper (Blixen 1991, 3-5).

24. Another concern of the United States is the continued use of Paraguay as a safe haven for laundering drug money (Aquino 1991; Amarilla 1992). The only instruments that exist for controlling this activity are recent measures adopted by the Paraguayan Central Bank and the Executive which force financial institutions to report any transaction beyond US$10,000 (Banco Central del Paraguay 1989; Paraguayan Executive 1989).

References

abc color (Asuncion). 1992. "Lucharán contra narcodólares." February 25:11.

abc color. 1991. "Coordinarán lucha contra narcos." April 14:22.

abc color. 1990a. "Tres países firman acuerdo para la lucha anti-narcóticos." June 13:28.

abc color. 1990b. "Paraguay es puente para tráfico de drogas hacia Europa, dicen." January 24:6

abc color. 1989. "Utilizan glifosato para destruir marihuana." April 3:44.

Abente, Diego. 1988. "Constraints and Opportunities: Prospects for Democratization in Paraguay." *Journal of Interamerican Studies and World Affairs* 30, 1 (Spring):73-104.

Adams, Nathan. 1973. "The Hunt for Andre." *Reader's Digest* March:223-259.

Alexander, Andrew, and Jeff Nesmith. 1988. "U.S. Envoy Thwarted 'Sting' in Paraguay: Ex-ambassador Says He Blocked DEA." *Sun-Sentinel,* November 5:16A.

Amarilla, José María. 1992. "Comercio y finanzas: La nueva cultura económica." *Hoy,* February 8:18-19.

Aquino, Miguel Angel. 1991. "Claves sobre el lavado del narcodinero." *Acción,* August:11-13.

Atlanta Constitution. 1988a. "Drug Probe Blocked to Shield Top Paraguayans." November 13:23A.

Atlanta Constitution. 1988b. "Florida Lawmaker Vows 'Bitter Fight' to Expose Paraguayan Link to Drugs." December 18:18A.

Bagley, Bruce Michael. 1989. "Narco-Diplomacy: Drug Trafficking and U.S.-Latin American Relations." Testimony before the U.S. House of Representatives Committee on Narcotics Abuse and Control. *Drugs and Latin America: Economic and Political Impact and U.S. Policy Options.* Proceedings of a seminar held by the Congressional Research Service, April 26.

Banco Central del Paraguay. 1989. "Resolution No. 9, Act No. 28."

DOPI/Circular No. 9/89, February 28 and DOPI/Circular No. 12/89, March 9.

Bird, Kai, and Max Holland. 1985. "Paraguay: The Stroessner Connection." *Nation,* October 26:401.

Blixen, Samuel. 1991. "El Presidente Rodríguez lava narcodólares." *Brecha,* 7, 314 (November 6):2-5.

Bouvier, Virginia. 1988. *Decline of a Dictator: Paraguay at a Cross-roads.* Washington, D.C.: Washington Office on Latin America.

Brinkley, Joel. 1985a. "Paraguay Pledges Action on Cocaine: Reportedly Tells Congressmen It Will Destroy Chemicals Used to Produce Drug." *The New York Times,* January 23:A4.

Brinkley, Joel. 1985b. "U.S. Aides Suspect Paraguay Officials of a Narcotics Link." *The New York Times,* January 3:A1, A8.

Brooke, J. 1989. "Paraguay Voting in Open Elections." *The New York Times*, May 1:A3.

Boveda, Rafael. 1985. "El tráfico de drogas." *Nuestro Tiempo* (Asuncion), October 3:39-49.

Burr, J. Millard. 1988. "Narcotics Trafficking in Paraguay: An Asuncion Perspective." U.S. Department of State, Bureau of Intelligence and Research, Office of Terrorism and Narcotics Analysis.

Cagliotti, Carlos Norberto. 1985. "The Role of the South American Agreement on Narcotics Drugs and Psychotropic Substances in the Fight against Illicit Drug Trafficking." *Bulletin on Narcotics*, 35, 4:83-95.

Cagliotti, Carlos Norberto. 1987. "Cooperation between South American Countries in the Struggle against Drug Abuse and Illicit Drug Trafficking." *Bulletin on Narcotics*, 39, 1, 61-67.

Cambio (Asuncion). 1989. "El negociado de las drogas: y seguimos siendo el 'trampolín..," April 21:19.

Carrizosa, Agustin. 1991. *Reordenamiento institucional en la lucha contra el narcotráfico y el uso indebido de drogas*. Asuncion: Secretaría Nacional Anti-Drogas (SENAD).

Clark, Evert, and Nicholas Horrock. 1973. *Contrabandista!* New York: Praeger.

Cohen, Roger. 1989. "Paraguay Ousts Its Aging Dictator, But Democracy May Take Longer." *Wall Street Journal*, February 6:A6.

Cohen, Roger. 1988. "Paraguay Provides a Haven for Smugglers." *Wall Street Journal*, December 23:A8.

Diario de Noticias (Asuncion). 1990a. "DINAR y DEA coordinan la lucha contra narcotráfico." July 28:49.

Diario de Noticias. 1990b. "Balance de un año de guerra al narcotráfico." April 18:20.

Diario de Noticias. 1990c. "El narcotráfico se extiende." April 11:48.

Diario de Noticias. 1989a. "Guerra frontal al narcotráfico." November 2:35.

Diario de Noticias. 1989b. "Rodríguez y Thurman trataron sobre drogas: en apoyo de la campaña de George Bush." November 1:12.

Diario de Noticias. 1989c. "Vicedirector de la DEA en diputados: Plantean acción directa contra narcotráfico." August 8:2.

Diario de Noticias. 1989d. "Lucha internacional contra el narcotráfico en Asunción." July 11:32.

Diario de Noticias. 1989e. "Nuevas 'armas' contra drogas." March 6:4.

Diario de Noticias. 1989f. "Narcotráfico: Uno de los peores flegelos. Así lo calificó el presidente Rodríguez, anunciando que abogará por leyes más severas." February 7, Special Supplement:4-5.

Diario de Noticias. 1988. "Salvidar réplica: 'Qué de nombres.'" March 12:8.

Gelbard, Robert. 1988a. Prepared Statement to the Subcommittee on Western Hemisphere Affairs. Committee on Foreign Affairs, U.S. House of Representatives, Washington D.C., March 29.

Gelbard, Robert. 1988b. Prepared Statement to the Task Force on International Narcotics Control. Committee on Foreign Affairs, U.S. House of Representatives, Washington, D.C., March 17.

Goshko, John M. 1985. "U.S. Prods Paraguay on Cocaine." *Washington Post*, January 4:A18.

Hoy (Asuncion). 1992. "Existen cerca de 1500 pistas de aviación." February 11:23.

Hoy. 1989. February 10:6.

Hoy. 1988a. "Sobre supuesta protección a narcotráfico expresada por Taylor: Terminante rechazo de la Cancillería," March 12:8.

Hoy. 1988b. "Altos funcionarios protegen el narcotráfico, según Taylor." March 11:11.

Hoyer, Hans. 1975. "Paraguay." In *Latin American Foreign Policies: An Analysis*, eds. Harold E. Davis and Larman C. Wilson. Baltimore: Johns Hopkins University Press, 294-305.

Labra, Fernando. 1990. "Paraguay: Nuevo perfil internacional." *Perspectiva Internacional Paraguaya*, 2, 4 (July-December):7-33.

Laino, Domingo. 1979. *Paraguay: represión, estafa y anti-comunismo*. Ediciones Cerro Cora.

Latin American Bureau. 1980. *Paraguay Power Game*. London: Russell Press.

Latin American Report. 1974. "Paraguay: 1001 nights." 8, 34 (August 30):270.

Latin American Report. 1972. "Paraguay: Two for the Pot." 6, 34 (August 25):269-270.

Latin American Report. 1971a. "Paraguay: A Second Look." 5, 47 (November 19):370-371.

Latin American Report. 1971b. "Paraguay: Turning on with General Stroessner," 5, 42 (October 15):329-330.

Latin American Regional Report. 1985. "The Guarani Connection." August 6:6.

Latin American Weekly Report. 1985. "Cocaine Route Turns North," January 18:5.

Latinamerica Press. 1988. "Paraguay Officials Blamed for Condoning Drug Trade." March 24:1.

Lee, Rensselaer. 1987. "The Drug Trade and Developing Countries." *Policy Focus*, 4 (June).

Lewis, Paul. 1980. *Paraguay Under Stroessner*. Chapel Hill: University of North Carolina Press.

Martínez, Nelson. 1990. "El narcotráfico amenaza al país." *El Diario de Noticias*, January 7:10.

Masi, Fernando. 1991. "Relaciones internacionales del Paraguay con Stroessner y sin Stroessner." Working paper of the Instituto Paraguayo para la Integración de América Latina (IDIAL). Asuncion.

Masi, Fernando. 1990. "Paraguay: Hasta cuando la diplomacia presidencialista?" Paper presented for the 1990-1991 issue of PROSPEL-CERC's foreign policies of Latin American and Caribbean countries. Santiago de Chile.

Masi, Fernando. 1989. *Stroessner: la extinción de un modelo político en Paraguay*. Asuncion: Intercontinental Editora.

Miami News. 1988. "Fugitive in Miami Cocaine Case Is Son of Paraguayan Dictator's Pal." November 4:4A.

Mora, Frank. 1990. "Relaciones Estados Unidos-Paraguay: conflicto y cooperación." *Perspectiva Internacional Paraguay*. 2, 3 (January-June):79-94.

Mora, Frank. 1988. "Política exterior del Paraguay: a la búsqueda de la independencia y el desarrollo." *Revista Paraguaya de Sociología*. 25, 73 (September-December):253-271.

Narcotics Control Digest. 1985 "Paraguay Refuses to Destroy Cocaine Production Chemicals." January 9:10-11.

Ne-engatu. 1991. "Narcotráfico y adicción a drogas ilegales." 9, 53 (December):17-18.

Newsweek. 1972. "Heroin: Now It's the Latin Connection." 79, 1 (January 24):24-26.

Nuestro Tiempo. 1988. "La Dirección de Narcóticos acusada de traficante." 3, 28 (May):44.

Oppenheimer, Andres. 1989. "Paraguay's New Ruler Had Disputes with Stroessner." *Washington Post*, February 4:A19.

Organization of American States. 1986. *Socio-Economic Studies for the Inter-American Specialized Conference on Drug Traffic*.

Inter-American Specialized Conference on Traffic in Narcotic Drugs. OEA/Ser.K/XXXI.1, CEIN/Doc. 7/86. February 12.

Paraguayan Executive Branch. 1989. "Regimen de cambios para las importaciones y exportaciones de bienes y servicios y el movimiento para bancos." Executive Decree No. 216, February 27.

Patria (Asuncion). 1990. "Paraguay y Estados Unidos intensificarán lucha contra drogas." June 16:9.

Patria. 1988. "Narcotráfico, Reagan y cooperación." March 11:2.

Riding, Alan. 1989. "Paraguay's Leader Denies Ties to Drugs." *The New York Times*, February 7.

Roett, Riordan. 1989. "Paraguay after Stroessner." *Foreign Affairs*, 62, 2 (Spring):124-142.

Roett, Riordan, and Richard Scott Sacks. 1991. *Paraguay: The Persona-list Legacy*. Boulder: Westview Press.

Rosenberg, Tina. 1987. "Smuggler's Paradise." *New Republic*. 196 (June 8):14-15.

Sendero (Asuncion). 1987. "Entrevista con el embajador Clayde Taylor." August 24.

Simon, José Luis. 1992. *El narcotráfico en el Paraguay. Condicionantes externos e internos, y sus repercusiones locales y para las relaciones internacionales del país*. Asuncion: Centro Paraguayo de Estudios Sociológicos.

Simon, José Luis. 1991. "La política exterior Paraguaya en 1991: Modernización insuficiente, carencia de una visión global y condicionamientos de un estado prebendario en crisis." Paper presented for the 1991-1992 issue of PROSPEL-CERC's foreign policies of Latin American and Caribbean countries. Santiago de Chile.

Simon, José Luis. 1990a. "La lucha contra el narcotráfico en la transición a la democracia." Prepared statement to the Committee on the Fight Against Narcotics of the Paraguayan Chamber of Deputies.

Simon, José Luis. 1990b. "El Paraguay y el narcotráfico." *abc color*, March 24:26.

Simon, José Luis. 1989. "Del aislamiento a la reincorporación internacional: El Paraguay de la inmediata transición post-stronista." *Perspectiva Internacional Paraguaya*, 1, 1-2 (January-June and July-December):163-200.

Simon, José Luis. 1988a. "El despotismo republicano de Paraguay en su hora cero." *Nueva Sociedad*, 95 (May-June):25-41.

Simon, José Luis. 1988b. "El autoritarismo paraguayo teme su `panamenización.'" *Nuestro Tiempo*, 3, (March 25):4-7.

Simon, José Luis. 1988c. "Narcotráfico vía Paraguay irrita a Washington." *Sendero 15*, January 15.

Simon, José Luis. 1987. "El narcotráfico afecta nuestras relaciones internacionales." *Sendero 15*, October 16.

Sun Sentinel. 1989. "Paraguayan Ruler Tied to Drugs: Secret U.S. Report Says Gen. Rodríguez 'No. 1 Trafficker,'" February 5:17A.

Surret, W.R. 1988. "The International Narcotics Trade: An Overview of its Dimensions, Production Sources, and Organizations." Washington, D.C.: The Congressional Research Service, October 3.

La Tarde. 1988. "Altos funcionarios protegen narcotráfico." March 11:9.

Tokatlián, Juan G., and Bruce M. Bagley, eds. 1990. *Economía y política del narcotráfico*. Bogota: CEI/UNIANDES/CEREC.

U.S. House Foreign Affairs Committee. 1988. Hearing. "Narcotics Review in South America." One Hundredth Congress, Second Session. Washington, D.C.

United States Department of State-Bureau of International Narcotics Matters. 1989. "Paraguay." *International Narcotics Control Strategy Report*. Washington D.C., March.

United States Department of State-Bureau of International Narcotics Matters. 1990. "Paraguay." *International Narcotics Control Strategy Report*. Washington, D.C., March.

U.S. News and World Report. 1989. "The Last Tango in Paraguay," February 13:14.

Ultima Hora. 1988a. "Investigaciones sobre las drogas están en su inicio," March 12:12.

Ultima Hora. 1988b. "Según embajador, Paraguay es fuente significativa," March 11:13.

Ultima Hora. 1988c. "Taylor citó puntos críticos en la relación con Paraguay." February 23:13.

(El) *Universal*. 1990. "Apoyar iniciativa de Bush acordó el Grupo de Rio." Caracas, Venezuela, October 13:12.

Vinocur, John. 1984. "A Republic of Fear: Thirty Years of General Stroessner's Paraguay." *The New York Times Magazine*, 134 (September):21-32, 36-40, 93-94, 101.

Washington Post. 1989. "Coup Leader Denies Drug Link, Schedules Election," February 7:A7

Washington Post. 1988a. "Something Rotten in Paraguay," June 14:A23.

Washington Post. 1988b. "U.S. Drug-Trade Allegations Anger Top Paraguayans," March 31:A33.

Washington Post. 1988c. "U.S. Presses Paraguay to Fight Drug Trade," March 7:A23.

Wrobleski, Ann. 1988a. Testimony to the Subcommittee on Western Hemisphere Affairs. Committee on Foreign Affairs, U.S. House of Representatives, Washington, D.C., March 29.

Wrobleski, Ann. 1988b. Testimony to the Task Force on International Narcotics Control. Committee on Foreign Affairs, U.S. House of Representatives, Washington, D.C., March 17.

Yopo, Mladen. 1991. *Paraguay Stroessner: La política exterior del régimen autoritario, 1954-1989.* Santiago de Chile: PROSPEL.

Bibliographical Note

Since 1986-1987 Paraguayan newspapers and magazines have published an extensive number of news reports and unauthored articles on drug seizures, public drug policy, and joint operations with the United States and other Southern Cone countries. A number of these news articles, which have not been used specifically for this chapter, have appeared in the following Paraguayan periodicals:

Newspapers: abc color, Cambio Auténtico, Diario de Noticias, Hoy, Patria, La Tarde (not in circulation since 1988), and Ultima Hora.

Magazines: Acción, Análisis del Mes, Nuestro Tiempo, and Ne-engatu.

Mexico

Chapter Nineteen

Drug Trafficking in U.S.-Mexican Relations: What You See Is What You Get

Jorge Chabat

"Economic embargoes historically haven't worked," Richard G. Darman, the budget director, said. "The international trade system does not respond to declarations of embargo or the closing of borders," he added. "The market responds to price, and in an embargo, the price goes up and the incentive to violate the embargo increases."

"Right," the President said. "Iraq would just find a new middleman. Where there was a buck to be made, someone would buy and sell the oil," Bush said. "Like my Texas friends."

— Bob Woodward, *The Commanders*. New York: Simon & Schuster, 1991, 228.

Introduction

Until the 1970s drug trafficking was not a major consideration in the U.S.-Mexican relationship, despite the growing traffic in opiates and marijuana across the border since the late 1940s (Walker 1989).[1] In fact, until the late 1960s when signs of friction in the bilateral relationship over drugs surfaced, Washington and Mexico had maintained very cordial relations. In 1969, however, the Nixon administration's unilateral imposition of Operation Intercept on the border with Mexico underscored not only the end of the

---

The author would like to thank Bruce M. Bagley, William O. Walker III, Jeffrey Stark, Adrian Bonilla, and Eileen Scott for their valuable comments and their help in the final version of this article.

"special relationship"[2] but also the emergence of a new issue in the bilateral agenda: drug trafficking.

Since Operation Intercept, drug trafficking has been present in the U.S.-Mexican relationship with differing degrees of conflict. However, the friction which appeared during the 1980s surpassed all previous levels and led many observers to speculate about the "poisoning effect" of narcotics on the relationship. According to this thesis, the level of conflict between the two countries is a direct consequence of the volume of drugs smuggled from Mexico into the United States:

> . . . the relationship's tone depends on Mexico's share of the U.S. illicit drug market, particularly its heroin and cocaine components. The larger Mexico's share, the greater Washington's pressures to eradicate. The greater the pressure, the more confrontational U.S.-Mexican narcopolitics and bilateral relations in general. Conversely, when market share indicators are favorable so too are relations (Craig 1989, 78-79).[3]

This explanation supposes that the natural tendency toward friendship and cooperation between both countries can be seriously affected by a criminal enterprise to which the Mexican government is highly vulnerable. It further assumes that the inability of Mexico to stop the flow of drugs to its neighbor — and the accompanying undesirable effects of this traffic, like Enrique Camarena's assassination — cause retaliation by the U.S. government. From this perspective, Mexican governments would be unfairly punished because of a phenomenon for which they are not responsible and which they cannot control. Behind this position lies the assumptions that drug trafficking is a real problem of national security for Mexico and the United States, that both governments have the political will to fight it, and that if the Mexican government fails to stop the flow of narcotics, it is because of the weakness of its institutions and the corrupting effect of narcodollars.

Notwithstanding the popularity of these theses in academic and journalistic literature,[4] a closer analysis of the phenomenon over the last decade suggests that this explanation is not entirely accurate: a) higher levels of conflict do not always correspond to higher levels of narcotics introduced into American territory and vice-versa; b) undesirable effects of drug trafficking do not necessarily poison the bilateral relationship; and c) drug trafficking is not a matter of the "actually existing national security,"[5] and it serves to hide other "real" national security concerns for Mexico and the United States.

From this perspective, it seems that drug trafficking acts only as an amplifier of the general tone of the relationship: if the relationship is good, the drug issue serves as a pretext to praise Mexico's will for cooperation and the U.S. government's respect for Mexican sovereignty; if the relationship is bad, it serves to highlight U.S. allegations of the corruption and ineffectiveness of Mexican administrations and, conversely, to cause Mexican governments to raise the flag of nationalism.

The first part of this chapter will look briefly at the role played by drug trafficking in the bilateral relationship before 1980. The second part will refer to the conflict in the bilateral relation associated —wrongly, in our perspective — with drug trafficking in the mid-1980s. We will then analyze the recent era of open cooperation between both countries in the last part of the 1980s. Finally, we will develop some conclusions.

Background: The Unwelcome Guest in the Bilateral Relationship

During the 1970s, the drug issue in the U.S.-Mexican relationship seemed to behave according to the "poisoning effect" theory. After pressures from the United States to make the Mexican government fight drug trafficking, the results were very successful. As we have mentioned, in 1969 the U.S. government implemented Operation Intercept.[6] This operation, which entailed the inspection of vehicles coming from Mexico to search for drugs, seriously affected tourism to Mexico and provoked an immediate response from the Díaz-Ordaz government, which declared its disposition to collaborate decisively in the fight against drug trafficking. This gave birth to the so-called Operation Cooperation. As a consequence of this operation, the Echeverría government implemented in the mid-1970s the most successful campaign against drug trafficking developed by Mexico: Operation Condor.

The effects of this campaign on the two drugs for export —heroin and marijuana— were clearly visible. According to U.S. State Department sources, in 1974 the "brown" heroin produced in Mexico represented 85 percent of the total volume of this drug arriving on U.S. territory. In 1976, the percentage was 53 percent, and in 1980, it was only 37 percent.[7] In the case of marijuana, the decrease was even clearer: the Mexican share in the American market fell from 90 percent in 1974 to around 5 percent in 1981.[8] The effectiveness of this campaign has, over the years, served as an example of what a Third World country could achieve with effort and good will[9] and, doubtless, nurtured the "poisoning effect" theory. During these years, the topic was not a point of friction in the bilateral relationship, and the Mexican government treated drug trafficking as a national security matter.[10]

Why was Operation Condor so successful? Craig (1980) mentions several factors that combined in the mid-1970s to boost drug production and trafficking:

1) campesino desperation and the resort to drug cultivation and trafficking; 2) arming of the campesino and professional trafficker with weapons often superior to those of local and national law enforcement officers; 3) open and increasingly violent defiance of law and authority; 4) infusion into the Sierras of enormous sums of money from narcotics sales that came to dominate local and regional economies, politicians, judges, and police; and 5) the merging of these trends in areas that have traditionally been the breeding grounds for rural guerrilla movements (360-361).[11]

Without entering into a discussion of the weight of every factor in explaining the commitment of Mexico's government in the fight against drug trafficking, it seems that drug trafficking posed "a threat to the control by the government and the all-pervasive Partido Revolucionario Institucional (PRI) over the entire country from Tijuana to Merida."[12] Thus, it seems that there was a clear determination in the Mexican government to combat drug smuggling in a context where drug trafficking could develop links with forces acting outside the system, like the guerrillas in the southern part of Mexico.

All this suggests that during the 1970s the "poisoning effect" theory explains the U.S.-Mexican relationship, since the assumption that the topic was considered a matter of national security was, in fact, true. In this sense, the relation of drug trafficking to the Mexican political system during the 1970s — acting outside of political parameters — is closer to the "Colombian model,"[13] which explains the confrontational response of the government. However, the military defeat of the guerrilla forces combined with a political openness — which allowed the legal participation of some forces who were operating clandestinely during the 1970s — built during the 1980s a more propitious environment for a different insertion of drug trafficking into the Mexican political framework. As we will see below, by the mid-1980s, drug traffickers were no longer a threat to the "actually existing" national security[14] but a tolerated actor in the Mexican political system.

Drug Trafficking in the Bilateral Relationship: The Poisoned Years

There are many factors that explain the revival of drug trafficking in Mexico in the early 1980s. Among them we can find an increase in the production of narcotics for climatic reasons (1984 was a year with high precipitation); a greater difficulty in the spraying of the drug plantations with herbicides (there were more cloudy days which obstructed the operation); great ingenuity on the part of peasants who learned to plant poppy in a very dispersed way; an increasing incapacity and poor administration in the Mexican bureaucracy in charge of the fight against drug trafficking; the resurgence of Colombia as a major producer of cocaine, which increased the importance of Mexico as a point of transit for drugs on the way to the United States; the deterioration of the Mexican economy, which made it more attractive for peasants to cultivate narcotics; the corruption of Mexican forces in charge of the antidrug campaign; and the deterioration of this campaign as a result of the bureaucratic inertia of the Mexican offices involved.[15] We can also mention the "balloon effect" explanation: the success of the Florida Task Force's interdiction campaign against Colombian marijuana favored the resurgence of Mexican production of cannabis.[16] Another reason that has been suggested as a cause for this increase in drug trafficking is the "oil boom," which "spread funds throughout the government-PRI apparatus, increased the incomes of the middle and upper classes, and whetted the appetite for corruption at high levels."[17]

If all of the above-mentioned factors can explain the resurgence of narcotics smuggling in Mexico, what explains its prosperity in the years to follow is a change of attitude in the Mexican government. The complacency — and, in many cases, complicity — of the Mexican officers supposedly in charge of combating drug trafficking during the 1980s suggests that the determination to fight drug trafficking had decreased substantially[18] (because it was not perceived as a threat to the "actually existing national security") and that drug traffickers were tolerated — but not legal — actors in the Mexican political system.[19]

In this sense, the Mexican government's reluctance to fight drug trafficking frontally is quite coherent with its traditional perception of the phenomenon as a demand-side problem. If the origins of drug trafficking are in the insatiable appetite of American drug addicts, it makes no sense to combat it where drugs are produced. In other words, if the origins of the problem are on the *other* side of the border, it does not seem very reasonable to spend vast economic and human resources, threatening Mexican stability, by fighting the war on *this* side of the border.

The conflict in the U.S.-Mexican relationship in the mid-1980s found fertile terrain upon which to grow in the issue of drug trafficking. However, the friction between both countries during de la Madrid's government can hardly be explained *only* or even *principally* by drug trafficking. In reality, what provoked the growing concern of the United States about its southern neighbor was, as Cornelius suggests, a feeling of vulnerability with respect to the consequences of an economic and political collapse in Mexico.[20] This feeling had its origins in the 1982 Mexican financial crisis and provoked the most severe pressure from the United States in recent decades.

The list of concrete forms that the conflict assumed from 1985 to 1987 is long, but perhaps the most serious incident was indeed associated with drug trafficking: the kidnapping and assassination, in February 1985, of the Drug Enforcement Administration (DEA) agent, Enrique Camarena, by Mexican drug traffickers, with the complicity of several members of the Mexican police in charge of the fight against drugs and, probably, of high Mexican government authorities.

After Camarena's assassination, the drug issue contributed significantly to the open deterioration of the U.S.-Mexican relationship. On February 17, 1985, only ten days after the disappearance of Camarena, the American government implemented the so-called second Operation Intercept. One week later, the strict inspection of vehicles crossing the border was replaced by the partial closing of the border with the same purpose: restricting the flow of drugs into U.S. territory (González 1985, 24-25).[21]

In 1986 tension escalated. In January of that year, the DEA decided to enact its own form of justice and sponsored the kidnapping of René Verdugo Urquídez to U.S. territory for his alleged involvement in the assassination of Camarena (Shannon 1989, 350).[22] On March 8, 1986, the American government closed 75 percent of the customs houses on the border with Mexico, arguing that this was in order to search for drugs and arms introduced by Libyan terrorists. One month later, on April 16, the American embassy in Mexico City suspended the issuing of visas until August, arguing that this was for security reasons related to possible terrorist actions (González et al. 1986, 8).[23] On May 12 and 13, 1986, Senator Jesse Helms (R-N.C.) chaired a hearing at the Senate Foreign Relations Subcommittee on the Western Hemisphere to analyze the Mexican situation. In those hearings, prominent members of the Reagan administration accused the Mexican government of continuous "electoral fraud" and corruption on a "massive" scale. As one might suppose, the drug issue was not absent, and the U.S. Customs Commissioner, William Von Raab, accused the governor of the Mexican state of Sonora of growing marijuana and opium poppies on his farms, which were guarded by the Mexican army.[24]

Actually, during those years, the implication of high members of the Mexican government in drug trafficking by the American media was a constant occurrence. Thus, the names mentioned included also the Mexican Minister of Defense, General Juan Arévalo Gardoqui; his son, Juan Alejandro Arévalo, who worked in 1986 as a federal prosecutor in Baja California; the head of the Mexican Security police, José Antonio Zorrilla Pérez; Miguel Aldana, head of Mexico's Interpol Office; and even a cousin of President de la Madrid.[25] The incarceration of Zorrilla Pérez and Aldana in 1989 and 1990, charged with drug trafficking, indicated that some measure of these accusations was right and that the embedding of drug traffickers in the political system was not merely a suspicion.

Although it may appear obvious, it is worth emphasizing that the avalanche of pressures that Camarena's murder provoked was due to the anger and frustration of the DEA over the killing of one of its agents and not because of the amount of drugs introduced into the United States. The pressures of the U.S. government were not directed toward the drug lords but rather toward the participants in the crime. The non-publicized kidnapping of Verdugo Urquídez and the highly well-publicized kidnapping of Humberto Alvarez Macháin are related to the assassination of Camarena, not to the traffic of narcotics in itself. The American interest in Verdugo or Macháin — who were not known as big drug dealers — contrasts with the benevolence toward the "big fishes," like Miguel Angel Félix Gallardo, who was circulating freely in Mexico despite repeated media reports about his involvement in drug trafficking, until the Salinas government arrested him in 1989.

If one looks at the amount of marijuana and heroin produced in Mexico (see Table 1), there is, indeed, a continuing increase from 1982 to 1987. The net production of marijuana increased from 750 metric tons in 1982 to 5,933 tons in 1987 (an increase of around 800 percent), while the net production of heroin increased from 17 metric tons in 1982 to 50 tons in 1987 (an increase of around 300 percent). However, the penetration in the American market of both drugs did not increase in the same way.

In 1986 Mexico was the source of 38 percent of the heroin sold in the United States (Morganthau, Shannon, Contreras 1986),[26] practically the same percentage it represented in 1980 (37 percent).[27] The growth of marijuana exports was more evident: the Mexican share of the U.S. market increased from 5 percent in 1981[28] to 32 percent in 1986.[29] Even though these figures are not conclusive, the "poisoning effect" theory could be successfully applied to explain the conflict that characterized the bilateral relationship during those years. From the perspective of this theory, what caused friction between both countries was the lack of effectiveness in the battle against drug trafficking by the Mexican government. As one American senior official said in 1986, "the trouble is, even though they are doing more, the problem is growing at an even more rapid rate" (Brinkley 1986).[30]

However, as we will see below, the enormous increase in drug production in Mexican territory from 1987 to 1991, combined with the near-disappearance of conflict in the diplomatic relationship between both countries, suggests that the "poisoning effect" theory is not sufficient to explain the impact of drug trafficking in the bilateral agenda.

Drug Trafficking in the Bilateral Relationship: The Happy Years

By 1988, after three years of conflict without precedent in U.S.-Mexican relations, the tone changed abruptly. In 1987, there were some signs of improvement with the replacement of Ambassador John Gavin. By mid-1988, there was no doubt about it. The poisoned years were over. In July 1988

President Ronald Reagan hastened to congratulate PRI candidate Carlos Salinas de Gortari. This attitude contrasts clearly with the previous critiques of Mexico's electoral processes. The reason for this change in American policy toward Mexico are probably related to the poor success of the policy of pressures over the prior three years to promote stability in Mexico, as well as due to the fact that the main opponent of the PRI presidential candidate was the moderate leftist Cuauhtémoc Cárdenas, who presumably was not a better alternative in the eyes of the White House.

Whatever the motivations for this change, the impact on the visibility of the drug issue was substantial. It practically disappeared as a conflictive topic on the bilateral agenda. The proclaimed "spirit of Houston," which arose from the meeting between the elected presidents Bush and Salinas on November 1988, proved to be the defining characteristic of the relation between both presidents. The will to emphasize the positive aspects of the relationship, in order to achieve common goals like the North American Free Trade Agreement (NAFTA), was enough to isolate the conflictive consequences of some incidents which, in previous times, could have been the cause of serious diplomatic breakdowns.

From this perspective, the broadcast on American television of the NBC series related to Camarena's murder, "Drug Wars," on January 1990, did not affect the bilateral relationship, despite the fact that it added the name of de la Madrid's Attorney General, Sergio García Ramírez, to the list of the government officials involved in drug trafficking.[31] Although this series could only have been watched by a small segment of the population because it was transmitted by an American network accessible in Mexico only through cable or satellite dish, the Mexican government sponsored a combative counter-program which accompanied an avalanche of nationalistic statements from official sources. In the counter-program, it was suggested that Camarena himself was a drug trafficker and that the DEA was a human rights abuser in Mexico.[32] After the transmission of this program, the American Senators Dennis DeConcini (R-AZ) and Pete Wilson (R-CA) sent a letter to U.S. Attorney-General Richard Thornburgh, saying that Mexican authorities did not fully cooperate with the American investigators and that the explanation for Camarena's murder was not sufficient.[33] One month later, a federal jury accused nineteen Mexicans of having been involved in Camarena's death, including Zorrilla Pérez and Aldana (Berke 1990; Bressey 1990).[34] Although this accusation was not well received by the Mexican government, and despite the fact that it was practically ignored by the Mexican Attorney-General, this incident did not significantly affect the relationship. Even more, at this time the Mexican government showed clearly its will to cooperate in the fight against narcotics by allowing an American radar airplane to fly over Mexican territory in the pursuit of a Colombian plane carrying cocaine (Jehl and Miller 1990).[35]

It is also surprising that this cordial relationship was maintained after a monitoring report made by an American satellite suggested that the Mexican production of marijuana was ten times larger than estimated (Jehl and McManus 1990).[36] This insinuation, rejected by the Mexican Ambassador to Washington, could have been, in other times, a strong reason for an increase in the pressures concerning Mexico. However, it seemed that both governments had other priorities, like NAFTA, and that a climate of conflict was in contradiction to them.

In this context, and despite all the problems mentioned above, President Bush acknowledged the Mexican efforts in the struggle against drug trafficking and asked Congress to maintain the financial assistance given for this purpose.[37] As an aside, the assistance authorized for 1990 was $15 million, which was only exceeded by that given to Colombia ($20 million), the biggest recipient. However, the amount for 1991 and the estimate for 1992 contain an increase in the assistance to Mexico: $19.1 million for 1991 (still exceeded by that of Colombia) and $26 million for 1992, the biggest amount received by any single country in the world from the U.S. State Department Bureau of International Narcotics Matters for that year.[38]

Notwithstanding, in April 1990, the harmony in the bilateral relationship faced the most serious threat since the assassination of Camarena. At the beginning of that month, the DEA sponsored the kidnapping from Mexican to American territory of the Mexican doctor, Humberto Alvarez Macháin, for his alleged involvement in the murder of Camarena.[39] Despite the fact that President Salinas and other Mexican officials protested vigorously over this incident, the U.S.-Mexican relationship proved to be highly resilient. By June 1990, a military unit in the U.S. Embassy at Mexico City was created apparently in order to provide information about drug trafficking and to help in the planning of Mexican actions (Jehl and Miller 1990).[40] Despite some poorly coordinated explanations by the Mexican Ministry of Foreign Relations, which ranged from the total denial of the fact to the explanation that the American embassy only provided informational support,[41] this Tactical Analysis Team was reported as an accomplishment in the U.S. Department of State *International Narcotics Control Strategy Report* of March 1991.[42] Mexican cooperation went even further by authorizing that DEA agents could carry guns and receive diplomatic immunity (Ostrow and Jehl 1990).[43]

However, the publication of the list of DEA agents in Mexico by a Mexican magazine — after the kidnapping of Alvarez Macháin — presumably with information furnished by the Mexican government,[44] suggests that the Salinas government wanted to send a clear message to the Bush administration: do not attempt to undermine the internal legitimacy of your partner.[45] In this sense, the Salinas administration was playing its role conscientiously: it was projecting an image of collaboration in the fight against drugs, which was essential to the American government vis-à-vis its own public opinion (obviously the motivation of the Mexican government was to address other goals like the Free Trade Agreement); it was not fair that the American government did not play its role in the same way.

It seems that, in the following months, both governments acted according to the rules of the game. The Mexican government collaborated in projecting an image of cooperation in the fight against drugs, increasing significantly the seizures, even when the veracity of some of them could be questioned.[46] The indictment of a general, the commander of a military zone where seven Mexican policemen were shot by the Mexican army during an antidrug operation at the end of 1991,[47] has to be analyzed from the same perspective. Once it had been made obvious for the American public that the Mexican military was acting to protect drug traffickers, the Salinas government decided to arrest the general in charge.[48] This was the first time in decades that Mexican authorities implicated a high-level military officer publicly in the drug trade.

From the American side, the Bush government was very conscious of the rules of the game. Referring to the Mexican will to cooperate, the State Department declared that "Mexico's sensitivity to perceived infringements on its sovereignty, however, may still threaten that cooperation" (Cody 1991).[49] In this context, it is worth mentioning that despite the fact that a Supreme Court decision in June 1992 authorized the kidnapping of foreign suspects abroad to prosecute them, even if such actions violate international law (U.S. Department of State 1992),[50] the Bush administration excluded Mexico explicitly from this policy in the future.[51] The Mexican reaction to the Supreme Court decision, which nullified the possibilities of extradition of Verdugo Urquídez or Alvarez Macháin, was to ban temporarily DEA activities in Mexican territory (for 24 hours)[52] to limit legally DEA's role in Mexico, including carrying guns, to increase the penalties for Mexicans who participate in kidnapping of persons to be delivered abroad,[53] and to reject U.S. assistance on drugs,[54] whose request for 1992, as we have mentioned, was the highest for Latin America.[55]

From this perspective, it is not difficult to see the differences in the White House policy toward Mexico and the policy toward other source countries, like those of the Andean region. The pressures toward militarization in the "Andean strategy" contrast clearly with the permissiveness in the Mexican case.[56]

What deserves attention is the fact that despite the existence of an ambiance of cooperation between the United States and the Mexican governments, in the drug issue and in the rest of the bilateral agenda, the Mexican production of marijuana and opium has increased significantly since 1989 (see Table 1). It is true that seizures also have increased substantially, but they still represent a minimal part of the worldwide and Mexican production of drugs (see Tables 2, 5, and 6). Moreover, Mexico is still the major producer of marijuana imported into the United States (70 percent in 1990 and 63 percent in 1991), an important producer of heroin consumed in the United States (one third in 1990 and 23 percent in 1991), and the main point of transit for the cocaine which enters the United States (more than 50 percent in 1990 and 1991).[57] This did not stop the U.S. government from praising the Mexican effort against drug trafficking: "Since the inauguration of President Carlos Salinas de Gortari in 1988, Mexican drug control efforts have improved significantly. His leadership has ushered in a period of closer cooperation between Mexico and the United States" (U.S. Department of State 1992).[58]

It seems evident that there is an explicit will to give priority to the positive aspect of the U.S.-Mexican relationship. The emphasis is placed on Mexican efforts to fight drug production and traffic, not on the effective diminution of the volume of drugs produced or entering the United States. Consequently, the Mexican government is carrying out seizures and arrests in order to project the image required for a good relationship with the United States and is not declaring total war on a phenomenon that does not seem to be considered a matter of national security and whose direct combat could transform it into that category. From this point of view, it seems that the Mexican approach to the topic is pervaded by an "olympic spirit" where what is important is to compete, not to win.

The American acceptance of this approach is a de facto recognition of the ineffectiveness of the drug war on the territory of source countries. In other words, despite its strong embargo rhetoric toward drugs, the real behavior of the United States suggests an acceptance of the law of supply and demand, as it happens in the rest of its commercial policy.[59] The probable high political cost for the White House of such a recognition is what explains the pathological persistence of this "olympic approach."

Conclusions

As we have seen, the level of conflict in the U.S.-Mexican relationship is not always related to the volume of drugs produced or imported into the United States. This suggests that the "poisoning effect" theory regarding the role of drug trafficking in the bilateral relationship is only useful if both governments place effectiveness as the defining criterion in the battle against drug trafficking. However, during the most recent years, what matters to both governments is the image of cooperation projected by the Mexican government. One possible explanation of this phenomenon is that, as we have suggested, drug trafficking is not perceived by both governments as a threat to the "actually existing national security" of Mexico. Further, the reluctance of the Mexican government to declare total war on drug traffickers, as in the

"Colombian model," derives from a fear of forcing a powerful group that is now moving inside the parameters of the political system to go out of it, posing in that way a real threat to political stability.

The specific insertion of drug traffickers into the Mexican political system has clearly established the limits of tolerance in the bilateral approach to the topic. Although some misunderstandings in the beginning of the Bush and Salinas administrations threatened these limits, it seems that both governments have understood the rules of this game well. The limits on the Mexican side are the projection of an open image of non-collaboration. The limits on the American entail jeopardizing Mexico's sovereignty in the eyes of the Mexican public. The acceptance of these rules has resulted in a diminution of the relative weight of the drug issue on the bilateral agenda, despite an increase in the amount of drugs smuggled into U.S. territory. Consequently, drug trafficking has proven in recent years to be a dependent variable in the relationship, reflecting its general tone, more than an independent variable capable of establishing its general tendencies.

It seems that this "olympic approach" to the drug issue by both governments can be maintained in the near future, until internal developments in Mexico force a different kind of insertion of drug trafficking into the political system or until the United States decides to change its approach to the issue. Meanwhile, what the United States sees in Mexican counternarcotics policy is what it gets.

Table 1. Mexico: Drugs Net Production (metric tons)

Year	Cannabis (usable)	Opium
1979	1,100-1,500	9-12
1980	800-1,300	17
1981	300-500	16
1982	750	17
1983	1,300	17
1984	2,500-3,000	21
1985	3,000-4,000	28.4
1986	3,000-4,000	20-40
1987	5,933	50
1988	5,655	.50
1989	30,200	66
1990	19,700	62
1991	7,775	41

Sources:1979-1989, National Narcotic Intelligence Consumers Committees, *The supply of illicit drugs to the U.S. from foreign and domestic sources*, 1980, 1982, 1983, 1984, 1985 and 1986, from *Estados Unidos, Informe Trimestral*, Mexico: CIDE, Vol. I, No. 2, April-June, 1991, 43. 1990-1991, U.S. Department of State, Bureau of International Narcotics Matters, *International Narcotics Control Strategy Report*, March 1992, 177.

Table 2. Mexico: Seizures
(metric tons)

	1987	1988	1989	1990	1991
Opium	—	0.16	—	0.40	0.10
Heroin	0.04	0.07	0.93	0.18	0.15
Cocaine	9.30	15.40	38.10	48.50	50.26
Marijuana	400	278	412	408	254.90

Source: U.S. Dept. of State, Bureau of International Narcotics Matters, *International Narcotics Control Strategy Report*, March 1991, 165 and U.S. Dept. of State, *International Narcotics Control Strategy Report*, March 1992, 177.

Table 3. Drugs Worldwide Net Production 1987-1991
(metric tons)

	1987	1988	1989	1990	1991
Total Opium	2,242	2,881	3,948	3,520	3,819
Total Marijuana	13,693	17,455	36,755	25,600	13,465

Sources: U. S. Department of State. Bureau of International Narcotics Matters, *International Control Strategy Report*, March 1991, 30 and U.S. Dept. of State, *International Narcotics Control Strategy Report*, March 1992, 27.

Table 4. Mexico: Share of Drugs
Worldwide Net Production
(percent)*

	1987	1988	1989	1990	1991
Opium	2.23	1.73	1.67	1.76	1.07
Marijuana	43.32	32.39	82.16	76.91	57.74

*Calculated from Tables 1 and 3.

Table 5. Mexico: Seizures
(percentage of world production)*

	1987	1988	1989	1990	1991
Opium	—	0.0055	—	0.011	0.0026
Marijuana	2.92	1.59	1.12	1.59	1.89

*Calculated from Tables 2 and 3.

Table 6. Mexico: Seizures
(percentages of Mexican production)*

	1987	1988	1989	1990	1991
Opium	—	0.32	—	0.64	0.24
Marijuana	6.74	4.91	1.36	2.07	3.27

*Calculated from Tables 1 and 2.

Notes

1. For a characterization of the "special relationship" between Mexico and the United States, see Olga Pellicer de Brody and Esteban L. Mancilla, *El entendimiento con los Estados Unidos y la gestación del desarrollo estabilizador*. Historia de la Revolución Mexicana No. 23. Mexico: El Colegio de Mexico, 1980, 75-96.

2. These theses are supported, among others, by Miguel Ruiz Cabanas, "Mexico's Changing Illicit Drug Supply Role," in Guadalupe González and Marta Tienda, *The Drug Connection . . . ,*:

The bilateral agenda will grow over the next fifteen to twenty years, not diminish, and the necessity of maintaining a workable relationship is real. The drug problem totally contradicts this requirement, vitiating an adequate negotiating environment for many other very important issues (62).

See also Samuel Del Villar, "Drogas: El nudo gordiano," *Nexos* (126), June 1988, (7). According to Del Villar, the American strategy on drugs "breaks the relationships between Mexico and the U.S., instead of uniting them in the protection of common values and national interests." José Luis Reyna qualifies drug trafficking as "a most irritating point in Mexican-U.S. relations," in his article "Narcotics as a Destabilizing Force for Source Countries and Non-source Countries," in Donald J. Mabry (ed.), *The Latin American Narcotics Trade and U.S. National Security*, New York: Greenwood Press, 1989, 123-135. For a journalistic point of view, see Flora Lewis, "Mexico's Drug Poison," *The New York Times*, May 12, 1990, 15A. For this author, the kidnapping of Humberto Alvarez Macháin for his supposed involvement in Camarena's murder "threatens to poison the whole relation, although diplomats on both sides are desperately eager to prevent that."

3. I refer here to "actually existing national security" as the governmental formulation and implementation of the concept of national security in a certain period of time, as opposed to some theoretically desirable national security described by others outside the government.

4. See Richard Craig, "Operación Intercepción: Una Política de Presión Internacional," *Foro Internacional*, Vol. XXII, No. 2, October-December, 1981, 203-230.

5. Craig, "U.S. Narcotics Policy . . . ," 75.

6. Craig, "U.S. Narcotics Policy . . . ."

7. See Craig, "U.S. Narcotics Policy . . . ", 75. For praise of the Mexican effort, see Peter A. Lupsha, "El tráfico de drogas: México y Colombia. Una perspectiva comparada," in Juan G. Tokatlián and Bruce M. Bagley, *Economía y Política del Narcotráfico*. Bogota: Fondo Editorial CEREC, 1990, 235-264.

8. For a broader discussion of the changes in the concept of national security in Mexico, see Sergio Aguayo Quezada and Bruce Michael Bagley (eds.), *En busca de la seguridad perdida. Aproximaciones a la Seguridad Nacional Mexicana*, Mexico: Siglo XXI Eds., 1990.

9. Craig, "Operation Condor . . . ," 361.

10. The "Colombian model" could be characterized as one in which drug traffickers act out of the established political rules and confront the state openly, in some cases associating themselves with other actors outside the system, like guerrillas. In this model violent manifestations, like terrorist actions, are common and the government considers drug trafficking as a real threat to national security. Also, although corruption associated with drug trafficking is not absent, it is present to a minimal degree and the government has the *political will* to fight traffickers to the last. A defining outcome in this model is the phenomenon called "narcoterrorism."

By contrast, the "Mexican model" could be characterized as one in which drug traffickers are tolerated — but not legal — actors in the political system since they do not defy the state. Consequently, there are no violent actions against the government, like terrorism, and the degree of official corruption derived from drug trafficking is very high. A defining outcome in this model is the phenomenon called "narcopolitics."

11. It is worthwhile to mention that drug trafficking has been explicitly defined as a threat to national security by Presidents de la Madrid and Salinas de Gortari. See Sergio Aguayo Quezada, "Los usos, abusos y retos de la seguridad nacional mexicana, 1946-1990," in Sergio Aguayo Quezada and Bruce Bagley (eds.), *En busca de la seguridad perdida*, Mexico: Siglo XXI Eds., 1990, 107-145; and Jose Luis Reyna, "Narcotics as a Destabilizing Force . . . ."

12. These reasons are mentioned by Richard B. Craig, "U.S. Narcotics Policy . . . ," 75-77.

13. See Bruce Michael Bagley, "U.S. Foreign Policy and the War on Drugs: Analysis of a Policy Failure," *Journal of Interamerican Studies and World Affairs*, Vol. 30, Nos. 2 and 3, Summer/Fall 1988, 199.

14. Peter Reuter and David Ronfeldt in their work "Quest for Integrity: the Mexican-U.S. Drug Issue in the 1980s," A Rand Note, N-3266-USDP, 1992, 13, mention this element, although they do not consider it as the main explanation for the phenomena but only a factor that may have facilitated the increase in drug trafficking.

15. Even in the 1970s some doubted the existence, in the Mexican government, of the will to combat drug trafficking. However, the evident success in the antidrug operations allow us to suppose the existence of this will. For the U.S. perception of the Mexican efforts at that time, see William O. Walker III, *Drug Control...*, 193.

16. Celia Toro does not see drug trafficking as a threat to national security but as a public order problem. However, she does not consider that drug traffickers have "prominent positions" in the society. She does not think that drug dealers are recognized as interlocutors by the state or the society. María Celia Toro, "México y Estados Unidos: el Narcotráfico como Amenaza a la Seguridad Nacional," in Sergio Aguayo Quezada and Bruce Michael Bagley, *En busca de la seguridad perdida . . .* , 367-387.

17. Wayne Cornelius, "Mexico/EU: Las fuentes del pleito," *Nexos* No. 118, October 1987, 26. Since 1985 the CIA was warning about the dangers of political instability and widespread violence in Mexico. See Joel Brinkley, "Concern Growing Among U.S. Aides on Mexico Future," *The New York Times*, May 25, 1986, 1.

18. For the Helms hearings, see Juan González, "El impacto de las Audiencias . . . "; Tom Morganthau and Elaine Shannon, "Presumption of Guilt," *Newsweek*, May 26, 1986, 17-18; Joel Brinkley, "U.S. Aides Accuse Mexico as Drug Trade Surges," *The New York Times*, May 12, 1986, and from the same author, "U.S. Aides Harshly Assail Mexico on Drugs, Immigration and Graft," *The New York Times*, May 14, 1986, A-1 and A-8.

19. See Joel Brinkley, "Mexico and the Narcotics Traffic: Growing Strain in U.S. Relations," *The New York Times*, October 20, 1986, 1.

20. See Richard Craig, "U.S. Narcotics Policy toward Mexico . . . ," 75.

21. Craig, "U.S. Narcotics Policy . . . ."

22. Tom Morganthau, et al., "Presumption" . . . , 17.

23. See Jorge Chabat, "Mexico's Foreign Policy in 1990: Electoral Sovereignty and Integration with the United States," *Journal of Interamerican Studies and World Affairs*, Vol. 33, No. 4, Winter 1991, 7-8.

24. See Jane Bussey, "Mexico Escalates War of Words over Agent's Murder," *The Miami Herald*, January 16, 1990, 13-A; and Larry Rother, "Mexico is Accusing a Slain U.S. Agent: Tension Grows Between the Two Nations on Fight Against Narcotics Trafficking," *The New York Times*, January 16, 1990, 7-A. The allegations that the DEA violated human rights in Mexico was based on a clear manipulation of the series scenes. The Mexican counter-program chose some parts of the program where DEA agents arrive at the "Rancho El Mareño" in Michoacán after a massacre of innocent people perpetrated by Mexican agents to suggest that these crimes were committed by the DEA itself. This incident was broadly covered by the Mexican press at that time. See also Elaine Shannon, *Desperados*, Chapter 10.

25. Jorge Chabat, "Mexico's Foreign Policy . . . ", 8.

26. Jorge Chabat, "Mexico's Foreign Policy . . . ", 8.

27. "Fact Sheet: US Economic, Military, and Counter-Narcotics Program Assistance," *U.S. Department of State Dispatch*, March 2, 1992, 167-168.

28. See Jorge Chabat, "Mexico's Foreign Policy . . . ", 8-9.

29. See *UnomásUno*, June 13 and 15, 1990.

30. The magazine *Proceso* published the list on April 23, a couple of weeks after the Macháin's kidnapping. See Jorge Chabat, "Mexico's Foreign Policy . . . ", 9.

31. Reuter and Ronfeldt refer to the limits of toleration in the Mexican antidrug effort: "The limits are apparently breached when the activity jeopardizes the revolutionary mystique and Mexico's image at home and abroad, embarrasses Mexican leaders in power, weakens central government or party control in some significant area, or gets subordinated to non-Mexican actors," Reuter and Ronfeldt, "Quest for Integrity" . . . , 11.

32. According to the magazine *Proceso*, the fact that there were neither arrests nor police activity in the region of two seizures at the end of 1990 suggests that those seizures were not real. See *Proceso*, No. 731, November 5, 1990, 18-23.

33. Ignacio Gutiérrez A. "Por Error, Balacera de Judiciales y Soldados," *Excélsior*, November 8, 1991, 5-A. Rafael Medina Cruz, "Filmó EU la Balacera en Veracruz: Negroponte," *Excélsior*, November 23, 1991, 5-A. Tim Golden, "Mexican Panel Faults Army in Death of Drug Agents," *The New York Times*, December 7, 1991, 3. Homero Campa, "Testimonios e investigaciones coinciden: los siete judiciales fueron acribillados a mansalva," *Proceso*, No. 785, November 18, 1991, 6-11. Carlos Puig, "Los soldados sabían que llegaban los narcos y tirotearon el avión norteamericano que filmaba," *Proceso*, No. 787, December 2, 1991, 6-9.

34. See Aaron Epstein, "Court Lets U.S. Kidnap Suspects," *The Miami Herald*, June 16, 1992, 1.

35. See "U.S. Pledges to Halt Abduction of Criminal Suspects in Mexico," *The Miami Herald*, July 3, 1992, 16-A.

36. "Mexico Lifts Ban on DEA," *The Miami Herald*, June 18, 1992, 24A, and Lucía Luna, "Energía efímera: el gobierno suspendió las actividades de la DEA durante 24 horas," *Proceso* No. 816, June 22, 1992, 10-15.

37. Roman Orozco, "Carlos Salinas de Gortari. Los secuestros de EE.UU. en México son inaceptables," *Cambio 16*, No. 1078, July 20, 1992, 6-8. "Mexico y EU buscan reanudar esfuerzos contra las drogas," *El Nuevo Herald* (Miami), September 2, 1992, 7A.

38. Tim Golden, "Mexico Says It Won't Accept Drug Aid From U.S.," *The New York Times*, July 26, 1992, 8.

39. The amount of financial assistance from the Department of State Bureau of International Narcotics Matters (INM) requested for Mexico for 1992 was $26 million, followed in Latin America by Colombia with $20 million. These figures do not include military assistance, which in the case of Mexico is practically nonexistent and which for some South American countries is a substantial amount, even bigger than the INM assistance. "Fact Sheet: US Economic, Military, and Counter-Narcotics Program Assistance," *U.S. Department of State Dispatch*, March 2, 1992, 167.

40. For a comprehensive analysis of the U.S. "Andean strategy" and the politics of militarization, see Bruce Michael Bagley, *Myths of Militarization. The Role of the Military in the War on Drugs in the Americas*. Miami: North-South Center, University of Miami, 1991, 37 pp.

41. For the 1990 percentage, see United States Department of State, *International Narcotics Control Strategy Report*, March 1991, 155. For the 1991 percentage, see United States Department of State, *International Narcotics Control Strategy Report*, March 1992, 167. See also Carlos Puig, "Pese a la lucha contra las drogas, crece la actividad del narcotráfico en México," *Proceso*, No. 800, March 2, 1992, 8.

42. United States Department of State, *International Narcotics . . .* , 7.

43. See the quote from Bob Woodward, *The Commanders*, at the opening of this chapter.

References

Berke, Richard L. 1990. "Two Ex-Mexican Officials Charged in 1985 Murder of U.S. Agent." *The New York Times.* February 1:A1, A10.

Brinkley, Joel. 1986a. "Concern Growing Among U.S. Aides on Mexico's Future." *The New York Times.* May 25:A1.

Brinkley, Joel. 1986b. "U.S. Aides Accuse Mexico as Drug Trade Surges." *The New York Times.* May 12.

Brinkley, Joel. 1986c. "U.S. Aides Harshly Assail Mexico on Drugs, Immigration, and Graft." *The New York Times.* May 14:A1.

Brinkley, Joel. 1986d. "Mexico and the Narcotics Traffic: Growing Strain in U.S. Relations." *The New York Times.* October 20:A1.

Bureau of International Narcotics Matters. 1991. *International Narcotics Control Strategy Report.* Department of State Publications, 9853-A.

Bussey, Jane, 1990a. "Mexico Escalates War of Words over Agent's Murder." *The Miami Herald.* January 16:13A.

Bussey, Jane. 1990b. "Mexico Ignores Bombshell Drug Indictments." *The Miami Herald.* February 2:8A.

Campa, Homero. 1991. "Testimonios e Investigaciones Coinciden: Los Siete Judiciales Fueron Acribillados a Mansalva." *Proceso.* No. 785. November 18:6-11.

Cody, Edward. 1991. "Drug Bust Goes Awry in Mexico." *The Washington Post.* November 29:1.

Cornelius, Wayne. 1987. "Mexico/E.U.: Las Fuentes del Pleito." *Nexos.* No. 188. October.

Craig, Richard. 1989. "U.S. Narcotics Policy toward Mexico: Consequences for the Bilateral Relationship." In *The Drug Connection in U.S.-Mexican Relations,* eds. Guadalupe González and Marta Tienda. San Diego, Calif.: Center for U.S. Mexican Studies, University of California, 78-79.

Craig, Richard. 1981. "Operación Intercepción: Una Política de Presión Internacional." *Foro Internacional.* 22(2):203-230.

Craig, Richard. 1980. "Operation Condor: Mexico's Antidrug Campaign Enters a New Era." *Journal of Interamerican Studies and World Affairs.* 22(3):235-264.

Del Villar, Samuel. 1988. "Drogas: El Nudo gordiano." *Nexos.* 126 (June).

Epstein, Aaron. 1992. "Court Lets U.S. Kidnap Suspects." *The Miami Herald.* June 16:1.

Golden, Tim. 1991. "Mexican Panel Faults Army in Death of Drug Agents." *The New York Times.* December 7:3.

Golden, Tim. 1992. "Mexico Says It Won't Accept Drug Aid From U.S." *The New York Times.* July 26:8.

González, Guadalupe. 1985. "El Problema del Narcotráfico en el Contexto de la Relación entre México y Estados Unidos." *Carta de Política Exterior Mexicana.* 5 (2-3) April-September.

González, Guadalupe, and Marta Tienda, eds. 1989. *The Drug Connection in U.S.-Mexican Relations.* San Diego: Center for U.S.-Mexican Studies, University of California.

González, Juan J., et al. 1986. "El Impacto de las Audiencias Helms en la Relación Bilateral." *Carta de Política Exterior Mexicana.* Mexico: CIDE. 6(2), April-June, 8.

Gutiérrez A., Ignacio. 1991. "Por Error, Balacera de Judiciales y Soldados." *Excélsior.* November 8:5A.

Jehl, Douglas, and Marjorie Miller. 1990a. "U.S. Planes Help Mexico Head Off Drugs at the Border." *Los Angeles Times.* April 9:A1, A10-11.

Jehl, Douglas, and Marjorie Miller. 1990b. "U.S. Military Unit on Mexico Aides Drug War." *Los Angeles Times.* June 7.

Jehl, Douglas, and Doyle McManus. 1990. "Mexico Rejects Report on Its Marijuana Crop." *Los Angeles Times.* March 1:A30.

Lewis, Flora. 1990. "Mexico's Drug Poison." *The New York Times.* May 12:15A.

Luna, Lucía. 1992. "Energía Efímera: el Gobierno Suspendió las Actividades de la DEA durante 24 Horas." *Proceso.* No. 816, June 22:10-15.

Medina Cruz, Rafael. 1991. "Filmó EU la Balacera en Veracruz: Negroponte." *Excélsior.* November 23:5A.

The Miami Herald. 1992a. "Mexico Lifts Ban on DEA." June 18:24A.

The Miami Herald. 1992b. "U.S. Pledges to Halt Abduction of Criminal Suspects in Mexico." July 3:16A.

Morganthau, Tom, Elaine Shannon, and Joseph Contreras. 1986. "Presumption of Guilt." *Newsweek.* May 26:17-18.

El Nuevo Herald (Miami). 1992. "Mexico y EU Buscan Reanudar Esfuerzos contra las Drogas." September. 2:7A.

Orozco, Roman. 1992. "Carlos Salinas de Gortari: Los Secuestros de EE.UU. en México son Inaceptables." *Cambio 16.* No. 1078. July 20:6-8.

Ostrow, Ronald J., and Douglas Jehl. 1990. "Mexico Says U.S. Agents May Carry Guns." *Los Angeles Times.* June 29:17A.

Pellicer de Brody, Olga, and Esteban L. Mancilla. 1980. *El entendimiento con los Estados Unidos y la gestación del desarrollo estabilizador.* Historia de la Revolución Mexicana. No. 23. México: El Colegio de México, 75-96.

Proceso. 1990. No. 731. November 5.

Puig, Carlos. 1991. "Los Soldados Sabían que Llegaban los Narcos y Tirotearon el Avión Norteamericano que Filmaba." *Proceso.* No. 787. December 2:6-9.

Puig, Carlos. 1992. "Pese a la Lucha Contra las Drogas, Crece la Actividad del Narcotráfico en México." *Proceso.* No. 800. March 2:8.

Reuter, Peter, and David Ronfeldt. 1992. "A Quest for Integrity: The Mexican-U.S. Drug Issue in the 1980's." *A Rand Note.* N-3266-USDP. Santa Monica, Calif.: Rand Corporation.

Rother, Larry. 1990. "Mexico Is Accusing a Slain U.S. Agent: Tension Grows between Two Nations on Fight against Drug Trafficking." *The New York Times.* January 16:A7.

Shannon, Elaine. 1989. *Desperados.* New York: Penguin Books, 350.

Tokatlián, Juan, and Bruce M. Bagley, eds. 1990. *Economía y Política del Narcotráfico.* Bogotá: Fondo Editorial CEREC.

United States Department of State. 1992. "Fact Sheet: U.S. Economic, Military, and Counter-Narcotics Program Assistance." *U.S. Department of State Dispatch.* March 2:167-168.

United States Department of State. 1992. *International Narcotics Control Foreign Assistance Appropriation Act. Fiscal Year 1992.* Budget Congressional Submission. Washington, D.C.: U.S. Department of State, 7.

United States Department of State. 1991. Bureau of International Narcotics Matters. *International Narcotics Control Strategy Report.* Department of State Publication 9853-A. March:157.

UnomásUno. 1990. June 13-15.

Walker III, William O. 1989. *Drug Control in the Americas.* Albuquerque: University of New Mexico Press, 189-192.

Woodward, Bob. 1991. *The Commanders.* New York: Simon & Schuster.

Chapter Twenty

After Camarena

William O. Walker III

Introduction

On February 7, 1985, Enrique Camarena Salazar was abducted in Guadalajara, Mexico, and subsequently tortured and killed. Like no other incident before or since, the assassination of Drug Enforcement Administration (DEA) agent Camarena and his sometime pilot, Alfredo Zavala Avelar, exposed the latent tensions in U.S. relations with Mexico over drugs. The response to the killings was one of outrage in the halls of Congress and in the executive branch. At a press conference in Mexico City, U.S. Ambassador John Gavin, flanked by then-DEA Administrator Francis M. Mullen, described an extensive drug business in Mexico; in doing so, Gavin probably shocked many Mexicans — for what he knew as well as for his audacity. Mullen, about to be replaced by John C. Lawn, would soon denounce the widespread corruption that, he believed, countenanced rampant drug trafficking out of Mexico.[1]

Four years later, the U.S. State Department's International Narcotics Control Strategy Report (INCSR) spoke with comparative optimism about the prospects for effective drug control by the administration of the new Mexican president, Carlos Salinas de Gortari. Salinas had described drug trafficking as a threat to his nation's economic health and security and had termed better control a national priority.[2] Even John Lawn, still serving as head of the DEA early in the administration of President George Bush, was encouraged about developments in Mexico regarding drug traffic in general and the Camarena case in particular.[3] Further, at the seventh meeting of the U.S.-Mexico Binational Commission held in Mexico City in August 1989, Secretary of State James A. Baker III, accompanied by Lawn, key members of the Bush cabinet, and other top administration officials, praised Mexico's antidrug activities.[4]

At the least, the apparent transformation of Mexican drug policy indicated remarkably amicable relations. To those not privy to the details of negotiations over drugs between the two nations, it was not altogether clear what had taken place. Had relations between the two neighbors really improved? And was the bilateral U.S.-Mexican relationship, as President Bush suggested, as important as any other? Could Baker be taken at his word when he claimed that the United States was fully committed to creating common opportunities for stronger relations? Jorge Castañeda of the National Autonomous University of Mexico and co-author with Robert A. Pastor of the important book, *Limits to Friendship: The United States and Mexico*, rightly warned that a new era "has been hailed every six years more or less" but significantly added that "the difference this time is [that] Mexico is much more willing to accommodate American concerns than it has [been] in the past."[5]

Another possibility was that the two nations had begun to share a common perception of drugs as a serious threat to their security. President Ronald Reagan's National Security Decision Directive No. 221 of April 8, 1986, made such a determination for the United States. And both Salinas and his predecessor, Miguel de la Madrid Hurtado, had defined drug trafficking as a security matter.[6] Arguably, the most plausible interpretation was that convergence over drug policy was in the offing between Washington and Mexico City. On two earlier occasions, when the two nations adopted similar antidrug perspectives, in 1940 and in the wake of Operation Intercept in 1969, it was clear that the United States essentially dictated Mexican policy. That did not seem to be the case in 1989.[7]

There is another related explanation. Both nations appeared to recognize that the narcotics problem exposed a mutual, though differing vulnerability that called for an interdependent, yet asymmetrical response. Mexican authorities under Salinas were demonstrating greater concern about the drug trade than at any time since early in the *sexenio* of José López Portillo. Nearly one-half of the budget of the attorney general's office went for drug control as did one-third of the budget for national defense. Moreover, some 25 percent of Mexico's armed forces were engaged in that country's war on drugs.[8]

For its part, the United States seemed willing to address the issue of domestic demand for drugs — as de la Madrid all but insisted upon in his farewell speech. Movement in Washington beyond a supply-side analysis of the drug problem was central to the passage by Congress of the 1988 Anti-Drug Abuse Act (P.L. 100-690). Most revealing of all was the emphasis on domestic law enforcement rather than merely crop eradication and interdiction in the National Drug Control Strategy prepared by Director of National Drug Control Policy William J. Bennett and unveiled by Bush on September 5, 1989. How the new strategy would apply to Mexico remained unclear at the time, particularly because of its emphasis on the Andes, but it is worth noting that Salinas, who attended a meeting of Latin American leaders at Ica,

Peru, in mid-October, was given no role to play in connection with a U.S.-Andean drug summit planned for Cartagena, Colombia, in February 1990.[9]

Even if Washington's relations with Mexico markedly improved in 1989, differences over drugs were virtually certain to recur. Mexico then was producing some fifty metric tons of opium, more than 5,600 metric tons of marijuana, and was serving as a transit country for possibly one-third of the cocaine reaching the United States. (That figure apparently exceeded 60 percent in 1990 and remained at that level or higher well into 1993.) In fact, in April 1988, the DEA had suspended its participation in Operation Vanguard, a bilateral reconnaissance and eradication verification program.[10] Members of Congress, dubious about the sincerity of Mexico's antidrug campaign, regularly questioned the wisdom of providing Mexico with aircraft for crop eradication operations. One of the favorites of congressional critics of the Reagan and Bush administrations, and a strident critic of Mexico as well, William von Raab, resigned his post as U.S. customs commissioner at the end of July 1989. Upon leaving office, von Rabb acidly condemned the Department of State, the attorney general, and the Treasury Department for failing to wage more than a halfhearted war on drugs flowing across the border.[11]

Drug Trafficking and U.S.-Mexican Relations in Historical Perspective

Journalists, scholars, and other informed observers of the political economy of drug control have portrayed a multifaceted relationship between the United States and Mexico. Both Elaine Shannon in *Desperados* and James Mills in *The Underground Empire* condemn Mexican policy makers for ineptitude, corruption, and probable complicity in the drug trade.[12] Their emotion-laden books lack an appreciation of the complexity of drug trafficking as a major issue in domestic and foreign policy in either Mexico or the United States. Such a conceptual debility has long been typical of a supply-side analysis of drug trafficking.

More incisive evaluations come from Richard B. Craig, who demonstrates the inherent coerciveness of an antidrug policy that depends upon control at the source, and Samuel I. del Villar, who concludes that the inability of U.S. officials to reduce demand at home has made scapegoats of the peasant growers of opium and marijuana. In an analysis of the Camarena incident, Juan David Lindau notes the historic asymmetry of objectives in the drug control policies of the United States and Mexico. Raphael F. Perl has underlined this important reality in an essay on U.S.-Mexican relations appearing in the journal *Cuadernos Semestrales*. Gregory F. Treverton of the Council on Foreign Relations observes that U.S. authorities have been quite insensitive to the economic conditions conducive to peasant involvement with drugs. William O. Walker III, in *Drug Control in the Americas*, describes how historical and cultural differences have made difficult a common approach to drug control.[13] More recently, Peter Reuter and David Ronfeldt have made a case for Mexico's defense of national sovereignty as the motivating force behind that country's drug policy and narcodiplomacy.[14]

Given what is known about the narcotics relationship across the Rio Grande, it is relatively easy to identify the problems that have chronically bedeviled that relationship. Del Villar persuasively argues that corruption will continue to impair Mexican antidrug efforts so long as the demand for drugs remains high in the United States.[15] Instead of analyzing further such interrelated dilemmas, this chapter will explore the structural limitations of U.S. narcotics policy by looking closely at the policy-making process as it related to the Camarena affair. To begin, drug policy must be located within its larger foreign policy context.

Soon after the Reagan administration took office in January 1981, potentially discordant issues, including immigration, petroleum prices, the Mexican economy, and drugs were minimized in comparison to the major importance given to Mexico's position regarding U.S. policy in Central America.[16] Constantine C. Menges, a special assistant to President Reagan for national security affairs, supported the carrying out of a "persuasion campaign" to prevail upon Mexican leaders to revise their Central American policy — with which the White House strongly disagreed. Never formally implemented, Menges's plan underscored Reagan's firm belief that hemispheric security was directly at stake in the Central American drama.[17]

Mexico's unwillingness to accept U.S. leadership on such a major foreign policy issue as Central America brought into question the premises upon which the United States had based security policy in the hemisphere since the Second World War.[18] This independence of action in the early 1980s was previously explained with reference to the dictates of Mexican sovereignty, traditional suspicion of U.S. motives, or simply differing foreign policy priorities. Importantly, structural limitations in U.S. policy are basic to a comprehensive understanding of the differences with Mexico. Put differently, distrust of Mexico was inherent in the logic of U.S. security policy. It comes as no surprise, therefore, that the United States has long insisted that its conception of security should dominate the bilateral relationship; that threats to security should be met directly, with force if need be; and that adversaries were identifiable and had to be contained. In short, U.S. officials believed that the so-called realist perspective should guide Mexico's foreign policy just as it did their own.[19]

The great irony is that authorities in Washington failed to implement a drug policy derived from their own primary operating assumptions. The strategy of reducing drug supplies in the United States, therefore, lay open to criticism from even its would-be supporters. Congressional critics began to charge, for example, that the Reagan administration never really went to war against drugs. These same critics further claimed that the White House virtually coddled source- and transit-country governments because of a reluctance to decertify countries not fully cooperating with the United States. As played out in the public arena, such disputes illuminated the limits of a drug policy based on realist assumptions. First, the realist emphasis on national actors was misplaced since the largely uncontrollable drug business remained primarily in the hands of non-national actors. In turn, market forces rarely received the attention they should have from drug control officials. Second, the United States overemphasized into the 1980s the importance that Latin American nations, including Mexico, placed on curbing illicit narcotics traffic. Finally, the use of force could not be taken for granted as an effective weapon against purveyors of the illicit drug trade.[20]

A Critique of U.S. Hardliner Policies

Notwithstanding the preceding analysis, a critique of U.S. drug policy as it relates to Mexico must go further and identify stasis or change in the attitudes of policy makers after 1985. A critique focused largely on the decision-making level of analysis will lead to a better understanding of why U.S. policy makers could at the same time acknowledge the interdependence that drug problems brought to U.S.-Mexican relations and could also decry Mexico's less than equivalent response.

It is important to emphasize that U.S. officials and members of Congress have long seen Mexico as the linchpin of a successful drug policy in the Americas. By the mid-1980s, U.S. objectives in Mexico included destruction of opium and marijuana crops, with eradication by aerial spraying where possible; interdiction of traffic in heroin, marijuana, and cocaine; prosecution of major drug traffickers; effective use of U.S.-provided equipment; and close cooperation of the government of Mexico with the Department of State's Bureau of International Narcotics Matters (INM), the DEA, Customs, and the Border Patrol.[21] Prior to 1985, the State Department and DEA officials in Washington assumed that these goals were realizable through Mexico's "permanent campaign" against drugs, an assessment that DEA personnel in Mexico had started to doubt even during the López Portillo presidency.[22]

By the time of Camarena's murder, Washington's faith in Mexico's antinarcotics programs had all but eroded. Officials reluctantly concluded that Mexico was not similarly committed to stopping narcotics trafficking. In fact, U.S. objectives did not define Mexico's frame of reference for antidrug activity any more than Mexico accepted U.S. presumptions about security policy and Central America. The 1985 annual report of the House Select Committee on Narcotics Abuse and Control found "serious problems in the drug control effort in Mexico" and lamented the "almost total lack of effective and meaningful cooperation by the MFJP [Mexican Federal Judicial Police] and the DEA."[23]

The blame for strained relations in 1985 should not rest entirely on Mexican shoulders. As congressional critics of the Reagan administration frequently pointed out, the president and his top aides did not seem interested either in developing a comprehensive antidrug strategy or in adequately funding a war on drugs.[24] As a result, expectations regarding what Mexico ought to accomplish in reducing the drug problem were quite incongruent with what the administration itself was willing to do at home. The considerable extent to which the United States assumed that Mexico should adopt a comparable drug control strategy showed both the delusion and limitations inherent in U.S. policy. Washington's egocentricity ـd to wishful thinking about Mexican policy and further diminished respect for Mexican sovereignty.[25]

Even so, it remains inadequate for analytical purposes to conclude that most U.S. policy makers held a jaundiced view of Mexico beginning in 1985. Such a characterization uniformly applied only in the immediate aftermath of the Camarena murder. Thereafter, various members of the executive branch and prominent individuals in Congress differed markedly over what the United States should do regarding Mexico and narcotics. For analytical purposes, three points of view can be identified: hardliners who wanted to punish Mexico in some way because they doubted Mexico's willingness to move against drugs; advocates of constructive engagement who knew that a major dispute over drug policy would be counterproductive both to control at the source and to the interdiction of illicit traffic; and others who were skeptical, if not contemptuous, of Mexico's narcotics control record but recognized the need to maintain relatively cordial relations.

An often acrimonious interplay between these factions soon complicated the policy-making process. What set the hardliners apart from the others was not just their belief that the Mexican government lacked the political will to initiate effective action against drugs; others involved in deliberations over policy had reached a similar conclusion. Rather, the hardliners, primarily DEA agents in Mexico, the Customs Service under von Raab, and such members of Congress as Representative Lawrence J. Smith (D-FL), the chairman of the Foreign Affairs Committee's Task Force on International Narcotics Control, and Senator Jesse Helms (R-NC), a member of the Foreign Relations Committee's Subcommittee on Terrorism, Narcotics, and International Communication, started by assuming that Mexico deliberately was seeking to impede U.S. drug control programs related to the situation across the border. As noted, doubts about the efficacy of Mexican policy arose in the midst of the permanent campaign under López Portillo.[26]

DEA agents in Mexico understandably felt endangered when cooperation was neither forthcoming nor consistent from their host government. Shannon's book portrays their situation in the most sympathetic terms and shows how agents inexorably became involved in the labyrinth of Mexican narcopolitics far in excess of their mission to gather information.[27] Von Raab's antipathy is less easily explained. As Shannon writes, the highly volatile commissioner "was no bureaucrat," but he possessed an unswerving commitment to accomplish what he perceived to be his "primary mission," drug interdiction. More than any other nation, Mexico was obstructing the realization of that objective.[28] Von Raab portrayed Mexican failure to work more closely with his agency as purposeful and, hence, a threat to U.S. security.[29] In testimony before Congress in March 1988 over whether or not to decertify Mexico, he declared that "the ante must be raised in the war on drugs."[30]

Von Raab doubtless knew that interdiction could not be an effective drug control measure. Historically, no U.S. official has claimed much more than a 15 percent rate of success for interdiction. At best, interdiction has served as one means of compelling traffickers to cease smuggling; far more often, it has provided a public relations device in a desperate attempt to bolster a flawed antidrug strategy. Decision makers often relied upon such quixotic efforts instead of reexamining their basic assumptions when those assumptions produced defective policies. Reliance upon compensating mechanisms of whatever sort, which political psychologists have identified as a kind of defensive avoidance, in stark contrast to the ideal of patient, vigilant policy making, may have induced von Raab's negative assessment of Mexico.[31]

The positions taken by Helms and Smith were motivated by little more than political opportunism couched in the language of security concerns (by Helms) and opposition to drugs (by Smith). That is, their views were derived from the self-arrogated roles they elected to play. Mexican political and economic instability greatly worried Helms and his ideologue associates who feared that Mexico's ruling Institutional Revolutionary Party, the PRI, would turn even further leftward in domestic and foreign policy than they assumed it already was.[32] Smith, whose understanding of Mexican politics scarcely surpassed von Raab's own limited knowledge, questioned whether Mexico should continue to receive antinarcotics assistance from the United States.[33] A close reading of the public record, as contained in congressional hearings, suggests that Smith believed that Mexican officials, "corrupt up to their eyeballs" as he once put it, were mostly predisposed to ignore U.S. entreaties about drug control. He accordingly headed the drive in the House of Representatives to decertify Mexico in 1988 for lack of compliance with Washington's standards for antidrug activity.[34]

Constructive Engagement

At the opposite end of the spectrum from the hardliners resided the proponents of constructive engagement. No less angry than other policy makers about the Camarena killing and bothered by what too often seemed to be an obstructionist response by the Mexican government to U.S. antidrug activities, they considered it foolhardy to couple antinarcotics assistance directly to Mexico's narcotics control perfomance.[35] On the whole, they reasoned, the Mexican record was more praiseworthy than not. Chief among those favoring constructive engagement in the Reagan years were officials in the Department of State, although it was not altogether clear what importance Secretary of State George P. Shultz or Elliott Abrams, the assistant secretary for inter-American affairs, attached to narcotics relations with Mexico.[36] Surely, policy makers at INM worked assiduously to make the case for maintaining cooperative relations, and as we have seen, they defined Mexico as essential to the success of U.S. drug control policy in the hemisphere.[37]

Just as instrumental as INM in trying to keep U.S.-Mexican relations from going sour over drug control were Attorney General Edwin W. Meese III and Stephen S. Trott, the associate attorney general. In fact, the Mexican government greatly appreciated Meese's role in trying to smooth relations in the immediate wake of the Camarena assassination. Although some in the DEA below Lawn and various critics in Congress may have found the attorney general's office too "soft on Mexico," Trott made it clear in an appearance before the House Select Committee that "we absolutely do not fingerpoint." As such, despite the furor over Camarena, the top law enforcement officials of the United States, with the approval of the president, convened on a regular basis with their counterparts in Mexico in charge of drug control.[38] That this solicitude for Mexico miffed Representative Smith, a member of the House Select Committee, was evident in an exchange he had with Trott in September 1986 — about which more later.[39]

The government of Mexico did not, however, receive carte blanche to ignore concern about lax narcotics enforcement from those advocating a policy of constructive engagement. It was one thing to acknowledge the economic roots of Mexico's difficulties with drugs,[40] but quite another to assume, as did some critics of the administration, that a laissez-faire approach dictated White House and State Department policy. Von Raab and Smith, to name only two, were too biased to admit that a policy which took into account a troubled domestic, economic, and political situation was other than a policy of surrender to drug traffickers and corrupt authorities within the Mexican government. Though believing that President de la Madrid and his attorney general, Sergio García Ramírez, were well intentioned, INM (and perhaps DEA officialdom in Washington) may have argued in March 1988 against certifying Mexico as complying with provisions of the 1986 Anti-Drug

Abuse Act.[41] President Reagan's special certification on grounds of national interest for Mexico in that year's INCSR likely came at the behest of the National Security Council.[42]

Dissenting Realists

In the vast middle ground between the hardliners and the conciliationists, who might fairly be termed realists, were found those persons whose perspective on Mexico was neither doctrinaire nor defined by broader issues of foreign policy. Essentially falling within this group, for which the phrase "dissenting realists" might be an appropriate description, were the important House Select Committee on Narcotics Abuse and Control and top-level DEA officials. Since its inception in 1976, the committee had injected itself into deliberations over domestic and foreign narcotics policy. Under the leadership and domination of Charles B. Rangel (D-NY) in the 1980s, the committee continually prodded the administration to adopt a comprehensive antidrug strategy and urged the development of better working relations with countries like Mexico.[43]

Into the 1980s, Mexico received reasonably fair treatment from Rangel's committee, which recognized both the problems confronting Mexico, including economic hardship and corruption, and the commitment of key federal officials to combat narcotics production and trafficking.[44] To be sure, Camarena's murder moved the committee to judge more critically than before Mexican drug control performance, but it never elicited the vituperation that marked the posturing of Helms, Smith, and von Raab.[45] The salient question, of course, was why not. Superficially, Rangel and Benjamin A. Gilman, the ranking Republican member of the committee, were highly motivated by domestic political needs and organizational interests — as were the hardliners. Moreover, the House Select Committee had not enjoyed permanent standing and, therefore, had to have its mandate renewed by each Congress; an aggressive, public stance against foreign sources of drugs would accordingly seem to make good political sense.[46]

Instead of denouncing further the Mexican antidrug effort, a plausible reponse given the increasingly limited effectiveness of U.S. drug control policy — as manifested in the crack plague,[47] for example — the committee attempted instead to influence the policy-making process in the White House. Rangel, possessing good political instincts and genuinely desiring to control drugs, cultivated cordial relations with the executive branch by knowing when to criticize and when to praise. During the Reagan years, he evidently got along well with von Raab and INM officials.[48] His committee consistently called for better policy coordination in the executive branch.[49] Only then could the United States hold to account producing and transit countries like Mexico. In early 1989, the committee adopted a wait-and-see attitude about

Bush's naming of William J. Bennett as national drug policy director and awaited the developments promised by President Salinas during its study mission to Mexico City in December 1988.[50]

As major participants in the policy-making process, DEA officials in Washington were not able to enjoy the House Select Committee's luxury of being detached from, yet also involved in, that process. The potential for conflict over policy with other U.S. agencies, particularly the State Department and Department of Defense, increased after Camarena's killing.[51] The task after 1985 for the dissenting realists of the DEA in Washington became the difficult one of seeking redress for agent Camarena's death from Mexican authorities, some of whom were reportedly complicit in drug trafficking at the least, without jeopardizing the status of DEA personnel in Mexico. That Lawn more or less succeeded in taking a direct, yet generally conciliatory approach toward Mexico arose from the realization that the U.S. government could not afford to ignore for a moment the drug situation south of the border.[52]

In other words, the mission at DEA headquarters was to implement existing policy — even if officials doubted the wisdom of a particular action by the White House or an agency of the executive branch. When questioned in March 1986 about Mexico's shortcomings, Assistant Administrator for Operations David L. Westrate told the House Select Committee: "We find that our eradication campaign is probably the best way in the short term to overcome this problem [of corruption] because the aerial spraying really is transparent to the corruption on the ground."[53] The suspension in 1988 of DEA participation in Operation Vanguard appeased domestic critics of administration policy and resulted in a productive review of the program.[54] To construe the hiatus in Operation Vanguard as a dramatic reversal in attitude toward Mexico would be a mistake, however. Taken in the context of DEA's (and INM's) actions since 1985, it confirmed the presumption that problems with drug control there resulted primarily from situational constraints. In that light, reports surfacing in August 1989, November 1991, and again in March 1993 of drug-related corruption in the Mexican military and the MFJP did not seriously threaten the improvement in narcotics relations with Mexico since the inauguration of Salinas.[55]

Clashes in Strategy and Policy Failure

The recurring presence of essentially unalterable differences over the Camarena case, however, would continue to plague the two countries, especially in the second year of the Bush presidency. Also, given the divergent, often opposing, perspectives over drug policy between Congress and the executive branch, there existed a clear need for strong leadership on the part of the White House. Whether or not President Reagan ever exercised such leadership can be debated,[56] but several influential committees acted as though he had not. For example, the 1987 annual report of the House Select Committee reiterated its earlier calls for the development of a comprehensive antinarcotics strategy.[57]

That a clash over strategy was imminent became evident in Trott's appearance before Smith's Foreign Affairs Committee task force in September 1986. Trott avidly defended the existence and activities of the National Drug Enforcement Policy Board (NDEPB) in questioning by Smith and Gilman. The board, which had begun operating in January 1985 under the jurisdiction of the Justice Department, coordinated national as well as international law enforcement activities. The two congressmen, subsequently joined by Rangel, doubted whether the board was overseeing anything resembling a viable antidrug strategy and pointed to conditions in Mexico to demonstrate the inherent weakness of the board.[58] Significantly, the State Department acknowledged the lack of an overall strategy so far as Mexico was concerned. And Francis A. Keating II, Trott's successor as chair of the Enforcement Coordinating Group at the NDEPB, admitted as much when he spoke with the House Select Committee about the transformation of the NDEPB into the National Drug Policy Board (NDPB), as accomplished by executive order in March 1987.[59] Yet not until more than one year later, in mid-April 1988, would the NDPB begin to draft a comprehensive antinarcotics strategy.

By then, it was too late to deflect congressional anger about either the absence of executive leadership on drug policy or the lack of progress, as many in Congress saw it, in relations with Mexico over drugs. In response to the administration's special certification in the State Department's 1988 INCSR, the Senate voted on April 14 to decertify Mexico. Smith's effort to press for decertification failed in the House, where Rangel, along with Gilman and other influential members, opposed such a move but made it clear that the White House had seriously misconstrued the certification requirements of the 1986 antidrug law.[60] Even so, Rangel believed that it was premature to worsen relations with Mexico over drugs.

That Mexico strongly denied the right of the United States to decertify its conduct was irrelevant to the political battle in Washington.[61] The hardliners had failed in their effort to force the Reagan administration to hold Mexican officials to strict accountability for their drug control performance, but the strident critique of U.S. policy by the irreconcilables continued unabated. Advocates of a more conciliatory approach, whether in the executive branch or Congress, realized that a rethinking of counterdrug policy was in order. A report published in March 1988 by the General Accounting Office on international control activities emphasized the various constraints limiting U.S.-sponsored programs abroad. And the 1988 Anti-Drug Abuse Act stressed the need to devise a workable strategy to cope with domestic demand for drugs.[62]

The preparation in 1989 of a new antidrug plan by Bennett's office did not mean, however, that the structural flaws in U.S. policy had been eliminated. Indeed, this chapter's critique of the strategy's realist assumptions suggests otherwise. Available evidence leads inevitably to the conclusion that disputes in the policy-making process largely reflected domestic political needs rather than attempts to alter the fundamentals of relations with Mexico over narcotics. Should the demand for drugs not decline markedly by the mid-1990s, as the Bush-Bennett plan envisioned, then Mexican peasants and politicians could again become the scapegoats of a failed policy. Ironically, in the late 1980s, the hardliners were asking a fundamental question: Should not drug control operations receive greater prominence in establishing hemispheric security concerns? The lack of a clear response in the case of Mexico was indicative of the several complex issues that were already beginning to define the future of U.S.-Mexican relations.[63]

The recurrence of scapegoating after late 1989 remained a distinct possibility but was not a certainty. The emphasis in U.S. policy on curbing demand for drugs promised to promote better bilateral relations with Mexico City. Yet for a smoother relationship quickly to flourish, a thorough reconsideration of priorities should not have been dismissed as readily as it apparently was. Reliance on law enforcement as a solution to the drug problem has long created a self-perpetuating situation at home and abroad in which the expected standard for drug control performance was remarkably high. As such, there existed little room in the United States for a dispassionate evaluation of the conditions in Mexico.

After Camarena: Ramifications for U.S.-Mexican Relations

Events in 1990 did not significantly alter this state of affairs. The conviction on July 31, by a jury in Los Angeles, of Ruben Zuno Arce for crimes related to Camarena's death was one of the year's highlights. This development followed the conviction in December 1989 in Mexico of Rafael Caro Quintero, Ernesto Rafael Fonseca Carrillo, and twenty-six others for orchestrating the Camarena assassination.[64] Even so, the Camarena murder case continued to strain U.S.-Mexican relations. Symbolic of this situation was the airing in January of a melodramatic three-part miniseries, "Drug Wars: The Camarena Story," based on Shannon's book, *Desperados*, and produced with the cooperation of the DEA. The Mexican government found the NBC docudrama to be "slanderous" and an affront to national dignity.[65] Perhaps in response, unidentified sources in Mexico raised questions about Camarena's possible ties to drug traffickers in the Guadalajara region.[66] Then in mid-April, the magazine *Proceso* printed the names of forty-nine DEA agents operating in Mexico, an action which DEA officials termed "irresponsible" and a threat to the safety of the agents.[67] The strain in relations was palpable.

What construction should be placed on these developments? First, the dissenting realists of the DEA, it could be argued, had finally tired of stumbling through the thicket of Mexican narcopolitics and had joined forces with the hardliners. As always, that turn of events was conceivable on the operational level of agents in the field. Available evidence points to a different interpretation, however, for senior DEA officials and, perhaps, for some agents in Mexico as well. That is, although complete resolution of the Camarena case would remain a matter of the utmost concern to the DEA, it was equally important not to jeopardize the cordial relations to which presidents Salinas and Bush were committed. At the same time, the DEA would continue to expect from Mexico unwavering allegiance in the fight against drugs.

The value of the narcotics relationship to both countries could hardly be doubted. First, the State Department's annual narcotics report, released on March 1, praised the Salinas government for pursuing "an aggressive antinarcotics program" and for declaring the war on drugs a matter of national security. Cooperation with U.S. agencies also merited special mention, and the arrest of several major drug traffickers was characterized as "an important accomplishment."[68] It seems unlikely, therefore, that DEA and State Department officials were fundamentally at odds in 1990 over the proper course of policy toward Mexico, no matter the travail agents in Mexico were experiencing.

In addition, the office of Attorney General Enrique Alvarez del Castillo in Mexico City announced in May the creation of a new investigative division, the "General Coordination for Special Affairs," which would handle troublesome issues in the bilateral relationship such as the Camarena case. Alvarez was endeavoring to lower the rhetoric attendant to the Camarena affair, claimed one official, but an unnamed, skeptical U.S. source called the action essentially an effort at "damage control." (The attorney general himself was subsequently suspected of involvement in the Camarena murder; he had been serving as governor of the state of Jalisco at the time of Camarena's death.)[69]

For the most part, such predictable cynicism may have been unwarranted in view of a subsequent development. The Justice Department concluded an unprecedented provisional agreement with the Salinas government to permit MFJP officers to operate in the United States on terms similar to those guiding DEA activities in Mexico. In return, all DEA agents in Mexico, not merely those operating directly out of the U.S. embassy, would be accorded the protection of diplomatic immunity. The State Department lauded the agreement, noting that Salinas's government "repeatedly has demonstrated its commitment to narcotics control."[70] Department INCSRs for 1992 and 1993 echoed this conclusion.[71]

In assuming conceptual convergence with Mexican officials on the matter of drug control, U.S. authorities put themselves in a position to overlook the substantial differences that still could affect relations.[72] That is,

Salinas and his subordinates may have viewed the differing emphasis given to the Camarena affair in the State Department and the DEA as a difference in kind rather than in degree — as was the case in the United States. In that regard, it is worth recalling that the vital question of Mexican sovereignty has never been far removed from bilateral relations over all issues, including drugs.[73] For example, early in 1990, the Mexican government expressed considerable alarm at the growing militarization of the border between the two nations. Authorities in Washington had previously announced the creation of Joint Task Force Six, a drug-fighting unit based in El Paso, and the potential for problems, which could arise in the pursuit of drug traffickers, became a matter of concern in Mexico. Not surprisingly, most officials on the U.S. side of the border discounted such a possibility.[74]

Differences of opinion over the task force and complaints about use by the United States of satellite technology[75] to chart areas of drug production in Mexico paled in comparison to the furor set off by the seizure of Dr. Humberto Alvarez Machain. Alvarez, a gynecologist who reportedly served as physician to several major drug kingpins, allegedly participated in the torture and murder of Camarena and his pilot, Alfredo Zavala Avelar. Indicted by a grand jury in Los Angeles on January 31, he was seized in Mexico in April by persons evidently acting on behalf of the Justice Department, flown to El Paso, and arrested. At once, the government of Mexico charged that a Mexican citizen had been kidnapped, and Alvarez del Castillo indicated that narcotics relations with the United States might be "at risk."[76]

The Salinas government rightly suspected that the DEA had a hand in Alvarez Machain's capture; the Justice Department made it clear that Alvarez Machain would not be returned to Mexico. U.S. Attorney General Dick Thornburgh, who happened to be in Mexico for an international drug control meeting on April 19, spoke with his Mexican counterpart and was assured by Alvarez del Castillo that "cooperation on drug law enforcement would continue."[77] Yet, had the DEA's dissenting realists gone too far and posed an unacceptable challenge to Mexican sovereignty? At a meeting with Vice President Dan Quayle on April 26, Salinas gave his visitor "unshirted hell" about the kidnapping and demanded that there be created "new rules of understanding" about cooperation on drug control.[78] Salinas, however, did accept, for the time being, Quayle's assurances about President Bush's respect for Mexican sovereignty. And Alvarez del Castillo told a press briefing that Alvarez Machain evidently had maintained close contacts with suspected drug traffickers.[79]

When Mexico at length decided to do nothing more than seek extradiction of the former MFJP officer who carried out the seizure of Alvarez Machain,[80] it appeared that the DEA's gamble to keep the Camarena case in the forefront of U.S.-Mexican narcotics relations had paid off. The creation of the special investigative division by Alvarez del Castillo in May and the signing of the provisional agreement in June regarding the rights of Mexican police in the United States seemed to support such a conclusion. Nevertheless, at least two domestic political considerations may have prevented the Salinas administration from reacting more decisively to Alvarez Machain's abduction. First, the human rights group, Americas Watch, released a report charging that rights abuses by police and security forces in Mexico had become institutionalized. Among the abuses mentioned were those committed in connection with drug control activities. Squads of elite MFJP officers, who once may have been associated with illegal narcotics trafficking, were now the backbone of the government's antidrug effort, operating "with near absolute impunity."[81] Thus, Mexico found itself in the international spotlight over an issue that caused it great embarrassment and that could no longer be ignored.

Second, the question of economic stability directly affected how the government responded to all contentious issues with its northern neighbor. As head of the third-largest trading partner of the United States behind Japan and Canada, Salinas could not afford to jeopardize U.S. help in revitalizing his country's economy. The prestigious newspaper *Excélsior* responded positively to Bush's overtures to Latin America at a June meeting of the Organization of American States. Speaking for Bush, Carla Hills, who was the U.S. representative to the Uruguay Round of the General Agreements on Tariffs and Trade, and Lawrence Eagleburger of the State Department emphasized the importance of removing barriers to trade as a fundamental part of the process of strengthening democracy in Latin America. Without a doubt, Salinas's legacy in his country was linked to the success of his economic measures since the day he assumed power — as, perhaps, was the survival of the PRI. That the Camarena affair ultimately was not truly damaging to relations between the two nations seemed apparent from the warm reception that Bush received in November on a special visit to Salinas's ancestral home in the midst of the crisis with Iraq over its occupation of Kuwait. The two presidents focused on questions of free trade and discussed as well other matters of mutual concern, including drugs.[82]

Not only was Mexico constrained from turning the seizure of Alvarez Machain into a major issue with the United States; so, too, was the DEA unable to focus just on indications of official Mexican complicity in the death of Camarena. In preparing for the trial of Zuno Arce and others in Los Angeles, the DEA learned from an informant that the Central Intelligence Agency (CIA) may have used Caro Quintero's ranch for training Guatemalan guerrillas in the early 1980s; to what end was not apparent. Denials were issued at once by the CIA and by Caro Quintero's lawyer.

The important point for present purposes is that public airing of the dispute indicated that DEA and CIA were considerably at odds over U.S. foreign policy objectives in Mexico and Central America. Evidently, the CIA for some time had cultivated ties with Mexico's Federal Security Directorate, some agents of which were implicated in Camarena's death. "The CIA didn't give a damn about anything but Cuba and the Soviets," explained a retired DEA agent, James Kuykendall, who had worked with Camarena in Guadalajara.[83] Given the apparent rift in the policy-making community in Washington, the uncompromising defense of the seizure of Alvarez Machain by Robert C. Bonner, Lawn's successor at the DEA, had no discernible impact on U.S.-Mexican narcotics relations. It is worth noting, moreover, that the September update of the State Department's INCSR did not even mention the problems caused by the abduction.[84]

Conclusions

In late 1990, the ending of the Cold War significantly altered the nature of the security threat previously posed by the Soviet Union and its allies. As a result, relations between the United States and Mexico concerning issues of mutual importance could be dealt with strictly on their own terms. In a sense, authorities in Washington were, therefore, free to invest customary declarations of friendship for Mexico with real meaning. Particularly with the removal from power of the Sandinista government in Nicaragua by means of elections earlier in the year, no single issue existed that could test the reality of the Bush administration's professed friendship for Salinas.

Nevertheless, there did remain a measure of uncertainty in the U.S.-Mexican narcotics relationship. To what extent was the United States actually prepared to wage war against drugs? If a war of sorts were to be fought, on whose terms would it be conducted? What would the Mexican role be in planning and prosecuting a drug war? How would U.S. action against drugs take into account the issue of Mexican sovereignty? And how would a bilateral struggle against drugs complement other antinarcotics operations in the Americas? Indeed, what could the drug warriors do that had not already been previously attempted to restrict the production of and trafficking in drugs?

Questions such as these admitted of no easy answers but led instead to an even more crucial question: was drug control really a security concern for the United States? Without a clear answer, the narcotics relationship across the Rio Grande would continue to be strained as hardliners and dissenting realists in the United States maneuvered to set the contours of that association. The calls have been many to recognize the need for an interdependent, even multilateral, approach to the scourge of drugs.[85] Yet to be more successful than their predecessors, U.S. policy makers will have to reduce political wrangling at home and work with their Mexican counterparts in carrying out the antinarcotics agenda. The House Select Committee has argued, perhaps without fully realizing the implications of its position, that an asymmetrical, interdependent approach is essential to improved narcotics control across the border.[86]

Real cooperation offers no magic solution; it is a process of agreement and discord.[87] Law enforcement will have a role to play in a regime of actual cooperation; crop eradication and interdiction will continue; and the laundering of money will be vigorously attacked. Nevertheless, these measures can offer only temporary gains in the struggle against drugs unless they are part of a foreign policy that also supports innovative educational and development projects. So reasons a 1989 study by the Arms Control and Foreign Policy Caucus of the U.S. Congress, *The Developing World: Danger Point for U.S. Security.*[88] To ignore its findings may well lead to far more troubling relations over narcotics between the United States and Mexico. Sergio García Ramírez, Alvarez del Castillo's predecessor, issued a comparable warning about the impact of drugs and addiction on future generations should cooperation fail: "What for us is an enemy will be an oppressor for them. [Drugs] lead to gradual, inevitable demoralization."[89] As the painful memories of the Camarena murder slowly fade, there remains much work to be done on both sides of the Rio Grande.

Notes

1. Elaine Shannon, *Desperados: Latin Drug Lords, U.S. Lawmen, and the War America Can't Win* (New York: Viking, 1988), 204-13.

2. U.S. Department of State, Bureau of International Narcotics Matters, *International Narcotics Control Strategy Report, March 1989*, 10, 22, 25, 107-14. *New York Times*, November 23, 1988, D20; *New York Times*, December 12, 1988, A7; *New York Times*, March 1, 1989, A8. In his statement of explanation for the certification of Mexico in 1989, President George Bush called for "a period of calm, cooperative actions against narcotics."

3. Statement of John C. Lawn, administrator, Drug Enforcement Administration, before the Subcommittee on Crime, Committee on the Judiciary, House of Representatives, April 12, 1989 (copy in possession of the author). On August 13, 1989, the *Washington Post* reported that agents of the Immigration and Naturalization Service had arrested Ruben Zuno Arce, a brother-in-law of former Mexican President Luis Echeverría Alvarez, in connection with the Camarena murder; *Washington Post*, August 13, 1989, A5. By mid-September, a number of new indictments pertaining to the Camarena case were expected in Los Angeles — the prospect of which greatly concerned Mexico City; *New York Times*, September 14, 1989, A34.

4. *Washington Post*, August 8, 1989, A10, A13.

5. *Washington Post*, August 8, 1989, A13. See also Robert A. Pastor and Jorge G. Casteñada, *Limits to Friendship: The United States and Mexico* (New York: Knopf, 1988), 242-53, 264-77.

6. INM, *INCSR, Mid-year Update, October 1986*, i; Pastor and Castañeda, *Limits to Friendship*, 250-51.

7. William O. Walker III, *Drug Control in the Americas*, rev. ed. (Albuquerque: University of New Mexico Press, 1989), 119-33, 192; Shannon, *Desperados*, 47-55; Richard B. Craig, "Operación Intercepción: una política de precisión international," *Foro Internacional* 22 (October-December 1981): 203-20.

8. INM, *INCSR, March 1988*, 131-32.

9. *Excélsior* (Mexico City), September 2, 1988. For early indications of the content of the plan, see *Washington Post*, August 16, 1989, A1, A16; *New York Times*, August 16, 1989, A1, A8. For the plan itself, see The White House, *National Drug Control Strategy, September 1989* (Washington, D.C.: Government Printing Office, 1989). Perhaps instrumental in turning the focus of U.S. planning somewhat away from interdiction were the findings of a study conducted by the General Accounting Office; U.S. General Accounting Office, *Drug Smuggling: Capabilities for Interdicting Private Aircraft Are Limited and Costly*, GAO/GGD-88-93 (Washington, D.C.: Government Printing Office, June 1989). On the drug summit, see *Washington Post*, October 11, 1989, A31; *Washington Post*, October 13, 1989, A29; and *Washington Post*, November 21, 1989, A20.

10. INM, *INCSR, March 1989*, 109, 113; *INCSR, April 1993*, 163.

11. *Washington Post*, August 1, 1989, A19.

12. Shannon, *Desperados*, 425, writes of U.S. policy that "lies, delusions, and wishful thinking [have] characterized two decades of the war on drugs." Much of her ire, however, is directed at the government of Mexico. See also James S. Mills, *The Underground Empire: Where Crime and Governments Embrace* (New York: Dell, 1986), 1148-61.

13. Richard B. Craig, "Illicit Drug Traffic and U.S.-Latin American Relations," *Washington Quarterly* 8 (Fall 1985): 105, 118-24; Richard B. Craig, "United States Antidrug Policy with Mexico: Consequences for American Society and U.S.-Mexican Relations," (unpublished ms.; copy in possession of the author); Samuel I. del Villar, "The Illicit U.S.-Mexico Drug Market: Failure of Policy and an Alternative," in *Mexico and the United States: Managing the Relationship*, ed. Riordan Roett (Boulder, Colo.: Westview, 1988), 191-208; Juan David Lindau, "Percepciones Mexicanas de la Política Exterior de Estados Unidos: el caso Camarena Salazar," *Foro Internacional* 27 (April-June 1987): 562-75; Raphael Francis Perl, "Narcopolítica: la ley norteamericana contra el abuso de drogas y las relaciones Estados Unidos-México," *Cuadernos Semestrales* No. 20 (second half of 1986): 239-56; Gregory F. Treverton, "Narcotics in U.S.-Mexican Relations," in *Mexico and the United States*, 209-20; Walker, *Drug Control in the Americas*.

14. Peter Reuter and David Ronfeldt, "Quest for Integrity: The Mexican-U.S. Drug Issue in the 1980s," *Journal of Interamerican Studies and World Affairs* 34 (Fall 1992): 89-153.

15. Del Villar, "The Illicit U.S.-Mexico Drug Market," 194-97.

16. Bruce Michael Bagley, "Interdependence and U.S. Policy Toward Mexico in the 1980s," in *Mexico and the United States*, 223-41; Treverton, "Narcotics in U.S.-Mexican Relations," 191ff.

17. Constantine C. Menges, *Inside the National Security Council: The True Story of the Unmaking of Reagan's Foreign Policy* (New York: Simon and Schuster, 1988), 118-23, 131-35. *New York Times*, April 28, 1983, A1, A11-A12 for Reagan's speech to a joint session of Congress on security and Central America.

18. Lars Schoultz, *National Security and United States Policy toward Latin America* (Princeton: Princeton University Press, 1987).

19. Bruce M. Bagley, "U.S. Foreign Policy and the War on Drugs: Analysis of a Policy Failure," *Journal of Interamerican Studies and World Affairs* 30 (Summer/Fall 1988): 189-212.

20. Bagley, 196-204.

21. Despite subsequent plans for a drug summit with Mexican participation, it is hard not to conclude that the Bush-Bennett antidrug strategy of September 5, 1989, played down the importance of Mexico in U.S. strategy. Yet U.S. officials have long made statements about the signal importance of drug control in Mexico; see, for example, U.S. Congress, House of Representatives, Select Committee on Narcotics Abuse and Control, *Annual Report for the Year 1986*, 99 Cong., 2 sess. (Washington, D.C.: Government Printing Office, 1987), 89; also, *Hearing before the Select Committee*

on Narcotics Abuse and Control, "International Narcotics Control: Provisions of the Anti-Drug Abuse Act of 1986 and Budget Decisionmaking," 100 Cong., 1 sess., March 25, 1987 (Washington, D.C.: Government Printing Office, 1987), 28. And see James W. Van Wert, "The U.S. State Department's Narcotics Control Policy in the Americas," *Journal of Interamerican Studies and World Affairs* 30 (Summer/Fall 1988): 6.

22. Shannon, *Desperados*, 69, 108-09; Walker, *Drug Control in the Americas*, 193-94, 213-14; Richard B. Craig, "La Campaña Permanente: Mexico's Antidrug Campaign," *Journal of Interamerican Studies and World Affairs* 20 (May 1978): 107-31.

23. House Select Committee, *Annual Report, 1985*, 99 Cong., 2 sess. (Washington, D.C.: Government Printing Office, 1986), 66-71; Craig, "Illicit Drug Traffic and U.S.-Latin American Relations," 118-23.

24. Walker, *Drug Control in the Americas*, 213-16. At the end of October 1987, Senator Alphonse M. D'Amato (R-NY) declared, "There is no major drug crusade. It is a sham." *New York Times*, October 26, 1987, 1.

25. The analysis of decision making in this chapter is informed by the extensive literature on psychology and decision making. Because policy matters such as drug control are so affect-laden, insights from cognitive and motivational psychology provide considerable guidance in understanding the actions of policy makers. Generally, see Irving L. Janis and Leon Mann, *Decision Making: A Psychological Analysis of Conflict, Choice, and Commitment* (New York: Free Press, 1977); Alexander L. George, *Presidential Decisionmaking in Foreign Policy: The Effective Use of Information and Advice* (Boulder, Colo.: Westview, 1980), 58-61; Janice Gross Stein, "Building Politics into Psychology: The Misperception of Threat," *Political Psychology* 9 (June 1988): 251-56.

26. House Select Committee, *Annual Report, 1985*, 69; Shannon, *Desperados*, 69, 108-09.

27. Shannon, *Desperados*, 399.

28. Shannon, *Desperados*, 212. U.S. Congress. House of Representatives, *Hearing before the Select Committee on Narcotics Abuse and Control*, "Impact of Gramm-Rudman on Federal Drug Programs," 99 Cong., 2 sess., March 18, 1986 (Washington, D.C.: Government Printing Office, 1986), 4-6.

29. House Select Committee, "Impact of Gramm-Rudman," 5. U.S. Congress, House of Representatives, *Hearing before the Committee on Foreign Affairs*, "United States-Mexican Cooperation in Narcotics Control Efforts," 99 Cong., 2 sess., July 17, 1986 (Washington, D.C.: Government Printing Office, 1986), 98-99; also, *Hearing before the Committee on Foreign Affairs*, "Review of Latin American Narcotics Control Issues," 100 Cong., 1 sess., March 18, 1987 (Washington, D.C.: Government Printing Office, 1987), 2.

30. U.S. Congress, House of Representatives, *Hearings before the Select Committee on Narcotics Abuse and Control*, "U.S. Foreign Policy and International Narcotics Control—Part II," 100 Cong., 2 sess., March 29, 1988 (Washington, D.C.: Government Printing Office, 1988), 43.

31. Regarding defensive avoidance and the strategies of satisficing and bolstering, see Janis and Mann, *Decision Making*, 52-59; Richard Ned Lebow, *Between War and Peace: The Nature of International Crisis* (Baltimore: Johns Hopkins University Press, 1981), 107-11.

32. Shannon, *Desperados*, 320-27. At a hearing on the 1989 INCSR, held on April 4, by the Senate Foreign Relations Subcommittee on Terrorism, Narcotics, and International Communications, Helms asserted that "Mexico has the worst record of cooperation with the U.S. government" and that "narcotics corruption has run rampant at the highest levels of the Mexican government." Helms's position on Mexico would seem to contradict Robert Jervis's contention that "beliefs about the most important issues of foreign policy — those involving war and peace — are usually unrelated to roles." (The subcommittee's hearing aired on the C-SPAN television network.) Yet since Helms's role was a self-arrogated one, which placed ideology over organizational duties, his was the exception that proved the rule. Robert Jervis, *Perception and Misperception in International Politics* (Princeton: Princeton University Press, 1976), 26.

33. Shannon, *Desperados*, 326-27. Smith evidently did not understand why Mexican surnames are formulated as they are. See Foreign Affairs Committee, "United States-Mexican Cooperation," 30, 34, 51. Given the tenor of Smith's statements regarding Mexico, his position stood out as an example of what some political psychologists describe as motivated bias. See Richard Ned Lebow and Janice Gross Stein, "The Limits of Cognitive Models: Carter, Afghanistan, and Foreign Policy" (unpublished ms.; copy in possession of the author). In hearings on the 1989 INCSR, Smith asked INM and DEA officials about their confidence in the reliability of crop eradication statistics provided by Mexican authorities: "How do we know that they are not lying?" U.S. Congress, House of Representatives, *Hearing before the Committee on Foreign Affairs*, "Review of the 1989 International Narcotics Control Strategy Report," 101 Cong., 1 sess., February 28: 7, 9, 14, 15, and March 22, 1989 (Washington, D.C.: Government Printing Office, 1989), 166, 168.

34. Foreign Affairs Committee, "United States-Mexican Cooperation," 122; U.S. Congress. House of Representatives, *Hearing before the Committee on Foreign Affairs*, "The Worldwide Drug Situation and International Narcotics Control Programs," 100 Cong., 1 sess., March 5, 1987 (Washington, D.C.: Government Printing Office, 1987), 50; U.S. Congress. House of Representatives, *Hearing before the Committee on Foreign Affairs*, "Worldwide Review of the 1988 International Narcotics Control Strategy Report," 100 Cong., 2 sess., March 3, 1988 (Washington, D.C.: Government Printing Office, 1988), 10 for the quote from Smith. See also House Select Committee, "U.S. Foreign Policy and International Narcotics Control—Part II," 54-55; U.S. Congress, House of Representatives, *Hearings and Markup before the Subcommittee on Western Hemisphere Affairs of the Committee on Foreign Affairs*, "Presidential Certifications Regarding International Narcotics Control," 100 Cong., 2 sess., March 29 and April 13, 1988 (Washington, D.C.: Government Printing Office, 1988), 34-35.

35. Jon R. Thomas, "Controlling International Narcotics Production and Trafficking," March 19, 1985, U.S. Department of State, Current Policy, No. 675.

36. George P. Shultz, "The Campaign Against Drugs: The International Dimension," September 14, 1984, U.S. Department of State, Current Policy No. 611; "Narcotics: A Global Threat," May 4, 1987, U.S. Department of State, Current Policy No. 967; Elliott Abrams, "Drug Wars: The New Alliance Against Traffickers and Terrorists," February 10, 1986, U.S. Department of State, Current Policy No. 792. Abrams's speech to the Council on Foreign Relations in New York City can be seen as a prelude to President Reagan's national security decision directive of early April. Importantly, Abrams linked drug trafficking with guerrilla groups in South America.

37. Note 20 above. John C. Whitehead, "U.S. International Narcotics Control Programs and Policies," August 14, 1986, U.S. Department of State, Current Policy No. 863.

38. Sergio García Ramírez, *Narcotráfico: Un Punto de Vista Mexicano* (México, D.F., México: Miguel Angel Porrúa, 1989), 100; U.S. Congress. House of Representatives, *Hearing before the Select Committee on Narcotics Abuse and Control,* "Drug Interdiction," 100 Cong., 1 sess., April 30, 1987 (Washington, D.C.: Government Printing Office, 1987), 13. Trott also served for a time as chairman of the Enforcement Coordinating Group of the National Drug Policy Board. As for the attorney general's office being "soft on Mexico," see Shannon, *Desperados,* 311, 335-39.

39. U.S. Congress. House of Representatives, *Hearing before the Select Committee on Foreign Affairs,* "The Role and Activities of the National Drug Enforcement Policy Board," 99 Cong., 2 sess., September 30, 1986 (Washington, D.C.: Government Printing Office, 1986), 35-39. Smith, no doubt, was also upset by the release in October 1986 of the INCSR update in which the State Department claimed that discussions with Mexico had improved drug control performance there. INM, *INCSR, Mid-Year Update, October 1986,* i, 10.

40. For example, see INM, *INCSR, March 1986,* 112-13, 116; House Select Committee, *Annual Report, 1984,* 98 Cong., 2 sess. (Washington, D.C.: Government Printing Office, 1984), 136-37.

41. Foreign Affairs Committee, "Worldwide Narcotics Review of the 1988 INCSR," 69-71, 74-75, 79; House Select Committee, "U.S. Foreign Policy and International Narcotics Control—Part II," 31-32. About the 1988 INCSR, Smith declared: "This is a joke."

42. Although Mexico did not receive a national interest certification, a reading of the report suggests that security considerations played a key role in the certification of Mexico. INM, *INCSR, March 1988,* iii.

43. See, for example, House Select Committee, *Annual Report, 1985,* 69-71.

44. House Select Committee, *Annual Report, 1985,* 136-37, 145; House Select Committee, *Annual Report, 1985,* 66-71. Compare the almost uniformly critical view in U.S. Congress, House of Representatives, *Report of a Staff Study Mission to Southeast Asia, South America, Central America, and the Caribbean (August 1984 to January 1985 to the Committee on Foreign Affairs),* "U.S. Narcotics Control Programs Overseas: An Assessment," 99 Cong., 1 sess., February 22, 1985 (Washington, D.C.: Government Printing Office, 1985), 34-40.

45. House Select Committee, *Annual Report, 1985,* 105-07, 113-17.

46. Rangel and Gilman refused to join Smith in calling for the decertification of Mexico in 1988. Foreign Affairs Committee, "Worldwide Narcotics Review of the 1988 INCSR," 81; Foreign Affairs Committee, "Presidential Certifications," 3, 160.

47. The conflict-theory model of decision making as described by Janis and Mann is pertinent to the analysis here. The leaders of the House Select Committee could have resorted to the strategy of defensive avoidance and put the onus on the Mexicans for causing drug problems in the United States. Instead, they sought to maintain a cordial working relationship.

48. U.S. Congress, House of Representatives, *Hearing before the Select Committee on Narcotics Abuse and Control,* "International Narcotics Control," 99 Cong., 2 sess., September 12, 1985 (Washington, D.C.: Government Printing Offie, 1985), 2; U.S. Congress, House of Representatives, "Drug Interdiction," 10, 33.

49. U.S. Congress, House of Representatives, *Hearing before the Select Committee on Narcotics Abuse and Control,* "Narcotics Control Conference," 99 Cong., 2 sess., February 10, 1986 (Washington, D.C.: Government Printing Office, 1987), 3; U.S. Congress, "Provisions of the Anti-Drug Abuse Act of 1986 and Budget Decisionmaking," 3, 25; U.S. Congress, *Hearing before the Select Committee on Narcotics Abuse and Control,* "Narcotics Control in Mexico," 100 Cong., 1 sess., August 5, 1987 (Washington, D.C.: Government Printing Office, 1988), 1-13.

50. House Select Committee, *Annual Report, 1988,* 100 Cong., 2 sess. (Washington, D.C.: Government PrintingOffice, 1989), 121-27, 131. Interview with House Select Committee Staff Director Edward H. Jurith by William O. Walker III, January 23, 1989; *New York Times,* December 12, 1988, A7; *New York Times,* November 23 1988, D20.

51. Foreign Affairs Committee, "U.S. Narcotics Control Programs: An Assessment," 39; Shannon, *Desperados,* 188-91, 236-39.

52. Shannon, *Desperados,* 238. In the 1988 debate over the certification of Mexico, Lawn defended aspects of Mexico's drug control record; House Select Committee, "U.S. Foreign Policy and International Narcotics Control—Part II," 45. It appears likely that the DEA (and INM) were not convinced that Mexico merited a presidential certification in 1988 but accepted Reagan's finding and defended the decision-making process before Congress. Foreign Affairs Committee, "Worldwide Narcotics Review of the 1988 INCSR," 69-71, 74-75, 79-84; House Select Committee, "U.S. Narcotics Foreign Policy and International Narcotics Control_Part II," 54-58.

53. House Select Committee, "Impact of Gramm-Rudman," 28.

54. INM, *INCSR, March 1989,* 109. For a defense of Operation Vanguard, see House Select Committee, "U.S. Foreign Policy and International Narcotics Control—Part II," 32-35.

55. *Washington Post,* August 15, 1989, A1, A14. And see a report on corruption within DEA ranks, *Washington Post,* August 17, 1989, A1, A13. See also *Washington Post,* November 29, 1991, A1, A42; *New York Times,* March 8, 1993, A3.

56. Walker, *Drug Control in the Americas,* 202-23.

57. House Select Committee, *Annual Report, 1987,* 100 Cong., 2 sess. (Washington, D.C.: Government Printing Office, 1988), 19-20. The committee had long argued that the lack of a strategy had a telling impact on the Mexican situation; House Select Committee, *Annual Report, 1985,* 68-69; House Select Committee, *Annual Report, 1986,* 89, 107, 109-13.

58. Foreign Affairs Committee, "The Role and Activities of the NDEPB"; House Select Committee, "Narcotics Control in Mexico," 1-6.

59. House Select Committee, "Narcotics Control in Mexico," 12-16; U.S. Congress, House of Representatives, *Hearing before the Select Committee on Narcotics Abuse and Control,* "National Drug Policy Board Strategy Plans," 100 Cong., 2 sess., April 14, 1988 (Washington, D.C.: Government Printing Office,

1988), 5-10; U.S. Congress, *Hearing before the Select Committee on Narcotics Abuse and Control*, "U.S. Foreign Policy and International Narcotics Control," 100 Cong., 2 sess., March 16, 1988 (Washington, D.C.: Government Printing Office, 1988), 7, indicates that Attorney General Dick Thornburgh realized that developing for the NDPB was essential to better drug control decision making.

60. *New York Times*, April 15, 1988, A6; Foreign Affairs Committee, "Presidential Certifications," 3; House Select Committee, "U.S. Foreign Policy and International Narcotics Control—Part II," 31-32. A report by the General Accounting Office likely raised Congressional concern over the situation in Mexico; U.S. General Accounting Office, *Drug Control: U.S.-Mexico Opium Poppy and Marijuana Aerial Eradication Campaign*, GAO-NSAID-88-73 (Washington, D.C.: Government Printing Office, January 1988).

61. *Excélsior* (Mexico City), April 15, 1988.

62. U.S. General Accounting Office, *Drug Control: U.S. International Narcotics Control Activities*, GAO-NSAID-88-114 (Washington, D.C.: Government Printing Office, March 1988); Raphael Francis Perl, "The U.S. Congress, International Drug Policy, and the Anti-Drug Abuse Act of 1988," *Journal of Interamerican Studies and World Affairs* 30 (Summer/Fall 1988): 19-51 details the provisions of the 1988 act as they apply to international control.

63. A brief survey of the multifaceted nature of the U.S.-Mexican relations can be found in the seven articles comprising "Mexico," *Current History* 92 (February 1993).

64. *New York Times*, August 1, 1990, A10; *Washington Post*, December 13, 1989, A32.

65. *Washington Post*, January 11, 1990, E1; *Washington Post*, January 13, 1990, A17.

66. *New York Times*, January 16, 1990, A12. Also, Miguel Aldana Ibarra, formerly the head of Interpol in Mexico and cousin of Manuel Ibarra Herrera who previously headed the MFJP, claimed that Camarena worked with drug traffickers and, in fact, was living in La Jolla, California. *Washington Post*, February 10, 1990, A14. See also countercharges made in a memorandum by the U.S. Attorney's office in Los Angeles to the effect that Salinas's chief of police in Mexico City, Javier García Paniagna, was aware of plans to kidnap Camarena; *Washington Post*, May 8, 1990, A30.

67. *New York Times*, April 24, 1990, A5.

68. INM, *INCSR, March 1990*, 185, 187.

69. *Washington Post*, May 16, 1990, A13; *New York Times*, March 31, 1993, A5.

70. *New York Times*, June 30, 1990, A25; INM, *INCSR, Mid-Year Update, September 1990*, 28.

71. INM, *INCSR, March 1992*, 167-70; *New York Times*, April 2, 1993, A4.

72. See the discussion about decision making in Chapter 3.

73. Jorge Chabat, "Mexico: So Close to the United States, So Far from Latin America," *Current History* 92 (February 1993): 55-58.

74. *New York Times*, February 25, 1990, 18.

75. *New York Times*, March 17, 1990, 3.

76. *New York Times*, April 17, 1990, A2; *Washington Post*, April 17, 1990, A14; *New York Times*, April 20, 1990, A1, A8. The DEA denied that it had agreed to pay bounty hunters up to $100,000 for the doctor's capture; *New York Times*, April 21, 1990, A3.

77. *Washington Post*, April 21, 1990, A18.

78. NBC Nightly News, April 26, 1990; *New York Times*, April 27, 1990, A8; *Washington Post*, April 27, 1990, A3.

79. *New York Times*, April 27, 1990, A8; *New York Times*, April 29, 1990, 9.

80. *Washington Post*, April 29, 1990, A21.

81. Americas Watch, *Human Rights in Mexico: A Policy of Impunity* (New York: Americas Watch, June 1990), 1-2, 11-16 (the quotation is from page 2). See also *Washington Post*, June 13, 1990, A33, A34; *New York Times*, July 5, 1990, A6. One week before the release of the Americas Watch report, Salinas issued a decree creating a National Commission of Human Rights under the Interior Secretariat. The establishment of the commission seemed to be consistent with the president's pledge to bring a true democracy to Mexico, along with a modern economy, but critics understandably wondered what authority the commission would possess.

82. *New York Times*, June 10, 1990, E4; *Excélsior* (Mexico City), June 14, 1990; *Washington Post*, November 27, 1990, A14; *New York Times*, November 27, 1990, A3; *New York Times*, November 28, 1990, A6.

83. *Washington Post*, July 5, 1990, A8; *Washington Post*, July 6, 1990, A4; *Washington Post*, July 16, 1990, A1, A16-A17 (the quotation is from page A1).

84. *Washington Post*, August 24, 1990, A23; *New York Times*, August 29, 1990, A12; INM, *INCSR, Mid-Year Update, September 1990*, 28-29.

85. Report of the Bilateral Commission on the Future of United States-Mexican Relations, *The Challenge of Interdependence: Mexico and the United States* (Lanham, Md.: University Press of America, 1989); more generally, see World Peace Foundation, *Collective Security in the Americas: New Directions* (Boston: World Peace Foundation, 1988).

86. House Select Committee, *Annual Report, 1988*, 121-27.

87. Robert O. Keohane, "International Institutions: Two Approaches," *International Studies Quarterly* 32 (December 1988): 380-81.

88. U.S. Congress, Arms Control and Foreign Policy Caucus, *The Developing World: Danger Point for U.S. Security* (Washington, D.C.: Government Printing Office, August 1, 1989), 1-8, 65-72.

89. García Ramírez, *Narcotráfico*, 11.

References

Abbott, Michael H. 1988. "The Army and the Drug War: Politics or National Security?" *Parameters*. December: 95-112.

Bagley, Bruce M. 1992a. "Myths of Militarization: Enlisting Armed Forces in the War on Drugs." In *Drug Policy in the Americas*, ed. Peter Smith. Boulder, Colo.: Westview Press.

Bagley, Bruce M. 1992b. "After San Antonio." *Journal of Interamerican Studies and World Affairs*. Fall, 1-12.

Bagley, Bruce M. 1988. "U.S. Foreign Policy and the War on Drugs: Analysis of a Policy Failure." *Journal of Interamerican Studies and World Affairs*. Summer/Fall, 189-212.

Chernick, Marc W. 1990. "The Drug War." *NACLA: Report on the Americas*. April, 30-38.

Craig, Richard B. 1977. "Operation Intercept: The International Politics of Pressure." Paper presented at the Organization of American Historians Convention. Atlanta, Georgia. April.

Craig, Richard B. 1978. "La Campaña Permanente: Mexico's Antidrug Campaign." *Journal of Interamerican Studies and World Affairs*. May, 107-131.

Epstein, Edward Jay. 1977. *Agency of Fear: Opiates and Political Power in America*. New York: G.P. Putnam's Sons.

Gellman, Irwin F. 1979. *Good Neigbor Diplomacy: United States Policies in Latin America*. Baltimore: Johns Hopkins University Press.

Green, David. 1971. *The Containment of Latin America: A History of Myths and Realities of the Good Neighbor Policy*. Chicago: Quadrangle Books.

Green, David. 1970. "The Cold War Comes to Latin America." In *Politics and Policies of the Truman Administration*, ed. Barton J. Bernstein. Chicago: Quadrangle Books.

Gutiérrez-Noriega, Carlos, and Vicente Zapata Ortiz. 1947. *Estudios Sobre la Coca y la Cocaina en el Peru*. Lima: Ministerio de Educacíon Pública.

Healy, Kevin. 1988. "Coca, The State, and the Peasantry in Bolivia, 1982-1988." *Journal of Interamerican Studies and World Affairs*. Summer/Fall, 105-126.

Keohane, Robert O. 1984. *After Hegemony: Cooperation and Discord in the World Political Economy*. Princeton, N.J.: Princeton University Press.

Kinder, David Clark. 1981. "Bureaucratic Cold Warrior: Harry J. Anslinger and Illicit Narcotics Traffic." *Pacific Historical Review*. May.

Kinder, David Clark, and William O. Walker III. 1986. "Stable Force in a Storm: Harry J. Anslinger and United States Narcotic Foreign Policy." *Journal of American History*. March.

Klare, Michael T. 1977. *Supplying Repression: U.S. Support for Authoritarian Regimes Abroad*. Washington, D.C.: Institute for Policy Studies.

Langguth, A.J. 1978. *Hidden Terrors: The Truth about U.S. Police Operations in Latin America*. New York: Patheon Books.

Lee, Rensselaer W. III. 1989. *The White Labyrinth: Cocaine and Political Power*. New Brunswick, N.J.: Transaction Publishers.

Levinson, Jerome, and Juan de Onís. 1970. *The Alliance That Lost Its Way: A Critical Report on the Alliance for Progress*. Chicago: Quadrangle Press.

McClintock, Cynthia. 1988. "The War on Drugs: The Peruvian Case." *Journal of Interamerican Studies and World Affairs*. Summer/Fall, 127-142.

McCoy, Alfred W. 1991. *The Politics of Heroin: CIA Complicity in the Global Drug Trade*. Brooklyn, N.Y.: Lawrence Hill Books.

McWilliams, John C. 1990. *The Protectors: Harry J. Anslinger and the Federal Bureau of Narcotics, 1930-1962*. Newark: University of Deleware Press.

Menzel, Lt. Col. Sewall H. 1989. "Operation Blast Furnace." *Army*. November, 24-32.

Morales, Edmundo. 1989. *Cocaine: White Gold Rush in Peru*. Tuscon: University of Arizona Press.

Musto, David F. 1987. *The American Disease: Origins of Narcotic Control*. Expanded ed. New York: Oxford University Press.

Poitras, Guy. 1990. *The Ordeal of Hegemony: The United States and Latin America*. Boulder, Colo.: Westview Press.

Rabe, Stephen G. 1988. *Eisenhower and Latin America: The Foreign Policy of Anticommunism*. Chapel Hill: University of North Carolina Press.

Scott, Peter Dale, and Jonathan Marshall. 1991. *Cocaine Politics: Drugs, Armies, and the CIA in Central America*. Berkeley and Los Angeles: University of California Press.

Shafer, D. Michael. 1988. *Deadly Paradigms: The Failure of U.S. Counterinsurgency Policy*. Princeton, N.J.: Princeton University Press.

Sheahan, John. 1991. "Economic Forces and U.S. Policies." In *Exporting Democracy*, ed. Abraham F. Lowenthal. Baltimore: Johns Hopkins University Press.

Skidmore, Thomas E., and Peter H. Smith. 1989. *Modern Latin America*. New York: Oxford University Press.

Slotkin, Richard S. 1973. *Regeneration Through Violence: The Mythology of the American Frontier, 1600-1860*. Middletown: Wesleyan University Press.

Tokatlián, Juan Gabriel, and Bruce M. Bagley. 1990. *Economia y Politica del Narcotrafico*. Bogotá: CEREC.

Trask, Roger. 1977. "The Impact of the Cold War on United States-Latin American Relations, 1945-1949." *Diplomatic History*. Summer, 271-284.

U.S. Congress. House of Representatives. 1982. *Annual Report for the Year 1981 of the Select Committee on Narcotics Abuse and Control*. Washington, D.C.: GPO.

U.S. Congress. House of Representatives. 1986. *Hearing Before the Committee on Foreign Affairs*. "The Role of the Military in Narcotics Control Overseas." August 5.

U.S. Congress. House of Representatives. 1990. *Hearing Before the Committee on Foreign Affairs*. "Operation Snowcap: Past, Present, and Future." May 23.

U.S. Congress. House of Representatives, Committee on Government Operations. 1990. *Thirty-Eighth Report by the Committee on Government Operations.* "United States Anti-narcotics Activities in the Andean Region." November 30.

U.S. Congress. House of Representatives, Committee on Government Operations. 1990. *Thirteenth Report by the Committee on Government Operations.* "Stopping the Flood of Cocaine with Operation Snowcap: Is It Working?" August 14.

U.S. Department of State, Office of Inspector General. *Report of Audit: International Narcotics Control Programs in Peru and Bolivia.* Memorandum No.9CI-007. March.

U.S. Department of State, Office of Inspector General. 1991. *Report of Audit: Drug Control Activities in Bolivia.* Memorandum No. 2-CI-001. October.

U.S. General Accounting Office. 1991. *Drug War: Observations on Counternarcotics Aid to Colombia.* GAO/NSIAD-91-296. Washington, D.C.: Government Printing Office. September.

U.S. General Accounting Office. 1991. *Drug War: U.S. Programs in Peru Face Serious Obstacles.* GAO/NSIAD-92-36. Washington, D.C.: GPO, October.

U.S. General Accounting Office. 1992. *The Drug War: Counternarcotics Programs in Colombia and Peru.* GAO/T-NSIAD-92-9. February 20.

U.S. General Accounting Office. 1988. *Drug Control: U.S.-Mexico Opium and Marijuana Aerial Eradication Program.* GAO-NSIAD-88-73. January.

Walker, William O., III. 1989a. *Drug Control in the Americas.* Revised ed. Albuquerque: University of New Mexico Press.

Walker, William O., III. 1989b. "U.S. Drug Control Policy and Drug Trafficking in the Americas: An Unwitting Alliance." Paper presented at the American Society of Criminology Annual Meeting. Reno, Nevada. November.

Walker, William O., III. 1991a. *Opium and Foreign Policy: The Anglo-American Search for Order in Asia, 1912-1954.* Chapel Hill: University of North Carolina Press.

Walker, William O., III. 1991b. "Decision-making Theory and Narcotic Foreign Policy: Implications for Historical Analysis." *Diplomatic History.* Winter, 31-45.

Chapter Twenty-one

U.S.-Mexican Border Drug Control: Operation Alliance as a Case Study

Gabriela D. Lemus

Introduction

D rug trafficking from Mexico, which is both a supply and transit country, into the United States has increased in direct correlation to the decrease of trafficking in the Caribbean/South Florida area. Since 1986, the net effect of this increased traffic has prompted the United States to implement a more stringent drug interdiction policy along its border with Mexico, characterized by Operation Alliance. The policy has been surprisingly inconsequential to the overall relationship between the two countries except in isolated instances — for example, the case of Enrique Camarena and the kidnapping of Alvarez Machain — because of the importance Mexico has placed on its economic recovery, which has increasingly affected the United States.

The issue of drug trafficking, though long important to the domestic agenda of the United States, tends to experience highs and lows in terms of public perception and, consequently, as a foreign policy issue. In general, U.S. response has been to consider Mexico's role as a drug producing and transit country outside the primary bilateral relationship, particularly when the United States considers other matters more important to its bilateral relationship, such as the North American Free Trade Agreement (NAFTA). Nevertheless, the U.S. border strategy, in accordance with the national drug control strategy, has resulted in large investments of money for a vast network of drug law enforcement and interdiction across the U.S. border area. Thus far, the resulting strategy has not affected the foundation of the overall relationship between the United States and Mexico; however, in the future, it could result in a foreign policy problem for the United States, especially in light of the 1993 NAFTA ratification. NAFTA will engender increased movement between the two countries and, accordingly, increase the likelihood of drug trafficking. The possibilities for bilateral problems would be greater because of the accompanying enhanced focus on Mexicans crossing into the United States which could lead to an upswing in human rights violations.[1]

Background of U.S. Drug Policy and the U.S.-Mexican Border

In order to demonstrate that the drug issue is rarely central to the overall quality of U.S.-Mexican relations, it is first useful to place U.S. drug strategy into a historical context. Since World War II, the energy and efforts of U.S. security officials were almost solely concentrated on the Cold War with the Soviet Union. However, when the Berlin Wall fell in 1989, so did the reasons to maintain Cold War policies, and the focus of U.S. national security broadened to include a number of social issues that, despite affecting the United States over a prolonged period of time, were formerly suppressed because East-West ideological concerns were viewed as more important by the various U.S. administrations. In the late 1960s, in reaction to the "turned-on generation," the Nixon administration responded to the problems of narcotics control by seeking out the source of drugs and placing drug control on the U.S.-Mexican agenda in 1969 with Operation Intercept.[2] In subsequent years, the issue of drug trafficking was treated as a minor but contentious one that escalated in importance when the overall fabric of the relationship would snag. Prior to the 1961 Single Convention and the efforts of the Nixon administration, the 1920s marked the last long-range effort that had been made to control illicit narcotic substances at a national and international level with any consistency or seriousness.[3]

In recent years, particularly since 1988, economic conditions in the United States have steadily worsened. The American people are feeling the pinch after many years of allowing credit to escalate and savings to decrease, and they have responded with insecurity as their basic livelihoods became threatened. U.S. domestic public reaction toward the establishment of a North American Free Trade Agreement that includes Mexico and Canada, for example, represents a wide range of feeling. In response to the increasing evidence of drug smuggling, the border area has been targeted as an interdiction point by the U.S. public and policy makers. In the past, the border held considerable notoriety because of its connection with illegal immigrants crossing over from Mexico. The border is once again the center of attention given the increase in traffic, of both commerce and illegal substances such as opium, cocaine, and marijuana. The U.S.-Mexican border, because of its very nature, forcibly places the relationship between the two countries at a premium. The border is the acute representation of the interdependence between the two countries on many levels, particularly in social and economic terms.

U.S. policy responses to domestic consumption of illegal drugs and to their supply directly reflect the confusion that a touchy issue like drugs generates when placed in the arena of foreign policy. The United States has attempted to restrict illegal trafficking for generations. Still, large quantities of illegal drugs get through the ever-porous border area. It has been estimated that between 50 to 80 percent of the cocaine entering the United States is smuggled across the Southwest border with Mexico.[4] The border is long and presents enforcement efforts with the challenge of a rugged, mountainous terrain as well as an arid desert. There are many pockets and long stretches of unguarded emptiness available to smugglers to practice their activities. Traffickers merely find alternative routes for their shipments when a particular route is discovered by U.S. law enforcement officials, engendering what is commonly referred to as the "balloon effect." In a special report to the U.S. Senate Committee on Finance, the General Accounting Office (GAO) expressed its concern over the adequacy of the law enforcement infrastructure currently in place along the border.[5] Even though both the U.S. and Mexican Customs Offices have attempted to improve their oversight procedures, serious problems remain. The GAO proposed that even if capital improvement projects were completed, staffing the expanded structure adequately could remain problematic.[6]

The Transition from Reagan to Bush

The explanation of asymmetrical responses to the drug issue on both sides of the border is one of different agendas. Mexican perceptions of drug trafficking have traditionally been less stringent than U.S. perceptions. Mexico has continuously stated that more emphasis should be placed on demand-side strategies. The Mexican government has had other problems to contend with that are politically more important for the survival of the ruling party, the Partido Revolucionario Institucional (PRI), headed de facto since his election in 1988 by President Carlos Salinas de Gortari. The economic situation has dominated the Mexican security agenda for the last three administrations. Economic growth has been the vital issue for PRI survivability; the cessation of drug smuggling, a negligible one. Furthermore, Mexico does not suffer from the same extensive drug addiction problems as the United States. Its drug problems primarily stem from legally available substances such as inhalants and alcohol. Mexican assistance to U.S. law enforcement efforts is more of a response to U.S. domestic pressures than an acknowledgment that drugs pose a security problem for Mexico.

At the end of the 1980s, Phase I in U.S. drug policy, the Reagan supply-side strategy received much criticism because it apparently did little to impede either the availability of drugs or the prices. The strategy was even referred to as being "an abysmal failure."[7] As a foreign policy initiative, Reagan's strategy was perceived negatively by the countries affected by it, since the policy considered the drug problem as essentially belonging to the country supplying the illegal substances without much concentration on their primary marketplace — the United States. In order to put this assessment into perspective, it must be noted that the United States has the largest drug consuming population in the world. According to some U.S. government estimates, approximately 60 to 70 percent of cocaine finds its way to the U.S. market through the Mexican border.

In 1985, Mexico was in the process of being decertified by the U.S. Congress, when DEA agent Enrique Camarena Salazar and a Mexican pilot, Alfredo Zavala Aguilar, were abducted, tortured, and subsequently murdered. The event was extensively covered by the U.S. media and cast a temporary shadow over the otherwise cordial U.S.-Mexican relationship. Responding to perceived Mexican foot-dragging in the Camarena case, on February 16, 1985, the United States announced strenuous U.S. Customs inspections along the border in order to find Camarena should the kidnappers attempt to transport him back into the United States. Mexicans received this news skeptically because it seemed improbable the kidnappers would ever attempt to do that, but much more negative was the Mexican perception that the action was merely another U.S. attempt to compel Mexico to comply with U.S. efforts at drug enforcement in spite of Mexico's difference of opinion with regard to the proper focus of that very policy.

The Mexican people reacted to U.S. pressure with outrage. The Mexican Left accused the United States of seeking points on which to attack Mexico. This sentiment was exacerbated when Mexico was further attacked by the media in the United States as not working hard enough to bring the killers to justice, and claims appeared accusing senior Mexican officials and police of being corrupt and having sold out to the drug traffickers. Mexicans were incredulous that such rage over one DEA agent developed, particularly since dozens of Mexican police and DEA informants had been tortured and killed for the U.S. drug war while the U.S. government stood by silently.

Unfortunately, the U.S. accusations were credible given the proof that periodically appeared regarding the Mexican police's lack of organization, as well as the obstacles that were apparently placed to block the Camarena investigation. An often cited example was that of an investigation being conducted on Juan Ramón Matta Ballesteros, a known trafficker who had been apprehended, but whose investigation was delayed for one day by the Chief of the Federal Judicial Police of Mexico, in which time Matta disappeared.

Mexico's reaction to U.S. allegations was to counterattack by issuing negative reports on the drug addiction problems in the United States. Relations between the two countries became icy as accusations were traded, and U.S. disappointment grew as Mexico's response to the Camarena affair was deemed inadequate, not lending the matter sufficient importance, particularly in the eyes of the Justice Department and its DEA branch.

In response to Mexico's perceived foot-dragging, the United States sent DEA agents into Mexico. Furthermore, the United States issued a "travel advisory" that placed Mexico in a bad light by warning tourists to be careful in Mexico, which, in turn, gravely damaged the Mexican tourist industry — one of the country's chief sources of badly needed foreign exchange. The timing of the report was particularly harmful given Mexico's economic collapse. Mexicans perceived this action as a concerted effort on the part of the United States to pressure them into further compliance with the parameters U.S. officials had set regarding the Camarena investigation.

During 1986, the principal communications media in the United States systematically transmitted news that repeatedly doubted Mexico's efficiency, morality, and sincerity in its approach not only to the drug war but also to U.S.-Mexican bilateral relations. In sum, the Mexican government's legitimacy and its right to govern itself were placed into question.[8] Mexicans perceived this reaction in the press and in the Travel Advisory as a slap in the face and a direct reflection of the views held by the White House. However, this was a misperception and reflected Mexico's erroneous belief that the U.S. government controlled the American media, much in the same manner as it is controlled in Mexico.

Since Mexico did not place the Camarena situation as a high priority issue, it assumed that U.S. reaction was so strong only because Washington disagreed with Mexico's Central American policy which ran counter to that of Reagan and the United States.[9] But Mexico had committed a tactical error in judgment and had misperceived the actual importance of the "Camarena affair," which would henceforth periodically rise from the ashes as the Justice Department and its DEA operatives refused to let the issue slide into oblivion.

When George Bush became president, he continued with Reagan's antinarcotics campaign and zero-tolerance policy and unveiled Phase II of the drug war. The focus of his plan was external. It did not contain any major departures from the first phase of the antidrug fight, but it requested a substantial increase in funds by raising the budget to $10.6 billion, roughly $1.1 billion more than what had been previously assigned to it. About 29 percent of the money spent was designated to provide supply reduction and interdiction aid to Latin American nations. In a matter of weeks, it seemed, the United States switched from fighting the Cold War to fighting the "drug war." After invading Panama in December 1989, Bush promised to pay $2 billion over the next five years to fight drugs in the region. Traditionally, the DEA had been assigned responsibility for controlling the U.S. domestic drug trade, but with Phase II of the declared drug war, the DEA further strengthened its presence in Latin America. More than 150 agents began working in 17 countries and were primarily involved in paramilitary actions in the coca-rich regions of South America where they accompanied or orchestrated helicopter raids on processing labs and clandestine airstrips.

Domestically in the United States, a new National Drug Control Strategy was announced by President Bush in 1990 that designated five areas of the country as "high-intensity" drug trafficking regions, therefore making them eligible for additional federal resources and special aid: the U.S.-Mexican border, Los Angeles County, Houston, Miami, and New York. The high-intensity drug designation of these areas was not as impressive as it initially appeared since it brought with it only a slight increase in funding[10] and was but one element of the overall strategy. In order to assign the designation of "High-Intensity Drug Trafficking Area," in 1989 Congress directed that the administration consider six criteria. The most important were the amount of local resources spent on drug control, the seriousness of each area's drug problem, and the degree to which each area's drug problem had impacted other areas of the country. There was also a provision that involved the powers of U.S. Customs agents. Customs officials had wanted all their roughly 2,600 agents to be given the full powers of a DEA agent. The DEA objected and drug czar William J. Bennett developed a compromise under which 1,000 Customs agents would be "cross-designated."[11]

In 1990, the California National Guard embarked on its most wide-ranging effort ever to interdict illegal drugs being smuggled across the U.S.-Mexican border. The initiative, officials said, would basically duplicate 1989's much-publicized Operation Border Ranger II, which involved the posting of unarmed guards to assist in inspections at commercial ports of entry, including the huge Otay Mesa port in San Diego, and the deployment of armed Guard officers at observation posts set up along the border. The deployment of troops along the U.S.-Mexican border drew criticism from both the Mexican government, which viewed such actions as a possible threat to its sovereignty, as well as from immigrant representatives concerned about a possible increase in human rights abuses along the heavily traversed border zone. The guards' mission was to crack down on drug trafficking, but officials said Guard observations in 1990 also resulted in the arrests of several hundred undocumented immigrants. The border is crossed each night by hundreds of foreigners without official entry papers as well as by illegal drugs.

The primary thrust of the operation was to take place along California's 150-mile border with Mexico. The U.S. Department of Defense allocated approximately $70 million in drug fighting money to National Guard units nationwide during Fiscal Year 1990. Texas received the largest share, about $11 million, while California received $10 million.[12] Though these events signified an increase in income for these economically depressed areas, they also implied a recognition by the United States that Mexico's interest in the drug issue was not as great as its own and demonstrated that the United States was finding new uses for its military in the post-Cold War era.

As a direct result of U.S. fortification of its radar network in Florida and the Caribbean, Mexico became an increasingly popular transshipment point for the smuggling of cocaine. During the period 1989-1990, bilateral tensions increased to such a degree that Mexico was forced to bend to U.S. pressure. Indeed, U.S. pressure was so successful that Mexican federal police adopted more aggressive tactics and shot down four drug-laden planes in 1989 and declared that they would continue to fire at suspicious planes that would not respond to their warnings. The orders to shoot down the planes were given to the police from the office of Mexico's Assistant Attorney General, Javier Coello Trejo, who was in charge of the country's narcotics investigation unit. The orders were explicit: to open fire when there was absolute certainty that any doubtful aircraft was about to land in one of the unauthorized airstrips that dot Baja California Norte, Chihuahua, Sinaloa, Michoacan, and Oaxaca.[13]

The shooting down of the unresponsive aircraft occurred at a time when Mexico had stepped up its overall drug enforcement effort. Mexico seized approximately 75,000 pounds of cocaine in 1989. Still, U.S. officials claimed that the flow of South American cocaine through Mexico was greater than ever, and some believed that small planes, which are virtually undetectable, flying by way of Mexico had become the major means of shipping cocaine into the United States. The proportion of cocaine that was entering the United States through Mexico increased from about 30 percent in the early 1980s, to more than 50 percent by 1990, according to Charles J. Gutensohn, chief of the DEA's cocaine investigation unit in Washington. It was at this point that aerostat radar units were to gain prominence in the drug war.[14] Mexican Attorney General Coello stated that his office, along with the Army, had begun to update their radar system. The first phase, which cost $70 million, was to be completed by February 1990. The radar system was activated in December 1991 to track aircraft suspected of illicit activities heading north from South America.[15] A Western diplomat disclosed that a drug-interdiction system was also being built along the Guatemalan border with Mexican support.[16]

Even as Mexico demonstrated willingness to aid the United States in its drug war, it still refused to allow any joint operations with the United States on the grounds that these would violate Mexico's sovereignty. Furthermore, U.S. chase planes could not, and still cannot, engage in hot pursuit of suspected smugglers into Mexico. Mexican police continue to rely mostly on tipoffs from U.S. sources to intercept drug-laden flights. Planes began flying from Colombia through the Yucatan peninsula and then into northern Mexico, where cocaine was then smuggled overland into the United States.[17]

The transition from Reagan to Bush really made no difference to the overall U.S. policy for drug control, despite Bush's new National Drug Control

Strategy, and did not much affect Mexico. During the Bush administration, the drug issue ceased to be a point of contention between the United States and Mexico, because drug trafficking responses became much more manageable and other issues were placed in the limelight. In fact, the United States and Mexico improved their levels of communication and the coordination of antidrug efforts, although events such as the Camarena affair, Mexico's refusal to participate in joint drug projects, and the U.S. Congress' periodic threat to decertify Mexico were provocative.

The result of these vexations was attention, and resources were removed from issues which Mexico considered important to its very survival, such as its economic restructuring and the North American Free Trade Agreement. Mexico, therefore, encouraged the United States to place its drug war in diplomatic limbo in favor of helping Mexico improve its economic situation. U.S. officials arrived at the conclusion that since there were no guarantees of absolute Mexican compliance with the drug war, the United States would have to adopt a more aggressive stance within its own borders, thus accepting a policy of interdiction from the inside.

The U.S. Southwest Border Response: Operation Alliance

The U.S. government initiated Operation Alliance in 1986. It was in this general context that the United States considered its drug problem to be one of the worst problems that the country faced. The Reagan administration responded by promoting the drug war domestically, with antidrug campaigns with catchy slogans like "Just Say No," and internationally, by placing pressure on countries (especially source countries) to do something about the supply issue. Interdiction efforts in the Caribbean increased, and drug smugglers simply sought a different port of entry: the Southwest border area was the chosen alternative. The primary U.S. government response to this shift was code-named "Operation Alliance." Until 1986, the National Drug Enforcement Policy Board had devoted little or no attention to the U.S.-Mexican border area as a smuggling route, as all efforts were concentrated on the Florida Coast and Gulf areas.

The Nature of Operation Alliance

In short, Alliance evolved as a coordinated effort between fifteen agencies and four state and local agencies. It is composed of a joint command group from Arizona, California, New Mexico, and Texas and has Senior Field Representatives from the following Federal agencies: U.S. Customs Service; Immigration and Naturalization Service; DEA; Federal Bureau of Investigation (FBI); U.S. Coast Guard; Alcohol, Tobacco, and Firearms; Internal Revenue Service (IRS); U.S. Marshall Service; U.S. Attorney's Office; Federal Aviation Administration; and the Secret Service with support provided by the National

Narcotics Border Interdiction System, the Department of Defense, and National Guard units from different states. The primary actors are the DEA, the U.S. Customs Service, and the Immigration and Naturalization Service in the form of the U.S. uniformed Border Patrol.

The original purpose of Alliance was to coordinate operations bilaterally with Mexico to control known smuggling routes more effectively. But Alliance became a much more unilateral project once it became obvious that the Mexican government was having problems coordinating its own drug control policy and was not willing to participate in joint projects. Under Alliance, Mexico is viewed as a transit country for cocaine shipments, though it also monitors Mexico's exports in heroin and marijuana. It has been estimated that approximately one-third to one-half of all illegal narcotics trafficking occurs across the U.S. Southwest border. However, the Office of National Drug Control Policy (ONDCP) has no direct responsibility to command Alliance or to run it.

Operation Alliance Tactical Procedures

Alliance's principal tactics are to use available strategic and tactical intelligence to its full advantage. The main source for intelligence information is the DEA's El Paso Intelligence Center, commonly referred to as EPIC. EPIC is the main repository and distributor of narcotics law enforcement intelligence. EPIC was established in 1974 by the INS and the DEA and its composition is basically the same as that of Operation Alliance. It has an around-the-clock watch that handles inquiries from member agencies and the placement of law enforcement alerts on aircraft and people that might be smuggling drugs into the United States. EPIC places approximately 6,000 warnings per year.[18]

The intelligence information is based on an historical analysis of smuggling trends and practices and is an essential component when placing law enforcement assets and personnel in the field. Intelligence is used primarily for mobile corridor operations that involve the various agencies. A mobile corridor operation is, in essence, the practice of using the U.S. Border Patrol, DEA, and Customs officers along with local law enforcement officers to interdict a particular smuggling route. Due to the high level of coordination required between all the agencies in order to implement a mobile corridor operation, problems have arisen on two levels.

On one level, insufficient cooperation of operational security or the integration of intelligence between the competing agencies has hampered the interdiction process. And on a tactical level, its primary problem has been the high visibility of the agents as large groups temporarily move into areas that are sparsely populated and where people know each other, at least by sight. The net result has been situations where all the different agencies would arrive at a designated spot and pull guns on each other without ever catching the smugglers.

Division of Labor

There are three primary aspects of Alliance that operate separately from the DEA. First, at legal ports of entry, Alliance primarily utilizes Customs agents in tandem with the National Guard working together with canine units to inspect all incoming cargo. Customs also participated in at least 14 different major multi-agency task forces and combined border smuggling groups. The strategy was multi-agency enforcement through the utilization of Customs Agency cross-designated state and local officers, who in task forces would foster the exchange of intelligence information and ideas "between [our] Customs Service and the land, air, and marine resources of other agencies."[19]

Also distinctive is Alliance's use of the U.S. Border Patrol which is different from the Patrol's original mandate of preventing illegal migrants from crossing the border into the United States. The U.S. Border Patrol has been helpful to the project because of the uniqueness of its knowledge of the terrain. The regions along the border are both mountainous and open. The Border Patrol was granted authority from both the DEA and Customs to seize drugs in 1986. By 1988, 60 percent of all cold hits were seized by the Border Patrol. (A cold hit occurs when traffickers are interdicted by chance and without any prior use of tactical and strategic intelligence.)

The third, and perhaps most controversial, element is the use of military assistance. For the most part, the military provides equipment, such as radar, aerostats, planes, and helicopters, but occasionally participates in joint ventures. The primary concern with the use of the military in drug interdiction efforts along the U.S.-Mexican border concerns Mexico's perception of violations of its national security and sovereignty. To place military units strategically along the border can only serve to invite problems.[20] Furthermore, doing so is technically illegal because after the Civil War Congress passed a law, the *posse comitatus*, that prohibits the military from enforcing civilian law that involves arrest. Given this law and the lack of enthusiasm of the military itself for involvement in the drug war, its role is being redefined. Now, the military primarily provides equipment, thus greatly increasing the effectiveness of the operation.

The Border Patrol specifically began using Department of Defense (DOD) assets in the 1960s, acquiring access to laser equipment that was being phased out of the Indochina war. At present, the Border Patrol receives aircraft, other specialized equipment training, instruction, and help from the photographic commission. There is a general feeling within the Border Patrol that the primary role for the military is one of assistance and that actually to employ U.S. soldiers, untrained in the field, to interdict drugs directly could seriously damage U.S. law enforcement relationships with Mexican officers with whom the Border Patrol and other agencies deal on a regular basis and from whom they have gained trust with difficulty.

At a Congressional hearing held in May 1988 on "The Role of the Military in Drug Interdiction," the Border Patrol requested more strategically placed sensors along the border area. At the time of the hearing, there were only 300 radar units in place, and Border Patrol officials felt they could use an additional 1000. Requesting that the military upgrade equipment that was already in place and suggesting the development of transportable sensor systems, the Border Patrol also suggested that a surveillance network linking interagency intelligence and interdiction efforts should be established and that strategic and tactical intelligence be developed, analyzed, and distributed to support interdiction and investigative efforts of all civilian law enforcement agencies along the border.[21]

The hesitation expressed by the Border Patrol actively to employ military units in interdiction efforts is also shared by many of the other branches of the Federal agencies. There seems to be general agreement that the role of the military should be limited to supplying necessary equipment but also, more importantly, to providing intelligence because its resources and capabilities are greater than any other organization within the structure of the U.S. intelligence community. It is estimated that in the period from the 1970s through the late 1980s, the DOD's intelligence operations received approximately $10-13 billion.[22] In a hearing held before Congress on February 6, 1991, discussions concerned who would receive what resources and the question was asked why the military was receiving more money than the Coast Guard, whose primary job was to interdict drug traffickers.[23]

Overall, Operation Alliance appeared to be a band-aid over the problem. Though its coordination of the different agencies is impressive, the program has not proven to be successful. Drugs continue to enter the United States through Mexico. The border is simply too large to secure effectively. Furthermore, it appears that even though Mexico has shown more concerted efforts at attacking the drug transit problem, it still does not believe drugs to be so important as to merit regular coordinated efforts along the border.

Drug Trafficking in the 1990s: The Mexican Perspective

Political and Economic Environment

The primary concern of Mexican President Carlos Salinas de Gortari is and continues to be the recovery of stability and the reformation of Mexico's economy. Under his guidance, Mexico privatized stated-owned industries, repatriated Mexican capital, and attempted to restore business confidence by opening the country to foreign capital. As a result, interest rates dropped, foreign investment grew substantially, exports increased, and the country's capacity to generate employment has been on the rise, though it still falls short of desired goals.

Salinas' economic plan lowered the external debt of the public sector from 54 percent of the country's gross domestic product (GDP) in 1987 to 23 percent in 1991.[24] But Salinas has repeatedly demonstrated that it is time for change. In his own words, "Modernization is a strategy that calls for change in keeping with our own needs and at a rate that matches the pace of world events. But its overriding goal is to ensure Mexico's continuing existence as a sovereign nation. Modernization is, as is evident from the facts, nationalistic."[25] Salinas' long-term goal has been to establish a free trade agreement among the United States, Mexico, and Canada that would probably entrench his programs so that they could not be easily dismantled by his opposition.

On the political spectrum, the Mexican government controlled by the Partido Revolucionario Institucional (PRI) since 1929 is facing serious opposition as its very legitimacy is being questioned by the Mexican electorate. Electoral fraud has become a constant theme, and Salinas is valiantly struggling to maintain his party in power. Salinas does maintain that democratic opening is only second to the demands of economic restructuring.[26] Overall, Salinas has given indications that there exists a mandate for change and a need to promote the diversification and consolidation of links with other countries.

There have been increasing accusations of human rights abuses by both the Mexican police and the military. Salinas responded to these allegations by establishing the National Commission for the Defense of Human Rights which has since become very active, though to what extent it will be effective is to be determined in the future. He addressed the issue in his third State of the Nation report when he proposed to "strengthen the capacity of law enforcement agencies, promote the earliest possible response to the decisions of the Federal Judiciary, and...raise to the constitutional level the protection provided by the national Commission."[27] It should be noted that nowhere in Salinas' 1992 national address does he mention the issue of drug trafficking, not even within the agenda of Mexico's bilateral relationship with the United States. Drug control, therefore, would appear to have lost its saliency as a priority issue for the Salinas administration, as was evidenced in his original 1988 address.

The Mexican Narcotics Control Agenda

The Mexican government has traditionally not perceived itself as having a major drug problem. This has been repeatedly reflected in Mexico's attitude that the problem with drugs is primarily a demand-side one. The primary drug problem for Mexico is with alcohol and inhalants (glue, ether, paint thinner), drugs of choice due to their low cost and easy availability. Mexico is, however, a producer of heroin and marijuana. Approximately 30 percent of the heroin and 75 percent of the marijuana consumed in the United States can be directly traced to Mexican growers.[28] In addition, U.S. officials estimate that between 50 and 70 percent of the cocaine entering the United States is transshipped through Mexico, approximately 250 to 550 metric tons annually.[29]

In spite of the traditional attitude that Mexico does not really have a drug problem, Mexico has increased its antinarcotics activities in response to U.S. pressure. Salinas increased spending on narcotics control from $23.1 million in 1988 to $63 million in 1990.[30] Mexico's traditional posture has been to maintain a low profile in drug enforcement, and in line with this attitude, Mexico has not made any efforts to increase its engagement or to head any multilateral efforts in drug enforcement except in reaction to U.S. pressures. The basic attitude is to keep what mechanisms are already in place and only to strengthen them by making them more efficacious.[31]

Conclusions

Despite the Bush administration's commitment to the drug war, contradictions remained between what the National Drug Control Strategy originally set out to do, in addressing the problem of drug abuse at its core, and the allotment of funding. The actual result was an emphasis on interdiction and law enforcement without adequately balancing these with drug prevention and recovery programs within the United States. Though some demand-side programs were in existence, these were mostly the result of individual state, not federal, efforts.

The Bush administration was not consistent in its treatment of the drug issue. Its emphasis was mostly on short- and medium-term goals, ignoring the need for long-term policies that met more than political needs. Billions of dollars were invested in these interdiction operations that emphasized military tactics and disregarded the social aspects of the drug problem. The U.S.-Mexican border, in particular, is one of the most unusual areas in the world, not only geographically but culturally and symbolically as well. It is also one of the poorest areas in the United States with some of the worst environmental and health problems in the country. At best, the conditions on the border are survivable for those who remain at the margins.

Furthermore, the possible impact of militarizing the border at the same time that commerce is increasing between Mexico and the United States could lead to uncertain instability. If the United States continues to treat drug trafficking as a national security issue, using the military against drugs could worsen relations with Mexico. In late 1992, Mexico appeared to have no problems with U.S. drug control policy, but that could change, especially if

Mexico improves its economic situation and gains leverage in its asymmetrically interdependent relationship with the United States.

Operations such as Alliance can, and do, serve a purpose. They are a show of force that serves as a warning to those who wish to operate outside of the law of any country. Alliance, in particular, has achieved something that is unusual in a country that requires its agencies to lobby for funding. The levels of cooperation between the different law enforcement organizations has, indeed, been unusual. They have managed to dissolve some of the animosity and competitiveness for the greater goal of controlling narcotics trafficking and the violence that results from it. But if the government does not properly use a project such as Alliance in combination with programs for the improvement of economic and living standards of the impoverished border area, any benefit the project might engender will inevitably be diminished.

In sum, drug war policy can be traced to the very serious national malaise and economic crisis that the country has been suffering in the last ten years. In certain sectors, poverty has increased, and in overall terms, the standard of living has decreased. Unemployment has reached an all-time high. The evidence points to a correlation between the two factors. Only when domestic issues become manageable can relationships with other countries improve. The Mexican government has continually stated that drug trafficking is a domestic problem and that the United States should attempt to resolve it by concentrating on its demand-side problem.

Which leads to the last point: much debate has been generated regarding how best to remedy the drug problem in the United States. Repeatedly, it has been stated — not just by Mexico, but by U.S. experts in the field — that the problem is one of demand. Regardless, the strategy currently in place continues to be supply-side-oriented. How much longer can the debate go on without it being more clearly addressed? Rigid adherence to policies that have been proven to be insufficiently effective is not the answer. The problem of drugs on the border will not go away by itself, and in fact, the adoption of a zero-sum attitude to drug control is unrealistic. The U.S. government needs to increase its responsibility not only to its citizens but to those on the other side of the border. Attention to demand cannot be continuously ignored. It is not enough to acknowledge that there is a problem, without tackling it at its roots.

Notes

1. Americas Watch issued a report in the summer of 1992 showing an increase in human rights violations being committed by U.S. Border Patrol officers.

2. William O. Walker III, *Drug Control in the Americas* (Albuquerque, New Mexico: University of New Mexico Press, 1989), 192.

3. It is important to note that the period of 1936-1940 and subsequently World War II also marked phases when the United States applied great pressure on Mexico to meet their needs. In the former because the United States was concerned over a burgeoning domestic drug abuse problem, and in the latter because cultivation of the illicit opium poppy was needed in order to aid the allied efforts. See Richard Craig, "U.S. Narcotics Policy toward Mexico: Consequences for the Bilateral Relationship," in Guadalupe González, María Tienda, eds., *The Drug Connection in U.S.-Mexican Relations* (San Diego, CA: Center for U.S.-Mexican Studies, UC, 1989), 72, as he cites William O. Walker III, "Control across the Border: The United States, Mexico, and Narcotics Policy, 1930-1940," in *Pacific Historical Review*, 47 (1978), 92 and William O. Walker III, "The International Politics of Drug Control," paper presented at the LASA conference, in Bloomington, in October 1980.

4. U.S. Congress, House, Select Committee on Narcotics Abuse and Control, Study Mission to Brownsville, Texas; Mexico City, Mexico; and Guatemala City, Guatemala, dated December 9-13, 1990. Washington, U.S. Government Printing Office, 1991, 3. (101st Congress, 2nd Session, House).

5. GAO, *U.S.-Mexico Trade: Concerns About the Adequacy of Border Infrastructure*, Report to the Chairman, Committee on Finance, U.S. Senate, (GAO/NSIAD-91-228, May 1991).

6. This report details the problem of Customs control along the U.S.-Mexican border in terms of increase in commerce. GAO, Report to the Chairman, Committee on Finance, U.S. Senate, U.S.-Mexico Trade: Concerns About the Adequacy of Border Infrastructure, (GAO/NSIAD-91-228), (Washington, D.C.: May 1991).

7. For an incisive commentary on the Reagan drug strategy, see the remarks made by Bruce M. Bagley in the Proceedings from a Congressional Research Service Seminar held on April 26, 1989. "Drugs and Latin America: Economic and Political U.S. Policy Options," *Report of the Select Committee on Narcotics Abuse and Control*, 101st Congress, 1st session, SNAC-101-1-12. (Washington, D.C.: 1989), 42.

8. Mario Ojeda, "El Papel de los Medios de Comunicación en las Relaciones México-Estados Unidos," *Foro Internacional*, XXVII-4, April-June 1987.

9. Juan David Lindau, "Percepciones Mexicanas de la Política Exterior de Estados Unidos: El Caso Camarena Salazar," *Foro Internacional*, XXVII-4, April-June 1987.

10. David Lauter, "Bush Seeking $1.1 billion more for Drug War in 1991," *The Los Angeles Times*, January 26, 1990, A1, A18.

11. David Lauter and Ronald J. Ostrow, "U.S. to Designate Los Angeles as a Major Drug Center," *The Los Angeles Times*, January 24, 1990, A1, A14.

12. Patrick McDonnell, "State Guard Plans Larger Role in Drug War,"*The Los Angeles Times*, January 15, 1990, A3.

13. McDonnell.

14. An aerostat is a type of radar that is located in a balloon above the ground.

15. Kate Doyle, "The Militarization of the Drug War in Mexico," *Current History*, (February 1993), 88.

16. McDonnell.

17. Eric Weiner, "Mexico Shooting Down Drug Planes, Officials Say," *The New York Times*, December 8, 1989, Y11.

18. U.S. Congress, House, Committee on Armed Services, The Role of the Military in Drug Interdiction, Statement made by Larry L. Orton, Special Agent in Charge, El Paso Intelligence Center, Drug Enforcement Agency, Washington, U.S. Government Printing Office, 1988 (100th Congress, 2nd Session, House Committee), 178.

19. U.S. Congress, House, Select Committee on Narcotics Abuse and Control, The Federal Strategy on the Southwest Border, Hearing, December 10, 1990; Testimony of James C. Platt, Regional Commissioner, United States Customs Service, Southwest region, Washington, U.S. Government Printing Office, 1991 (101st Congress, 1st session), 92-99.

20. For a detailed analysis of the role of the military in drug enforcement, see Bruce M. Bagley, *Myths of Militarization* (Miami, FL: University of Miami, 1991).

21. U.S. Congress, House, Committee on Armed Services, Narcotics Interdiction and Use of the Military: Issues for Congress; comments about cooperation between the U.S. Border Patrol and the DOD prepared by James E. Bower, Deputy Tactical Coordinator, Operation Alliance, Border Patrol, El Paso, TX. Washington, U.S. Government Printing Office, 1988 (100th Congress, 2nd session, House, Committee), 174-184.

22. For an overview of the role of the Defense Intelligence Agency (DIA) in the Intelligence community, see Charles W. Kegley, Jr. and Eugene R. Wittkopf, *American Foreign Policy: Pattern and Process*, (New York: St. Martin's Press, 1991), 383-386.

23. U.S. Congress, House, Select Committee on Narcotics Abuse and Control, National Drug Control Strategy, Hearing, February 6, 1991. Washington, U.S. Government Printing Office, (102nd Congress, 1st session), 22-24.

24. BANAMEX Direct Foreign Investment Report, (Mexico City, Mexico: Banamex, 1991).

25. President Salinas de Gortari's 3rd State of the Nation Report, (Mexico, DF: Novedades Editores S.A. de C.V., November 2, 1991), 1.

26. Salinas, 4-5.

27. Salinas, 10.

28. U.S. Congress, Study mission to Brownsville, Texas; Mexico City, Mexico; and Guatemala City, Guatemala, 11.

29. U.S. Congress, Study mission.

30. U.S. Congress, Study mission, 30.

31. The former Procurator General of Mexico, Sergio García Ramírez, came out with a book in 1989 that gives the explanation of the Mexican viewpoint of drug trafficking and the drug enforcement efforts of the de la Madrid administration. Though the book is essentially a memoir, it does impart the essence of the Mexican government's feelings with regard to the narcotics problem and does contain some information on operational problems Mexico has encountered with regard to drug enforcement. *Narcotráfico: Un punto de vista mexicano,* (Mexico, DF: Miguel Angel Porrua Eds., 1989), 579p.

References

Banamex. 1991. *Direct Foreign Investment Report.*

Bagley, Bruce M. 1991. *Myths of Militarization.* Miami: University of Miami.

Bagley, Bruce M. 1989. Remarks made during proceedings for a Congressional Research Service Seminar: "Drugs and Latin America: Economic and Political U.S. Policy Options." *Report of the Select Committee on Narcotics Abuse and Control.* 101st Congress, 1st session. SNAC-101-1-12.

Craig, Richard. 1989. "U.S. Narcotics Policy toward Mexico: Consequences for the Bilateral Relationship." In *The Drug Connection in U.S.-Mexican Relations,* eds. Guadalupe González and María Tienda. San Diego: University of California Center for U.S.-Mexican Studies.

GAO. 1991. *U.S.-Mexico Trade: Concerns about the Adequacy of Border Infrastructure.* Report to the Chairman, Committee on Finance, U.S. Senate. GAO/NSIAD-91-228. Washington, D.C.

García Ramírez, Sergio. 1989. *Narcotráfico: Un punto de vista mexicano,* ed. Miguel Angel Porrua. Mexico, DF.

Kegley, Charles W., and Eugene R. Wittkopf. 1991. *American Foreign Policy: Pattern and Process.* New York: St. Martin's Press.

Lauter, David. 1990. "Bush Seeking $1.1 Billion More for Drug War in 1991." *The Los Angeles Times,* January 26:A1.

Lauter, David, and Ronald J. Ostrow. 1990. "U.S. to Designate Los Angeles as a Major Drug Center." *The Los Angeles Times,* January 24:A1.

Lindau, Juan David. 1987. "Percepciones Mexicanas de la Política Exterior de Estados Unidos: El Caso Camarena Salazar." *Foro Internacional,* 27(April-June):4.

McDonnell, Patrick. 1990. "State Guard Plans Larger Role in Drug War." *The Los Angeles Times,* January 15:A3.

Ojeda, Mario. 1987. "El Papel de los Medios de Comunicación en las Relaciones México-Estados Unidos." *Foro Internacional,* 27(April-June):4.

Salinas de Gortari, Carlos. 1991. *Third State of the Nation Report.* Mexico, DF: Novedades Editores S.A. de C.V., November 2.

U.S. Congress. House Armed Services Committee. 1988. *The Role of the Military in Drug Interdiction.* 100th Congress, 2nd session.

U.S. Congress. House. Committee on Armed Services. 1988. *Narcotics Interdiction and Use of the Military: Issues for Congress.* 100th Congress, 2nd session.

U.S. Congress. House Select Committee on Narcotics Abuse and Control. 1991. *Study Mission to Brownsville, Texas; Mexico City and Guatemala City,* December 9-13. 101st Congress, 2nd session. Committee Print.

U.S. Congress. House Select Committee on Narcotics Abuse and Control. 1991. *The Federal Strategy on the Southwest Border.* 101st Congress, 1st session.

U.S. Congress. House Select Committee on Narcotics Abuse and Control. 1991. *National Drug Control Strategy.* Hearing, February 6. 102nd Congress, 1st session.

Walker, William O., III. 1989. *Drug Trafficking in the Americas.* Albuquerque: University of New Mexico Press.

Walker, William O., III. 1980. "The International Politics of Drug Control." Paper presented at LASA Conference, Bloomington, IN.

Walker, William O., III. 1978. "Control Across the Border: The United States, Mexico, and Narcotics Policy, 1930-1940." *Pacific History Review* 47:92.

Weiner, Eric. 1989. "Mexico Shooting Down Drug Planes, Officials Say." *The New York Times*, December 8:Y11.

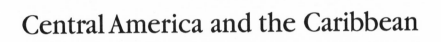

Central America and the Caribbean

Chapter Twenty-Two

Central America
and Drug Trafficking

Linda Robinson

Overview

My task is to present a review of what is known about Central America's involvement in drug trafficking. *U.S. News & World Report* is known for having one of the best clip collections among the Miami news bureaus, but not one file for an individual Central American country and drugs before 1990 was found. Aside from some isolated, notorious cases in the 1980s, the explosion of trafficking in Central America (excepting Panama, of course) did not occur until the end of the decade, and we are just now realizing how massive that explosion is.

During the 1980s, the incidence of trafficking in Central America was, no doubt, greater than reporters and researchers discovered, and greater even than law enforcement officials realized. Attention during the 1980s was focused on the wars and the Cold War battle for Central America. With the exception of reporters who probed the possible drug trafficking connections of the Nicaraguan contras, most non-official attention was focused on the revolutionary tide sweeping the region.

But even if we were asleep at the wheel during the 1980s in terms of tracking the incidence of drug trafficking in Central America, it is clear that there has been a vast expansion of that activity since the closing years of the past decade. The exponential growth of trafficking in Central America is due to a shift in drug transit patterns during the late 1980s. Law enforcement efforts focused on the Caribbean and Florida throughout the 1980s, causing traffickers to shift to what DEA officials call the "western pipeline." Now most cocaine entering the United States comes through Mexico, and Central America has become an important way-station for traffickers using this western pipeline.

As will be outlined below, Guatemala has become a major transit route and also a center for opium growing for heroin. But no country is immune, and the consequences are especially grave for Central America for two reasons. First, except for the Caribbean islands, no region has less capability to respond to the drug threat. The region lacks professional law enforcement forces and basic equipment such as radar. Second, the political institutions of these countries are notoriously weak, making them extremely vulnerable to corruption. However much the abilities of the Andean governments are criticized, they are far greater than those of the Central American governments. The case studies from the 1980s signal both of these dangers quite clearly. No doubt the traffickers' inroads were greater than realized at the time. But putting together what was known then and the signs of endemic trafficking now, the trajectory of an unending and worsening epidemic can be charted.

Now it is clear that drug trafficking is one of the principal threats to Central American stability in the 1990s, if not the primary threat. But aside from a few reports, this phenomenon has not received the attention that it might have were the region still commanding the attention of editors, policy makers, and other opinion shapers. Even though law enforcement officials have awakened to the new monster in Central America, the U.S. government as a whole does not treat this problem as one equally as serious as the guerrilla threat of the 1980s. Central America has, for all purposes, been forgotten.

This is also true of news organizations. Reporters are leaving the region in droves. This means less information about Central America is available today than at any time in the past twelve years. This waning attention does not only apply to Central America: Latin America and the drug issue as a whole receive far less attention than they did even two years ago. The momentous events in Europe and the former Soviet Union, of course, must assume top priority in U.S. foreign policy, but the dearth of information about what is occurring in Central America — the aftermath story — will, in all probability, come back to haunt Washington.

What We Learned in the 1980s

I will first review the celebrated cases of trafficking in Central America in the 1980s, which made clear that traffickers were making inroads then and that they were able to corrupt the region's politicians and military men. These cases involve the Nicaraguan contras, Nicaragua, Costa Rica, and Honduras.

The Contras

The most exhaustive research in contra associations with trafficking was conducted by Senator John Kerry's Subcommittee on Terrorism, Narcotics, and International Communications beginning in 1986. While its final report concluded that "individual contras accepted weapons, money, and equipment from drug smugglers," it failed to establish an intimate ongoing relationship between traffickers and the top leaders of the contras: "The subcommittee did not find evidence that the contra leadership participated directly in narcotics smuggling in support of their war against the Sandinistas."[1] The Iran-contra congressional investigation also failed to turn up evidence of a more tight-knit association. But a marriage of convenience was certainly consummated, by both the northern and southern armies fighting the Sandinistas.

Eden Pastora's contra army, which operated from Costa Rica, got mixed up with traffickers in 1983. A Pastora aide named Karol Prado bought five airplanes from a Cuban exile named Alfredo Caballero, a trafficker who smuggled cocaine through Costa Rica who was eventually convicted in the United States. The other known episode implicated Pastora's army more clearly. In 1984 Pastora's army needed larger planes. Two Pastora aides, Octaviano César (brother of current National Assembly president Alfredo César) and Adolfo "Popo" Chamorro (now Miami consul for the Nicaraguan government) bought a C-47 plane from Colombian trafficker George Morales. At that time, Morales was already under U.S. indictment for marijuana smuggling and later testified to Congress that he told Chamorro and César that he hoped they could help get his indictment dropped. The two deny it. Nevertheless, one of Pastora's pilots, Gerardo Durán, regularly carried cocaine as well as arms for the contras. As Pastora's personal pilot, many assume that Durán's activities had to be known to Pastora before a 1986 indictment led to a break in the association.

The northern front of the contras, based in Honduras, also found that the trafficking network provided convenient transport services. Four of the firms that the State Department contracted in 1986 to deliver $27 million in contra aid were found to be owned and operated by traffickers.[2] After the $100 million in contra aid was approved in 1987, two free-lance arms merchants named Ron Martin and James McCoy were hoping the contras would buy the tons of weapons they had shipped in Honduras. But the State Department and the CIA nixed the plan, saying the weapons had been bought with drug money. The Honduran chief of the armed forces, Gen. Humberto Regalado, tried to insist that Martin and McCoy's arms be used, leading U.S. officials to assume that members of the Honduran military had a stake in the project and were determined to reap some benefit from it. It took a visit to Honduras by Assistant Secretary of State Elliott Abrams and Alan Fiers, chief of the CIA's Central American Task Force, to force the Honduran military to permit the landing of planeloads of arms from the United States.[3]

Nicaragua

Perhaps the most publicized case of Nicaragua's trafficking connections during the 1980s was that of Barry Seal and the Sandinistas. In the spring of 1984, the Medellín cartel told Seal, one of its drug pilots who turned informant for the DEA, that it was moving its operations to Nicaragua in the aftermath of Panama's raid on the cartel's lab in Darien. In June, Seal flew 750 kilos into Los Brasiles military airfield outside Managua, where Federico Vaughan, an aide to Interior Minister Tomás Borge, supervised the unloading by uniformed Sandinistas. Upon takeoff, Seal's plane was shot down, and he was arrested. Vaughan, who had earlier briefed Seal on how to conduct his operation, got him out of jail and took him to Pablo Escobar, who was staying in Managua.[4] When Seal went back to Nicaragua to pick up the load, he photographed Vaughan and Escobar loading his plane. These pictures were widely used by the Reagan administration to argue that the Sandinistas were involved in ongoing trafficking activities, but no such continuing pattern was ever established. The Medellín cartel may have reverted to its former reliance on Panama as a way-station once its problems with Noriega were worked out.

Yet the charges of ongoing Sandinista complicity were raised during Noriega's trial in Miami by convicted Medellín trafficker Carlos Lehder, testifying for the prosecution. At the instruction of Cuban intelligence agent Manuel Piñeiro, Lehder said, the Sandinistas allowed drug flights through Nicaragua in the mid-1980s and were paid for their services.

Costa Rica

The airstrips and refueling points used by the Sandinistas during their war to oust Somoza were taken over in subsequent years by pilots who had worked for the Sandinistas and others in the trafficking business.

One of the episodes in the 1980s suggested some official Costa Rican complicity with traffickers. In 1985 the head of the Guadalajara, Mexico, cartel, Rafael Caro Quintero, fled to Costa Rica to escape U.S. and Mexican authorities, who were hot on his trail after the death of DEA agent Enrique (Kiki) Camarena. The Costa Rican pilot who flew Caro Quintero to Costa Rica had been involved in drug trafficking and was subsequently arrested. He flew Caro Quintero and his gang into the San José airport and a limousine met them, whisking them away without having to pass customs.[5]

Honduras

Three damaging cases came to light in the 1980s involving Honduran military links to drug trafficking. This limited evidence suggests that the institution is in need of a thorough house-cleaning. The State Department Bureau of International Narcotics Matters 1990 report said that the government was dragging its feet on antidrug cooperation.

The former chief of the Honduran armed forces, General Humberto Regalado, has been accused of participating in trafficking and other illegal activities, and in 1988 his half-brother was arrested in the Miami airport for smuggling cocaine. General José Bueso Rosa was accused of involvement in

a 1984 drug trafficking and assassination plot and was tried and convicted for
the latter charge. The plot was reportedly financed by a $40 million cocaine
shipment, but no narcotics convictions were obtained. Oliver North inter-
ceded to help Bueso Rosa, on grounds that he had helped the contras, but
North's notes also say he wanted to keep Bueso from "spilling the beans." This
led some to speculate that Bueso knew of a contra-drugs connection, and
North wanted to keep him quiet.[6] Colonel Said Speer, an ambitious officer
who led a mutiny in 1989, was arrested in Colombia driving a Porsche
registered in the name of a Medellín cartel member.

What Was Learned in the 1990s

Guatemala

By all accounts, no Central American country has been harder hit by
drugs than Guatemala, paralleling the increase in trafficking through Mexico
in the late 1980s. And, in a further demonstration of what is called the
"balloon" or "doughboy" effect, as Mexican effectiveness at interdiction has
improved, traffickers have increasingly turned to Guatemala. In 1990, the DEA
estimated that 48 tons of cocaine were coming through Guatemala annually.[7]
In 1991, cocaine seizures in Guatemala amounted to 17 metric tons, leading
the DEA to consider this country the largest transshipment point in the isthmus,
surpassing Panamanian traffic. By comparison, Mexico seized 45 tons in its
much larger territory.[8]

From Guatemala, the cocaine is either flown or trucked over the border
into Mexico, flown directly into the United States, or sent via container ships.
Just as in Panamá, private airstrips abound in Guatemala — over 1,000, mostly
on large farms in the southern coastal region. Although a slower route, it was
more secure, since Guatemala had no functioning radar outside the international airport, in contrast to the direct flight path from Colombia into Mexico,
which was being monitored by U.S. radar planes and Mexican radar. The DEA
chief in Mexico, Ralph Saucedo, has said that the Guatemalan route was
proving to be very difficult to interdict since by the time they identified the
flight, the drugs were usually already inside Mexico.[9]

In 1990, even after the new "western pipeline" trend became widely
known, U.S. DEA and other officials ran into bureaucratic resistance in their
efforts to shift some of the drug-fighting resources from the Caribbean-Florida
theater to address the growing Mexico threat. Getting additional resources to
address the concomitant Central American problem was even more difficult.
DEA-Guatemala had been signalling the rapid increase in transshipment, but
only after three years of pleading was the DEA staff there increased by two
agents, for a total of four. One intelligence analyst was also added. In 1991,
an additional six agents were temporarily assigned to confront the blizzard
of cocaine.

The principal transit points for drugs in Guatemala are the southeast of the country, Puerto Barrios, and the northern border province of Petén. Without radar, law enforcement is dependent on human intelligence to make busts. The Guatemalan entity responsible for counternarcotics action is CIPROSI, a joint police-military unit. Four tons of cocaine were seized in 1989 and over eight tons in 1990. But CIPROSI has only six cars and four motorcycles, leading the U.S. government to turn increasingly to the Guatemalan military for antidrug assistance. This has been an extremely controversial policy, especially in its reliance on intelligence from the G-2, since the Guatemalan military has perhaps the worst human rights record in the hemisphere. In fact, the Bush administration cut off military assistance to the Guatemalan military at the end of 1990, before the newly elected president, Jorge Serrano, took office. The case that precipitated the cutoff was the killing by Guatemalan soldiers of U.S. citizen Michael (CK) Devine, a tour guide who lived in the Petén. Arrests were made, but no one has been prosecuted. Rumors suggest that Devine was a DEA informant, which would explain the sudden U.S. decision to draw the line after a decade of overlooking the military's human rights record.

Guatemalan Lt. Fernando Minera, arrested by the United States for cocaine smuggling, said that Guatemalan G-2 officers and the military-run immigration service were involved in trafficking. But rumors also circulated that former President Vinicio Cerezo protected friends and associates who were involved in trafficking, and U.S. officials said that Alfonso Cabrera, the foreign minister (also the party's presidential candidate for the 1990 elections), was himself a major narcotics figure.[10] Cerezo's government was clearly implicated in a number of non-narcotics-related corruption cases, but few of the allegations about trafficking by officials have been fully confirmed. One exception was Guatemalan army Col. Carlos Ochoa Ruiz, whose extradition was requested by the United States, along with two civilians. The United States also requested the extradition of Arnoldo Vargas Estrada, former mayor of Zacapa, who allegedly smuggled several tons of cocaine monthly to the United States.

U.S. antidrug officials say that the real problem with corruption in Guatemala is with civilian, not military, officials. "If a Panama happens here," one official said, "it will be the civilians not the military."[11] Citing the inroads that Colombians have made, this official said many Colombians have established residence in Guatemala and are investing heavily in farms and businesses with the aid of false documents.

Finally, Guatemala is witnessing an explosion of opium cultivation, as the demand for heroin increases. It is now the seventh- or eighth-largest opium producer, and production between 1989 and 1990 quadrupled. The U.S. State Department's Bureau of International Narcotics Matters runs aerial spraying eradication programs directed at opium poppies and marijuana fields in Guatemala and Belize. These are the only producer countries in the isthmus, although in Panama, officials cite unconfirmed reports of cocaine laboratories in the jungles of Darien.

El Salvador

After Guatemala and Panama, El Salvador ranks next in Central America as a storage and transfer point for drugs. The 1991 report of the State Department's Bureau of International Narcotics Matters said that El Salvador's importance as a drug route is growing. In October 1991, three metric tons were found in a ship that stopped at the port of Acajutla in El Salvador, and five Salvadorans were among those arrested.

Only 343 pounds were seized in 1990, but that same year, a 175-man Salvadoran antinarcotics police force was formed.[12] El Salvador has also passed some of the region's toughest drug laws, with penalties of 20 years for trafficking and 15 years for money laundering.

The U.S. response to signs of growing trafficking through El Salvador has been slow; only in early 1992 did the DEA send its first agent there to open an office. U.S. officials expect that the end of the guerrilla war and the consequent unemployment of soldiers and combatants will lead to a significant increase in trafficking as Salvadorans seek new sources of income.

Nicaragua

A DEA agent, Fred Villareal, said that in the 1980s traffickers shied away from Nicaragua, relying instead on Costa Rica and Honduras as refueling points, out of fear that if captured by the Sandinista authorities, traffickers would be branded as U.S. agents.[13]

In October 1991, 750 kilos were found in Managua, and police chief René Vivas estimated that some 5,000 kilos transit Nicaragua every few months, mostly by air en route to the United States. One report said that some returning exiles from Miami were involved in the narcotics trade, including sale of drugs in Nicaragua, where drug use has increased by an estimated 85 percent since 1980.[14] The Atlantic Coast and especially the port of Bluefields has reportedly grown since 1987 into one of the main areas of trafficking in Nicaragua.

There is no U.S. DEA office in Nicaragua, but the Nicaraguans do have a special police force assigned to counternarcotics duty, and it reportedly cooperates with U.S. authorities. The United States is providing $40,000 for counternarcotics assistance in Nicaragua.

Costa Rica

Costa Rica's role as a way-station was established in the 1980s, as the effects of Panama's substantial traffic spilled over U.S. northern borders. But Costa Rica's policing efforts have been more concerted than elsewhere in Central America, and a DEA office has long been operating in that country.

Three loads of cocaine were found off Costa Rica's Pacific coast in May 1991, and a helicopter apparently used for trafficking was found along the country's border with Panama.

Belize

An eight-year spraying campaign in Belize, financed by the United States, has reduced the marijuana crop by some 90 percent. But opium cultivation is reportedly on the rise, and Belize has been a refueling and distribution center since the 1980s. A paved road in northern Belize is reportedly used openly as a landing strip. The Belize Defense Force has only 750 members. A DEA office is planned for Belize but had not been opened as of early 1992.

Honduras

Honduras has cooperated with aerial reconnaissance (that show no evidence of marijuana cultivation) and with joint interdiction missions backed by the antinarcotics intelligence unit of the armed forces joint staff. But the September 1990 report of State's Bureau of International Narcotics Matters listed indications of Honduran government recalcitrance: U.S.-supplied drug-sniffing dogs were not put to effective use, and radio equipment provided for the national police's drug squad was not installed. A drug prosecutor's office was promised but not installed.

Conclusion

The documentary evidence of trafficking in Central America, represented by number of seizures and the amounts seized, clearly indicates a vast expansion in drug transit through the region, particularly in Guatemala. As for official complicity in the trade, the evidence is still slim, but, at a minimum, it shows that corruption of public officials has not abated and may well be worsening. Particularly in Guatemala, drug money is in evidence and politicians appear to be benefitting. All over the region and especially in Guatemala and Honduras, efforts to gain official cooperation in antinarcotics programs have run into controversy and reluctance. The existing problem of corruption may be exacerbated by U.S. efforts to draw the militaries of the region into the drug war. At a minimum, the United States faces the same dilemma it did in Panama: is it seeking help from forces that have already been corrupted by the other side?

Notes

1. Senator John Kerry, Chairman, Senate Subcommittee on Terrorism, Narcotics, and International Communications, *Drugs, Law Enforcement and Foreign Policy,* Washington, D.C.: G.P.O., 1989, 136.

2. Kerry report, 41-49.

3. Glenn Garvin, *Everybody Had His Own Gringo,* New York: Brassey's, 1992, 199-200. According to Garvin, the money behind the Martin-McCoy operation came from the brother of Panama's then-vice president Arturo Delvalle, 165.

4. Guy Gugliotta and Jeff Leen, *Kings of Cocaine,* New York: Simon & Schuster, 1989, 154-156.

5. See Elaine Shannon, *Desperados,* New York: Penguin, 1988, 284-291, 345-346.

6. Francis McNeil, *War and Peace in Central America,* New York: Scribner's Sons, 1989, 229-231.

7. *U.S. News & World Report,* December 3, 1990.

8. *The New York Times,* December 16, 1991, A6.

9. Personal interview.

10. *The Los Angeles Times,* May 7, 1990, A8.

11. Personal interview with privileged sources.

12. *Miami Herald,* December 3, 1991.

13. *El Nuevo Herald,* December 2, 1991.

14. *El Nuevo Herald,* February 9, 1992.

References

Garvin, Glenn. 1992. *Everybody Had His Own Gringo*. New York: Brassey's.

Gugliotta, Guy, and Jeff Leen. 1989. *Kings of Cocaine*. New York: Simon & Schuster.

Miami Herald. 1991. "El Salvador Role as Drug Stopover Grows." December 3: A8.

McNeil, Francis. 1989. *War and Peace in Central America*. New York: Scribner's Sons.

The New York Times. 1991. "Central America a New Drug Focus." December 16: A10.

El Nuevo Herald. 1991. "Narcos amenazan costas nicas." December 2: A4.

El Nuevo Herald. 1992. "Droga gana terreno en la nueva Nicaragua." February 9: A1, 18.

Shannon, Elaine. 1988. *Desperados*. New York: Penguin.

U.S. News & World Report. 1990. "The New Frontier in the War on Drugs." December 3: 52-54.

U.S. Senate Subcommittee on Terrorism, Narcotics, and International Communications. *Drugs, Law Enforcement, and Foreign Policy*. (The Kerry Report). Washington, D.C.: Government Printing Office.

Chapter Twenty-Three

Costa Rica and the Drug Trade

Carol Weir

Costa Rica's involvement in the international drug trade, primarily as a transshipment point for South American cocaine bound for the North American market, has not been widely studied. Although production of illicit drugs is limited to the cultivation of cannabis and domestic consumption of narcotics has not been a major social problem, Costa Rica's increasing importance as a transit country should be of interest to scholars, journalists, law enforcement professionals, and policy makers who study drug trafficking. Money laundering, although of limited scope in Costa Rica, is a further area for concern. The purpose of this chapter is to assess the state of current research dealing with Costa Rica and drug trafficking, to detail the current situation inside the country with respect to criminal activity and enforcement efforts, and to suggest some areas in need of further exploration. A review of the literature will be followed by analysis and some preliminary conclusions.

Review of the Literature

Anyone attempting to assess the state of current research on Costa Rica's involvement in the international drug trade will be initially frustrated by the lack of books and scholarly articles relating to the topic. Since the majority of work done on the Costa Rican drug trade has been investigative rather than analytical, reports by journalists largely constitute the basis of this study. The principal Costa Rican daily newspaper, *La Nación*, and *Esta Semana*, a weekly magazine of news and opinion published in San José, operate independently of the government and in an environment free of censure. Both publications have been supportive of the government's antidrug campaign and regularly feature pieces on drug trafficking, drug-related corruption, and the effects of drug abuse on society.

Several English-language publications have proven valuable in the search for information relating to Costa Rica and drugs. *Mesoamerica*, a non-profit magazine published monthly in San José and affiliated with the Institute for Central America Studies, includes feature articles, often related to drug trafficking, and monthly summaries of events in each Central American country. *Mesoamerica* is similar in focus and tone to the *Christian Science Monitor. Central American Report*, which is published in Guatemala City by Infopress Centroamérica, identifies regional trends and addresses the Costa Rican drug trade in an international context. The *Miami Herald, Los Angeles Times*, and *New York Times* have occasionally featured stories about drug trafficking in Costa Rica, but generally U.S. media attention to the issue has been scarce.

Less than a half-dozen books have been published which deal seriously with the Costa Rican drug trafficking situation. Perhaps the most comprehensive of these is Peter Scott and Jonathan Marshall's *Cocaine Politics* which includes a detailed account of U.S.-contra drug connections established in the early 1980s in Costa Rica. Based on the U.S. Senate Subcommittee investigation initiated by Senator John Kerry in 1986, Scott and Marshall's book limits itself to discussion of a short period of time (1983-1988), is investigative rather than analytical in nature, and does not attempt to imbue the discussion of CIA wrongdoings and Costa Rican and U.S. government complicity in the drug trade in any type of socio-political, institutional, or economic framework.

Two book-format reports, one compiled by Verny Quiros and the other by the 1989 Costa Rican Legislative Commission, are perhaps the most complete published accounts of both drug trafficking activities in Costa Rica and the response of Costa Rican institutions and civil society to this societal menace. As recommendations made to the Costa Rican Legislative Assembly, both documents are semi-official treatises concerned primarily with the investigation of allegations against prominent politicians and private individuals associated with the drug trade. Although the main purpose of these reports is to provide policy suggestions to the executive and legislative branches of Costa Rican government, the Commission also addresses issues of political culture and international relations. The thorough and unflinching examination of the problem presented in these widely circulated reports is an example of democracy in action and should be read as such by those who doubt Costa Rica's commitment to the battle against drug trafficking.

The final source of information deserving discussion is U.S. government documents. Congressional and Senate hearings since 1985, including reports by the Senate Subcommittee on Terrorism, Narcotics, and International Operations (headed by John Kerry and begun in April 1986), are well worth reading. These supplement the Costa Rican Legislative Commission reports by examining the role of U.S. agencies, private citizens, and official U.S. foreign policy with respect to the Costa Rican drug trade. In addition, valuable statistics concerning arrests, seizures, and levels of international assistance can be found in the Department of State's Bureau of International Narcotics

Matters' *Annual International Narcotics Control Strategy Report.* This publication is particularly useful for examining the evolution of Costa Rican efforts to control drugs since the mid-1980s.

Taken together, these sources suggest that the drug industry is growing in Costa Rica due to a combination of domestic and international factors. Drug trafficking in Costa Rica takes place in a context of domestic economic difficulties and increasing international preoccupation with drug issues. During the 1980s, poor growth performance by the Costa Rican economy created economic preconditions inside the country that currently induce people to be attracted to illegal activity. The rising cost of living, low prices for traditional export crops, and under- and unemployment (especially among youth and residents of the Atlantic Coast, where the combined rate may be as high as 40 percent) have led many people to join both the informal and illegal sectors of economic life.

Costa Rica is, however, making a valiant attempt to reduce its huge foreign debt (most of which dates to the 1970s) and to liberalize and diversify the national economy, which has traditionally been both extremely dependent on the export of bananas and coffee and inward-looking in orientation. The search for international sources of credit and finance led Costa Rican President Rafael Angel Calderón to sign an agreement with the International Monetary Fund (IMF) in 1989. The austerity package currently in place has led to massive public sector lay-offs, cuts in social programs including those dedicated to drug rehabilitation and education efforts, a rise in street crime, and the decline of real wages. Recent natural disasters in Limón, the country's major area of involvement in the drug trade, exacerbated economic hardships there and have left many looking for any way to feed their families.

International factors also play an important role in the analysis of drug trafficking in Costa Rica. Due to changes in the international environment, the last five years have seen dramatic increases in official estimates of the amounts of cocaine passing through Costa Rica, cocaine-related seizures, and arrests. Primarily, increased efforts to control the drug trade in major source and transit countries (especially Colombia) caused South American drug cartels to look for new bases of operation in Central America.

Until the late 1980s, General Manuel Antonio Noriega's cooperation with drug traffickers, the permissive banking system in Panama, the proximity of the Caribbean to the United States, and the lack of a broad opposition to the international drug trade in Mexico made these locations more attractive to drug traffickers than Costa Rica. Since 1985, stepped-up interdiction efforts along the Mexican border, the installation of a radar system as part of a U.S. Drug Enforcement Administration (DEA) campaign to "clean up" the Caribbean, and the fall of General Noriega in Panama have caused South American drug traffickers to seek alternative locations to carry out money laundering operations, refuel planes, and store their product for short periods of time. In this context, both Guatemala and Costa Rica have been increasingly penetrated by drug traffickers.

The international environment has also been instrumental in shaping Costa Rican perceptions of and responses to the drug threat. Due to the involvement of former Costa Rican president Oscar Arias in the international arena, self-identification with other democracies, and the extreme vulnerability of the national economy to international fluctuations in commodity prices, world events assume a special significance in Costa Rica. Panama has provided a glaring example of the chaos and ruin that result when a country's political and law enforcement elites become sympathetic to drug traffickers. Colombia's battle against violence and corruption is a warning to Costa Ricans of the corrosive effects of the drug trade on democratic institutions.

Costa Rica's attempts to deal with the threat posed by drug traffickers are both constrained and facilitated by international cooperation in drug control matters. The United States, under the auspices of the "war on drugs" declared by Ronald Reagan and continued by President George Bush, has, since the mid-1980s, provided increasing levels of technical assistance, training, and aid to Costa Rican antidrug law enforcement authorities. Unlike many other Latin American source and transit countries (e.g., Colombia and Peru), Costa Rica has received largely intelligence and support equipment rather than the military-style assistance currently favored by the United States. However, fear of Costa Rica's police becoming "militarized" as a consequence of the war on drugs remains a source of tension in U.S.-Costa Rican relations.

The existence of a unique political culture has led Costa Rica to respond differently to the drug-trafficking threat than many other Latin American source and transit countries. Since 1948, mass participation in a representative democracy that includes most social groups has allowed Costa Rica to develop economically while maintaining a fairly equitable distribution of income, to create a social welfare system that rivals many in Western Europe, and to escape the social violence, repression, and polarization of society that has plagued Nicaragua, El Salvador, and Guatemala. Ticos, as Costa Ricans call themselves, are extremely proud of their system of government and recognize the threat that the illegal drug trade poses to their institutions and processes. This analysis strives to give proper weight to domestic and international factors to account both for the increasing ability of drug traffickers to carry out operations in the country and for Costa Rica's relative success in protecting its institutions and civil society from the drug trafficking threat.

Due to space constraints and the desire for a unity of focus, this study will deal primarily with the cocaine industry in Costa Rica. Although cannabis production and domestic consumption will be treated briefly, neither problem merits as much concern and attention as cocaine trafficking, drug-related corruption (almost all of which is associated with cocaine), and cocaine-linked money laundering.

Marijuana

Cannabis is the only drug currently produced in Costa Rica. The cultivation of cannabis began in Costa Rica in the 1970s and quickly expanded due to a favorable climate and the lack of enforcement capacity by authorities. Most Costa Rican marijuana is grown in the Atlantic Coast area, where it is essentially a small enterprise operation typically carried out by individual farmers who have been led by economic hardship to abandon the cultivation of traditional crops (Bureau of International Narcotics Matters 1988, 118-120).

Due to the results of a 1988 aerial survey (the first in Costa Rica), figures citing cannabis production and the extent of marijuana exports were adjusted downward from earlier estimates. The Bureau of International Narcotics Matters now estimates that 100 tons of cannabis are cultivated annually (INM 1990, 141). Based on calculations of domestic consumption (discussed below), authorities believe that 75 percent of marijuana produced is exported, although processing of marijuana remains rudimentary. Largely due to the success of increased eradication efforts since 1985, cannabis production seems to be declining in importance as an economic activity and a national problem.

Domestic Consumption

The most recent national drug abuse survey, conducted in 1988 by the Costa Rican Institute of Alcoholism and Chemical Dependence (IAFA) in cooperation with the Government of Costa Rica and private groups, reported that only 3.5 percent of Costa Ricans had ever used illicit drugs, with use being concentrated among young men ages 20-29. Ninety-one percent of the respondents identified marijuana as the drug of choice, with use reported highest in Limon where cannabis smoking is traditional in some communities (INM 1989, 99). Alarmingly, reports now indicate that a variation of crack cocaine is now available in Limon (*The Miami Herald* 1990). This development indicates that the domestic consumption problem is growing.

Cocaine

Historically, Costa Rica has not played a substantial role in the hemispheric cocaine trade. A review of U.S. government documents for the years 1900-1971 reveals no investigations, studies, or reports dealing with Costa Rica in conjunction with the narcotics industry. In 1973, a U.S. congressional report entitled "The World Narcotics Problem: the Latin American Perspective" does not mention Costa Rica in its detailed account of source and transit countries.

Drug trafficking became significant in Costa Rica in the late 1970s when private airstrips in the north of the country began to be used as part of the effort by sympathizers from many nations to deliver arms to the Sandinista rebels in Nicaragua. The airstrips and territory used to coordinate the rebel supply effort belonged to private Costa Rican citizens and resident foreign nationals (including U.S.-born rancher John Hull), whose efforts proceeded with the complicity if not the overt cooperation of the Costa Rican government (*The Christian Science Monitor* 1989). The covert nature of the rebel supply effort, pre-existing connections between arms and cocaine dealers involved in the international black market, and the participation of many South Americans in the delivery of weapons to the Sandinistas facilitated the development of drug trafficking in Costa Rica during this period.

Costa Rica's lack of an army, its small and ill-equipped police force, and rugged geography meant that drug traffickers were able to disguise their criminal activities as legitimate operations and to remain hidden in jungles and mountain regions. Members of Colombian cartels, Venezuelans, Cuban-Americans, and other U.S. citizens involved in the cocaine trade increasingly found Costa Rica attractive as a refueling, warehousing, and reloading site for private planes carrying arms and drugs. The Bureau of International Narcotics Matters' *International Narcotics Control Strategy Report 1986* notes that few Costa Ricans were involved in the cocaine trade before this time (INM 1986, 96).

The establishment of linkages among residents of Costa Rica, drug traffickers, and the Nicaraguan Resistance (contra) movement after 1983 led to a surge in the amount of cocaine traveling through the country. In *Cocaine Politics*, Scott and Marshall report that drug trafficking pervaded the entire contra war effort, that the smuggling involved individual contras, contra suppliers and pilots, contra supporters throughout the region, CIA agents, and allegedly senior U.S. policy makers including Oliver North. According to Scott and Marshall, the Reagan administration chose to do business with individuals and companies already known for their involvement in the drug trade and failed to address the drug issue for fear of jeopardizing the war effort against Nicaragua (Marshall and Scott 1991, 104-120). A 1989 U.S. Senate Subcommittee on Terrorism, Narcotics, and International Operations reached basically the same conclusions and serves as the basis for their book.

Costa Rica Responds to the Cocaine Menace

In 1985, the arrest and subsequent expulsion from Costa Rica of Mexican drug trafficker Rafael Caro Quintero by Costa Rican authorities, acting in conjunction with the U.S. Drug Enforcement Agency (DEA) (following the murder of DEA agent Enrique Camarena in Mexico), served as the catalyst for increased national attention to drug trafficking (*The Miami Herald* 1989). Four years later, in response to a public outcry against drug trafficking motivated by the April 1988 arrest of suspected heroin trafficker Roberto Fionna (who was revealed to have ties to several elected officials), the Costa Rican legislature in 1989 appointed a six-member bipartisan commission to study the problem of narcotics trafficking and make recommendations, which then might be voted into law (*The Miami Herald* 1989).

The members of the committee took their jobs extremely seriously and produced a report which indicated that international drug traffickers had gained influence in all three branches of government. Implicated in the report were high-ranking members of both major political parties (Partido de Liberación Nacional and Partido de Unidad Social Cristiana), three supreme court judges, the homicide chief of the judicial police, an ambassador, several prominent private citizens, and a number of foreigners. Since 1989, three subsequent commissions have endorsed the recommendations made by the 1989 commission and have urged speedier action to implement them.

The 1989 Legislative Commission's report included condemnation of some of the country's most important elected officials. Counterallegations increased the publicity of the report and left the country mired in scandal. In a bizarre twist, the chairperson of the Legislative Commission himself was accused of questionable fund raising in Panama for the 1982 presidential campaign of Luis Alberto Monge; two other Legislative Deputies were implicated in the case against Singaporan Sheik Sahib Tajundeen, who had been sentenced to twenty years in prison in France on drug trafficking charges (*Regionnews-Managua* 1989).

Former Costa Rican president and then-PLN President Daniel Oduber was also reported by the commission to have been involved with U.S. citizen Lionel James Casey, a lawyer and financial backer of the Arias campaign who was extradited to the United States in 1988 on drug possession and trafficking charges. The report recommended that Oduber resign from his position as chairman of the PLN and return the donation to Lionel James Casey. Oduber eventually did both. Also included in the commission's document was a call for the resignation of the manager of the state-owned Bank of Costa Rica because of alleged improprieties in the approval of a loan (*Esta Semana* 1989).

The commission's ability publicly to release damning findings that touched individuals representing the most powerful factions in Costa Rican life without violent reprisals, bribery, or challenges to the regime is a testimony to the strength of democracy and the rule of law in Costa Rica.[1] Partially due to the importance of moral issues in the Costa Rican political debate, drug trafficking and drug-related corruption became issues in the 1990 presidential campaign. The principal 1990 presidential candidates committed themselves to supporting even stronger antidrug legislation, the ratification of the U.S.-Costa Rica extradition treaty signed in 1982, and the strengthening of law enforcement operations. In part due to the discrediting of PLN party chairman Daniel Oduber, the Partido de Liberación Nacional lost the 1990 election and power passed to the opposition PUSC (Partido Unidad Social Cristiana), led by Rafael Angel Calderón.

The release of the 1989 Legislative Commission's report prompted the passage of tougher narcotics legislation with respect to seizure of assets, money laundering, precursor chemicals, plea bargaining guidelines, and revocation of business licenses for involvement in trafficking or sale of narcotics. The 1989 Narcotics Law (as the new legislation came to be known) also called for the establishment of a permanent Narcotics Commission, which in turn established a Joint Center for Intelligence on Narcotics (CICAD) to serve as a central oversight and planning body for what had previously been a loosely coordinated, multiple-agency effort at battling drug trafficking. The legislature's rapid decision to fund CICAD with a generous budget of 50 million colones (US$625,000) was an indication of the political will that exists to support antidrug efforts (INM 1991, 138-139).

Money Laundering

Although banking laws in Costa Rica have historically been lax and easily manipulated, the country lacks significant numbers of the offshore banks which are traditionally considered essential to money laundering efforts. Nonetheless, money laundering activity has expanded (apparently, without the cooperation of the government) as the cocaine industry has grown in Costa Rica. The first major money laundering case in Costa Rica occurred in 1988 with the arrest and prosecution of suspected Costa Rican money launderer Ricardo Alem (a financial backer of the Arias presidential campaign) following an airport seizure of US$750,000 (INM 1989, 97).

By 1990, Costa Rica ranked third among Latin American countries in terms of money laundering, mainly due to the migration of traffickers' accounts from Panama in the aftermath of the 1989 U.S. invasion. Due to enhanced enforcement efforts and passage of new legislation after the release of the 1989 Legislative Commission report (and the reemergence of Panama as a haven for traffickers), money laundering is believed to have decreased in Costa Rica in the last two years.

Under the 1989 Narcotics Law, the Costa Rican Central Bank's Office of Bank Examiners implemented new regulations aimed at money laundering operations in domestic financial institutions. All financial institutions are now required to report transactions involving foreign currency in amounts equal to or larger than US$10,000. These regulations apply to all transactions within Costa Rican financial institutions on behalf of domestic or foreign corporations or individuals and transactions undertaken on behalf of other financial institutions (*La Nación* 1989).

Bilateral and Multilateral Cooperation

The primary foreign bodies involved in the antidrug effort are the U.S. Drug Enforcement Administration, which conducts investigations and provides the Costa Rican judiciary with evidence against individuals suspected in conjunction with drug trafficking crimes, and the Bureau of International Narcotics Matters, which are funded through the U.S. State Department and provides financial resources and material and technical assistance to Costa Rican law enforcement bodies. Radios and communications equipment, computers and office equipment, vehicles, and spray kits for cannabis eradication are the main components of the material aid received.

Less significant in terms of dollar amounts, the United States Agency for International Development (USAID) supports the Department of Justice's International Criminal Investigative Training Assistance Program and the United Nations' Latin American Institute for the Prevention of Crime effort in Costa Rica. The Organization of American States (OAS) has also funded antidrug programs in Costa Rica. In the last few years, the Costa Rican Coast Guard has conducted joint operations off the Pacific Coast with the U.S. Coast Guard, and the Rural Guard has undertaken joint exercises with the U.S. Seventh Special Forces Unit. The U.S. Customs Service has also visited at the request of the Costa Rican government to give training courses to Costa Rican customs authorities. These various programs have substantially aided Costa Rican antinarcotics activities, which focus on interdiction efforts, eradication of cannabis fields, and preventing traffickers from setting up cocaine processing labs. Cooperation with Nicaragua (since 1990) and Panama (since 1989) have also been important in controlling the movement of illegal drugs across Costa Rica's borders (INM 1991, 138-141).

Since 1985, the Costa Rican government has been described as "dedicated" and "committed" to antidrug activities in the annual *International Narcotics Control Strategy Report* published by the Bureau of International Narcotics Matters, which in 1986 described relations between Costa Rican authorities and the DEA as "excellent" (INM 1986, 98). Strains have, nevertheless, surfaced in the relationship between the two countries over drug matters. On several occasions in the last few years, Costa Rican law enforcement authorities and the DEA have been at odds over jurisdictional and procedural issues. However, the most serious challenge to U.S. interests in Costa Rica's antidrug effort came in 1990 when, despite pressure from the United States, Costa Rican courts declared the use of wire-tapping devices for gathering evidence illegal. The law is retroactive until 1973 and allowed dozens of traffickers to request reviews of their cases by the Supreme Court, many of which resulted in releases (INM 1991, 138-39).

It cannot be expected that the interests and desires of various U.S. agencies charged with implementing drug policy and their Costa Rican counterparts will always coincide. Costa Rica's extreme dependence on U.S. goodwill in the areas of trade, finance, and aid means that local policy makers have little room to maneuver vis-à-vis the United States. Despite a history of close relations between the two countries, tensions remain in Costa Rica as to whether the effort to fight drug trafficking will be imported from outside the country or will be locally produced and managed to suit the specifications of those on the ground.

Publicity Campaigns

Since 1989, both the government and the private sector have mounted aggressive publicity campaigns against drug abuse. Prominent Costa Ricans from the sports and entertainment worlds are regularly featured in professionally produced television spots that emphasize the dangers of substance abuse. Relatively high levels of public awareness have facilitated this effort, and the vigorous response of the many voluntary organizations to the drug threat is, perhaps, the most encouraging component of the Costa Rican antidrug effort. In March 1990, USAID signed an agreement with the Association of Professionals for Integral Development (ADIFAC) funding a $500,000 grant to establish a community awareness program on drug abuse. The project is designed to train community leaders to lead prevention programs in both rural and urban areas. Eight thousand community leaders in 91 communities will be trained (INM 1991, 140).

Conclusions and Recommendations

The evidence presented in the preceding analysis suggests several preliminary conclusions. There seems to be no question that the government of Costa Rica and the vast majority of its citizens are fully committed to eradicating drug trafficking from their society. The scope of public mobilization and political debate, of legal reform and enforcement efforts suggests a consensus against illicit drugs that largely transcends partisan, clientelistic, or institutional interests. However, as a full and participatory democracy, Costa Rica may be uniquely vulnerable to the influence of drug traffickers as the pressures of increasingly expensive political campaigns have led both major parties to accept funds from questionable sources.

Given both continued demand for cocaine in the United States and the immense resources available to drug traffickers, Costa Rica cannot realistically hope to diminish substantially the amount of cocaine passing through the country. The most local authorities and their international counterparts can expect is to prevent drug trafficking from expanding or leaking into an internal market and to diminish the corrupting influence of the illegal narcotics industry over the political and legal system. With this as a premise, I would like to suggest several areas for further research.

First, the community of scholars concerned with the international drug trade should consider investigating Costa Rican civil society's response to the drug threat. Doing so may find that voluntary, private sector, and neighborhood antidrug efforts currently underway in Costa Rica could serve as models for the United States and other consumer countries in their search for effective demand reduction strategies. Second, social science might benefit from a more thorough investigation of the particular vulnerabilities of democracies to the corrupting influences of drug trafficking and should further study the effects of such influences on regime legitimacy. Third, greater study of U.S.-Costa Rican antidrug relations could contribute to understanding challenges and opportunities presented by regional and international cooperation in drug control efforts. Finally, the relationship between the growth of the illicit drug industry in Costa Rica and the pronounced and rapid domestic economic decline (particularly since the signing of the 1989 IMF stabilization agreement) should be of interest to those who approach the study of drug trafficking from the perspective of political economy.

Notes

1. Death threats were received by members of the Legislative Commission.

References

Asamblea Legislativa. 1989. *Segundo Informe de la Comisión sobre el Narcotráfico*. San Jose: EUNED.

Bureau of International Narcotics Matters. 1985-1992. *Annual International Drug Control Strategy Report*. Washington, D.C.: Government Printing Office.

Esta Semana, July 21, 1989, 4-5.

La Nación, July 20, 1989.

Marshall, Jonathan, and Peter Scott. 1991. *Cocaine Politics*. Berkeley: University of California Press.

Miami Herald, June 25, 1989, 12A.

Miami Herald, October 16, 1990, 27A.

Quiros, Verny, ed. 1989. *Informe Sobre El Narcotráfico*. San Jose: Editorial Marti.

Regionnews-Managua, July 15, 1989, 18.

The Christian Science Monitor, January 30, 1989, 1-2.

Chapter Twenty-four

The Drug Trade in the Caribbean: Policy Options

Anthony P. Maingot

Introduction

The Caribbean, although only a minor player in the production of illicit drugs, is not at all a small player in the total picture of the U.S. drug problem. Yet, it has taken Caribbean societies far too long to become aware that drugs are not purely an American problem but one that affects them as well. A recent survey of those arrested for possession of cocaine in the Jamaican resort Negril discovered that only 15 to 20 percent were tourists. Jamaica is not alone: drug use has become a major social problem throughout the region.[1] Similarly, third parties have underestimated the general consequences to the region of the drug trade. These facts stem, in part, from the fact that the Caribbean has been studied — and thought of — under much the same agenda used for the study of major drug producing countries.

The purpose here is to suggest that the study of the drug trade in the Caribbean requires a different agenda and analytical framework. I propose six different points or issues for such an agenda. The formulation of an appropriate conceptual framework should follow an agreed definition of the problem.

Issue No. 1: The Geopolitics of Being "Offshore"

Only two Caribbean countries have been involved in any substantial drug production: Jamaica and Belize. In both cases, that production has been decreasing. U.S. State Department figures indicate that Jamaica reduced marijuana production from between 625 and 1,280 tons in 1985 to 300 tons in 1988. Its share of the U.S. marijuana market was a mere 1.7 percent in 1987. Belize's production of marijuana went from 645 tons in 1985 to 180 in 1988, supplying 1.6 percent of the U.S. market. There is no known, significant production for export elsewhere in the islands, of marijuana or of other types of drugs. The importance of the Caribbean lies in two other assets it possesses that are vital to the drug business: 1) geographical location and 2) expertise in the culture, language, finances, and consumption preferences of the United States and Europe.

This fact, being "offshore," requires additional research.

One way to formulate the problem is as follows: The Caribbean region is experiencing a dramatic increase in a wide array of transnational or "offshore" activities at a time when its capacity for collective, region-wide responses is at a low point. Certainly, not all offshore activities are nefarious or detrimental. It is a plausible hypothesis, however, that any and all of the individual activities which are presently affecting the well-being of these small societies take full advantage of the generally beneficial arrangements and "milieu" created by the bulk of offshore activities. In fact, the very character-istics which make the islands attractive to one set of activities, make them attractive to the more nefarious other part. It is not an issue of either-or but of margins and opportunity costs. The offshore activities described here — the drug trade, offshore banking, and tax havens — illustrate this point.[2]

An immediate question which emerges from this geopolitical reality relates to the issue of state capabilities vis-à-vis the enormity of the tasks involved. Capabilities have to include the capacity to discriminate the good from the bad — a task not even larger societies seem capable of performing — and then both to promote and defend healthy development initiatives. Since, by definition, transnational and offshore activities are largely beyond the authority of states or international agencies, policing such activities is nowhere easy.

It is even more intractable and slippery when geopolitical factors favor those who place a premium on secrecy and evasion. This clearly is the case in the Caribbean where three vital characteristics of transnational develop-ment are present: 1) a sending society with the clients (whether as tourists or drug users) and the money, 2) a receiving society with the geographical location and commodities (sun, sand, and relaxed banking and company laws), and 3) native elites with the will and the talent to exploit one or the other — and in some cases, both. The issue is not an absence of public opinion, but the fragmentation of that opinion typical of archipelagal areas.

Issue No. 2: Are the Problems New?

There is growing evidence that this situation in the Caribbean is not new. In fact, the history of piracy in the Caribbean is ancient, merely going through costume changes.

There is a real need to pursue historical research into the networks established by the U.S.-based mafia in Cuba and elsewhere in the Caribbean.

A Havana-Medellín connection has been traced back to the 1930s and, even stronger, in the 1950s. Andres Oppenheimer does a superb job of demonstrating those links in the 1980s.[3]

While the pirates of old, and their networks, pale by comparison with the contemporary types, it is vital to inquire whether and where there are continuities in illicit behavior. We understand the possible future transformations of present piracy by understanding this evolution.

In many ways, Robert Vesco is prototypical of the modern-day pirate operating in the Caribbean. He certainly has a long trajectory in the Caribbean. A fugitive from U.S. justice, his status as a "felon in flight" in no way prevented him from establishing the closest of relationships with political elites, first in Costa Rica, then in the Bahamas, Antigua, and finally, as a guest of Fidel Castro in Cuba. Clearly, aside from money, Vesco has had a variety of talents and skills which different national elites, of diverse ideology, have found useful. There is — in the Caribbean Basin and elsewhere — no shortage of sovereign states ready to give such pirates safe haven.

Indeed, there are even states which purposefully encourage and facilitate the granting of a safe haven as a significant source of income in convertible currency. Panama under the Noriega dictatorship was one such case. Citizenship, passports, visas, all were for sale and governments as diverse as the United States and Cuba found the Panamanian "arrangement" quite suitable to their wider geopolitical goals. It is now revealed, by the director of Panamá's Technical Judicial Police (PTJ), that fully 75 percent of the criminals sought by INTERPOL entered or settled in Panamá at some point.[4]

In other words, transhipment of drugs is not the only issue or threat.

The discovery on January 6, 1989, of a container in the port of Kingston with US$8 million in arms demonstrates that the problem had wider ramifications. Of West German manufacture, the weapons were shipped from Portugal on a Panamanian registered ship and were destined for an unspecified group in Colombia. It took a joint effort of Jamaican, British, U.S., and Colombian intelligence to break the Jamaican link of what was called "an international network of drug traffickers and terrorists."[5] The Panamanian ship was owned by Bluewater Ship Management Inc. of Panama. Both the company and its British-naturalized Panamanian president had previously been tied to illegal arms shipments, cocaine distribution, and the laundering of drug-related monies.[6]

What was happening in Jamaica was symptomatic of a regional crisis. The region-wide alarm over the links between the corruption wrought by the drug trade and violent threats to the region was slow to develop. Meanwhile, the infrastructure of a much more complex offshore environment was quickly taking shape.

Issue No. 3: The Challenge of High Technology

The Caribbean Sea acts as both a barrier and a bridge. Both functions favor the new internationalization of corruption and violence. By "balkanizing" the region into relatively weak nation states — while, at the same time, facilitating the flow of international commerce and transnational activities of some of the world's great procedures and exports — this sea puts many an international activity beyond the reach of nation states. The result is often an asymmetry in maneuvering capabilities between national and international actors. This asymmetry is augmented and perpetuated by the technical and electronic revolution which gives even private parties enormous capacities of communication, including the electronic transfer of capital. The international cartels tend also to have preferential access to human talent. Indeed, as ex-President López Michelsen of Colombia has noted, the transferability of skills and technology from legitimate industry to the drug trade has made the latter a truly modern and transnational industry.[7] The Caribbean not only provides the bridge between the producer and the consumer in that industry, its modern banking system provides virtually impenetrable shelter to its profits.

The importance of all this is that the drug trade both contributes to and is facilitated by widespread and enduring corruption which permeates key elements — though certainly not all — of the public and private sectors. Combatting specific aspects of the drug trade (cultivation, transportation, distribution), difficult as that is, is a great deal simpler than uprooting corruption. The problems are both conceptual and practical.

Issue No. 4: The Need for Understanding the Role of Corruption

What these changes point to is the need for a more self-conscious understanding of the nature of corruption.

It is the awareness of the realities wrought by these issues that led newly elected Jamaican Prime Minister Michael Manley to tell the United Nations that drug traffickers and criminals "have the globe to play with":

> You are dealing with a level of international criminal organization that is probably without precedent. Those who manipulate produc-tion, transport, distribution, and marketing operate in a global framework.[8]

What Manley was addressing was the internationalization of corruption which made such a "global framework" possible. What makes this corruption international is the fact that it invariably involves actions and transactions in more than one national jurisdiction. A whole series of actions, generally referred to as "layering," makes the tracing of money flows and principal actors virtually impossible. This type of corruption is beyond the control or supervision of any one state. Manley's concern was, of course, with how this process would affect his native Jamaica. "I certainly can't conceive," he told the press, "of what kind of Jamaica our people could build on the basis of a drug culture or a society massively corrupted by drug trafficking."[9]

Neither traditional (vi. nepotism) nor bureaucratic-administrative (viz. jobbery) corruption are new to the Caribbean. From the Bahamas through Cuba, all the way down the island chain to Trinidad, the region has had a reputation for both. Nor is it the case that the region is necessarily more corrupt than other areas. When Walter Lippmann noted that in the United States corruption was "endemic," he could well have spoken for many another country.[10] Lippmann also made a universally valid methodological point when he maintained that no history of corruption was possible, only the history of the exposure of corruption. Exposure, he maintained, invariably was merely one sequence in a cycle which alternated between "unsuspecting complacency and violent suspicion." Clearly, however, empirical and conceptual elusiveness should not deter attempts at a more systematic understanding of the phenomenon. It is the central argument of this chapter that the greatest menace to the security of the states in the Caribbean Basin stems from a new form or level of corruption which should best be called the internationalization of corruption and violence.

The assumption here is that, to the extent that the situation is qualitatively new, it has to be understood in the context of a widely practiced type of corruption: a corruption which is "functional" to the internationalization of capital, labor, and labor movements which characterize the region's (and the world's) economy. In other words, it suits the logic of the marketplace. "A corrupt civil servant," writes Jacob van Klaveren, "regards his public office as a business, the income of which he will...seek to maximize. The office then becomes a 'maximizing unit.' The size of his income depends...upon the market situation and his talents for finding the point of maximal gain on the public's demand curve."[11] The definition is similar to that of Robert Tilman's which sees corruption in terms of a rational choice, a "free market" type calculus: they may "decide that it is worthwhile to risk the known sanctions and pay the higher costs in order to be assured of receiving the desired benefits."[12] It should be evident that in the context of a new corruption, fostered by the enormous amounts of drug-related monies, the concept of "maximization," or any other utility function, cannot be measured in "normal" terms. Even if historical standards of corruption are incorporated in the calculation, the phenomenon defies measurement. Robert Klitgaard's sound recommendation, that administrative corruption be combatted through material and other incentives, clearly fails on the material (i.e., wages) side; and up to now, no one has figured out which "other" incentives will work.[13]

Interestingly enough, the logic of the "rational" corruption of the individual civil servant can also operate at the level of major state actors or foreign policy designs. What else — if not the maximizing of geopolitical advantages — would lead an administration to "marry" a corrupt dictator such as General Manuel Antonio Noriega?

Again, the calculus might not be financial gain but rather an attempt to avoid the discomfort of being called "colonialist" or imperialist by a corrupt "Third World" tyrant such as Suriname's Col. Desi Bouterse. Whatever the motivations or fears, the fact is that there has been a very belated awareness that corruption affects national security directly.

Issue No. 5: The Need for a New Conception of Security

It is a fact that in general terms Caribbean leaders' perceptions of threat have not been grounded in any broad ideological or theoretical conception of national security but on hard experiences related to their immediate political fortunes. None of the important politician-writers of the Caribbean in the 1960s, 1970s, and even early 1980s had even intimated that the threat to Caribbean security would come largely from corruption, internal to their societies and external in the Caribbean as a whole. Even the prolific Michael Manley was totally absorbed by the North-South issue. Academic scholars tended to follow suit; their concern was with issues of "revolution" and dependency. Even one as moderate and well-informed as Carl Stone refused to confront the issue of the international criminal threat. As late as April 1988, Stone wrote that he found it distressing that in a year when Jamaicans were electing a new government, "we are spending as much time agonizing over petty U.S. gossip about supposed mafia-type links between local politics and drug dons."[14] He called for a discussion of "the real issues."

Neither the right's versions of a communist menace nor the left's versions of imperialism, nor, indeed, the various enumerations of discrete — and short-lasting — incidents of violence address the true nature of the contemporary threats. Much more promising is the approach of Peter Calvert who divides the threats to small states into four categories:[15]

1. Attack by external forces, including mercenaries

2. Coups d'etat

3. Subversion by narcotic traffickers

4. Generalized corruption in government and/or the private sector.

It is not that there has been no awareness that the threats of the Cold War had been displaced by a new type of threat. Note the exchange between Senator John F. Kerry (D-Massachusetts), chairman of the Subcommittee on Terrorism, Narcotics, and International Communications of the Senate's Committee on Foreign Relations, and Nestor D. Sánchez, former Deputy Assistant Secretary for Latin American Affairs, Department of Defense:[16]

Senator Kerry: You are familiar with the assessments that General (Paul) Gorman made...that the national security of the United States was threatened by Latin drug conspiracies dramatically more successful at subversion in those areas than the subversion efforts from Moscow.

Mr. Sánchez: Absolutely, it's a national security threat to one country, because of the countries and individuals involved.

Senator Kerry: Now, General Gorman also testified that if you want to move weapons or munitions in Latin America, the established networks are owned by the cartels.

Senator Kerry could have mentioned that the cartels not only control networks of gun running but also of illegal aliens. While the vast majority of illegal aliens are law-abiding, there are key "pipelines" used by the cartels to bring distributors, "enforcers," and others into the United States. Much attention has been focused on the Jamaican "posses" (called "yardies" in the U.K.), but the so-called "Sandoval Pipeline" brought into South Florida some 175 illegals a week, at US$1700 per head, via Panama, Nassau, and Bimini.

The critical methodological point, however, is that events in the Caribbean demonstrate that hardly ever do Calvert's four points operate as discrete or "independent" events. They are interconnected and related and require a framework which encompasses those interrelations.

Conclusion

Despite the absence of a Caribbean-wide conception of threat from corruption and violence, it is a fact some Caribbean leaders — though, certainly, not all — emerged from the 1980s fully aware that pirates, mercenaries, and terrorists responded to more than just Marxism-Leninism, that the issue of security was broader than the North-South confrontation which had taken up so much intellectual attention and energy in their nations and region. "In 1982," wrote Prime Minister James F. Mitchell of St. Vincent, "although the United States might be single-minded in its position, the Caribbean with its political diversity cannot agree on a common enemy."[17] Not that West Indian leaders were innocent about Cuban actions, wrote Mitchell, but there were other threats. Those who disparage the menace posed by the mafia, he noted, "are already victims." And, then, there was white-collar crime. "In St. Vincent's case," he noted, "more money is swindled through our offshore banks from U.S. accounts than our total annual budget."

"We are threatened," Michael Manley told an audience in Toronto, Canada, in April 1990, "by an international criminal network in drug trafficking that has no precedent in history."[18] Manley's words were being thoroughly corroborated by investigators and by events in the Caribbean. Not only did

Manley make the war on drugs priority number one of his administration, he carried his call for collective action to the United Nations. Similarly, Trinidad's Prime Minister A. N. R. Robinson called for the establishment of a special international court to try drug dealers.[19] Unfortunately, not everyone was ready for Manley's or Robinson's ideas on how to combat the trade: traditional conceptions of sovereignty had still to be overcome in the Caribbean.

Because the internalization of corruption means that so much occurs beyond the national jurisdiction, national actors will have only limited scope over its elimination. This reality is evident in Prime Minister Mitchell's description of one of the shady sides of the growing offshore banking industry, a rare official Caribbean statement about that business, easily one of the fastest growing sectors in the Caribbean. The small Caribbean state is fortunate, therefore, that the offshore tax havens have recently attracted increased attention from British and U.S. law enforcement authorities. But since any corruption involves a giver and a taker, national actors can at least hold the local takers accountable. The rest will require international, collective action which all nations should encourage.

That world awareness about the threat posed by the drug trade, the internationalization of corruption and violence, has reached new levels is evident in the language of the 1987 UN Draft Convention Against Illicit Traffic in Narcotic Drugs and Psychotropic Substances, a multinational agreement designed to increase the effectiveness of law enforcement efforts against illicit drug trafficking.

That convention's language showed that the threat is perceived in quite broad terms. It calls for seven areas of action, five of which fall directly into any new agenda for the study of the drug trade in the Caribbean (items 3 through 7):

1. Eradicate illicitly cultivated narcotic crops.

2. Monitor chemicals and equipment used in the processing of drugs.

3. Identify, seize, and forfeit illicitly generated proceeds.

4. Improve international legal cooperation by such means as extradition, mutual legal assistance, and exchange of information relating to trafficking activities.

5. Improve "controlled delivery" procedures (a term referring to law enforcement cooperation through which the movement of an illicit drug consignment can be monitored so that arrests are made at the time of ultimate delivery).

6. Require commercial carriers to take reasonable precautions to avoid use of their facilities and means of transport for illicit trafficking.

7. Prevent illicit traffic by sea, through the mails, or by abuse of special rights prevailing in free trade zones and free ports.

As broad as these seven areas are, they do not fully address the central problem facing the Caribbean. In fact, they omit any reference to the underlying structures and practices which make the drug trade possible: corruption, nationally and internationally.

Quite evidently, as aware as the leaders of the world are of the threats posed, they still resist any outside "interference" with "internal" political and administrative affairs. Any notion of extraterritorial jurisdiction being located in an international body is stiffly resisted. It is still regarded as an absolute precept that each nation should be left to govern its own territory and apply its own laws within that territory, never outside it. Corruption — to the extent that it is so regarded and punishable by a nation's laws — is clearly a national matter. And, yet, can any major inroads against the cartels be made without effective, and worldwide, sanctions against it? It is to the credit of the U.S. Senate's Caucus on International Narcotics Control that they believe not. As their report on the UN Draft Convention notes (and I quote it at length), the absence of any charge on corruption is a major weakness:[20]

> Official corruption and complicity in the drug trade by some governments, particularly the laundering of illicit drug profits, has been one of the biggest obstacles to effective bilateral and multilateral drug enforcement efforts. The draft convention, however, contains no language addressing this aspect of the international drug control problem, nor have any proposals been seriously discussed by any participating nation. There are several options that could be considered to address the gap in the draft convention's language: 1) including sanctions similar to those included in the 1961 Single Convention on Psychotropic Substances against governments found participating in the drug trade and 2) prohibiting any such government from participating in cooperative drug enforcement efforts with all signatory countries. While this convention may not be the most appropriate vehicle to address the corruption problem, *international narcotics control efforts will never adequately attack the trafficking problem until official government corruption in the drug trade is eliminated,* so that the efforts of the international community can be focused solely on prosecuting the criminal syndicates directly involved in the international drug trade.

The United States, for instance, wants money laundering to be considered as serious a crime as narcotics trafficking. In a region where offshore tax havens are thriving, there is resistance to any such suggestion. In short, the Caribbean — like much of the rest of the world — knows what the poison is, and many have ideas about what its possible antidote might be; yet they are not prepared to take full dose of any remedy.

Notes

1. *Jamaican Weekly Gleaner*, April 1, 1994, 4.

2. Further on this in Anthony P. Maingot, *The U.S. and the Caribbean: Challenges of an Asymmetrical Relationship*. London: Macmillan, Chapters 7 and 8.

3. Andrés Oppenheimer, *Castro's Final Hour*. New York: Simon and Schuster. 1992.

4. Interview with Don Bohning, *The Miami Herald*, February 8, 1993, 6.

5. *Jamaican Weekly Gleaner*, January 16, 1989, 1.

6. Anthony P. Maingot. "The Drug Menace in the Caribbean," *The World and I*. (July 1989), 128-135.

7. Alfonso Lopez Michelsen. "Is Colombia to Blame?" *Hemisphere*, Vol. 1, no. 1. (Fall 1988), 35-36.

8. Michael Manley. Speech to the UN. Office of the Prime Minister. Kingston, June 9, 1989.

9. Quoted in *The Miami Herald*, June 10, 1989, 8.

10. Walter Lippman, "A Theory About Corruption," *Vanity Fair*. Vol. 35. (November 1930), 61.

11. The quotes from van Klaveren and Robert Tilman are taken from Arnold T. Heidenheimer (ed.), *Political Corruption* (New York: Holt, Rinehart, and Winston, 1950).

12. Heidenheimer, *Political Corruption*.

13. Robert Klitgaard, "Incentive Myopia," *World Development*, Vol. 17, no. 4 (1989), 447-459.

14. Quoted in the *Jamaican Weekly Gleaner*, April 18, 1988, 5.

15. Peter Calvert, *The Central American Security System: North-South or East-West?* Cambridge: Cambridge University Press, 1988, 195.

16. Hearings, Subcommittee on Terrorism, Narcotics, and International Communications, One Hundredth Congress, Second Session, Part 4 (July 11, 12, 14, 1988), 196.

17. James F. Mitchell, *Caribbean Crusade* (Waitsfield, Vt.: Concepts Publishing, 1988), 155.

18. *The Miami Herald*, April 16, 1990, 8.

19. In Trinidad, the opposition to A.N.R. Robinson's government ridiculed the call. In 1992, that opposition, now in government, expressed "shock" at the extent of corruption in the society. Prime Minister Patrick Manning, quoted in the *Trinidad Guardian*, September 17, 1992, 1.

20. A Report on the Status of the Draft Convention, the U.S. Negotiating Position, and Issues for the Senate. Senate Caucus on the International Narcotics Control. 100th Congress, 1st Session, October, 1987, 10. Emphasis added.

Chapter Twenty-five

Politics and U.S.-Jamaican Drug Trade in the 1980s

Antoinette Khan-Melnyk

Introduction

Among the major problems confronting the Jamaican government in the 1980s and 1990s were the substantial increase in domestic marijuana production and the adverse impact of drug trafficking on the economy. Considered the single most significant threat to security, drugs endangered the nation's export development strategy, communications system (ports, airports, mail), and international relationships and facilitated a new wave of crime throughout the country and abroad. Moreover, Jamaica became a priority theater in the U.S. war on drugs as it exported marijuana on a larger scale. From 1981 to 1983, this small Caribbean island was ranked the second largest supplier of marijuana (or *ganja*, as it is locally known) to the U.S. market — an issue that complicated political and economic relations between the two countries.

For over a decade, the government has been faced with a dilemma: drugs earned considerable income for individuals living in a highly indebted economy where joblessness and poverty were rampant. At the same time, the United States was pushing hard for antidrug efforts on the part of foreign drug producers. The bottom line was that Jamaica simply could not mobilize the kind of resources necessary to wage an effective war on the illegal trade. But the United States kept up the pressure, linking to antidrug enforcement other issues that were important to the island's leaders.

This chapter presents a case study of the drug trade in Jamaica. Although the island is now known to be a transshipment point for cocaine, the focus here is on drug trafficking as it relates primarily to marijuana. Unlike ganja which has been grown in Jamaica for decades and is an integral part of the local culture, the presence of cocaine is a recent phenomenon; the dearth of Jamaican statistics and information on the subject precludes any meaningful assessment of its domestic impact. The objectives of this study are to 1) examine the controversial issues in the Jamaica-U.S. drug traffic; 2) assess the social, political, and economic impact of drug smuggling on Jamaica; 3) determine the degree to which the "war" on illegal substances inside Jamaica was a predominantly *Jamaican* initiative; and 4) address questions relating to Jamaica's ability to achieve its goals in spite, and in light, of U.S. attention to the drug menace. Here, relative autonomy is measured by the extent to which Jamaica was able to circumvent U.S. policy objectives not perceived to be in its interest, while reaping the economic rewards from the relationship and protecting its political interests at home. In effect, the attempt to resist U.S. pressure depended on political costs. Hence, both the Seaga and Manley administrations sought policies that could satisfy local pressure for an improved standard of living (thereby guaranteeing their own power) and obtain considerable foreign economic benefits without incurring the displeasure of the United States.

Background to the Problem

The emergence of ganja as a profitable industry inside Jamaica can be seen as a creative response to pressures such as a declining standard of living, fewer formal sector jobs, and an ever-growing demand for drugs in the United States. But, the persistence of the drug as an influence in contemporary life, despite more than 75 years of criminal legislation, must be attributed largely to sociocultural factors. The existence of the marijuana plant *cannabis sativa* is often traced to the period following the emancipation of slaves in 1838. Brought to the island by East Indian indentured workers, it was adopted by, and reworked into the cultural framework of, the black lower class. A contemporary influence in this process was the Rastafarian movement, a religiopolitical group advocating "black pride" and social justice. Among its most prominent teachings were the worship of Ethiopian Emperor Haile Selassie as God, rule of the black race in the after-life, and repatriation to Ethiopia as the ultimate goal of the faithful. "Rastas" also claimed that ganja was found growing on the grave of the biblical King Solomon and, therefore, was a holy weed and gift from God. Not surprisingly, smoking of the weed became religious practice. To a large degree, this doctrine appealed to the poor as it lent dignity to their subjugated status in society. By the late 1960s, the middle class had begun to experience elements of the Rasta subculture, particularly the use of ganja and the music known as Reggae.

In Jamaica, the cannabis culture has so thrived and proliferated throughout society that it has become something of an institution exhibiting "a series of definable and repetitive activities, characteristic social groups, and an integrated body of beliefs and values," or what Rubin and Comitas (1975) call a "ganja complex."[1] This complex is conditioned by the belief that the drug is beneficial to the individual. Consequently, use of the drug is linked to most aspects of working class social structure:

> cultivation, cash crops, marketing, economics; consumer-cultivator-dealer networks; intraclass relationships and processes of avoidance and cooperation; parent-child, peer and mate relationships; folk medicine; folk religious doctrines; *obeah* [magic] and gossip sanctions; personality and culture; interclass stereotypes; legal and church sanctions; perceived requisites of behavioral changes for social mobility; and adaptive strategies.[2]

Of particular significance is the situational use of, and reaction to, the drug. That is, ganja serves multiple purposes in accordance with the various needs of its users: it may be drunk in teas, taken as medicine, cooked in foods, or simply smoked to facilitate meditation and relaxation. Likewise, the tradition of ganja use in Jamaica must be seen as an adaptive mechanism by which many poor people cope with limited economic opportunities. Some small farmers cultivate cannabis for household purposes, and for years it has been a source of additional income. Because government policies have not substantially improved the standard of living of the peasant population, many try to utilize their lands as best they can by growing both food crops and marijuana. Food specialization is seen as too risky an undertaking since much of the land villagers have access to is ill-suited for agriculture, often steeply sloped, and subject to drought and floods.[3] The market for food crops is unstable, prices fluctuate, and sometimes these cash crops are not even enough on which to subsist. Thus, for the majority who have no other means of eking out a living due to lack of education and technical skills, ganja growing becomes an attractive enterprise. Not only does the plant grow easily — like a weed even in subpar soils — but market prices are also relatively stable, providing a steady (though illegal) source of revenue for poor households. Up until the internationalization of the drug trade, domestic cannabis cultivation was a small-scale operation, partly for family consumption and partly for the cash market.

The importance of rural sector ganja use lies in the nature of the Jamaican social structure in which the black peasantry and working class comprise the great majority of the population. This means that well over half the total number of Jamaicans who may be found in country settlements are likely to be influenced by the ganja complex in some way. In the early 1970s, it was estimated that between 60 to 70 percent of the lower income section of the rural population (including children) used marijuana in some form. By 1986, one out of five Jamaican youths was a regular user, and more than half the adult population had smoked the drug.[4] With the proliferation of cocaine in the 1980s, drug consumption patterns changed as the incidence of persons using ganja for the first time declined moderately in favor of coke and crack.

Surveys reveal that 27 percent of ganja users began taking the drug after 1986, compared with 41 percent who started prior to 1980. In this same period, cocaine use quickly rose to 55 percent, up from 12 percent. A predominantly "upper class" drug in the 1970s, cocaine is gradually becoming more popular in urban ghetto settings among lower income males. Fortunately, use of this narcotic is still marginal; by mid-1991, only 0.9 percent of the total population were consumers.[5]

The national debate on ganja use and the drug traffic is indicative of the public psyche and must be linked inevitably to the success of any government attempt to cut back on the industry. A number of polls conducted by political scientist Carl Stone since the 1970s reveal an interesting shift in perceptions of the drug in society. In 1972, as many as 71 percent of persons interviewed were opposed to the legalization of ganja smoking. Four years later, public opinion was evenly divided on the issue: 46 percent for, 46 percent against. By February 1981, two out of three Jamaicans disagreed with government legitimizing the ganja trade, although in July 1981, a majority (61.8 percent) rejected the view that a cutback in the trade was desirable. Interestingly, one of the reasons given by respondents in the February poll was that such a development would depress prices and the income earned by those involved in the trade.

These statistics show great public acceptance for the presence of ganja in society and highlight what proportion of the people themselves favor the trade, regardless of whether or not they are connected with ganja.[6] Opinions have shifted over the years away from the view that the drug causes mental illness, brain damage, non-productivity, and criminal behavior. Significantly, Jamaicans differentiate between marijuana and other "hard drugs." The belief is that when taken in moderation, and when compared to narcotics such as cocaine, ganja is not a dangerous drug. As far as drug use is concerned, cocaine poses the real threat to the country and its youth. No doubt, this has been influenced by 1) the spread of the Rastafarian culture throughout society and the consequent increase in drug users among the upper classes, including government and business leaders, and 2) the expansion of the ganja trade and its importance as a source of income and hard currency for some Jamaicans.

The background to the current problem of ganja in Jamaica is quite significant to the success of any antidrug program. Indeed, it raises a number of questions. *First,* with roots in pharmacopoeia, the essentially pragmatic purposes of the use of the drug and the social motivations for smoking seem to suggest that criminalization will not succeed. Aubrey Fraser explains: "It will not be easy to persuade the rural dweller in Jamaica by enforcing punitive legislation that the habit of consuming ganja tea is a crime."[7] However, while ganja use is integral to a way of life, it is not vital to survival, suggesting the possibility of change.[8] *Second,* while a change from the ganja habit is possible in theory, the difficulties in actually doing so are great. This is because change is dependent upon finding a suitable alternative commodity that is legitimate and that possesses all the perceived advantages of marijuana. *Third* is the distinction frequently made by Jamaicans between the "menace" of ganja and its simple economics. This mode of thinking asserts that the corrupt individual dealing in the lucrative commodity for personal gain at the expense of others is a problem and a just enough reason for any government to fight drug activity. On the contrary, the role of the peasant is not considered criminal, and even though the cultivation and use of marijuana is outlawed, penalties are seldom enforced. These issues bring to light the peculiarities of the ganja complex and must be addressed in any analysis of the drug in contemporary Jamaican society.

Issues in the Jamaica-U.S. Drug Trade in the 1980s

The Jamaican election of 1980, which brought to an end nearly a decade of left-leaning socialist rule, was hailed throughout the Western world as a triumph for democracy. The anti-communist and free market thinking of the new Jamaica Labor Party (JLP) government quickly resulted in Jamaica's emergence as America's closest political ally in the Caribbean. At the same time, however, the U.S. drug problem worsened, and the Reagan administration declared "war" against narcotics an essential part of its foreign policy toward drug producing nations. The reality of Jamaica's heavy contribution to the U.S. drug dilemma soon created serious political and economic strains in what was hoped would be a harmonious relationship between the two countries.

At the start of his administration, Jamaican Prime Minister Edward Seaga pledged to eliminate the illicit production and traffic of ganja, but his government's efforts to deal with the problem in the early 1980s were little more than "cosmetic." In other words, the outward appearance of trying to wrestle with the drug trade belied the actual attention being paid domestically. This policy course may have been the logical outcome of two factors: 1) Jamaica's need to earn valuable foreign exchange, the ability of which was contingent upon antidrug action, and 2) the recognition of the futility of trying to stop the formidable trade. Despite this reality, Washington did not pressure Jamaican officials, mainly because its attention was focused on the South American cocaine producers, but also because of the island's status as "friend." As a result, the Reagan administration was heedful in its approach to that country's handling of the drug traffic, a policy that reflected a number of concerns: 1) Jamaica's representation as an important counter-example to leftist experiments in the region and designation as "showpiece" of what U.S.-aided capitalism could achieve, 2) the conservative prime minister's strong pro-U.S. leaning and his leadership role in the Caribbean,[9] and 3) the recognition that serious differences in foreign policy had eroded the relationship in the late 1970s.

By the mid-1980s, the quantity of Jamaican marijuana being imported into the United States had reached such alarming proportions (see Table 1) that the Reagan administration was forced to reassess its policy of tolerance toward that country. More important, the catalyst for concerted action against ganja was the increasing use of the island by Colombian narcotraffickers as a transshipment point for cocaine en route to the North American market.[10] The belief in Washington was that lax attention to Jamaica as a drug producer, plus the island's unenforced laws and ineffective interdiction efforts, made it easy for South Americans to move cocaine through Jamaica and on to the United States. Suddenly, Jamaica became a high priority country in the U.S. drug war as pressures mounted on both sides to deal with the issue that was quickly becoming a matter of controversy between Washington and Kingston.

In 1983, the U.S. House Select Committee on Narcotics Abuse and Control visited the island to observe first-hand the magnitude of the problem. The concern lay with the lack of an effective government program to destroy widespread cultivation and to curb the traffic. The prime minister's strategy was to prevent smugglers from transferring ganja from growers to distributors — which would cause the industry to collapse due to lack of a market — and to recommend the cultivation of legitimate crops. But the committee considered this "a restatement of the strategy followed by the Government of Jamaica...with no success since the late 1960s."[11] Indeed, the evidence was clear by 1983: Jamaica furnished roughly 13 percent of the total supply of marijuana available on the U.S. market; almost 3/4 of those passengers arrested for marijuana smuggling mainly in New York and Miami airports were Jamaicans, and about 80 percent of 84 seizures of air cargo in the United States originated in Jamaica. Furthermore, a total of 163 illegal aircraft supposedly had crashed on the island between 1979 and 1983.[12]

While the situation up to that point suggested failure on the part of the Jamaican government to deal effectively with an extensive drug traffic, it also revealed the imbalance of the national drug plan. Seaga may have centered his attention on encouraging and expanding interdiction efforts to deter ganja traders, but the most cost-effective and efficient approach to narcotics control in the eyes of Washington was crop eradication, hence the dispute over demand and supply. According to James Van Wert, the U.S. rationale behind a supply-oriented approach was that it would 1) lessen the incidence and prevalence of drug abuse in the United States since drugs would be hard to find, 2) reduce the level of organized crime, and 3) preserve the security and stability of friendly countries from powerful narcotraffickers. A more realistic assumption was that "it [was] easier to locate and destroy crops in the field than to locate the subsequently processed drugs in the smuggling routes or on the streets of U.S. cities."[13] Naturally, the prescription of a supply-oriented policy was crop eradication. However, by adopting a policy geared toward reducing the flow of narcotics from the Caribbean and South America, the United States was, in fact, blaming its drug problem on outside forces.

Although Jamaica acknowledged that it was a major international producer and exporter of marijuana, like other Western suppliers, it criticized the insatiable U.S. demand for the drug. The argument was that lower American demand would decrease the inflow of narcotics and reduce prices. The trade itself would gradually diminish as traffickers would have little incentive to ship the drug to the United States. The Jamaican government also complained about what they saw as American citizens corrupting Jamaicans to grow marijuana on their behalf. Indeed, their role in the trade was key. In a May 1988 address to a drug conference in Kingston, U.S. Ambassador Michael Sotirhos admitted:

> We Americans are not without blame. On any given day, some 80 Americans are serving time in Jamaican jails for narcotics violations. About 350 Americans are arrested annually on drug charges. In addition, to the extent that marijuana smuggling is done by small aircraft, most of the planes and pilots involved come from our country [the United States].[14]

Jamaican attempts to eradicate ganja in the fields were conducted on a small scale, involving rudimentary methods which had virtually no impact in the United States. Still, said Seaga, there were practical considerations of which the government had to be cautious. Citing an incident in 1983 in which ganja growers had retaliated by burning sugar cane fields after government squads eradicated their crop, he stressed that without the means to prevent a repetition of this, innocent cane farmers would be hurt financially. Furthermore, the matter of crop substitution compensation begged the obvious question of how to convince rural farmers to cultivate alternative legitimate commodities after they had witnessed the kind of wealth associated with growing ganja. Even if such a move were possible, it would be dislocating to farmers and require huge amounts of financial assistance which could not be provided by the state. While these concerns touch on the issue of the meager resource base on which to fight the Jamaican drug war, they are also indicative of the deeper questions of internal economic and political hazards to the party in power.

Prime Minister Seaga understood the country's economic dependence on the drug trade. With a fall in national revenue from the dwindling prices of sugar and bauxite, and mounting joblessness — about one half of the work force was unemployed by 1984 — more and more Jamaicans relied on ganja cultivation and sales to cushion themselves financially. Inasmuch as inflows of direct foreign investments and large international aid packages encouraged growth, however modest, in the economy, a majority of the Jamaican people did not feel the effects. This was largely due to the government's International Monetary Fund (IMF) austerity policies in the 1983-1985 period which made life tougher and doing legitimate business in Jamaica riskier. Although outside factors such as low world commodity prices and the U.S. recession were invisible contributors to the country's economic decline in the first half of the 1980s, the crunch of layoffs, high prices, and goods not selling in the local market was very real for the petty commodity sector which represented some 42 percent of the work force. Notwithstanding the socioeconomic motivations for growing marijuana, there were significant profits accruing to the industry, some of which percolated very rapidly to the grass roots level. This was especially important in light of the government's failure to create additional jobs and the lack of other meaningful sources of national revenue shy of bauxite and tourism. The trade had become a source of steady income for even the smallest element in the drug network and, therefore, was indirectly crucial to the legitimate economy. Though it is difficult to estimate the contribution ganja made to the gross domestic product, it is probably enough to know that it was the largest cash crop, worth somewhere between J$1-2 billion annually — well above the combined total for bauxite, sugar, and other licit exports.[15] Unlike the United States, then, Jamaica did not consider the traffic a moral danger to society.

On the political side, eliminating the trade had direct implications for the governing party. On one hand, Seaga knew that in order to stabilize the economy he would have to implement measures that would sharply escalate the cost of living; on the other, he was cognizant of the ganja industry's ability singlehandedly to keep the country afloat. As early as the end of 1982, disillusionment with "deliverance"[16] had begun to grip all sectors of society, causing a swift erosion of the JLP's base of support and disaffection among voters and critical business groups. Significantly, a good portion of the JLP's followers in the 1980 election comprised traditional supporters of the opposition People's National Party (PNP) who could swing back at any time. For political parties, a highly politicized electorate comprising a large percentage of nonpartisan voters means that the traditional safety net of an assured number of seats in Parliament based on strong voter allegiance can no longer be taken for granted.[17] Thus, to save political face and to keep dissatisfaction at a minimum while pursuing the harsh IMF stabilization program, Seaga would have to turn a blind eye to the ganja trade for the advantages his government could not provide otherwise.

The kind of "war" Jamaica was expected to wage overwhelmed the small country. The extensive domestic cultivation of marijuana and the burgeoning traffic of drugs, by air and sea, presented such a formidable challenge that the government simply did not have the means even to cope with the dilemma.

Legislation notwithstanding, Jamaica's defense establishment was handicapped through severe shortages of manpower, equipment, and operating funds — a factor which proved self-defeating in the battle against drug dealers. Consequently, the four aging boats used by the Coast Guard to patrol some 80,000 square miles of sea, the lack of helicopters and pilots, efficient vehicles, and other basic equipment (which, in some cases, meant nothing less than uzi submachine guns or M-16 rifles to match the firepower of the ganja men) were major obstacles to police and security forces. In contrast, their adversaries possessed low-profile, high-speed boats that could outrun anything in the water; made use of sophisticated radios, rental cars, motorcycles; and were licensed holders of at least one heavy caliber firearm.[18] Most important, the enormous wealth of the drug dealers presented a powerful deterrent to the many underpaid police and soldiers. Capable of offering huge bribes, and wielding influence over whole communities, the drug lords successfully lured many law enforcement agents down the path of corruption. Even with U.S. assistance, the stark inequalities of the two forces continued to put the Jamaican government at a disadvantage in its war against drugs.

Still, there was the problem of U.S. pressure to take drastic action against Jamaica if something were not done about the illegal ganja trade. In 1981, Congress passed an amendment to the Foreign Assistance Act, establishing the annual requirement for a report by the president on the status of U.S. narcotics policy. This was strengthened in 1983 by making U.S. assistance partly contingent upon a country's efforts to reduce levels of drug production and by determining the "maximum reductions in illicit drug production which are achievable" in primary source countries. In 1986, a further amendment legalized the withholding of 50 percent of the economic and military assistance allocated to such countries.[19] Likewise, one of the prerequisites to receiving benefits under Edward Seaga's much-desired Caribbean Basin Initiative (CBI) became government cooperation with the United States in its offensive against the drug traffic. In effect, through these regulations and requirements, the United States was forcing major drug producers to take the U.S. drug war seriously. And by linking the question of financial aid and development assistance to that of the ganja trade, the Reagan administration sent a clear message to Jamaican leaders that their lack of effort would no longer be acceptable. The Jamaicans responded by giving drugs top priority on their political agenda.

Antidrug Efforts in the 1980s: Interdiction

The goals of the Seaga administration's antidrug effort in the 1980s were 1) to eliminate Jamaica's involvement in the international drug trade through strict legislation and strengthened law enforcement, 2) to raise public awareness as to the dangers narcotics — especially cocaine — posed to society, and 3) to eradicate permanently the cultivation of marijuana on state lands. At first, the problem was tackled from two angles: legislation and enforcement, both of which required considerable improvement to be effective in the war on drugs and demonstrated the government's emphasis on a strategy of interdiction. By preventing smugglers' boats and planes from leaving Jamaican territory, securing known points of entry and exit, and apprehending traffickers themselves, the Jamaican authorities believed they could curb the ganja trade. Initially, the campaign depended on the police and security forces but, as this proved ineffective, later stretched to include the Airports Authority, the Port Authority, and Jamaican Customs.

Pointing to an increase in ganja cultivation from approximately 1400 hectares in 1981 to more than 1800 hectares in 1983, and an estimated 1750-2500 metric tons of Jamaican marijuana on the U.S. market in 1982, the United States accused the island's government of foot-dragging. But the latter insisted that in 1983 local police teams eradicated twice as much hectarage as in 1981, seized and destroyed nearly 77 percent more reaped ganja than in 1981, and arrested over 10,000 nationals and foreigners for smuggling during the 1981-1983 period (see Table 2). The contradiction in these statistics indicated a lack of success on the part of the Jamaican government in restricting the outward flow of drugs. This was attributed to 1) the severe shortage of personnel, equipment, and funds required to wage a rigorous battle; 2) the rudimentary eradication methods — cutting, uprooting, burning — which did not always end in the permanent elimination of cannabis cultivation; in other words, crops were replanted the following season; 3) the inadequacy of Jamaican drug laws and the infrequency of their enforcement (drug dealers could easily get around these); 4) the confining austerity budget under which the government operated, implying that its attention was focused elsewhere; and 5) the distinction frequently drawn between marijuana and other "hard drugs," which amounted to a lack of government and public will to deal with the trade.[20]

In short, the strategy of interdiction did not deter traffickers, though it did bring into sharp focus the extent of the drug trafficking network in Jamaica. Some 60 to 70 percent of the marijuana and cocaine leaving the island was supposedly transported by small airplanes also engaged in the movement of banned goods and weapons. For that matter, illegal airstrips and the wrecks of such planes were literally scattered across the island. In 1984, Parliament amended the Civil Aviation Act to tighten control over the movement of illegal aircraft utilizing aerodromes and some 70 clandestine airstrips — a significant link in the drug trade. Under the new regulations, aircraft could only operate in and out of licensed aerodromes, and international flights were restricted to a customs airport. For violation of these laws, the operator and crew of the aircraft faced fines of up to J$100,000 or three times the value of the carrier, its engines, accessories, and equipment, and five years in prison. No doubt, the prime targets of the new law were the many U.S.-owned aircraft and U.S. pilots involved in the shipment of drugs to the United States. The amendment also sought to counter the incidence of airstrips being put back into operation after they had been demolished by security forces. Thus, it made unlawful the construction of an aerodrome without the written permission of the Minister of Transportation, the operation of an unlicensed aerodrome, and the preparation of land for use as an airstrip. As an added penal measure, Seaga announced that 28 suspected drug dealers would be required to pay more than J$117 million in taxes. This dramatic move was criticized by as many as 54 percent of those interviewed in a Stone poll who saw the tax as a harassment of ganja traders trying to earn valuable foreign exchange. But the announcement should be viewed more as a response to U.S. threats to decrease aid by providing a mechanism by which to seize drug assets and force traffickers out of business, rather than an effort to control the formidable trade.[21]

As the government intensified its campaign to disrupt traditional routes used by small aircraft and boats, drug traffickers began hiding marijuana in containerized cargo shipments of legitimate exports, in unmanifested baggage placed on Air Jamaica (the national airline), and in letters and packages bound for the United States. Whether an act of sabotage, or merely a commitment to drug smuggling, the discovery of marijuana by U.S. Customs on carriers originating in Jamaica became a frequent occurrence. The boomerang effect was so powerful that it not only hurt the credibility of the airline and shipping industries but also jeopardized the whole economic structure of Jamaica as well as its connection with the outside world. Political relations between the two countries became strained on the issue, as U.S. pressure sent the small country scrambling to resolve its domestic ganja problem in the midst of other weighty concerns. Between 1984 and 1986, the government stepped up its enforcement capacity in response to the marijuana trap now facing the country, a trap which also caused the United States to intensify its own war against Jamaican drugs.

In a political move to clamp down on the drug trade, the United States threatened, in 1984, to confiscate Air Jamaica's license to fly into U.S. gateways and imposed a fine of US$25 for every ounce of marijuana found on any Air Jamaica plane. When the airline was fined J$13 million (US$2.4 million) in March 1985 for having 5,940 pounds of compressed ganja on board, Minister of Transportation Pearnel Charles fired all airport workers who were on shift when the plane left for Miami. Concerned about the high costs to the government and the bad image drugs was giving the country, the minister instituted new measures to increase security at airports, including the arrest of any unauthorized persons found in restricted areas of the airport and sniffer dog patrols of planes before they were loaded with passengers and after maintenance crews had gone through. In addition, an accord was signed in August 1985 between Air Jamaica and U.S. Customs to cooperate fully in the crackdown on drugs. This resulted in a security checklist to protect Air Jamaica's fleets traveling to the United States, added security personnel at the airports, and increased vigilance on the part of employers and employees. Charles assured U.S. Customs that anyone found to be involved in smuggling would be removed from any position they held with the airline and shipping services and warned foreign traffickers to "stay out of Jamaica." Over 160 security guards and ramp handlers were fired and replaced by new workers at the Kingston airport. In a companion move, all goods being shipped on Air Jamaica were to be accompanied by the photo ID of the exporter.

 Yet, in spite of the strict rules governing cargo on the national airline, the traffic continued. The services of foreign airlines (Air Canada, British Airways, for example) were also jeopardized. In December 1986, Eastern Airlines stopped flying cargo out of Jamaica after a shipment was found on one of its jets at the Miami International Airport. If it had not resumed operations a month later when stricter security measures were implemented, Jamaican exporters in the garment and agricultural industries would have been adversely affected by the cutoff of transportation for their goods. By 1987, the steep fines threatened to ground Air Jamaica; some $35 million had already been extracted from the government to pay penalties. For that matter, the airline did not even own a permit to fly and operated on emergency licenses. Security costs to the airline were so high, it ran second behind fuel costs. The potential effect on tourism could be particularly damaging as air transportation was important to that sector. As a result, all airlines were given permission to hire their own security in an effort to save the country's travel and export industries.

A find of 500 cartons of ganja in a shipment of green peppers and cucumbers in April 1985 — and other such incidents in which marijuana appeared under the guise of agricultural and manufactured products — compromised the export effort as a development strategy. When U.S. Customs examined shipments to ensure they were free of narcotics, this caused disruptions and delays of legitimate shipments to the American market and heavy losses to Jamaican farmers. It was estimated that ganja trafficking had caused export products to suffer a 20 percent disadvantage against the products of other countries[22] as delays ran as high as 38 days in some places. To counter the situation, Foreign Minister Hugh Shearer repeatedly urged farmers and exporters to ensure that their products were loaded under very secure conditions. In July 1986, U.S. Customs implemented a pilot project that involved stripping containers arriving in New York from Jamaica. Charged to the importer, the estimated cost was US$1200 per container. This was regarded as a necessary step since the normal tailgate inspection proved ineffective and Jamaica was considered a "high risk area." The Seaga government objected to the excessive costs being passed on to its products, further eroding Jamaica's export earnings. The intense U.S. surveillance led to a concerted drive by the private sector, government, Port Authority, and Shipping Association to increase vigilance on their part. The Jamaica National Export Corporation had already begun striking off individuals and firms from their list of registered exporters because of loose security procedures and noncompliance with the regulations. Between 1985 and 1987, approximately 166 thousand pounds of illegal drugs were seized in consignments originating in Jamaica, and some 367 exporting entities had their registration canceled because of failure to meet the statutory requirements. The result was that exporters were unable to ship their goods to overseas markets, and workers were laid off because their employers were out of business. Fortunately, the quantity of drugs found in exports fell from 98 thousand pounds in 1986 to 38 thousand pounds in 1988.[23]

Drugs also threatened the survival of Jamaica's ports and shipping industry. A large ganja find disguised as a cargo of cement in May 1986 resulted in steep fines to the shipping line, but the implication of the after-effect worried the government. The danger of foreign shipping lines ceasing to call on Jamaican ports because they were afraid to expose themselves to criminal proceedings and heavy fines if drugs were found on their vessels was a legitimate concern. Foreign companies were a critical component not only in shipping Jamaica's products but also in expanding and developing the infrastructure of Kingston's seaport. In 1987, this port handled some 161,200 containers, 60 to 70 percent of which was accounted for by Evergreen Line — one of the largest shipping companies serving the island. But, in mid-1988, the company drastically reduced berthing after U.S. Customs levied a US$60 million fine (later reduced to US$29 million) against it for marijuana discovered in three containers aboard one of its ships coming from Jamaica. By July, the company threatened to pull out of the country altogether, but the government appealed the decision on the grounds that it would lose up to US$45 million annually. Evergreen consented to remain, though it would not conduct any transshipment business in Jamaica apart from simply unloading cargo brought by other ships. Later, the problem resurfaced when both Kirk Lines and Sea-Land Service threatened to cease operations due to similar situations involving ganja.

At this time, the government believed it had done everything possible to curb the traffic and complained that U.S. authorities were not taking its efforts into consideration. A large slice of the national budget being used to finance security at airports and wharves ranked second to what was being spent on national security, and it was believed that this money could be better utilized for health, education, and local transportation needs. By early 1988, the budget was almost depleted, and government now looked to other sources for funds.

Eradication

Close collaboration between Jamaica and the United States on eradication methods was not always forthcoming. Early Jamaican efforts were modest, with very little impact in the United States. Nevertheless, Seaga's ongoing pledge to eradicate, and his insistence that the country was doing all it could to stop ganja cultivation, was enough to forestall any possible cutbacks in U.S. aid, even though his commitment did not thoroughly convince the Reagan administration. Locally, the destruction of crops by government teams had only served to disrupt the activities of farmers, who hit back by burning sugar cane fields and brutally murdering three policemen in December 1983. Seaga had been reluctant to tackle the thorny issue of drugs at the source, but the increasing incidents of ganja aboard Air Jamaica and the pressures mounted on the government by the seizure of airplanes and the imposition of fines led to an aggressive eradication program commencing in 1985. Named "Operation Buccaneer," the campaign relied on mechanical eradication using U.S.-supplied motorized brushcutters; aerial search and destroy missions which targeted harvesting, packing, and shipping operations; and helicopter transportation to growing areas inaccessible from the ground. Furthermore, the creation of a joint Jamaica Constabulary Force/ Jamaica Defense Force (JCF/JDF) task force that year to develop eradication and interdiction strategies, determine resource needs, and serve as liaison with the State Department's Bureau of International Narcotics Matters (INM) helped to institutionalize Jamaica's antidrug program. These efforts, along with a three-fold increase in the quantity of marijuana destroyed in 1984, saw a dramatic jump in total INM funding from $49 thousand in Fiscal Year (FY) 1984 to $430 thousand in FY 1985.[24]

For some time, it had been the view in Washington that Jamaica should develop a program of aerial spraying of ganja fields, for which they would provide the funds. But the Seaga administration refused to use the herbicide paraquat to spray fields, citing the toxic nature of the compound and the dangers it posed to domestic food production. Furthermore, they argued that in the United States an environmental impact statement was required before herbicides were used and that Jamaica proposed to do the same. Even without spraying, the Jamaica antinarcotics force had achieved some semblance of success as the number of hectares eradicated rose between 1984 and 1986. This left ganja growers and dealers hurting, though not deterred, as the drug continued to be grown and taken out of the country.

Just as the interdiction campaign had resulted in a shift in drug trafficking methods, so did government eradication force ganja farmers to rethink cultivation strategy. Instead of the traditional rest period in between the spring and fall growing seasons, ganja was now being planted year-round and interspersed with food crops to prevent detection. The large fields (5 to 50 acres) had given way to small plots of one acre or less, and there was a change in the traditional places of production from the wet and flat lands of western and central Jamaica to the more remote sites deep in mountain valleys, on the sides of ridges, or at the top of steep hills. The inaccessibility of these sites from the ground and the demand for helicopter transportation further complicated the task of eradication squads. Many farmers were harvesting their crop before it reached full maturity and before it could be destroyed by soldiers. Consequently, the production of hashish oil increased as it could be made from any stage of the plant's growth. Farmers were also going to great pains to store the reaped ganja and usually whisked it miles away from the growing areas to different locations for drying and packaging.[25]

Although the eradication drive left growers complaining bitterly about the loss of their product, it did force the price of ganja high, and dealers were willing to pay anything for whatever quantity of marijuana farmers could supply. Since the start of the "Buccaneer" program in Fall 1985, cultivation the following year had more than doubled (see Table 3). This symbolized a forceful reaction on the part of traffickers who were suffering losses to government and who were encouraging growers to expand production exponentially. In turn, Seaga responded by announcing his intention in December 1986 to use the herbicide glyphosate to spray fields. The recognition of a rapidly deteriorating domestic situation and its adverse effect on legitimate exports and tourism — as well as its concomitant political problems — no doubt influenced the new government decision. More important were the recent U.S. threats to withhold 50 percent of the economic and military assistance given to drug producing countries; to vote against any loans by the multilateral development banks (World Bank, Interamerican Development Bank, and the IMF); and to deny preferential tariff treatment for products under programs, such as the CBI and the Generalized System of Preferences, unless serious action was taken by primary source countries.[26] In view of this, and if the eradication program was to have the desired effect, said Seaga, manual and mechanical destruction would have to be complemented by chemical eradication.

The herbicide otherwise known as "Round-Up" had been licensed for use in Jamaica since 1971 as a harvest aid and ripening agent in the cultivation of sugar cane, tobacco, and coffee and was considered as mild as table salt. It was to be applied only by backpack to immature ganja plants well in advance of reaping, at the same time ensuring that damage to adjacent foliage was avoided. As a result of this new undertaking, INM narcotics funding once again increased, this time to US$1.5 million. But spraying generated new problems. In some places, legitimate food crops were mistaken for ganja, livestock were killed by herbicide-carrying winds, and small homes within close range of ganja fields were deliberately torched by soldiers.

According to the U.S. State Department, the year 1987 was the turning point in the Jamaican battle against marijuana as net production reached its lowest point (roughly 460 metric tons) since the start of Seaga's drug war (see Table 4). This was also reflected on the U.S. market — Jamaica's supply had declined from about 12 percent in 1986 to a mere 1.7 percent (see Table 1). However, local eradication teams actually had destroyed roughly the same hectarage as the previous year. This indicated only a slowdown in the industry, although business continued as usual. In the first half of 1986, successive drought and flood rains had wiped out thousands of ganja seedlings and scorched substantial acreage of land used for drug cultivation, resulting in a scarcity of cannabis seeds. Farmers and dealers were also expressing concern at the 1987 amendment to the Dangerous Drugs Act which put more teeth into the law by imposing stiffer fines of up to J$500 per ounce of marijuana if convicted of possession. Recognizing that the large quantities dealt with by some people could add up to hefty sums and certain jail time, dealers in one western parish forced down the price of ganja to such low levels so they could quickly sell their supply.

In general, the downward trend in the industry made life tougher for whole communities of peasants dependent upon illegal ganja farming. Seaga's assurances to the United States that he would encourage a movement away from cannabis toward lawful enterprises was not met with any practical effort until 1986, and even then, little was actually accomplished. In fact, the question of crop substitution seemed moot. When it came up, it lacked consensus among members of the prime minister's own cabinet. At a November 1986 meeting of the Caribbean Congress of Labor, Jamaica's Labor Minister J.A.G. Smith stated that whereas assistance was forthcoming in destroying ganja plants, none was being made available for helping peasant farmers enter into legitimate enterprises. The main reason was the lack of the necessary capital structure. He suggested that small projects, which conceivably could be funded from national savings, be implemented. On the other hand, Pearnel Charles opposed such compensation, saying that those involved in an illegal activity "should be told to stop and if they didn't, the laws of the country should put an end to their activities." Instead, he argued, compensation should go to farmers to improve their legitimate businesses.[27] Since the issue of substitution was debatable and the question of eradication politically sensitive, the answer would have to be found through implementation of formal agricultural projects and improved social services for the poor.

In October 1983, the Jamaican government had launched its "Agro-21" project — a commercial-type approach to agriculture, featuring a whole new range of nontraditional crops. The hope was that the industry's earning potential would be maximized through the application of modern technology and mobilization of some 200 thousand acres of unused and underutilized land for production over the 1983-1987 period. It is possible that these measures were also aimed at creating new agricultural opportunities for rural areas and deterring the many small-scale growers from using public lands for ganja cultivation. But the period 1983-1985 was a difficult one for Jamaica's poor, many of whom experienced the high cost of economic stabilization. The 1986 upturn in the country's investment, employment, and production levels came too late to diffuse widespread anti-JLP sentiment which culminated in the party's defeat in local government elections that year. While this did not amount to public repudiation of JLP policies,[28] it did demonstrate the extent to which the PNP — by capturing 56.6 percent of the vote or 44 of the 60 parliamentary constituencies — had strengthened its position since its massive defeat in 1980.

In an attempt at rebuilding the JLP's image, Seaga adopted a new policy — the "Social Well-Being Program" — to ease the burden on the poor and the marginally poor who had felt the brunt of the IMF policies. Emphasis was placed upon improving health care and education, fixing roads and water supplies, and creating jobs. There is little question that the program also would have benefited whole communities of peasants whose only means of livelihood had been destroyed by the various "Buccaneer" programs. However, the crackdown on small producers and the spraying of ganja fields remained a bitter issue in Jamaican politics, fueled by popular belief that eradication was cutting the economic lifeline of many poor farmers, that the Seaga government was paying less attention to cocaine and the rich middlemen, and that the United States was forcing Jamaica to eradicate in order to fight its own drug use problem. This reality implied that the war on marijuana in Jamaica could not be won solely on the basis of eradication and interdiction.

Concluding Analysis

The Seaga administration's war on the illegal ganja trade was ostensibly successful insofar as it reduced net cultivation in Jamaica. However, the general battle seemed to have been lost as the enormous costs to the country far outweighed the achievements and the balance continued to be tipped in favor of the traffickers. The domestic milieu of adverse balance of payments, 50 percent unemployment, and austere IMF measures made the drug trade far more formidable than it would have been otherwise and the need for U.S. economic assistance essential. But, cooperation with the Reagan administration resulted in a severe backlash for the government, as drug smugglers turned to legitimate carriers to transport their goods. This activity threatened every productive sector in the country at a time when Jamaica struggled to meet even its basic needs. At the same time, noncollaboration with the United States may have produced an economic whiplash in terms of cutbacks in U.S. aid and privileges under one of the most important trading arrangements, the Caribbean Basin Initiative. In short, the government faced a binding situation. The question is, to what degree did costs matter to the Seaga administration?

Foremost among the long-term goals of the government was the establishment of a well-functioning market system which was seen as the key to Jamaica's economic development. The immediate concern was to procure a greater flow of trade, aid, and credit to the island in order to overcome problems of foreign exchange unavailability and to withstand the shocks of the transition to free enterprise. And while the political leadership sympathized with the poor, it could do little to ease their plight since from the start, it was realized that economic hardship would be unavoidable. Therefore, Seaga chose to toe the U.S. line, and in complying politically, he was rewarded by the Reagan administration even in the face of a burgeoning marijuana trade. For this reason, the costs incurred by Jamaica in its drug war did not matter quite as much since economic benefits from the United States were forthcoming.

The degree of the small country's apparent compliance must not be overstated. Ganja is illegal there, and antidrug laws have existed since the early 1900s to counter the incidence of crime, public unrest, and substance abuse. Any government is constitutionally obliged to deal with situations involving marijuana. More important, as economic conditions worsened in the country, it became in Jamaica's own interest to deal with the problem since it threatened to strangle the legitimate economy. In other words, the ganja war inside the country became a predominantly *Jamaican* initiative. Therefore, the question of a meaningful antidrug effort hinges less on the fact that Jamaica acted in line with U.S. wishes and more on the *timing* of those actions.

In the early 1980s, the government lacked the political will to deal with the drug traffic, an important source of income for many Jamaicans. Public opinion very much favored the industry. By the end of 1982, the JLP's popularity had declined because the electorate could see little tangible economic improvement. In Jamaica this is critical to guaranteeing the continued power of the ruling party. The following year, the island became caught up in the events of Grenada, boosting government support and prompting Seaga to call snap elections which, in turn, were boycotted by the PNP. Seaga may have been firmly reinstated as prime minister, but 1983-1985 were to be difficult, austere years. Up to that point, Washington did not consider the country a high priority in its narcotics war, and Kingston was able to circumvent U.S. anger by promising to deal with the problem. In the meantime, the government pursued a makeshift ganja policy at home that had little effect on the massive international drug trade. By 1986, positive growth returned to the economy, employment rose, and there was buoyancy in the business and investment climates. But, the JLP captured only 43.2 percent of the vote in local elections that year, as against the PNP's 56.5 percent. By this time too, U.S. support was slipping slowly away, and the country was no longer spared the intense pressures of U.S. drug control policy. Only then did Seaga turn to the question of eradication by spraying — the most important supply-oriented policy of the U.S. administration.

To address the issue of foreign policy autonomy is to ask the question, did Jamaica have the capacity to confront the drug trade on its own? If not, to what extent were Jamaica's actions dictated by the United States? The discussion has shown that the local drug situation proved too formidable for a small country like Jamaica to handle, given the paucity of resources. Congress' use of the "carrot-and-stick" approach — first threatening Jamaica with reductions in aid and later rewarding it with financial support once it executed meaningful steps toward eradication — was very effective in extracting cooperation from the island's government. Furthermore, the relationship between Air Jamaica (and the shipping industry) and U.S. Customs illustrates how, by raising the costs of drug trafficking, the United States was successful in forcing Jamaican compliance. It may be argued, too, that voluntary collaboration with Washington reflected the island's stake in its own civil and economic well-being.

In the face of U.S. pressure and Jamaican economic goals, the extent to which Seaga was able to circumvent U.S. objectives and placate the Reagan administration (rather than defy it outright) is the key to measuring small state autonomy within the issue of the Jamaica-U.S. drug trade. This is because conformity can soften U.S. disapproval of a small country's internal policy, thereby widening its political space for action.

Furthermore, Seaga's continuous linkage of this issue to others that were important to the Reagan administration — mainly, the security of the Caribbean Basin — was an attempt to maximize Jamaica's own maneuverability in the area of drug policy. American unwillingness to punish Jamaica the way it did Bolivia by cutting off aid is significant. A mere pledge on Seaga's part to do something about the trade, even in the absence of concrete plans, was satisfactory to the U.S. administration. The fact is, Jamaica did have greater leeway than many other countries of the region because it was the United States' closest political ally in the Caribbean. Because of this, it was able to get away with cosmetic policies in the earlier part of the decade. When the United States stepped up pressure to adopt a program of aerial herbicide spraying, the Jamaican government refused to use the prescribed chemical paraquat, settling only for backpack spraying with a milder substance.

Critics may argue that although Jamaica's privileged standing made a difference, the fact remains that the United States did force the small country to take stronger action at a time when the latter was interested in pursuing a softer policy. What this constitutes are the limits to autonomous foreign policy. Even within the drug issue, Jamaica operated under certain constraints. The challenge, however, was to gain maximum mileage out of whatever space could be created in the relationship. The argument can be made that the Seaga administration cleverly exploited its new-found status by effectively manipulating the principal resource at hand — U.S. security fears in the Caribbean Basin. This was possible insofar as the former realized that it did not have a powerful negotiating stance or great leverage vis-à-vis the United States, but that it could enhance cooperation and expand its degree of freedom by capitalizing on the importance of drugs to the interests of the Reagan administration. In this regard, the country proved to be quite an effective actor, helping to set the agenda of the Jamaica-United States drug war.

Epilogue: The Drug War in the 1990s

In February 1989, the People's National Party (PNP) led by Michael Manley (and now P.J. Patterson)[29] assumed office. The government has been firmly committed to an active antidrug policy with a good degree of success. However, its unavoidable obligation to an IMF/World Bank economic path and to an overwhelming debt which consumes roughly 40 cents of every dollar earned by the state has drastically limited its range of options, both domestic and international. Furthermore, the diminished threat of Soviet adventurism in the region has rendered the "security card" invalid in its diplomatic arsenal. A parallel development is the high-profile attention being given Eastern Europe by the United States — an anticipatory sign that the Caribbean will occupy a lower place on the U.S. agenda.

Nevertheless, Manley won Jamaica quick approval from the George Bush administration as well as multilateral lending institutions by moderating his political stance and accelerating the pace of economic reform (mainly, privatization and liberalization). Shortly after his election, the U.S. Export-Import Bank extended its short-term credit facility to Jamaica from US$45 million to US$60 million, a sign that Washington was willing to assist the fragile Jamaican economy. In the area of drugs, the prime minister pushed for multilateral cooperation through the creation of an international antidrug organization to 1) gather intelligence; 2) train narcotics agents; 3) conduct programs in public education, demand management, and rehabilitation; and 4) offer advice in the planning and administration of income substitution programs. Most controversial was his call for a multilateral strike force under the command of the United Nations.[30] The initiative promised to resolve considerations of not only resource constraints but also sovereignty. Manley argued that Third World countries — by virtue of their dwindling capability to combat poverty and underdevelopment — were locked into a vicious cycle of drug production since these very characteristics made them natural areas for such activity. On the question of sovereignty, a multinational response would prevent strong nationalistic outbursts such as occurred when the United States sent antidrug forces into Peru and Bolivia. In this way, the plan catered to all interests.

At home, the Manley government's antidrug policy proceeded beyond Seaga's own initiatives. In particular, it finally ratified and put into effect (on July 7, 1991) an extradition treaty signed between Jamaica and the United States in 1983. It also drafted conspiracy and asset forfeiture legislation, though its implementation may be problematic since the Jamaican Constitution shields against unlawful seizure of property without due compensation. Furthermore, the National Council on Drug Abuse (NCDA) was commissioned to develop a demand reduction program which included drug treatment and rehabilitation facilities, and crop substitution projects were actually encouraged, in one case, with financial assistance from the European Community. It is clear that Manley addressed a number of important U.S. issues, but he did not yield on the question of aerial spraying as a more efficient method of eradication.

Table 3 outlines the trends in marijuana production and harvesting for the years 1988-1992. The figures show that in 1992 cultivation was at its lowest level since 1984. Of significance, however, is the resiliency of Jamaican farmers. It is true that many businesses have been wiped out completely and that farmers have turned to alternative commodities, yet others continue to grow the crop despite numerous losses to eradication. In many cases, crop destruction has kept pace with cultivation, but it is still hampered by lack of aviation resources. Like Seaga, Manley tried to shift attention away from the politically sensitive topic of eradication. Since he was regarded by many as someone who cares for the poor, a false move on his part could have weakened his base of support. Moreover, the sharp devaluation of the Jamaican dollar following the abolition of exchange controls in September 1991 caused a record inflation rate of 80 percent during 1991 and price hikes of basic foodstuffs. Previously, the country endured drastic cuts in food subsidies and crucial public sector programs, as well as heavy taxation. In short, his government found itself in as precarious a situation as Seaga.

Table 1
Estimated Sources and Quantities of Marijuana Available
For Use in the United States, 1981 - 1987

	Country	Quantity (metric tons)	% of Total Imports*	% of Total Supply*
1981	Colombia	7,500-11,000	86	79
	Jamaica	900-1,200	10	9
	Mexico	300-500	4	3
	Domestic	900-1,200	0	9
	Other	-	-	-
	Total	**9,600-13,900**	**100**	**100**
1982	Colombia	7,000-8,000	67	57
	Jamaica	1,750-2,500	19	16
	Mexico	750	6	6
	Domestic	2,000	0	15
	Other	840	8	6
	Total	**12,340-14,090**	**100**	**100**
1983	Colombia	6,900-9,300	66	59
	Jamaica	1,750	14	13
	Mexico	1,300	11	9
	Domestic	1,500	0	11
	Other	1,150	9	8
	Total	**12,600-15,000**	**100**	**100**
1984	Colombia	4,100-7,500	48	42
	Mexico	2,500-3,000	24	20
	Jamaica	1,500-2,250	16	14
	Belize	1,100	8	8
	Domestic	1,700	0	12
	Other	500	4	4
	Gross Marijuana Available	11,400-16,050	100	100
	Less U.S. Seizures, Seizures in Transit, & Losses ¯	4,120-5,290		
	Net Marijuana Available	7,280-10,760		
1985	Mexico	3,000-4,000	40	32
	Colombia	2,600-4,000	38	31
	Jamaica	350-850	7	6
	Belize	550	6	5
	Domestic	2,100	0	19

Continued next page

Country	Quantity (metric tons)	% of Total Imports*	% of Total Supply*
1985 (Continued)			
Other	800	9	7
Gross Marijuana Available	9,400-12,300	100	100
Less U.S. Seizures, Seizures in Transit, & Losses "	3,000-4,000		
Net Marijuana Available	6,400-8,300		
1986 Mexico	3,000-4,000	37	30
Colombia	2,200-3,900	32	27
Jamaica	1,100-1,700	15	12
Belize	500	5	4
Domestic	2,100	0	18
Other	800-1,200	11	8
Gross Marijuana Available	9,700-13,400	100	100
Less U.S. Seizures, Seizures in Transit, & Losses "	3,000-4,000		
Net Marijuana Available	6,700-9,400		
1987 Mexico	3,100-4,200	37.1	27.9
Colombia	2,300-6,600	43.3	32.5
Jamaica	145-285	2.2	1.7
Belize	200	2.0	1.6
Domestic	3,000-3,500	0	24.9
Other	1,000-2,000	15.4	11.4
Gross Marijuana Available	9,545-16,585	100.0	100.0
Less U.S. Seizures, Seizures in Transit, & Losses "	3,000-4,000		
Net Marijuana Available	6,545-12,585		

* The percentage reflects the midpoint of the quantity ranges, rounded to the nearest 50 metric tons.

" U.S. seizures include coastal, border, and internal (not domestic eradicated sites); seizures in transit include those on the high seas, in transit countries, from aircraft. The loss factor includes marijuana lost because of abandoned shipments, undistributed stockpiles, and inefficient handling and transport.

SOURCE: U.S. Department of State, INM, *International Narcotics Control Strategy Report* (Washington, D.C.: INM), compiled for the various years.

Table 2
Jamaica: Cannabis Cultivation, Eradication, Arrests
1981-1983

	1981	1982	1983
Cultivation (mt)*	1913.00	2459.70	2459.7
Hectarage	1417.00	1822.00	1822.0
Hectares Eradicated	203.60	221.00	350.5
Crops Eradicated (mt)	274.80	298.40	473.2
Arrests"			
Nationals	3135.00	3068.00	3397.0
Foreigners	170.00	460.00	413.0
Seizures			
Cocaine (gram)	56.70	317.52	2757.0
Marijuana (mt)"	21.97	11.36	50.5

* Yields are calculated at an estimated 1.35 metric tons per hectare (1200 pounds per acre).
** Arrest figures for 1983 cover the period January-November only.
*** Marijuana seizures are defined as reaped ganja found in bulk, prepared for export, which was seized while in possession of persons arrested.

Source: U.S. Department of State, INM, *International Narcotics Control Strategy Report* (revised ed.) (Washington, D.C.: INM, March 1984).

Table 3
Summary of Jamaica's Production of Marijuana
1984-1988

Cannabis	1984	1985	1986	1987	1988
Cultivation (ha)	1400-2400	2365	4800	1330	1257
Eradication (ha)	390	955	2200	650	650
Harvested (ha)	1205-2205	1410	2600	680	607
Yield (mt)	1627-2977	950	1755	460	405
Loss Factor (mt) (.05)	81-149	48	88	23	20
Seized-in-country (mt)	200	—	—	215	53

Source: U.S. Department of State, INM, *International Narcotics Control Strategy Report* (Washington, D.C.: INM, March 1989).

Table 4
Jamaica: Cannabis Production, Seizures, Arrests
1984-1988

	1984	1985	1986	1987	1988
Gross Cultivation (ha)	2575	2365	4800	1330	1257
Gross Potential Production (mt)	1740	1595	3240	900	850
Hectares Eradicated (ha)	260	955	2200	650	650
Crops Eradicated (mt)	175	645	1485	440	445
Net Cultivation (ha)	2315	1410	2600	680	607
Net Production (mt)	1565	950	1755	460	405
Seizures					
Cocaine (mt)	—	0.40	0.55	8.60	0.01
Marijuana (mt)		—	—	215.00	0.53
Arrests					
Nationals	3346	2272	3341	3400	3100
Foreigners	167	—	782	567	625

Source: U.S. Department of State, INM, *International Narcotics Control Strategy Report*
(Washington, D.C.: INM, March 1989).

Table 5
Jamaica's Production of Marijuana
1988-1992

Cannabis	1988	1989	1990	1991	1992
Cultivation (ha)	1257	1790	2250	1783	1200
Eradication (ha)	650	1510	1030	833	811
Harvested (ha)	607	280	1220	950	389
Yield (mt)*	405	189	825	641	263
Seized-in-Country (mt)	53	38	29	43	35
Seizures					
Cocaine (mt)	0.01	0.13	0.76	0.06	0.49
Marijuana (mt)	0.53	38.00	29.00	43.00	35.00
Hash Oil (ltrs)	—	—	—	171.00	165.00

* Yield is based on 675 kilograms per hectare.
Source: U.S. Department of State, INM, *International Narcotics Control Strategy Report*
(Washington, D.C.: INM, March 1992 and April 1993).

Notes

1. Vera Rubin and Lambros Comitas, *Ganja in Jamaica: A Medical Anthropological Study of Chronic Marijuana Use* (Paris: Mounton & Co. Publishers, 1975), 36. For a more in-depth look at the empirical evidence of the Jamaican ganja complex, see Melanie Creagan Dreher, *Working Men and Ganja: Marihuana Use in Rural Jamaica* (Philadelphia: Institute for the Study of Human Issues, 1982).

2. Rubin and Comitas, *Ganja in Jamaica*, 161.

3. Small farmers interviewed for the Rubin/Comitas study claimed that poor land conditions forced them to cultivate ganja and that if that were no longer the case, they would abandon their illegal activity.

4. Bureau of International Narcotics Matters (INM), *International Narcotics Control Strategy Report* (Washington, D.C.: INM, March 1, 1987), 198. In 1986 there were over 2.3 million Jamaicans living on the island, half of whom were between the ages of 0-19. When one considers this larger picture, marijuana use is quite extensive.

5. Carl Stone, "Hard Drugs Use in a Black Island Society," *Caribbean Affairs* 4, 2 (April-June 1991), 154, 151.

6. Carl Stone, *The Political Opinions of the Jamaican People, 1976-81* (Kingston: Blackett Publishers, 1982), 56-58.

7. H. Aubrey Fraser, "The Law and Cannabis in the West Indies," *Social and Economic Studies* 23, 3 (September 1974), 383.

8. Barry Chevannes, *Background to Drug Use in Jamaica.* Working Paper No. 34 (Mona, Jamaica: Institute of Social and Economic Research, University of the West Indies, 1988), 14.

9. The anticipation in Washington was that Seaga would exert strong pro-American influence on his Caribbean colleagues and develop cooperation among the moderate governments.

10. Joseph Treaster, "Jamaica, Close U.S. Ally, Does Little to Halt Drugs," *New York Times*, September 10, 1984, A12.

11. U.S. Congress. House. Select Committee on Narcotics Abuse and Control, *International Narcotics Control Study Missions to Latin America and Jamaica, Hawaii, Hong Kong, Thailand, Burma, Pakistan, Turkey, and Italy* (Washington, D.C.: U.S. Government Printing Office, 1984), 104. The absence of numerical targets or fixed timetables on the part of the Jamaican government seemed to justify the Committee's concern.

12. *Daily Gleaner*, "Airlines Face U.S. Ban due to Ganja," March 17, 1984, 1; and *Daily Gleaner*, "All-Out War on Drugs Here," February 13, 1984, 3.

13. James Van Wert, "The U.S. State Department's Narcotics Control Policy in the Americas," *Journal of Interamerican Studies and World Affairs* 30, 2-3 (Summer/Fall 1988), 8.

14. Lloyd Williams, "State of the Illegal Ganja Industry in Jamaica," *The Daily Gleaner*, August 23, 1988, 13.

15. Scott B. MacDonald, *Dancing on a Volcano: The Latin American Drug Trade* (New York: Praeger Publishers, 1988), 89. Many analysts believe that a major portion of the ganja earnings do not enter the Jamaican economy at all. Instead, it is invested in offshore banks in the Caribbean or laundered through legitimate enterprises in Miami and New York. However, some profits have been used inside the country by way of real estate purchases, rural community projects, and political party campaign contributions.

16. This is a reference to the JLP's 1980 election campaign slogan.

17. See Carl Stone, *Politics Versus Economics: The 1989 Elections in Jamaica* (Kingston: Heinemann Publishers Caribbean Limited, 1989), chapters 1 and 2.

18. *Daily Gleaner*, "Ganja Eradication: Security Forces Hampered by Lack of Equipment," December 3, 1986, 25.

19. Government Accounting Office (GAO), *Drug Control: International Narcotics Control Activities of the United States* (Washington, D.C.: GAO, January 1987), 36.

20. These problems are pointed out in INM's annual *International Narcotics Control Strategy Report.*

21. Carl Stone, "Taxing the Drug Dealers," *The Daily Gleaner*, September 26, 1984, 8.

22. Errol Anderson, "Drug Smuggling: Its Effects on Shipping and the Nation," *Daily Gleaner* November 22, 1988, 22.

23. Figures were obtained from the Jamaica National Export Corporation (JNEC), *JNEC Export Security Service Manual* (Kingston, Jamaica: JNEC, 1988).

24. INM, March 1987, *International Narcotics*, 195.

25. INM, *International Narcotics Control Strategy Report* (Washington, D.C.: INM, March 1988), 137; *The Daily Gleaner*, "Ganja Farming, Corruption Problems," December 1, 1986, 26.

26. *The Daily Gleaner*, "Ganja Fields to be Sprayed," December 10, 1986, 1, 3.

27. *The Daily Gleaner*, "Ganja Farming, Corruption Problems," December 1, 1986, 26.

28. See Carl Stone, *Politics Versus Economics*, chapter 3, for a thorough analysis of the elections.

29. In March 1992 Manley resigned due to poor health and was replaced by Patterson. The transition has been smooth, with no change in policy direction, as the new leader is himself a firm supporter of Manley's domestic and foreign policies.

30. See full text of Manley's address at the opening of the Caribbean Ministerial Narcotics Law Enforcement Conference in Kingston on October 2, 1989. The speech was the topic of JAMPRESS News bulletin No. 2090/89 (Kingston, Jamaica).

References

Anderson, Errol. 1988. "Drug Smuggling: Its Effects on Shipping and the Nation." *The Daily Gleaner.* November 22:22.

Bureau of International Narcotics Matters (INM), *International Narcotics Control Strategy Report.* Washington, D.C.: INM.

Chevannes, Barry. 1988. *Background to Drug Use in Jamaica.* Working Paper No. 34. Mona, Jamaica: Institute of Social and Economic Research, University of the West Indies.

The Daily Gleaner. 1984. "Airlines Face U.S. Ban Due to Ganja." March 17:1.

The Daily Gleaner. 1984. "All-Out War on Drugs Here." February 13:3.

The Daily Gleaner. 1986. "Ganja Eradication: Security Forces Hampered by Lack of Equipment." December 3:25.

The Daily Gleaner. 1986. "Ganja Farming, Corruption Problems." December 1:26.

The Daily Gleaner. 1986. "Ganja Fields to be Sprayed." December 10:1,3.

Dreher, Melanie Creagan. 1982. *Working Men and Ganja: Marijuana Use in Rural Jamaica.* Philadelphia: Institute for the Study of Human Issues.

Fraser, H. Aubrey. 1974. "The Law and Cannabis in the West Indies." *Social and Economic Studies* 23 (3).

Government Accounting Office (GAO). 1987. *Drug Control: International Narcotics Control Activities of the United States.* Washington, D.C.: GAO, January.

Jamaica National Export Corporation. 1988. *JNEC Export Security Service Manual.* Kingston.

MacDonald, Scott B. 1988. *Dancing on a Volcano: The Latin American Drug Trade.* New York: Praeger Publishers.

Rubin, Vera, and Lambros Comitas. 1975. *Ganja in Jamaica: A Medical Anthropological Study of Chronic Marijuana Use.* Paris: Mouton & Co. Publishers.

Stone, Carl, 1982. *The Political Opinions of Jamaican People, 1976-1981.* Kingston: Blackett Publishers.

Stone, Carl. 1991. "Hard Drug Use in a Black Island Society." *Caribbean Affairs* 14 (2).

Stone, Carl. 1989. *Politics Versus Economics: The 1989 Elections in Jamaica.* Kingston: Heinemann Publishers Caribbean Limited.

Stone, Carl. 1984. "Taxing the Drug Dealers." *The Daily Gleaner* September 26:8.

Treaster, Joseph. 1984. "Jamaica, Close U.S. Ally, Does Little to Halt Drugs." *New York Times* September 10:A12.

U.S. Congress. House. Select Committee on Narcotics Abuse Control. 1984. *International Narcotics Control Study Missions to Latin America and Jamaica, Hawaii, Hong Kong, Thailand, Burma, Pakistan, Turkey, and Italy.* Washington, D.C.: U.S. Government Printing Office.

Van Wert, James. 1988. "The U.S. State Department's Narcotic Control Policy in the Americas." *Journal of Interamerican Studies and World Affairs* 30 (2-3).

Williams, Lloyd. 1988. "State of the Illegal Ganja Industry in Jamaica." *The Daily Gleaner* August 23:13.

International Dimensions

Chapter Twenty-six

International Cooperation and the War on Drugs

Fernando Cepeda Ulloa

I must confess it was quite difficult to identify something new to say; therefore, I decided to rely on my old thinking about drugs and also to reinforce it with my most recent experience at the United Nations. Then it occurred to me that all this should be wrapped up as new thinking. It will be most heartening to find out that most of you already share the same style of thoughts.

An acute observer of international politics notes that there is a strong analogy between the present situation and the period after the Second World War. The difference is that rather than fear and hope, we now have hope and fear, with hope being much stronger but fear by no means entirely dispelled. This is what is happening in the fight against drugs. Also, hope is now stronger, but fear does not vanish. What I mean is that we have moved forward. Without all that has been achieved, the situation would be catastrophic. If we learned the lessons of the past ten years of intense fighting, we have real possibilities of getting the threat under control.

The balloon syndrome has diminished the merit of the important partial successes already achieved. No wonder many are the scholars, no wonder we hear that the effectiveness of the fight in some places means that now others are the new target, target for the production, trafficking, money laundering. It is high time to seek a strategy that will give full efficacy to achievements

---

Although the rest of the chapters in this edited volume were first presented as papers at the State of the Art Drug Trafficking Research Conference, the editors felt that the event's keynote speech was too important to be left out. The speech by Ambassador Fernando Cepeda appears as delivered, without footnotes or references. As Colombian Minister of Interior, Minister of Communications, Ambassador to the Court of St. James, and Permanent Representative of Colombia to the United Nations, he provides a valuable perspective of one who has lived very close to the issue of international cooperation in the war on drugs.

attained and which will prevent the demoralizing effect of the balloon syndrome. I do not anticipate that credibility will persist if consumption declines in the United States but increases in other countries; if the seizures of drugs increase substantially, but production grows much more; if each day more countries are involved in some stage of the criminal business; if new drugs come to substitute for the previous ones or to enrich the variety of the menu; if corruption affects more countries, more institutions, more individuals.

To quote extensively from the *International Narcotics Control Strategy Report 1991*:

> Seizure data shows that drug trafficking takes place throughout Europe and is increasing. Cocaine seizures more than doubled in 1990 to over 13 tons from 6 tons the previous year. Cocaine laboratories were detected in southern parts of Europe during 1990. In western European countries, the number of abuses of cannabis and heroin is declining. However, abuse of cocaine is increasing. Cannabis abuse is beginning to spread to several central and eastern European countries.

> Seizure data shows that trafficking routes have proliferated throughout Latin America and Caribbean regions, and virtually all countries are now being used for transiting drugs and precursors. It is also worrisome that illicit production now in more countries involves not only cocaine but also opiates. However, traffickers are using increasingly sophisticated means to launder money derived from their illicit activities.

The same report highlights positive development in some countries of the region: "Attacks by the Bolivian and Colombian authorities against trafficking organizations have achieved impressive results."

"In east and southeast Asia, seizure data shows that traffickers may be seeking to establish markets for cocaine in this region. Assistance to Africa," adds the report, "to combat drug abuse is more necessary than ever in light of the abuse and trafficking of both narcotic drugs and psychotropic substances."

It is true that more has been done, more is being done, and that is recognized, but it does not seem that such important efforts are enough. Yes, we have to do more, much more. But it is essential that we know how to do it. As President Cesar Gaviria requested in the San Antonio summit, clear objectives and measurable targets should be established. Otherwise, credibility will soon vanish and skepticism will become the fashionable perspective. In the fight against drugs, Colombia continues to be an admirable example. Based on the brave tactics achieved by President Virgilio Barco, President Gaviria took advantage of momentum already attained in order to assure very important progress. I will now mention some of the main results.

Reformulation of the Colombian judicial drug policy which has made possible the surrender of key figures of the Medellin cartel. This successful policy was also a big defeat to the international campaign projecting the image of members of the cartels as lawless, invincible, untouchables able to bribe or intimidate anyone, laws of state within the state. I believe the psychological impact of this victory is enormous and just for that could it be validated, but, of course, it is much more than that. Narcoterrorism has been brought to an end. The frontal defiance of governmental authority has disappeared. The so-called lawless are now dead, or in jail, or extradited. The Colombian judicial system has now to prove that it will be able to put to trial the most dangerous drug offenders. In order to accomplish that, it needs international judicial cooperation. From the Colombian side, traffic has suffered to the point that Colombian advantage is no longer an indisputable fact.

More coordination has been obtained in the antidrug policies of the producer, transit, and money laundering countries in Latin America. The European Community, first, and then the United States Congress have come out in support of the Colombian economy as a token of compensation for the invaluable losses incurred by Colombia and for the substantial economic cost of a struggle that is helping many nations. It is also a recognition, in President Gaviria's words, "that trade opportunities and economic aid are decisive if the drug problem is to be overcome."

Even though it may sound academic, a new thinking is required as an essential part of this effort. Here, as in many other cases, nothing is more practical than a good theory. Reports like *Seizing Opportunities* and *Global Connections* are opening a new and constructive approach. To begin with, we have to admit that none of the national legal systems was well prepared to face the criminal business. The international instrument adopted in December 1988, the UN Convention Against Illicit Drugs and Psychotropic Substances, now in force requires such complex adaptation of the domestic laws that its usefulness will be delayed for some time yet. The critical inefficiency of the international legal system has given a great advantage to the drug people to consolidate and expand, which makes the problem more and more intractable. It is not true that only the Colombian legal system was inadequate; it was a failure of the law enforcement system against drugs everywhere. The mechanisms of judicial cooperation that are being designed, which were highly improved at the San Antonio summit, are being substituted for the international legal system that Colombia and Venezuela and others have been requesting time and again. The international legal system, in my opinion, is the correct legal answer. I am not talking about its tradition, but about a core of duties that would allow us to face criminal behavior with effectiveness and fairness. With the present laws and the current international legal practices, we might be conducting a titanic effort to enforce the unenforceable. Giuseppe di Genaro, the former director of the UN program against drugs, conceived a less ambitious but very attractive proposal: the establishment of regional courts and jurisdiction of an international pool of justice with experience in investigating organized crime and drug trafficking. It was an idea to overcome the vulnerability of the judiciary in the Andean region. This scheme was suggested by Giscard d'Estaing and elaborated by di Genaro and other European jurists during the wave of the 1970s' terrorism, the so-called "espace judiciare Europeanne."

The new thinking has to go much further. A serious transnational response to oppose the ominous phenomenon of transnational organized crime is required. Drugs are one of the most evident manifestations of the phenomenon of globalization that characterizes this historic moment. The fight has to be globalized here more than in other aspects. Here the incoherence between diagnosis and response is obvious, and one of the clearest lessons we still have to learn is that a gradual approach is not only ineffective, but it could be tragic.

It is accepted that there are critical situations that do not allow avoiding social strategy. It is recognized as well that a perfect global strategy is beyond our possibilities, but "in medio estar virtus," in between could be the second best option. This is an option that has to be identified and then improved as much as possible.

Up to now, we have suffered the problems of a two-speared strategy. Where countries like Colombia are committed to a frontal fight, in other parts of the world, the action is less determined and in some parts there is only well-intentioned debate. We have endured the consequences of a desperate, although often inescapable, tactic. If we learned the lessons of previous experiences, we must globalize the procedure. If we learned from recent experiences of international action, we should resolve to follow the coalition-building approach.

I want to be more precise in the presentation of the outline of this global strategy that must reflect the universal political will cum financial resources for the eradication of drugs. At least four principles should preside these actions: co-responsibility, cost sharing, mutual cooperation, synchronization. Consequently, it should contain at least the following elements: a unit that establishes the basic outlines of the integral fight against drugs and should refer to producers of the natural ingredients as well as to producers of the chemicals, to the carriers, to money laundering, to those who make available the financial system for these transactions, to the consumers, to those who produce an amicable culture for drug consumption, suppliers, providers of arms, exporters of expertise in violence. Education and prevention should play a key role. Seizure and confiscation of assets and the mechanisms for its fair distribution have to be effectively addressed. At some moment, priorities have to be emphasized.

Let me mention other elements of this global strategy: national, subregional, and regional strategies in harmony with a basic global outline; global, subregional, and regional units for the coordination of intelligence service as proposed by the Inter-American Dialogue in 1989; cooperative mechanisms for sharing information and for monitoring what works and what does not should be strengthened and expanded; inventory of financial, physical, legal, and human resources; and an independent auditing over results and performances of different countries and actors leading to permanent review and refinement of their methodology.

Allow me to elaborate on the idea of the coalition-building approach in today's international actions. The new international politics are characterized more than ever by the coalition-building approach. These coalitions are made up of actors who have a paramount interest in the solution of the respective problem. That is how the core group for the coalition is formed. The coalition is extended to actors who, for some reason, can not be excluded, sometimes because they are international institutions that give legitimacy to the decisions or because they express interest in being part of the coalition, thus helping to project a broader characteristic and, in some cases, the aura of universality. In any event, the coalition usually seeks to interpret the universal feeling. Therefore, it looks for declarations, even merely rhetorical, in support of its objectives and actions. That is why it is useful to include the multilateral bodies in the decision-making process. Thus, the new spirit of international cooperation takes shape and, in some way, the desire of some countries to participate in international politics is satisfied. The coalition approach implies that concessions must be made and that, as a result of the consultation process, delays are to be expected. However, all these nuances are worldwide in view of advantages that this context of cooperation and compromise has, if the objectives of the coalition are to be obtained.

The system of coalitions allows for the materialization of the principles of co-responsibility, cost sharing, synchronization, mutual cooperation, and participation in the international decision-making process. This does not mean that there is equality between the actors. In the dynamics of the coalition, the functions of the actors vary, but it is also probable that there will always be an inner power group. It is also probable that the distribution of the costs will not be co-relative to the level of influence or level of participation of different actors. This brief and, no doubt, incomplete description serves well the purpose of explaining the nature of what I personally believe could be the approach that should be used in the fight against drugs.

By all means, something similar is happening in the Western Hemisphere. The coalition of the United States, Colombia, Peru, and Bolivia initiated in Cartagena during the Barco administration was a good beginning. Now in San Antonio, it was extended to Mexico, Ecuador, and Venezuela.

Without a doubt, the Cartagena coalition responds so far to the requirements of a subregional system. It is now in process of being harmonized with a continental and global strategy. The San Antonio summit is a novel step forward in that direction. If these regional coalitions are articulated with continental and global strategies, then the dynamic of the coalition will determine the composition and nature of the inner group and the proper distribution of responsibilities, costs, and compensations.

The coalition model in the case of Iraq is very illustrative. The United States had the leadership. The Security Council assumed the commitment of the political will of the entire international community. Only a small group of nations, some more powerful than others, participated in the military action. Colombia participated in the decision-making process only. Others, like Japan and Germany, made substantial financial contributions. Some countries received high compensation for the risks they took and for their cooperation. The case of Egypt is prominent.

To mention other recent examples of international coalition building: the universal condemnation of the coup in Haiti and the embargo ordered by the international community. Some countries took the leadership. The Organization of American States adopted the strategy. The Security Council operated as a sounding board. The General Assembly of the United Nations gave universal support to the OAS resolution, and an inner group is in charge of the plan implementation.

At other levels, there are two interesting cases: the quasi-global coalition for repealing the infamous UN resolution on Zionism as racism and the quasi-global coalition for not considering the resolution submitted by Cuba to the General Assembly demanding the lifting of the so-called U.S. embargo.

The final stages of the negotiation process for peace in El Salvador is another illustrative case. This successful political negotiation counted and continues to count on the support of the former Soviet Union and the United States, on the sympathy of Cuba, and the full backing of the Security Council, General Assembly, and yes, on the active participation of the group of four friends of the Secretary General. In the new era of cooperation at the United Nations, the Security Council is involved in most of the critical situations. As a consequence, the constructive participation of the five permanent members is assured, plus that of Japan and, through the consultation process, the cooperation of Germany and Canada is obtained. This is particularly true when there is a military threat to international peace and security.

In the case of drugs, there is no role for the Security Council. We already have the universal consensus of the General Assembly. There is a global commitment. The United Nations agencies related to drugs have been reformulated. Then it seems clear that the bilateral approach continues to play the most prominent role. As a consequence, we are suffering both the limitations of the bilateral approach even when it was via subregional strategies and the weakness of the multilateral, the expected global approach which, to say the least, is notoriously underfunded and in the process of reorganization. The global program of action adopted by the special session of the UN General Assembly in February 1990 is a universal aspiration to be fulfilled. In political life, it is relatively easy to reach consensus with regard to the main objectives. The difficulties arise when discussing how to reach the objectives. This is the real moment of truth.

As you realize, most of this presentation has been related to how to fight drugs, not to determine the course to be pursued. Synchronization is preached with regard to the methodology to obtain objectives which have been universally accepted. The predicament emerges when it must be decided who should do what and when a bilateral, multilateral, national, regional, or global strategy. It is in this gray area between conceptualization and action that political constraints and ambiguities, financial and human limitations, and the objective intricacies of the drug abuse problem have their most negative impact.

Having been close to these processes and on occasions deeply involved in some of them, I believe that the coalition-building approach is effective and, therefore, should be used in the case of strategies against drugs.

President Gaviria, in a speech he delivered before the American newspaper publishers association in 1991 in Miami, pointed out that, unfortunately, in the fight against drugs our coalition in comparison with the one built for the Persian Gulf War was not as strong as our enemy. Colombia has offered an example to be followed. Barco and Gaviria have been successful in preventing the establishment by the drug mafias of an alternative society pretending to offer employment, protection, social and welfare benefits to the submissive and lead and death to the clean and law-abiding citizens and officials. As Barco and Gaviria did, we all should prefer substance over show. They have preserved the moral legitimacy that gives us strength to fight drugs. The British Secretary of State for Foreign and Commonwealth Affairs in his speech to the General Assembly of the United Nations special session on drugs was very right when he said, "no country is immune from this plague, neither rich nor poor, neither capitalist nor socialist, neither nuclear superpower nor tiny island state. This enemy makes allies of us all. The Cartegena summit showed the results of both developed and developing nations. Let the results serve as an example to us all."

It is not, I believe, an exaggeration to say that the whole of humanity will benefit if we together implement the correct global strategy against drugs. It is our duty to promote and strengthen the kind of institutions and mechanisms which will actually make that possible. What a difference it would make if we gave proper thought to the effect that our actions will have on the welfare of our children and our grandchildren. Let me finish by conveying to you all this conviction. If we are able to build a coalition responding to the principles of globalization, for sure we will be in the position to claim as Winston Churchill did, in his finest hour, that this coalition was the most capable we have ever had. This is the policy that can unite us the most. United and well synchronized in time and substance, success, real success is ours.

Chapter Twenty-seven

The International Nexus: Where Worlds Collide

William B. McAllister

The debate about drug control and drug trafficking in the Americas is intense. Tensions abound, policies clash, human tragedy and suffering continue on a massive scale. The present volume is eloquent testimony to the extent and depth of the problem. Yet, important questions fundamental to the framing of the debate often remain unexplored. Who defines exactly what a "drug" is and is not? Who decides which drugs should be controlled? What kinds of controls should be imposed on various types of drugs? Why do other addictive substances, equally if not more dangerous, remain outside the scope of control? Why do many governments actively promote the export of certain "licit" drugs? Who defines the parameters of licit and illicit use? Why has the "supply control" strategy been so persistently adhered to, in the face of voluminous evidence that it is unworkable and despite viable alternatives? For answers to those questions, one must look beyond the confines of the Western Hemisphere to the global arena. The search for answers takes us far away from the domain of the clinicians and deep into the realm of the politicians and the diplomats.

The current international drug control regime is embodied in three treaties, the 1961 Single Convention on Narcotic Drugs, the 1971 Convention on Psychotropic Substances, and the 1988 Convention Against Illicit Traffic in Narcotic Drugs and Psychotropic Substances. Those treaties make no attempt to impose a rational system of controls over drugs according to the dangers they pose to humans. Rather, the treaties are indicative of the power relationships extant at the time of their negotiation. Weaker states have to put

I should like to express my gratitude to William O. Walker III, not only for his critical commentary concerning this chapter but also for his unselfish support of all my endeavors.

I am also grateful to the Institute for the Study of World Politics and the American Institute of the History of Pharmacy for their generous support of my research.

up with stricter controls on substances indigenous to their societies. Stronger nations have avoided substantive controls on drugs they find unobjectionable or profitable. Various entities within the United Nations have had an impact on the creation and operation of the system. Non-governmental organizations (NGOs) and multinational corporations (MNCs) have also had a hand in shaping the present structure. Yet, little is known about the process by which all this happened.

In this chapter, I will suggest some profitable avenues within the discipline of history through which the issues discussed above might be explored. First, the present state of affairs will be examined briefly. Second, I will assess the successes and failures of the international drug control system since its inception at the beginning of this century. Finally, after a review of the literature, some suggestions for future historical research will be made, keeping in mind the interests of fellow travelers in the social sciences.

The Real Scope of the Problem: The Drug Pyramid

Figure 1 represents the levels of international control imposed on various types of drugs. What one notices immediately about this diagram is that international controls on drugs are applied in an inconsistent manner. The drugs that, at the global level, cause the most death and disease each year (alcohol and tobacco) are under no international controls whatsoever. Psychotropics, which are the cause of more drug abuse problems than those in category A, are inadequately controlled. They remain available in large quantities through both licit and illicit channels. Marijuana, generally conceded to be somewhat less dangerous than many of the drugs in categories A and B, remains under the strictest control regime.

FIGURE 1: THE DRUG PYRAMID

A Organics[1]
(strictest international controls)
B. Psychotropics[2]
(less stringent international controls)
C. Alcohol and Tobacco
(no international controls)
D. Inhalants[3]

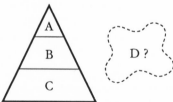

Only national and local controls exist over alcohol and tobacco. Plenipotentiaries attending meetings to draw up international drug control treaties have repeatedly exempted them from consideration. The worldwide trade in these highly addictive substances is immense, profitable, and dominated by Europe, North America, and Japan. That they should escape the attention of the international control community is evidence of the power relationships that animate the system.

Since the substances in category D are not really "drugs" at all, they can never be effectively controlled. They represent the "wild card" in the drug abuse/drug control equation. The number of people abusing these drugs is unknown, but it is almost certainly higher than any of the present estimates of usage.

Part of the purpose of this chapter is to survey the "drug problem" in its largest parameters. To put it bluntly, the problems associated with the substances in category A are only the tip of the iceberg. Even if we could concoct an airtight control system for organics, the majority of the problem would remain to be dealt with. This is a disturbing thought only if one considers the "drug war" as a conflict in which unconditional surrender is the only scenario for victory. If, on the other hand, we consider the realistic possibilities, we must conclude that some level of drug abuse will always be with us. The task is to decide how much abuse is acceptable. Sufficient resources must then be committed in order to reduce the "drug problem" to that level.

The Treaties[4]

The available evidence indicates that Western industrialized nations, and particularly the United States, have had paramount influence in the creation and operation of the international drug control regime. The system reflects Western cultural, social, economic, and religious biases about which drugs require control and how stringent those controls should be. To reinforce this point, we need only consider the alternate possibilities. One could easily imagine an entirely different regime of international drug controls if South American, Asian, or Muslim states were in a position to impose a set of restrictions according to their cultural, social, economic, and religious values.[5]

The 1961 Single Convention[6]

The control regime for the drugs in category A is embodied in the 1961 Single Convention on Narcotic Drugs. (Certain amendments of a relatively minor nature were made in a 1972 protocol.) The treaty categorizes substances into one of four "Schedules of Control," each with differing control provisions. Signatories are required to estimate their yearly needs in a report to the International Narcotics Control Board (INCB), which supervises the implementation of drug treaties. After the end of each year, states submit to the INCB a statistical report concerning imports, exports, production, usage, and reserve stocks. If there are any inconsistencies in the report, the treaty empowers the INCB to make inquiries and bring recalcitrants to the attention of the UN General Assembly. The INCB may even impose sanctions, such as an embargo on imports of drugs or precursor chemicals to the offending state, but the Board has never actually attempted to do this. In an interesting restriction of national sovereignty, the INCB is also empowered to make estimates for and impose sanctions on states not party to the treaty. Other articles in the treaty deal with extradition, enacting domestic legislation complimentary to the provisions of the treaty, procedures to amend the schedules, and the appeals process.

The 1971 Psychotropic Convention[7]

The control regime for the drugs in category B is embodied in the 1971 Convention on Psychotropic Substances. The provisions of this treaty are similar to, but weaker than, those of the Single Convention. Although certain statistical returns must be submitted, there is no requirement for the reporting of estimates of need. The control provisions of the four schedules (different from the schedules of the Single Convention) are less stringent, especially in the case of schedules III and IV. In general, more loopholes are available to those who wish to avoid substantive controls.

The 1988 Trafficking Convention[8]

The 1988 Convention Against Illicit Traffic in Narcotic Drugs and Psychotropic Substances requires signatories to fortify all aspects of their domestic drug control apparatus. It delineates offenses very specifically and includes provisions to combat money laundering, organized crime, and smuggling in related contraband items such as arms. States party to the convention are required to strengthen laws concerning financial reporting, extradition, and confiscation of assets. The treaty also calls upon adherents to improve international cooperation in the areas of information sharing, mutual legal assistance, and search and seizure operations. Two schedules of control are provided for a small number of precursor chemicals.

The three treaties provide the framework within which most of the drug control activities of the UN are carried out. Although dozens of agencies are involved in various aspects of drug control, the following section will deal only with the major ones.

The Roles of Key United Nations Agencies[9]

The League of Nations and the UN have historically concentrated most of their drug-related resources on law enforcement. Controlling the supply of organic drugs was and still is the main preoccupation. The official drug control apparatus has largely ignored alternative solutions to the problem. Preventive education, treatment, rehabilitation, and alleviating the social factors that create demand for drugs have received relatively little attention. In recent years, many UN directives and pronouncements have touted demand reduction as a priority equal to supply control. The lion's share of the money, however, is still spent on supply control. It remains to be seen whether the pattern of spending will be modified any time soon.

The International Narcotics Control Board (INCB)

As stated previously, the INCB is charged with supervision of the drug treaties. The Board is comprised of 13 members who are supposed to be appointed in their professional capacity rather than as national representatives. The Board has its own secretariat that gathers, collates, and disseminates the estimates and statistical returns. The Board may also advise the Commission on Narcotic Drugs as to what countries require funding and technical assistance in order to deal with their drug control problems.

The Commission on Narcotic Drugs (CND)

The CND is made up of 30 members, all political appointees. About ten seats are unofficially reserved for "permanent representatives" from the most important industrialized states. The CND is the chief policy-making organ of the international drug control apparatus. It creates the initial drafts of treaties and presents resolutions concerning drug control to the Economic and Social Council (ECOSOC). The CND amends the schedules, adding or deleting drugs from the lists. The Commission also acts as technical advisor to the ECOSOC on a variety of drug-related issues including where money should be spent for drug control and demand reduction programs. Of pivotal importance to the international drug control system, the CND attracts its share of "lobbyists." Many intergovernmental organizations and international non-governmental organizations attend the sessions of the CND.

The Division of Narcotic Drugs (DND)

The DND is the secretariat of the CND. It handles all the preparatory arrangements for plenipotentiary conferences. The DND also conducts research concerning dependence-producing drugs, national drug laws and regulations, the illicit traffic, and drug addiction. The DND publishes the journal *Bulletin on Narcotics* and disseminates information and advice on all aspects of drug control. It also acts as liaison with other international bodies with an interest in drug issues.

The World Health Organization (WHO)

Certain expert committees within the WHO structure act in an advisory capacity. Their main task is to make recommendations, based on medical criteria, about whether drugs should be added to, or deleted from, the schedules.

The United Nations Fund for Drug Abuse Control (UNFDAC)

UNFDAC is funded entirely by voluntary contributions. Its task is to fund programs for preventive education, technical assistance, rural development, income/crop substitution, assistance to reduce illicit trafficking, and rehabilitation and social reintegration of addicts. Almost all UNFDAC-funded programs are targeted for developing countries. About two-thirds of UNFDAC funding goes to various types of supply control measures. The balance is used for demand reduction.

Successes of the System

With respect to the drugs controlled by the 1961 Single Convention, the international drug control regime works about as well as can reasonably be expected, given the constraints imposed within a system comprised of sovereign states. Licit and illicit production, manufacture, and distribution of organics is clearly defined. Additionally, norms for state behavior are generally agreed upon. The same general assessment can also be applied to the drugs controlled by the 1971 Psychotropic Convention, but only with much greater circumspection. A modicum of controls exist, yet they are both limited in scope and relatively porous.

The international bodies of control, supervision, and aid are in place, functioning, and reasonably competent. They aid materially the efforts of regional, national, and local entities to deal with drug problems. Additionally, illicit production and traffic are harried. Supply control efforts do prove sporadically successful.

The greatest successes of the system, however, may be potential. Recent UN rhetoric favoring more emphasis on demand reduction may signal an important move toward the consumption side and away from the traditional emphasis on supply control. It remains to be seen if the UN and its member states are willing to support this position with increased funding.

Finally, the present drug control apparatus may set a precedent for expanded operations in other areas of international intercourse in the future. States have been willing, at least on paper, to give up a modicum of their sovereignty in order to combat the drug threat.[10] Proposed additions to the system include an international drug court and an international drug police force.[11] If such a comprehensive legislative, executive, and judicial system were to become operational, it might, over time, expand its competency into other areas of international conflict. Logical areas for consideration would include arms trafficking and peacekeeping, while more readily achievable possibilities might include international copyright protection, endangered species protection, prosecution of international environmental crimes, and so forth.

Failures of the System

The failures of the system are legion and manifest. Since many of the chapters in this volume deal with those failures in some detail, I will offer only a few general observations here. The most obvious failure is that the international drug control system has been profoundly unsuccessful in eliminating or even curbing the problem. Illicit production has merely been shifted from legitimate concerns into the hands of clandestine manufacturers. Demand continues unabated.

Another distressing failure of the system is one of vision. Policy makers and negotiators have consistently not dealt with the problem in its entirety. For example, regional approaches to drug control ignore the truly global nature of the traffic. Stamping out the illicit trade in one part of the world merely shifts the problem somewhere else. Furthermore, attention is all too often focused on a single drug or group of drugs, resulting in a switch of consumption from the targeted substance(s) to some less conspicuous substitution. Finally, international policy has consistently favored supply control over demand reduction, notwithstanding abundant evidence that supply control is, at best, an insufficient response. The fundamental realities of consumption underlying drug abuse remain unremedied and largely unstudied.

Moreover, the system is leaky. Diversions of psychotropics from licit to illicit channels are more frequent than is generally admitted. The control and distribution system for pharmaceutically manufactured drugs has too many loopholes through which unscrupulous middlemen can operate.

Additionally, the international drug control system continues to operate at the sufferance of sovereign states. The estimates and statistical returns collected according to the provisions of the 1961 and 1971 treaties are only as accurate as the information supplied by governments. There is much evidence to suggest that states do not always take their responsibilities seriously in this regard.[12] Incomplete adherence also prejudices the operation of the system. As of this writing, several important states had still not adhered to either the 1961 Single Convention, its 1972 amended form, or the 1971 Psychotropic Convention.[13] Although provisions exist within the system to discipline recalcitrant states, the preferred method to gain cooperation seems to be to sign another bilateral, regional, or multilateral treaty and hope for the best. There is little evidence to suggest that this strategy will be any more successful in the future than it has been in the past.

The international drug control system also holds the potential to do great mischief to national and international norms of jurisprudence. This is the converse of the observations made above about the potential of the regime to expand into new areas of competence. Many find the idea of an international corps of "drug cops" unpalatable. States have clearly proved willing to usurp fundamental human liberties in the name of fighting the drug war. Many Europeans, for example, interpret the 1988 convention and other recent international developments as a repressive turn to the right. They fear the blurring of traditional lines separating investigation of crime and processing of offenders. No provision is made for control over information sharing between regular police, secret services, and police authorities in other countries. No legal restrictions exist at present on the international operations of police — they can participate in actions that lead to prosecutions in jurisdictions other than their own.[14]

Finally, the present system has engendered many constituencies opposed to radical changes in policy. The international bodies of control, their secretariats, police organizations, NGOs, and many other entities have a stake in the system as it now exists. States wishing to attempt alternate solutions are hamstrung by the weight of the present apparatus.[15]

Literature Review

R esearchers wishing to uncover quite a bit of recent information quickly should consult the *P.A.I.S.* (Public Affairs Information Service). Although not exhaustive, it abstracts periodical articles, books, government documents, speeches, and reports in English, Spanish, German, French, and other languages. On computer, it covers 1972 to the present, although it is less comprehensive before the 1980s.

Readers interested in international views on various aspects of the drug problem should consult the *Bulletin on Narcotics* (quarterly through 1985, biannually thereafter). Published by the United Nations Division of Narcotic Drugs in Vienna, this journal gives a feel for the evolution over time of drug policy at the United Nations and around the world. In addition, articles frequently refer to important United Nations documents of which researchers should be aware.

The dearth of historical works on various aspects of international drug control leaves interested researchers with many avenues to explore.[16] Peter D. Lowes, in *The Genesis of International Narcotics Control* (Geneva, 1966), discusses the very early history of the international aspects of the issue.

As far as national histories are concerned, only the United States has received much attention, and even there the record is very incomplete. Readers should be sure to consult David F. Musto, *The American Disease: Origins of Narcotic Control* (New York, 1987); Arnold H. Taylor, *American Diplomacy and the Narcotics Traffic, 1900-1939: A Study in Humanitarian Reform* (Durham, N.C., 1969); William O. Walker III, *Drug Control in the Americas* (Albuquerque, New Mexico, 1989); Walker's second book, *Opium and Foreign Policy: The Anglo-American Search for Order in Asia, 1912-1954* (Durham, N.C., 1991); and John C. McWilliams, *Harry J. Anslinger and the Federal Bureau of Narcotics, 1930-1962* (Newark, Del., 1990).

For Great Britain, the record is even more sparse. S. D. Stein's *International Diplomacy, State Administrators and Narcotics Control* (Brookfield, VT, 1985) starts off well but turns to the story of the implementation of British domestic drug policy after 1920. An older work, David Edward Owen's *British Opium Policy in China and India* (New Haven, 1934), provides valuable background information.

After crossing the channel, the trail appears to peter out completely. France and Germany were the most active continental states in the creation of the international drug control system, but a fairly extensive search of the historical literature turns up no works on their role. Switzerland, the Netherlands, Russia/U.S.S.R, and Turkey have also been important players in international negotiations, yet there appears to be no work on the historical development of their policies either.

The role of various arms of the League of Nations and the United Nations in creating and operating the system seems also to have escaped the eye of the historian. The one work that does deal with certain historical aspects of this topic is Kettil Bruun, Lynn Pan, and Ingemar Rexed, *The Gentlemen's Club* (Chicago, 1975). Readers should be sure to consult this carefully crafted and insightful book for its cogent criticisms of the international drug control system.

Finally, the role of non-governmental organizations, multinational corporations, and other international interest groups remains unexplored territory. Three works that may be suggestive of the position of the pharmaceutical industry are Milton Silverman and Philip R. Lee, *Pills, Profits and Politics* (Berkeley, 1974); Milton Silverman, *The Drugging of the Americas* (Berkeley, 1976); and Milton Silverman, Philip R. Lee, and Mia Lydecker, *Prescriptions for Death* (Berkeley, 1982).[17]

Questions for Future Research

The paucity of historical literature leaves researchers with a wide choice of directions. If we are to have a fuller understanding of the genesis of the system, research must be done on the international policies of major players in creating and maintaining it. In addition to several European countries, the policies of other important states including Persia/Iran, Pakistan, India, the states of the golden triangle, and China should be investigated. What parties in each of those states were interested in strong control measures? Who wanted to see weak controls? Who was more successful in influencing state policy?

When states have come together to negotiate agreements, what have been the relative strengths and weaknesses of the protagonists? Who have been the winners and losers in the process of creating the international drug control regime? What role have the international secretariats and other agencies played in the process? How have non-governmental organizations attempted to influence the creation of the international rules of the game?

From the time the system became operational in the mid-1920s, how have the international bodies of control functioned? Have they acted in an entirely independent manner, or have various interest groups attempted to manipulate the operation of the system? If so, how successful have these interest groups been? Why has demand reduction received such short shrift at the hands of national and international policy makers?

With regard to all the questions posed above, the role of the United States is crucial. Has the United States been as successful in promoting its position as first appears? If so, what kind of ramifications has this had for domestic developments in states all over the world? If not, how have states parried the seemingly hegemonic power of the United States?

Dealing with the types of questions posed above will provide valuable insights about a variety of larger issues. The example of international drug control should enhance our knowledge of

1. The relative strengths and weaknesses of small and large states at the negotiating table;

2. The role that non-state actors play in the creation and execution of policy at the international level;

3. How international bureaucracies operate, take on new responsibilities, and retain old ones;

4. The relative value placed on high-profile action versus more mundane projects such as research and consideration of priorities;

5. The role of experts and expertise in international policy making; and

6. The transmission of legal principles and practices from one state to another.

As can be seen, the history of international drug control is fertile ground indeed. Researchers should, however, understand the risks in advance. Even in relatively small doses, they may find the topic addicting.

Notes

1. Due to the primarily natural, agricultural nature of the substances in category A, I refer to them as "organics." Included in this category are opiates (raw and smoking opium, heroin, morphine, codeine), coca products (primarily the various forms of cocaine), and cannabinoids (marijuana and hashish).

2. The drugs in this category are primarily hallucinogens and central nervous system stimulants and depressants.

3. Also referred to as "toxic solvents," inhalants are not actually drugs at all, but rather any chemical substance that contains toxic fumes. Examples include paint thinner, gasoline, fingernail polish remover, and various types of glues. These substances can be inhaled for a short, intense "high." Among other deleterious effects, repeated usage causes great damage to brain tissue.

4. For a more detailed comparison of the 1961 and 1971 treaties, see William B. McAllister, "Conflicts of Interest in the International Drug Control System" in William O. Walker III (ed.), *Drug Control Policy: Essays in Historical and Comparative Perspective* (University Park, Pa., 1992). (Originally appeared in *Journal of Policy History* [1991] IV, 3.)

5. For an insightful discussion of the role culture plays in the societal acceptance or rejection of a drug, see J. Westermeyer "Cultural patterns of drug and alcohol use: an analysis of host and agent in the cultural environment" *Bulletin on Narcotics* 39:2 (1987), 11-27.

6. For the text of the original Single Convention, see *United Nations Treaty Series* (UNTS), Vol. 520, no. 7515, 151 ff. For the text of the "Single Convention on Narcotic Drugs," 1961 as Amended by the 1972 Protocol Amending the Single Convention on Narcotic Drugs," see *UNTS*, Vol. 976, no. 14152, 106ff; see also *Commentary on the Protocol Amending the Single Convention on Narcotic Drugs, 1961 done at Geneva on 25 March* (New York, 1971); *Commentary on the Single Convention on Narcotic Drugs, 1961* (New York, 1973).

7. For the text of the 1971 treaty, see *UNTS*, Vol. 1019, no. 14956, 176ff. See also *Commentary on the Convention on Psychotropic Substances done at Vienna on 21 February 1971* (New York, 1976).

8. UN document E/CONF/.82/15 and Corr. 1 & 2.

9. For more detailed information on the present status and operation of the system, see *Declaration of the International Conference on Drug Abuse and Illicit Trafficking and Comprehensive Multidisciplinary Outline of Future Activities in Drug Abuse Control* (New York, 1988, Sales No. E.88.XI.1); *Political Declaration and Global Program of Action* (UN document A/RES/S-17/2, March 15, 1990); *United Nations System-Wide Action Plan on Drug Abuse Control* (UN document E/1990/39, May 1, 1990); *International cooperation in drug abuse control: Report of the Secretary General* (October 23, 1990, UN document A/45/542); and Kettil Bruun, Lynn Pan, and Ingemar Rexed, *The Gentlemen's Club* (Chicago, 1975).

10. An impressive example of this is a 1981 bilateral agreement between the United Kingdom and the United States allowing U.S. ships to board and search British vessels on the high seas without prior consent of Her Majesty's Government. See William C. Gilmore, "Narcotics Interdiction at Sea: US-UK Cooperation," *Marine Policy: The International Journal of Ocean Affairs* 15:3 (1991) 183-192.

11. For several examples, see Fazia Patel, "Crime Without Frontiers: A Proposal for an International Narcotics Court," *New York University Journal of International Law and Politics* 22:4 (1990), 709-747. See also "Drug menace to be focus of special session," *UN Chronicle*, 27 (March 3, 1990), 82; and Arlen Specter, "International crime requires international punishment," *USA Today*, 118 (May 31, 1990) 28.

12. See Bruun, et al., *The Gentlemen's Club*, Part II.

13. Partial list of states not adhering to

1961 Single Convention	1972 Protocol Amending the 1961 Convention	1971 Psychotropic Convention
		Austria
	Afghanistan	
		Belgium
Belize	Belize	Belize
	Bulgaria	
Cambodia	Cambodia	Cambodia
	Czechoslovakia	
Dominica	Dominica	Dominica
El Salvador	El Salvador	El Salvador
		Indonesia
	Iran	Iran
		Ireland
		Israel
	Laos	
		Luxembourg
		Netherlands
	New Zealand	
North Korea	North Korea	North Korea
	Pakistan	
	Poland	
		Romania
	Switzerland	Switzerland
	Turkey	
Viet Nam	Viet Nam	Viet Nam

Note: This list does not include states that have made reservations with respect to certain crucial articles in the treaties. From *Narcotic Drugs: Estimated World Requirements for 1991, Statistics for 1989* (UN document E/INCB/1990/2).

14. For a recent expression of various European positions, see Hans-Jörg Albrecht and Anton van Kalmthout (eds.), *Drug Policies in Western Europe* (Freiburg, 1989).

15. For an example of how European Community and international policies have limited the policy options of the Netherlands, see Anton van Kalmthout, "Characteristics of Drug Policy in the Netherlands" in Albrecht and van Kalmthout (eds.), *Drug Policies in Western Europe.*

16. Since my area of expertise encompasses modern European history and U.S. diplomatic history, I am able to comment only on sources in English, French, and German. I must leave discussion of Spanish sources to those familiar with the language and the literature.

17. A quick perusal of several works analyzing the roles of IGOs and INGOs turned up no specific references to their role in the creation and operation of the international drug control system. Works consulted: Vaubel and Willett, *The Political Economy of International Organizations* (Boulder, 1991); Morgenstern, *Legal Problems of International Organizations* (Cambridge, 1986); McLaren, *Civil servants and public policy* (Waterloo, Canada, 1980); Graham and Jordan, *The International Civil Service* (New York, 1980); Jacobson, *Networks of International Interdependence* (New York, 1979); Klepacki, *The Organs of International Organizations* (Warsaw, 1979); Barnet and Müller, *Global Reach* (New York, 1974); Cox, *The Politics of International Organizations* (New York, 1970); Kindleberger, *Power and Money* (New York, 1970); Sharp, *The United Nations Economic and Social Council* (New York, 1969); Higgins, *The Development of International Law through the Political Organs of the United Nations* (London, 1963); Hadwen and Kaufmann, *How United Nations Decisions are Made* (1960); White, *International Non-Governmental Organizations* (New Brunswick, NJ, 1951).

References

Albrecht, Hans-Jorg, and Anton van Kalmthout, eds. 1989. *Drug Policies in Western Europe*. Freiburg, Germany: Eigenverlag Max-Planck-Institut für Ausländisches und Internationales Straftrecht.

Bruun, Kettil, Lynn Pan, and Ingemar Rexed. 1975. *The Gentlemen's Club*. Chicago: University of Chicago Press.

Commentary on the Protocol Amending the Single Convention on Narcotic Drugs, 1961 done at Geneva on 25 March. 1971. Sales no. E.73.XI.1. New York: United Nations.

Commentary on the Single Convention on Narcotic Drugs, 1961. 1973. Sales no. E.73.XI.1. New York: United Nations.

Commentary on the Convention on Psychotropic Substances done at Vienna on 21 February 1971. 1976. UN document E/CN.7/589. New York: United Nations.

Gilmore, William C. 1991. "Narcotics Interdiction at Sea: US-UK Cooperation." *Marine Policy: The International Journal of Ocean Affairs* 15(3):183-192.

McAllister, William B. 1992. "Conflicts of Interest in the International Drug Control System." In *Drug Control Policy: Essays in Historical and Comparative Perspective*, ed. William O. Walker III. University Park, Pa. (Originally appeared in *Journal of Policy History*, [1991] 4(3).) Pennsylvania State University Press.

Narcotic Drugs: Estimated World Requirements for 1991, Statistics for 1989. UN document E/INCB/1990/2.

Patel, Fazia. 1990. "Crime Without Frontiers: A Proposal for an International Narcotics Court." *New York University Journal of International Law and Politics* 22(4):709-747.

Spector, Arlen. 1990. "International Crime Requires International Punishment." *USA Today*, 118 (May 31):28.

"Single Convention on Narcotic Drugs, 1961 as amended by the 1972 Protocol Amending to the Single Convention on Narcotic Drugs." *UNTS*. 976 (14152).

"Single Convention on United Nations Treaty Series, *UNTS*. 520 (7515).

UN Chronicle. 1990. "Drug Menace to be Focus of Special Session." 27 (March 3):82.

United Nations Treaty Series (UNTS) 520 (7515):151 ff.

UNTS. 1019 (14956):176ff.

van Kalmthout, Anton. 1989. "Characteristics of Drug Policy in the Netherlands" in *Albrecht and van Kalmthout*. Freiburg, Germany. Eigenverlag Max-Planck-Institut für Ausländisches und Internationales Straftrecht.

Westermeyer, J. 1987. "Cultural Patterns of Drug and Alcohol Use: An Analysis of Host and Agent in the Cultural Environment." *Bulletin on Narcotics* 39(2):11-27.

Chapter Twenty-eight

Who Are the Bad Guys?
Literary Images of Narcotraffickers

Pola Reydburd

Introduction

P erhaps it would be an exaggeration to state that foreign policy decision making is based on or shaped by the images and concepts that the media disseminate, but it is quite evident that public opinion is affected, guided, and shaped by magazines, movies, TV shows, and popular books. In the case of narcotrafficking, the American public has been deluged with images of dangerous, "Latin" drug dealers who are out to get them, and, as a consequence of these portrayals, entire countries and their populations have become the objects of discrimination.

It is the purpose of this chapter to explore this issue through the study of several works of fiction written by American writers. The works to be analyzed represent a cross-section of American contemporary popular fiction that should not be confused with American contemporary fiction. These novels, most of them examples of the suspense, detective-story genre, written within the last 15 years, deal with the topic of drugs and narcotrafficking.

Serial writers like Robert B. Parker and John D. MacDonald depict their fictional characters as heros in the midst of the dangers that arise from the drug trade. In several of Parker's novels from the 1980s, his protagonist Spenser (known mostly from the TV series *Spenser for Hire*) gets involved with narcotraffickers. This is the case in the novel *The Widening Gyre*, where Spenser is hired to try to find out who is blackmailing the wife of a Senate candidate who has "a little problem with sex and drugs," and in *Pale Kings and Princes*, where he travels to Wheaton, a small Massachusetts town and "the biggest cocaine distribution center above the Mason-Dixon line," to uncover the reasons for the murder of a young reporter from Boston.

Travis Mcgee, MacDonald's fictional hero, faces villains from the international cocaine trade in *The Lonely Silver Rain* as he searches for a wealthy friend's yacht in the middle of the Caribbean, and he also confronts drug smugglers in *Cinnamon Skin* as he attempts to discover the reasons for the violent explosion of a friend's boat off the Florida Keys.

Some novels place the topic of drugs and the character of the drug dealer or dealers at the center of the plot, as is the case in *Gulf Stream*, by Cherokee Paul McDonald, where the action is directly related to the business of importing marijuana and cocaine into the United States and in *White Cargo*, by Stuart Woods, to a one-man crusade against drug traffickers who have raped and killed the protagonist's wife and daughter. Other books, like *Under Cover of Daylight* written by James W. Hall, seem to deal with the issues related to drugs in a marginal way that is not central to the plot but which reinforces the common image of narcotraffickers.

Two other novels present a completely different picture of the problems related to drug trafficking. *Clear and Present Danger*, Tom Clancy's novel, describes the actions taken by an American government that feels threatened by drugs and responds with military actions to defend its "national security," while *Under Siege*, by Stephen Coonts, brings the War on Drugs to the United States and depicts its violent consequences in Washington, D.C.

Finally, I would like to point out that there are not many writers, outside of the United States, who explore the topic of drugs and narcotrafficking in contemporary fiction, although it is a current problem with serious consequences that have to be analyzed and, eventually, solved by the world. There has been ample speculation as to the reasons for this lack of production, and one of the most commonly given explanations has been the fear that a Latin American writer might feel if he gets too close to the truth in his description of imaginary characters.

Regardless of the motives, we will have to wait for Latin American fiction to tackle this theme. In the meantime, a comparison will be made of the American novels previously mentioned and two novels by Pedro Casals, a Spanish novelist who has approached the problems of narcotraffic. Two of Casals novels, *Disparando Cocaína* and *El Señor de la Coca*, deal basically with the financial aspects of the drug trade and, therefore, present a completely different outlook of the main issues related to narcotrafficking.

The Stereotype of the Narcotrafficker

The stereotypical image of the narcotrafficker is first established through the description of his physical characteristics. In *Gulf Stream*, he is shown as a "dark, Latin male," with "brown skin" who "speaks English with a heavy Latin accent" and wears clothes "with a very Latin look." In other novels, he is depicted simply as an "Hispanic man," or just a man "who appeared to be of Latin descent;" in other occasions, the description shows him as one of "those dirt balls who supply the drugs gladly with huge gold-filled smiles on their greasy faces."

The clothing comes next, from "iridescent acrylics" to "*lobo*-style synthetics." At times, he is one of several "well-dressed little Latin types," "very tan men with hard eyes and Dior shirts and Gucci shoes." Images taken from *Under the Cover of Daylight* and *Gulf Stream* show "them" wearing "black shiny shirts and mirrored sunglasses," that are worn despite the time of day and stay on even at night, perhaps "in case the moon flared up." The shirts are always worn open to show those "impressive gold chains and gold charms" and there is the ever-present Rolex watch.

Even the attorneys who represent them are "bemedaled with gold chains and bracelets." A stereotypical character's description would show him as a "carefully barbered Latino with a great deal of gold jewelry," who wears "rings the size of knuckles."

Frequently, the narcotraffickers are "lumped" together in the same "Latino bag" regardless of their national origin, and they are referred to as "Latino-Cuban-Colombians," "Hispanic Indians," or "Hispanic cowboys." They are called "creepy Cubans or Colombians or whatever the hell they were," and personal identity and nationality are seldom considered important except in the case of the Colombians who are all potential traffickers and the Cubans who are all potential subversive revolutionaries.

Special consideration will be given to the descriptions of Colombia and Colombians and the simplistic generalization that turns the country into a jungle and its people into wild savages. In *Pale Kings and Princes*, Colombia is depicted as a country where "coca was a part of life before Columbus" and where "cocaine was a heritage," statements that show utter disregard for the scientific and botanical differences between coca and cocaine. As one of the characters expresses it, Colombians are "savages" who have "been dealing with cocaine since your ancestors were running around Ireland with their bodies painted blue."

Remarks like these are made despite the fact that the action takes place in a New England town where close to five thousand Colombians had lived peacefully for several decades. The peace is apparently shattered when a young journalist starts "to screw" the wife of drug dealer Felipe Esteva, but it becomes evident that it is his search for the connection between drugs and police corruption that causes his death. This is a town where the police department has been bought by Esteva who also employs the son of the police chief to run his errands.

And yet, there are no harsh words to judge the corrupt public officials, no demeaning adjectives, no nasty epithets, just factual statements like "you've had three murders in the last month including your own chief and you haven't arrested anyone." As will be shown later, when the topic of corruption is analyzed, the indictment made is always of the "forces of corruption" that tempt the innocent American with hardly any criticism of the people who are easily bought.

But it is in *White Cargo* where the most stereotypical images of Colombia appear. The novel contains complete and thorough descriptions of the country and its people because most of the action occurs there. But even though this is one of the few books where the "bad guy" is an American involved in the drug trade as well as in the white slave trade, Colombia and Colombians are criticized from the beginning of the novel until the end.

As the protagonist travels in Colombia searching for his daughter who has been kidnapped by the American drug dealer, he encounters an "Indian woman who made breakfast for him," "toothless women on the street," "fat peasant women who carried baskets," "garishly painted American school buses," "people who live in seedy shacks," "pickpockets everywhere," and "street children with no family who would kill for a Rolex."

When he gets to Bogota, he finds it a modern city with high-rise buildings but not a "nice place to live in." In some instances, the author tries to offer a few positive impressions of the country, but they are so impersonal and detached that they seem to be taken out of a real estate brochure: "beautiful buildings, high skyscrapers, modern hotels with fancy pools," and "air-conditioned homes." But regardless of the modern and technological advances that he observes, the country is a "crazy place, full of thieves and drugs and people who'd just as soon cut your throat as look at you," "a country where everything can be fixed through bribery," in short, "a very dangerous place."

There is one Colombian character in the book who even has a proper name, María Eugenia García-Greville. She is the only Colombian the protagonist gets to know, but even she is not completely clean. She is "suspect" because her name appeared in the "black lists of the FBI and the CIA as a communist sympathizer." Everybody else is nameless: taxi drivers and street vendors are described by their racial characteristics and therefore assumed to be "Latinos," and Colombian public officials are seldom given any credit for their stand against drugs.

Although the villain is an American, there is no attempt to show any redeeming quality for Colombians or for Colombia. Woods adds an author's note at the end of the book that pretends to be a caveat in which he invokes the "courage of the people and the government to endure until these vermin have been imprisoned or expelled," but his book does nothing to encourage even the most modest recognition of the values and strength of the Colombian population and the Colombian government in their fight against drugs. After all, he writes, "it's a wonderful country, but it has drugs, poverty, and terrorism."

Drugs and Corruption

Corruption seems to be one of the main consequences of the excess of money that results from a profitable drug trade. Most writers acknowledge the problem of corruption as they describe "custom officers who have been on the take" since drug trafficking operations started. In *Gulf Stream*, "commissioners and Cabinet ministers" in the Bahamas not only received the bribes offered by the dealers, but, at times, they also took "the cache and sold it to other groups." This operation was known to the traffickers, but they could not afford to antagonize the officials who made a double profit on many deals.

For Parker, "small-town police departments are not normally equipped to stand up against the kind of money ... that cocaine represents." So, the typical American police officer who is corrupted by "dirty money" often seems to have an excusable motivation to receive the bribe. One officer's daughter is "ready to go to college," while another one's children need "orthodoncy," and a third one has to make "large alimony payments."

In *Under the Cover of Daylight*, a nice old lady from the Florida Keys is bringing marijuana to the United States to get enough money to continue her environmental work. As one of the characters observes, "last month, I had to bust the Baptist minister. Drying out a bale in his backyard. The sucker found it fishing, just brought it home. I mean, it gets so nobody thinks of the stuff as illegal. It's just this thing, like broccoli; only it's worth a bunch of money."

The implausible story details how trouble begins when drug dealers want to get into the act. The old woman is killed, and the logical conclusion seems to be that "marijuana is O.K., but cocaine is not," a shift in values that reflects the acceptance that marijuana has achieved in American society.

To complicate matters further, the corruption of public officials creates a judicial system that is characterized by its unfairness. Harsh penalties and sentences are given to the "little dealer" or the "casual user," the person who usually cannot afford to be protected by offering bribes to the arresting officers, while leniency is often provided for the dealer who had the established connections with the law enforcement authorities.

This view is expressed in *Gulf Stream*, where one of the protagonists, who is a policeman, watched "over and over again, when some young person, caught with a small amount of some stupid drug, would wind up fighting for his life, or at least some years of his personal freedom ... in a court system that at the same time could be so sickeningly lenient to a group of investors and participants in a multimillion dollar drug ring."

The novel *Under Siege* also emphasizes the problems of corruption. American dealers have several senators and other highly placed public officials on their payroll through regular contributions to their "political action committees." Since the accusation has frequently been made that "cartel criminals have bribed, threatened, bullied, and occasionally subverted the Colombian authorities," it is interesting to hear a fresh voice that reveals how the same kind of illicit activity can also take place in the United States.

As McNally, the crack dealer who handles a large operation in Washington, D.C., states, "the most serious threat to the health of [t]his enterprise was the authorities — the police, the DEA, the FBI. So he had systematically set about reducing that threat to an acceptable level. He found politicians, cops, and drug enforcement agents who could be bought, and he bought them."

And the indictment of public officials continues as a grocer who lives in the poorest housing project in the city reflects on life in the midst of crack addicts. "It's sorta like a tax, y'know? . . . The scumbags take my money at gunpoint and buy crack. The city takes my money legally and pays the mayor a salary he doesn't earn and he uses it to buy crack. The feds take my money legally and pay welfare to that crowd in the projects and they let their kids starve while they spend the money on crack. What the hell's the difference?"

But the most scathing attack on the honesty of American politicians is made when, in the same novel, a drug dealer confonts one of the senators who has received his bribes. "Get real! You politicians sold out to the country-club types who ran out and bought savings and loans. You let them shoot craps with government-insured money — five hundred *billion* dollars down the sewer. You've maneuvered like drunken snakes to get yourselves big pay raises. You've voted yourselves the best pensions in the nation while you've looted the Social Security trust fund. *You've damn near bankrupted America.*"

Drugs and Users

Here again, as in the case of corruption, American writers tend to justify the actions of the people who indulge in the use of drugs. In novel after novel, the character who consumes drugs is presented as a weak, problem-ridden individual who cannot get control of his or her life. In *the Widening Gyre*, Ronni Alexander, the "adoring wife" of a candidate for the United States Senate is a woman who "drinks too much and when she does she gets boisterous and sometimes mean." She finds herself entrapped in a video-sex scandal because of her addiction to cocaine. But, then, almost everyone in Washington "scores coke."

Usually, they are white, middle-class professionals who have no will power to stay away from drugs and who do not assume any individual responsibility for their actions. They are always depicted as victims: victims of the system and of society, victims of their parents and of their spouses.

Such is the case of Dell Catledge, an angry young man who hates his father, in the novel *White Cargo*, and blames him for the death of his mother and sister. Dell deals in drugs and uses them occasionally, and his punishment comes when he is killed after his father rescues his sister from the drug dealer who had kidnapped her.

However, the "victim" mentality of good, American normal people who must face the temptation of the "evil" drug dealers is questioned by Clancy when he states that "Colombia is a country with real democratic traditions, one that had put its institutions at risk fighting to protect the citizens of another land from themselves." And he reiterates his position when one of his characters states that "as long as your [American] citizens wish to destroy their brains, someone will make it possible."

Realistic descriptions of drug users also fill many pages of Coonts' novel *Under Siege*. He dares to show the problem of drugs not only as a middle-class diversion but as a social problem of a large segment of the population, mainly black people who live in government projects with poor housing, bad educational facilities, and minimum health care.

The country's capital, Washington, D.C., "has a drug mess" that needs to be cleaned and to "just say no" is not enough. In fact, "just say no is an obscene joke. Hell, the mayor of Washington couldn't say no. The chief of the Mexican federal police couldn't say no. The president of Panama couldn't say no. Professional athletes and movie stars can't say no. Cops can't say no. Congressmen can't say no."

The message presented by Clancy and Coonts is clear. The United States cannot continue to deny that the problem of drugs is a domestic problem. It cannot appeal to military solutions that might provide temporary relief by the partial interruption of drug supply. It cannot pretend that the reasonable behavior of its citizens will take them out of harm's way and save them from the evil temptation of drugs. It needs to address the problem of demand and begin to fight this "War on Drugs" in the domestic battlefield.

Drugs and National Security

In April 1986, President Ronald Reagan addressed the problem of drugs as an issue of national security. This new treatment shifted the focus of attention from one of many social problems in the domestic scene into a priority for international concern. As a result of this new perception, a clear difference was established between the "good" guys and the "bad" guys.

Americans, of course, were the good guys, and the others, the drug dealers and narcotraffickers who threatened national security, were the bad guys.

The message of several of the novels reviewed in this chapter is that the United States is being threatened from the outside by "evil forces" that are attempting, and succeeding in their efforts, to undermine and, eventually, destroy the underlying fabric of American life and American society by the gradual erosion of its values. Once this process is complete, the object of the task becomes to depose the democratic government and replace it, through a revolution, with an authoritarian, totalitarian, or dictatorial system or to allow anarchy and chaos to reign.

Many of the writers establish a direct relationship between narcotraffickers, regardless of their nationality, and Cuba. Sometimes, this connection appears to become an American obsession, and the paranoid fear of communism strikes the reader as a politically naive belief. Fidel Castro is portrayed as an evil character, one of the main forces behind the drug trade, bent on the overthrow of the American government. In *Gulf Stream,* he is described as someone "who has a penchant for smuggling cocaine into America in order to use the money not only to help Cuba's staggering economy but also to fund revolutionary fighters in other Latin countries"(107). In *Cinnamon Skin,* the explosion of a boat is attributed to "maybe some kind of Cuban terrorists,"(13) when, in fact, it had been perpetrated by a group called the Liberation Army of Chile. Here again, as was mentioned before, everything Latin appears to be equal: all Latin American revolutionary movements are linked regardless of their different political ideologies.

In *Clear and Present Danger,* Tom Clancy shows, with a critical attitude, the importance of invoking the idea of drug trafficking as a threat to the United States. Drug smuggling operations in the country were "a clear and present danger to U.S. national security." "That phrasing made everything legitimate" and allowed the American government to involve itself in Colombia in a military operation that could only be interpreted as an act of war.

Throughout the novel, U.S. officials try to justify their unilateral military actions against Colombia even though, as one of them points out, "we just invaded a friendly foreign country." But the "Constitution grants you [the President] plenipotentiary powers to use military force to protect our national security once it is determined — by you, of course — that our security is, in fact, threatened."

Clancy also addresses the Cuban connection, mainly through one of his protagonists, Felix Cortez, an ambitious and intelligent, KGB-trained, former Cuban DGI agent who works for one of the cartel's bosses. Cortez gets involved in a dangerous game as he tries to take advantage of the U.S. invasion of Colombia to play the drug barons against each other; his position as a trusted advisor allows him to succeed in creating a rift between them, but he is finally captured by the Americans and returned to Cuba.

The Business of Drugs

For novelist Pedro Casals, narcotraffic is a business; in fact, it is "the best business in the world as well as the biggest business of our time." He analyzes the economic implications of the deals in a financial setting "that moves more money than any other in the world — money, so much money that it can't be gotten in several lives by orthodox methods." In this process, Casals also reveals the different avenues that "black money, the money from drugs," takes to be laundered.

Narcotrafficking, then, is a source of wealth and in many cases is managed by people who have studied in the United States and who apply to it "American business school savvy." Drug negotiations are handled like Wall Street deals, and the lingo of "market, shares, quotas, and agents" could pass for the description of a legal transaction anywhere in the world.

Casals also approaches the financial impact of cocaine for the countries that grow it. He writes of the need of the peasant of the Andean countries to grow coca as a legitimate means of subsistence. "Many farmers," he states, "eat thanks to cocaine because the powerful industrialized nations have burdened [their countries] with a debt so enormous that they are not even capable of paying the interest."

The reserve of "Bolivian *divisas* is beginning to show improvement thanks to the cocaine trade," and it is ironic that "they will pay their debt to the gringos thanks to the *snow* which the same gringos buy at the price of gold." As one of Casals' characters says, "they screw us with the debt and we answer with cocaine."

Moreover, some of the Colombian characters who have entered the drug trade used to be coffee growers, but all the problems with the "crops and the coffee prices that went to hell" made them quit. They looked for another type of business and when "coca came up," they "hit it right in the head." After all, cocaine was a growing business, with consumption being doubled every year.

The novels also show the desires and ambitions of those who want to corner the cocaine market, be it in Colombia (*Disparando Cocaína*) or in Spain. One of Casals' main characters recognizes "that once someone is in the business, there is no way to get out of it," so he decides to "deal with coke the rest of his life." Since he cannot change his destiny, he might as well become *El Señor de la Coca*, Barcelona's biggest dealer.

The drug dealers portrayed by Casals are persons who have to come to terms with "the power of money," a power they can use in many ways. Some use it to enhance their life-style, while others take advantage of the money to "support political campaigns, to improve conditions of life in their country, or to aid revolutionary groups that oppose the system and seek to overthrow it."

Another interesting aspect of the drug business introduced by Casals is the recognition of increased security risks. This raises the "matter of protection," a new need that must be addressed in contemporary society. After all, the "best business of the century needs protection," and the people available to offer it are usually cops or former military-trained personnel.

These are people who have the experience and the training necessary to defend the drug barons from the "outside world" and from each other and who perform their duties for a fee. Often, they are "narcotics cops who were told to look the other way when [the dealers] started working with coke." Later, they "moved up to work with the organization earning a salary between that of a professor and an assistant professor at the university."

As they develop a highly sophisticated system of security, the narcotraffickers must make use of the most advanced tecnhology in communications and in warfare. Wire-tapping and scramblers are common tools, essential for the safe management of the operation, as are explosives and modern weapons. These devices were part of a "methodology practiced by coke distributors" which was "worthy of the most advanced intelligence services."

But the biggest challenge of all is to make the business grow. The organizational scheme is very simple: divide Barcelona's population in segments, set each one up in a different division, and address its specific concerns. Artists and beautiful people, executives and stock market analysts are all potential customers. After all, cocaine is *in* in Barcelona; "there is no party of a certain category where it is not given to the guests."

The marketing strategy includes the identification of people "who already belong to that world" so it will be easy to induce others to try cocaine. The individual must be very convincing, someone whose face is always on magazines and TV, and who can be successful *apalabrando* "grams and more grams of snow either in his office or in elegant parties," as he sets up the "beautiful people operation."

Finally, Casals does recognize that the drug trade is in the hands of a few Colombian providers, but they are always mentioned by name. In his novels, there are no derogatory comments, no stereotypical remarks, and no generalized judgments; he depicts individual characters, acknowledges the appeal of drugs, and does not indict a country or its people.

Conclusions

As has been suggested in this analysis, there have been changes in the direction taken by the authors to emphasize the problems of narcotrafficking and narcotraffickers. It is evident that the portrayals presented in the novels reviewed can be qualified as incomplete, if not distorted. Few writers present totally false images, but many simply draw simplistic and incomplete portraits of dealers and users. Some authors have not checked their sources and frequently misspell entire sentences in Spanish or confuse geographical locations.

Do these images that depict narcotraffickers in contemporary literature influence the perception that the average American citizen has of them, their country of origin, or their society? Is the American public in a position to ascertain the differences between fictional characters and real narcotraffickers? Have these generalized images resulted in the confirmation of racial and ethnic stereotypes that increase prejudices toward Colombians and other Latins? Most of these questions are not easily answered.

Prejudices are on the rise in many countries, and American contemporary society is not immune to this condition. Moreover, the United States has adopted ethnocentric, intolerant positions where fundamentalist attitudes prevail. This tendency is at odds with the pluralist and democratic values that have characterized this nation and served as ideal models for other countries of the world.

In the search for solutions, there has been a growing recognition of the complexity of the situation, leading to new approaches that seek to avoid stereotypes while they question the efficacy of the U.S. government's efforts to solve the problems of drugs and narcotraffic. After all, the political and military strategy of the War on Drugs has failed.

That is the opinion of Mathea Falco, author of *The Making of a Drug-Free America: Programs that Work,* who writes that "despite massive expenditures, we have not reduced either drug addiction or crime." And she adds, "we do not need a bigger drug war which pours even more resources into trying to seal the nation's borders, eradicate foreign crops, and lock up addicts. We need an entirely different approach built on what we have learned about reducing drug abuse and drug crime. The most promising strategies are not coming from Washington, but from communities working to find new solutions to their drug problems," and they include prevention, education, and treatment programs.

Another critical opinion expressed is that of Bruce M. Bagley whose monograph, *Myths of Militarization: The Role of the Military in the War on Drugs in the Americas,* states "To 'win' the war against drugs will require profound changes in both Latin American and American societies that cannot be achieved quickly or cheaply, certainly not by law enforcement and military tactics alone. The United States ... could best help ... by coming up with the resources needed to fund demand-reduction programs at home and by backing international economic assistance programs, multilateral cooperation, and institution-building efforts throughout the region."

In conclusion, some facts are incontrovertible. Drug trafficking is not a problem with an easy solution and cannot continue to be interpreted as the result of external efforts to subvert and corrupt American society. It is not by coincidence that the U.S. government has made use of the War on Drugs when domestic issues seem difficult to handle. This war has turned into a useful operation, a political strategy to generate popular support and a way to show interest in the improvement of the conditions of life of the citizens of the country who struggle against the corrupting influence of drugs.

Nevertheless, the problem of drugs is not a foreign conspiracy that need be attacked with military strategies. The use of drugs has been recognized as a domestic menace that has resulted in an increase in violence and corruption, two conditions that contribute to the deterioration and destabilization of society in both the United States and Latin America.

The United States must search for solutions with intelligence and resources, with educational programs and treatment facilities. The arguments used by Coonts and Clancy to express their disapproval of the War on Drugs confirm that the excuse of the bad guys is no longer relevant or valid. The accusations that place the responsibility on the source of temptation bring to mind the lines of a poem written by a Mexican nun, Sor Juana Inés de la Cruz, almost 350 years ago:

> O cuál es más de culpar,
> aunque cualquiera mal haga,
> el que peca por la paga
> o el que paga por pecar?

References

Bagley, Bruce Michael. 1991. *The Myths of Militarization: The Role of the Military in the War on Drugs in the Americas*. Coral Gables, Fla.: North-South Center.

Casals, Pedro. 1986. *Disparando Cocaína*. Bogotá: Plaza & Janes.

Casals, Pedro. 1987. *El Señor de la Coca*. Barcelona: Editorial Planeta.

Clancy, Tom. 1990. *Clear and Present Danger*. New York: Berkley Books.

Coonts, Stephen. 1991. *Under Siege*. New York: Pocket Books.

Falco, Mathea. 1992. *The Making of a Drug-Free America: Programs that Work*. New York: Random House.

Hall, James W. 1987. *Under Cover of Daylight*. New York: Warner Books, Inc.

MacDonald, John D. 1982. *Cinnamon Skin*. New York: Harper & Row.

MacDonald, John D. 1985. *The Lonely Silver Rain*. New York: Ballantine Books.

McDonald, Cherokee Paul. 1988. *Gulf Stream*. New York: Warner Books, Inc.

Parker, Robert B. 1983. *The Widening Gyre*. New York: Dell Publishing.

Parker, Robert B. 1987. *Pale Kings and Princes*. New York: Dell Publishing.

Woods, Stuart. 1988. *White Cargo*. New York: Avon Books.

Production Notes

This book was printed on 60 lb. Glatfelter Natural stock with a 10 point C1S cover stock, film laminated.

The text of this volume was set in Garamond for the North-South Center's Publication Department, using Aldus Pagemaker 5.0, on a Macintosh IIci computer. It was designed and formatted by Susan Holler and Lorenzo Pérez.

The cover was created by Stephanie True Moss using Aldus Freehand to create the illustration and exported to Quark XPress 3.3 for the composition and color separation.

This volume was edited by Jayne M. Weisblatt.

This volume was printed by Edwards Brothers in Lillington, North Carolina.